T0320101

Harvard Historical Studies, 116

Published under the auspices
of the Department of History
from the income of the
Paul Revere Frothingham Bequest
Robert Louis Stroock Fund
Henry Warren Torrey Fund

The Labor Wars in Córdoba, 1955–1976

Ideology, Work, and Labor Politics in an Argentine Industrial City

James P. Brennan

Harvard University Press
Cambridge, Massachusetts
London, England
1994

This book is printed on acid-free paper, and its binding
materials have been chosen for strength and durability.

Library of Congress Cataloging–in–Publication Data
Brennan, James P., 1955–
The labor wars in Córdoba, 1955–1976: ideology, work, and labor
politics in an Argentine industrial city / James P. Brennan.
    p. cm.—(Harvard historical studies; 116)
Includes bibliographical references and index.
ISBN 0–674–50851–3
1. Trade-unions—Argentina—Córdoba—Political activity—
History—20th century. 2. Labor movement—Argentina—Córdoba—
History—20th century. 3. Automobile industry workers—Argentina—
Córdoba—Political activity. I. Title. II. Series.
HD6605.C66B74   1994
322′.2′098254—dc20
93–46839
CIP

For my mother and father

Contents

Preface   vi

Abbreviations   x

Introduction   1

I   Córdoba

1   Industry, Society, and Class   23
2   Union Politics   54
3   The Factory, the Union, and the New Industrial Worker   85

II Rebellion

4   Córdoba and the "Argentine Revolution"   103
5   The Cordobazo   136
6   The *Clasistas*   170

III The Peronist Restoration

7   Tosco and Salamanca   209
8   Peronists and Revolutionaries   235
9   *Patria Metalúrgica, Patria Socialista*   274

IV The Politics of Work

10 Work and Politics in Córdoba   305
11 Conclusion: The Sources of Working Class Politics
        in Córdoba   343

    Source Materials   365
    Notes   371
    Index   433

Preface

This is a historical study of labor politics in the Argentine industrial city of Córdoba between 1955 and 1976. In those years Córdoba was the center of Argentina's automobile industry and the scene of an unusually active and militant working class. The city experienced rapid industrial growth in the decade following the overthrow of Juan Perón's government in 1955. The arrival and expansion of foreign automobile firms, principally IKA-Renault and Fiat, fostered a particular kind of industrial development and created a "new industrial worker" of predominantly rural origins, former farm boys and small-town dwellers who were thrust suddenly into the world of the modern factory and the industrial relations systems of the multinational corporation.

The domination of the local economy by a single industry, automobile manufacturing, and the prominent role played by the automobile workers' unions in the powerful local labor movement, which culminated in the greatest working class protest in postwar Latin American history, the 1969 Cordobazo, are analyzed in this volume in the context of the recent debates on working class politics in Latin America, particularly that of workers in the modern industrial sectors. I hope to demonstrate that the pronounced militancy and even political radicalism of the Cordoban working class were due not only to the changes taking place in Argentina's political culture, but also to the dynamic relationship between the factory and society during those years and to the specific shop floor conditions and workplace culture that are created by automotive production in a semi-industrialized country such as Argentina.

The structure of this book is alternately analytical and narrative, as the two do not seem to me to be incompatible modes of historical analysis.

Part I is primarily concerned with the formation of the working class and analyzes the factors contributing to the development of a militant trade union movement in the city. Parts II and III study the power politics of the Argentine and specifically Cordoban trade union movement between 1966 and 1976. Part IV provides a detailed shop floor study of the local automobile plants and advances my principal argument regarding the primacy of the factory as the crucible and locus of Cordoban working class politics.

Historians may note that relatively little attention is given to the relationship between the state and the local unions. Studies of working class politics in Latin America have tended to concentrate on the public history of trade unions, on the interaction between governments, labor ministries, and the trade union leadership. For reasons having to do with Córdoba's history, such a nearly exclusive preoccupation—questionable, I believe, for histories of working class politics in general—is clearly inappropriate for this trade union movement. The Cordoban unions were in large measure independent of the state, in open opposition to it, in fact, for most of this period, and were isolated from the center of political, economic, and trade union power in the country, Buenos Aires. The internal histories of the unions, their interaction with one another and with other groups and classes, and especially working class politics as it was forged and developed in the workplace are therefore my principal concerns.

I am indebted, as any academic historian invariably is, to the many people who helped me reconstruct a history in which I personally played no part. The many workers who shared with me their memories and, in some cases, lent me materials they had hidden during the years of military dictatorship from 1976 to 1983 are certainly the first people to whom I would like to express my gratitude. The assistance of the staff of the Renault company archive in Boulogne-Billancourt, France, and especially the intelligent advice and guidance given by Dr. Patrick Fridenson and Gilles Gleyze, two historians of Renault, during my research in France greatly contributed to whatever worth this book can claim. Similarly, Dr. Cristiano Buffa at the Fiat archive in Turin generously lent his time and advice and greatly assisted my research in Italy. In Argentina, the collaboration of Héctor Luti and Hernán Avendaño of the Renault Industrial Relations Department in Santa Isabel, and their assistance in accumulating the statistical material on the IKA-Renault factories between 1966 and 1976, was of invaluable help in illuminating the shop floor politics of those years. Naturally the arguments advanced in this book are my own and do not necessarily reflect the opinions of any of these people. All translations from Spanish, French, and Italian to English are similarly mine. To the staffs of the Biblioteca Mayor and the Biblioteca de la Legislatura (especially to Javier Troillo in the latter), as well as those of the Sindicato de Mecánicos y Afines del Transporte Automotor and Luz y Fuerza union locals in Córdoba, I also owe an enormous debt. The financial support given by the Harvard History Department, the Committee on Latin American and Iberian Studies at Harvard University, the Tinker Foundation, the Fulbright-Hays program, and the Social Science Research Council allowed me the luxury of devoting great amounts of time to research and writing. I hope this book is worthy of the confidence they showed in me.

I was fortunate during my years of research on this subject to have met and become friends with some exceptionally generous and intelligent people whose help I would also like to acknowledge. Ofelia Pianetto and Susana Fiorito, both of whom lived in Córdoba during the years under study and who are scholars of Argentine working class history, explained things that I would not otherwise have understood and, most important, extended to me their friendship. Mónica Gordillo likewise became both a good friend and an intelligent critic and shared her thoughts on this history as well as her time in assisting me in the research for the chapter on the Cordobazo. The early chapters of this book benefited greatly from our many discussions and from her important work on the Cordoban unions in the 1960s. Daniel James and Juan Carlos Torre offered me encouragement over the years and intelligent and useful criticisms of the manuscript, which I greatly appreciate. Three teachers especially need to be thanked. John Finan first taught me about Latin America, and Orlando Letelier, murdered by the Chilean secret police in Washington, D.C., in September 1976, opened my eyes about many things while I was an undergraduate at American University. John Womack, Jr., my graduate adviser at Harvard, has served for many years as a thoughtful and patient critic of my work, including this book, and is the person who taught me the most about history and what it means to be a historian.

My greatest thanks go to my mother and father, who always encouraged me to do what I wanted to do and who put up with my long absences during the years I was working on the manuscript, as did my brother and sisters. I hope that they and my wife, Olga Ventura, will forgive me for being such a bear at times while writing this book and that they know that I love them very much and have always appreciated their support.

Who can deny the essential role that Peronism has played in the "homogenization" of a class identity among Argentine workers . . . ? Who can close their eyes to this reality that the dynamic of Argentine politics presents of an almost absolute identification of the working class with Peronism . . . that displays an unmovable solidity and considerable resistance to attempts at political integration undertaken by the dominant classes in Argentina? . . . This then is the tragedy of the Argentine left, if action cannot begin there where the relations of production end, only at the risk of utterly isolating itself from the working class, there is but one conclusion that can be drawn: the need to reconsider the workplace, the factory.

José Aricó, *Pasado y Presente*

Abbreviations

AAA	Alianza Anticomunista Argentina
ATE	Asociación de Trabajadores del Estado
CGE	Confederación General Económica
CGT	Confederación General del Trabajo
CGTA	Confederación General del Trabajo de los Argentinos
EPEC	Empresa Pública de Energía de Córdoba
ERP	Ejército Revolucionario del Pueblo
FAL	Fuerzas Armadas de Liberación
FAP	Fuerzas Armadas Peronistas
FAR	Fuerzas Armadas Revolucionarias
FATLYF	Federación Argentina de Trabajadores de Luz y Fuerza
FREJULI	Frente Justicialista de Liberación
FUC	Federación Universitaria de Córdoba
GAN	Gran Acuerdo Nacional
GOCOM	Grupo Organizador de Comisiones Obreras Metalúrgicas
IAME	Industrias Aeronaúticas y Mecánicas del Estado
IKA	Industrias Kaiser Argentina
IME	Industrias Mecánicas del Estado
JTP	Juventud Trabajadora Peronista
MAS	Movimiento de Acción Sindical
MRS	Movimiento de Recuperación Sindical
MSC	Movimiento Sindical Combativo
MUCS	Movimiento de Unidad y Coordinación Sindical
PC	Partido Comunista
PCR	Partido Comunista Revolucionario
PRT	Partido Revolucionario de los Trabajadores
PST	Partido Socialista de los Trabajadores
SITRAC	Sindicato de Trabajadores de Concord
SITRAGMD	Sindicato de Trabajadores de Grandes Motores Diesel
SITRAM	Sindicato de Trabajadores de Materfer
SMATA	Sindicatos de Mecánicos y Afines del Transporte Automotor
UIA	Unión Industrial Argentina
UOM	Unión Obrera Metalúrgica
UTA	Unión Tranviarios Automotor
VC	Vanguardia Comunista

Introduction

In early 1944, Agustín Tosco left his family's dirt farm in Coronel Moldes, a small town in the central Argentine province of Córdoba, and traveled north to the province's capital city. The gangly, diffident farm boy's rustic origins were betrayed by his countrified Spanish, a Spanish laced with the Italian dialect spoken in his home, as well as by the mottled teeth acquired from years of drinking *agua de pozo,* the heavily limed well water that left dun-colored stains and scarred the smiles of Cordoban farmers and their families. Tosco's migration was a personal odyssey, but not remarkable for either his family or his generation. His father and mother had once made a similar journey of their own, down from the northern Italian mountains in Piedmont and across the sea to Argentina. These were also the years of the great rural migrations from the Argentine countryside to the urban centers, preeminently to Buenos Aires but also to smaller cities such as Córdoba. Like Tosco, many migrants were lured by a youthful sense of adventure, as well as by the hope of finding work in one of the city's industries, perhaps even in one of the larger military munitions or airplane factories that had initiated Córdoba's transition from an agrarian to a modern industrial economy.

Far from the austral depths of Tosco's Argentina, in what the Argentines still consider the centers of Western civilization and culture, events were transpiring in early 1944 that would one day affect Córdoba and Tosco's own life. In a winter of war, the industrial countries of Europe and North America glimpsed the changes that would follow the likely defeat of the fascist powers. In the United States, Henry J. Kaiser, a restless entrepreneur bent on expanding his already formidable industrial empire, was contemplating building an automobile company that he hoped would

1

win a place alongside Ford, General Motors, and Chrysler as a manufacturer in what had become the century's most prestigious, lucrative, and representative industry. Like other wartime automotive entrepreneurs, Kaiser hoped his Willow Run factories, near Detroit, would be able to exploit the domestic shortage of vehicles and gain a small share of the market. Nevertheless it was apparent that, with the conclusion of the war, competition would again favor the automotive giants. The automatic machine tools and transfer machines that their engineering departments were designing and already experimenting with threatened to transform the manufacturing process and create capital demands that smaller companies such as Kaiser's would have difficulty meeting.[1]

In occupied France, the empire of another industrialist was on the edge of ruin. Parisian socialite Louis Renault, through the combination of ambition and guileless optimism that sets the entrepreneur apart from the common businessman, had years before developed his once small, backyard workshop into a major automotive industrial complex in Boulogne-Billancourt, on the southwest outskirts of Paris. Unlike the American manufacturers, Renault had intended his cars primarily for a luxury market, and his plants had employed only modified Ford production methods. Yet by the thirties, the Renault factories had been comparable to those of the American companies and had made Louis Renault one of Europe's most successful automobile manufacturers. Renault had decided to continue production under German occupation, indeed to allow the use of some of his plants for the maintenance and manufacture of military vehicles and thereby avoid the threats of expropriation coming from the Germans. In 1944 this appeared to have been a first and fatal blunder. After the liberation of Paris, France's collective guilt for its role in the war was partly assuaged by the arrest of the more notable collaborators such as Louis Renault. In 1944, while awaiting trial, Renault died a prisoner of the French government—even as his company, newly nationalized, was making the transition from a private to a state-owned enterprise.[2]

Meanwhile, in the Fiat plants in Turin, the imminent defeat of the fascists caused confusion and fear in many and hope in a few. As the industrial heart of Italy's fascist state, Turin had many ties, emotional and practical, to Mussolini's expiring regime. The Agnelli family, founder and owner of the Fiat company, had been early supporters of Mussolini and principal beneficiaries of his economic program. The Turinese working class had partly abandoned its socialist and communist identity for a fascist one, mesmerized by the revolutionary and cultural imagery that fascism skillfully offered, as well as by the economic benefits of a regime committed to full employment and economic prosperity through industrial rearmament programs and imperial expansion.[3] Its factories heavily damaged by Allied bombing, Fiat barely survived the collapse of fascism, and the following decade would be one of unremitting crises and conflict, the company continually threatened with bankruptcy and the workers settling the score for the deceptions of fascism through reborn, militant socialist and communist unions. Fiat's hostility to union representation for its workers would remain unshaken, however, and management would take full advantage of the defeat of the communists and socialists in the 1955 union elections to sweep away whatever vestiges of union power had crept back into the company after the war.[4]

Despite the apparent change in the fortunes of the war, fascism was by no means as yet discredited in Argentina in 1944, the year Tosco arrived in Córdoba. The Argentine military retained great sympathy for the fascist powers, continued to believe in their imminent victory, and sought to imitate their methods and programs wherever possible. In the Cordoban armaments factories, military discipline and militarist sentiments permeated their entire operations. In the thirties, the armed forces' equation of national greatness with a powerful armaments industry had allowed them to win government approval for expanding weapons production and to enter into licensing agreements with the fascist powers for the manufacture of state-of-the-art military technology.[5] Several years later, the Ramón Castillo government (1940–1943) bowed to pressures from nationalist sectors of the military and in 1941 created a military industrial planning board, the Dirección General de Fabricaciones Militares, thereby acknowledging a permanent industrial role for the military. Out of that group of military nationalists emerged a secret military lodge with undisguised fascist sympathies, the Grupo de Oficiales Unidos (GOU), which seized power in 1943. One member of that group, Juan Perón, had studied in Turin in the thirties and served as a military observer in Mussolini's elite Alpine division. Perón's admiration for the fascists' reforms would find an outlet in his tenure as Argentina's minister of labor and especially after his election to the presidency in 1946.

In the years when the young Tosco was struggling to make his way in his adopted city, Perón was first coming to national prominence through his surprisingly effective and innovative performance in the Labor Ministry. Despite the deep personal impression made by his Italian experience, Perón as labor minister and as president was unable to recreate a fascist state in Argentina, partly due to the very different historical circumstances that existed in his country and partly to the discrediting of fascism internationally as a result of its defeat in the war.

Rather than as fascism, Perón and Peronism need to be understood and placed securely within the history of other populist political movements in Latin America in those years. As with those other movements, Perón's revolution would be essentially political and cultural, not economic or even social. Aside from the nationalization of the railroads and public utilities, Peronist economic policies did not affect the interests of the country's dominant economic groups, nor did they significantly depart from those followed by the conservative governments of the thirties and early forties, when a rickety alliance of the landed elite and the military ruled the country and restored government by the powerful, ending more than a decade and a half of contentious party politics. Public works projects, increased investment in industry, some tariff expansion, and the manipulation of exchange rates to discourage imports, as well as a deferential treatment of the landed elite—the latter policy only slightly modified by Perón with the establishment of a state monopoly on the commercialization of agricultural exports—were as much former President Agustín P. Justo's (1932–1938) policies as they were Perón's. Similarly, as with Justo, grandiose plans for using the state as a tool for economic development rarely translated into effective policy. Though Perón undertook a broad program of nationalization in such important sectors of the economy such as the railroads, the port works, telephones, and a major part of the electric power industry, the Peronist period (1946–1955) was characterized by a relatively consistent volume of production, modest investment in infrastructure, and little technological innovation in industry. Indeed, Perón proved to be far more effective in dividing the country's wealth than in promoting economic development.[6]

In only one respect did Peronist industrial policies significantly depart from those of the traditional elite, and even there it was a matter of degree rather than a qualitative change. As military pressure for industrial programs increased, Perón involved the armed services more directly in the modest development projects undertaken in select "strategic" industries during his presidency. Whereas light industry was promoted primarily through an expanding domestic market, heavy industry seemed to require significant state participation. The military was the primary advocate of such a role for government, demanding improvements in production methods and more advanced technology for its established arms and munitions factories, but also pressuring the state for the establishment of a heavy metals industry, specifically a copper smelter and a steel plant.[7] In response to pressures from the military, Perón expanded the activities of the Dirección General de Fabricaciones Militares, and under its auspices some progress was made in the chemical industry. More typical were showy projects such as the establishment of the Sociedad Mixta Siderúrgica Argentina (SOMISA) in 1947 to promote the greatly lagging steel industry, and the expansion and consolidation of the Cordoban military factories in the Industrias Aeronaúticas y Mecánicas del Estado (IAME) in 1951 for airplane and vehicle production. The bold plans of the military for industrializing Argentina were never realized by Perón. Even in the high-priority steel industry, Peronist planning produced few results. The country's first major steel plant in San Nicolás was not in operation until 1960, and the very nature of the Peronist state was such that light industries, not heavy, capital-intensive ones, were more likely to flourish.[8] Perón's loss of support among the armed forces in his second administration had much to do with the military's disillusionment with Peronist industrial policies and Perón's failure to promote those industries it equated with a modern economy and saw as essential to its own institutional interests.[9]

The industrial growth that took place during the Peronist years resulted more from changes in Argentine society and Perón's political incorporation of the working class than it did from effective state planning. The sustained growth of the urban working class in the thirties and forties encouraged a particular kind of industrial development. Urbanization and the concentration of a sizable market for a wide range of industrial goods stimulated the expansion of privately owned, light and medium-size industries. The growth was fastest during the Second World War, the crucial years for the formation of the Peronist industrial bourgeoisie, but it continued through the 1940s into the early 1950s.[10] This new class of industrialists, henceforth known as the national bourgeoisie, was characterized by having few links to international capital and a near complete dependence on domestic markets, serving largely as manufacturers and suppliers in the consumer goods industries. Grouped together after 1952 into the Confederación General Económica (CGE), their rivals were found in the Unión Industrial Argentina (UIA), an organization of exporters and industrialists with ties to international business and finance who increased their economic and political weight in the late 1950s and through the 1960s, giving the Argentine bourgeoisie even more of a dual character than was found in other Latin American countries.[11]

Perón's economic policies were predominantly an extension of his politics, tools used to garner political loyalties and cement political alliances. The vulnerability of an agrarian economy and stunted industrial development were of little concern so long as the exceptionally favorable conditions for Argentina's traditional exports and fat trade surpluses allowed Perón to bankroll his welfare state and buy political loyalties. The deteriorating terms of trade for those exports and the worsening fiscal problems that were apparent by the early 1950s forced a reluctant change. Perón courted foreign investment during his second administration (1952–1955) and eventually pushed through legislation that greatly eased restrictions on foreign capital, belatedly recognizing that his earlier economic policies had been ineffective. For example, shortly after his reelection Perón established contact with a number of European automobile manufacturers, among them Fiat, looking for possible investments in Argentina. Nationalist measures undertaken during the first administration had by then failed utterly to create a national automobile industry. Restrictions amounting to a near prohibition on profit remittances and difficulties in obtaining the mandatory exchange permits for imports had forced Ford and other American companies to shut down their Argentine assembly plants in the late forties. Perón's halfhearted attempt to create a national automobile industry with the establishment of the Automotores Argentinos S.A. in 1949 and the conversion of some of the Cordoban military factories to motor vehicle production had flattered nationalist sensibilities but produced few results.[12] In 1952, in the very days Agustín Tosco was finishing his first year as a union delegate in the electric power company where he had found work, Perón and the foreign automobile companies discussed terms that would be acceptable to both for investment in Argentina.

The negotiations with the companies were arduous, and their outcome remained unresolved for several years. Yet if Peronist economics had failed to create a modern industrial economy at the time the negotiations began, the regime's other effects on the country were clearer. After only a few years in power, Perón had bred a complex set of loyalties and alliances throughout Argentine society. Generally, the interests of the working class and, to a lesser extent, those of the new industrialists were favored at the expense of others. Support for and opposition to the regime did not always break down along simple class lines. Even in the middle class, generally presented as a bastion of anti-Peronism, there could be found the small renter, aspiring industrialist, or government functionary who benefited in some way from Peronism. The relationship between Peronism and the working class, though complex and not without tensions, was simply less ambiguous than that between other classes and the regime. The social base of Peronism was unquestionably the country's laboring classes. The uniqueness of Peronism in modern Latin American history, its peculiar genius, was its ability to wed the working class to a political regime determined to transform much of the workers' established political culture and forms of association to its own ends, thereby undermining their ability to take collective, independent action. The state's co-optation of organized labor is, of course, a leitmotiv in the history of Latin America in this century, but Peronism differed in both scale and character from other examples of the incorporation of the Latin American urban working classes in its massive and complete nature. Given Perón's political ambitions and the country's class structure, with the absence of either a large peasantry or a propertyless, drifting underclass, Peronism's courting of the working class was perhaps inevitable. The growth of the urban proletariat in the thirties and forties meant that any regime not wishing simply to prop up conservative interests would have to take it into account. The working classes' power was still only latent, however, the result more of numbers than of class consciousness or organizational muscle. Perón's political acumen allowed him to recognize its potential sooner than his rivals did. His ambitions and considerable gifts allowed him to translate its potential into power.

A career military officer, Perón remained fundamentally a conservative all his life. As with both the European fascist leaders and the Latin American populists, his vision of the working class, separate from its strict political utility to his movement, was essentially corporatist. Perón attempted to include the working class in an alliance with the country's other classes, to give it a stake in a capitalist Argentina and to exploit its latent political power. Above all, Perón hoped to replace the inchoate class loyalty of the urban proletariat with a clear identification with the state—a state increasingly synonymous with the Peronist movement. To achieve that, he had to make real concessions to the workers. As was the case with the new industrialists, working class's loyalties and support for the regime were tied to self-interest. The needs of both groups were served by expanding the domestic market, redistributing the country's wealth more equitably, and increasing the buying power of the burgeoning working class.

Markets for Argentina's agricultural exports boomed in the immediate postwar years, and Perón used the wealth, in part, to create the rudiments of a workers' state. The working class experienced a 20 percent increase in real wages between 1945 and 1948, a figure that translated into a rise in its share of the national income from 40.1 percent in 1946 to 49 percent in 1949 and an annual average increase in personal consumption of 7.5 percent.[13] Nor did the deterioration of the economy after 1949, when the working class experienced a significant decline in real wages, indicate a reversal of Peronist redistributive policies in favor of the propertied classes. The working class was perhaps less affected than most by the country's economic problems, and certainly there was no significant redistribution of national income away from it.[14] The workers' deep if less boisterous support for the regime in the leaner years of the 1950s reflected their recognition that the Peronist state had tended to their material needs in a way no government before had.

Increased wages and a greater share of national income, however, only partly explain working class loyalty to Perón and its increasing Peronist identity. The very personal kind of identification that Argentina's workers felt for the regime was due to Peronism's ability to articulate their frustrations, rancor, and hopes as a class into an idiom that reached them emotionally.[15] In part, its ability to do this was due to its novelty, to the fact that Peronism simply represented a new political style. The best representative of the change was Perón himself. His wit, earthy language, and informal dress, his reputation for street smarts, and his preference for the simple diversions of the common man, flaunted in well-publicized friendships with boxers and soccer players, in contrast to the aristocratic pretensions of the genteel, opera-attending political elite, contributed to his image as worker's politician.

Peronism's appeal was undoubtedly due in part to Perón's very strong and unique personality. Other aspects of his political image were more premeditated, if no less effective. The Peronists sought to cultivate a familiar political style. They used a new political vocabulary, less formal and stiffly rhetorical than that of the country's traditional parties. Similarly, the Peronists appropriated the term *compañero,* or comrade, stripping it of its Marxist and particularly communist connotations, and generally adapted bits and pieces of Argentine working class slang (*lunfardo*) to their own political argot. As Daniel James notes, Perón's personal political vocabulary, his sometimes mawkish and grandiloquent paeans to the *descamisados* and the *muchachos peronistas,* was strikingly different from the oligarchy's disparaging references to the *chusma* and even the Radical and Socialist parties' discreet and sometimes priggish political language. Indeed, none of the country's political parties had realized the power of language; they all aped the political style established by the elite and forfeited to Perón the use of a more popular vocabulary that helped him garner working class support. Bombastic and maudlin though it often was, it enhanced working class self-esteem and strengthened the workers' emotional ties to the regime.

Workers' loyalties were also courted through less subtle means, via the creation of a Peronist political culture. Though the Peronist state could not aspire to and did not attempt to establish an absolute control over Argentine life as practiced by the totalitarian regimes of Europe in the thirties, it did nonetheless establish a modified version of it. The dissemination of the *justicialista* doctrine in elementary and high school textbooks, the subsidizing and exhibiting of Peronist "art," the use of symbols and political imagery—the ubiquitous Peronist *escudo* and the obligatory portraits of Perón and Evita in all public buildings—collectively represented an attempt by the Peronist state to imbue the Argentine nation with the spirit and teachings of the Justicialist revolution.[16] The elaborate social welfare programs created by Perón also had their propagandistic value. Charity became a pillar of the Peronist state and perhaps its most representative working class institution. State beneficence was used to ameliorate class tensions and cement worker loyalties in a way that gains in wages or in the share of national income could not. This paternalistic impulse in Peronism was also expressed through a vast body of extensive and unquestionably laudable and welcomed social welfare legislation. Health insurance, pension plans, right-to-work laws, subsidized low-income housing, paid vacations, child labor laws, an annual bonus system, and other measures all date from these years.

The other side of Peronist paternalism was more unambiguously philanthropic and calculating. The Social Welfare Ministry and the Eva Perón Foundation touched workers' lives in a direct way that even the government's social welfare legislation could not match. Evita personally oversaw much of the regime's charity work and, together with her minions in the welfare bureaucracy, listened sympathetically to the small tragedies, bestowed favors, and resolved the individual problems of thousands of workers. Her food and clothing drives for working class families, the tireless supervision of relief work for earthquake and flood victims, even her more eccentric and gaudy schemes, such as the building of a miniature "Peronist city" as a recreational park for working class children on the outskirts of La Plata, all touched an emotional chord, which, whatever her personal ideals, had a clear political intent. Indeed, the handsome resources at her disposal, thanks to workers being subject to mandatory "contributions" to her charities through monthly salary deductions, not only gave Evita a monopoly on dispensing state charity, but they also allowed her to exploit her popular following and the deep, no doubt deserved, popular affection that surrounded her; she thereby established an emotional monopoly as well, hastening the working class's Peronization, especially the large numbers of workers who remained unorganized and outside the official trade union movement.

Perón's greatest legacy to the working class, the one that outlived Justicialist economics, the elaborate social welfare programs, and all the movement's propaganda campaigns, was the creation of a unified and powerful labor movement. The organization of the workers into national industrial unions bound together in a single labor confederation assured the survival of the labor movement in the country's political life long after the original Peronist coalition had disintegrated. Perón took a nascent working class, one that was largely apolitical and unorganized, and within a few years made it a formidable factor of power in the country.

The creation of such a powerful labor movement did not lack an element of coercion; union busting and intimidation tactics were resorted to when necessary. In this respect also, Peronism represented a continuation of the labor policies of the military and civilian governments of the thirties and early forties. Those governments had followed a policy of dialogue and compromise with the most powerful unions in the labor movement. They had also harassed the more militant unions, such as the communist-controlled construction and meatpacking workers' unions, while encouraging the split in the national labor confederation, the CGT (Confederación General del Trabajo), which had occurred in 1930. But unlike those earlier governments, the Peronist state chose to repress in order to build again, to remove the bumptious elements of the labor movement and replace them with a pliant and beholden leadership, but also to strengthen the union machinery and empower the labor movement to a greater extent than ever before, thus making it a formidable political ally.[17] In addition to being aided by the divisions within labor and the low level of unionization, Perón's task was made simpler by the fact that many of those unions that had a history of militancy and independence were in industries in crisis and had suffered a serious loss of membership in recent years. Perón thus found it relatively easy to establish rival labor organizations, to shower them with wage and benefit concessions, and to win rank-and-file support. As early as his stint as labor minister, Perón had resorted to these tactics to eliminate communist rivals in the textile and shoe workers' unions.[18]

The combined effects of state patronage; increased unionization under the Labor Ministry's auspices; the weeding out of the hard-bitten anarchist, socialist, and especially communist union leadership; and Perón's own attractive personality had already produced a considerable personal following for Perón by 1946. Nevertheless, Perón's hold on the labor movement was still tenuous, and a number of unions did not hesitate to voice their opposition to the ministry's interference in some spheres of union affairs. The balance of power, however, had definitively shifted away from organized labor toward the state. Argentina's independent union tradition and its historical suspicion of and often open hostility to the state was ending. Perón's strategy to eliminate the remnants of that tradition was thenceforth twofold: he continued to use the powers of the state to promote unionization and favorable collective bargaining agreements while he isolated the union holdouts that refused to recognize Peronist tutelage. The so-called *laboristas,* who wished to lend Perón conditional support while retaining the union autonomy necessary to establish an independent labor party, were to feel the brunt of the attacks, but nearly all the country's unions would be affected in some way.

Perón preferred to avoid confrontations, and he resorted to squaring off with uncooperative union leaders only after all else had failed. In those cases, the options at his disposal were many: he could withdraw the union's legal status, its *personería gremial;* withhold the Ministry of Labor's support in a collective bargaining dispute, thus assuring an unfavorable outcome for the established leadership; form rival union lists for union elections; and, as a last resort, suspend a union from the CGT. As president, Perón showed that he remained willing to employ strong-arm tactics when necessary, and from its birth Peronist trade unionism contained an element of thuggery in which intimidation, and on rare occasions even violence, was used to keep organized labor in tow. But this was not a dominant tendency during the Peronist presidencies of the forties and fifties. It was as a benefactor and protector rather than a union buster that Perón was most effective in undermining the old union leadership and building a new generation of loyal Peronists in the labor movement.

For the most part, the unions flocked willingly to Perón. They also flocked quickly. Within two years of the start of his first administration, Perón had managed to get control of virtually all the unions that had maintained their independence during his stint as labor minister. Former communist unions, such as the meatpackers and construction workers, were solidly in Perón's camp, while unions that had historically been socialist or syndicalist had either a Peronist leadership or a working relationship with the government by 1948. As president, Perón was able to offer unions a range of benefits that had been beyond the means of the more circumscribed Labor Ministry. He was also willing to use the institutions of the state to back up the unions. For example, Perón empowered workers on the shop floor to a greater extent than ever before. The creation of a powerful shop stewards' movement, the factory *comisiones internas,* provided workers with effective advocates on all questions relating to work and production and ensured that Peronist labor legislation was followed by the owners, a fact that explains the latter's almost uniform hostility to it. Similarly, the shop stewards provided the workers with organic links to their national unions and the labor confederation and were a means of instilling worker identification with the unions and increasing worker interest in union affairs. Thus, the benefits of cooperating with the regime were many. After 1946, nearly all the country's unions were reporting pressure from their members to affiliate with the reunified CGT and to accept a place in the ranks of the Peronist labor movement.[19]

The sporadic opposition Perón encountered thereafter, most famously from the crusty old socialist leadership of the railroad workers' union, La Fraternidad, was almost completely confined to his first term as president. The intransigence of that particular union, which was broken in May 1951 when its socialist leadership was replaced by loyal Peronists, was exceptional during the first presidency and would have been unthinkable by the second. After 1952, Perón was in an unassailable position with regard to organized labor, and despite sporadic strikes in those years, the labor movement's Peronization was fully consummated. As the labor movement's dependence on Perón increased, so did his on it. Labor's influence grew as the original Peronist coalition disintegrated and the military, the Catholic Church, and the industrialists, each for different reasons, drifted away from the regime. Labor increasingly became Perón's sustaining institution, and the unions were relied on more than ever to undertake the propaganda work and membership drives for the myriad Peronist organizations in existence. The direct involvement of union leaders in politics also evolved. During his first presidency, Perón had discouraged labor leaders from running for political office. In 1951, however, with Perón's blessing, numerous union men were candidates at both the provincial and national levels. The Peronist state took on an increasingly syndicalist character as the other members of the alliance that had brought Perón to power joined the opposition.[20]

Obviously this represented the consolidation of a political movement that had been heavily improvised from the start. Perón had always known that the political base of his regime was weak. The loyalties of the Church and the military were unpredictable and provisional, and neither, at any rate, could provide the mass following that the labor movement could. Since the working class was the social base of Peronism, it was necessary to ally its interests closer to those of the state, to incorporate it institutionally. That was made possible by the great unionization drives of the first presidency. The Peronists claimed five million workers with union affiliation by 1951, though more credible calculations showed an increase in union membership from 434,814 in 1946 to 2,334,000 in 1951, which was still remarkable. Increases were most notable in the unions that were to become the bulwarks of Peronist labor: the textile workers (from 2,613 members in 1946 to 123,000 in 1951), the state workers (from 41,471 to 472,000), and the metal workers (from 5,992 to 120,000).[21] The hierarchical and highly centralized structure of the Peronist movement, *verticalismo* as it came to be called, was facilitated by the strengthening of the principle of one union per industry *("sindicatos de rama"),* which allowed Perón to establish a rigid chain of command and discourage dissident movements from developing within labor. Nevertheless, the regime's sponsorship of industrial unionism, whatever the future abuses of *verticalismo,* also made possible the unity of the labor movement and assured it an influence in the nation's political life that had been elusive in the past.

For all its contributions to organized labor and the sense of empowerment and dignity it instilled in the working class, Peronism ultimately had deeply conservative priorities and in many ways finally failed the workers' movement. Preaching class harmony, Peronism sought to consolidate support for a political regime unwilling to disrupt existing property relations or even to undertake genuine economic reform and hence to oversee meaningful social and political change in the country. Argentina's extraordinarily favorable and exceptional position in the world economy in the immediate postwar period allowed Perón briefly to pull off the masterful sleight of hand of appearing to subvert the country's established order while in fact supporting much of it. In this sense, Peronism was uniquely successful in implementing ideas that had been in vogue in Latin American conservative and even fascist circles since the thirties. It was significant that Perón's greatest imitators in Latin America, General Marcos Pérez Jiménez in Venezuela and General Carlos Ibáñez in Chile, were both military presidents who drew their support from the right.

Perón succeeded in no small part by appearing to be more than he really was, employing the language of the truculent nationalist to convince those sectors of Argentine society he depended on for support, chiefly the working class, that the country was en route to both economic independence and social justice. His regime fell not because of working class disenchantment with his regime, but because of a failure to fashion an economic program that fit its political needs. Perón himself stubbornly refused to ignore the existing international and domestic economic realities and tried to force the capitalist world to live on his own terms, to let bluster and cant solve the country's structural weaknesses. The conceits of Peronism were its undoing, and the belated recognition of its failures as expressed in the changing policies of the second presidency were unable to amend past errors. Yet Peronism was always much greater than Perón himself, and the movement survived proscriptions and persecutions precisely because it had been rooted in the lived history of the Argentine working class and better expressed its needs as a class at a determined historical moment than any of the country's left-wing parties.

Perón fell under the weight of his own contradictions as much as under the plottings of the oligarchy, the military, the Church, and the political opposition. The military and civilian governments that followed his overthrow in 1955 moved first to strengthen the country's traditional role as an agricultural exporter and then turned to an almost desperate hope that the new Latin American positivism, *desarrollismo,* would lead the country out of its social and political morass. The initial popularity of *desarrollista* ideas was widespread in Argentina and reflected a deep concern for the country's economic malaise, but it also exposed the conservative nature of Argentine society and the limited range of political options there. The ideas of Raúl Prebisch and the economists of the Economic Commission on Latin America (ECLA) commission who influenced *desarrollismo* stressed efficient capitalist economies and industrialization to avoid the deteriorating terms of trade that afflicted the Latin American economies. The state was to work to eliminate the bottlenecks that were hindering accumulation and investment by performing three basic functions: acting as a financial intermediary between developed creditor nations and local borrowers; providing a mechanism to effect minimum income redistribution and thereby stimulate demand; and serving as a source of public investment.[22]

The *desarrollista* program in Argentina established certain priorities that represented a break with the Peronist state and thus began an assault on the interests of classes and groups nurtured by Perón's regime. There was much of *desarrollista* theory, of course, that any good Peronist could have agreed with, and the use of the state as a tool for development along capitalist lines had long been part of Peronist dogma, if ineffectually applied. In actual practice, the implications of the theory were more unsettling. Interests that had emerged during the Peronist years, specifically those of the working class but also those of the more protected and uncompetitive industrialists and of the public sector generally, were threatened by plans to court foreign capital, to reduce state subsidies of all sorts, to repeal protective tariffs, and to increase worker productivity. Arturo Frondizi came to power in 1958 with a pledge to end the ban on the Peronists' participation in the country's political life, and he lifted the union interventions and repealed measures that weighed heavily against the labor movement, but the government's overall program and the interests of the working class as they had developed under Peronism would ultimately prove to be irreconcilable.

The influence of ECLA ideas and the *desarrollista* strategy to eliminate the legacies of Peronism and modernize the Argentine economy pervaded not only Frondizi's government (1958–1962) but also nearly all others that followed. Since there was obviously no thought among the elites, and little as yet among other classes, of socializing private property or of anticapitalist economics—the absence of socialist and communist parties of national standing being one of the hallmarks of Argentine politics—*desarrollista* ideas were initially received with enormous sympathy in the country. Despite their resentment of the continued political proscription of the Peronist movement, even the unions were initially reluctant to criticize such policies or to resort to arguments of economic autarky, which Perón had himself had abandoned in the final years of his regime.

The area of greatest policy change was foreign investment. Foreign capital, particularly American, swept into the manufacturing sector with the same enthusiasm with which the British had earlier moved into transport, banking, and insurance. By 1969, American investments in Argentine industry totaled $789 million out of a total foreign investment of roughly $2 billion in manufacturing. This meant that the American stake in Argentine industry had tripled in less than fifteen years, up from the $230 million invested in 1955.[23] The greatest foreign investment came in the capital intensive industries, automobiles and transport production most notably, while the traditional, light industries remained in Argentine hands. Industrial growth surpassed the modest achievements of the Peronist decade and put Argentina on an equal footing with the other principal industrial economies of Latin America. In the automobile industry alone, production climbed from a total of 13,901 vehicles manufactured between 1951 and 1955 to an annual production of 136,188 as early as 1961.[24]

Argentina's abrupt introduction into the era of multinational capitalism strained the country that Perón had created. Frondizi's *desarrollista* project centered on an almost personal obsession with eliminating the obstacles to capitalist development left by Perón. The Frondizi government's devaluation of the peso, the major cutbacks in public spending, including the elimination of all price controls and subsidies, the abandonment of rigid wage guidelines, and other measures were aimed at attacking the remnants of the Peronist state and restoring the country's standing with foreign creditors. Frondizi and his minister of economy, Rogelio Frigerio, sought to break free of the agrarian basis of the Argentine economy by devising an economic program in which certain key industries, with the support of foreign capital, would be openly encouraged. In this respect, the automobile industry was particularly prized for its presumed ability to establish industrial "linkages." Its hoped-for benefits included the spawning of a hearty steel industry, the growth of a parts industry, and greater petroleum production, as well as its presumed ability to develop the managerial expertise associated with a modern industrial economy.[25] In truth, all the governments of the period regarded automobiles as the key industry in Argentina's transition to a modern industrial economy. Between 1958 and 1969, 20 percent of the foreign investment approved by Argentine government's went into automotive production, and by 1970 the industry accounted for 37 percent of the royalty payments made for foreign technology, usually in the form of licensing agreements, in Argentine industry.[26]

The *desarrollista* program did not produce the hoped-for results, however, and it stalled seriously in the early 1960s. Agricultural export earnings and foreign investment had been unable to keep pace with the increasing import bills for capital goods and thus created serious problems with the balance of payments, causing Frondizi to turn to foreign finance. The government's economic problems soon scared away the foreign banks, as did the hint of political uncertainty following the Peronist upset victories in the 1962 elections. As repayment of the original loans came due, most of them having been short-term, five-year loans, the *desarrollista* program lost steam; this was followed by a recession and the fall of Frondizi's government. Nevertheless, Frondizi's program had committed the country to a certain kind of development, with a concrete vision of Argentina's role in the postwar capitalist order. Thereafter all civilian and military governments, even the short-lived and ill-fated attempts by

Arturo Illia's Radical government (1963–1966) to resurrect some of the nationalist shibboleths of Perón, would accept certain *desarrollista* assumptions about economic policy, the role of the state, and an overall vision of Argentina's place in the world economy.

Following the fall of the Illia government to a military coup in 1966, Argentina entered an exceptionally tempestuous period in its history. The military governments that ruled the country from 1966 to early 1973 sought to deepen the *desarrollista* strategy, but they only managed to precipitate an even deeper polarization of society, a polarization that was also the product of complex changes in the intellectual life and political culture that had been germinating in Argentina since the fall of Perón. These new forces gave rise to an ideological and political opposition that threatened to go beyond reformism and rhetorical radicalism. The Peronist governments that came to power between 1973 and 1976 confronted the legacy of these changes as the country exhibited all the signs of ineluctably drifting toward prolonged civil violence if not civil war. In the midst of the upheavals of the late 1960s and early 1970s, organized labor and the military were the institutions that determined the course of the country's national political life. With the proscription of political parties between 1966 and 1972, organized labor continued to perform the dual role of the working class's institutional interlocutor with the state and with business as well, as the voice of the outlawed Peronist party. The politics of the labor movement since 1955 had been more than just that of the working class—it had been the politics of society at large, as opposition to regimes and government policies were more effectively expressed in the labor movement than in any other institution in the country. With the onset of military rule in 1966, the labor movement's internal politics, as well as its relationship to civil society, became perhaps the most decisive elements in the country's national political life.

Labor's leadership role in national politics continued after 1966, but after that year it also more deeply reflected the divisions in society. Both support for and opposition to the programs and policies of the governments of the period had their strongest institutional base in labor. The opposition of other classes and groups remained dispersed and contradictory, and among the other corporate powers in Argentine society, the military and the Church, opposition failed to develop into more than minor rumblings within the ranks. Though the military was divided ideologically between liberals and nationalists, and practically between rivals for power and influence, as the governing institution and the chief architect of the country's economic programs after 1966, it was generally hostile to reformist or revolutionary solutions. The Church might have offered some institutional support to those disaffected by the military governments of the period, but its historic break with Peronism during Perón's first presidency, as well as an innate conservatism born of its own history, frustrated any political alignment other than support for the forces of order and stability. Dissident currents would emerge within the Church, but as an institution it remained a staunch defender of the establishment and the status quo.

Thus, an important part of the country's political history between 1966 and 1976 was played out within the labor movement and in the working class's relationship to civil society. After General Juan Carlos Onganía's seizure of power in 1966, sectors of organized labor became alternately defenders of the regime, targets of the government's modernization programs, and sources of its most effective opposition. Similarly, after 1973, the unions were both the supporters and the chief adversaries of the Peronist governments, as dissident currents emerged and challenged Peronism's hegemony over working class loyalties and especially its quotidian handling of union affairs.

The years of violence and dissent from 1966 to 1976—when there were strong revolutionary currents at work under the surface, never dominating but always influencing the political climate—were perhaps most tellingly played out in the labor movement. The events had their epicenter in Córdoba, soon to become Argentina's second industrial city. The split in organized labor that became apparent immediately after the Onganía coup, between the old guard Peronist labor bosses and the more militant Cordoban unions, and the subsequent confrontation between the Peronist labor movement and the *clasista* movements, some of whose supporters openly identified with revolutionary, anticapitalist programs, typified struggles that were going on at other levels of Argentine society. In the late 1960s, Argentina entered an era of revolutionary politics, and given the configuration of its class structure and the power of organized labor in the city, it was natural that Córdoba would play a decisive role. Organized labor obviously was not the only institutional actor in the period, and the history of the working class as expressed in the labor movement is inseparable from its interaction with the country's other classes and institutions. Yet the polarization of political life in Córdoba was more acute, the struggles were more eloquent and probably more significant for the historian, and their outcome was certainly clearer.[27]

The events of those ten years would be particularly momentous for Agustín Tosco. In 1955, however, as he finished his first stint as a union shop steward, it was talk of other politics and revolutions that most concerned him. Perón's fall from power in September filled Tosco and workers all over the city with apprehension, as they waited for a reaction against the labor movement that had supported Perón's regime.

Life in formerly soporific Córdoba was also upset by the sudden appearance of groups of English- and Italian-speaking foreigners, the consultants, engineers, and managers from the Kaiser and Fiat plants that were being built on the city's outskirts. The years of haggling between Perón and the foreign motor vehicle manufacturers had finally produced results in 1954 and 1955, and Fiat and the American company Kaiser-Frazier Automobile Company had agreed to invest in Argentina. Overnight Córdoba became the site of the country's new automobile industry. By the year's end, machinery was arriving, workers were being hired, and Kaiser was looking at potential licensors, among them Renault, to provide additional models for the company's limited line of cars. But the full meaning of all these changes was as yet invisible to Tosco. More real to him were his job in the local electric power company, his responsibilities in the union, and the daily hardships and pleasures of life in the city on which he had staked his future more than a decade before.

· I ·

Córdoba

Just as in a *factory* the workers are formed—being ordered in accordance with the production of a particular object that unites and organizes metal and wood workers, masons, electricians, etc.—so in the *city* the proletarian class is formed in accordance with the predominant industry, which through its existence orders and governs the whole urban complex.

Antonio Gramsci, *Program of L'Ordine Nuovo*

Industry, Society, and Class

Domingo Sarmiento's often quoted characterization of the paradox in Argentine history, of the conflict between civilization and barbarism, the port and the provinces, was not a merely literary portrayal of the antagonisms between Buenos Aires and the rest of the country. The uneven nature of Argentina's capitalist development had meant the monopolization of trade, business, and culture by Buenos Aires and had established a historical rift between the city and the hinterland, or *el interior* as the Argentines would call it. Some provinces were more fortunate than others in this division of wealth and power. Among them Córdoba, with its rich agricultural lands in the south, managed to get a share of foreign export markets and to imitate some of the changes that, late in the nineteenth century, were transforming Buenos Aires Province, and particularly the port city, into the economic hub of the South Atlantic. Córdoba's provincial capital, renowned for its cathedrals, university, and severe Hispanic morality, a city of erudite, rhetoric-loving barristers, censorious ecclesiastics, and prideful university dons, all drawn from the old aristocratic families and tightly knit through ties of blood and kinship in what the more worldly *porteño* elites referred to somewhat disparagingly as the *"aristocracia doctoral,"* reluctantly exchanged its medieval ambience for the cosmopolitan ways prosperity brought.

As Buenos Aires had drawn immigrants, so Córdoba's agricultural wealth drew peasants and workers from Mediterranean Europe, some of whom abandoned the ruder life of the countryside and found work in commerce and industry in the city. Though still a middling urban center of roughly 135,000 in 1914, its workshops and industries, notably the Anglo-Argentina brewery and the Farga Hermanos shoe factory, had created a working class that numbered an estimated 11,708 by the start of the First World War.[1] Also as in Buenos Aires, the greatest challenge to elite rule at this time came not from the workers but from the burgeoning agrarian and, especially, urban middle classes. Their assault on the symbol of elite privilege and exclusiveness in Córdoba, the university, culminated in the 1918 university reform movement. The Radical party committees to which they flocked were also, in their moment, centers of sedition that expressed the resentments of the excluded and snubbed in Cordoban society. Like the *porteño* elites, the Cordoban aristocracy responded to the middle class challenge by adapting rather than repressing. The elites allied with the followers of Marcelo T. de Alvear, leader of the patrician, *alvearista* wing of the Radical party, the *azules,* against the local *yrigoyenista* wing, the *rojos.* Political talent was recruited and class resentments were assuaged by letting new blood in to the old families. The Cordoban aristocracy abandoned some of its traditional clannishness and recognized the suitability for marriage of able middle class men with university degrees, provided the aspirant's university education was complemented by evidence of Catholic piety and was untainted by any anarchist or socialist association from the young man's student days.[2]

Córdoba's history, with the permutations the special character of its society determined, thus mirrored many of the changes occurring in Buenos Aires during the half-century of liberal rule (1880–1929). It was only toward the end of that period that an element was introduced that strayed from Buenos Aires's example. In 1927 Alvear's Radical government, responding to pressures coming from the military, awarded federal monies for the establishment of an airplane factory in Córdoba. The decision to locate the factory in Córdoba had been a mere sop for Alvear's political allies there, but his casual decision would have immense implications for the city's future. By 1929 the factory was one of the largest industrial operations in the country, employing some 600 workers, although with a precarious existence and with production periodically suspended owing to the government's niggardliness with the federal funds necessary to keep the factory running.[3] The airplane factory, soon to be building German Focke-Wulff planes and Rhoen-Bussard gliders, was the country's first experience with continuous-flow mass production in the mechanical industries. By 1932 it was a major industrial complex covering 160 acres, comprising some 23 separate buildings, and employing production processes that used specialized machinery and up-to-date testing laboratories.[4]

The airplane factory set a precedent for establishing other armaments and munitions factories in the province. In the 1930s additional military factories such as the Fábrica Militar de Pólvora y Explosivos in Villa María, the Fábrica de Armas Portátiles in San Francisco, and an artillery ammunition factory in Río Tercero were constructed. These armaments and munitions factories laid the region's base in engineering expertise and gave the military a vested interest in assuring the continued viability of Córdoba as an industrial center in the mechanical industries, with military industrial planners hopeful that their factories would benefit as supplier and buyer for other plants in the city. State intervention and government support accompanied Córdoba's industrialization from the start. The Río Tercero ammunition factory owed its establishment to the existence of cheap electricity supplied by the nearby Río Tercero dam, then the largest hydroelectric operation in South America.[5] The dam was just one of many public works projects initiated by Governor Amadeo Sabattini (1934–1940). Sabattini, the son of Italian immigrants, revived the apparently moribund *yrigoyenista* tradition in the Radical party and forged an effective local party organization with a faintly nationalistic program, one at odds with the philosophy and policies of the conservative governments of the 1930s. The depression in the Cordoban countryside was more severe than that faced by the Buenos Aires *estancieros* who supported the conservative restoration, and *sabattinismo* urged a more activist role for the state in promoting economic recovery.[6]

Among the measures adopted during Sabattini's years as governor were a series of public works projects that allowed Córdoba to undertake the most comprehensive system of road construction, hydroelectric development, and light industrialization of any province in the country. The success of Sabattini's programs did not always match their ambitions, but the results were a significant step in the subsequent industrial development of Córdoba. The road-building programs, for example, were immensely successful, and the road gangs that were set to work throughout the province gave Córdoba one of the most extensive road networks of any province in the country. The industrialization programs had less spectacular but still respectable results, and the textile, cement, and armaments industries especially showed notable growth. The number of industrial establishments in the province as a whole increased from 2,839 in 1935 to 5,319 in 1940, and the industrial working class grew from 20,189 to 37,649.[7]

Although Córdoba retained its agrarian character and the province's share of industrial production was a modest portion of the 43,613 industrial establishments that existed nationally in 1940, given the depressed state of the Cordoban countryside, the results of the state's industrial programs were significant. The most important of Sabattini's programs were undoubtedly the hydroelectric projects. The dikes and dams built in the Cordoban *sierra* in the 1930s ensured that the production of electric power would, at least for the immediate future, keep pace with industrial needs. The establishment of discount rates for industry was a principal reason for Córdoba's industrial growth during the Sabattini years and thereafter. Later, Perón's acrimonious and ongoing disputes with the electric power companies would prompt their piecemeal nationalization in the 1940s and 1950s, and the Cordoban power industry would be one of the most affected. In 1946, the province would assume control of all electric power production and establish the public power company EPEC (Empresa Pública de Energía de Córdoba), the company where Agustín Tosco would find work in 1948.

The Córdoba that Agustín Tosco discovered on his arrival in 1944 was thus something in between the small commercial and bureaucratic city it had been through the 1930s and the major industrial center it would become in the 1950s. The industrial growth of the 1950s would be a legacy of the Sabattini public works projects and also of Peronist policies.

Córdoba was an exception to the general ineffectiveness of Peronist industrial programs, due not so much to Perón's planning as to the intense pressures coming from the military, which he could not ignore. Perón's minister of aeronautics, Brigadier General Ignacio San Martín, served as a spokesman for the military interests in the province and managed to convince Perón to increase state investment in the military factories on the city's outskirts. In 1951 the government created the Fábrica de Motores y Automotores to build the engines that had formerly been imported and assembled in the airplane factories. A year later, the Justicialist government agreed to consolidate Córdoba's factories and create a major military industrial complex, the Industrias Aeronáuticas y Mecánicas del Estado. IAME, renamed Dirección Nacional de Fabricaciones e Investigaciones Aeronáuticas (DINFIA) in 1957 and finally simply Industrias Mecánicas del Estado (IME), established Córdoba as the premier industrial center in the interior, ending its reputation as a predominantly agrarian province and its dependence on agricultural exports for economic sustenance. The mechanical factories of the IAME complex profoundly transformed the local industrial culture, introducing new technologies and labor processes, and the modern managerial practices of factory production. Its effects on the labor market and even on Córdoba's notoriously hidebound traditionalism and social conservatism were also considerable. The new industries established demands for engineering skills that in turn prompted a reform of its universities' venerable and slightly outdated classical education and the upgrading of their engineering departments.[8] Revealingly, the *ingeniero* would become in the 1950s a figure of prestige in the city, competing with the liberal professionals in law and medicine as a paradigm of upper and middle class respectability and achievement.

IAME's operations were concentrated in the outlying industrial complex, but the military had factories and workshops spread all over the city and its outskirts. One of its operations, for example, was a tractor factory in Ferreyra, a sparsely populated district on the city's southeast corner, where cows still grazed (see Figure 1). The Ferreyra factory would later

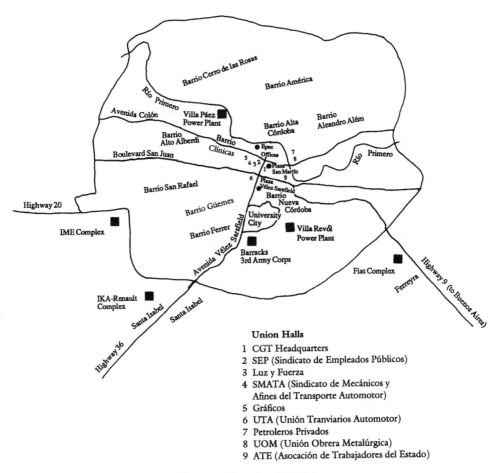

Union Halls

1 CGT Headquarters
2 SEP (Sindicato de Empleados Públicos)
3 Luz y Fuerza
4 SMATA (Sindicato de Mecánicos y Afines del Transporte Automotor)
5 Gráficos
6 UTA (Unión Tranviarios Automotor)
7 Petroleros Privados
8 UOM (Unión Obrera Metalúrgica)
9 ATE (Asocación de Trabajadores del Estado)

Figure 1 The city of Córdoba.

emerge as one of the centers of the Cordoban automobile industry, but in the early 1950s it was just one of IAME's some 55 industrial establishments, which collectively employed 10,000 workers.[9] The major site of IAME's production and the principal source of factory employment in the city remained the industrial park in the city's southwest corner, where almost 9,000 workers and an administrative staff numbering several hundred was found. By the time of Perón's overthrow in 1955, the IAME factories were producing a wide range of transport vehicles: commercial and military planes, the Graciela car—nicknamed the Justicialista, it was sparingly produced and had few sales but was important for its symbolic value—jeeps and army trucks, and the Puma motorcycle. By the mid-1950s, Córdoba was the second largest producer of motorcycles in the world, after Milan, and the city streets swarmed with droning Pumas built in the IAME factories until the automotive boom at the end of the decade made affordable, domestically produced cars available to the city's middle and, briefly, working classes. Within the IAME complex there existed a military-staffed and administered technical school to train workers needed for the more specialized jobs in the plants. For the military managers of the IAME works, the factories were an extension of the barracks, and the strict military discipline that had always characterized the IAME operations continued throughout the years of Peronist rule. Unionization was prohibited, management's authority on the shop floor was absolute, and the IAME factories gained a reputation as one of the country's few modern and efficient industries, although it was notorious in the local working class for the harshness of its dealings with its labor force.[10]

IAME had many effects on Córdoba's subsequent economic development. First, it reinforced the view of Córdoba as an attractive site for industrial investments, one that could successfully compete with Buenos Aires in certain areas. The development of local engineering expertise and of the core of skilled workers needed in the continuous-flow mechanical factories explained part of this appeal; so did the preponderant role played by the military in the industrialization of the city. The formation of an experienced labor force, one subject to the rigors of military discipline and renowned for its tractability, was a major enticement for companies that wished to avoid the labor disputes and personnel problems that they had come to associate with Perón's Argentina. Industrial development was further aided by the experience Cordoban political leaders had gained in what might be called the politics of industrialization. Government officials learned the value of boosterism and industrial promotion; they learned how to court investment through tax breaks, subsidies, and the lax enforcement of labor codes. Sabattini's electric power projects especially brought benefits, as Córdoba could lure industrial investment through the discount rates made possible by ample hydroelectric power. Cheap electric power had been one of General San Martín's principal arguments in convincing Perón to establish the Fábrica de Motores y Automotores, and the importance of electric power carried over into the IAME expansion and the era of multinational investment in the mechanical industries. In a 1964 survey of the leading thirty-two industrial establishments in the province, the great majority of which were located in the capital city, most pointed to the availability of cheap electric power as the principal reason for establishing their plants in Córdoba rather than in the other provinces or even in Buenos Aires.[11]

Electric power proved to be the midwife of Córdoba's postwar industrialization. Sabattini's hydroelectric projects of the 1930s were complemented by the provincial government's 1959 Plan Ansaldo, which permitted Italian capital to finance two great power plants, Dean Funes and Pilar, and gave Córdoba what was indisputably the most extensive electric power industry in the country outside of Buenos Aires. In the early 1960s, thermal energy sources were tapped and EPEC undertook a rapid expansion program and constructed new plants, transforming substations, and powerlines. Though its resources were already being overtaxed by then and the demands of the new mechanical industries and consumers soon threatened the province's economic base, Córdoba still had a relative advantage in courting industrial investment via discount electric rates. In 1965, Córdoba was the second province after Buenos Aires in yearly electric power generated. In that year it produced 865,086 kilowatts (kw) of power while its closest competitors, Santa Fe and Mendoza, lagged considerably behind with 443,865 and 667,918 kw, respectively.[12]

The success of the IAME factories established Córdoba as the country's favored site for investment in the mechanical industries. The subsequent transformation of the local economy occurred with extraordinary swiftness. In 1946, 47.9 percent of the industrial jobs in the city were concentrated in the light, traditional industries: slaughterhouses, breweries, flour mills, and a few small textile plants. Another 9 percent were found in what could be termed intermediary industries, primarily in cement production. Although the remaining 43 percent were in "nontraditional" sectors, almost all of those jobs were concentrated in two enterprises: the Fábrica Militar de Aviones and the workshops of the Ferrocarril del Estado, a collection of repair shops not engaged in manufacturing at all. Just seven years later, the impact of the IAME factories was obvious in the changes in industrial employment. In 1953, 63 percent of the industrial labor force was found in the nontraditional sector, overwhelmingly in the city's military factories. The IAME complex had begun a process later continued and intensified by the automobile firms. By 1961, 75 percent of the industrial labor force was in the "dynamic" sector, synonymous in Córdoba with the mechanical industries, while the light and intermediate industries absorbed only 20 percent and 5 percent, respectively, of industrial workers. Similarly, by 1961 the mechanical industries were accounting for 83 percent of the value of total industrial production in the city.[13]

In the 1950s, Córdoba became the center of a new kind of industrial development in Latin America, one characterized by extremely rapid rates of growth but concentrated in a single, technologically complex industrial sector and lacking the range of economic, social, and political changes generally associated with a genuine process of industrialization. Building on the province's tradition in the aeronautical and mechanical industries, the military and Cordoban Peronist politicians encouraged Perón to court foreign automobile companies and to get them to establish their plants in Córdoba. The automobile industry, for Perón just as it would be for Frondizi, was prized as much for its symbolic as its economic value, automotive production being considered the sine qua non for advancement into the ranks of the developed nations. In addition Perón was faced with the failure of his recent industrial policies. The strict controls on imports and the abandonment of Argentina by Ford, General Motors, and other automobile assemblers had led to a severe shortage of new vehicles and a deterioration of the existing stock. Perón was thus forced to either negotiate with foreign automotive manufacturers or see valuable foreign exchange lost to automobile imports.[14]

Fiat signed an agreement with the Justicialist government on September 24, 1954, to purchase IAME's tractor factory in Ferreyra as its first step toward building a major motor vehicle complex there. In the negotiations, Fiat played skillfully on the government's vulnerability, and Perón, his regime by then in full crisis, had to accept the terms laid down by the Italian company. First, the Argentine government facilitated Fiat's purchase of the tractor factory by awarding the company a credit through the Banco Industrial that greatly reduced the final cost of purchase. In addition, to raise its working capital Fiat received permission to import some 2,000 of the model Fiat 1400 at an undervalued exchange rate and to sell the cars at a price that was higher than what they were sold for in Italy. Fiat was thereby able to defray a significant amount of the costs of importing machinery and retooling the tractor factory and acquired a significant foreign investment at minimal risk and for a capital investment of only $1.5 million.[15]

Perón's negotiations with the American industrialist Henry J. Kaiser, and later with Kaiser's son, Edgar, produced an agreement similarly advantageous to the investor. The agreement signed on January 19, 1955, for the construction of a Kaiser automotive complex in Santa Isabel, on the southwest outskirts of Córdoba, established a joint state-private venture between Kaiser-Frazer Industries and IAME, with $10 million and $5.7 million, respectively, to be invested while majority investment was expressly guaranteed to individual Argentine stockholders through private subscriptions sold on the Argentine stock exchange. The final division of stock was to be Kaiser-Frazer Industries 32 percent, IAME 20 percent, private stockholders 48 percent. Kaiser's junior partner status, however, was a mere formality, a ruse designed to protect the government from the criticism of economic nationalists over the agreement. Kaiser set as a condition for investment the promise that IAME would support Kaiser candidates and that the American company would thereby be assured control of the board of directors.[16]

The arrangement worked for the duration of Kaiser's participation in the company. The Americans never lost control of Industrias Kaiser Argentina (IKA), and Kaiser's management philosophy and business practices permeated the entire operation. Furthermore, like Fiat, Kaiser also received a loan under favorable terms from the Banco Industrial and wrangled concessions from Perón to minimize the cost of its original investment, among them the right to sell 1,000 Kaiser cars in the Argentine market. Kaiser's capital investment consisted largely of the transfer of used and even outdated equipment and machinery from its American operations to Córdoba. IAME received the right to produce some of the necessary tools, dies, jigs, and fixtures for IKA in return for its capital investment.[17]

The companies' only significant compromises in their negotiations were regarding the final site of investment. Both Fiat and Kaiser voiced some reservations about Córdoba as a suitable location for their plants. In the negotiations with Perón, Fiat had expressed interest in setting up its factories in Mendoza, thereby giving the company access to the promising Chilean market as well as to Argentina's. One of Kaiser's chief negotiators and the future president of IKA, James McCloud, preferred Rosario, which is closer to the country's principal market in Buenos Aires, to Córdoba as the site for the Kaiser plants.[18] The existence of a sizable

labor force with experience in the mechanical industries was an enticement to them but a minor one, as the companies well knew that their
production processes would require a predominantly unskilled labor
force and that even many of the skilled and semi-skilled workers they
needed would have to be retrained for their new jobs.[19] Córdoba was
finally agreed on as the site for investment mostly because of two factors:
the low cost of electric power and Perón's insistence, at the behest of
General San Martín and other military and civilian interests in the city,
that Córdoba be the site of the new plants.

IKA's stock subscriptions and IAME's investment were in Argentine
pesos, which were being devalued at an alarming rate after the agreement
was signed. This forced IKA to move quickly to start production as soon
as possible. By the end of 1956, the company had already completed
construction of a number of plants, was negotiating manufacturing licenses with automobile companies in Europe and the United States to
add new models, and was well advanced in the first stages of screening
the more than 12,000 applications it had received for jobs.[20] Kaiser's own
line of jeeps and cars was running off the assembly lines by early 1957.
At the end of 1958, the company signed an agreement with the Italian
company Alfa Romeo to manufacture the Alfa Romeo 1900, paying
$375,000 for the dies and agreeing to pay future royalties for the manu-
facturing license, the first such license IKA negotiated.[21] IKA would subsequently sign similar agreements with Volvo, American Motors, and,
most important, with Renault in 1959, as it attempted to diversify its
models and tailor production to local market tastes by moving beyond the
oversized and slightly garish line of Kaiser cars.

The Kaiser plants introduced concentrations of capital, labor, and technology on a scale that had been unknown in Argentine industry. Kaiser
had essentially transferred its Detroit operations to Argentina, and it
divided the Santa Isabel complex into separate units of production: forge,
press department, tool and die facilities, engine plant, vehicle assembly,
paint department, and electroplating plant. The large tool and die (or
matrices) plant produced all the press dies used for building Kaiser's own
line of cars; the engine plant and the forge, the largest in the country,
employed manufacturing and work processes that revolutionized the local
industrial culture, though they were increasingly outdated by the standards of the American and European automobile industries. Work in the
Kaiser plants had many idiosyncrasies—notably the ubiquity of batch
work as opposed to moving line production, a high incidence of model
tinkering, and, eventually, an extreme product mix—all of which required

considerable flexibility from the work force.[22] But generally IKA established a modern, mass production industry in Córdoba that encouraged the kind of industrial development begun by the IAME factories and helped to shape the peculiar character of life, work, and working class politics in Córdoba.

The Kaiser plants influenced the local industrial culture in myriad other ways as well. Because it operated on a scale larger than Fiat's and was up and running at an earlier date, IKA had a more direct effect on the city's subsequent industrial development. The combination of government legislation establishing minimum domestic content requirements in automobile production and IKA's lack of a parent company to act as source for components and industrial inputs led the company to undertake a radical program of vertical integration. IKA decided not to rely on the city's small bootleg parts manufacturers who made high mortality parts for motor vehicles (axle shafts, some gears, brake drums, simple machine castings and forgings), as it was suspicious of the metallurgical origin of these products and especially of their engineered tolerances. Instead, IKA began to set up its own parts manufacturers, factories that used "tooled-up" production processes as opposed to "job shop" processes—that is, factories that employed machine tools with the formal work rhythms and exacting quality control of mass production industries.[23]

The result of this policy was an improvement in the quality of the Kaiser cars, but it also reinforced the unusually concentrated nature of Córdoba's industrial development. Hundreds of small metallurgical workshops did emerge in the shadow of Córdoba's automotive industry, operating as suppliers of basic parts and accessories (speedometers, mirrors, spark plugs) to IKA and Fiat and as direct parts manufacturers on the replacement market. Nevertheless the owners of the metal-working establishments were generally small-time operators, and a local industrial bourgeoisie worthy of the name in the metallurgical industry never emerged in the city.

IKA's various component plants—Transax (axles), sold to Ford in 1967; the ILASA factories (cables, electrical components, and carburetors); Pajas Blancas; the various Santa Isabel plants—as well as independent foreign manufacturers, such as Thompson Ramco and Associated Spring, that were eventually attracted to the lucrative local market and established factories in the city, fulfilled most of IKA's manufacturing needs. They also later sold to Fiat and other companies, the interdependence and interchangeability of the automobile companies' parts and components having been one of the outstanding characteristics of the Argentine industry.[24] For example, the Transax plant for many years would be the sole supplier of rear axles for all the automobile companies operating in Argentina, and IKA's transmission shop in the Santa Isabel complex was the supplier of the transmissions used by all the companies save Chrysler. IKA's vertical strategy advanced so far that in 1961 it could claim that the first Renault model built under license, the Dauphine, had a domestic content of 72 percent.[25]

Despite the enormous demand for sheet metal in automotive production, a steel plant was never established in Córdoba. As would other automobile firms operating in Argentina, in the first years of production IKA and Fiat imported all their body sheet metal. In the early 1960s, however, IKA also began to purchase some sheet steel from the state-owned Sociedad Mixta Siderúrgica Argentina (SOMISA) mill in San Nicolás. Eventually IKA's vertical strategy came to include forged metals, and in 1965 it purchased Metalúrgica Tandil, the largest foundry in the country, in Buenos Aires Province. Then, with its acquisition in 1966 of the Perdriel plant to build high-precision machine tools, IKA's vertical strategy was finally complete.[26]

One unintended effect of all these acquisitions was, as I mentioned, the highly fragmented character of the local metallurgical industry. The typical metallurgical establishment in Córdoba was a precarious undertaking, using primitive technologies and generally employing no more than a dozen workers, a situation that would have important repercussions later for the politics of the local Unión Obrera Metalúrgica (UOM).[27] IKA's vertical strategy, in a city that was already losing its industrial diversity, limited prospects for the development of a local industrial bourgeoisie and profoundly influenced industrial politics in Córdoba. Among other effects, for many years IKA's policies denied the metal trades' employers' association, the Cámara de Industrias Metalúrgicas, from acting as a serious interlocutor with the automotive firms or with the provincial government. Such policies deepened the rift between the automobile companies and the dependent metallurgical industry, triggering acrimonious confrontations in the city, and in the country generally, that would reach their climax during the Peronist governments of 1973 to 1976.

IKA had initially aspired to more than vertical integration of its industrial operations. The Kaiser executives and managers had brought with them a set of typically American attitudes toward work in a foreign culture—seeing themselves as a mixture of the missionary and the plantation owner—and these attitudes were soon inflated by the small vanities that their exalted position in Cordoban society brought them. The first years of sales were promising, and their status as representatives of the largest and most profitable company in the city bred a kind of stern but benevolent paternalism among company officials. Independent of the sobering control that was exercised over the other automobile manufacturers in Argentina by their headquarters back home, IKA executives briefly had delusions of transforming Córdoba into their own version of the company town, to be centered around the IKA industrial park in Santa Isabel. IKA threw itself into a wide variety of community affairs for this purpose. An extensive program to build low-cost worker housing was drafted by the company, though this plan was one of the first casualties when the palmy days of the late 1950s and early 1960s came to an end. The company did manage to establish its own medical clinics for its workers as well as various educational institutions open to the community at large. In 1960 it set up the Academia Arguello and Instituto IKA, the former a private elementary school and the latter a technical institute.[28] The Instituto IKA was the cornerstone of the company's community service program, and its activities distilled much of the company's paternalist intent. Offering a three-year work-study program, the institute served the purposes of forming a new core of skilled workers for the local mechanical industries; indoctrinating its students with a slightly puerile, but in the company's eyes no doubt uplifting, "IKA philosophy" of sobriety, thrift, and company loyalty; and probably screening undesirables from employment in the IKA plants. It was also a masterful public relations gesture and won the company endless encomiums in the Cordoban press. IKA's sponsorship of numerous cultural and recreational activities, particularly sports clubs, completed its community service programs.[29]

The ambitions behind the community service program did not outlive slumping sales and Renault's buyout of IKA in 1967. The French company, scornful of what it viewed as IKA's moralizing and paternalism, abandoned what remained of IKA's community programs, retaining only the technical school and giving it a more Gallic and professional personality. IKA's fanciful schemes had been born of the unquestionable success it enjoyed as a purely business venture in the early years of automotive production in Argentina. IKA had not only dominated but also nearly controlled the motor vehicle industry for the first half-decade of its existence. The company had increased its volume of annual production from a modest 16,082 vehicles for the 1957–58 fiscal year to 36,047 vehicles three years later. Industrial employment had risen from 2,709 in June 1958 to more than 9,500 in July 1962.[30] Its daring investments in parts and components plants in those years, and its attempt at industrial diversification, expanding beyond vehicle production to produce hydraulic presses, soldering machinery, and other nonautomotive products via licensing agreements with various foreign companies, were a testimony to vigorous entrepreneurship. Until 1962 IKA had been the annual industry leader in profits, and it was the annual leader in total sales until 1967.[31]

In addition to the IAME and IKA complexes, Córdoba's other industrial establishments in the mechanical industries were Fiat's Ferreyra plants and a small Perkins factory. Perkins, a British engine manufacturer, established its factory in the early 1960s as a supplier of motors for a variety of uses—tractors, cars, and air compressors, among others. Located in Ferreyra near the Fiat complex, it began production in 1963 with a work force of 280 production workers, 80 administrative employees, and 20 supervisors.[32] The Perkins plant thus entered the market just as the Cordoban automotive boom was starting to falter, a fact that may have discouraged the company from undertaking costly expansion plans and thereby have allowed it to better adapt to new conditions by virtue of its specialization and reputation for high quality. As in the other mechanical establishments, its labor force comprised predominantly unskilled workers engaged in mass production who shared a common workplace culture that permitted their participation in the labor militancy of the 1970s.

IKA's major competitor and the second locus of economic power in Córdoba was the Fiat complex in Ferreyra. In the early years, Fiat was more of a potential rival than an actual one, as the Italian company held back from car and truck production until 1960. The two principal Fiat factories, Concord and Materfer, were initially devoted to tractor and railroad equipment production, respectively, and a third plant, Grandes Motores Diesel, manufactured the heavy diesel engines used in trucks, buses, and railroad engines.[33] In 1958, Fiat retooled its Concord plant— the former IAME Pampa tractor factory and the progenitor of Fiat's investment in Córdoba—to convert it to car and truck production. Though at first the Concord factory was an integrated production unit, with all the mechanical and assembly operations of the IKA complex, it always operated on a much smaller scale and was more heavily dependent on outside suppliers (among them IKA's own factories) than was Kaiser. Fiat also had a much more muted impact on the city, being somewhat more discreet in the civic role it, too, assumed and more reluctant than IKA to undertake the same type of bold and long-range planning.

Despite an initial timorousness with its investment, Fiat's operations were a major industrial undertaking and the Ferreyra plants represented the second largest concentration of manufacturing might and industrial labor in the entire Argentine interior, second only to IKA. The figures on production and industrial employment for the Grandes Motores Diesel (GMD) plant are the most complete prior to 1960 and show a modest but steady growth. GMD began production in 1956 and by January 1958 had a labor force of 133 production workers and 74 administrative employees, numbers that would rise to 331 and 110, respectively, by the end of that year.[34] Despite sales figures that were notably inferior to those of IKA, the number of production hours—hours directly related to the elaboration and assembly of motors and engines—rose considerably. By late 1959, GMD had a labor force of 432 production workers and 120 administrative employees. Production hours, which were 60,000 in 1957 and 247,000 in 1958, jumped to 430,000 in 1959.[35]

The hydraulic presses in the forge, the machine tools that manufactured the engine parts in the Concord factory, and the large and fully mechanized assembly sections and elaborate quality control procedures all indicated a production process that, in terms of technology and organization, was comparable to IKA's. The scale of production, including a labor force that always remained about half the size of IKA's, and the degree of vertical integration were what made Fiat's operations humbler. Thus annual production figures were initially more modest, though they would overtake IKA's in the late 1960s. Fiat's smaller scale, in fact, proved to be an advantage as competition in the industry grew more severe in the 1960s. Between 1962 and 1976, Fiat's annual profits surpassed IKA's in every year but one, 1965.[36] Fiat's greater resiliency in the market was due to multiple factors: lower labor costs owing to the absence of effective union representation in the plants; smaller financial burdens thanks to the financing done directly through the company's Turin headquarters; and greater flexibility due to the fact it was building its own models and not bound to cumbersome, costly licensing agreements, as IKA was until the 1967 Renault buyout.[37]

Fiat's decision to begin to manufacture its line of diminutive cars was not strictly a response to IKA's promising sales figures. The government was actively promoting the development of a national automobile industry. Despite the IKA and Fiat contracts, the industry continued to be hampered by the vestiges of Peronist nationalist economic legislation for several years. In 1958, Frondizi pushed through the Argentine Congress law 14.780. The new law guaranteed equal juridical treatment for foreign and local capital and repealed the protectionist thrust of Peronist industrial policy by allowing foreign companies to make their investments in the form of goods, equipment, or patents, a policy Perón himself had already accepted in principle with the Kaiser agreement but had been reluctant to acknowledge publicly. Most important, it allowed foreign companies to remit their profits without restrictions, something Perón had not been willing to accept. Another of Frondizi's measures, decree 3.693, gave tax breaks to companies that submitted production plans for the local manufacture of cars and trucks that met quotas on the use of locally produced parts.

Frondizi's industrial strategy generally envisioned a high degree of regional specialization in which federal and provincial policy would be coordinated to encourage production in certain favored industrial sectors. The priority he gave to the establishment of a national automobile industry, and the comparative advantages that Córdoba offered, meant that federal policy initially contributed to the industry's growth there. However, the Frondizi legislation also planted the seeds of the city's future industrial decline. The tax breaks, liberal licensing agreements, and incentives offered to automobile manufacturers were not extended to other industries, and Córdoba was thenceforth tied to a regional form of industrial specialization characterized by a modern, technologically sophisticated, capital-intensive but undiversified industrial base. More important, the legislation did not allow even that specialization to prosper, as Frondizi's measures quickly attracted other automobile companies, companies that were by then less worried about potential labor problems and therefore chose to locate their operations closer to the principal domestic market in Buenos Aires. Córdoba's motor vehicle industry was growing at a fast rate, but there were already signs of impending difficulties. As early as 1959, more American and European car manufacturers were planning the establishment of manufacturing facilities as a result of Frondizi's legislation.[38] Within the next three years, Ford, Chrysler, General Motors, Citroën, and Mercedes Benz would all have manufacturing establishments in and around Buenos Aires.

The long-range effects of the Frondizi government's economic policies were nonetheless disguised by the great industrial explosion that was taking place in Córdoba in the late 1950s and early 1960s. The swiftness of Córdoba's economic transformation was evidenced in all the leading economic indicators—electricity consumption, levels of industrial production, and industrial employment—which show that industrial growth was concentrated between 1947 and 1965.[39] Between 1947 and 1960, industrial employment alone grew at an annual rate of 3 percent a year and then was only slightly lower until 1963, the year that marks the first serious stalling of the local economy.[40] The mechanical industries were literally the engines of industrial growth in these years, and they turned a sleepy provincial city into an industrial metropolis in less than two decades. For five years in particular, from 1957 to 1962, Córdoba was an anomaly in Argentina, a thriving industrial center at a time of widespread industrial stagnation in the rest of the country. Córdoba was an island of prosperity and opportunity during the years it enjoyed its unassailable position in motor vehicle production—of cars especially but also jeeps and trucks, as well as the airplanes and military transport vehicles that the IAME factories continued to produce. With the market temporarily cornered, the companies were able to reinvest, expand production, and turn their industrial complexes into the hubs of the local economy. Thenceforth, the fate of the local mechanical industries directly affected all aspects of the city, not only its economy and class structure but also its politics.

The end of the boom in the local mechanical industries was apparent by the middle of the 1960s and was an established fact by the end of the decade. The Córdoba-based companies had gone from near total control of the market in 1958 to less than a 40 percent share by 1969.[41] Moreover, when the crisis in the mechanical industries came, Córdoba was still an industrial neophyte, and its economy in many ways had changed only superficially. More than a decade of intense industrial activity certainly had failed to produce an industrial revolution in the city, and after the mid-1960s the local economy returned to its original, more lethargic pace. Only increased production in the traditional industries, particularly textiles and food processing, sustained modest industrial growth. In 1961, the traditional industries had contributed between 17 percent and 33 percent of the value of total industrial production. By 1969 they again contributed one-half.[42]

The ultimate result of the Frondizi legislation for the automobile industry generally was consolidation and internationalization. Throughout Argentina the small, domestically owned, and undercapitalized automobile companies that had mushroomed during the first years of the Frondizi presidency simply shut down their operations, while others were bought out by local manufacturers, as happened when Siam di Tella was purchased by IKA in 1965. Of the completely Argentine-owned motor vehicle manufacturers, only the state-owned IAME complex remained in production after 1966.[43] Other companies with complete or partial Argentine ownership, IKA and a company called IAFA most notably, were taken over by the multinationals whose licenses they had been using (Renault and Peugeot, respectively). In the IKA buyout, Renault broke with its traditional distaste for direct involvement in foreign manufacturing, having historically preferred the safer and lucrative licensing arrangements. With its decision to buy the IKA empire came a determination to assert complete control of the Cordoban subsidiary. Between 1967 and 1970, Renault bought out IKA's Argentine public and private stockholders to gain a majority share of the company and integrated its operations into the French multinational's organization.[44] Nationalist legislation passed in 1971 and 1973 that established stricter domestic content requirements and quotas for Argentine members on the automobile companies' boards of directors and professional and technical staffs could not reverse what the market had determined. Bankruptcies, multinational takeovers, and industrial consolidation were the inevitable responses in an industry that had developed artificially, was overextended, and was producing far more than the domestic market could consume.

Given the undiversified nature of the city's industrial development, Córdoba was perhaps more affected by these changes than any other part of the country, yet the local economy appeared to adapt. The IAME military factories were greatly insulated from the decline, given their access to government funding and their near total dependence on defense contracts. Moreover, the decline of the mechanical industries was relative—an adaption to a smaller share of the market, not an absolute collapse. Córdoba's unemployment figures, for example, remained relatively low, and the growth of the traditional industries somewhat compensated for the slowdown in IKA-Renault's and Fiat's hiring (Tables 1.1 and 1.2). Nor did the automobile companies undertake massive layoffs to compensate for their declining market share. In 1970, 35 percent of the labor force

Table 1.1 Participation of the industrial sector as an employer

Year	Workers employed in traditional industries (%)	Workers employed in mechanical industries (%)
1946	74.2	25.8
1953	53.2	46.8
1959	43.2	56.8
1964	34.2	65.8
1969	43.6	56.4

Source: Aldo A. Arnaudo, "El crecimiento de la ciudad de Córdoba en el último cuarto de siglo," *Economía de Córdoba,* vol. 8, no. 2 (December 1970), pp. 8–9.

Table 1.2 Growth of employment in industry, shown as percent change

Years	Traditional industries (%)	Dynamic industries (%)
1947–1960	7.3	129.8
1960–1965	76.4	84.1
1965–1970	50.4	−32.6

Source: Aldo A. Arnaudo, "El crecimiento de la ciudad de Córdoba en el último cuarto de siglo," *Economía de Córdoba,* vol. 8, no. 2 (December 1970), pp. 8–9.

was employed in service occupations; 19 percent in commerce, banking, and insurance; 10 percent in miscellaneous occupations; and a healthy 35 percent in industry, a figure indicative of a thriving industrial city and not a declining one. Most notably, 40 percent of this industrial labor force was still found in the mechanical industries, and unemployment actually declined in the city, from 9.5 percent in 1964 to 4.4 percent in 1971.[45] The labor force in the IKA-Renault plants remained relatively stable through the 1970s, and problems with layoffs were episodic, not part of a systematic company policy of hiring and firing to adjust to changes in the business cycle.

The growth in industrial employment in the traditional industries was thus not primarily the result of unemployed automobile workers finding work in the city's textile plants, breweries, and other traditional industries. Those industries seem to have been more prone to absorbing younger workers just entering the labor force rather than unemployed auto workers, though they did not hire at a pace fast enough to avoid a notable rate of teenage unemployment.[46] Although after 1966 there would be periodic layoffs in the Cordoban automobile industry and even a few attempts at mass firings, notably at IKA-Renault in 1970 and 1974 and at Fiat in 1971, they were bitterly and effectively resisted by the unions and were generally responses to prolonged confrontations and strikes rather than attempts on the part of the companies to correct slumping sales and rising costs. The cyclical reduction of their labor forces became the automobile companies' policy only after 1976, when the military governments suspended collective bargaining, prohibited the right to strike, and suppressed the unions.

The malaise of the local economy that underlay the labor militancy after 1966 was not fully recognizable in aggregate figures of unemployment or even industrial production. Rather, it was revealed in the deterioration of the working conditions in the two major automotive complexes and, to a lesser extent, in the dependent metallurgical industry. In the case of the dozens of small metallurgical shops that supplied the automotive plants with the simpler parts and accessories that the companies found more cost-effective to job out, the new market conditions often meant bankruptcy. For the few that managed to hold on, the market prompted them to tighten up their work rules and take a harder line in all their dealings with workers. A similar but more aggravated condition existed in the Fiat and IKA-Renault plants, and there the city's economic difficulties would be played out most tellingly.

The automobile companies and their workers were part of a distinct social environment in Córdoba and as such were subject to certain influences, apparently exogenous but in reality closely linked to events in the plants. Among those influences were rapid urbanization and the peculiarities of the class structure that resulted from the city's sudden industrial development. Urban growth occurred rapidly after 1955 and was fastest in the city's southern fringes, the new working class neighborhoods surrounding the IKA-Renault and Fiat factories (see Figure 1). In the city's eastern districts, site of the food processing, textile, and other light industries, Córdoba's traditional working class neighborhoods experienced little growth, and limits on housing and population density seemed to have been reached well before the industrial boom of the 1950s. Nor did the older, downtown neighborhoods close to the Plaza San Martín change. Neighborhoods such as Barrio Clínicas, once a patrician stronghold and now the preserve of Córdoba's huge student community, and Alto Alberdi remained the most densely populated and demographically dormant parts of the city, absorbing just enough new workers to keep pace with declining birth rates and a steady death rate.[47]

The city's population increases were concentrated in the exclusive north and northeast districts and especially in the new southern working class zones. Surrounding Fiat were the Ferreyra, San Lorenzo, Dean Funes, and Empalme neighborhoods where the Fiat automotive proletariat now lived. Those neighborhoods had been transformed from open lots and cow pastures in 1950 into a collective community of 12,503 in 1970. Similarly, the Villa el Libertador, Barrio Comercial, and Santa Isabel neighborhoods adjacent to the IKA-Renault complex had a working class population of 23,565 in 1970, compared with only a few families who had lived there two decades before.[48] The formation of young working class neighborhoods and the concentration there of workers from the automotive industries partly shifted the locus of working class power to the south of the city. The problems of work in the automotive plants were thus a shared, lived experience and gave the neighborhoods their own identity. Though participation in community affairs was low and few neighborhood organizations appear to have existed in the new residential zones, bonds of sympathy and solidarity were nonetheless established. Among other effects, this gave the automotive proletariat a mobilizing power that made them a far more formidable adversary than if they had been, like the Buenos Aires working class, occupationally heterogeneous and dispersed over a wide geographic area.

The swiftness of urbanization stretched the availability of existing housing in the city, and Córdoba's industrial boom had its counterpart in a construction boom in two- and three-room dwellings during the same years. Housing construction generally kept pace with demand, and Córdoba managed to absorb its population increases; though there were housing shortages, they lacked the severity of housing shortages that generally characterized postwar Latin American urbanization. In 1960, of the existing housing in Córdoba, 55,389 of the family dwellings, or 43.8 percent, had been constructed between 1947 and 1960.[49]

Much of this housing consisted of makeshift bungalows built by the workers themselves. Thanks to easy credit available in the first years of the automotive boom and, especially, to low property values, workers would typically buy a small lot in one of the new neighborhoods, put up the frame and roof of the house, and then buy materials and finish the work over a period of several years. Such houses were generally overcrowded; the problem in Córdoba was less the scarcity of housing than it was the quality of housing. Figures for 1965 indicate that 8 percent of the occupied housing in the city could have been classified as "substandard," and 35.5 percent had a density above the average recommended 1.3 persons per room, but such figures were still well under those of Buenos Aires.[50] Housing receded even further as a major urban problem in the years that followed. By 1970, the number of inhabitants per housing unit had decreased from 4.62 in 1947 to 4.22 in 1970, and Córdoba experienced only mildly the urban squatter problem so common in Buenos Aires; the *villas miserias* that surround the city today are the legacy of the military governments of 1976 to 1983 and not of the industrializing Córdoba of the 1950s and 1960s.[51]

In this light, arguments that posit social anomie and working class alienation resulting from rapid industrialization as the explanations for the labor militancy and urban insurrections in Córdoba in the late 1960s and early 1970s certainly appear questionable.[52] Other indexes offer slightly more grounds for such assumptions, but they too are hardly conclusive.

The problems of rapid urbanization seem to have been most acutely felt in the inadequacy of certain basic public services, conditions that were particularly severe in the new working class neighborhoods. As early as 1960 there were problems in the city due to the lack of an adequate urban transport system to serve the needs of the commuting industrial workers.[53] There were many complaints about inadequate municipal services such as street cleaning, trash disposal, urban lighting, and street paving. Water shortages became commonplace by the late 1960s, with frequent cutoffs, some of them lasting several weeks, and poorly constructed sewage systems that caused backups and periodic flooding. Air pollution and traffic congestion were notoriously bad, though they were problems that mostly afflicted downtown residents, as air pollution from vehicle exhaust was a greater problem than industrial pollution from the automotive complexes. No conclusions can be drawn from urban problems, however. The problems were not unique to Córdoba. They affected to a greater or lesser degree all the major cities in Argentina; housing problems, for example, seem to have been less severe in Córdoba than in other urban centers. The Cordoban working class made only occasional passing reference to urban problems in their protests of the late 1960s and early 1970s, being far more concerned with problems directly related to work and politics.

The impact of demographics on the social contours that shaped relations between business and labor in the city was more direct and significant for working class politics. Between 1947 and 1970, Córdoba was the fastest growing city in Argentina. The city's reputation as the "Argentine Detroit," a city that offered abundant work, technical education at the plants, and some of the highest wages in the country, drew workers from the Cordoban countryside and surrounding provinces, as well as a sizable number of immigrants from neighboring countries. The migrations to Córdoba had actually begun in the thirties and early forties and Agustín Tosco's trek to the city from Coronel Moldes was part of a massive flow out of the Cordoban countryside to the provincial capital during the depression years. These migrations gained momentum and grew more varied with the expansion of the mechanical industries. Population increases in the postwar years were great and seem to have lost impetus only once the local mechanical industries lost their dynamism as industrial employers. After 1970 Buenos Aires would regain its preeminence as the city of opportunity, and Córdoba thenceforth would have to rely largely on the birth rate among its own citizens for its comparatively modest population increases. Yet from 1947 to 1970, Córdoba was the scene of one of the major demographic revolutions in twentieth-century

Argentina. In those years, Córdoba had the greatest number of migrants ever received by a city of the interior. Between 1947 and 1966 alone, the city's population increased by some 300,000, of whom more than 152,000 were migrants who had left their farms and small towns for a chance at jobs and a new life in one of Córdoba's factories (Table 1.3).[54]

Additional figures break down the migrations further and give a clearer picture of the character of Córdoba's demographic growth. The first and most notable trend, repeating the previous experience of Buenos Aires and that of other Latin American cities, was the preponderance of women in these migrant flows. The figures for migrants to Córdoba between 1947 and 1966 reveal 48 percent were men and 52 percent were women, a significant balance in favor of the women (Table 1.4). However, this was not as great a difference as has generally been the case in other examples

Table 1.3 Demographics, Córdoba, 1947–1966

Year	Total population	Births	Migrants	Deaths	Net increase
1947	386,828	6,870	2,491	2,930	6,431
1948	393,259	11,089	8,495	4,237	15,347
1949	408,606	11,711	5,842	4,305	13,248
1950	421,854	12,310	8,700	4,267	16,743
1951	438,606	12,400	8,258	4,510	16,148
1952	454,745	12,648	5,317	4,576	13,389
1953	468,134	12,687	4,647	4,555	12,779
1954	480,913	12,620	6,143	4,534	14,229
1955	495,142	12,751	8,817	4,015	17,553
1956	512,695	13,301	10,320	4,907	18,714
1957	531,409	14,787	7,078	5,640	16,225
1958	547,634	13,651	7,053	5,097	14,607
1959	563,241	13,940	5,492	4,119	14,313
1960	577,554	14,196	10,096	5,445	18,847
1961	596,401	14,319	7,970	5,437	16,852
1962	613,253	13,643	9,689	5,779	17,553
1963	630,806	14,293	8,439	5,307	17,425
1964	648,231	14,949	8,835	5,501	18,283
1965	666,514	14,873	8,372	6,131	17,114
1966	683,628	14,615	10,422	6,200	18,837

Source: Carlos E. Sánchez and Walter E. Schulthess, Población e inmigración en la ciudad de Córdoba, 1947–1966, Facultad de Ciencias Económicas, Universidad Nacional de Córdoba, 1967, p. 7; Dirección General de Estadística, Censos, e Investigaciones, Ministerio de Hacienda, Economía y Previsión Social, "Estadísticas Demográficas y Vitales: Población, 1901–1970."

Table 1.4 Migrations to Córdoba, 1947–1966

Year	Total no. of migrants	Men (%)	Women (%)
1947	2,491	65.4	34.5
1948	8,495	51.4	48.6
1949	5,842	51.5	48.5
1950	8,700	42.5	57.5
1951	8,258	57.3	42.7
1952	5,317	41.7	58.3
1953	4,647	46.0	54.0
1954	6,143	46.7	53.3
1955	8,817	47.7	52.3
1956	10,320	50.7	49.3
1957	7,078	56.4	43.6
1958	7,053	52.8	47.2
1959	5,492	51.8	48.2
1960	10,096	43.2	56.8
1961	7,970	45.8	54.2
1962	9,689	44.5	55.5
1963	8,439	47.1	52.9
1964	8,835	47.4	52.6
1965	8,372	41.2	56.8
1966	10,422	30.6	69.4
Total	152,476	48.0	52.0

Source: Carlos E. Sánchez and Walter E. Schulthess, *Población e inmigración en la ciudad de Córdoba, 1947–1966,* Facultad de Ciencias Económicas, Universidad Nacional de Córdoba, 1967, p. 3; Dirección General de Estadística, Censos, e Investigaciones, Ministerio de Hacienda, Economía y Previsión Social, "Estadísticas Demográficas y Vitales: Población, 1901–1970."

of rapid urbanization in twentieth-century Latin America. Furthermore, considerably heavier male migrations took place between 1955 and 1959, at the height of the industrial boom. The character of Córdoba's industrial development determined its particular attraction for male migrants. Labor forces in the automobile industry have historically been predominantly male, and Córdoba was an extreme example of the preference of automobile companies for male workers. There were virtually no women found in the Cordoban plants nor indeed in any of the automotive manufacturing operations in Argentina; even in the trim shops, where women were hired in significant numbers in other countries, men operated the sewing machines used in upholstery manufacturing.[55] The nature of the city's industrial opportunities, specifically the companies' preference for male workers and the scant possibility women had of finding work in the plants, best explains the unusually high participation of men in the migrations to Córdoba in those years. The greater total number of female migrants simply reveals the even bleaker prospects for women in the countryside. Though women would find few jobs in the automobile plants, they would fare better in the expanding government bureaucracies, in commerce, and in domestic service, as well as in the industries such as textiles where they had always found work.

The outstanding feature of these migrations was their regional character. Demographic statistics show that in almost every year approximately half of the new arrivals were from Córdoba Province (Table 1.5). Presumably the province's predominantly agrarian economy encouraged many like young Tosco to try their luck in the city, as conditions in the Cordoban countryside remained difficult through the 1960s. But the later migrations were also more varied than they had been in Tosco's day. The migrants of the 1950s and 1960s were a heterogeneous group, with migrant flows in given years greatly depending on the local economic conditions in the migrants' own provinces or countries. Generally, however, there was a tendency for greater migration from Buenos Aires Province, the northwest (Catamarca, Jujuy, La Rioja, Salta, Santiago del Estero, Tucumán), and especially from the littoral provinces (Chaco, Corrientes, Entre Ríos, Formosa, Misiones, and Santa Fe) as well as from neighboring countries (Paraguay, Uruguay, and Bolivia) than from the Cuyo (Mendoza, San Juan, San Luis) or the sparsely populated south (Chubut, La Pampa, Neuquén, Río Negro, Santa Cruz, Tierra del Fuego). The heavy influx of migrants from Santa Fe and Entre Ríos especially represented a fundamental shift in the country's migratory patterns. Both provinces had historically been major contributors to the population flows from the Argentine countryside to Buenos Aires, and their attraction to Córdoba in the 1950s and 1960s attest to the powerful enticements that the new mechanical and ancillary industries were then offering. Immigration from bordering Latin American countries, though relatively modest, was another innovation in Cordoban demographic history. Of the waves of Spanish and Italian immigrants that had arrived in Argentina in the late nineteenth and early twentieth centuries, some had made their way across the pampa to Córdoba. Nevertheless, this was the city's first experience with one of the great population movements between Latin American countries, and for a brief period its fame as a prospering town with jobs and good money diverted many of the Paraguayans, Uruguayans, and Bolivians who might otherwise have gone to the major urban centers in their own countries or even to Buenos Aires.

Table 1.5 Origins of migrations to Córdoba, 1947–1966

Year	Córdoba (%) (province)	Buenos Aires (%) (province and city)	Littoral provinces (%)[a]	Northwest (%)[b]	Cuyo (%)[c]	South (%)[d]	Foreign countries (%)
1947	46.9	12.5	15.6	6.3	—	3.1	15.6
1948	43.5	7.9	10.5	17.1	1.3	2.6	17.1
1949	25.9	9.3	9.3	7.4	—	—	48.1
1950	60.5	3.7	8.6	11.2	1.2	6.2	8.6
1951	42.7	9.3	9.3	14.7	1.3	—	22.7
1952	62.2	6.1	8.2	2.1	—	4.0	18.4
1953	64.3	11.9	7.1	2.4	2.4	—	11.9
1954	50.0	8.6	8.6	5.2	3.5	—	24.1
1955	60.2	3.6	20.6	6.0	3.6	—	6.0
1956	47.9	9.6	20.2	3.2	1.0	2.1	16.0
1957	59.7	6.0	16.4	1.5	4.5	—	11.9
1958	49.2	9.2	7.7	10.8	7.7	6.2	9.2
1959	41.5	11.3	18.9	—	9.4	—	18.9
1960	41.8	11.2	19.4	12.2	2.0	3.2	10.2
1961	34.6	12.8	16.7	25.6	1.3	1.3	7.7
1962	49.5	6.3	21.1	20.0	—	—	3.1
1963	49.4	14.1	12.9	12.9	7.2	1.2	2.3
1964	49.4	7.9	20.2	16.9	2.2	—	3.4
1965	48.2	15.3	5.9	10.6	15.3	—	4.7
1966	39.7	4.3	22.4	24.1	4.3	.9	4.3

Source: Carlos E. Sánchez and Walter E. Schulthess, Población e inmigración en la ciudad de Córdoba, 1947–1966, Facultad de Ciencias Económicas, Universidad Nacional de Córdoba, 1967, p. 5; Dirección General de Estadística, Censos, e Investigaciones, Ministerio de Hacienda, Economía y Previsión Social, "Estadísticas Demográficas y Vitales: Población, 1901–1970."

a. Chaco, Corrientes, Entre Ríos, Formosa, Misiones, Santa Fe.
b. Catamarca, Jujuy, La Rioja, Salta, Santiago del Estero, Tucumán.
c. Mendoza, San Juan, San Luis.
d. Chubut, La Pampa, Neuquén, Río Negro, Santa Cruz, Tierra del Fuego.

The migratory patterns closely followed the fortunes of the local economy and slowed down considerably after 1966. The increase in the city's population from 666,514 in 1965 to 798,663 in 1970 revealed the fastest growth in its history and was well above the national average for those years, but the stagnation in the local labor market and the greater employment opportunities by then offered in Buenos Aires indicate that this population growth was primarily due to an increased birth rate. Whatever the source of this final spurt of rapid growth, it was the legacy of the previous twenty-five years of migrations that mattered as Córdoba entered a new period in its history after 1966. The salient demographic characteristic was the rapid creation of an industrial proletariat, much of it concentrated in a single industry. Córdoba had become the "youngest" city in Argentina, with 54 percent of its population under the age of 30, compared with 46 percent in both Buenos Aires and Rosario, also industrial centers that absorbed great numbers of young migrants.[56] In Córdoba, most of this young population was in the 18-to-30 age group, and in 1970, out of a population of nearly 800,000, an astounding 337,600 were working full- or part-time.[57] Moreover, the unusually high percentage of workers employed in the industrial sector and their concentration in the mechanical industries—in the IAME, Fiat, IKA-Renault, and Perkins plants, as well as in the city's numerous parts and components workshops—despite plodding growth and only slow increases in employment after 1965, remained a constant of the Cordoban class structure until the post-1976 military governments.

The Cordoban automotive boom had created the greatest concentration of industrial workers in the country outside of Buenos Aires. Of course the local working class was not confined to the mechanical industries. Spread over a wide range of activities, it included a core of highly skilled workers in the automotive complexes, the city's railroad repair shops, and the local electric power industry; common day laborers in the construction industry; print workers using technologies that had barely changed in half a century; and the great mass of unskilled assembly line and production workers on the IKA-Renault and Fiat payrolls. "Working class" was also a somewhat arbitrary distinction in a city with a poorly remunerated middle class in the government and university bureaucracies and in commerce. Workers and the white-collar class often lived side by side and shared a similar standard of living and life-style. Still, the concentration of Córdoba's industrial working class in the mechanical sector and the near lack of an identifiable proletarian culture in the city, and even of forms of association beyond those of the workplace and the unions, attest to a particular kind of economic development in which the mechanical industries and their labor forces established an unmistakable dominance, not only over the Cordoban economy, but in social and political arenas as well.

Córdoba's accelerated and concentrated industrial growth abruptly and incompletely introduced into a traditional society the workings of industrial capitalism. The boom in the mechanical industries transformed the city's rhythms and colonial ambience, but its effects were actually more superficial than the effects of industrialization in Buenos Aires. The industrial growth that had occurred in Buenos Aires in previous decades, despite its limitations and heavy dependence on the state, resembled a more genuine process of industrialization than what took place in Córdoba did. In Buenos Aires investment in industry, diversification, the formation of a heterogeneous working class and a native industrial bourgeoisie all repeated the experience of earlier industrializing economies. In Córdoba, the process was more abrupt and less complex, closer perhaps to one of the classic Latin American mining or agricultural booms than to a real process of industrialization. Indeed industrial Córdoba was to share many of the characteristics of an industrial mining town: the concentration of economic activity in essentially one sector; a near complete control of that sector by foreign capital; a heavily male, unskilled, young labor force; rapid growth and sudden decline.

The most significant result of Córdoba's industrial boom was unquestionably the formation of a strong factory proletariat. The Cordoban working class became a political actor of note between 1966 and 1976, and it had an immediate ability not only to affect local politics but also to exercise considerable influence at the national level, due at least partly to the nature of the city's recent economic development. Whereas in Buenos Aires the working class and its organizations had the competing influence of a powerful bourgeoisie, a bourgeoisie that was not without its contradictions but was on the whole hostile to working class interests, in Córdoba the workers had no serious class rivals. The old Cordoban aristocracy was little more than an identifiable social elite. Aristocratic names still dominated the lists of university deans and judgeships and appeared occasionally on the local boards of IKA-Renault, but the aristocracy's presence as a class in politics had been greatly diminished. In addition, the local industrial bourgeoisie was weak and divided; only the local metallurgical interests, grouped into the Cámara de Industrias Metalúrgicas, had any kind of unity, but their influence paled alongside the automobile firms. Industrialists in this and other traditional sectors had meager capital resources and never participated as investors or partners in the mechanical industries. The middle class was similarly weak and divided, comprising a minority of reasonably privileged liberal professionals and a majority of struggling school teachers, government and university functionaries, clerks and salespeople. Indeed of all the classes in Córdoba, only the university students, whose numbers often reached 10 percent of the city's population, had a sense of identity and power comparable to that of the working class.

Though some managerial positions were created by the industrial boom, the development of the automobile industry did not spawn a sizable new white-collar administrative class, nor did it favor the development of a local financial bourgeoisie.[58] The companies' character as essentially foreign entities with minimal Argentine participation, as in the case of IKA, or as multinational subsidiaries, as in the case of Renault and Fiat, meant that many managerial positions were staffed by their own nationals and that a major part of the financial work was done through their home offices or by the big Buenos Aires banks. The administrative offices for the automobile companies were in Buenos Aires, and except for some involvement with local parts and components factories, provincial banks watched most of the finance being handled by outsiders. Managerial positions in the plants themselves offered slightly better opportunities for the local middle class, but there were hardly enough jobs to satisfy everyone's needs. At IKA-Renault, for example, it was company policy to reserve all the major decision-making and technical positions for French nationals while leaving the positions in personnel and public relations for Argentines.[59] Fiat followed a similar policy and was even more predisposed to put its nationals in positions of authority, given the complete ownership of the Ferreyra complex by Turin, though the majority of its administrative staff by the late 1960s was Argentine. Cordoban professionals, trained at the local university, generally could not aspire to anything more than work as legal counsel or as *ingenieros* in lower-echelon managerial positions in the automobile companies.

The legacy of Córdoba's economic and social development was thus a working class that had a sense of power—a sense of confidence in its ability to confront authority and influence political events—that was rare in Argentina. The creation of this proletariat meant that Córdoba was ripe for labor militancy when the city was faced with the simultaneous onset of military dictatorship and problems in the local automobile industry. As the companies, backed by the repressive powers of the state, began to suspend collective bargaining agreements and attempt to remain competitive and increase labor productivity through plant rationalizations, speedups, and general attacks on labor costs, resentment grew among the autoworkers. To this was added the increasing politicization of Cordoban society and the success of the left in winning over young labor activists to revolutionary parties.

As the automobile companies' relations with their labor forces worsened, workers' developing rancors, grudges, and frustrations found political articulation, inchoate and incomplete as it was, in a new kind of unionism and in a more widespread militancy among all the autoworkers. Revolutionary trade unionism, *clasismo,* began to appeal to some automobile workers who were disenchanted with what they saw as a totemic Peronism and a corrupt Peronist trade union movement, but for the majority of workers who supported the militant tactics of the *clasistas* the issue was not *clasismo* versus *peronismo* but rather honest and effective union representation versus dishonest and ineffectual unions. There was no simple link between problems in the local automobile industry or conditions in the automobile plants and Cordoban labor history in these years. Labor militancy was a citywide phenomenon and many of the most committed union activists were, like Agustín Tosco, in unions that were relatively protected from the vagaries of the car industry. Nevertheless, both labor militancy and the *clasista* movement were centered in the automobile factories, and the problems in that industry formed the essential setting for the ideological and political heresies that thrived in Cordoban labor after 1966.

Córdoba's unusual industrial development pushed the locus of labor conflict in the city into the automotive factories, and their unions acquired a political weight that was simply not available to workers employed in the local textile plant or metallurgical workshops. The conflict between two kinds of unionism, partly expressed in political terms as *peronismo* and *clasismo* but also, more important for the majority of workers, as two distinct approaches to running unions, was most bitter in the IKA-Renault and Fiat plants. For the Cordoban car worker, the adversary was not the small-time industrialist who could employ a panoply of intimidation tactics and enticements to manipulate and control the labor force. Rather, after 1966 the enemies were the impersonal foreign automobile companies, the invisible production managers, and even their shop floor collaborators in the unions, who collectively appeared to be making working conditions increasingly onerous, as well as the state, which upheld the companies' antilabor policies. The automobile workers had a wealth of shared experience from their work lives that drew some to *clasismo,* an ideology that would have carried less weight had Córdoba experienced a more diverse industrial development and had the working class been less concentrated in the mechanical industries. For most workers, however, their collective identity drew them toward a militancy that did not require them to reject their Peronist loyalties.

Broad sociological explanations for Córdoba's labor history can suggest only the nature of the relations between labor and capital in the city and not their specific dynamics. Far more revealing and analytically useful are the problems that were experienced at the factory level. It was in its work life that the city's young automobile workers played out the legacy of Córdoba's industrial development and the idiosyncrasies of Cordoban society. In addition, the Cordoban car workers were part of a regional and a national labor movement, and just as they influenced developments outside of Córdoba, so were they affected by factors that were removed from the day-to-day problems on the shop floor.

The local labor movement's relationship with the state, the CGT, and the union centrals sometimes opened new opportunities for the unions and at other times restricted their freedom to maneuver. Rivalries, political ambitions, and personal vendettas also played a part in labor politics. The unique configuration of the local labor movement, the specific nature of the relations between capital and labor in the city, and the individuals and the balance of power within the trade union movement—the latter continuously in a state of flux and responding to multiple influences—collectively made up the world of Cordoban working class politics and for nearly a decade made Córdoba the center of the country's dissident labor movement.

· T W O ·

Union Politics

As in most labor movements, working class politics in Córdoba was always operating on two levels. One arena was centered on the shop floor and the workers' relationship to production, and the other involved the internal power struggles and institutional interactions of the workers' labor unions, as well as the unions' relationship with the state. The shop floor politics was a homier and almost hermetic kind of labor politics in which the workers' varied interests, represented individually by their shop stewards and collectively by the union, confronted the more uniform interests of capital. The workplace relationships determined by the nature of the enterprise, by its markets, technology, and management practices, were a fundamental part of the history of all the Cordoban unions in this period. It was most important, however, in those industries in which both labor and capital were present on a scale to make their confrontation consequential for the entire working class. In Córdoba, that meant the automobile industry. Only in that industry were the stakes high enough and the relationships so contentious that they were able to influence the city's other unions. Moreover, it was only after the mid-1960s that the familiar skirmishing between labor and management in that industry developed into open war and the ripples spread beyond the confines of the automotive complexes to affect other unions and the Cordoban labor movement in general.

The second kind of labor politics, though equally complex, was more public and involved a greater number of unions at an earlier point in time. Union politics was a looming presence in the history of the local working class. It was only incompletely represented in the manifestos or institutional acronyms that so often preoccupy labor historians, and the unions'

54

motivations, in fact, were often only scarcely visible in the written evidence of the historian. The internal politics of the unions and the political rivalries between them responded to many influences: personal, strategic, and ideological. It was a political realm that involved all the workers, but which was represented most tangibly by their leadership. The Cordoban labor movement became something both singular and significant in recent Argentine working class history only once the two kinds of labor politics meshed to produce a new kind of unionism. But a long and intricate history preceded the birth of the dissident Cordoban trade union movement, and knowing that history is crucial for its later understanding and explanation. It is a history that can best be described as the underground power politics of Cordoban labor.

The history began in the final years of Perón's presidency. In the early 1950s, as the Peronist state showed its first signs of exhaustion, groups of young workers were starting to cluster in a number of Cordoban unions and question the old guard Peronist leadership. Their challenge was partly ideological. A handful, like Agustín Tosco, through study and reflection had begun to look critically at Peronism's relationship with the workers' movement. Tosco and others like him eventually sought out the unreconstructed anarchists, socialists, and communists in Córdoba, most of them now little more than elderly spectators in the local labor movement, to learn something of the working class traditions that had preceded Perón.[1] Largely, however, their nascent rebellion involved more mundane issues than ideology and centered on disagreements with Peronist approaches to collective bargaining or simply on generational displeasure with the established union leadership.[2]

As a result of this growing discontent, by 1955 a number of key unions in the city were ideologically and politically pluralist to a much greater extent than was common in Peronist Argentina. Such pluralism was no doubt made possible by Córdoba's comparative isolation from the centers of working class politics and trade union power in the Peronist labor movement, Buenos Aires and Rosario. Córdoba's isolation, for example, had allowed a core of non-Peronist, left-wing union activists in the light and power workers' union, collectively known in the union's history as the "generation of 1953," to elect their leader, Agustín Tosco, to a position on the executive council in the heyday of Peronist orthodoxy, and in 1957 to the office of secretary general of Luz y Fuerza at the tender age of twenty-seven.[3] Similar situations existed in other local unions, such as the print workers' and the railroad workers' unions. Córdoba was also unique in that the workers who would make up the backbone of the labor movement, those in the automobile industry, were still a class in the making and thus were unorganized when the Peronist government fell in 1955. For those workers Peronism was a received working class tradition rather than a lived experience, and their loyalty to that tradition, though strong, often had to compete with equally potent attachments to their province and, eventually, to their unions.

Despite these local idiosyncrasies, the Cordoban working class was indeed overwhelmingly Peronist in 1955. Founded in 1949 at the height of the Peronist union drives, the Cordoban Confederacíon General del Trabajo (CGT) grouped an assorted collection of the pluralist, mostly nonindustrial unions, the most important of which were light and power, the print workers, and the railroad workers, with other solidly Peronist unions such as the bus drivers, public employees, textile workers, mill workers, and carpenters. In the labor movement's resistance campaign against General Pedro Aramburu's (1955–1958) anti–working class and, more specifically, the anti-Peronist government, Córdoba's unions played a particularly prominent role. The Peronist Resistance in Córdoba was one of the fiercest of the entire Argentine interior. The Cordoban delega- tion drafted two documents that emerged from separate labor congresses held in the province, one to coordinate the resistance and the second to keep its tradition alive—in La Falda in 1957 and in Huerta Grande in 1962, respectively—that stood as the most radical programs offered by any sector of the labor movement until the emergence of revolutionary cur- rents in the unions in the early 1970s.[4] The *línea dura* tendency within Peronist unionism, advocating a militant opposition to the state and em- ployers in the demand for the return of Perón from exile and for the lifting of the proscription of their movement, remained strong in the city. It effectively resisted encroachments from Buenos Aires on local union autonomy and thereby preserved a uniquely Cordoban identity for the local labor movement that both Peronists and non-Peronists thenceforth sought to uphold.

Union politics in Córdoba were also influenced by the character of its recent industrial development. In the first moves to organize the automo- tive proletariat, the Aramburu government sought to weaken the Peronist presence in Cordoban labor, and it partly succeeded. The tardy arrival of the mechanical industries allowed Aramburu to award jurisdiction of the IKA workers to the Sindicatos de Mecánicos y Afines del Transporte Automotor (SMATA), then a small and inconsequential union that essen- tially represented service station mechanics. The decision was a blow for Peronist labor and especially for the Unión Obrera Metalúrgica (UOM), which was the leader of the Resistance and was emerging as the dominant union and final arbiter in the Peronist labor movement. The following year, with Peronist candidates proscribed, a communist slate stressing work-related issues won the first union election and the right to represent the IKA workers. In January 1957, the communists negotiated IKA's first collective bargaining agreement. It established a number of substantial gains for the union, among them the extension to the IKA workers of the *"sábado inglés"* law, a provincial measure that granted workers in select industries 48 hours' pay for a 44-hour work week, while also winning numerous job safety and benefits clauses.[5]

The effect of the communist slate's 1957 victory was to galvanize a small group of Peronist militants in the IKA plants to back a program that stressed bread-and-butter issues at the expense of the broader political concerns of the proscribed Peronist movement. For several months, the SMATA Peronists disputed among themselves the leadership position of their union-recovery movement until one man, Elpidio Angel Torres, emerged as their recognized spokesman. The burly, swarthy Torres had built on his notoriety as a local tough from Alta Gracia, a small town near the Santa Isabel complex, to start a union career at IKA and assert control over the badly disorganized Peronists there. Torres's campaign to create a stronger Peronist presence in the IKA plants had been hindered both by the continued ban on Peronist participation in union affairs and by the weak union tradition among the young IKA labor force. To circumvent the legal impediments on union activity, Torres and the circle of Peronist militants who surrounded him had adopted a conciliatory attitude toward the company and the provincial authorities. In the midst of the Peronist resistance, Torres maintained a cordial but aloof relationship with the unions most actively involved.

As he was to do throughout his union career, Torres attempted to further his own interests and those of the Cordoban SMATA while remaining independent of the Buenos Aires labor bosses who controlled the CGT and what was known as the 62 Organizaciones, the political wing of the Peronist labor movement. The SMATA Peronists embraced a moderate position during the Resistance, arguing for restraint and the abandonment of sabotage and other militant tactics so as not to delay the reestablishment of Peronism in the nation's political life.[6] More important, by distancing themselves from the most militant elements in the Resistance, Torres and his circle had a freer hand to challenge the communists' control of the union. Management and provincial authorities spared them at least some of the pettier harassments that were hindering Peronists in other unions, and Torres and his collaborators were soon able to operate with relative freedom in the IKA plants, despite the proscription of their movement and the restraints on Peronist union activity elsewhere.

Torres's great problem was worker apathy. Few of the IKA workers had previous union experience. The company had craftily chosen to recruit its labor force from the nonunionized Industrias Aeronaúticas y Mecánicas del Estado (IAME) factories, from first-time industrial workers in the city, and from the newly arrived rural migrants.[7] Despite the gains won by the union in 1957, worker registration did not significantly increase. Union drives and even talk of unions were received sullenly by the labor force. Although the IAME workers were familiar with factory life, most of the labor force was not. IKA's workers were a motley collection of former agricultural laborers, handymen, independent mechanics, plumbers, even waiters from the resorts in the nearby Cordoban *sierra*.[8] The minimal skills demanded by much of automotive production enabled the company to hire a largely inexperienced labor force and then train the workers for the simple and repetitive tasks required by assembly-line production. These nonskilled workers were especially indifferent to Peronist overtures, and presumably to those of the communists as well, and many seemed to fear that union involvement would in some way threaten their job.[9]

The year 1958 was a turning point for the SMATA Peronists and for unionism in general in the IKA complex. Torres began with a mordant propaganda campaign against the 1957 contract and the communists' lack of vigilance in holding the company to compliance on several of its provisions. The recent Perón-Frondizi pact, and the impending relegalization of the Peronist labor movement in return for its support of Frondizi's candidacy, encouraged Torres to move up his bid for control of the union and to adopt more aggressive tactics. Torres made a bold effort to displace the communists and win the union elections scheduled for later that year, first by discrediting his rivals and then by capitalizing on his Peronist ties. Partly he was counting on a combination of the methodical and lackluster character of the communist union leadership, the divisions within the communist ranks that forced them to form separate slates, his own powers of persuasion and personal charisma, and workers' sympathy for the underdog to help him defeat the communists. Mostly he was relying on his status as the representative of a movement increasingly mythologized by the Argentine working class to put him and his fellow Peronists in charge of the Cordoban SMATA. His hesitancy to claim Peronist loyalties in 1957 gave way to a realization that those ties could be a distinct advantage in the changed political circumstances of 1958.[10]

Torres opened his attack against the communists on the issue of effective union representation. By goading the communists into hasty and poorly organized strikes in March over stalled collective bargaining negotiations, Torres contributed to worker disaffection. Grumbling on the shop floor became widespread. By the end of April, most of the workers were ignoring the communists' strike calls, and the union's president, Alejandro Brizuela, had lost much of his former popularity among the small number of workers active in the union and angered the great majority who had simply tolerated it.

From Buenos Aires came other pressures on Torres to act. Throughout the history of Cordoban labor, union decisions were often made in response to pressures coming from union centrals and the CGT, and especially in response to the political machinations of the principal powers in Peronist labor who controlled the union centrals and dominated the CGT and the 62 Organizaciones. Such decisions generally sought to maintain the independence of the Cordoban unions and resist the encroachments of the *porteño* Peronist labor bosses on local union autonomy. In this particular case in 1958, Torres sought to head off a UOM campaign pressuring Frondizi to allow the metal workers' union to assert jurisdiction over the IKA workers. The UOM had recently been awarded such jurisdiction over the Fiat workers, and control of the city's second automotive complex would assure the union a dominant position in the Cordoban labor movement and also frustrate the union aspirations of young Cordobans such as Torres who rightly feared that affiliation with the highly centralized UOM would mean absolute control from Buenos Aires. Rumors of the UOM's intentions became an open challenge in the second half of 1958, when UOM representatives began a campaign at the factory gates to sign up workers, the first step toward presenting a formal petition to the Ministry of Labor to recognize its jurisdiction. The IKA workers proved to be as indifferent to the UOM advances as they had been to previous union drives, but there was a general feeling among the SMATA Peronists that they were being pushed aside and that the loss of prestige recently suffered by the communist leadership threatened to redound to the benefit of the UOM.[11]

Shortly after the first appearance of the UOM canvassers in Santa Isabel, Torres and his supporters put together the first Peronist slate to run against the two communist slates competing in the December

SMATA elections. The election results were close and also illustrative of the extent to which worker apathy still existed in the plants. Out of a total work force of more than 3,000, fewer than half chose to vote, with Torres's Peronist slate receiving 588 votes and the two communist slates 411 and 274 each.[12] Torres's election as secretary general put the Peronists in control of the Cordoban SMATA for the first time, but the narrow margin of victory and widespread worker indifference toward the elections and toward the union in general meant that the Peronists' mandate was more apparent than real. Moreover, a number of the departments in the IKA plants remained in communist hands and Torres found himself on the defensive, with a resentful and capable core of communist activists prepared to criticize his handling of the union at every turn.

To consolidate his control in Santa Isabel, Torres continued to follow an independent approach and concentrate on building his support among the IKA rank and file. Torres and the other SMATA Peronists realized that the union still occupied a precarious position. The shallow union tradition and the palpable suspicion toward union activists threatened to turn indifference and even begrudging support into open hostility at a moment's notice. The SMATA leaders needed to build rank-and-file support through concrete gains and not subordinate union decisions to the dictates of Buenos Aires. Their public demonstrations of fealty to the *porteño* labor bosses were therefore infrequent. Torres himself became adept at making florid speeches in praise of Perón, threatening in menacing tones the union's participation in Peronist-sponsored labor mobilizations and general strikes, and effectively ignoring orders coming from Buenos Aires. The two years following the union victory were spent building alliances, resolving problems on the shop floor, putting together a solid union organization, and remaining largely indifferent to the political maneuvering of the Peronist labor movement.

Torres was encouraged to pursue bread-and-butter unionism by changes taking place in the plants. The relatively tranquil management-labor relations that had characterized the first few years of IKA's history had begun to deteriorate just as the Peronists were assuming control of the union. Though the company's sales figures were high and jobs in the plants were plentiful, there were signs that the young labor force was starting to react to the regimentation and stringencies of factory life. The first company acknowledgment of labor problems reported an increased surliness of workers toward management and foremen, and even occasional incidents of outright insubordination on the lines, problems that the company attributed to labor agitators on the shop floor.[13] Workers in some of the more onerous departments grew restless. The painting tunnels were already notorious—for the workers, because of their reputedly slipshod design, which left lingering eye- and lung-damaging paint fumes; for management, because they were a nest of sedition. When workers there began a campaign to have their jobs classified as hazardous, and thus made subject to the six-hour work day required by Argentine labor law, the company held firm, seeing the move as an intrusion into management's control over the productive process and as an unwelcome precedent for other departments.[14] However, a special commission from the Labor Ministry found not only poor ventilation in the paint tunnels but also increased production rhythms that were unacceptable, and it forced the company to improve ventilation, distribute better masks and suits for protection, and reduce both the work day and the production rhythms.[15]

Similar sorts of problems were festering in other departments, and Torres and the Peronist union leadership capitalized on them to establish the kind of solid union organization and rank-and-file participation that had eluded the communists. The Peronists used union funds to build a union headquarters in downtown Córdoba and set up training courses for newly elected union shop stewards. They also undertook a major organizational drive in all the departments, offering the union's commitment to resolve the specific problems in each. A clear chain of command began to emerge, with Torres playing the part of the labor *caudillo* while relying on a group of tough, young Peronist union activists to win the workers over. Progress was painstaking. The union won some worker support through such measures as establishing a lavish union medical program to compete with the company's more modest health services and through the resolution of small problems in individual departments. But affiliations still lagged. What was needed was a prestige-winning victory, and in the hopes of obtaining one, Torres and the union, on February 26, 1959, voted to unilaterally rescind the contract reached with the company in 1958 and declare a strike.

The 1959 strike was an important event in the SMATA's history, and it established precedents that would influence labor politics in the future. First the 1959 strike established what would become a hallmark of the Cordoban labor movement for years to come: the *paro activo* (active strike). After the waning of the Resistance and the institutionalization of the labor movement, the major Peronist unions, particularly in Buenos Aires, would discourage any rank-and-file participation that threatened to move beyond clearly circumscribed limits. Increasingly, strikes would tend to be carefully orchestrated and controlled affairs, such as the lackadaisical *paro matero* or *paro dominguero* (Sunday strike), in which workers simply stayed home while the labor bosses negotiated with their interlocutors of the moment—the employers, the state, or, more frequently, both. In contrast, the *paro activo* was a militant statement of worker intransigence, a provocative throwing down of the gauntlet, undertaken deliberately to increase participation in the work stoppage. Such strikes brought the workers into the streets and always threatened to erupt into violent confrontations with the police. The tendency in coming years for the Cordoban unions' work stoppages to resemble popular mobilizations—and frequently to trigger citywide protests that sometimes escalated, as in 1969 and 1971, into full-fledged urban insurrections—was born with the *paro activo* and the 1959 strike.

The SMATA Peronists were not so much interested in establishing a trade union precedent or even a more combative union style as they were in overcoming the stubborn indifference, even antipathy, to the union among the IKA workers.[16] Torres recognized that the strike was a formidable acculturation and union-building mechanism, much as the United Auto Workers union organizers had in Detroit in the 1930s. In the 1959 conflict, Torres also made use of what would thenceforth be another practice of the Cordoban SMATA: he held open assemblies at a local boxing ring, the Córdoba Sport Club, to bring workers together to vote on all strike calls. These assemblies became important socializing events and were a deliberate attempt to instill an identification with the union and a class identity in workers who previously had felt little of either.[17]

The 1959 strike failed in the short-term, but it ultimately garnered Torres and the neophyte Peronist leadership a crucial union victory. As a result of the strike, IKA management realized it had to negotiate seriously with the union, and in the next contract it met nearly all of the union's demands. The 1960 agreement recognized the union as the sole legitimate representative of the IKA workers in all dealings with management and allowed the SMATA to increase the number of shop stewards in the plants, an invaluable tool in increasing the union's profile among the workers. Procedures were also established for the *paritarias,* the collective bargaining talks that, in the automobile industry, were held directly between the automobile companies and the SMATA local and not between a single employers' association and a national union, as in the case of the metal trades. In the March 11, 1960, agreement Torres also won a major concession with regard to the workers' three-year contracts: a wage adjustment clause *(cláusula gatillo)* that provided for automatic cost-of-living increases every four months. He obtained a series of benefits and a significant wage hike over that in the 1958 agreement, as well.[18] On the basis of the 1960 agreement, Torres would build his rank-and-file support and a formidable union machine that would dominate union affairs for more than a decade.

The significance of the strike and of the first few years of Torres's and the Peronists' control of the SMATA was that they established the tenor of management-labor relations in the IKA plants and staked out the responsibilities and limits of the union's relationship with the workers. By the end of the formative period, the Peronists were in firm control of the union apparatus, with open lines to IKA's executives and managers. The union had also established certain democratic practices at a time that the Peronist labor movement was moving toward a more bureaucratic, deliberative union style, *vandorismo* as it came to be known in honor of the metallurgical leader, Augusto Vandor, who inspired many of its practices.[19] The 1959 strike also contributed to a nascent SMATA identity—a mixture of provincial pride, suspicion toward Buenos Aires, and shared values born of a common work experience and, to a lesser extent, neighborhood familiarity—that gave the IKA labor force a special character. Finally, there was the continued presence of a group of carping, vigilant, left-wing union activists in the plants. All these factors combined to prevent the consolidation of a petrified union bureaucracy in the union. Though Torres began to assume all the characteristics of an archetypical Peronist labor boss, alternately the fixer of problems and the dispenser of favors, and though the union's executive committee gradually took on an administrative as opposed to a class character, the Cordoban SMATA was, within the limits of Peronist trade unionism at that moment, a democratic organization and an effective advocate of workers' interests.

The Fiat workers similarly had an early history that established them as independent actors in Cordoban labor politics, though in Ferreyra such independence was a result of company machinations rather than union struggles. Fiat's labor policies from the start were severe and intransigent, and company officials in Ferreyra oversaw a meticulously orchestrated campaign to quash any signs of serious union activity in its plants. Fiat had established its Argentine operations just as a nearly ten-year struggle with the communist and socialist Confederazione Generale Italiana de Lavoro (CGIL) alliance representing the Fiat workers in the Turin plants was coming to an end. The defeat of the CGIL in the 1955 union elections brought union activity to a standstill in Turin. The Fiat workers, subject alternately to the paternalist and intimidation tactics of the company, returned to a state of affairs that had characterized union representation at Fiat from the rise of fascism in the 1920s and through the war. The Italian Fiat workers did not participate in any significant work stoppages again until the great 1970 strikes.[20]

Fiat was predictably unwilling to tolerate in Córdoba what it had found unacceptable in Turin. Unlike the case at IKA, the early union organizing efforts by the communists were unwelcome at the Italian company, and union activity was virtually banned until 1958. In that year, and in response to the ill winds blowing from Santa Isabel where the SMATA had already emerged as a formidable union adversary, Fiat briefly yielded to government and worker pressures and allowed an affiliation with the local UOM. Fiat's decision to keep the local automobile workers divided proved judicious, and the UOM, a union whose strength was concentrated in Buenos Aires, was a more attractive option in 1958 than it had been in Aramburu's day, when IKA was first deciding the union affiliation issue, due to the waning of the Peronist Resistance and Peronist labor's support for Frondizi. A 1959 company report gleefully noted the absence of labor problems in the complex, a tranquility it compared to conditions that existed "outside" Ferreyra, in an oblique reference to Santa Isabel.[21] The scarce impact in Ferreyra of the bitter metal workers' strike the following year was evidence of an at least initially timorous union representation and vindicated Fiat's decision to keep its labor force away from what it considered the corrupting and more menacing prospect of a SMATA affiliation.

In 1960, Fiat went a step further with its labor policies and withdrew its workers from the mainstream Argentine labor movement altogether by forming plant unions. Although the UOM central and the Peronist labor movement in general gave every sign of a willingness to cooperate with business, the resuscitation of Peronism was still an unsettling prospect for most employers, and Fiat management was aware that the Cordoban UOM was likely to embrace more combative tactics to forestall any rank-and-file movement to join the local autoworkers' union. Both considerations convinced Fiat company officials that more drastic measures would have to be taken if union representation were to remain weak in Ferreyra. Since the UOM affiliation was no longer seen as a guarantee for future labor peace, and with the SMATA anathema to the Italian company, in early 1960 Fiat proposed to Frondizi and his conservative finance minister, Alvaro Alsogaray, that *sindicatos de planta* be formed in the Fiat complex. Although the formation of such unions was a flagrant violation of Argentine labor law, the government partially approved the company's request. Under the auspices of the company-controlled Federación Sindical de Trabajadores Fiat, plant unions were formed for the Concord factory (Sindicato de Trabajadores de Concord, or SITRAC), the Materfer factory (SITRAM), and the Grandes Motores Diesel factories (SITRAGMD), though legal recognition, *personería gremial,* would not actually be granted until 1964 under the Radical government of Arturo Illia.[22] Thus, in 1960, as the independently minded Peronists under Torres's leadership in the SMATA were consolidating their control in Santa Isabel, an even more radically separatist union representation was germinating in the city's other automotive complex.

While the great automotive and mechanical complexes were wrestling with the problems of union representation, establishing the parameters in the relationship between labor and management in the IKA and Fiat plants that would endure for many years, other local unions were passing through their own formative period. Unlike workers in the mechanical industries, the workers in the city's other unions were not found in concentrated, capital-intensive industries but were dispersed throughout the government bureaucracies, the service industries, and in light, technologically simple industries. Theoretically they shared a class identity with the workers in the mechanical industries, but in reality the nature of their work, their product markets, and their relationships with their employers made them as different from the IKA and Fiat workers as they were from one another. Among this heterogeneous group, three broad political tendencies were beginning to emerge. Each not only represented discrete ideological positions but also formed part of local and national alliances in the power politics of the labor movement. A renegade Peronist group, a formally mainstream but effectively independent Peronist tendency, and an explicitly non-Peronist current comprised the power blocs in Cordoban labor outside the IKA and Fiat complexes.

The old guard Peronist unions had slipped from the majority status they had enjoyed before 1955 and through the Resistance to a minority position by 1960. The repression they suffered at government hands during the Resistance was only partly responsible for their decline. More important were the changes that had taken place in the Cordoban economy, specifically the creation of the new automotive proletariat and the corresponding increase in the strategic power of the light and power workers' union, a union servicing the industry that was now the lifeblood of Córdoba's industrial economy. In Córdoba, the union that inherited the right to represent the emerging mainstream *vandorista* position in Peron-

ist labor was the local branch of the UOM. During the Peronist governments of the 1940s and 1950s, the Cordoban metalworkers' union had
actually been a small union with little influence in a local labor movement
whose expansion took place only after 1955.[23] Under Perón, the powers
of Peronist labor in Córdoba had been in the textile industries and food
processing industries (slaughter houses, flour milling, and the like), as
well as in the urban transport union, notably the bus workers, and the
public employees' unions. Though at a national level Vandor's metalworkers' union was passing from its role as principal union protagonist of
the Resistance to become the mainstay of the new business unionism
obliquely espoused by *vandorismo,* the Cordoban UOM refused to ally
itself with this current, partly because of regionalist pride and unwillingness to subordinate local interests to the dictates of the highly centralized
UOM, but largely because the *línea blanda* approach that Vandor's followers, the so-called *legalistas,* represented did not serve the Cordoban
UOM's own tactical needs.

The Cordoban UOM was in a stage of growth, not consolidation, and
conciliatory, *línea blanda* tactics were only appropriate for a union that
had already been accepted as an interlocutor with business. The Cordoban UOM's recent loss of the Fiat workers had driven home how tactics
that stressed negotiation rather than militancy, while they might be appropriate for Buenos Aires, could not yet be accepted by Córdoba's fledgling industrial unions. From that point on, the UOM represented a faction
within Cordoban labor termed initially the *auténticos* and subsequently
the *ortodoxos,* a faction that professed unquestioning fealty to Perón but
that was in reality, most importantly, a power rival and foil to Vandor. The
ortodoxos allied with the Peronist unions of José Alonso, Vandor's chief
rival in the labor movement, and they stressed their *línea dura* credentials
via their insistence on Perón's return as the prerequisite for labor peace
and by their adoption of more intransigent, combative positions with
respect to the state and the employers.

Besides the UOM, many of the other unions found in the Cordoban
ortodoxo ranks were simply local has-beens itching to reassert control
over what had become a suddenly and disconcertingly transformed trade
union movement, both in Córdoba and nationally. A good number were
controlled by an older generation of Peronist union leaders, the same
ones who had wielded power under Perón's governments of the 1940s
and 1950s, and they resented the upstarts, the younger generation of
Peronists—best represented by Vandor himself—who had emerged dur-

ing the Resistance and in its aftermath were quietly urging a pragmatic *"peronismo sin Perón,"* which assured the continuance of their recently won union careers. The Cordoban *ortodoxo* union leaders were also largely drawn from the nationalist and proclerical sectors of Cordoban Peronism and, ironically, included many of the labor leaders who had actually turned against Perón in the final years of his government, as a result of his partial abandonment of a nationalist economic program and especially because of Perón's feuding and historic break with the Church.[24] The Cordoban UOM allied with this current and indeed assumed leadership of Vandor's local rivals, not because of ideological affinity but because they served the union's strategic needs and preserved its independence from Buenos Aires. Ideology was not the issue and would, indeed, never matter much to the Cordoban metalworkers' union. The local UOM sought to increase its power, and it alternately followed policies, then and in the future, that would assure its strength as a union and promote the influence of the Cordoban UOM leadership in the Peronist movement. The UOM's behavior was not, as the union leadership repeatedly claimed, attributable to a more faithful adherence to the combative labor tradition of the Resistance, but rather was due to a sharp sense of the union's own self-interest and to tactical considerations.

The combative Cordoban unions of the Resistance, in fact, had not been drawn from the *ortodoxo* ranks but belonged mainly to its rival in the Cordoban Peronist labor movement, the *legalistas.* This faction in Peronist labor was comprised of those unions that were nominally supportive of Vandor's negotiating priorities, but that in practice also sought to maintain a certain distance from Vandor to avoid any interference from Buenos Aires that would hamper their ability to conduct union affairs effectively. A typical *legalista* union was the transport workers' union, Unión Tranviarios Automotor (UTA), under the leadership of Atilio López. López, who had been a firebrand leader in the Cordoban Resistance, was a union man loyal to Peronism and to Perón but suspicious of Vandor and skeptical of a Peronist labor movement that promoted negotiation by the select few and discouraged rank-and-file militancy. Like the SMATA, a union that had not participated notably in the Resistance but that would eventually assume leadership of the Cordoban *legalistas,* the UTA and other *legalista* unions were more sensitive to conditions in their industries and less concerned in these years with the grander institutional and political designs or power struggles within the Peronist labor movement. Some, such as the SMATA, were immersed in efforts to build their union apparatus, an undertaking that made independence of action essential. A number were passing through crises that required the kind of tactics that Vandor appeared about to abandon.

López's transport workers' union, one of the city's largest, with a membership of more than 1,000, was concentrated in the municipal bus company and since 1957 had faced a privatization scheme that threatened the jobs of hundreds of its members.[25] The publicly owned urban transport system, Compañía Argentina de Transporte Automotor (CATA), was a product of the nationalizations in the first Peronist presidency and was a natural target for privatization under Frondizi, given what even the bus drivers recognized was a deplorably ill-administered system. The union resisted the privatization schemes and countered with a proposal of its own to establish a worker cooperative to administer the company. In late 1962, however, a military governor finally carried out the long-threatened privatization of the bus company. The CATA was dissolved, the bus lines were sold off to private investors, and López, the UTA, and the *línea dura* position within the *legalistas* were momentarily eclipsed—though the UTA would reemerge several years later, again under López's leadership, in the events surrounding Cordobazo and would serve as the haven for left-wing and militant Peronists in the early 1970s.[26]

As had been the case with the UOM, López and the *legalista* unions had been pushed into independent positions with respect to Vandor by hard-headed tactical considerations, rather than woolly ideological ones. As unions that were predominantly found in unstrategic industries that carried little weight in the Peronist labor movement nationally, the *legalistas* realized they had scant possibilities of winning support from Buenos Aires in their local struggles with employers and the provincial government. Neither Vandor nor the CGT would be willing to become embroiled in disputes that, to them, were minor affairs deep in the Argentine hinterland. A full integration into the Vandorist fold, on the other hand, could mean a subordination of local union needs to those of Vandor and the other *porteño* labor bosses. The *legalistas* thus insisted on their independence and resisted creeping *vandorismo*. Though they had no wish to ally with the old guard, which comprised the majority of the *ortodoxo* unions (nor would they have been welcomed), they could cooperate with them for the sake of Cordoban trade union autonomy. Their Peronism was a powerful emotional bond, but it was subordinate to their strategic needs. Tactical alliances were made to guarantee some protection from union intervention, to ward off the freezing of union funds, and to defy the panoply of intimidation tactics Vandor had at his disposal.

Throughout their history, what most distinguished all the Cordoban Peronists was their concern with maintaining their independence and maximizing their bargaining muscle without being forced to abandon Peronism altogether. Working through the SMATA, Vandor would slowly gain control of the *legalista* unions, tame them, and make their unions a bona fide *vandorista* current in the Cordoban CGT for several years. But the *legalistas'* subsequent emergence as the principal voice in Córdoba for a combative, militant Peronist labor movement would be unfortuitous, and Vandor's victory would turn out to be a short-lived one. Both wings of the Peronist labor movement in Córdoba consistently sought to minimize outside interference. The UOM joined the *ortodoxos* and the SMATA the *legalistas* precisely because their union centrals belonged to the opposing faction. Vandor's attempts to integrate the Peronist labor movement and transform it into a labor party independent of Perón's control but subordinate to his own was thus rejected by both the *legalistas* and the *ortodoxos*.

That such a maverick Peronist labor movement was possible in Córdoba was due in no small measure to the presence of other unions beyond the reach of the *verticalismo* that Alonso and Vandor alike wanted to reestablish. The Tosco-led "Independents" were the city's most consistent and vociferous defenders of Cordoban trade union autonomy. Some 20 unions were in this bloc, among them the print workers, postal and telegraph workers, sanitation workers, and other small unions. They were abetted in their insubordination by the fact that nearly all were federal unions, one of two forms of organization in Argentine trade unionism. Unlike unions such as the UOM, the SMATA, and indeed nearly all the country's principal industrial unions, the minority of federal unions enjoyed control over their union funds, administered their own union elections, and were less vulnerable to intimidation than those unions that belonged to centralist structures. The presence of one particular federal union in their ranks, Luz y Fuerza, made the Independents a power in local labor politics. The light and power workers' union was a force partly due to its size—after the SMATA, the UOM, and the Fiat unions, it was the city's biggest and wealthiest union—but largely due to its power, both literal and figurative. Through its ability to control power cutoffs and blackouts, the electricians' union was the only one in Córdoba capable of immediately shutting down the city and unleashing a provincial and even a national crisis. It was a strategic union in a strategic industry in industrial Córdoba, a fact that would be demonstrated tellingly in two great working class protests, the 1969 Cordobazo and 1971 *viborazo*.

Most of the Independents, however, were found in strategically inconsequential industries that owed allegiance to the bloc because of their long traditions of radical, socialist, or communist loyalty previous to the Peronist years. A number of them had converted only reluctantly to Peronism. Several, notably the print workers' and sanitation workers' unions, had been taken over by the Peronist government for their intractability. Nearly all had a core of visceral anti-Peronist sentiment that fed on a complex web of personal grudges and vendettas as well as genuine ideological and political differences.

The print workers' union and its secretary general, Juan Malvár, were as representative of the Independents as Atilio López and the UTA were of the *legalistas*. The print workers, spread out in dozens of small printing houses all over the city, had a membership of never fewer than 800 and never more than 1,200 between 1955 and 1976. The chain-smoking Malvár, whose finely clipped moustache and melancholy air gave him the appearance of a tango singer rather than a union leader, brought a Radical party slate to power in the 1958 union elections and remained one of the city's most active non-Peronist labor leaders until the 1976 coup. Malvár and other Independents watched with bemused satisfaction as local Peronists bickered. They preferred the *legalistas* in their tactical alliances because of what was seen as the latter's greater loyalty to the working class over simply personal interests, but they allied with them only when it seemed to further the chances of maintaining a politically pluralist Cordoban labor movement.

Unions such as the print workers never questioned Luz y Fuerza's leadership of the Independents, partly because the light and power workers' strategic importance left little doubt as to their rightful claim to authority in the alliance, but largely because of Agustín Tosco's prestige in local labor circles. Tosco had risen from being just one of several Luz y Fuerza non-Peronist union activists in the early 1950s to become the leading spokesman for a pluralist labor movement in the city by the end of the decade. He would be the commanding figure in the Cordoban labor movement for the next fifteen years and would oversee the Independents' ideological development as they moved from a vaguely anti-imperialist perspective to more of a genuinely socialist position on questions of national economic planning and political reform.

Monkish by nature, after his arrival in Córdoba Tosco had devoted his time off from his job in the Empresa Pública de Energía de Córdoba (EPEC) electromechanical workshop to immersing himself in the literature of socialism, showing an asceticism and self-discipline that was certainly part of an Argentine working class tradition, but that clashed in his own day with the Peronists' general scorn of intellectuals and book-reading workers. Perhaps his imposing physical size prevented their taunts, the gangly teenager having turned into a broad-shouldered and powerful-forearmed man whose strength revealed his early hard years spent in the fields. More likely his indifference to approval and his obvious intelligence discouraged them. *El gringo* Tosco quickly gained a reputation as one of the labor movement's most able and articulate spokesmen, and he commanded great respect and affection in Cordoban union circles, Peronist and non-Peronist alike. With the certainty and some of the obstinacy of the autodidact, Tosco never wavered from the moral assumptions and political ideology of his early acquired Marxist culture. To a great extent the Independent movement was Tosco's personal creation, and he and his closest collaborators in Luz y Fuerza carefully supervised its political development.

Yet Tosco's undoubted gifts might have come to nothing had he been in any other union but Luz y Fuerza. The light and power workers were then the only union really capable of leading an anti-*verticalista* current in Cordoban labor. Luz y Fuerza had begun to distance itself from the Peronist trade union hierarchy shortly after Tosco's election as secretary general in 1957. This was possible because the union was in a favorable position compared with most of the city's working class organizations. Its energies were not spent on exhausting union-building programs, nor was it preoccupied with outstanding work-related problems. The union and its relationship with EPEC were issues that had been decided during the Peronist years. As a state company engaged in a public service that depended on federal and provincial budgets and not annual profits, EPEC had less to fear from its labor force than IKA, Fiat, the owners of the city's metal-working shops, and all other privately owned industries in the city, for that matter.

The light and power workers enjoyed a relatively privileged status in the local working class in these years. Layoffs were rare, and the rapid expansion that had been under way in the industry since the 1930s translated into increasing job opportunities, mobility within the company, and some of the highest wages in the country. In 1960, the light and power workers were the fourth highest paid category of workers in Argentina, and eventually they came to trail only workers in the automobile and chemical industries.[27] Tosco and his closest collaborators in the union thus had their hands freer to deal with problems that were essentially political. Such political projects could include everything from opposing a government plan that would end the state's monopoly on electrical power, a campaign the union successfully mounted in 1958 and framed as an anti-imperialist issue, to building a pluralist working class alliance in Córdoba.

As in all the city's unions, there was an intense political life within Luz y Fuerza. Intra-union politics always needs to be taken into account in the history of Cordoban labor, since it influenced union behavior as much as a union's relationship with other unions, the CGT, and the state. Luz y Fuerza's most salient characteristics were its high degree of union affiliation, which reached 98 percent by the early 1970s; the union's political pluralism; the democratic spirit that permeated it; and the relative weakness of its Peronist activists. The Peronists' monopoly on union offices had ended in 1957 with the victory of Tosco's heterogeneous slate, which brought to power the circle who would steer the union, either from the union hall or clandestinely, until the 1976 coup. The majority of the Luz y Fuerza workers in the union certainly identified themselves as Peronists. Yet Tosco's nonpartisan slates won by wide margins in all subsequent union elections, and the light and power workers obviously were able to reconcile their Peronist identity with support for Tosco. Moreover, for the core of Peronist activists eager to build union careers of their own, there was the sober realization that no help could be expected from outside. The light and power workers' national organization, the Federación Argentina de Trabajadores de Luz y Fuerza (FATLYF), was controlled by a mixed group of Independents, communists, and antiverticalist Peronists until 1961. As a federally structured union, Luz y Fuerza led a relatively autonomous union existence, and there was little chance of unseating Tosco without deep rank-and-file support.

Union politics therefore did not unleash a bitter internal power struggle within Luz y Fuerza, and an exceptionally cooperative and generally amicable relationship existed between the Peronist and non-Peronist union activists. Unlike the SMATA, where the rivalry between the Peronists and the left was fierce and only attenuated by Torres's gradual isolation of the Marxist unionists, Luz y Fuerza would not for many years have a polarized political life. Indeed the balance of power had shifted so heavily in Tosco's favor that the Peronists in the union chose to ally with him and thereby gain influence by winning positions on the executive council. The leader of the Luz y Fuerza Peronists, Sixto Ceballos, understood that Tosco's personal prestige and his reputation as a skilled negotiator counselled against anything but a decorous, restrained opposition. Throughout the 1960s and early 1970s, the Peronists often chose not even to run a slate of their own, and they never seriously contested Tosco's leadership until the restoration of Peronist government in 1973.

Ceballos's and the other Peronists' acceptance of pluralism in the union and of their own status as a merely formal opposition was not born only of their pragmatism. As with much of the Cordoban labor movement, their identification with the union and their suspicion and hostility toward Buenos Aires informed much of their behavior. Their stance was also the product of an internal democratic structure. Of all the city's working class organizations, Luz y Fuerza was the one that most practiced a participatory union democracy, holding frequent open assemblies to debate issues of consequence and to vote on collective bargaining agreements, strike calls, and union affairs in general. In a union that never numbered more than 3,000 and that had an elected shop steward for every twenty workers, the levels of hierarchy between the leadership and the rank and file were few, a situation strengthened by the absence of paid union positions and the need for all union officials, Tosco included, to keep their jobs and work full days.[28] All the *lucefuercistas* identified with this union tradition and jealously guarded the union's independence from Vandor and other *porteño* labor bosses, many of whom had Peronist credentials that appeared suspect to the combative Peronists in the union, after Vandor and his disciples traded the incendiary rhetoric and militancy of the Resistance for boardroom meetings with industrialists and army officers.

The power balances within and between the Cordoban unions that existed by 1960 underwent important changes over the following six years, but the fundamental character of Cordoban labor politics remained the same. The changes were the result of conditions existing in individual industries and of the vicissitudes of national politics. Nationally, Vandor and the Peronist labor bosses in Buenos Aires strengthened their verticalist campaign and became more persecutory in their dealings with dissenting opinion and rivals in the unions. Vandor also sought to build his own political career and furthered preparations to free the labor movement from its Peronist moorings, at least those extending from Madrid, where Perón remained in exile. For the next six years, the Peronist labor movement would be wracked by internecine feuding, splits, and breakaway organizations—presented by some as conflicts between collaborative and combative Peronism, but in reality a more ignoble struggle for power and influence as the union leadership fought for control of Perón's proscribed but still formidable movement.

The Cordoban unions were affected by these rifts and power struggles, but they were also insulated from them to a greater degree than any other provincial group. The peculiar configuration of Cordoban labor, the presence of the left-wing unions grouped in Tosco's Independents, the existence of the Fiat plant unions, and the independent ways of the Peronist leadership in nearly all the other unions obstructed Vandor's designs. Cordoban Peronism had a different character, and even local UOM leaders such as Jerónimo Carrasco and Alejo Simó continued to exhibit a degree of independence that was unthinkable elsewhere in the country. The pluralism of the Cordoban labor movement, so long as it did not threaten them in their own unions, benefited the local Peronists and made their independence possible. On the one hand, the vigilance of the Independents and the left kept them from practicing a highly bureaucratic style—*"sindicalismo del sillón,"* or "armchair trade unionism," as Tosco derisively referred to it—and increased their legitimacy among the rank and file. On the other, coexistence gave them local allies and protected them from Buenos Aires.

For Vandor, the SMATA loomed as the principal obstacle to a unified and obedient Cordoban labor movement fully integrated into the Peronist union hierarchy. The national UOM also coveted the Fiat unions and began a campaign to reestablish a UOM affiliation for the Ferreyra workers, but Fiat was not a priority. The Cordoban UOM retained an important foothold in the complex, given its jurisdiction over the Concord workers, and a premature affiliation of remaining Fiat workers would serve no purpose other than to buttress the strength of an already too independently minded union. The local UOM would not bolt from the *ortodoxo* fold until changes in the balance of power in the Cordoban labor movement forced it to do so. The bigger problem for Vandor was Torres's SMATA, which was by 1962 clearly the most powerful union in the city. Vandor, moreover, could not rely on a powerful autoworkers' union central to control its wayward Cordoban branch. The SMATA central, a young union in a young industry, was still relatively weak in the early 1960s and was, at any rate, allied with Vandor's rival, Alonso. Since a powerful, centralized SMATA bureaucracy did not yet exist, and since collective bargaining agreements in the automobile industry were worked out on a company-by-company instead of an industrywide basis, there was no way to discipline the Cordoban SMATA effectively or to force it to follow directives from Buenos Aires. Torres took advantage of the situation to keep as much power in his hands as possible, and he skillfully avoided compromising entanglements while continuing to pursue an independent unionism that was more Peronist in its political vocabulary and public displays of respect for the movement's iconography than in its active involvement in Peronist trade union politics. Between 1960 and 1962, the Peronist leaders in the Cordoban SMATA tended to matters in their own union. Despite the gains won in the 1960 contract, they were still in a precarious position. Leftist union activists from the Communist party and the few outspoken Trotskyists (Fracción Trotskista de Obreros Mecánicos) from the small Partido Obrero Trotskista, maintained a vigilant and captious opposition, especially critical of the Peronists' handling of the union on the sensitive issue of job control, and were generally prepared to exploit any slip by the union leadership to their advantage.[29]

After signing the 1960 agreement, Torres's chief preoccupation remained the continued strengthening of the union apparatus, not Peronist labor politics. Following their victory later that year in the November 1960 union elections, Torres and the SMATA Peronists set about tightening their hold on the union machinery and garnering rank-and-file loyalties. The union leadership needed to win concessions from management to increase its standing among the workers as an effective, indeed indispensable, overseer of their welfare. To further that end, Torres began to cultivate personal ties with company officials. In addition to IKA president James McCloud, Torres established a close working relationship with the director of personnel, Manuel Ordóñez. Torres's friendship with Ordóñez allowed him to consult on and directly negotiate the SMATA contracts between 1960 and 1966. He privately submitted the proposals of the *comisiones paritarias* (collective bargaining committees) to Ordóñez, apprising him of the limits of concessions on the part of the union, and often winning substantial wage increases for the IKA workers peacefully and without resorting to strike action.[30]

Yet there were limits to compromise, and Torres relied more on his and the union's own resources to win gains from the company and thereby increase the SMATA's standing among the workers. Personalism became a tactic of the union leadership generally. The open assemblies at the Córdoba Sport Club had already become a SMATA institution, but after 1960 Torres showed a new fondness for calling these open assemblies. The motive could only have been to increase Torres's own visibility and the workers' identification with the union, since the issues of real consequence were decided through the formal procedures of union deliberation in the shop stewards commission or in private consultation between Torres and the union leadership, not in open assembly. Such gestures were not, however, without effect, and they helped to foster a sense among the workers of direct participation in running union affairs.

The once apathetic young workers were increasingly identifying their interests with the SMATA, thanks in no small measure to Torres's enormous abilities as a union organizer.

Torres and the executive council had become permanent fixtures on the shop floor in the IKA plants. They adopted a solicitous, comradely but paternal posture that was in the true tradition of Peronist labor. Cultivating personal ties in a labor force that already numbered in the thousands was not easy, but Torres seems to have established an extraordinary degree of familiarity with the IKA workers in these years, aided by his own great personal energy and remarkable power of recall, which allowed him to remember the names, family history, and even health problems of individual workers with prodigious accuracy. Even more tellingly, Torres adopted a combative Peronist style of discourse that made every union struggle appear hard fought and each gain, whether painlessly acquired from company officials in amicable negotiations or bitterly won through strikes, the result of the SMATA's vigilance and verve. The farm boys, former IAME workers, and others who had entered the SMATA plants just years before were learning the value of union representation—were never allowed to forget it, in fact—as Torres and his collaborators, now called the *torristas* by the workers with more affection than enmity, set about instilling perhaps not a class consciousness but certainly a union consciousness.[31]

Torres's visits to the shop floor became increasingly infrequent after the early 1960s, but his drum-beating tactics, together with the prestige even only a formal Peronist affiliation granted him and the significant gains in wages and benefits won under his union's stewardship, allowed the SMATA Peronists not only to build rank-and-file support but also gradually to neutralize the left-wing opposition in the IKA plants. An outright purge was unfeasible; the probable negative reaction of the city's other unions always weighed heavily in Torres's calculations. Still Torres was effectively achieving their isolation without a frontal assault, and only the company's actions jeopardized his success.

Torres and the Peronist union leadership had proved adroit in negotiating and winning favorable contracts for the SMATA workers, but they were hesitant and ineffective in challenging management's prerogatives on the shop floor. IKA reacted to the first signs of a tighter domestic car market partly by attempting to increase worker productivity and generally reduce labor costs. IKA's initial approach was not to undertake massive layoffs, being aware that the union would react with strikes and perhaps even factory occupations. Instead, IKA chose at first to peck away at its labor costs and begin a productivity campaign intended both to pare down the labor force through attrition and to maximize its cost-effectiveness.

Only in 1961 did company reports begin to complain of inflated labor costs and to bemoan the greater efficiency, real or imagined, of their new competitors in Buenos Aires. Most common were complaints of gold-bricking by the workers on the assembly line *(densas líneas de proceso continuo)* who reputedly failed to keep up with established production rhythms. To increase worker productivity, in late 1961 IKA began to install a series of warning lights *(señales luminosas)* along the assembly lines to indicate any interruption in the work flow.[32] These warning lights and the productivity campaign in general were responsible for greater tensions on the shop floor, and they placed new demands on Torres and the union leadership. When IKA decided in late 1962 that its labor costs were still excessive and began layoffs in the Santa Isabel plants that reached 1,500 by December, prompting a violent response from the IKA workers, Torres was forced to respect the vote of workers on the three company shifts in favor of a strike.[33]

IKA refused to negotiate the layoffs, emboldened as it was by popular disapproval of the violent tactics adopted by some of the workers, and the prospect of a prolonged and possibly fatal strike eventually persuaded Torres to accept help from Vandor. The independent union-building work of more than five years was suddenly jeopardized by IKA's intransigence. Vandor's support and that of other unions would apparently be needed to prod the government to intervene and bring IKA to the bargaining table. Vandor responded to Torres's plight, and under the threat of a UOM general strike in a dispute that was entirely the affair of the Cordoban autoworkers, the government exerted pressure for a solution and the company relented and began negotiations.[34] With the weight of Vandor and the UOM behind him, Torres managed to win an agreement in April 1962 that rescinded the layoffs in return for a reduced work day and thereby saved the SMATA leadership from a potentially humiliating defeat. The cost for Torres would be a closer alignment with Vandor and, at least for a while, a loss of the SMATA's jealously guarded independence.

As Torres and the SMATA Peronists sought to recover from these events, the Cordoban UOM attempted to strengthen its position in the local labor movement. The UOM's leader, the laconic, methodical Alejo Simó, had established his control of the union in the wake of the loss of the Fiat workers. Simó and others in the UOM reacted negatively to union secretary general Jerónimo Carrasco's less than spirited defense of the

UOM's jurisdiction over the Fiat workers and to the recent closing of the Conarg factory, one of the larger metalworking establishments in the city.[35] Simó won the 1963 union elections largely on the Fiat affiliation issue and shortly afterward began a campaign to revoke the government's decision to recognize the Fiat company unions, initiating one of his many episodic flirtations with Vandor to win the backing of the UOM *caudillo* in the affiliation drive. Simó was soon the dominant figure among the *ortodoxos,* and along with Torres, Tosco, and López, he would represent over the next fifteen years a distinct tendency in the local labor movement—distinct in terms of tactics, political alignments, and union practices. His phlegmatic ways seemed out of place in the rough and tumble world of the metalworker's union, where rivalries often ended in violence and where thuggery and *pistolerismo* were a constant part of union life, revisionist interpretations of Peronist labor notwithstanding. Simó's placid exterior hid a sharp sense of the political realities and opportunities of the moment and a naked ruthlessness that could be employed when the situation seemed to require it. He nimbly changed alliances and retained power while others in the labor movement fell victim to their idealism and political innocence.

The SMATA and the UOM had become the closest things Vandor had to local allies in Córdoba. Since each led one of the two currents in Peronist labor in the city, the *legalistas* and the *ortodoxos,* respectively, the unification of Cordoban Peronism and the integration of Córdoba into the verticalist structure appeared obtainable to Vandor. But two factors conspired against *verticalismo* in Córdoba: the continued efforts of Peronists such as Torres and Simó to retain as much independence from Buenos Aires as possible and the presence of Tosco and the Independents. Neither Torres nor Simó was anxious for a showdown with Tosco or willing to participate in a campaign to dismantle the Independents. As a result, Vandor and the labor bosses in Buenos Aires had to rely on their own resources and could count on only the neutrality of the local Peronists in their attempt to bring Córdoba into the verticalist fold. In 1963, for example, Vandor funded a press campaign to discredit Independent labor leaders, such as Tosco and Malvár. Rumors of murky foreign connections and membership in sinister foreign cabals, particularly of participation in a putative international Jewish conspiracy called the *sinarquía internacional,* long a Peronist bugaboo, appeared in the Cordoban newspapers, and similar stories ran rife in union circles throughout the year, but Torres and Simó refrained from joining the attacks.[36]

Tosco responded to the attacks by effectively withdrawing Luz y Fuerza and the Independents from national labor politics. For the length of the Illia presidency, from late 1963 until the June 1966 Onganía coup, the Cordoban Independents concentrated on a provincial strategy to protect the integrity and ideological pluralism of Cordoban labor. On November 4, 1963, the CGT central in Buenos Aires intervened against the Cordoban CGT in the first step toward establishing a wholly Peronist local CGT. Simó was named regional delegate to oversee the restructuring of the local CGT and to coordinate the national CGT's *plan de lucha*—country-wide factory occupation and a general strike against the Illia government.[37] Torres was expected to cooperate in his new position as secretary general of the Cordoban CGT. However, neither Simó nor Torres completely fulfilled Vandor's expectations. Tosco and the Independents reacted frostily to Vandor's *plan de lucha* against the Illia government and gave only tepid support to the May 27, 1964, general strike, thereby serving notice that the Cordoban Independents intended to remain outside the boundaries of *verticalismo,* although willing to cooperate with local Peronists who respected the diversity of the local labor movement.[38] The *ortodoxos* and *legalistas* made no move to discipline the Independents at the time of the strike, which they supported actively with factory occupations, nor in the remaining two years of the Illia government. Tosco, Malvár, and other non-Peronist labor leaders continued to participate actively and as voting members in the Cordoban CGT.

Torres and Simó were reluctant partners in the verticalist campaign, not out of any sense of fair play or even respect for ideological plurality in Cordoban labor, but rather as a result of a cold assessment of the campaign's scant chances of success and their own wish to remain free of Vandor. The former was demonstrated convincingly just two weeks prior to the May 1964 general strike when Tosco, running on a platform extremely critical of Vandor, won reelection in Luz y Fuerza. With the Peronist slate offering only formal opposition, Tosco's *lista azul* received 1,114 votes compared with the Peronists' 298.[39] Furthermore Tosco's slate was the most pluralist to date and contained many of the men—Ramón Contreras, Simón Grigatis, Felipe Alberti, and Tomás Di Toffino—who would be Tosco's closest collaborators in the coming years. Any verticalist campaign would thenceforth have to take into account the fact that the light and power workers could not be tamed simply by eliminating Tosco, that the strength of pluralist sentiment within the union ran deep.

There were other factors that also cautioned restraint. By the end of the Illia government, there were already signs that Luz y Fuerza was straying further from the traditional boundaries of the Argentine labor movement and gaining stature nationally as the voice for dissidents and the disgruntled in the workers' movement. At the 1965 national labor congress held at La Cumbre in the nearby Cordoban *sierra,* the Luz y Fuerza representatives, Tosco in particular, launched scathing attacks against the *burocracia porteña* and, for the first time, made explicit reference to their conception of the labor movement as an instrument of "national liberation."[40] The more prominent the union became, and the more outspoken in its opinions, the more reluctant local Peronists were to participate in any plan to isolate and eliminate it as a force in Cordoban labor. On the other hand, the Cordoban Peronists' ties to Vandor and the Peronist labor movement meant, for the time being, that an alliance with Tosco and the Independents was out of the question. The result was paralysis, an unwillingness to carry out the wishes of Buenos Aires and yet a reluctance to join with Tosco and make the Cordoban CGT the source of their strength in conflicts in their respective industries.

The baleful consequences of the local Peronist unions' inability to control their own fate were highlighted in the 1964–65 Fiat affiliation controversy. This incident proved once again that Vandor was as intent on limiting the power of potential rivals among the Cordoban Peronists as he was on integrating Córdoba into the national labor movement. And as in the past, the SMATA represented a potential threat. Vandor had targeted the Fiat company unions as part of his verticalist campaign, but there were risks involved. Though Torres and the SMATA were no longer completely free of Buenos Aires, they retained considerable independence, and recent events had suggested an even more important role for Torres and the Cordoban autoworkers' union.

One development was that the SMATA Peronists no longer looked as vulnerable as they had just one year before. Rank-and-file participation was growing and the position of the leadership had been buttressed, making the Cordoban SMATA the most powerful industrial union in the Argentine interior and a worthy rival to the UOM.[41] Torres's slate, moreover, had won a decisive victory in the April 1964 SMATA elections. Nevertheless the Cordoban SMATA remained loyal to Vandor for the moment and supported, unsuccessfully, the *vandorista* slate in the election of SMATA central authorities held that same month.[42] Torres was by this time fully immersed in the politics of the Peronist labor movement, grooming himself for a national leadership role and being referred to in the labor press as the "Cordoban Vandor." He was a consummate union negotiator and an able political horse trader, alternately combative and conciliatory as necessary to assure his trade union base and advance his personal ambitions. Thus there were signs in early 1964 that Torres and the Cordoban SMATA were recovering some of the ground lost since 1962 and that the autoworkers' union, in a rapid state of growth in Buenos Aires as well Córdoba, might threaten to develop into a serious rival to the UOM.

This new state of affairs presented a predicament for Vandor. The campaign begun in 1964 to abolish the Fiat company unions might strengthen the position of the SMATA even more. With the company's Concord plant now fully reconverted to automobile production, an affiliation with the SMATA, not the UOM, would be the logical choice, and Torres was now publicly demanding jurisdiction over Ferreyra and had already sent his men to the Fiat factory gates with affiliation cards. The situation was further complicated by the Cordoban UOM's wish to continue to represent the workers in the Concord plant and Simó's demand that any agreement with Fiat should restore the pre-1960 status quo in which the UOM had the sole representation of the Fiat workers. In 1964, a group of Radical and Christian Democrat activists in the Concord plant, unhappy with the UOM representation and compelled, no doubt, by an anti-Peronist animus, began to agitate for an affiliation of the Concord workers with the company union, SITRAC. With a sympathetic Radical government in power, *personería gremial* was awarded to SITRAC, and the UOM lost its last bailiwick in Ferreyra.[43]

The Fiat affiliation controversy raged through late 1964 and much of 1965 in the midst of stalled collective bargaining negotiations and a bitter 1965 strike in the Ferreyra plants. The inability of SITRAC to negotiate effectively with the Italian multinational's vastly more powerful management discouraged even the most enthusiastic early supporters of the plant union. Worker sentiment by 1965 was overwhelmingly in favor of a SMATA affiliation, and the first step toward that goal was taken on April 1, 1965, when workers in the Grandes Motores Diesel plant voted almost unanimously for affiliation with the autoworkers' union, a vote subsequently upheld by the Ministry of Labor.[44]

The SMATA was still anathema to the company, though Fiat continued to recognize the difficulty of maintaining labor peace in the plants without some Peronist union representation. To avoid the long-feared prospect of affiliation with the SMATA, Fiat appears to have cut a deal with Vandor and Simó, the latter now serving as a Peronist congressional deputy and dividing his time between Córdoba and Buenos Aires. The UOM transferred some 80 UOM union activists from Fiat's UOM-affiliated plants in

Buenos Aires to Córdoba. The company let them enter the Ferreyra plants as newly hired workers, and despite initial worker suspicion of the newcomers, they quickly established control over the fledgling SITRAC union—at least this was the widespread belief of the Fiat workers, especially those who would lead the factory rebellions in the Ferreyra plants several years later.[45]

The UOM activists' unexpected leadership of the 1965 strike, a gamble on the part of Vandor to reestablish the prestige of the metalworkers' union among the labor force and to force Fiat's formal recognition of the UOM's jurisdiction, caught the company by surprise. The strike ended in an ignominious defeat for SITRAC, and Fiat banished the UOM from its plants, though the UOM's collective bargaining agreements would be used as the model for Fiat's own in-house contracts for the remainder of the decade. Fiat recognized that at least formal, perfunctory union representation would be necessary in the plants to avoid a SMATA affiliation and the company decided to retain SITRAC and transform it into an appendage of its industrial relations department, to be at the bidding of the company rather than the workers. Fiat preserved the two company unions, SITRAC and SITRAM, as the institutional representatives of the Fiat workers while relying on its traditional mix of paternalist and authoritarian policies, rather than genuine union representation, to handle the labor force. Fiat's paternalism, expressed in its sports clubs and in a well-publicized campaign to give employment to Argentines of Italian descent along with a symbolic partnership status as *"socios,"* deepened after the 1965 strike.[46] The company demanded that SITRAC-SITRAM maintain a quiescent labor force and adherence to Ferreyra's traditional isolation from local and national labor politics, a task that the *sindicatos de planta* would perform obediently for the following half decade. Torres did not abandon his campaign to incorporate the Concord and Materfer workers. However, he saw that the company was not prepared to give in on the issue, and he was unwilling to undertake a prolonged and probably futile fight that might jeopardize the affiliation of the GMD workers. Torres temporarily conceded the loss of the Fiat workers to their plant unions.[47]

The continued existence of Fiat's company unions protected the Independents and revealed the already peculiar character of Cordoban trade unionism. For Tosco's Independents, their survival meant the preservation of an unusually heterogeneous labor movement, one that hindered Vandor's verticalist campaign. Though Fiat preserved its company unions, they remained a nullity in the power politics of Cordoban labor for years. Vandor could keep the Fiat workers away from the SMATA but could not use them either to strengthen his hand in Córdoba or to isolate the Independents. The entire Fiat affair had shown just how propitious local conditions were to a pluralist labor movement and how inappropriate Vandor's tactics were, given his twin preoccupations with buttressing the Cordoban Peronists and assuring they could pose no threat to his control of the Peronist labor movement nationally. Vandor could hardly call for strict verticalism and ideological purity if he were willing to acquiesce in the continued isolation of the second largest concentration of industrial workers in the city. Tosco and the Independents criticized the UOM's interference in the Fiat affiliation controversy and later denounced the "yellow" unionism of Fiat's company unions, but they were also aware that the arrangement protected them and hindered Vandor. For the Cordoban Peronists, it was further evidence that their individual interests needed to be protected from Buenos Aires. In this particular instance, Simó, the UOM, and the *ortodoxos* had lost more than Torres, the SMATA, and the *legalistas,* but no one was happy with the interference from Buenos Aires nor with the necessity to sacrifice local needs to the strategic calculations of Vandor, and each would seek to increase his independence in the coming years.

In the first months of 1966, as Vandor had to confront a series of new challenges to his leadership from his erstwhile adversary José Alonso as well as from trade unionists, subsequently dubbed the *participacionistas,* intent on taking *"peronismo sin Perón"* a step further and looking for organic links with the next probable military government, local union politics returned to a less agitated state. The balance of power within and between unions now seemed to be established; it appeared that only some providential and momentous force would be capable of disrupting it. Yet the alignments were less firm than they seemed and more supple than those of any other labor movement in the country. Tosco's Independents and the Fiat company unions introduced elements that were absent elsewhere. The Cordoban CGT continued to follow a more independent course, a situation that presented opportunities in the city for Peronist and non-Peronist trade unionists alike. In the April 1966 election of national SMATA leadership, the Cordoban local, alone among the country's autoworkers, voted for the *lista celeste* slate backed by Vandor, thus indicating that Torres's alliance with the UOM leader remained firm.[48] If it was an alliance that restricted Córdoba's independence in some ways, it was also one that enhanced the local's autonomy in others, since it protected the union from the threat of interference from a meddlesome autoworkers' union central.

However, Cordoban labor autonomy, and the dissident union movement it helped to produce, was the result not only of the tug and pull of local union politics but also of the particular kind of industrial development the city had experienced and of the trade union practices that had resulted from it. In the automobile industry especially, there existed a different relationship between the leadership and the workers, an alternative union tradition fashioned from the influences of work and the respective management philosophies of the local firms. That alternative union tradition underlay the great labor mobilizations in Córdoba between 1966 and 1976.

· T H R E E ·

The Factory, the Union, and
the New Industrial Worker

In the first great wave of historical scholarship dealing with industrial working class, labor historians such as E. P. Thompson, Herbert Gutman, David Montgomery, and Michelle Perrot persuasively argued that the cultural traditions of peasant and artisan had impinged significantly on working class formation—that industrialization, at least in England, the United States, and France, did not encounter individuals without established modes of behavior and thought, folkways and traditions that greatly influenced the workers' subsequent forms of association and political comportment.[1] Yet as these historians themselves often explicitly acknowledge in their writings, such arguments seem more appropriate for the working class formation of early industrialization, for the transition from the peasant and artisanal world to that of nascent industrial capitalism, rather than for the workers of the "second industrial revolution," born in the era of mass production and during the full maturation of capitalism. Even less do they seem to apply to a newly industrialized country such as Argentina.

The modern factory, though it was never the entire universe of the workers' experience in Argentina or anywhere else, shaped class consciousness more directly and completely than early factories had affected those first industrial workers subject to the competing influences of peasant and artisanal traditions, which facilitated resistance to the discipline of factory life. In Córdoba, by contrast, a new industrial worker had emerged, uprooted from the farm or small rural town and thrust suddenly into the workings of mass production and the industrial relations systems of the modern corporation. The new industrial worker felt little of the pull and tug of competing traditions and was certainly unable to resist, individually, the overwhelming power of the factory.

In the automobile plants, a new set of relationships and a new view of the world were fashioned. Córdoba's industrial boom introduced a young, largely inexperienced and unskilled labor force to a particular workplace environment, to the peculiar ambience and demands of work in a mass production industry. Life in the factory became the workers' principal social link, even overshadowing the importance of other working class institutions such as the family and the neighborhood. Through their work lives, the Cordoban autoworkers acquired a view of society and their own place in it, a complex set of attitudes formed by the experience of work and given meaning by the country's political culture and the union's political and ideological interpretation of the workers' status as producers in a country divided sharply along class lines. The dynamic relationship between factory and society in Córdoba in those years underlay the history of the workers' movement in the city. It is in examining that relationship that the historian's search for the explanations of recent Cordoban working class history will be the most fruitful.

The gradual emergence of the Cordoban autoworkers as a militant and leading sector of the Argentine labor movement, and their increasing prominence in national politics after the 1969 Cordobazo, called into question what had been the conventional wisdom among postwar scholars of the Latin American working classes. In the 1960s, sociologists and political scientists had begun to apply to Latin America arguments made popular in the United States by Herbert Marcuse, Seymour Lipset, and Daniel Bell, who themselves had merely restated Lenin's and Gramsci's labor aristocracy theories with regard to the conservatism of at least the more privileged sectors of the American working class, to their growing embourgeoisement and concern for higher wages and social mobility over politics. Most studies of Latin American labor written before the Cordobazo seem to suggest, if not openly assert, that workers in the modern industrial sectors in Latin America, among them autoworkers, were destined to become a kind of labor aristocracy in the region, potentially combative on economic issues but apathetic politically and indifferent toward the fate of other, less privileged sectors of the working class. These "new industrial workers," who were outside the populist labor structures and pragmatic in their outlook, were believed to be fully integrated into the companies for which they worked. Higher wages, lavish benefits, and more autonomous and effective industrial relations systems caused the workers to direct their aspirations within the company rather than toward one form of politics or another, whether oppositional or collaborative.[2] On the left, a small but outspoken minority argued that just the opposite was the case: that these modern industrial workers, inserted in the most advanced sectors of capitalism, were in a better position to perceive the contradictions of that system and to develop demands of a more advanced and ultimately political nature, thus serving as a kind of vanguard within the workers' movement.[3]

In the late 1960s, a team of sociologists working under the direction of French sociologist Alain Touraine carried out surveys of worker attitudes in various Latin American countries, among them Argentina. The surveys revealed that workers in the most advanced sectors of Argentine industry, while displaying certain "integrative" attitudes toward their company—as expressed in their perception of their relatively privileged status and their desire to stay in the employment of the firm, as well as in the widespread belief that their individual interests depended on the company's fortunes, not the conquest of political power—also expressed skepticism about their employer's willingness to satisfy their demands without the vigilance of the state and their unions. Moreover, a sense of relative privilege did not necessarily ameliorate class tensions; nor did it cause workers to abandon their identity as a group that was in some way in conflict with the company, or to perceive their interests as necessarily different from those of other sectors of the working class. Economic integration thus existed alongside a continued sense of social distinctiveness, even a kind of class identity.[4]

In truth, workers in the modern industrial sectors had the potential to behave as either a labor aristocracy or a labor vanguard, depending on the historical conditions that existed at a given moment. At least in Argentina, and it would appear to be the case in Brazil and Mexico as well, the autoworkers' unions initially fulfilled the expectations of the social scientists and behaved more as an aristocracy than a vanguard. Union efforts were directed toward strengthening the union machinery through improved wages and benefits. Collective bargaining took place directly with the company and with minimal union involvement in politics and even limited interference from the state. The SMATA central's failure to participate in the reorganization of the CGT in 1963 or in the factory occupations during the 1964 *plan de lucha,* indeed the early union-building years of the SMATA local itself, did seem to indicate a nascent business unionism in that particular industrial sector. However, high wages, elaborate company social welfare programs, and paternalist labor policies put forth by the companies did not necessarily make labor militancy impossible or prevent an eventual involvement in politics. After 1966, when the Onganía dictatorship suspended collective bargaining privileges and thereby adversely affected the Cordoban autoworkers' wages and working conditions, the leadership role autoworkers assumed in labor's opposition to the regime was not merely a reaction to a loss of privileged status; rather, it drew heavily on the autoworkers' own sense of class identity, something forged through a complex mix of industrial and cultural factors and merely triggered by the government's assault on their incomes and benefits.

Scholars who have studied Latin American autoworkers have given priority to state policy as the determinative factor in the leadership role assumed by the auto industry's unions in the Latin American labor movements of the 1960s and 1970s. John Humphrey, Ian Roxborough, and Kevin Middlebrook have all emphasized such factors as government wage and labor policies, the breakdown of populist-corporatist labor structures, and the autonomous industrial relations systems of the automotive multinationals in their attempt to explain the sudden emergence of the Latin American autoworkers as the principal powers within their trade union movements and as important political actors in their own right—certainly the most important within the ranks of organized labor. None of these scholars, however, has considered fully the complex process of class and the formation of class consciousness in all its facets in the industry—specifically the precise shop floor and cultural contexts in which it developed, and which state policies it interacted with to shape the autoworkers' attitudes and influence their political behavior.[5]

The specific nature of automotive work in Latin America and the ideological and political interpretations given to factory life by unions and by society at large are elements either ignored or considered only in passing in these studies. Paying attention exclusively to the effects of state policies on this industrial sector has certainly simplified the sources of the autoworkers' militancy and underestimated how disruptive, confusing, and formative factory life was for this new working class. Specifically, scholars have failed to acknowledge the importance of such diverse industrial influences as labor processes, management philosophies, and union practices in establishing the autoworkers as a militant sector of the postwar Latin American working class.

In Córdoba, these first-generation workers were abruptly introduced to the unique rigors of work in an automotive plant. At both Fiat and IKA-Renault there were three 8-hour shifts, and the plants were ceaseless centers of activity. For the handful of skilled workers who had passed through the IAME factories, the rhythms and demands of mass production were familiar and reasonably comfortable terrain. But for the majority of autoworkers, the noise, the rush, and the physical and mental strain of eight hours on the line was something completely new, and they were greatly affected by all the influences of work in the factory. It is thus necessary to understand not only the interaction of the unions with the state, but also those of the workers and their unions with the companies, and the particular conditions that surrounded work in the Cordoban car plants.

There were essentially three kinds of workers in the Fiat and IKA-Renault factories. The first were the highly skilled maintenance workers (electricians and machine repairmen) and the toolmakers and set-up men who made and assembled the dies, jigs, fixtures, and form tools that went on to the specialized machine tools for the production of parts. The second were the operatives: the semiskilled machine operators who performed drilling, grinding, boring, and other tasks on the engine blocks, cylinder heads, crankshafts, and other complicated mechanical components. Finally, there were the unskilled workers— the majority of employees—who were engaged in final assembly and who performed simple operations such as mounting, tightening, filing, and similar repetitive tasks. For the semiskilled workers standard output, or "ratings," were established, and chronometers were used to time jobs and establish the rates required of the workers. For semiskilled and unskilled workers alike, job categories were loosely defined in the early years of the Cordoban industry; only after Renault's buyout of IKA in 1967 did the French company establish more precise job categories. For the unskilled workers, job categories ultimately depended more on the nature of the job performed than the attributes or skills of the worker himself. Job categories were thus determined by such factors as monotony of the work, effort expanded (dépense musculaire), and dexterity demanded, and by the comparative unpleasantness and the health hazards of the workers' department (noise level; incidence of respiratory and skin irritants caused by dust, steam, or gas; intensity of light and heat) rather than skill, just as they were in Renault's French plants.[6]

The production process in the Fiat and IKA-Renault plants shared the general characteristics of automotive manufacturing found at the time in other parts of the world, but with important variations resulting from the nature of the city's belated automotive industrialization and the local market conditions. As in plants in Europe, the United States, and Japan, in the Cordoban factories' forge operations the sheet metal and bar stock were worked into component parts or dies. (A die is a high-precision tool used in body stamping, a heavy metal form, designed for a specific car model, that presses the sheet steel to produce body panels.) The dies themselves were designed and cut with high-precision tools in the Fiat and IKA-Renault plants, including all types of hammers, upset forging machines, and vertical forging machines. Die makers in this and other departments in the Cordoban factories still retained a high degree of skill, unlike those in the industrialized countries where large consumer markets and standardized production processes had greatly reduced the need for skill and job discretion in the manufacturing of dies. In Córdoba, the workers who produced the specialized dies, jigs, and fixtures used on the machine tools were more skilled and retained a considerable degree of control over their work until the mid-1960s, when the companies began to increase the number of models produced annually and production processes were brought closer to those existing in the industry internationally.

Typical of the die operations in the early years of automotive manufacturing in Córdoba was the process used to create the dies for the different parts of the body. Such a die started out as a heavy steel casting that was molded into shape, initially by workers using general, all-purpose tools; only later did workers employ profiling machines, which had a stylus that automatically moved over a model of the part and directed the milling cutter to grind the steel to produce the precise shape of the die. The dies were then ground further by hand to prevent any imperfection after the sheet metal had been pressed into shape. Hundreds of dies were used for just one automobile body.[7]

After the tool and die shops, the production moved into various departments. The body dies, for example, were taken to the power presses, where they were locked on and used to stamp, bend, and perforate sections of the auto body. The body then passed through various subassembly departments where spot welders and assembly workers fastened the body shell together. In the body welding departments in the IKA-Renault complex, special jigs held the parts in place while the workers welded the body together using electric welding machines. After spot welding, the body moved down the assembly line where additional welding, sanding, and polishing jobs were performed. Solderers used blowtorches to join the seams and then smoothed them down with hand tools. The body then moved into the paint tunnels where the frames were coated, sprayed twice by hand, baked, and then painted again before being moved on to various lines where trim and finish work was performed, after which some would move on to the next production department while others would go into storage as reserve stock in case of any disruption in production. Every department had its own occupational hazards. For the solderers it was the hot, dripping solder that fell from each car. For the workers in the painting tunnels, a department "full of poisonous vapors, damaged lungs, benzene poisoning and blood diseases," as Robert Linhart described it in his famous account of work inside the French Citroën plants, goggles and gas masks could not prevent the inhaling of noxious fumes, which led to some of the highest rates of industrial disease in automotive work.

The special nature of work in the Cordoban car plants was perhaps best shown in the production machining departments. By the time of Cordoba's automotive boom, work in the machine shops of most automobile factories had gone the way of other jobs and been effectively "deskilled." Indeed, the jigs and fixtures used to set up and position the work in car plants were called "farmers' tools," since inexperienced, green hands could turn out work better and faster than those of a skilled machinist. In the North American and European factories, this process had gone even further, and work on the engine blocks by the late 1950s was being largely performed by automated machinery, transfer machines with work-feeding devices that were monitored by the workers and that moved work down the line by coded, punched, or magnetic tape.[8] In Córdoba's factories, by contrast, engine blocks continued to be moved manually, in small trucks, rather than by conveyor belts or transfer machines, and they were worked on by workers using various all-purpose machine tools. Indeed, Kaiser had moved his operations from the United States to Argentina largely because he was unable to invest in automated machinery.

The workers in the machine shops in Córdoba performed hundreds of broaching, honing, drilling, tapping, and milling operations. In the Fiat Concord plant, which in the late 1950s had begun experimenting with automobile production, and especially in the IKA-Renault plants an unusually high degree of informal, nonautomated work was performed, evidenced by the great number of general, all-purpose tools in the plants' machining departments, the slower pace of work, the poor quality control, and the higher than normal incidence of defects.[9] These machinists were largely experienced workers who had learned their trade in the IAME plants, though a fair number of new, inexperienced workers made it into the machining departments and showed a remarkably high degree of innate mechanical ability, a fact that oral testimony indicates was due, in the case of many, to their experience using and repairing the antiquated farm machinery that was still employed on many Argentine farms, especially in Córdoba.

Most of the production machining was performed on the automobiles' cylinder blocks, cylinder heads, and crankshafts. In the Fiat plants, Cincinnati milling machines were used for mounting the cylinder block and then for drilling in a series of cutting and boring operations, after which the cylinder block would receive manually applied perforations. The block was then pressure washed, and bearings and cramshaft holes were rough-bored. Further machining operations, such as milling for the oil gauge and ignition distributor, operations that were performed manually in Córdoba, were performed in Fiat's Italian plants by automatic drilling machines that also transferred the block; the worker in Italy only loaded and locked the work into position.[10] Similarly, automatic drilling machines were used in Turin to drill the spark plug holes and to make the necessary tappings on the cylinder head, operations that were performed manually in the Concord plant. The absence of automatic drillers in the Concord factory worried company officials, because of the excessive dependence then placed on more highly skilled labor for basic machining work.[11] Nevertheless, low production volumes in the early years discouraged investment in the machines, and in the line-bearing machines also used in Fiat's Turin plants to perform lathe work on the crankshafts and to feed and make the cuts on the shaft axis, in what was there a completely automatic process.

Elsewhere in the Córdoba plants work was a modified, more informal variant of Fordist production practices. Since production was carried out on a low-volume basis, the machinery imported from Kaiser's Michigan plants for many departments stood idle or underutilized, a fact that raised their capital costs and quickly encouraged IKA to adopt more flexible and effective work practices for its labor force.[12] Engine assembly at both Fiat and IKA was done by hand, the first assembly workers putting in the pistons, crankshafts, wrist pins, valves, oil pumps, flywheels, connecting rods, water pumps, and spark plugs, while the next would add the alternators, fuel pumps, water hoses, and other parts that would allow the engine to pass the inspection station and meet up with the finished chassis for final assembly. Final assembly was performed in the Fiat complex only until the mid-1960s, after which the assembly lines were moved to Fiat's El Palomar plants in Buenos Aires Province. Final assembly in both Santa Isabel and Ferreyra in the early years of the industry was nevertheless a similar process. Different assembly lines existed for the various models being produced (at IKA-Renault there were three separate lines; at Fiat there were two), and workers had more tasks to perform on lines that moved at speeds well below those found in automobile plants in Europe and North America.[13]

Final assembly began in the chassis shop, where workers would lower the engine onto the frame with overhead cranes and then hook up the drive shaft. As the finished chassis moved down the line, other workers would bolt the engine into place with power tools. This "engine drop" process was followed by the "body drop," in which the car body, suspended above the line and held there by huge mechanical "hands," would be slowly lowered by the workers onto the chassis. Once in place, the body moved down the line where it would be bolted down securely and the steering wheel, horn ring, and other parts would be added. Meanwhile, subassembly work in the nearby upholstery department would be coming to a conclusion, and the finished seats would be added. Upholstery was widely regarded in the industry as the "finesse" department, which required nimble hands and great dexterity, a fact that perhaps explains the sizable numbers of women in that particular department in other automobile industries, though not in Córdoba's. Industrial sewing machines were used to sew the heavy cloth and vinyl, while special compressing machines squeezed the seats and backrests to allow the upholstery to be pulled over them, and steam machines were used to take out the wrinkles and make the seat covers fit tautly.

Subassembly on the front end of the body was also proceeding simultaneously. There dozens of additional parts, such as the headlights, turn signals, horn, grille, and radiator, were added, as was the electrical wiring needed to make the dashboard operate. The front end was then fed into the main assembly line, where it was dropped into place on the body. The "trimming" process then began, where the finished seats were installed and the ornamental chrome was added, along with further electrical wiring, the glass, interior hardware, the radio, the heater, and other accessories. Workers would bolt the front end in place, hook up the water hoses, and connect the wires of the electrical systems. The finished car would then go through the final test and inspection departments and be delivered to the lots for shipment.

Though the precise nature of the plants' production processes and shop floor relations would eventually impinge greatly on the politics of the local autoworkers' unions, automotive work in Córdoba in the early years was, if not a value-neutral experience for the labor force, certainly given political and ideological meaning only by the unions. The prolonged militancy of the Cordoban working class and the leadership role assumed specifically by the city's autoworkers in Argentine working class politics in the 1960s and 1970s cannot simply be explained by particular working class conditions. They were, rather, the products of the multiple influences of Argentine, and especially Cordoban, society at that time, and of the special character of the local trade union movement.

The proscription of Peronism during these years was certainly a factor of enormous influence in shaping workers' perceptions of their condition. With the union-building drive complete, Elpidio Torres had abandoned his initial aloofness and involved the SMATA in Peronist trade union politics to an increasing degree in the early 1960s. The union's active participation in the 1964 *plan de lucha,* culminating in an unprecedented occupation of the IKA plants by the workers, was just one of many examples of the SMATA's increasing involvement in the politics of the Peronist trade union movement.

The Peronization of the young automotive proletariat, its growing self-identification as a disenfranchised class, the strength of nationalist and anti-imperialist sentiment within its ranks and among individuals who had previously thought little in such terms, were part of a process of acculturation that took place under the union's tutelage. A deepening Peronist identity naturally served to strengthen the position of Torres and the Peronist SMATA leadership, but the process was not simply or cynically orchestrated from above. Indeed many *torrista* union activists were themselves a product of this Peronization, and the workers were drawn toward a Peronist identity and eventually to a high degree of militancy by factors beyond the control of Torres and the union hierarchy. One such factor was certainly the unique character of the Cordoban trade union movement, a product of the city's late industrialization.

I have already discussed the significance of the greater autonomy that recent industrial development had allowed the Cordoban labor movement, specifically in its independence from Buenos Aires. However, the effects of this autonomy on the internal practices of the unions, particularly the autoworkers' unions, has only briefly been alluded to, and understanding these effects is essential to understanding the Cordoban autoworkers' history.[14] The considerable degree of independence that decentralized collective bargaining fostered, for example, gave union activity in an industry such as automobile manufacturing a concrete focus, and ultimately drew workers' into a closer identification with the union and union affairs. The key variable was not the formal structure of the union but the specific management philosophy and practice; that is what gave expression to Cordoban autonomy, that either allowed or discouraged union activity and worker participation in union affairs. The existence of plant unions, in the case of the Fiat workers, and industrial unions, in the case of the IKA workers, were not in themselves determinative of either greater internal union democracy or working class militancy.[15]

By accepting the union as an independent interlocutor for its labor force, IKA allowed the particular characteristics of the autoworkers' union structure—its somewhat greater control over union funds and especially the decentralized nature of union elections and collective bargaining negotiations—to have expression locally. Specifically, it contributed to the adoption of more democratic and participatory internal union practices. These practices ultimately contributed to the creation of a highly militant labor force.[16] The daily skirmishing between labor and management in the integrated, mass-production industry increased the union presence in the plants and strengthened its standing among the workers. The existence of union institutions such as the shop stewards' commission *(comisiones internas)*, which gathered on a weekly basis to discuss union matters, or the collective bargaining committees *(comisiones paritarias)*, which were drawn from the shop stewards and met on a quarterly basis to adjust the wage levels provided under the *cláusula gatillo* (wage adjustment clause) of the 1960 collective bargaining agreement, gave workers a sense of their own ability to influence issues relating to their income and, to a lesser extent, working conditions. They greatly raised participation in union affairs, as evidenced by the increasingly high percentages of workers who voted in union elections.[17]

The elections themselves were generally honest and free from the intimidation and fraud that more and more often would characterize Peronist trade unionism. Unlike the case of the SMATA locals in Buenos

Aires, for example, the Peronists in Córdoba were always faced with rival slates. Thus the SMATA union statute requiring that representatives from opposition slates be given seats on the local's electoral committee was not the dead letter it was in Buenos Aires; some degree of internal union democracy was assured in the Cordoban local.

The actual effectiveness and independence of many of these union institutions and practices under the Peronist leadership should not be exaggerated. Objections to Torres's backroom negotiating style and his links to the company must not be dismissed as merely the carping of the Peronists' left-wing opposition in the SMATA plants, as events after the Cordobazo would make abundantly clear. Yet it is also clear that the conditions created by automotive production, combined with presence of opposition within the union, both that of the Marxist left and eventually that of dissident Peronists, caused Torres to adopt union practices and a style of leadership that had the ultimate effect of instilling in the IKA autoworkers a strong sense of their rights and a heightened sensitivity to the injustice of their status as a disenfranchised class.

Torres's attempt to cultivate a combative union image and establish a union tradition among the labor force involved both style and practice. The union leadership tapped into the political imagery and vocabulary of anti-imperialism and the widespread hostility toward capitalism that was so potent in Argentina in the 1960s and was the common property of Peronism and the Marxist left. The SMATA's diatribes against the oligarchy and the capitalist firm had a clear and recent precedent in—and perhaps an outright descent from—the working class traditions in the Peronist Resistance. As one historian has noted, the constant representation in union publications of IKA as the "octopus," the ubiquitous, voracious predator exploiting the country and the workers, indifferent to the national interest, was merely the most graphic example of the union's at least publicly contentious relationship with the company.

Similarly the union's challenges to the company's absolute control over certain managerial functions, among them IKA's unilateral discretion in assigning overtime work, had the intended effect of staking out ever widening parameters of authority for the union and increasing its prestige among the workers. With the first signs of doldrums in the automotive market, IKA began to attempt to reduce costs through layoffs and, especially, reduced work days, measures that had an obviously deleterious effect on the workers' monthly earnings. The vigorous union response against layoffs and reduced work hours, and perhaps even the feebler, sporadic, and somewhat disingenuous union calls for shared worker participation in planning and managing the company *(cogestión)*, fed class animosities and heightened worker identification with the Cordoban local.[18]

At Fiat, in contrast, the potential that existed for developing a similar working class tradition, thanks to independence from the bureaucratic structures of Peronist trade unionism, was not realized, because of the very different managerial philosophy and union practices there. The difference was not simply Fiat's paternalism versus IKA's more modern industrial relations practices, since IKA, through its sports clubs and community service programs, also had adopted elements of a paternalist managerial philosophy. Rather, the crucial difference was that Fiat relied exclusively on paternalist practices to handle its labor force and to confront the problems that emerged in the workplace. The company's distribution of school uniforms for the children of Fiat workers, its annual Christmas parties with presents ostentatiously distributed by the wives of company officials, the maternity clinic it established in Ferreyra in 1967, and the activities of Fiat's Centro Cultural, which sponsored everything from public lectures to sports clubs to vacation colonies, were all within a well-established Fiat tradition of attempting to ameliorate the animosities, grudges, and discontent created by work on the line through company paternalism, thereby building worker loyalty and undermining any resort to worker solidarity or unionism. Official union discourse in the Fiat plant unions was free of any hint of the class animosities so prevalent in the SMATA and tended to preach cooperation, even integration, with the company. More important, the absence of any of the SMATA-type participatory practices in the Fiat plants, where the shop stewards were not renewed after 1965 and were practically powerless after the failure of the great 1965 strike, discouraged union participation and undermined labor militancy. In plants where wages and working conditions were determined unilaterally by the company and merely rubber-stamped by the plant unions, workers were unconvinced of the utility of participating in union affairs, a situation that naturally bred apathy among the labor force.[19]

The greater significance of the formative decade in Cordoban labor history following Perón's overthrow was therefore not only the resilience of the various ideological and political currents at work in the city's unions, but also the development of internal union practices that gave Cordoban labor particular characteristics within the Argentine labor movement. One reason for the emergence and survival of those currents and union practices was the interplay of national and local labor politics in the city. Another was the particular character of Córdoba's sudden industrialization, which introduced new and powerful actors in Cordoban trade unionism and established a certain degree of autonomy for the local trade union movement. That local autonomy encouraged more democratic practices and a greater propensity to use militant tactics in a number of the city's most important unions than was seen in other parts of the country. The Cordoban labor movement was operating in a setting very different from that in other parts of the country, especially in Buenos Aires. Labor politics in Buenos Aires was by the mid-1960s largely limited to rivalries for control of the CGT and the 62 Organizaciones, as well as to an overriding concern with protecting the Peronist labor movement's bargaining position with the state, which ultimately arbitrated in all industrial disputes.

In Córdoba, labor politics was an ongoing struggle for collective bargaining muscle, independence from Buenos Aires, and rank-and-file support. There the Peronists were more vulnerable, and their control over labor was never secure. Given their isolation from Buenos Aires, the center of economic and trade union power in Argentina, the Cordoban unions' ability to deal and horse-trade directly with the Labor Ministry and the government was minimal. This situation kept the union's leaders closer to the workers and made it more difficult for them to adopt the bureaucratic style and rigid hierarchies that were especially becoming characteristic of the bigger Peronist industrial unions in Buenos Aires, including the autoworkers' union. It also gave the Cordoban labor movement a vitality unmatched in the country. Labor politics in Córdoba was not a benumbed and hollow ritual but a vital part of urban life in which union leaders and workers alike, and even other groups and classes, were beginning to take an active interest and to participate with greater frequency and resolve. The union tradition that had crystallized in Córdoba by 1966 was thus a combination of a strong sense of regional identity and an almost visceral animosity toward Buenos Aires, combined with an acceptance, born of pragmatism in some unions and independence and opposition in others, of the need to uphold the ideological pluralism of the local labor movement. Finally there was a growing confidence in

Córdoba's ability to participate in national labor politics as a force in its own right. This local working class tradition underlay the subsequent decade of struggles when the Cordoban unions influenced not only the politics of the labor movement, but that of the entire country as well.

· II ·

Rebellion

From that time the youth of Córdoba began to experiment with new ideas, and it was not long before the effects were felt.

Domingo Faustino Sarmiento, *Facundo*

· F O U R ·

Córdoba and the "Argentine Revolution"

The military coup that overthrew the Illia government on June 28, 1966, was intended as the first step toward making a final and irrevocable break with the many legacies of Peronism. The military and civilian groups that had argued for the coup, and found an appropriately willing and guileless figure to lead the "Argentine Revolution" in the dour General Juan Carlos Onganía, offered a comprehensive program to halt what they saw as the country's obstinate decline. Their ideas were heavily influenced by the policies, even the style, of the military regime in neighboring Brazil that had been in power since overthrowing the country's civilian government in 1964. Like their counterparts in Brazil, the Argentine apostles of the new order had contempt for the inefficiencies of parliamentary politics and the reputed venality of civilian politicians who put individual and party interests before those of the nation. Also like the Brazilian generals, they were determined to break the structural obstacles, whether economic, social, or political, that were hindering successful capitalist development. They sought to establish order and discipline, coerced if necessary, in the country's inconstant political life.[1]

But the legacy of populist policies weighed particularly heavily on Argentina. They were even more vexing than in Brazil, owing to the collapse of the mechanisms of control that followed the fall of the Peronist government and to the unbroken power of the labor movement there. Whereas Brazil's president Vargas and his successors had incorporated labor into the state to a considerable degree through the many tentacles of that country's Labor Ministry and the labor courts, in Argentina the labor movement had a more adversarial relationship with the state after 1955, and it preserved an institutional role that more faithfully protected

103

working class interests through a mixture of negotiation and militancy than did the Brazilian unions. The Argentine labor movement had become more bureaucratized after the collapse of the Resistance, but it was a bureaucracy that essentially operated outside the state, and its ability to satisfy the workers' aspirations through lobbying and influence peddling was considerably less than that of its Brazilian counterpart working from inside government ministries. The result was a more bitter stalemate among business, the state, and the working class than in Brazil and a greater ability and willingness on the part of the labor movement to protect and advance the workers' interests, to ensure that the gains in wages and living standards made during the Peronist years were not altogether abolished.

Onganía took power and offered no timetable for returning it to the political parties. As Mónica Gordillo has noted, the dictatorship spoke of *"los tres tiempos"*—the economic, the social, and the political—with a Comtian certainty in the evolutionary sequel of its authoritarian program. Similarly, it employed the term *revolution* not only for its connotations of systemic change but also for its sense as a social process with no temporal limits. All forms of popular participation were suppressed. The Argentine Congress was shut down, political parties were proscribed, the universities suspended, and the country's intellectual and cultural life was intimidated into silence. The linchpin of the Argentine Revolution was an economic program that sought to deepen the *desarrollista* project and insert Argentina into the international postwar economic order through continued industrial development and a close association with multinational capital. Onganía's economics minister, Alberto Krieger Vasena, abandoned Illia's attempt to promote industrialization along neo-Peronist lines by encouraging the domestic market and supporting the small and midsize industrialists who sold to it. Modernization was instead to be achieved by eliminating the drag on capital accumulation, reducing the public spending that fed inflationary pressures, and increasing worker productivity, none of which seemed possible to Onganía's military and civilian planners in Argentina's pluralist, democratic political system.[2]

One key goal in Onganía's program was to redefine the working class's role in the country's economic, social, and political life. The need to create a flexible labor market and to eliminate the considerable power that organized labor wielded in civil society was a priority for the new regime. In Brazil, this goal had been achieved almost effortlessly through the 1966 labor legislation that had further reduced the independence of the labor courts and abolished laws that complicated firing procedures or provided for costly indemnities for dismissed workers. The sine qua non of a successful capitalist economy, a fluid labor market, was achieved in Brazil through government decree, with little resistance after 1968 from the tame Brazilian labor movement.[3] Breaking the strength of the vastly more formidable Argentine labor movement would be far more difficult. Virtually all the post-1955 governments had sought to tame labor, and each had foundered on the shoals of the unions' mobilizing powers and the government's own lack of legitimacy and authority in what was a tightly hemmed in democratic system. Illia's administration had been the latest to show the risks involved with such a policy. His Radical government had attempted to weaken the ties between the workers and the Peronist labor movement and had skirmished with the unions on many fronts. Illia had used the Labor Ministry to monitor union elections closely, to keep tight controls on the disbursement of union funds, to encourage rival union slates and feed the internal feuding in Peronist labor, all of which had kept the labor movement off balance and seemed to offer the promise of discrediting the entrenched leadership and perhaps even weaning the country's working class away from Peronism.[4]

Illia's labor policies had had some unexpected results for unions, however, among them the protection they afforded the maverick Cordoban labor movement and the stalling of the verticalist campaign there. But Illia's running feud with Augusto Vandor and the labor bosses had created so much bad blood that the labor movement had been among the most enthusiastic supporters of the 1966 coup. Relieved that the obdurate, exasperating Illia was toppled, Peronist labor, encouraged by Perón's own initially positive response to Onganía, maneuvered to curry favor with the new regime. Both Vandor's and José Alonso's factions of Peronist labor praised the change of government, and the Confederación General del Trabajo, under Vandor's control, released a document the day following the coup with policy suggestions for Onganía, a clear overture of its willingness to work with the regime.[5]

While the Peronists fantasized about the restoration of a military-union alliance, Agustín Tosco and Luz y Fuerza emerged as the sole dissenting voice in the country's labor movement. In May, shortly before the coup, Tosco's slate, with Ramón Contreras running for union president, had commandingly won reelection. Nagging health problems and perhaps some curiosity about seeing the inner workings of labor movement politics in the place where it most mattered encouraged Tosco to take a two-year leave of absence to serve as the Cordoban union's representative to the light and power workers' central, the FATLYF, in Buenos Aires.

Following the coup, Tosco returned briefly to Córdoba to apprise the Luz y Fuerza leadership of recent events. To the surprise of all those present at an impromptu meeting he called, Tosco urged caution and called for a grace period to see what kind of policies Onganía was really going to follow.[6] The president of the FATLYF, Félix Pérez, and the president of the local Buenos Aires light and power workers' union, Juan José Taccone, though relatively free of Vandor's pressures by virtue of the strategic power of their union, also believed Onganía's government offered new possibilities and had gone so far as to assume the leadership of the *participacionistas,* that sector of the labor movement most supportive of the new government.

However, neither Tosco nor the Cordoban Luz y Fuerza hesitated once it became clear what the real intent of Onganía's policies were. Within two months of the coup, the government had passed law 16.936 establishing obligatory arbitration, a measure that effectively eliminated the right to strike. Onganía had also begun a series of rationalization programs in various state-owned or state-subsidized industries, affecting everything from the country's ports to the railroads to the Tucumán sugar *ingenios.* Mass firings, job reclassifications, and the shutting down of whole industries altogether were the outcome of the Argentine Revolution for the country's public sector workers.[7] Shortly thereafter, through decree 969, the *comisiones paritarias* were suspended and collective bargaining was effectively abolished. Krieger Vasena soon announced a stabilization plan that included a devaluation of the peso by 40 percent and a freezing of all wages for a period of twenty months.[8]

On August 18, 1966, Luz y Fuerza published a notice, "Signos Negativos," in the Argentine press and became the first union to criticize publicly the new regime. The plight of the railroad, sugar, and dock workers' unions became a symbol of the government's anti–working class character and the issue around which a dissident labor movement was beginning to rally. Vandor and the Peronist labor bosses meanwhile held back, unwilling to sacrifice a potential partnership with the government for unions such as the dock workers and railroad workers, whose influence in the labor movement had long been on the wane, and utterly indifferent to the lot of the sugar-working *mestizos* and Indians in a distant province as foreign to Vandor, Alonso, and their kind as Paraguay or Bolivia. The government's ban on collective bargaining and other measures were more troublesome, as they struck at the very heart of the labor movement's power. Pressures built on the leadership, but Vandor, Alonso, and others clung for several months to a policy of qualified support for Onganía.

The Peronist leadership in the big industrial unions that controlled the CGT vacillated for the remainder of 1966. At an October 20 "Congreso Normalizador" orchestrated by the government to restructure the CGT, in a rump session that excluded all the militant unions, a pliant and wheedling leadership was elected that offered only the mildest criticism of the regime.[9] It thus fell to the unions feeling the brunt of the anti–working class measures to respond to the government. Lorenzo Pepe of the Unión Ferroviaria, Amado Olmos of Obras Sanitarias, and other union leaders in the affected industries, mostly in the public sector, formed the Comité Central Confederal as a resistance committee, and they eventually gained enough strength to force a December 14 strike out of the CGT—a strike that was organized in a slapdash fashion and that had only moderate success, but it was important symbolically as the first protest against Onganía. The government responded to the provocation with greater intransigence. Dialogue was effectively suspended with even the most craven unions. Vandor and other labor bosses meanwhile had reached the limits of prudent patience. Worker unrest was simmering, and the CGT drafted a Plan de Acción that called for separate general strikes to be held on March 1 and March 21.[10]

The March 1, 1967, general strike, despite its massive character, ended as a tactical rout for the labor movement. The Onganía regime was at the pinnacle of its strength, with the authority to confront organized labor in any manner short of outright violence or physical intimidation. The day following the strike, Onganía stripped six unions, among them Unión Ferroviaria and the Unión Obrera Metalúrgica, of their legal status, their *personería gremial,* and then suspended all collective bargaining until December 31, 1968.[11] Vandor and other labor leaders retreated into a morose silence while they secretly attempted to rebuild the bridges to the regime they had burned with the March 1 strike. Over the course of the next year, the hardline labor leaders who remained, Pepe, Olmos, and the young charismatic leader of the Buenos Aires print workers' union, Raimundo Ongaro, slowly built their influence in the CGT.

A labor convention, the Congreso Amado Olmos (named in tribute to Olmos, who was killed in an automobile accident shortly before the meeting), was to be held in Buenos Aires on March 28, 1968, for the purpose of regrouping the unions and the CGT, which were both in a state of disarray since the previous year's general strike, and to draft a new program to deal with the government. The boyish-looking Ongaro had won the leadership of his union in 1966 and come to national prominence after leading a bitter January 1968 strike against the Haynes publishing house and preventing the lay offs of some 900 workers there. That strike or something in Ongaro himself had caught Perón's eye in early 1968. Searching for an heir to Olmos, the exiled leader encouraged Ongaro in a private meeting in Madrid just shortly before the March congress to take charge of the militant unions and establish their control of the CGT at the upcoming congress.[12]

Vandor's relationship with Perón had long been strained, and in the wake of the UOM leader's loss of prestige and real power following the 1967 general strike, Perón all but ignored him and the other union leaders who were still searching for a dialogue with Onganía. The Labor Ministry, Vandor, and the labor bosses all sensed the danger that Ongaro represented and followed obstructionist tactics in the days leading up to the congress. Onganía's minister of labor, Rubén San Sebastián, refused to allow the participation in the congress of any unions that were still under government supervision. Since these unions were the core of the hard-line position and Ongaro's support, the ban would have effectively assured Vandor control of the CGT. Ongaro and the hardliners ignored San Sebastián's ruling, however, and crowded into the Unión Tranviarios Automotor headquarters in Buenos Aires on March 28 for the congress. Among the participating CGT regionals was Córdoba's, the largest of the provincial CGTs. Tosco attended as Luz y Fuerza's representative, and he quickly assumed control of the entire Cordoban delegation when Vandor called in his debts and forced the unions in his camp—including Elpidio Torres's SMATA and Alejo Simó's UOM—to withdraw from the congress on the basis of a minor procedural infraction by the Ongaro forces.[13]

Vandor had hoped to deny Ongaro the quorum he needed to hold the congress but was frustrated by the last-minute defection of the municipal workers' union. The alignments in this incident were revealing. The major industrial unions and more privileged nonindustrial unions allied with Vandor and walked out of the congress. The UOM, SMATA, Luz y Fuerza (save the Cordoban branch), and the construction and petroleum workers' unions all boycotted the proceedings. Not by coincidence, they were the very unions that had parlayed their special position as representatives of workers in the key, strategic sectors of the Argentine economy into a favored status. These were the bread-and-butter men, the chief exponents of business unionism, the *burocracia sindical* that was to be the target of so many attacks in the coming years. Under normal conditions, their position as the final arbiters for the labor movement would have been unassailable. But the exceptional conditions that existed in the country, the severity of the government's attack on some unions, and the perception of its overriding hostility to working class interests put the momentum into the hands of the firebrands, not the conservatives.

On March 29 Ongaro was elected secretary general of the CGT. The executive committee members represented precisely those unions feeling the full brunt of the government's policies: Antonio Scipione (Unión Ferroviaria), Julio Guillán (the telephone workers), Salvador Manganaro (the state gas workers), Alfredo Lettis (the merchant marine), Pedro Avellaneda (the state workers), Benito Romano (the sugar workers), Enrique Coronel (La Fraternidad), and Ricardo De Luca (the shipyard workers).[14] Except for Romano's sugar workers, all the unions represented on the executive committee were public sector unions based in Buenos Aires. Tosco refused a position on the executive committee, a decision he never explained but which can most likely be attributed to a reluctance to commit himself to another prolonged absence from Córdoba. Instead he devoted his energies at the congress to winning support for the new CGT, soon redubbed the CGT de los Argentinos (CGTA), and especially to strengthening its position among the union delegations from the provinces. His efforts were successful: Córdoba, La Plata, Rosario, Santa Fe, Paraná, Corrientes, Chaco, Tucumán, Salta, Mendoza, and the other principal CGTs of the interior all adhered to the new CGTA.[15]

This provincial strategy, an unshakable belief in the greater combativeness of the unions of the interior, would become a hallmark of Tosco's tactics in the coming years. The provinces did appear to be a promising area of recruitment for the CGTA. Though Onganía's measures had affected greater numbers of *porteño* workers than provincial ones, the dead hand of Peronist trade unionism also weighed more heavily in the capital city and hindered the development of new tactics there to combat the dictatorship. In the interior the collapse of Vandor's leadership and the old guard was more absolute, and it permitted new individuals, many with ties to the left but most simply renegade Peronists, to emerge in positions of authority. One of the most important radicalizations was that of the Tucumán sugar workers, who came under the leadership of left-wing Peronists and became a guiding spirit in the CGTA in the provinces. There was a shared indignation—if not as desperate as that of the Tucumán sugar workers—among a number of provincial unions that vindicated Tosco's faith in the necessity of a provincial strategy, a unity of the interior to resist the counterattack from Vandor and the labor bosses that he rightly predicted.

The crucible of the provincial strategy was Tosco's own Córdoba. As the country's second-largest industrial city, its labor movement had both a symbolic and strategic importance that none of the other provincial CGTs could match. The imperfect integration of the Cordoban Peronists into the national labor movement and the continuing strength of the non-Peronist unions there offered certain possibilities that were absent elsewhere. Córdoba was also, coincidentally, a province in a state of severe unrest as a result of the government's economic program and the generally weakened position of Vandor and Peronist labor. Though Onganía's rationalization programs had fallen hardest on the public sector unions, the support given to business over labor, the specific legislation prohibiting strikes and collective bargaining negotiations, and the general climate such measures created had emboldened private companies to attack their labor costs. The automobile industry was the most affected of all the privately owned industries. Layoffs, increased production rhythms, and a general deterioration of working conditions in the plants sparked major labor protests in IKA-Renault, Chrysler, Ford, Citroën, and Peugeot factories throughout 1967 and 1968.[16]

The most serious of these labor protests took place in the IKA-Renault complex. In Santa Isabel, IKA management faced the twin problems of dealing with a declining share of the automotive market and convincing Renault of the attractiveness of a proposed buyout of the company. In 1966, IKA had begun to implement periodic reduced work weeks to compensate for slumping sales. By early 1967, it had already made the decision to reduce its executives' salaries by 20 percent and to lay off some 1,000 workers out of a total labor force of 7,200, as a first step to assure a jittery Renault of its intent to reduce its labor costs and put its finances in order.[17] Stalled collective bargaining negotiations had given IKA the pretext to begin to lay off the workers on January 20. Then, in reprisal for the bitter and often violent SMATA strike that followed the first wave of layoffs, IKA fired an additional 4,000 workers, though only as an intimidation tactic and with the full intention of hiring them back. The tenor of labor-management relations by then had so deteriorated that a Renault investigative mission sent to the Cordoban plants was urging the home office in Paris to withdraw its licenses and buy the company out only when the situation had improved.[18]

Though the union managed to get the layoffs rescinded, in return it had to accept reduced work days for the entire labor force. Torres and the SMATA were now on the defensive. The lines of communication to James McCloud and other company officials were broken, and the comfortable arrangement SMATA had worked out with IKA over the years, with labor stability guaranteed and handsome wage increases awarded in every new contract, crumbled. Additional blows followed the strike. In May 1967, under government pressure, the SMATA central took control of the Cordoban local, a control it lifted only in March of the following year, presumably in return for Córdoba's good behavior at the March 1968 labor congress. With labor peace restored, Renault bought out the Kaiser stock in September of that same year and began a campaign to reduce labor costs even further. The French company believed it had to lower its wage bill, break with the IKA's 1960 to 1966 policy of granting pay increases, and generally weaken the union as well as reduce the size of the work force.[19] With collective bargaining frozen by Onganía in March and with the right of the company to reduce the work week in accordance with market conditions fully supported by the government, Renault began to reduce wages in all job categories and to eliminate jobs in select departments.[20] The company's plans changed only after government pressure won from Renault a pledge not to undertake massive layoffs or prolonged suspensions of production.[21] Such gestures of goodwill, however, gave Renault an even freer hand to handle its labor force as it saw fit, including instituting a major rationalization program of all the Santa Isabel plants in 1968.

The deteriorating conditions at IKA-Renault meant that at least one sector of the Cordoban automotive proletariat had propitious grounds for future labor militancy. The other pillar of Peronist labor in Córdoba, the UOM, was also passing through a period of crisis. Shortly after the Onganía coup, the UOM central had won a favorable national collective bargaining agreement, wrangling a 25 percent wage increase from the industry's negotiators as well as a suspension of the *quitas zonales,* a system of remuneration that gave metalworkers in the provinces a lower pay scale than their *porteño* counterparts. The agreement enhanced the UOM's standing in Córdoba, and Simó, his political career apparently ended by Onganía's closing of the Argentine Congress, returned to Córdoba to reassert his control of the union. He immediately faced the grim reality of Onganía's Argentine Revolution. As in the automobile industry, the owners of the country's metalworking factories and workshops disregarded collective bargaining agreements once they saw the state had weakened labor's ability to resist an employer offensive. Simó led September 1966 strikes against the Luján Hornos and Gerardo Seel factories, two of the more important metalworking establishments in the city, but owners in the local industry and elsewhere in the country were undertaking firings, and suspensions and closing down establishments at a pace that threatened the very survival of the UOM.[22]

Vandor and the labor movement's weakness after the 1967 general strike put Simó in a defensive position similar to Torres's stance with the SMATA. Successful resistance to company firings and rationalization plans increasingly appeared to require some kind of alignment with Tosco and the Independents. Torres and Simó had already found themselves in the curious position of siding with Tosco when the local CGT declared Onganía persona non grata during his August 1967 visit to Córdoba, at the very time that their union centrals were attempting to salvage a working relationship with the regime. Two weeks later, at the general assemblies of the Cordoban CGT on September 15 and 19, they had supported the Independents' *plan de movilización* to resist the government's anti–working class measures through militant tactics.[23] Their estrangement from Vandor had limits, however. Neither had been willing to challenge openly Vandor's authority at the Congreso Amado Olmos or to support Ongaro, as they showed by joining Vandor's boycott. Each was also worried by the apparently deepening radicalization of the labor movement and the leftward drift of politics in the Córdoba, a particularly ominous development for Torres given the continued presence of left-wing activists in the IKA-Renault plants. At an April 26, 1968, union general assembly called by Torres, Ongaro's supporters, who included nearly all the leftist activists in the plants, had shouted down the secretary general and physically threatened the SMATA leadership in attendance.[24] The prospect of a Tosco-led, *ongarista* Cordoban CGT was clearly a sobering prospect for both Torres and Simó. Outside support was necessary in their conflicts with the companies, but there were risks in a premature alliance with Ongaro, and for the time being they remained in Vandor's camp.

Ongaro and the CGTA had established a stronghold in Córdoba in the first months of the rebellion against Vandor, largely through the efforts of Tosco and Luz y Fuerza. The light and power workers' union was unrelenting in its hostility to Onganía following the publication of the "Signos Negativos" advertisement two months after the coup. Before the March 1968 labor congress, Luz y Fuerza had already broken with its national union on the issue of support for the government. At the October 1967 national congress of the country's light and power workers' unions held in Río Hondo, the Cordoban delegation had attacked the FATLYF policy of dialogue and cooperation with the dictatorship.[25]

The FATLYF, dominated as were most union centrals by its Buenos Aires branch, was assailed for its coziness with Onganía and its refusal to support those unions adversely affected by the regime's policies. The Cordoban union's championing of general working class interests rather than strictly union ones was unusual. The unity of the working class and its organic relationship with the state had been broken with Perón's overthrow. Collective bargaining since 1955 had taken place on an industry-level and in the case of some industries, such as automobiles, on a company-by-company basis. As Argentina's economy had diversified and the working class was divided into different sectors, some with considerable bargaining power and others with none, a hierarchy of unions had developed in which the more privileged unions rarely thought in broad working class terms, unless to further their own bargaining position. The Peronist labor movement as it developed in the 1960s can best be described as an attempt to maintain the institutional integrity of organized labor as a tactical and political necessity while pursuing individual union interests as a pragmatic reality. A general strike by the CGT in support of a weak, unstrategic union involved in even the most bitter labor dispute had become an extremely rare event. Tosco and Luz y Fuerza union seemed to be calling for the kind of altruism that the Argentine labor movement had not shown since the days of anarchist idealism and revolutionary general strikes early in the century.

The ideological and political formation of the Cordoban light and power workers' union that explains this stance involved a complex series of personal, structural, industrial, and historical factors. Certainly the importance of Tosco and the core of union militants closely associated with him cannot be underestimated. The most important study of the union has posited there were roughly 200 *tosquista* activists closely tied to Tosco, out of a total membership of 2,500, and has attributed to them and especially to Tosco's personal influence the central political role the union would play in local and national labor politics between 1966 and 1976.[26] Personal factors alone, however, seem an inadequate explanation for the union's history. The Cordoban Luz y Fuerza was a unique union in a unique industry. Among other things it was unique for the highly skilled, even professional, nature of its membership, the character of its work, and its relationship to its industry, its employer, and its union central.

On paper the Cordoban light and power industry appeared to have an exceptionally diverse labor force. The Empresa Pública de Energía de Córdoba recognized ten broad job categories, with numerous job classifications within each, that included everything from university-trained engineers working out of the EPEC offices in the city center to the unskilled workers *(peones)* who assisted the line workers out on the job.[27] In reality, however, the labor force was more homogeneous than it appeared. Luz y Fuerza was a union characterized by a high percentage of skilled and semiskilled workers, with only a very small percentage of members, generally between 15 and 20 percent, performing unskilled work.[28] It was also a union in which nearly all employees of the company were eligible for union membership. Only the EPEC directors, their private secretaries, and contracted and part-time workers could not join the union.[29] It was exceptional among the Cordoban unions in that engineers, technicians, and administrative staff were nearly all affiliated with the union and among its most active members. Though there was no domination of union affairs by a "professional" wing, its white-collar members did play an active role and had considerable influence in determining the political orientation of Luz y Fuerza.[30]

The kind of work performed also influenced union politics. For the most part, workers in the power industry were spared the hardships experienced by those involved in industrial production. Positions in EPEC were considered, in workers' circles, the plum jobs in the city, not only for the high wages but also because of the nature of the work involved. The work was both more stable and less grueling than it was in other industries. As a public service industry, the labor force was also less directly affected by the vagaries in the local and national economy. Work-related grievances that were endemic in the automobile industry and common in others such as the metalworking industry were less common here. Unlike with the automobile workers, complaints of excessive work demands or hazardous working conditions are virtually absent from the union record. The workers in the power industry, many in EPEC offices and the remainder performing repair and maintenance tasks in the company's workshops or out on the job sites, had nothing comparable to the rigors of factory life. Work discipline was lax, and even the line workers were able to do their job with little supervision.[31]

The most common work-related complaints concerned the failure of EPEC to supply the workers with enough of the necessary tools. The company failed to restock its inventory to cover the usual losses through overuse and the increased demand resulting from line expansion. It was also niggardly in its provision of some materials and supplies, such as wire, fuses, and the like, that were necessary to do the job. The most serious complaints involved faulty equipment directly related to work safety. Worn safety belts and gloves were occasionally singled out for the dangers they represented for the men working on the power lines. Similarly, the union criticized the company for faulty functioning of the cherry pickers *(grúas)* used to hoist the workers up to the lines and for the inadequate fleet of company trucks used to transport the workers to the job sites.[32] Such problems were more irritating than they were provocative. The light and power workers had minor job annoyances to contend with, but working conditions were not the major issue that they were for other unions in the city, and they never figured prominently in the collective bargaining negotiations with EPEC.

Luz y Fuerza was unique among the city's unions in its relationship with its employer. Though there were tensions that occasionally flared and the relations were not as idyllic as the company claimed in its official publications, labor-management relations were certainly more harmonious than in most Cordoban industries. As a state company, budgetary considerations, not profitability, determined EPEC's well-being. The company was therefore more concerned with lobbying for increased state subsidies than with protecting its control over the workplace, a fact demonstrated by its willingness to grant the union a major say in hiring policies. In effect, the union controlled the hiring of new workers through the labor exchange, or *bolsa de trabajo*. EPEC also had a policy of giving preference to applicants with family members already working for the company, leading to generations of families in the company's employ and workers' close personal identification with EPEC. The company reserved the right of final approval over all job applicants and was frequently criticized for its slowness in filling vacancies, but its delegation to the union of what was a jealously guarded prerogative in other industries revealed a different kind of relationship with its labor force. With its control over hiring, the union could prevent an erosion of wages and benefits by manipulating the supply of labor and regulating entry into the company in guildlike fashion. Job turnover was low, and the union frequently called hiring freezes and closed job inscriptions, as it did from 1964 to 1967 and periodically in the early 1970s.[33] In wage negotiations the union had an exceptional degree of influence as well. The relationship between management and labor was generally amicable, almost obliging, as the company representatives on the arbitration boards were often executives who had worked their way through the ranks and still retained strong union sympathies.[34] In general the union's demands were fully met, and strikes over wage and benefits issues were rare.

When union demands could not be satisfied and negotiations did break down, it was most often due to pressures from the provincial government to reduce company expenditures rather than to any intransigence on the part of EPEC officials. This situation gives the first clue to the politics of Luz y Fuerza, for conflicts with the company took on an inherently political meaning. The union attributed EPEC's financial problems to political regimes and government policy rather than to mismanagement by the state company. EPEC as an entity, in stark contrast to the automobile companies, was never criticized by its union. As a state company, it represented the ideal for the Peronist and leftist members alike. Though not under worker control, at least it was a public company with a recognized role for the union in important areas of planning and administration, and it was therefore regarded as being more responsive to worker needs. Though there is some evidence that union sentiment existed for *cogestión*, codified worker participation in administering the company, the privileges enjoyed by the union built up strong loyalties to EPEC all the same.

Though denied outright *cogestión,* the light and power workers wielded an extraordinary degree of influence, which nearly amounted to shared responsibility with management. The union's participation in the *planteles,* the job classifications and work assignments decided in the departments, afforded it the kind of partnership that existed in no other Cordoban industry. Partly for these reasons and partly because the union executive committee, and specifically Tosco, refused to push for what they considered a premature demand for worker control—in an economy that was still capitalist—EPEC was largely immune from union criticism. The same was not true for the company's directors and subdirectors, however, who were political appointments and were considered the executors of government policy. But the union's practice was generally to avoid attacks against such individuals and direct its displeasure with company policies directly against the government in political terms, first from a nationalist perspective and eventually from a genuinely socialist one.

A final sign of the close ties between the company and the union was the financial support given by EPEC to Luz y Fuerza. In 1950 the union had won a concession in its collective bargaining agreement that pledged the company to contribute regularly to a special union fund, the Mutual Unión Eléctrica, which financed Luz y Fuerza's medical plan. EPEC also contributed sizable sums to the union's housing, vacation, and retirement programs. Problems periodically arose as a result of EPEC's tardiness with contributions, but the extent, indeed the very existence of such support was unusual in Argentine industry, where union programs were generally solely dependent on the union dues *(descuentos)* paid by the members.[35]

Company financial support for the Mutual and other union benefits programs contributed to the union's political involvement by freeing it from a dependence on its union central. By subsidizing programs usually financed and administered through the central, EPEC made the union less vulnerable to intimidation tactics from Buenos Aires. The union was also aided by the fact that Luz y Fuerza, unlike UOM and many other unions, was a federative organization. Under the federative structure, the branch unions controlled their own monies and the dispersal of union funds. The FATLYF could threaten and suspend uncooperative unions, as would happen to the Cordoban local on numerous occasions over the next decade, but outside of being banned from the FATLYF's hotels and vacation colonies, the ramifications of expulsion were not serious and could not effectively hamper the union local's actions.

The tenor of labor-management relations, the fewer demands on the union to resolve work-related problems or to haggle with hostile company officials over wage and benefit issues, freed the union's more politically inclined members to devote time to politics. The work-related problems that did occasionally arise could generally be resolved without resorting to strike action. When negotiations broke down, the union resorted to partial work stoppages that were usually adequate to prod EPEC into action.

EPEC's status as a public company attenuated the kind of financial tensions that were so manifest in the local automobile industry. Though the company was periodically threatened with insolvency, there was always a fiscal alternative—a rate hike or increased government subsidies—that allowed the company to avoid the risky alternative of playing with its labor costs. On the few occasions when the company tried such actions, when it enacted a small number of layoffs in 1972, the resolute response of the union exposed the dangers of such a policy. As a result the company was remarkably accommodating to the labor force's demands, and there was a dearth of reasons for union representatives to perceive the union as strictly a collective bargaining tool.

All these factors contributed to the creation of a union prepared to assume the leadership of the dissident labor movement in 1968, but none can be said to be the determining factor. The fact that other light and power workers' unions in the country, most notably Taccone's Buenos Aires branch, were supporting dialogue and even collaboration with the dictatorship at the very same moment indicates that there were elements peculiar to Córdoba that drew the union toward militancy and eventually radicalized its political positions. One crucial factor, as has been discussed, was the unusual configuration of the local labor movement and the protection it afforded Tosco and other left-wing activists in the union, allowing them to adopt maverick political positions without fear of reprisals from Buenos Aires. Tosco and his circle were thereby able to adopt independent positions and preside over a never doctrinaire or coerced, but still discernible, political education of the union members. The main vehicle for the political education of the union was the Luz y Fuerza weekly publication, *Electrum,* which would remain the most coherent and cogent expression of independent left-wing unionism in the city until its closure by the Peronist government in 1974. But the force of Tosco's personal example, the stoic resolve with which he would accept long months of imprisonment and the national prominence he would gradually gain, were at least as important as *Electrum* in that political education and in building support within the union for its dissident positions. Loyalty to Tosco, the near mythic status he achieved in the labor movement even in his own lifetime, explains much of the members' willingness to withstand the years of turmoil and persecutions that the union would suffer as a result of its political involvement.

It would be wrong to assume, however, that the light and power workers were passive recipients of an ideological and political praxis conceived and executed from above. Rather, the history of the union was a dynamic process involving the interplay of institutional and industrial influences that predisposed the union's workers to left-wing positions and informed a certain political comportment. Tosco and the leadership's ability to transform Luz y Fuerza into a markedly political organization relied on more than the tacit approval of the rank and file. One influence was the union's aforementioned democratic character. Worker identification with the union was strong, and participation in union affairs was high. Favored by its relatively small size and by Tosco's scrupulous respect for the union's democratic apparatus, Luz y Fuerza practiced a genuine union democracy.

It was union policy to get as many members involved in union affairs as possible. In addition to the executive council the union machinery consisted of the *cuerpo de delegados,* elected shop stewards who, like those on the executive council, served two-year terms. Shop stewards existed in virtually all Cordoban unions, even the most undemocratic, but their influence was greater in Luz y Fuerza than in any other union in the city. The greater number of shop stewards in the union, the frequency with which shop stewards' assemblies were called and matters of real weight were discussed, and their ability to make decisions independently of the executive committee gave them positions of real power. The Luz y Fuerza shop stewards chose the union's delegates to the FATLYF and national CGT congresses as well as nominated all the union delegates to the Cordoban CGT. The union members chosen to represent Córdoba at the FATLYF headquarters in Buenos Aires were rotated to guarantee that the greatest number of workers as possible would have occasion to serve. Delegates for the two CGTs tended to be chosen from Tosco's seasoned circle, but the decision ultimately remained with the shop stewards and not the executive committee. Finally, participation in union elections for the period from 1962 to 1973 averaged 75 percent of the membership, an unusually high figure in Argentine trade unions.[36]

The *lucefuercistas'* identification with their union was also the result of its importance to their lives beyond work. Union activities were greatly expanded after its move in 1967 to new headquarters on Deán Funes Street. The headquarters, in fact, became something more than a union hall and developed into a focal point of Cordoban working class life, with Luz y Fuerza union members drawn into its many activities in myriad ways. Volunteers from the union served on committees to administer a range of community service programs, among them a weekly children's film series, literacy classes, and a credit union with low-interest loans available for members of any of the city's legally recognized unions.[37] The sense of being in a better kind of working class organization and the pride workers felt in the union translated into support for Tosco and his circle. Not until the early 1970s would some rank-and-file discontent over the heavy costs the union was being forced to pay for its political involvement develop into an organized opposition to Tosco. But even then it would be a minority position, the result of the political ambitions of the core of conservative Peronists in the union, not any profound dissatisfaction with the leadership, as the overwhelming electoral majorities won by Tosco's slates in those years consistently proved.

The politics of any union is also informed by its industry, and the Luz y Fuerza workers' support for the union's dissident positions was firmly rooted in the character and problems of the electric power industry in Córdoba. The leadership role that the Cordoban light and power workers' union assumed in Argentina's militant labor movement had numerous sources, but as in the case of the local automobile workers, the specific influences of the workplace helped shape ideology and create a certain kind of political activism. By the early 1960s, Córdoba's once formidable electric power resources were in a state of near crisis. Córdoba had possessed the country's most extensive hydroelectric power network, a network that was so well developed that, as late as the 1950s, there were no shortages of generating capacity or restrictions on consumption. This situation stood out starkly among the power scarcities that existed in other parts of the country—especially in the interior, where demand generally far outstripped supply. As has been discussed, the abundance and cheapness of Córdoba's electric power had been a major enticement for the establishment of the automobile industry in the city.

The increased demands that resulted from the great wave of automotive, mechanical, and metalworking industrialization in the late 1950s and early 1960s, however, had begun to overtax available power production. Despite its impressive hydroelectric resources—the numerous fast-running streams, rivers, and falls with which nature had endowed the nearby *sierra,* and the dikes and dams built by Sabattini's Radical government in the 1930s—the province's power isolation threatened its economic base. As early as 1960 engineers were warning of Córdoba's vulnerability as a result of limited transmission facilities. Single-circuit lines connected all the province's substations to their respective transforming stations, and none was tied into a larger grid. Electric power throughout the province thus depended on a limited number of highly vulnerable and increasingly inadequate power lines.[38]

With its central location and abundant hydroelectric resources, Córdoba was the logical nexus for any future nationally integrated power system. Perón's swift nationalization in 1946 of the two American Foreign Power Company utilities that had poorly supplied the province with its electricity had not been coincidental; nor was the strategic importance of the province lost on Luz y Fuerza. Their work exposed union members to the contradictions between the country's electric power potential and its increasing inability to meet its needs. The union newspaper, *Electrum,* became a forum in which workers from all job categories discussed, often in homely but very insightful terms, the particular nature of the country's power problems and the role of Córdoba in their resolution, as well as the relationship between national models of economic development and electric power production. Throughout its history, the Cordoban union dismissed attacks against the deficitary public power companies as politically inspired. It frequently noted that such deficits were generally the result of the preferential rates given to private industry. In the case of EPEC, big energy purchasers such as IKA-Renault, Fiat, and local parts producers were essentially receiving state-subsidized power. The association between models of economic development and the problems in their industry, the ideological trappings placed on the pursuit of private interests, were understood by much of EPEC's highly skilled labor force.[39]

The perception existed among the light and power workers in Córdoba that the problems in their industry were not merely budgetary or technological, but that they formed part of a larger problem with the character of Argentina's capitalist development and the structural obstacles to energy independence in a semideveloped country. Their exposure to the politics of rate setting gave them an understanding of the real workings of the industry and especially of the incestuous relationship between business and the state in their country. This critical understanding, buttressed by the other ideological and political influences at work in Argentine, and especially Cordoban, society at the time, built sympathy in the union for socialist positions. The union members most able to form an elaborated analysis of the industry's problems in this regard were naturally the EPEC engineers. But the problems of the industry were common knowledge in the union, and many of the most articulate critics of the role of private enterprise in electric power development were workers, like Tosco, employed in one of the EPEC repair shops or on the lines.

The concrete experience of the Onganía dictatorship was the final factor that pushed the Cordoban light and power workers to the forefront of labor resistance. Onganía's suspension of all collective bargaining was naturally resented in a union that had become accustomed to periodic and generally favorable contracts negotiations. As president of the FATLYF's collective bargaining committee (Comisión Paritaria Nacional) in 1966 and early 1967, Tosco perhaps had a better opportunity to appreciate the real intent of the government toward the working class than did Taccone and the other union leaders urging dialogue with the government. Luz y Fuerza also felt the full brunt of Onganía's rationalization plans sooner than other light and power worker locals. Suspension of personnel, reduced work weeks, and plans to transfer EPEC jurisdiction over nuclear power development in the province to the central government, believed by many in the union to be a ruse to permit subsequent privatization of the company, rallied union sentiment in opposition to the government.[40]

The combined weight of such personal, structural, industrial, and historical factors explains the union's steadily building tradition of involvement in politics after 1966. The tendency toward political strikes, as opposed to merely work-related ones, had become apparent by 1964. The only major work stoppage of that year was the union's adherence to the CGT's general strike of December 17 and 18. Similarly, the most important strike of 1965 was the twenty-four-hour work stoppage to protest the murder in Buenos Aires of two labor activists. After 1966, this tendency increased markedly, and the union showed a proclivity for political strikes that was unique in Cordoban labor and most likely in the entire country. The major work stoppages of 1966, two twenty-four-hour strikes, were undertaken to protest Onganía's anti–working class measures. The three major strikes of 1967 were similarly political in nature.[41] Between 1968 and 1972, strikes to protest the government's economic policies, to demand the restoration of democratic rule and the release of political prisoners, to protest the *porteño* labor bureaucracy's disregard for local union rights—in a word, politics—dominated the strike record (see Table 4.1). After 1972, when the union allied itself even more closely with the left and broke with the Peronist government in power, strikes were almost completely of a political nature.

The Cordoban light and power workers thus assumed an almost predictable role in the CGTA mobilizations of 1968, drumming up support not only in the city but throughout the Argentine interior. Unquestionably Córdoba was the epicenter of labor's rebellion against the government, Vandor, and the labor bosses. All over the city, the talk was of CGTA secretary general Raimundo Ongaro. Overnight he emerged from relative

Table 4.1 Work stoppages, Luz y Fuerza de Córdoba, 1964–1972

Year	Number	Work-related	Political
1964	5	1	4
1965	6	2	4
1966	5	2	3
1967	3	—	3
1969	8	—	8
1970	6	1	5
1971	24	2	22
1972	13	4	9
Total	70	12	58

Source: Carlos E. Sánchez, "Estratégias y objetivos de los sindicatos argentinos," Instituto de Economía y Finanzas, Facultad de Ciencias Económicas, Universidad Nacional de Córdoba, p. 86.

obscurity to widespread notoriety in labor, student, and underground left-wing circles, momentarily eclipsing even the commanding figure of Tosco. Ongaro's Peronist loyalties were particularly attractive to those sectors of the left that saw in the CGTA a more authentic and homegrown example of working class militancy than that promoted by the familiar and slightly tarnished mainstays of the Argentine left, such as the Communist party. The CGTA secretary general's biography provided the attractive mix of a Christian mystic and a combative Peronist that was more in tune with the tenor of the times—at the height of revisionist interpretations of the Peronist movement and the birth of the Peronist left—than was the traditional Marxist left.

Ongaro was something genuinely new in the labor movement. A former seminary student who laced his calls for class struggle and national liberation with biblical allusions and occasional rambling monologues on Christ's social message. He had a messianic streak that immediately set him apart from other labor leaders in the country. Young and wide-eyed, pious and courteous in manner, he provided a strong contrast to the scarcely concealed arrogance, power-loving displays, and lordly pretensions that workers had come to expect from many of the Peronist labor bosses. For Tosco, Ongaro's personal charisma and the appeal he had for broad sectors of the labor movement temporarily compensated for what he saw as a whimsical and somewhat moony personality, as well as for his political ingenuousness. Intent on winning the local CGT to the new labor confederation, Tosco allowed Ongaro to serve as the symbol of working class resistance to Onganía. Meanwhile Tosco began to weave alliances among Peronist and non-Peronist unions for the purpose of unifying Córdoba behind the CGTA rebellion.

Ongaro's dramatic victory at the March 1968 labor congress and the euphoria that followed it hardly meant that the old guard of Peronist labor had been eliminated. Vandor's unions were powerful and prepared to fight for control of the CGT. The first indication that they would resist Ongaro was their refusal to hand over the CGT headquarters to the victorious new leaders. Unperturbed, Ongaro declared that thenceforth the CGTA would operate out of the print workers' union hall on Paseo Colón, and in fact Ongaro's organization was alternately known as the CGT de Paseo Colón for the first several weeks of its existence. The ousted *vandoristas* at this point could only harass Ongaro with minor nuisances such as the headquarters scuffle, however, and the CGTA continued to win new adherents through the month of April.

At Tosco's urging, Ongaro named Julio Guillán, president of the telephone workers' union, as the CGTA's special emissary to the provinces. The warm reception that Guillán received in Rosario, Córdoba, and other provincial cities indicated there was deep grass-roots support for the CGTA in the interior. Even if Ongaro and the organization itself proved ephemeral, the damage being done to the old guard leadership's reputation was serious. The CGTA activists made unrelenting and mordant attacks on the *vandoristas,* accusing them of Mafia tactics, red-baiting, corruption, and collusion with the dictatorship. By the end of April calls from the old guard for a new CGT congress to halt Ongaro's advance were increasingly frantic. The rift between the *ongaristas* and the *vandoristas* widened further when Ongaro sought to use the traditional May Day celebrations to launch a counterattack and make the CGTA's position as the legitimate representative of the workers' movement unassailable. The executive committee laid careful preparations for CGTA-sponsored May Day demonstrations throughout the country and for a speech by Ongaro in Córdoba. Writer and political journalist Rodolfo Walsh and the circle of intellectuals who had flocked to Paseo Colón in the weeks following the March congress also planned to release the new *ongarista* weekly, *CGT,* to coincide with the May Day demonstrations.[42]

On April 29 Ongaro left for Córdoba with a speech he had written with Walsh that was intended to be the clarion call of the nascent dissident labor movement. Tosco and other union activists, drawn mainly from the Independents, had been tilling the ground for several weeks, and the city was expecting more than another mundane May Day celebration. The importance of the provinces and particularly Córdoba to the success or failure of the CGTA meant that Ongaro's words and the reception they received here would be carefully observed by the rest of the country. On May 1, some 5,000 workers crowded into the Córdoba Sport Club to hear Ongaro. Torres's SMATA, Simó's UOM, and the handful of unions still loyal, many halfheartedly, to the *vandorista* line were absent, as were the Fiat company unions.

Ongaro's Cordoban speech, dubbed later the "Programa del 1º de mayo," showed any doubters that the CGTA rebellion was something other than just another internal Peronist power struggle like those that had wracked the labor movement throughout the 1960s. The speech itself was revealing. Ongaro articulated the significance of the CGTA rebellion, its repudiation of *verticalismo,* and its intention to practice a combative, nonsectarian unionism.[43] Using language that harkened back to the heady times of October 17, 1945, to Evita's incendiary speeches from the balcony of the Casa Rosada, and to the revolutionary writings of John William

Cooke and other militant Peronists of the Resistance, Ongaro seemed to be rescuing the always minority and by then apparently moribund revolutionary tendencies within the Peronist labor movement. The May 1 program was replete with the traditional vocabulary and imagery of the combative, *línea dura* stance of Peronist trade unionism, excoriating the *traidores* and *vendidos* within labor's ranks. It went beyond Peronism's traditional positions on economics and class relations only in the stridency of its anticapitalist language. Nevertheless, in Ongaro's direct, provocative repudiation of the Onganía government, and especially in his proposal for an alliance between the workers' movement and the country's university students and the activist clergy, the CGTA was clearly straying from the mainstream Peronist trade union movement. The CGTA rebellion now unquestionably represented more than a factional union opposition to Vandor and *vandorismo*. It was also an ideological and political one.[44]

The following day, Ongaro left for a speaking tour of the provinces, hoping to capitalize on the enthusiasm displayed by the Cordoban working class at the May Day rally and to cement his support in the interior. In late April, nine CGT regionals had voted to affiliate with the CGTA. The principal provincial CGTs of the interior, Rosario, Santa Fe, Tucumán, and Salta, were among those that had voted in favor of Ongaro. The May Day celebrations had indicated deep support for Ongaro in all those places, and the CGTA rebellion soon took on something of the character of a revolt of the provinces against Buenos Aires. But even in the capital city, the CGTA was gathering momentum. A rally held for the *porteño* working class in La Matanza, an industrial suburb of Buenos Aires, was attended by masses of workers despite the *vandoristas'* calls to boycott it. The *vandoristas'* hope that the CGTA rebellion would prove ephemeral was appearing more unfounded. Ongaro's hand was strengthened further when Perón in late May dissolved the 62 Organizaciones, the political wing of the Peronist labor movement that was still in Vandor's hands. The decision was a clear gesture of support from Perón for Ongaro and a repudiation of the *vandoristas'* plans to hold a rump congress to impose their slate on a reorganized CGT.[45]

It was the *ongaristas,* not Vandor, who were on the offensive and making the greatest advances in these months. From the offices of the *CGT,* Walsh and his staff began a press campaign that was designed to discredit the old guard Peronists and win rank-and-file support. Walsh devoted a weekly column to documenting incidents of thuggery and corruption by the unions opposing Ongaro's election. His study of

Vandor's personal involvement in the murder of a union rival in the UOM, *¿Quién mató a Rosendo?*, which was published the following year, was part of this attempt to expose the dark side of Peronist labor as practiced by Vandor and other Peronist labor bosses. Moreover, the CGTA was attracting volunteers from student and left-wing circles throughout these early months to work on the newspaper and to proselytize among the workers. The CGTA rebellion, in fact, marked the rebirth of two important and closely linked rapprochements, the first between the working class and the left and the second between the working class and the student movement.

The solidarity shown and alliances established by student organizations and the workers' movement in the 1918 University Reform movement and in countless other incidents in the early decades of the century had been shattered by Perón. Among the antipathies Peronism had bred in Argentine society was a relatively novel one of the workers for the students. Perón portrayed the students as a group of *niños bien,* a privileged caste drawn mainly from the country's upper and middle classes, in an act of political vindictiveness against the students further opposition to his candidacy in the 1946 elections. The Peronists' October 17 cry of *"¡alpargatas sí, libros no!"* had stood as a symbol of the broken tradition of solidarity between both groups. The students' decade-long opposition to the regime, their participation in the Revolución Libertadora, and the delirium they had displayed at Perón's overthrow in 1955, had sowed suspicion and rancor between the country's Peronist working class and university students that had remained potent for years afterward.[46]

The reconciliation between the workers and students had at least its symbolic commencement in Córdoba. A second-year engineering student and part-time IKA worker, Santiago Pampillón, had been killed by police gunfire in Barrio Clínicas on September 7, 1966, in one of the early student protests against Onganía. The death of Pampillón served as an early link between the university students and the Cordoban labor movement, an alliance which would grow stronger over the coming months as both felt the full weight of the government's repression. The CGTA rebellion, in fact, provided the first institutional outlet for a rekindled sympathy, both in Córdoba and nationally, between the country's workers and students. In Córdoba specifically, Ongaro had become a kind of cult figure within the city's large and powerful university student population, a figure likened in folk songs and student poetry to Che Guevara, Córdoba's native son whose death in the Bolivian jungle the year before had greatly affected the local student population and contributed to its increased politicization. The student *peñas,* weekly dances held at the university, became fund-raisers for the CGTA, and student volunteers at the CGTA headquarters made photocopies, ran errands, and did much of the spade work for the new organization. The unions reciprocated with solidarity strikes to protest Onganía's university policies and by making union halls available for classes in those departments closed down by the regime as well as for students preparing for the new university entrance exams.[47]

The Argentine left was similarly reborn with the CGTA rebellion. Great changes in the country's Marxist parties and political organizations had actually preceded 1968. At the start of the decade, the Cuban Revolution and the Sino-Soviet rift had unleashed a debate in left-wing circles that ultimately ended the monopoly of the Socialist and, especially, Communist parties within the country's anticapitalist forces. Two anti-Communist party, Maoist groups, the Vanguardia Comunista (VC) and the Partido Comunista Revolucionario (PCR), emerged and broke with the pro-Soviet Partido Comunista's insistence on the formation of a revolutionary party, offering instead the model of the Chinese Revolution, the revolutionary general strike and popular insurrection. The Guevarist Partido Revolucionario de los Trabajadores (PRT), the result of a fusion in 1963 of the Trotskyist Palabra Obrera and the Frente Revolucionario Indoamericano Popular, also rose from obscurity as a left-wing fringe group to become a real force in the left, with especially strong support among university students. The Peronist left, still nascent in the mid-1960s, appeared in the form of the first guerrilla organizations such as the Fuerzas Armadas Revolucionarias (FAR) and the Fuerzas Armadas Peronistas.[48]

A revitalized left was also manifested in institutions other than Marxist parties and Peronist guerrilla organizations. An increasingly radicalized Catholic church accompanied the birth of the CGTA. After the 1966 Latin American bishops' conference in Mar del Plata, the Third World priests' movement began to make inroads, at the parish level notably, in Argentina's famously conservative Catholic church. In the very days when Ongaro was present in Córdoba for the May Day celebrations, the first congress of the Movimiento de Sacerdotes del Tercer Mundo was also being held in the city, an event regarded by many as the birth of a liberation theology movement in Argentina.[49]

All these currents—the student movement, the Marxist and Peronist left, a radicalized Church—were, due to factors in the city's historical development, stronger in Córdoba than anywhere else in the country, and it was there that CGTA's fate was being decided. Córdoba's fame as

Argentina's "red city" was in many ways justified. The city's rebel ethos, which drew on its venerable rivalry with Buenos Aires, was impregnated by the intellectual currents of the time and produced the country's most distinguished Marxist publication, the Gramscian *Pasado y Presente*. Córdoba had a political life of extraordinary effervescence and creativity, and generally provided a sympathetic ambience in which a dissident labor movement could flourish. After the May Day celebrations, Ongaro's support in the city steamrolled. On May 2, a delegation presented the Cordoban CGT's secretary general, Julio Petrucci, with a petition signed by thirty-three of the city's unions, demanding an immediate general assembly to vote on CGTA affiliation.[50] The petitioners included not only all the Independent unions but also such unions as the construction workers' and others that had traditionally been allied with Vandor. The most notable defection was Simó's UOM. With his customary political acumen and opportunism, Simó jumped sides when it appeared Ongaro could not be stopped in the city and added his union's name to the list of the petitioners. That same day, in a move designed to contribute to the sense of Ongaro's unstoppable momentum, Tosco called an extraordinary session of Luz y Fuerza, and the union voted unanimously in favor of a CGTA affiliation.[51]

The last union holdout of strategic significance in Córdoba was Torres and the SMATA. Though the pressures on the IKA-Renault labor force increased to almost unbearable levels and his leadership looked vulnerable and shaken, Torres remained distantly loyal to Vandor, suspicious of Ongaro, and thus immobile. The local SMATA was one of the few unions that did not attend the May 7 CGT general assembly when the Cordoban labor movement voted overwhelmingly to affiliate with the CGTA and gave Ongaro his most important victory to date.[52] Torres was now virtually alone and isolated in the city in his opposition to Ongaro, while Córdoba was in a state of political ferment that was to last more than a year and would culminate in the Cordobazo.

The CGTA had breathed new life into the labor movement and unleashed all the frustrations and rancor pent up during two years of dictatorship. The alignments in Cordoban labor and the very temperament of the labor movement seemed to have been transformed overnight. The unions appeared ready to confront Onganía directly, and a few were ready to embrace the CGTA's more ambitious proposals for a fundamental reform of if not revolutionary change in Argentine society. Yet there were already signs that the CGTA had some fatal flaws. Particularly for many of the Peronists, the changes had been unsettling. Miguel Correa, head of the local carpenters' union and elected president of the Cordoban CGTA, felt the unease of many Peronists at the sudden appearance of students, radical priests, Trotskyists, and assorted left-wing activists at the CGTA headquarters.[53] Elpidio Torres believed the CGTA was putting unreasonable pressures on the union leadership throughout the city, creating expectations among the rank and file that could not be met, given the weakened state of the unions and the employers' general offensive against them. This fear no doubt heightened by the formation of a rank-and-file movement within his own SMATA in support of an autoworkers' affiliation with the CGTA.[54]

Doubts such as Torres's did not yet increase opposition, however, and enthusiasm in the city for Ongaro remained high. With Tosco's reelection as secretary general of Luz y Fuerza in the very month of Córdoba's affiliation with the CGTA, Ongaro was assured of an important ally in a strategic and influential union, but in the heady days of May, not even Tosco's help was necessary to sustain Ongaro's rebellion. Córdoba quickly became the most important center of CGTA agitation in the country, the spiritual capital of the new labor movement. Throughout June and early July, the remaining *vandorista* loyalists straggled in to join what now appeared to be an irresistible force. Of the city's principal working class organizations, only the Fiat company unions and Torres's SMATA continued to hold back. Defections and dissent within SMATA over the CGTA issue had much to do with the perception that Perón himself had cast his lot with Ongaro. Throughout June Perón released public statements and revealed correspondence that indicated unqualified support for the CGTA rebellion.[55]

The most significant defection from Vandor's camp had undoubtedly been that of Alejo Simó's UOM. Simó's initial hesitation and wish, like that of Torres, to remain free of Ongaro were overcome by his customary pragmatism. Simó had already moved away from Vandor in early 1966, when in January the Cordoban UOM had sided with José Alonso's faction against Vandor's in the split of the 62 Organizaciones. Nevertheless the Alonso and Vandor factions had reached an understanding and a virtual alliance after the June 1966 coup, first in their decision to support the Onganía government and then in their opposition to Ongaro and the CGTA. But Simó could no longer afford to remain loyal to the Peronist labor hierarchy's tactical stratagems and overlook the possibilities that an affiliation with the combative CGTA offered him.

In making their decision Simó and the Cordoban UOM leadership certainly felt the unrelenting pressure of their industry's current crisis. In

May the Electrometálica plant had stopped production and laid off its entire labor force, an event that capped a series of bankruptcies and firings in the local metalworking industry that had been taking place since early in the year.[56] Simó's decision to bring his union and its *ortodoxos* into the CGTA was therefore a strategic necessity. The UOM leader sensed that affiliation to the more combative CGT was essential to palliate the grumbling and discontent among the workers the union, and perhaps to even resist more effectively the owners' offensive moves. By June Simó was among Ongaro's most important local allies. He was one of the driving forces behind the June 28, *día de protesta,* a twenty-four-hour general strike organized by the CGTA to protest both the second anniversary of the Onganía coup and Vandor's ongoing machinations to frustrate the results of the March congress. The crisis in his industry and the changing winds in national labor politics compelled Simó to promote an unlikely alliance between his *ortodoxos*—the local bastions of the verticalist, nationalist, and conservative right-wing tendencies in Peronist labor— and the CGTA, as well as to embrace an uncharacteristically outspoken militancy.

In Buenos Aires, the unions still loyal to Vandor witnessed Simó's defection and others with increasing bewilderment. By late June Ongaro's CGTA could claim 650,000 members, with its greatest strength in the provinces, while Vandor's unions, their power base in the great Buenos Aires industrial unions that were under siege but still intact, claimed some 785,000.[57] Signs were everywhere of a bandwagon effect, especially in the interior, and of creeping disarray in the Vandor camp. Ongaro had simply ignored the rump labor congress Vandor held in late May, where he had attempted to reunify the CGT and reestablish the *vandoristas'* authority. As the prospects increased for a permanent split between two apparently irreconcilable factions in the national labor movement, Vandor adopted a more aggressive strategy. Interventions against individual unions, again over quibbling, sometimes fabricated statutory infractions, and even more blatant intimidation tactics became commonplace. Vandor hoped that he could eliminate the CGTA by neutralizing the more troublesome unions and then achieve an only thinly veiled coerced reunification of the labor movement through formal electoral procedures. In late June Vandor presided over a national congress of the Azopardo unions in Rosario to serve notice that he would combat the *ongarista* unions in their very bailiwick, the interior.[58]

Córdoba, a fortress that not even Vandor was prepared to scale, remained untouched. The presence of Tosco's Independents in the city, of a powerful non-Peronist labor bloc, meant that *verticalismo* could not be reestablished simply by isolating and eliminating recalcitrant *ongarista* unions. The union that continued to sustain both the Independents and the CGTA was Luz y Fuerza. Given Ongaro's rebellion, the light and power workers' union articulated an ideological and political strategy with greater clarity than they had in the past. Ideologically the union moved closer to genuinely socialist positions, as opposed to the anti-imperialist positions it had espoused in the past. Politically Tosco and the union adopted a strategy of defending the pluralism of the local labor movement and promoting the Cordoban CGT as the leader of working class–led change. The union aimed neither at the conquest of state power by the working class nor at the formation of a separate workers' party. Tosco's conviction that the democratization of the labor movement had to precede any meaningful working class participation in a socialist project meant a twin strategy: protect Córdoba as the redoubt of an alternative, dissident labor movement and encourage movements, such as the CGTA, that sought to undermine the power of the labor bosses.

Ongaro relied greatly on Luz y Fuerza and Córdoba to sustain his rebellion through the Argentine winter of 1968, but the CGTA was already beginning to falter. One problem was Ongaro himself. Quixotic and impulsive, he was undertaking projects that revealed an impractical personality, one that made many wonder about his ability to lead a movement that would represent a realistic alternative for the country's workers. The worker-student alliance also brought liabilities. The eager participation of the students gave the CGTA greater mobilizing power as well as a cadre of student volunteers to perform the necessary canvassing and administrative work, but it also exposed the unions to accusations of apostasy that played on the workers' latent antipathy toward students. The *vandoristas* began to refer scornfully to Ongaro's organization as the "CGT de los Estudiantes" and to sow doubts about Ongaro's real intent and loyalties. Ongaro responded to such accusations imprudently, defending the CGTA as a *"frente civil"* and a *"movimiento de resistencia popular,"* thereby giving credence to rumors of manipulation by the left and by student organizations. Ongaro's close relations with the Third World priests' movement and liberation theologians were also unsettling. In many Peronist unions there remained a visceral anticlericalism, and Ongaro's efforts to win Church support were received with undisguised suspicion by many union men.

More disturbing to Ongaro's allies in Córdoba was his tendency to be distracted by causes that drew his attention away from the building of an alternative labor movement. Ongaro expended great energy, for example, on organizing cooperatives and defense leagues, again with the prominent participation of student organizations and activist clergy, in the *villas miserias,* the urban slums that ringed Buenos Aires. In the year of the CGTA rebellion, the *villas miserias* problem had certainly become a national issue. The failure of Onganía's "Plan Nacional" to eliminate the *villas* through the construction of public housing and the provision of low-interest loans for the *villeros,* a program that basically remained on the blueprints in the government ministries where they were drawn, had been replaced by the more expedient approach of evicting the squatters and bulldozing their shacks and makeshift dwellings. In July, Ongaro had thrown himself into a laudable but impolitic campaign for the defense of the *villas miserias.*[59] The campaign seemed to occupy an inordinate amount of the CGTA's time and at a particularly crucial moment, contributing to Ongaro's growing fame as a well-intentioned but dreamy leader and to perceptions that the CGTA was a collection of eccentrics and assorted political malcontents instead of a serious trade union alternative.

Despite uncertainty in working class ranks over Ongaro's tactics and even his judgment and loyalties, the CGTA remained a serious alternative to *vandorismo* through the Argentine winter. The Cordoban CGTA was able to oversee a major affiliation campaign in the provinces in early July that assured Ongaro the support of most of the interior. The CGTA rebellion had reached its high-water mark. With the provincial unions solidly in the CGTA camp and progress made in such *vandorista* strongholds as La Plata, Berisso, and Ensenada, confidence was high. The organization made a serious play for Vandor's unions in Buenos Aires.[60]

The campaign to win over the big *porteño* industrial unions failed utterly. Ongaro had underestimated the powers of intimidation and coercion—and overestimated the degree of rank-and-file discontent with the established leadership in Vandor's unions. Perón also contributed to the CGTA's failure. From Madrid came calls in late July and throughout August to reunify the divided labor movement, calls that were understood by many Peronist unions as an order to realign with Vandor. In Córdoba, some Peronist unions began to suspect that their support for Ongaro had been premature. Simó went so far as to hold a series of meetings with Vandor that were widely publicized in the Cordoban press and generally interpreted as negotiations to resolve their differences and bring the Cordoban UOM back into the *vandorista* fold.[61]

Córdoba was momentarily safe for Ongaro nonetheless. Though Tosco himself had begun to express frustration with Ongaro's whimsical character, everything had been staked on the CGTA rebellion and there was no going back. In early September Ongaro's Cordoban supporters, including doubters such as Simó, approved the recently drafted CGTA *plan de acción,* a program for resistance to the government that would keep Córdoba in an almost continuous state of agitation over the next nine months while *ongarismo* languished in Buenos Aires. The price the Cordoban unions continued to pay for their loyalty to the CGTA was sometimes ostracism from their union centrals and sometimes more direct forms of intimidation. The FATLYF finally carried out on a long-threatened expulsion of the Cordoban Luz y Fuerza in early November, along with expulsions of other light and power union locals, such as those in San Nicolás and Pergamino, that continued to support the CGTA.[62] Other unions suffered similar or worse reprisals, but Córdoba remained loyal to Ongaro. In the final months of 1968, local CGTA supporters fanned out into the provinces to support and advise striking unions, such as the sugar workers in Tucumán and Salta and the print workers in Santa Fe, while Ongaro heeded Tosco's advice to stay closer to union affairs and threw the CGTA behind the strike of the Ensenada oil workers.

Massive support shown by the unions in Córdoba, Rosario, and Tucumán in an October solidarity strike for the oil workers reaffirmed the CGTA's provincial strategy.[63] Ongaro carried the Ensenada oil workers' strike to Mendoza and other oil-producing parts of the country and briefly recaptured the momentum the CGTA had lost in recent months. He raised the protests of the Ensenada workers, initially a purely local dispute involving the union's opposition to the awarding of exploration and drilling contracts to foreign companies, to the status of a national issue, thereby making the CGTA appear as the defender of the national patrimony. The oil workers' strike proved to be only a brief revival for the CGTA, however. In coming months, as the strike dragged on and Ongaro appeared to lose interest, Vandor ordered union centrals to take control of a number of CGTA unions in Buenos Aires and cajoled others into deserting, and Ongaro lost what little support remained to him in Buenos Aires.

After the collapse of the oil workers' strike on December 10, Tosco's doubts about Ongaro turned into bitter disillusionment. To prevent further damage to the CGTA, Tosco convinced Ongaro to undertake a speaking tour of the provinces, where his personal popularity remained high, to keep him away from Buenos Aires where the hemorrhaging of the labor confederation continued unabated. Ongaro now stood as a serious liability to the dissident labor movement, the symbol of what the Peronist labor bosses were now skillfully portraying as a more muddled than malevolent attempt to divide the country's labor movement. For the next several months, Tosco worked to salvage what remained of the CGTA by more clearly defining its political positions and by strengthening its ties with the left, particularly in the Cordoban student movement, to compensate for its weakened working class base.

Vandor reconciled with Perón in early 1969, and Perón ordered Ongaro to disband the CGTA, eliminating whatever hope remained of the CGTA's holding on to a sizable number of Peronist unions. Meanwhile Ongaro's erratic behavior was alienating even his staunchest supporters.[64] Perón received Vandor in Madrid and urged him to make greater efforts to reunite the labor movement, ostensibly to combat the progovernment *participacionista* unions, but also to eliminate Ongaro's rebellion, a movement that had outlived its usefulness to Perón and appeared to be a haven for the most radical tendencies in the country, both within and outside the labor movement. What hindered the reestablishment of *verticalismo*, particularly in Buenos Aires, was in fact no longer *ongarismo* so much as it was the swelling ranks of *participacionismo*. Led by such union leaders as Taccone of the Buenos Aires light and power workers' union and Roger Coria of the construction workers' union, these unions worked closely with Onganía's labor minister, San Sebastián, and had become a major force within the labor movement by early 1969. In Buenos Aires the desertions from the CGTA became a virtual retreat as former *ongarista* unions chose to rejoin Vandor or even to affiliate with the *participacionistas* in the hope of being better positioned to negotiate with the government.

In the provinces, the collapse of the rebellion was not so complete, but the CGTA had clearly lost some of its appeal and desertions were taking place even in former *ongarista* strongholds. Only in Córdoba did the core of the CGTA's support remain intact. On January 10 and 11, 1969, the Cordoban unions sponsored the Congreso del Peronismo Combativo to keep the CGTA rebellion alive in the city. The city's state of agitation was highlighted several days later when the Cordoban CGT issued its "Declaración de Córdoba," in which *participacionismo* was again repudiated and all the "popular sectors" were called on to oppose the government.[65] In Argentina's second industrial city, a working relationship between the Independents and the Peronist unions continued to exist that held the promise of cooperation on at least local problems. This was the real significance of Ongaro's rebellion for Córdoba. The CGTA had mobilized most of the Cordoban working class behind a common banner.

Those unions, such as the SMATA, that did not join Ongaro had at least not actively supported Vandor but had followed a neutral policy. The result was a further breaking down of the barriers between Peronist and non-Peronist unions and greater opportunities for dialogue and cooperation. Ongaro's rebellion had also forged a worker-student alliance in Córdoba that, though it caused dissent in some unions, offered tactical advantages that greatly enhanced the local labor movement's independence. The changes occasioned by the CGTA transformed the balance of power in Cordoban labor and made possible the broad cooperation among the city's working class organizations that led to Argentina's greatest working class protest in half a century.

The Cordobazo

In 1963 Pablo was working in the local airplane factory when he heard that Industrias Kaiser Argentina was hiring and paying better wages than he received as a mechanic on the public payroll in the Industrias Aeronaúticas y Mécanicas del Estado complex. On a day off, he took a bus to Santa Isabel and applied for work in the Kaiser plants. There the IKA personnel office gave him a simple mechanical aptitude test and informed him that his chances of getting a job in one of the factories was good. He was hired shortly thereafter. Pablo was soon disenchanted with his new job, however as he found that the mechanical skills he had acquired in the airplane factory were of little use on Kaiser's assembly lines. When he was transferred to a line in the paint department, a job for which he had little experience and where he felt out of place, his frustrations grew. Pablo also quickly realized that the higher wages came at a price and that he was working "three times more" than he had in the airplane factory, where the production rhythms and pace of work were relatively slow compared with what he found at IKA-Renault.

Juan Baca had also been enticed by the higher wages and reputedly better working conditions in the IKA complex, where the workers enjoyed the protection of a "real union," one that represented their interests rather than the company's. From 1959 to 1966, he had worked in the Fiat complex, but in 1967 he was able to enter Kaiser's Perdriel plant as a skilled tool and die maker. He was generally pleased with the new job, though to his surprise he found himself uneasy with the large number of union activists he encountered in the plant, many of whom he suspected of being leftists rather than Peronists, the group with which he proudly identified himself. In May 1969 Juan Baca was working overtime almost

136

every chance he could. The numerous strikes over the previous two years and the resulting lost work days had cut down his take-home pay. Like Pablo, he had learned that despite the apparent advantages, a job with IKA-Renault also had its drawbacks. In this case, a more independent and responsive union also meant more strikes, a loss of work days, and financial problems for his family.

In 1966 Alberto left his home in Villa María, a prosperous agricultural town in the province of Córdoba, to begin his university studies in architecture. The day of his arrival in the city, he was confronted with a bewildering display of angry autoworkers in Córdoba's streets, the first time he had ever seen one of the union strikes that Argentine newspapers continuously spoke of. He joined the marching column without fully understanding what the workers were protesting. Alberto's political education was interrupted the following year when he performed the *colimba,* the obligatory military service that ironically helped to instill in him a hatred of the military, as it would in many of the young leftists of the 1970s. When he returned to Córdoba the following year, he found the city greatly changed. The political climate had hardened, and in the school of architecture, what had once been friendly political disagreements were now acrimonious ideological disputes. The reformist student groups that had dominated university politics when he left Córdoba had been eclipsed by the newer Peronist left and Marxist organizations, organizations interested not simply in protecting university autonomy as the student groups had been in the first days of the Onganía dictatorship, but also in advocating a complete transformation of Argentine society, some of them even calling for a socialist revolution.

Eduardo also hoped to begin studies in architecture. Unlike Alberto, he arrived in Córdoba after the coup and was faced with the entrance exam that Onganía had established for the universities in the first year of his government. Onganía had claimed the entrance exam was necessary to improve the quality of higher education in the country, though many like Eduardo believed it to be nothing more than a brazen attempt to abrogate the legacy of the university reform movement begun in Córdoba in 1918, to restore the elitist nature of the Argentine university and undermine its character as the principal institution of social mobility in the country. Eduardo failed the exam, a bitter disappointment and a source of wounded pride if not exactly shame for himself and his family. The failure to gain admission to the university meant Eduardo spent a lost year working part-time in the local telephone company and studying for the entrance exam for the following year. In 1968 he passed the exam and gained admission to the school of architecture, but he continued to work part-time for the telephone company, and the frustrations and anger of the lost year would fester for years as a personal grudge against a government he considered elitist and illegitimate.

Erio Vaudagna, a parish priest in the working class neighborhood of Los Plátanos and one of the most important figures in the local "Third World priests movement," noticed important changes in his barrio by 1969. His neighborhood was populated almost completely by workers employed in the mechanical industries. More than half, he estimated, worked at the IAME complex, another large fraction in the IKA-Renault plants, and a small number in the more distant Fiat factories. Despite the neighborhood's working class character, the traditional barriers between students and workers had been partially broken down there. Students had begun to volunteer in parish activities, traveling from their own neighborhoods to Los Plátanos to participate in its community service programs as well as to organize debates, lectures, and political discussions in the church hall. The workers at first received them with more suspicion than gratitude, but the students' presence had become a part of parish life.

The very different lives of Pablo, Juan Baca, Alberto, Eduardo, and Father Vaudagna found an exceptional, historical link in their participation in the uprising of May 29 and 30, 1969, that would later be known as the Cordobazo. All would, for their own reasons, join the revolt and feel varying degrees of identification with the furious nature of the protest of those days, as would thousands of other residents in the city, each with their own personal history. The complexity of the Cordobazo, and its character as a distinctively Cordoban event, was revealed in such diversity. The Cordobazo would also mark a turning point in all their lives, because of the profound effects it would have on their country.

The Cordobazo uprising stands as one of the genuinely seminal events and historical watersheds in twentieth-century Argentina. Its immediate political effect was to discredit the Onganía dictatorship and weaken the foundations of what had once appeared to be the strongest of all the post-Peronist regimes. It unleashed forces both within and outside the government that would force Onganía to resign less than a year later, dismantling the government's economic program and certain of its authoritarian pretenses, and paving the way for the restoration of democratic rule in 1973.

Yet rather than as a precipitant of yet another political crisis and change of regime, the Cordobazo's most significant legacy was as a symbol. The effect of the uprising on the local working class and the Argentine left was nothing short of revolutionary. Quickly mythologized by both, it became the touchstone, the benchmark by which Peronist left and Marxist organizations and parties, as well as certain sectors of the labor movement, evaluated all subsequent working class mobilizations in the city. It eventually encouraged those both within and outside the labor movement who were unhappy with Peronism and Peronist trade unionism to elaborate an alternative political project, *clasismo,* for the Argentine working class. The unfulfilled promise of the Cordobazo and the remarkable hold the uprising had on the minds of the workers and those in leftist groups, particularly the Cordoban left, influenced events for years after. To a certain extent, all the furious labor agitation of the next six years occurred in the shadow of the Cordobazo. Some unions consciously tried to recreate the experience and others used it as an edifying example of the latent power of the working class, but all took their cue from it in some way.

The great significance of the event unfortunately has not been matched by accuracy in the accounts of it, nor by cogency or fullness in the explanations offered by those who have analyzed it. Studies of the Cordobazo have often been marred by overly schematic interpretations, syllogistic and sociological for the most part, that have paid insufficient attention to the historical complexity of the uprising. Such explanations have generally presented the Cordobazo as a kind of metaphor for the contradictions of postwar Argentine capitalist development. The disruptive effects of sudden, capital-intensive, and technologically sophisticated industrialization, as it was promoted through the activities of the foreign automobile firms, are often presented as a complete explanation for the uprising. Such interpretations have dwelt on the great sense of deprivation and loss of privilege felt by the highly paid automotive proletariat whose mobility aspirations were rudely frustrated by the decline of the Cordoban automobile industry, and on problems exacerbated by a political regime that gave the dynamic sectors of the economy a free hand to attack their labor costs. Given the absence of electoral alternatives, the Cordoban working class, led by the automobile workers, was supposedly pushed toward what were effectively if unconsciously revolutionary positions. The Cordobazo was thus seen as a kind of working class assault, albeit frustrated and inchoate, on state power. In short, the protest was depicted as having been led by the most privileged sectors of the working class, in a city where class consciousness had developed more precociously due to its eccentric economic development.[1]

Unsatisfactory interpretations of the Cordobazo have been the result of two approaches: an inappropriate application of labor aristocracy theories, simplistically equating the higher wages of the automotive proletariat with privileged status and therefore with an unusual sensitivity to a deterioration in the local economy; and conversely, an assigning of "vanguard" status to the workers, thus a greater propensity to undertake a systematic critique of capitalist relations of production by virtue of their employment in a modern, multinational, industrial enterprise. There has also often been simple inaccuracy as regards to the very facts of the uprising. Existing studies of the Cordobazo have failed to recognize adequately the diversity of the working class that participated in the uprising, and they have also underestimated the social complexity of the event: the importance of the involvement of other classes and groups that was unique to Córdoba and which lacked the specific objectives of the unions. The destruction and loss of life caused by the protest, for example, cannot be explained simply by working class ire. The violence surrounding the event was certainly greater than the depth of working class discontent, and the centers of destruction and resistance, Barrio Clínicas and Barrio Alberdi, were student neighborhoods, not working class preserves. After the army entered the city late in the afternoon of May 29, the workers, perhaps frightened by what they had unleashed, largely withdrew from the protest, while students and snipers, the latter never identified but probably members of the underground left in Córdoba, resisted the army's advance. The Cordobazo was a popular protest with a predominantly working class character, but it also contained elements of a popular rebellion and an urban insurrection independent of working class control.

The Cordobazo obviously occurred within a unique economic and social setting. Córdoba's tardy and sudden industrial development had created a local working class and labor movement that were more independent, democratic, and combative than others elsewhere in the country and that had some very particular characteristics. Nevertheless, by itself the city's automotive-industry-led development offers an unsatisfactory explanation for the uprising. The Cordobazo was a complex event in which broad sectors of the working class, as well as other classes, participated under the weight of cultural, intellectual, and political influences that, collectively, were probably more powerful than the immediate problems of the automobile industry or the local economy. The Cordobazo had its immediate origins in local working class politics. The unions that took part in the protest were influenced by diverse factors, and the protest is best explained not as a result of Córdoba's socioeconomic singularity, but as a result of conditions existing in individual unions.

Córdoba was certainly propitious ground for a popular explosion with

heavy working class participation, but the reasons for that are complicated, involving not only the problems in the local economy and the
character of its working class, but also general political and cultural
influences in the city that affected the workers as well as many other
Cordobans. The working class's participation in the uprising thus was the
product of a particular history, with all the intricacies and nuances that
any history implies. Most important, it was the result of the accumulated
frustrations and grudges built up among all classes in the city over nearly
three years of authoritarian rule. That frustration meshed with the local
workers' tradition of resistance and militancy and with the specific strategies the Cordoban unions had devised to deal with the dictatorship.

It is first important to recognize the influence that the CGTA mobilizations had in making the Cordobazo possible. The failure of the Confederación General del Trabajo de los Argentinos to fulfill its early promise and offer a serious alternative to the conservative and increasingly
ineffectual business unionism practiced by Augusto Vandor and the Confederación General del Trabajo did not mean that the labor movement
returned suddenly to the status quo. Vandor was able, with Perón's blessing, to reassert control over much of the workers' movement, but pockets
of resistance remained, especially in the provinces. In Tucumán and
Rosario, the *ongaristas* were still a powerful force, and they obstructed
attempts to integrate their labor movements into Vandor's CGT. In Córdoba, CGTA supporters still dominated the local trade union movement.
Indeed, despite Alejo Simó's negotiations with Vandor and the rumblings
coming from other Peronist CGTA unions, the labor alliance was still
intact in the city. The very thing that had driven Peronist unions into the
CGTA, the inability or unwillingness of the mainstream Peronist labor
movement to protect local union interests, continued to be the decisive
factor holding the alliance together. A coincidence of interests and a
consensus on tactics among these unions prevented Vandor from breaking Córdoba and made labor militancy possible.

The continued vitality of the CGTA alliance in Córdoba met the immediate need to resolve new problems that were affecting certain sectors of
the Cordoban working class. Onganía's economic policies adversely affected working class interests in general, but certain local industries were
experiencing what could fairly be described as a crisis. The automobile
and metalworking industries were having the worst years in their histories; the companies were attempting to take advantage of the weakened
state of the Sindicatos de Mecánicos y Afines del Transporte Automotor

and the continued defenseless position of the Fiat workers to lower labor costs through reduced work weeks and temporary suspensions in production. For workers in the city's small parts and components workshops, there was the prospect of a permanent loss of livelihood as the always fragile metal trades went through a series of bankruptcies in early 1969. The owners of the workshops and the small parts factories that made up the local industry were unbending to all union demands, including those surrounding the *quitas zonales* controversy, an issue that emerged as a major grievance for the Unión Obrera Metalúrgica and encouraged its continued collaboration with the CGTA unions.

The owners' refusal to eliminate the *quitas zonales,* the differential wage rate used only in their industry that awarded lower wages to metalworkers in the interior, forced Simó to take a stand. There was little that the UOM could do to resist bankruptcies or even production suspensions, but the union leadership's credibility rested on its efforts to resolve the *quitas zonales* issue successfully. The controversy over the *quitas zonales,* a practice deeply resented by the Cordoban UOM workers for the privileged treatment it granted their *porteño* counterparts, had actually begun in 1966. In the national collective bargaining agreement reached several months after the Onganía coup, the owners had reluctantly agreed to begin the gradual elimination of the *quitas zonales,* a pledge that the Cordoban owners ultimately failed to keep. For Simó and the local UOM the problem threatened their leadership, as owners in other provinces unilaterally abolished the practice while their bosses remained immobile. In March 1969, as a concession to Vandor to aid in his attempt to win back the wayward Cordoban UOM, the Labor Ministry abolished the *quitas zonales.* The Cordoban owners once again cavalierly disregarded the ministry's order.[2] Vandor's reluctance to push the issue on Córdoba's behalf pushed Simó back into a close working relationship with the CGTA unions in the month of the Cordobazo.

The UOM's problems with the *quitas zonales* became one of the rallying points of the Cordoban labor movement in the weeks leading up to the Cordobazo. The SMATA workers also contributed a grievance to the mounting frustrations of the local working class. Unable to reduce its labor costs through layoffs, which would have been sure to elicit an immediate union response, IKA-Renault emerged as the major provincial advocate of the repeal of the "sábado inglés" law, a special concession in several provinces that granted workers in select industries a full day's pay in return for working half a day on Saturday. Since the law had never been passed in Buenos Aires, IKA-Renault could point to it as yet another factor responsible for the company's inability to compete with the newer, Buenos Aires–based firms and could argue convincingly for its repeal. The law was especially prized by the Córdoba's automobile workers, who were subject to more strenuous working conditions than most of the Cordoban working class, and union concern over a possible annulment was great.

In late March, representatives from the Unión Industrial Argentina presented a petition to Alberto Krieger Vasena requesting the abolition of the law in those provinces where the *sábado inglés* was still in force: Córdoba, Mendoza, San Luis, Santiago del Estero, and Tucumán. On May 12, the government abolished the *sábado inglés*. The SMATA immediately prepared to resist, and Elpidio Torres called a general assembly for May 14 at the Córdoba Sport Club. The May 14 SMATA assembly, broken up violently by police, ended with Torres playing the role of rabble-rouser, leading columns of SMATA workers into the city, where for some hours the workers controlled the downtown area.[3]

The confrontation with the police marked the end of Torres's aloofness from the city's other unions. The pressures his leadership had been subjected to over the preceding three years had come to a climax with the *sábado inglés* problem. Mizael Bizzotto, a worker in the IKA-Renault Perdriel factory, remembered that the anger in the plant increased palpably after the May 14 rally and that even the factory bathrooms became settings for political discussion, with a feeling of indignation and a resolve to respond to the government's provocations being the overwhelming sentiment. Torres, always sensitive to his union's changing moods, began to seek out Simó, and later Agustín Tosco, to coordinate a demonstration against the government. The result was a group of unions primed for a major protest, not because of any inexorable contradictions in Córdoba's automobile-based industrialization, but because of a confluence of factors, greatly influenced by the vicissitudes of national and local labor politics, that affected broad sectors of the local working class and opened certain possibilities for cooperation between unions with different political loyalties.

The mobilizations of the Cordoban labor movement were contemporary with an upsurge in student activism, much of which responded to the revitalized Cordoban left. The city's nearly 30,000 university students had reemerged as a political force with their collaboration in the CGTA union drives, and by early 1969 the university faculties on Obispo Trejo Street and in the nearby Ciudad Universitaria were the unofficial centers of local opposition to the regime. Isabel Rins, a university student in 1969, listened interestedly to the unfailing after-dinner political debates in the sprawling university dining hall where more than 5,000 students ate each night. For her, and for many students, these debates were their political initiation and the beginning of a personal interest in politics. For a minority of students, they marked the start of life as a left-wing activist; some even became guerrillas. For nearly all the students, many of whom came from conservative small towns and farms in the province, it was an experience that encouraged them to question the prejudices and preconceptions they had brought with them to the university—in Isabel Rins's case, eventually to reject the almost tribal anti-Peronism cultivated in her Radical home in Río Cuarto. At the student *peñas* (gatherings for folk music and political discussion), in their classes and dormitories, Peruvians, Bolivians, Paraguayans, and students from other neighboring countries mingled with the Argentines, and a uniquely Cordoban left-wing student culture took shape, born of a common Latin American identity and of the widespread reading and discussion of the classic texts of socialist thought.

Córdoba's university students had opposed Onganía almost from the very first days of the dictatorship. In the early months of the regime, student resistance to Onganía's faculty purges and to his university policies in general had been swift and spirited. The resistance reached an early climax in September 1966 when, in what amounted to a dress rehearsal for the Cordobazo, the students occupied Barrio Clínicas, the twenty city blocks of student boardinghouses and the historic center of university political life, as a protest against the regime. Onganía responded by banning the powerful Federación Universitaria de Córdoba (FUC), the organization that coordinated student politics, and all other student political organizations. Student resistance then moved underground, split between the Marxist Coordinadora Estudiantil en Lucha and the Peronist Frente Estudiantil Nacional, a rift that was healed only when the two found a common cause in the CGTA campaign.[4] In clandestinity, student politics became increasingly radicalized, and both the Marxist and Peronist left gained disciples. Gonzalo Fernández, a university student who had returned to Córdoba in late 1968 after two years of graduate study in the United States, found that student politics had greatly changed during his absence. Sympathy for revolutionary solutions had palpably increased, and the moderate student groups such as the Movimiento Universitario Reformista, which had coordinated resistance to Onganía in the early months of the regime, had been almost completely eclipsed by more radical groups. Many of his friends once active in Catholic student organizations were now left-wing Peronists.

The radical student movement in Córdoba was part of an international phenomenon and was undoubtedly influenced by a certain cultural mimicry, notably of French student politics, as well as genuine political disaffection. As with its counterparts in North America and Europe, there was an element of political dilettantism in the activism of Córdoba's university students. For many, political militancy was confined to the four or five years necessary to get the university degree, and participation in one or another of the student political organizations was almost an obligatory rite of passage for middle-class respectability. But in Córdoba there were also elements that gave the generational rebellion a historical significance rarely seen in other instances of student activism. One such element was the social weight the university carried in Cordoban life. Student organizations had traditionally been accepted as legitimate political interlocutors by local authorities, and university politics had never been confined just to educational issues, as the 1918 University Reform had first eloquently shown. Thus students had come to expect to exercise a political influence that was unheard of elsewhere in the country, a fact that undoubtedly made their subordinated status under Onganía more difficult to accept and precipitated student disaffection and eventually opposition to the regime. Despite Onganía's intervention, which forced the university students to work clandestinely, student organizations, revealingly, maintained an institutional integrity and effectiveness that was unmatched by the local political parties, which were proscribed and in disarray, and was surpassed only by the unions.

Since the 1918 University Reform, Córdoba's public university had also become a fairly egalitarian institution and the only meaningful mechanism of social mobility in the province. Though the student body was predominantly middle class, there were important gradations within that class, and a university student might be anyone from the son of prosperous businessman to the daughter of a penurious rural schoolteacher. Moreover, at a time when it was still possible in Argentina for an industrial worker to support a son or daughter who wished to study at the university, a small number of students were of working class origins, a fact that perhaps helps explain the sympathy of many students for the workers' struggles in these years.[5]

Another factor giving greater meaning to student activism was the role the Catholic church played in encouraging student militancy and dissent. After the 1968 Latin American bishops conference in Medellín and the meeting of the Third World priests movement in Córdoba, sympathy grew in the Argentine Church for an activist clergy. Liberation theologians, though still a minority, gained notoriety and centered their activities in Córdoba. Like the university, the Church remained a powerful force in the city and in Córdoba's traditional society. Though it lacked the support nationally of a powerful Christain Democratic party and therefore found its political influence circumscribed, the Church maintained power as a censorious and legitimizing institution. After Perón's overthrow, all the principal political parties, including the Communist party, had taken great pains to cultivate friendly relations with it, and anticlericalism in Córdoba was confined only to the more hard-bitten Marxist and Peronist activists in the labor movement. For example, during the Church's acrimonious conflict with the Illia government over plans to end certain tax exemptions for Catholic private schools and to abolish some anachronistic legal dispensations (*fueros*), local politicians had remained silent, and Tosco and other union leaders had emerged as the only public critics of the Church's opposition campaign.[6]

The political influence of the Church was reaffirmed, albeit in a very different guise, with the appearance of the liberation theologians. Led in particular by Milán Viscovich, local liberation theologians attempted to reformulate Church doctrine into what sympathetic local Catholics began to call *"socialismo cristiano."* Unable to participate openly in politics, students were able to find a forum for political debate and discussion in the Catholic study groups that mushroomed in various university departments after 1966. In Córdoba, there also existed another movement, the Movimiento de Reivindicaciones por los Derechos del Pueblo, led by two parish priests, Gustavo Ortiz and Erio Vaudagna—the same rector of the church in the Los Plátanos neighborhood where the students had become active. Ortiz and Vaudagna's movement was a liberation theology–inspired attempt to channel leftist student political sympathies into Church-sponsored organizations, especially at the neighborhood level. The significance of an activist Church generally was that it sustained the students at a time of repression and also that it infused many of them with political ideas that equated Christianity with socialism. The step from concerned Catholic to socialist revolutionary became shorter.

What contributed most immediately to the students' political transcendence, however, was the fact that their numbers and latent power made possible the worker-student alliance that would reach its apogee in the Cordobazo. Since the stalling of the CGTA Tosco, particularly, had courted student support. The light and power workers' secretary general appeared regularly as a speaker at student gatherings and had tempered his once frank anticlericalism, praising the new currents in the Church and thereby reassuring Córdoba's numerous Catholic students, who were still suspicious of the labor leader's reputed Marxist sympathies. Under Tosco's influence, the light and power workers called solidarity strikes in the worst moments of Onganía's repression of the student movement and generously allowed their union hall to be used by students for everything from entrance-exam prep courses to clandestine political meetings.[7] Tosco hoped to cement an alliance with a group he rightly suspected would be a natural ally in any future confrontation with the government. His long association with the student movement was undoubtedly partly due to the personal attraction he felt for an environment in which his intelligence and erudition, though highly personal and not academic, were received with interest and respect. Mostly, however, it was a calculated, strategical decision. Tosco was fully aware that the students were a factor of considerable power in the city and therefore worthy of his attention.

Workers and students also found common cause in their opposition to Córdoba's provincial government. Onganía's appointed governor, Carlos Caballero, sought to harness the city's unruly labor movement through a vaguely corporatist scheme to allow labor representatives to sit, along with those from business, the Church, and the military, on a purely ceremonial *consejo asesor* (advisory council)—a sop that Caballero rather naively believed would calm working class spirits. It had precisely the opposite effect. Though it was an issue that principally preoccupied the more politically sophisticated labor leaders, such as Tosco, all the city's major unions publicly spurned Caballero's offer.

From working class ranks came accusations of intimidation tactics used by the provincial government, of *brigadas fantasmas,* comprising off-duty police and local thugs, operating with official blessing to make the unions cower and force their cooperation with the government.[8] Caballero compounded working class and student disaffection by angering the city's middle class residents when he increased property taxes in early 1969, further alienating a large segment of the population already unhappy with the suspension of civil liberties and the loss of all political participation under Onganía's authoritarian regime. The popular character of the Cordobazo, the support it drew from diverse classes and groups, owed much to Caballero's clumsy handling of the provincial government at a particularly sensitive moment.

The Cordobazo of May 29 and 30, 1969, brought to a climax a weeks-long campaign of opposition to Onganía by the workers and students in the city. Many of Córdoba's major unions coincidentally faced serious problems in their industries in that same month. In addition to the ongoing problems for the IKA-Renault and UOM workers, workers in other industries were subject to new pressures from their employers. Atilio López and the Unión Tranviarios Automotor reemerged from a nearly seven-year retreat from local union politics to organize a series of strikes to protest a proposed reorganization of the urban transport system that would have seriously disrupted established retirement plans and job classifications.[9] In the weeks leading up to the Cordobazo the bus drivers, bitter over the failure of worker cooperatives that had been established for some lines after the 1962 privatization of the municipal bus company and uneasy with the prospects of the impending restructuring of the city's public transportation system, were among the most active members of the Cordoban working class. Luz y Fuerza, a union normally immune to such bitter conflicts with management, had reasons of its own to step up its militancy. A new government plan for the rationalization of Empresa Pública de Energía de Córdoba and the partial privatization of electric power in the province was seen as the first step toward the dissolution of the public company and eventually the complete privatization of the industry.[10]

That May was also an exceptionally tense month for the students, as the government redoubled its efforts to quell any sign of political activity in the country's universities. On May 15 a student strike in Corrientes at the Universidad del Nordeste was violently suppressed by the army, leaving one student dead and a number wounded. The events in Corrientes sparked a nationwide student protest in which the remaining CGTA loyalists and student protesters marched arm in arm in such cities as La Plata, Rosario, and Tucumán. Predictably Córdoba had the largest protests of all. The student demonstrations there were the most broad-based, with the Sacerdotes del Tercer Mundo, Tosco's Independents, and a number of Peronist unions participating in the marches as well. After separate confrontations with police, culminating in the students' May 23 barricading of the streets in Barrio Clínicas, the friendly relations between the labor and student movements became a virtual alliance, and the CGT headquarters on Vélez Sarsfield served as the meeting place both for unions and student political organizations. On May 25 Tosco made a speech at the university that publicly cemented the alliance between the workers and students and prepared both for the events of the Cordobazo.[11]

Meanwhile, within the labor movement, the ecumenical spirit of recent weeks deepened and opportunities for cooperation between unions increased. Even Torres overcame his traditional dislike of compromising entanglements and worked closely with other leaders, such as Tosco and Simó. Pressures from the provinces, especially from Córdoba's CGT, had prompted both the national CGTA and Vandor's reluctant CGT to coordinate a twenty-four-hour general strike for May 30. In Córdoba the unions negotiated to begin the strike on May 29 and make the local protest last forty-eight hours. Fernando Solís, an administrative employee in IKA-Renault forge, was one of many IKA-Renault workers who expressed support for a *paro activo,* an abandonment of work and march on the city center, instead of the *paro dominguero* or *paro matero* (stay-at-home strikes) urged by Vandor and the *vandorista* CGT. The union leaders shared that sentiment and, the forty-eight-hour strike decided, met on May 28 in the Luz y Fuerza headquarters, along with leaders of principal student organizations, to coordinate the protest. As a gesture of support for Córdoba's more ambitious protest, the CGTA dispatched Ongaro to the city to participate in the events.

Ongaro was arrested on his arrival in Córdoba on the morning of May 27. His arrest probably facilitated the coordination of the protest and increased cooperation between the unions, helping to make the protest a strictly Cordoban affair without partisan implications. At the May 28 meeting Tosco, Torres, Miguel Correa, López, Alfredo Martini (Simó's chief lieutenant in the local UOM), and various student representatives agreed to march the following day in separate columns: one comprising largely SMATA workers from Santa Isabel that would march up Vélez Sarsfield to the plaza, and another led by the Luz y Fuerza workers from the EPEC offices that would march up the Avenida Colón (for a map of the city, see Figure 1 in Chapter 1). They were to meet in front of the CGT headquarters and stage a rally there sometime around noon. The four principal unions participating in the protest—Luz y Fuerza, the SMATA, the UOM, and the UTA—were assigned separate sections of the city, where each was to coordinate resistance in the event that the police broke up the demonstration. (Although violent police repression and the ensuing confusion would prevent the smooth execution of this plan, attempts would be made in the early hours of the Cordobazo, particularly by Luz y Fuerza, to establish orderly resistance in the assigned districts.)[12]

In subsequent writings and interviews, Tosco stressed the premeditated political objectives of the unions; he insisted that interpretations positing the spontaneous nature of the Cordobazo were mistaken and that the unions and their student allies had well-defined tactical designs and a political purpose behind their protest.[13] Indeed in the first hours of the protest, events proceeded much as had been planned. Early on the morning of the twenty-ninth, Torres and his closest collaborators in the SMATA left the union's downtown headquarters and drove to the IKA-Renault factory gates. Torres arrived just as the night shift was leaving the complex; the morning shift was already in the plants and at work. Over the next hour and a half, word spread from department to department of an imminent abandonment of the factories. Francisco Cuevas worked in a machining shop and was one of many workers who saw Torres as a deal-cutter, a "bureaucrat" who negotiated with the company behind closed doors, *"por debajo de cuerda."* Nevertheless he and practically everyone else in his department abandoned their jobs to march behind the SMATA leader when their shop steward gave the word. Nino Chávez, working in the painting department, similarly saw his co-workers abandon their work stations en masse. As they left the plants, workers grabbed metal bars, tools, ball bearings, bolts, and whatever else was handy for defending themselves. Outside the factory gates, Torres made a brief speech. Sometime around eleven o'clock nearly 4,000 SMATA workers, among them Pablo and Juan Baca, followed Torres and left for the CGT headquarters on Vélez Sarsfield.

Oscar Alvarez, an administrative employee in EPEC, was meanwhile gathering with the light and power workers at their company offices several blocks north of the downtown district. The column to be led by the light and power workers was set to march directly to Vélez Sarsfield through the student neighborhood of Barrio Clínicas. In the Fiat factories, where company-controlled union representatives had not been included in the planning of the strike, word nonetheless spread of the downtown demonstration, and a few individual workers abandoned the plants to march from Ferreyra. Gregorio Flores was among those who were willing to risk suspension, perhaps even being fired, to leave their work stations to march down Highway 9 and into the city. The military foremen in the IAME factories, on the other hand, prevented any plant abandonments there, and Manuel Cabrera, a worker in the airplane factory, was forced to wait until the end of his shift at two o'clock to march with the handful of other IAME workers willing to trek the nine miles to the city center, which was by then a scene of confusion and tumult.

Workers from other unions that were normally passive also mobilized. Graciela García, a university student, was returning home when she was startled by the sight of the railroad workers marching in a column toward the downtown; it was the first time she had seen workers from that union participate in a protest in years. Juan, a metalworker, found that his co-workers' unhappiness with Simó, the local UOM's union representation, and its repeated failure to resolve problems with working conditions and job classifications in their small parts factory did not prevent them from supporting their union that day. Miguel Contreras and others working in a small metalworking workshop on La Rioja Street that supplied parts for IKA-Renault were also unhappy with their UOM representation and had tried, unsuccessfully, to affiliate with the SMATA. But despite their opposition to Simó, they too heeded the union's call to abandon work and march downtown. Some UOM workers did not. The owner of a small parts workshop in Barrio Mitre that was a supplier for Fiat's Grandes Motores Diesel factory drove his UOM-affiliated workers home after work, and in his neighborhood near the Fiat complex the day passed quietly. Those workers, who the owner said had never struck "a single day" in his workshop, were nonetheless the exception, as members of even the most dormant unions joined the protest.

The principal working class contingent meanwhile continued its march from Santa Isabel. The IKA-Renault column had been swelled by several thousand, joined by students and workers through whose neighborhoods they marched, as well as by columns from the UOM and other unions. As the marchers proceeded to the city center, word reached Torres from SMATA workers who had scouted the route ahead on motorbikes of a huge gathering of city police, mounted and with attack dogs, waiting for them in the plaza to prevent access to Vélez Sarsfield and the demonstration at the CGT. As they reached the plaza one worker, Aristides Albano, saw students release bands of stray cats and throw ball bearings into the streets, tactics he had seen them use in previous demonstrations to divert the attention of the police dogs and to frighten the horses. When the first tear gas canisters were released by the police as the columns neared the plaza, homemade tear gas bombs, reputedly manufactured by chemistry students, were thrown in reprisal.

As a result of the police presence, some workers fanned out into the adjoining neighborhoods—Barrio Nueva Córdoba, a student neighborhood to the east, and Barrio Güemes, a working class neighborhood to the west—where neighbors rushed out to give the protesters brooms, bottles, anything they thought could be used as a defense. Some of the marchers, such as Pablo, the disgruntled worker from the IKA-Renault painting department, believing the protest was going to be yet another uneventful demonstration, abandoned the column as it reached the city center and headed for home. Most, however, were prepared to see the protest through and marched on.

As the bulk of the column moved down Vélez Sarsfield toward Boulevard San Juan, the police panicked and opened fire, killing one worker, Máximo Mena, and wounding many others. After their initial panic, a wave of indignation and resolve spread through the ranks of the thousands who remained on Vélez Sarsfield. At the sight of thousands of now angry and menacing workers marching resolutely toward them, the police at first hesitated and began to withdraw, then they ran. From this point on, the protest lost its organization and became a spontaneous popular rebellion.

Within minutes of the clash between workers and police, panicked store owners rushed to close down for the day, boarding up windows and bringing all commercial activity to a halt. The workers who had marched through the adjacent neighborhoods rejoined the rest of the column and began building barricades and bonfires on Vélez Sarsfield and on nearby streets. The SMATA workers were soon joined by the downtown residents, who had watched the confrontation from their windows and balconies and were now sharing in the expression of collective indignation not only with the police's action but also with three years of intimidation and authoritarian rule. Luis Muhio, a university student, was surprised to see downtown middle-class residents bringing their mattresses, furniture, and other belongings to build the barricades and start bonfires. Countless gestures of such solidarity from all classes would be made in neighborhoods throughout the city that day.

Tosco's worker-student column had meanwhile been prevented from advancing toward the CGT headquarters by police units and had attempted to reach Vélez Sarsfield along the parallel street of La Cañada. Led by the light and power workers, this column also contained contingents from *legalista* unions such as the UTA and the state workers, the Asociación de Trabajadores del Estado (ATE), and had been attacked with tear gas by the police outside the EPEC offices where they had assembled for the march. To the rage of the SMATA workers was added the anger of these workers as they made their way to Vélez Sarsfield. Upon reaching the SMATA workers there, Tosco's column melted into the general protest. Some stayed on Vélez Sarsfield while others moved to the neighborhoods surrounding the SMATA and Luz y Fuerza union headquarters to begin another center of resistance. Elsewhere, as word spread of the police attack, the protest turned into a citywide rebellion. By one o'clock, barricades and bonfires sprang up in an area covering some one hundred fifty city blocks, from Barrios Alberdi and Clínicas in the west to Avenida Vélez Sarsfield in the east, and from the neighborhoods on the edge of the Río Primero in the north to Barrios Nueva Córdoba and Güemes in the south. In the neighborhoods east of Vélez Sarsfield roving bands of workers and students set fire to cars and moved at will while the police retreated to the *cabildo* (city hall) and the Plaza San Martín, shaken and confused about what steps to take next.

Since both the SMATA and Luz y Fuerza headquarters lay within the occupied zone, Tosco and, intitially, Torres attempted to establish some degree of organization and control over the protest. Students and workers moved from barricade to barricade on motorbikes, gathering intelligence to coordinate the resistance. Messengers shuttled between the two union halls, and Tosco visited the barricades he deemed strategic. Nevertheless the protest took on a spontaneous character, responding to the ebb and flow of the struggle in the streets without regard to any greater tactical design. The union leadership was largely working in the dark, barely able to follow the course of events, much less control them. By late afternoon, the protest had turned destructive. On the Avenida Colón, the city's principal commercial street, protesters had burned down the Xerox Corporation's offices, a Citroën dealership, and a number of other businesses. The destruction of foreign businesses such as Xerox and Citroën was not an accident. Whereas the *porteño* working class had vented its collective rage on October 17, 1945, against the Jockey Club and other symbols of aristocratic privilege, the Cordoban protesters targeted representatives of the government and imperialism. But the general mood in Córdoba was euphoric rather than vindictive. Lidia Alfonsina, owner of student boardinghouse in Barrio Clínicas, *la tucumana* as she was popularly known among the students, walked to the Avenida Colón and saw the atmosphere as festive, the destruction done with more joy than malice. *La tucumana* saw no wanton plundering of businesses, and indeed some of the distinguishing characteristics of the destruction surrounding the Cordobazo were the low incidence of pillaging and the preference for targets with some political and ideological symbolism. Though there were examples of lootings and some gratuitous violence, the character of destruction in the Cordobazo was more politically purposeful than the violence surrounding the October 17, 1945, rioting had been, or that of the 1948 Bogotazo and other urban protests in twentieth-century Latin America.

As the destruction spread to other parts of the city, however, the army prepared to intervene. Units from the Córdoba-based Third Army Corps were assembled, and they marched to the western edge of the city around one o'clock. Osvaldo, an engineering student performing his military service at the time of the Cordobazo, knew little of what was happening in the city center, like other conscripts, but by late afternoon he was armed and in uniform and being told to prepare to march on the convulsed city. The army commander, General Sánchez Lahoz, released several communiqués throughout the afternoon announcing an imminent occupation of the city and demanding that all the protesters abandon the barricades and return to their homes. The communiqués showed that the military was operating under the false assumption that the uprising was responding to a central command. Despite Tosco's intense efforts to reestablish discipline, it was proving impossible. Tosco, for example, had not been involved in the burnings on Avenida Colón, nor was he consulted in the decision to burn the junior officers' club in his district on San Luis and La Cañada, an act he would have particularly disapproved of, since it served no immediate tactical purpose and assured a harsh repression by the military.

By late afternoon there was a lull. Exhausted after nearly five hours of protest, students and workers rested on park benches and street corners and chatted about the day's events. Around this time, the ranks of the working class protesters began to thin. Though thousands of workers remained in the streets through the night of the twenty-ninth, more, like the SMATA worker Juan Baca, ended their protest at dusk. Many had families waiting for them at home, and the sense of having reached the end of a working day was a stronger pull than any interest in continuing what to many was an already consummated protest. It was only then, as they began to return to their neighborhoods, that many workers began to sense, some with remorse and others with apprehension, the consequences of their actions. The destruction unleashed had been the worst of any popular uprising in Cordoban history, the worst in the entire country since the 1919 *semana trágica*. Smoldering buildings and the charred frames of cars, streets strewn with shards of glass, and barricades and bonfires from one end of Córdoba to the other gave the appearance of a city at war. The spectacle was so shocking that many of the labor organizers began to lose their nerve, fearing that the protest had gone too far. The UOM leadership retreated to its headquarters in the safer eastern district of the city and ceased altogether to participate in the uprising. Juan Carlos Toledo, a journalist covering the events for a local newspaper, *Los Principios,* visited the CGT headquarters where Correa and other union leaders had sought refuge. He found the workers there frightened and the union leaders distraught, a sight that contrasted with the defiance and anger he had noted in the faces of the SMATA-led column of workers in the Plaza Vélez Sarsfield just a few hours before. Torres had been in his union's headquarters since the early afternoon and had passed from euphoria to petulance to gloom. From the time of the burnings on Avenida Colón he had sunk into a dark sullenness, and he had temporarily broken off communication with Tosco and withdrawn for a period of several hours from direct involvement in the uprising.

By evening, the protest began to assume a different character as the initiative passed from the workers to the students. The two student neighborhoods, Barrio Clínicas and Barrio Alberdi, became the centers of resistance, though other groups and classes participated there, notably those from the working class. Jorge Sanabria, a university student, was surprised to find himself in his neighborhood of Barrio Alberdi not only with fellow students, but also with neighbors who were homemakers, workers, and businessmen, none of whom had ever joined in one of the student protests before. Father Vaudagna had also arrived in the city center with his parishioners to join the protest. Barrio Clínicas, especially, attracted supporters from all over the city, a number Tosco subsequently estimated at 50,000, and a bloody confrontation with the army seemed unavoidable. By this time, snipers had taken positions on the rooftops of many of the buildings there, and caches of arms, rumored to be the hasty contributions of various underground left-wing organizations initially caught off guard by the protest, had started to arrive.

It was into this tense situation that the army marched, the first troops reaching the edge of Barrio Alberdi shortly before five o'clock. By six o'clock, they had moved into the barricaded zone up Avenida Colón, returning the fire of the rooftop snipers with machine guns. Despite stiff resistance, the troops steadily advanced, taking the streets one at a time. The snipers, armed mainly with low-caliber pistols, hunting rifles, and Molotov cocktails, were outgunned, and as the army slowly moved east up the parallel streets Avenida Colón and Santa Rosa, some protesters sought refuge in the neighborhood's boardinghouses and in private homes while the majority abandoned the neighborhood altogether and joined the thousands who were manning the barricades and building bonfires in Barrio Clínicas.

At another end of the city, Eduardo, the same architecture student who had been denied entry to the university in 1966 as a result of Onganía's new entrance exam, was working at his part-time job in the telephone company on the evening on May 29. He and other operators watched apprehensively while the army coordinated its suppression of the uprising by entering the telephone company and eavesdropping on calls, gathering intelligence from conversations of common citizens that provided valuable logistical information and helped the army pinpoint the precise location of the snipers.

Since there existed pockets of resistance elsewhere in the city, troops were also sent to neighborhoods other than Clínicas. In neighborhoods such as San Martín and Nueva Córdoba, students and neighbors built barricades of their own, and gunfire was exchanged between protesters and the army at various points throughout Córdoba. But these were minor affairs, sideshows to the more important events that were taking place in Barrio Clínicas.

Shortly before eleven o'clock, Luz y Fuerza commandos entered the Villa Revol power plant and blacked out the city, just as they had planned the night before. The blackout temporarily disoriented the army troops, allowing the protesters to regain the initiative. Fernando Solís, the IKA-Renault worker who had supported the idea of a *paro activo* and remained in the streets all day, was by evening back in his neighborhood in Barrio Parque Chacabuco, listening to the shortwave radio of a friend who had managed to pick up the transmissions of the Third Army Corps. Solís gained his first understanding of the magnitude of the protest then as he heard the frantic army radioman plead for reinforcements from Buenos Aires and characterize the situation in the city as critical, on the verge of being "uncontrollable." In the downtown police headquarters, Héctor Maisuls, a student who had been arrested several hours before, watched the police grow more angry and anxious, venting their frustration and humiliation at being unable to suppress the uprising by beating the captured protesters. In the Barrio Clínicas boardinghouse of *la tucumana,* the army troops entered looking for students, that status alone now implying culpability and inviting reprisal. Nevertheless, for the time being the momentum had returned to the resistance. For the next two hours the protesters were able to move about in relative freedom, setting more fires—including a failed attempt to burn down the Banco de la Nación—while the army remained paralyzed without communications.

Power was restored around one in the morning, and the army renewed with its assault, making dozens of arrests through the night and taking a heavy toll on snipers. Barrio Alberdi and especially Barrio Clínicas remained the centers of resistance through the night, though neighborhoods north and south of the contested downtown district became new areas of disturbance as the uprising apparently moved to the periphery of the city where the military presence was weak. At dawn, Córdoba was an occupied city. Though sporadic gunfire could be heard throughout the city and the snipers in Barrio Clínicas continued to offer resistance, the army had posted troops at strategic points throughout the city and moved in heavy tanks. As infantrymen mobilized for a final assault on Barrio Clínicas, the strategic center of the rebellion, protest marches previously planned for the national general strike that day drew the support of much of the populace and tied up downtown streets, forcing the military commanders to postpone their attack.

In the union halls of the SMATA and Luz y Fuerza, union leaders, the principal working class organizers of the Cordobazo—some amazed and others dismayed by what their protest had wrought—were planning the next step. Tosco and those light and power workers still in the city center were generally in favor of continuing the resistance. Torres simply hoped for an end to it, convinced it had already sealed his own fate—the loss of the union, perhaps even a long jail sentence—and had no chance of succeeding further. Neither Tosco nor Torres was forced to make the final decision to resist or surrender, however. Army troops entered both union halls late that morning and arrested all the union leaders present. Tosco and Torres were handcuffed and driven to the central police commissary in the Plaza San Martín. Later the next day, as he was being transported in an air force plane to the federal penitentiary in La Pampa, Torres would learn that his worst fears had been realized: a military tribunal had hastily condemned him to imprisonment for four years and eight months. Tosco had received a sentence of eight years and three months, and other Luz y Fuerza leaders, such as Felipe Alberti and Tomás Di Toffino, had also received stiff prison terms of several years.

After the arrests of Tosco and Torres, what remained of the working class participation in the Cordobazo diminished. Resistance was now confined to the Barrio Clínicas, but it was greatly weakened even there. Around six o'clock on the evening of May 30, the army made its final push into the neighborhood and within an hour had completely occupied it. New disturbances were reported in working class neighborhoods north of the city, particularly in the General Bustos and Yofre neighborhoods, and in Barrio Talleres the railroad workers set fire to the Belgrano railroad repair shops. But these were isolated and disorganized protests, the final tremors in the earthquake that had been centered in Barrio Clínicas. The labor leaders who remained free, Simó and Correa from the CGTA and Miguel Godoy from the rival *vandorista* CGT, agreed to an emergency session of the two CGTs to negotiate the release of Tosco, Torres, and other imprisoned labor leaders, but logistical problems prevented their meeting and the military rebuffed all the unions' inquiries on the status of the prisoners. By the evening of the thirtieth, the Cordobazo was over. The previous two days had left an official figure of twelve dead, but the actual figure was undoubtedly much higher—perhaps as many as sixty had been killed. Hundreds had also been wounded, at least ninety of them seriously, and over a thousand had been arrested. Much of the city was damaged, some of it destroyed.

The uprising had far exceeded the expectations of the organizers. Though Tosco alone of all the labor leaders had anticipated something more than a general strike and a peaceful demonstration at the CGT headquarters, not even he had foreseen the police reaction or the massive popular explosion it had triggered. From the time of the killing of the IKA-Renault worker, Máximo Mena, the Cordobazo had followed no plan. Facets of the uprising, certainly, had been decided beforehand. The decision to black out the city had been reached by the light and power workers independently of the other unions, as a contingency plan in the event of harsh repression by security forces. Following the retreat of the police, the dispersal into and barricading of the neighborhoods corresponded to the zones the various unions and student organizations had been assigned. Nevertheless the character of the Cordobazo was more one of improvisation than intent. The working class and student organizations that had planned the May 29 demonstration could not control the events that occurred when much of the city's population poured into the streets, some as intrigued or horrified spectators, but many as active participants in the protest. The Cordobazo had become a popular rebellion, a collective repudiation of the Onganía regime that resulted from the multiple frustrations of Córdoba's citizenry and was articulated in the exceptional behavior of otherwise ordinary individuals.

The egalitarian nature of the protest impressed nearly everyone who participated in it. Rodolfo, a parish priest in Villa Siburu and a member of the Sacerdotes del Tercer Mundo movement, had been in Paris as a seminarian during the May 1968 student uprisings there and had only recently returned to Córdoba. He was struck by the more popular character of the Cordobazo, a protest that seemed less confined to strictly student radicalism than what he had witnessed in Paris, with more frequent and genuine acts of solidarity between different groups and classes. His own working class parish, Villa Siburu, was made up of "poor workers" employed in construction and others who worked as handymen or as domestic servants, with very few employed either in the big automotive complexes or in EPEC. Nonetheless those workers had gone to the city center to participate in the protest. The incidents of middle-class support—of homemakers who brought food and drink to students and workers at the barricades and respectable, apparently apolitical families who hid protesters in Barrio Clínicas during the army searches on the evening of the twenty-ninth—were countless, and they were emblematic of a protest that had momentarily transcended class differences.

The working class had remained the principal protagonist in the uprising, but the unions' and particularly Tosco's attempts to establish some sort of discipline and organization throughout the twenty-ninth had been largely unsuccessful. The arrests of Tosco, Torres, and the other labor leaders on the morning of the thirtieth had spoiled any chance of mounting a more coordinated worker resistance and sealed the fate of the uprising. What had brought about the initial success of the Cordobazo—a spontaneous explosion of popular rage that quickly transcended its organizational framework and was so decentralized that standard police tactics could not suppress it—had become a liability once the army entered the scene. To stall the army's occupation of the city, the protesters would have needed organizational and tactical coordination and the ability and will to resist with weapons of their own, both of which were lacking. The tardy entry of the snipers, who were independent of the workers and never really in contact with them, had been a poor substitute for organized resistance by the working class.

The character of the working class participation in the Cordobazo becomes more clear when one throws aside broad sociological explanations and obfuscating theories of labor aristocracies or dependent industrialization and analyzes the bare facts. The greatest myth, which admittedly belongs more to the realm of political folklore than scholarly exegesis, is that the so-called privileged sectors of the local working class, the automobile workers especially, led a strike that had a deliberately subversive intent, that the unions in the modern industrial sectors planned a sort of revolutionary general strike that culminated in the Argentine equivalent of the Paris commune. The second myth, which indeed has the patina of scholarly respectability, is that the workers in the better paying, dynamic industries were simply responding to their loss of status and the economic hardships imposed by the Onganía dictatorship, that the Cordobazo was the societal result of the peculiar and fragile kind of industrial development that Latin America experienced in the postwar period. The problem with both interpretations is that they simplify the nature of the protest, failing to acknowledge the massive nature of the Cordoban working class's participation in the uprising while conveniently ignoring the fact that precisely half of the workers in the dynamic sectors played only a minimal role in the events of May 29 and 30. The Fiat workers, still under the tight control of their plant unions, had been largely absent from the protest. Though a small group of Fiat workers left the plants on the morning of the twenty-ninth, the overwhelming majority stayed on the job and returned to their homes following work. The testimony of Carlos Masera, a future president of the *clasista* Fiat union Sindicato de Trabajadores de Concord, who learned of the conflagration in the city center late on the twenty-ninth while at home and never joined the protest, is representative of the accounts of other Fiat workers. The role of the IAME workers in the military-administered complex was similarly minimal.

Most important, such interpretations ignore the role of the other working class participants and thus distort the nature of the protest. At some point in the Cordobazo, nearly all the other Cordoban unions were in the streets. Both CGTs had mobilized and prepared the workers beforehand for a major protest at the month's end, and the physical proximity of most of the workers to the city center, except for those in the more removed Fiat plants, facilitated the participation adherence of even the most sedentary unions. The groundswell of unrest that had existed throughout the local working class, stoked by the CGTA mobilizations and the labor hierarchy's tactical stratagems, had therefore been a factor of considerable importance in explaining the massive nature of the Cordobazo.

For the principal working class organizers, the intent and goals of the protest had certainly been modest and pragmatic. Immediate work-related problems, such as the revocation of the *sábado inglés,* the ongoing dispute over the *quitas zonales,* and other conflicts with the companies, were at the heart of the participation by the SMATA and UOM leaders. Their opposition to the Onganía government was also partly the result of nearly three years of an uninterrupted loss of bargaining power and influence; normally cautious labor leaders, such as Torres and Simó, hoped to reverse the situation through the militant tactics of protest, though they would have preferred, as in the past, the safer waters of negotiation and compromise.

But in the case of the IKA-Renault workers, the Cordobazo was also the consummation of the young automotive proletariat's integration into the union apparatus, a widespread and deeply felt expression of their identity as autoworkers, if not a class consciousness, born of a common workplace experience, that was manifested in their close personal identification with the SMATA. This new sense of identity was heightened by their perception of themselves as a disenfranchised group in Argentine society due to the proscription of Peronism, a perception Torres and the union leadership had been cultivating for more than a decade. For the IKA-Renault workers, especially, the union had become a repository of the values of solidarity and comradeship. Membership in the union rather than in a social class defined their shared status. The workers had reacted so furiously in the Cordobazo not simply because of a loss of pay or reduced possibilities of social mobility, but to protest the dictatorship's and IKA-Renault's disregard for their identity and the policies designed to limit the union's right to speak in their behalf. Torres's union-building campaign had succeeded perhaps more than he might have wished, since now he was expected to remain worthy of the union's stewardship; the SMATA was now an institution above the interests of the union leadership. Despite his wilting in the heat of the battle, Torres's participation in the organization of the May 29 strike, and especially his arrest and imprisonment, persuaded the SMATA workers he was indeed worthy of union leadership. But such legitimacy remained provisional, a duty entrusted and therefore subject to the workers' approval.

The Cordobazo clearly also had some of its genesis in a Peronist labor movement, in which considerations of self-interest and power politics and not class animosities or even political opposition were still, in the late 1960s, important motivations for union militancy. The importance of the Peronist labor hierarchy's contribution to the Cordobazo has been neglected—perhaps deliberately, perhaps due to the confusion that still surrounds the event—by the Marxist left, which later sought to appropriate the uprising and transform it into the point of departure for the socialist revolution in Argentina. Perhaps no better testimony to the importance of the Peronist labor movement's contribution to the Cordobazo was the subsequent assessment of one of its principal instigators, Governor Caballero, a man given to wild exaggerations of Marxist influence and the existence of sinister revolutionary cabals in the city. Though Caballero placed much of the blame for the uprising on the influence of radical priests and leftist political organizations on the local student population, he conceded that working class participation had been overwhelmingly Peronist-inspired.[14] Tosco and the Independent unions may have had more deliberately political intentions and envisioned the toppling of

Onganía, but they formed only a small part of the working class protest, a protest which drew its strength from unions under a decidedly unrevolutionary Peronist leadership.

However, in terms of the popular reaction that had followed Mena's death, and specifically the massive and enthusiastic working class involvement in the street resistance, other factors had been at work. In explaining the Cordobazo, it is important to avoid reducing the Cordoban workers' participation to their own class experience, to remember that the workers were also part of the larger society and therefore subject to the specific social influences at work in Argentina and in Córdoba at that particular moment. The Cordobazo in this respect was something very different from Latin America's other great urban protest of the twentieth century, the 1948 Bogotazo. The loss of human life and property, though considerable in the Cordobazo, was not comparable to that in the Colombian upheaval. The bacchanalian destruction and sanguinary terror of the Bogotazo had had firm roots in a rural society in which political violence was widespread and where the desperation of the growing ranks of the urban poor had reached dangerous levels. This was not the case with the Cordobazo. Violence was not yet an integral part of Argentine civil life, though the Cordobazo would be the starting point for the violence of the 1970s. Nor was there a growing urban lumpen proletariat in Córdoba; there was no powder keg of misery waiting to explode. The urban poor of the outlying *villas miserias,* a relatively small population in Córdoba in those years, did not participate significantly in the protest.

The work-related grievances in Córdoba were real and were a factor of considerable importance in explaining the workers' participation, but the Cordobazo can only be fully understood when one also takes into account the character of Argentina's politically active and politically literate culture. Argentina was a country in which participation in politics, in some form, was expected by all classes, and the authoritarian policies in the three years of Onganía's government had raised political frustration to an unsustainable level. Politics was a way of life especially in Córdoba, partly due to the role of the university in civic life and partly due to the city's small size and its history of opposition to Buenos Aires. Thus, though the working class did not respond to a revolutionary spirit, it did to a nonconformist and rebellious one, and that local working class *élan* was heightened by the specific grievances that workers had in their individual industries. In the events that had followed the police attack and the break up of the planned demonstration, the Cordobazo had become an eminently political protest. Beyond the tactical stratagems of labor leaders like Tosco, Torres, and Simó, without whose preparations the uprising admittedly never would have taken place, there had been a spontaneous explosion of opposition, a popular repudiation of the authoritarian regime, a political protest. This explains the Cordobazo's appeal to and active support from nearly all classes in the city.

Although the Cordobazo may have been something very different from what many have claimed, its significance has not been exaggerated. Its mythologization by the left and by Córdoba's working class served to galvanize much of the local labor movement, and it sparked the almost six years of labor militancy that followed. Ironically, the uprising did not enter the mainstream Peronist movement's pantheon as one of Peronism's sacred days, despite the crucial role played by the Peronist unions. The Cordobazo came to be associated almost exclusively with the other sectors in the local labor movement, to symbolize a new kind of working class protest, one that was presumed to herald a new role for that class in the country's political life. The truth behind the myth was not as important as the myth's existence and the fact that it encouraged tendencies within Cordoban labor that, though always powerful, had never been dominant.

Each of the underground left-wing parties and organizations saw the uprising through its own set of ideological precepts and built its revolutionary programs around its example. For the Partido Comunista Revolucionario and the Vanguardia Comunista, the Maoist left, it was proof of the latent power of the masses and of the efficacy of the revolutionary general strike and popular insurrection as the surest road to socialism. For the Marxist-Leninists, on the other hand, it confirmed the need to form a revolutionary party to give the working class the institutional and organizational discipline required to prevent its efforts from dissipating. For the neo-Trotskyists and Guevarists in the Partido Revolucionario de los Trabajadores and the Fuerzas Armadas de Liberación (FAL), it pointed to the need to devise a parallel military strategy, a revolutionary army, to confront the repressive powers of the state in future confrontations. For the Peronist left, it was a vindication of the revolutionary essence of Peronism and of the innate mettle of the Peronist working class, which only needed the return of its historic leader to wrestle it away from the corrupt and traitorous elements in the movement and restore its original revolutionary promise.

For many who had lived through the Cordobazo firsthand, the experience marked a political turning point. It helps explain the widespread sympathy that would exist in the city, particularly among university students but also among some workers, for one or another left-wing organization in the coming years. For some, the Cordobazo translated into an absolute conviction regarding the imminence and desirability of the socialist revolution in Argentina and a willingness to work actively toward it, often at great personal risk. For Alberto, for example, the architecture student from Villa María, it confirmed a growing involvement in politics and led to a later decision to join the PRT. Luis, a law student, had moved toward Peronism through his involvement in Catholic student organizations and had participated in the CGTA campaigns. He became convinced of the possibilities of revolution in Argentina but also of the need for a socialism that fit Argentina's national character and conditions; his later decision to join the Montoneros would be one repeated by many students in the law school who had similar Catholic backgrounds.

Despite the subsequent mythologizing of the Cordobazo, the immediate political impact of the uprising was less contradictory. The gravity of the events of May 29 and 30, the protesters' open defiance of both the provincial and national governments, unleashed a wave of repression by the regime that only deepened the opposition. Caballero's government fell shortly after the Cordobazo, but Onganía attempted to reestablish his authority by dealing harshly with the city. On May 31, police squadrons ransacked the CGTA headquarters and the SMATA and Luz y Fuerza union halls in spiteful retribution against the unions considered most responsible for the insurrection.[15] That same day, police and army units began to round up and arrest more labor and student activists in house-to-house searches throughout the city. The light and power workers' union was a particular target of government spite, and Luz y Fuerza became Onganía's official scapegoat for the protest. The large number of light and power workers arrested and the heavy jail sentences given to Tosco and other union leaders indicated the government's awareness of the union's strategic importance. Whatever value governments had seen in the past in the existence of a counterweight to Peronists in Cordoban labor ended with the violence of the Cordobazo. Thenceforth the elimination of Luz y Fuerza as a force in the labor movement became a priority for all Argentine governments, military and civilian.

The SMATA was another target. The union's prominence in the organization of the protest and the alliance it had worked out with Tosco and the CGTA unions was a sobering reminder of the power Cordoban labor could wield should it bury its sectarian rifts and undertake coordinated action. The stiffness of the sentence received by Torres was the first sign that the SMATA would be held as accountable for the uprising as the more militant Luz y Fuerza. However, the strategy adopted against the SMATA was not a wholesale purge of the union's leadership but an attempt to better control its activities. A ban on political activity on the shop floor, tighter factory discipline, and a large military presence in and around the Santa Isabel complex were intended to intimidate the automobile workers into passive acceptance of the regime's repressive measures. The policy had precisely the opposite effect, however. The SMATA workers took the measures as blatant provocations, and the union's fighting spirit was kept alive where it might have flagged had some of its outstanding grievances been resolved.

The government's retribution provoked continued militancy by the IKA-Renault workers, and Torres's lieutenants moved into the leadership void along with other *legalista* unions to lead the resistance to the post-Cordobazo reaction. On June 2, the smoke barely cleared from the destruction of two days before, the SMATA called a twenty-four-hour strike to protest the government's measures and demand the release of all the imprisoned labor leaders.[16] Over the next several weeks the union appeared to be inching closer to a break with Vandor and perhaps a permanent alliance with the city's more militant unions.

Almost immediately the Cordobazo had the effect of upsetting the established labor alliances in the city. The most important change was the rebirth of the *legalista* unions. The UTA, the ATE (state workers), and other Peronist unions that had lived under Vandor's shadow since early in the decade regained their independence and rediscovered a leader in the UTA's Atilio López. In the coming years López and the *legalistas* would move their alliance closer to the positions of the Peronist left and change their tactical priorities from alliance with the leaders of the Peronist labor movement in Buenos Aires to a more local strategy favoring Tosco's Independents and, to a lesser extent, the *clasista* unions. These moves would realize a long-held fear of the *vandoristas'* and tip the balance of power in favor of the non-Peronist unions in the country's second industrial city, and they help explain the special pains taken by the 1973 to 1976 Peronist government to discipline the local Peronist unions and break the Cordoban labor movement.

One of the reasons that the SMATA, the UTA, and other *legalista* unions decided to stick with the unlikely alliance that had developed in the city was the crisis in the *vandorista* ranks following the Cordobazo. Vandor's timorousness and the indecision displayed generally by the labor hierarchy during the escalation of events leading up to the Cordobazo had not been redeemed by the CGT's twelfth-hour call for a May 30 general strike. Beaten to the punch by the Cordoban unions, Vandor was once again on the defensive. The uprising had shown that, at least in Córdoba, the initiative lay in other currents in the labor movement, and that Vandor and the *porteño* labor bosses had no monopoly on the ability to mobilize large sectors of the working class. A similar uprising, though on a far smaller scale, in Rosario a week before the Cordobazo had indicated that the interior was still untamed and the CGTA alliance remained alive. Ongaro's own prestige had been restored by his impulsive but dramatic and well-publicized trip to Córdoba and his arrest there on the twenty-seventh; it was seen as a decisive gesture of solidarity, in contrast to Vandor's hectoring and stalling tactics. Unions such as the telephone, shoe, and state workers that had deserted Ongaro returned to the CGTA fold in the weeks following the Cordobazo, and the alternative labor movement gained one final burst of support.

In early June, with Ongaro released from jail, the CGTA undertook a new resistance campaign. Ongaro once again received his strongest support from Córdoba, where the labor protests continued unabated. On June 17 and 18, general strikes were held in Córdoba to demand the release of all political prisoners. Shortly thereafter Onganía appointed a military governor for the province, which was slowly drifting into a state of prolonged civil disobedience if not open insurrection. Tensions rose throughout the month as preparations were made for a July 1 general strike, a strike supported by Ongaro but opposed by Vandor. Then, on June 30, Vandor was gunned down in the UOM headquarters in Avellaneda. His murder was repudiated by the CGTA and has never fully been explained, but it certainly had as its background the acrimonious Peronist splits and rivalries that had resurfaced in the weeks following the Cordobazo.[17] Vandor's assassination provided the government with just the pretext it needed to eliminate the rejuvenated CGTA. The day of the assassination, the government declared a state of siege (which would not be lifted until May 1973), assumed control of several of the leading CGTA-affiliated unions, and imprisoned much of the CGTA leadership.[18]

The July 1 general strike proceeded as planned, but for the rest of the year the government's unyielding repression kept the labor movement on the defensive and reduced its chances for immediately capitalizing on the Cordobazo and constructing an effective working class opposition to the dictatorship. Only in Córdoba was the labor resistance unbroken. Though the CGTA was a useful ally, the Cordoban labor movement now had a power of its own and was capable of acting independently. The June

strikes called by the SMATA workers, for example, saw a massive out-
pouring of support from all the city's unions and suggested that the
Cordobazo had established a unified labor movement, one that was prepared to confront the government alone if necessary. From prison, Torres
supported militant tactics to increase pressure on the government.[19] Yet
even in Córdoba, the short-term prospects of union militancy were hindered, as the imprisonment of Tosco and other Luz y Fuerza leaders
crippled efforts to combat the government. Further resistance would have
to be led by the SMATA, a union accustomed to the role of leadership in
resisting the government, but now in the hands of Torres's inexperienced
union lieutenants.

Problems with the SMATA leaders' inexperience were compounded by
the union's recent history: its alliance with the traditional power brokers
in the labor movement against the young turks and firebrands in the
CGTA and thus its vulnerability to pressures coming from the CGT central. The union's natural proclivity for allying with the established powers
in organized labor was undercut, however, by the crisis and disorder that
followed Vandor's assassination. For several months the Peronist labor
movement was in a state of disarray and unable to help the Cordoban
SMATA resist the government's repressive tactics. Local conditions and
a cold assessment of the limited possibilities of resisting Onganía's campaign without support from other Cordoban unions, more than any interest in continuing a struggle against the government, encouraged the new
SMATA leadership to uphold the labor alliance born in the Cordobazo.
By October, as the government sought to "normalize" the national CGT
with the support of the *vandoristas* and *participacionistas,* the SMATA and
other unions in Córdoba were calling for a congress of regional CGTs to
explore the possibility of forming another rival CGT national, this one with
a provincial base and in opposition to Buenos Aires.[20]

The labor movement's ability to sustain its resistance depended greatly
on Tosco's release from prison. Without the Luz y Fuerza leader, the
chances for developing the union's cooperation into a disciplined labor
alliance were slim. Only Tosco held the loyalty of the Independent unions,
and only he could command the respect of much of the local Peronist
working class. Tosco's leading role in the Cordobazo had won him a
prestige that overshadowed that of all other labor leaders, including Torres. He was needed as an arbiter, as the catalyst who would prevent a
squandering of rank-and-file militancy and hold the local labor movement
together. Through his long months of imprisonment in Rawson Prison
Tosco attempted to preserve the unity of Cordoban labor with a common

program of opposition to the dictatorship. In letters smuggled out of prison and published in *Electrum* and local newspapers, he tried to encourage cooperation as best he could in absentia, hoping to regain his freedom before Cordoban labor cracked under the weight of its own diversity.

What Tosco could not see from behind his prison walls, deep in the Argentine Patagonia, was that new rifts were emerging in the labor movement that could not be overcome with words of encouragement, pleas to common sense, or even a unifying program of opposition to Onganía. At the heart of the conflicts that would soon appear were not, as in the past, personal and political rivalries or strategic calculations on the part of the union leadership, but genuine ideological differences. Following the Cordobazo, ideology became a major force in local labor politics. The local labor movement was soon speaking a new language, and many workers became concerned with notions of revolution, class struggle, and socialism, displaying a new political sophistication that had been absent just a few months before. Obviously this tendency was not miraculously born in the May uprising; it expressed influences that had long been at work in the city. In the labor movement, the continued presence of left-wing activists in Santa Isabel, unable since the late 1950s to seriously contest Peronist control of the union but still a major force, and the existence of a large bloc of non-Peronist unions in Tosco's Independents were factors that prepared Córdoba for *clasismo* and the labor struggles of the following decade. Intellectually, the revisionist interpretations of Peronism as a revolutionary movement by a generation of political activists and intellectuals, encouraged above all by Perón's own messages to his youthful followers, made possible a closer relationship between the Peronist working class and labor activists on the left. Politically, the influence of the Cuban Revolution and the impending victory of Salvador Allende's Unidad Popular coalition in neighboring Chile established a deep sympathy for socialism and belief in its inevitable triumph, not only among Marxist ideologues but also among a large sector of the Cordoban working class.

If the Cordobazo was not the progenitor of these changes, it was nonetheless a powerful stimulant for the latent tendencies that found expression in the 1970s. It was significant as a legitimizing myth, transformed by the left from a popular protest into an epic revolutionary event, but the Cordobazo was also important for the real changes it occasioned. It set in motion a process of dissent and opposition within the military against the regime—causing a fatal weakening of the dictatorship that would culminate with Onganía's removal in June of the following year.

Also, in terms of the local labor movement, it opened possibilities that had not existed before. One of the most significant changes took place in Ferreyra, where years of union collusion with the Fiat company and an ignominious passivity during the Cordobazo had left the workers particularly susceptible to the influences that the May uprising had unleashed. This susceptibility coincided, moreover, with renewed efforts by the Italian company to reduce its labor costs and increase its competitivity, encouraged by the progress it had made in recent years in the automotive market.[21] In early September 1969 Fiat fired more than 100 workers in its SMATA-affiliated GMD plant. The union took resolute action in defense of the fired workers, and the company's subsequent agreement to rescind the firings drove home the vulnerability of the workers in the other Fiat plants and the ineffectiveness of what they were increasingly referring to, disparagingly, as their *sindicatos amarillos,* the plant unions SITRAC and SITRAM.[22]

The Cordobazo contributed to a greater politicization of the entire Cordoban working class and gave it a sense (in retrospect, an exaggerated one) of its power. For those labor activists who identified with one or another of the programs of the left, it proved what many of them had long contended but had probably come to doubt: that the Argentine working class still had the potential to act as a political protagonist independent of Peronism's corporatist scheme.[23] For many others it was a starting point for a systematic critique of Argentine capitalism and the elaboration of a political program for the unions even more radical than that offered by Tosco and the Independents, who were ever reluctant to identify with any political tendency that might further divide the labor movement. Above all, however, the Cordobazo changed the dynamic of local labor politics. For the next six years it would exercise a profound influence on the imagination of Córdoba's working class and encourage many workers, some of whom had been absent from the uprising altogether, to build on its example as the first step toward achieving a revolutionary role for the working class.

· SIX ·

The *Clasistas*

The Cordobazo and the labor resistance that immediately followed the May 1969 uprising unleashed political changes at nearly every level of Argentine society. The most immediate effect was a deterioration in the government's ability to control political dissent, thereby allowing greater freedom for all forms of opposition. The Cordobazo especially revitalized the Argentine left and contributed to the radicalization of the country's political life that would find full and tragic expression in the following decade. The underground world of revolutionary politics, persecuted and clandestine from the early days of the *onganiato,* moved out of the shadows to occupy a central place in national life.

Argentina's heterogeneous left had never been fully tamed by the regime. The proscription of party politics had certainly adversely affected its most venerable and cautious member, the Partido Comunista (PC), but the repressive nature of Onganía's government had actually encouraged other tendencies. The Guevarist Fuerzas Armadas de Liberación (FAL), the Maoist Partido Comunista Revolucionario (PCR) and Vanguardia Comunista, the once Trotskyist but by 1969 Marxist-Leninist Partido Revolucionario de los Trabajadores (PRT), and numerous smaller parties and factions that made up the Marxist left became more active under Onganía. In clandestine meetings and secret party congresses, their members had worked out their respective revolutionary programs—programs that had been often little more than the whimsical yearnings of intellectuals in the years before the Cordobazo, but that became the guidelines for political action of determined revolutionaries in the years after it. The Peronist left, which had its roots in the Peronist Resistance and which had been represented before 1969 in guerrilla organizations

170

such as the Fuerzas Armadas Peronistas (FAP), grew even more powerful, as the Montoneros–Juventud Peronista (JP) axis was able to fuse the
increasing sympathy in certain sectors of Argentine society for revolutionary solutions with the Peronist masses' demand for the return of Perón
from exile and the relegalization of their movement.[1]

The Cordobazo marked an important shift in the tactics of nearly all
the country's left-wing organizations. The emphasis on strictly armed
strategies was abandoned or complemented by strategies that stressed
the need for the left to move into the labor unions and cultivate a revolutionary role for the working class. In this, the Cordobazo did not represent
a genesis so much as it did a deepening of changes that had already been
perceptible in the Argentine left. Most, though not all, of the country's
left-wing organizations had been reevaluating their tactics in the late
1960s, and at the time of the Cordobazo they had been hammering out
programs they hoped would allow them to become mass movements.
Nevertheless those on the left had still had doubts about their ability to
win over a working class that appeared, to their eyes, captivated by the
shibboleths and demagoguery, as well as the formidable intimidation
tactics of the Peronist labor movement. Those doubts, particularly in
Córdoba, were dispelled with the May uprising. At the PCR's first national
congress, held in December 1969, party members drafted a program that
presented the Cordobazo as the turning point in the class struggle in
Argentina. The strategy of any authentic revolutionary party was now to
build support in the working class, particularly in the industrial proletariat, through the formation of revolutionary cells in the factories and the
creation of a *"corriente sindical clasista."*[2]

From this point on, the term *clasista* would be used by groups on the
left to indicate a program of revolutionary change in alliance with the
working class. Not all of the left would embrace *clasismo,* however. The
Communist party's electoral strategy, and an innate conservatism born of
its long history in Argentina, made it initially hostile to the *clasista* movements. The PC preferred to align locally with Tosco's Independents, and
nationally it sponsored the Movimiento de Unidad y Coordinación Sindical (MUCS) in its attempt to win a working class following. But for other
left-wing parties, notably the PCR, the Vanguardia Comunista, and the
PRT, *clasismo* thenceforth defined their relationship with the workers'
movement and their vision of the working class's role in a revolutionary
socialist project.

Given the preponderance of the local automotive proletariat and its
unquestionable strategic and symbolic importance in the city, it was nat-

ural that the left in Córdoba placed a priority on the Fiat and IKA-Renault factories. It was to Ferreyra and Santa Isabel that their militants were sent, some merely as propagandists who distributed party literature at the factory gates and others as activists who entered the factories as workers and *clasista* militants. But in the city's automotive complexes it was not sympathy for *clasismo* or revolutionary change that occasioned the first great shop floor rebellion of the 1970s. Instead the disruption of authority locally and nationally and the social effervescence following the Cordobazo were what encouraged the workers in the Fiat plants to mount a union recovery movement, which initially was independent of the left's political tutelage; it was a genuine rank-and-file movement that sought above all to establish effective union representation for workers who had never known it. After years of formal and ineffective representation by their company-controlled plant unions, SITRAC and SITRAM, the Fiat workers rebelled. They initiated an experiment in workplace democracy that was improvised from the start and heavily dependent on the changing conditions in the plants. The movement would find political expression only belatedly and never in a uniform fashion among either the union leaders that emerged or the workers who sustained the movement.

Of all the members of city's working class, the Fiat workers seemed the least likely to mount a shop floor rebellion of such consequence. The weakness of the Fiat unions was notorious in the local labor movement. SITRAC and SITRAM were considered to be so hopelessly in league with Fiat that they had not even been approached by the labor leaders, such as Agustín Tosco, who had organized the May 29 strike that ended in the Cordobazo. The Fiat unions were known both to the workers they claimed to represent and to the rest of Córdoba's working class more as "yellow unions"—unions in which activists were singled out and word was passed to management about undesirables on the shop floor—than as effective advocates and protectors of workers' interests. The captive nature of the Fiat unions was demonstrated not only in their absence in the Cordobazo, but also more tellingly in the small treacheries and repeated failures of the SITRAC-SITRAM leadership to address the problems of the labor force. By 1970, a small clique of leaders with close ties to management was firmly ensconced in the union apparatus of both SITRAC and SITRAM. Union elections had become meaningless rituals in which single union lists were presented and few workers voted.

Thus collective frustration with ineffective unions and the problems of work was the genesis of the 1970 Fiat shop floor rebellion. In December of the previous year, the SITRAC union leadership had reached a preliminary collective bargaining agreement with the company. As contracts had in the past, the new contract failed to achieve an increase in wages or to propose any significant reforms to answer the numerous worker grievances related to production practices and working conditions in the Concord plant. As details of the contract became known—the sole gain being the company's agreement to provide a monthly bar of soap and roll of toilet paper in the factory bathrooms for each worker—grumbling spread in the plant about the union's failure to make even a perfunctory attempt to camouflage the fact that it was at the company's bidding.[3] Though most workers were resigned to yet another humiliating agreement, a small number began to talk about attempting to gain control of the union. In the January 1970 union elections, one such worker, Santos Torres, nominated himself as a shop steward and was elected by his production line. Within days of his election the company transferred him to another part of the factory in an attempt to prevent his assumption of shop steward duties. When Torres subsequently attended the first meeting of the recently elected *cuerpo de delegados,* the executive committee ordered his expulsion.[4]

At a March 23 assembly to rubber stamp the December contract, Torres and fellow worker Rafael Clavero publicly assailed the SITRAC leadership and unleashed the pent-up frustrations of the Fiat workers. SITRAC secretary general Jorge Lozano watched, bewildered, as workers from each of the three shifts present at the assembly demanded his resignation and called for new elections. Lozano, one of the many former Unión Obrera Metalúrgica men who had found a place in the Fiat company unions, was especially hated as he was the most visible representative of the years of union betrayals and company intimidation on the shop floor. Lozano and the union executive committee left the hall under a barrage of insults and threats. The rest of the meeting became the first of the great open assemblies that would take place in the Fiat complex over the next eighteen months. After Lozano's departure, order was re-established and motions were made by individual workers to reject the recent union elections and the collective bargaining agreement. The assembly lasted through the night, and a steering committee *(comisión provisoria)* was selected to represent the workers until new elections could be held. The committee included Torres, Clavero, and other workers, such as Carlos Masera, a machinist and former IKA-Renault worker, who would play leading roles in the Fiat rebellion.[5]

Between March 24 and May 13, the workers elected in the open assembly visited and petitioned the Ministry of Labor on repeated occasions, patiently following all the byzantine notarizing and legal procedures that government functionaries, under pressure from Fiat, could devise to prevent the formation of an opposition slate and new union elections in the Concord plant. For weeks there was no response. The ministry's silence gave Lozano time to counterattack. Aware that he would be vulnerable if he attempted to confront the rebellion directly in Ferreyra, Lozano attempted to use other means. In early May he asked the local Confederación General del Trabajo to admit SITRAC as a voting member, a move he obviously hoped would bestow a mantle of legitimacy on his tarnished leadership.[6] Lozano's request several days later to use the CGT headquarters for a SITRAC press conference was similarly intended to establish an air of authority, directed more toward the Ministry of Labor and other unions in the city than the Fiat workers, in the hope that their support would prop up his greatly weakened position in the Concord plant.[7] Masera, Clavero, Torres, and others meanwhile oversaw a campaign to keep spirits high on the shop floor. The new steering committee's first fliers reached the workers in these weeks. All addressed the issues of effective union representation, not politics or ideology, and promised an honest and democratic union through free elections.[8]

As the weeks passed and Lozano's machinations showed signs of having some effect, the Ministry of Labor remained alternately aloof and hostile, and the local unions were cautious. The Fiat rebels resolved to take direct action before they lost the momentum altogether. On May 14 members of the opposition met with Undersecretary of Labor Antonio Capdevila to learn the status of their petition. They were accompanied for the first time by their recently acquired legal counsel, Alfredo Curutchet. Curutchet was then one of the city's youngest and most promising labor lawyers, a brilliant advocate of workers' interests whose political sympathies for dissident trade unionists had already been shown by his previous work for the CGTA and for Tosco in Luz y Fuerza. The diminutive Curutchet, affectionately known as "Cuqui" to the workers, would play a crucial role in sustaining the Fiat rebellion over the coming months. The *compañero-abogado* would soon win the respect and trust of the workers through his tireless efforts to fend off the manifold harassments of the state and the company that the law made possible. At this first meeting, both Curutchet and the Fiat workers listened as Capdevila threatened reprisals if they persisted with their petition. The following day, at Curutchet's suggestion, the Fiat dissidents called an open assembly and urged that the workers occupy the Concord plant. The resulting *toma*, or takeover, lasted three days. Company officials were taken hostage and the workers abandoned the plant only after Curutchet had met with government emissaries and Lozano and had acquired the written resignation of the SITRAC executive committee. Fiat and the Labor Ministry agreed to hold new elections in thirty days.[9]

The Fiat rebellion had begun as a spontaneous repudiation of what the workers considered to be a traitorous union leadership, leaders who were in league with a company that was determined to deny the workers even the most minimal union protection. The Fiat workers had a long history of bitter defeats in their attempts to acquire effective union representation. The initial success of the 1970 Concord rebellion thus undoubtedly had much to do with the specific conditions in the city following the Cordobazo. The government was jittery over any sign of unrest in the local working class and was willing, once the alternatives became clear, to force concessions from Fiat in the hope of defusing further labor militancy. The victory also was due to the fortuitous presence of a group of exceptionally able workers who emerged to lead the reborn SITRAC. Some, such as Masera, Torres, and Clavero, had first come to the forefront in the March 23 assembly. Others, such as Domingo Bizzi, José Paéz, and Gregorio Flores, had only gained prominence in the weeks leading up to the taking of the Concord plant. None of these workers, save Bizzi, had participated notably in union affairs before, and none had any political affiliations, much less an elaborated political ideology. Their displeasure with Lozano and the SITRAC leadership, like that of the rest of the labor force, stemmed from personal frustrations with conditions in the plant and the unwillingness of the union to address them. Masera was especially aware of the ineffectiveness of the plant union in Concord, having spent several years in the IKA factories. Masera had entered the Concord plant in 1963 and quickly found working conditions there far below what he had known in at Kaiser, where Elpidio Torres's union machinery was an effective interlocutor with the company and where wages were significantly higher than those paid by the Italian company. But for the vast majority of workers the *toma* was simply the culmination of years of bitter work in the Fiat plants. Fiat's paternalistic style, expressed in everything from its stated preference for hiring workers of Italian descent to its public relations campaigns extolling *"la famiglia Fiat,"* was considered a poor substitute for a vigilant union and fair wages, and when the chance to act appeared, the workers seized it, not knowing what the outcome might be.[10]

Masera's personal history offers some clues to the nature of the workers who rose to prominence in the union recovery movement and to leadership positions in the *clasista* SITRAC and SITRAM in the months that followed. Like Masera, most had begun their work lives as Peronists. Their knowledge of Marxism was at best rudimentary, and few if any had attempted to critique their own status as workers in an automotive multinational in abstract, ideological terms. Also like Masera, many were first-generation industrial workers who had migrated to the city from the countryside. A number could read or write only with great difficulty. Though some were skilled workers who had been educated in one of the city's technical schools, many of the 21 members of the union executive committee and a majority of the 125-member *cuerpo de delegados,* were unskilled workers drawn largely from one or another of the factory's production lines.[11] In short, the Fiat *clasistas* began as simple workers who rebelled against the accumulated frustrations of work in a company that seemed intent on denying them what they felt was fair and honorable treatment. Though many of them would subsequently seek political explanations to make sense of the intense struggles they were involved in, none had been attracted to the rebellion that unexpectedly developed out of the March assembly for what could reasonably be called political reasons.

The success of the May 1970 factory occupation and the resignation of the SITRAC leadership encouraged a similar rebellion in the Fiat Materfer factory. The labor force at the Fiat railroad equipment plant had also been only nominally represented by its plant union, SITRAM. In the weeks following the fall of Lozano, a shop floor rebellion with a similar goal—honest and effective union representation—gained momentum. As had Lozano, the entrenched SITRAM leadership sought to shore up its beleaguered position by drawing other unions into the controversy. In late May SITRAM secretary general Hugo Cassanova hastily abandoned the Fiat union's traditional isolation from local labor politics and informed the CGT in Córdoba that it was adhering to the labor confederation's Plan de Acción and would support a May 29 general strike to commemorate the anniversary of the Cordobazo, which SITRAM it had missed the year before, due its notorious reputation in the local labor movement. Cassanova's suddenly discovered militancy was accompanied by a more revealing offer of 500,000 pesos to the CGT in support of the strike plan, an embarrassingly indecorous gesture that showed how isolated the SITRAM leadership was from a local labor movement in which financial support for striking unions was never publicly stated for fear that it would taint worker solidarity. SITRAM's real motivations for supporting the strike were also exposed by its warnings to the Cordoban CGT about extremists currently active in the labor movement, groups of Marxist activists attempting to use the workers for their own political ends, an obvious reference to recent events in the Concord plant.[12] Despite Cassanova's maneuvers the local unions remained chary of SITRAM, and the Materfer workers' factory occupation of June 3, a virtual reenactment of the *toma* at the Concord plant, precipitated Cassanova's resignation and that of the entire SITRAM leadership.

The two Fiat factory occupations coincided with yet another plant seizure in the city conducted by the Perdriel workers in Santa Isabel. The character of this plant rebellion, which seemed similar to those taking place in Ferreyra, was actually quite different and revealed early differences in the nature of the *clasista* movements that would soon emerge in both automotive complexes. Perdriel, a tool and die factory, had long been a center of opposition to Elpidio Torres. The labor *caudillo* had returned to the city in December 1969 after Onganía had commuted his prison sentence in the hope of calming the waters in Córdoba, where the local labor movement was now unquestionably the center of opposition to the regime. On his return Torres had found that his once-formidable SMATA union machinery had been greatly weakened and that left-wing candidates, organized in an anti-*torrista* union recovery movement, were now serious contenders in the upcoming union elections and had a particularly strong presence in the Perdriel plant. A core of militant workers in the factory had ties to the left and had originally belonged to the *grupo 1º de mayo,* the most powerful of Torres's left-wing opposition groups in the late 1960s. In the months following the Cordobazo, the PCR had singled out Perdriel as a weak link in the SMATA union machinery and made it a priority for its move into the local automotive proletariat, eventually managing to get some of its own members into the plant.[13]

The PCR activists were the principal promoters of the May 12 factory occupation, which included the taking of thirty hostages, many of them French supervisors employed by the powerful multinational. The occupation took place after the company had transferred four of the left-wing candidates in upcoming union shop steward elections to other plants, a move intended to strengthen the more conciliatory Peronist leadership among workers in the plant.[14] Like the the Fiat *tomas,* the Perdriel factory occupation represented an extreme union action, one that would become a characteristic tactic of *clasista* trade unionism and that indicated a deterioration of the relations between labor and management in the city's automobile plants. The lines of confrontation grew sharper and the possibilities for compromise more remote.

As a result of the occupation of Perdriel, IKA-Renault agreed to return the left-wing workers to the plant and allowed the two elected workers to retain their union posts. But Torres, for his part, had handled the affair clumsily by failing to protest the company's transfer of the Perdriel workers; indeed he was suspected of complicity in supporting the company's scheme. Torres had weakened his position in a union in which the workers, largely as a result of the continuous state of agitation in the local working class following the Cordobazo, were unusually sensitive to any action on the part of either the state or the company that could be interpreted as a provocation.

The Perdriel workers were not mollified by the company's concessions. Under pressure from the rank and file, Torres called a strike for all the IKA-Renault factories in early June to protest stalled contract talks, a strike he hoped would reestablish his credibility as a hard-line labor leader, but which he presented as a response to company intransigence on wages and work issues. Hostages were taken in most of the plants on June 3, and the local CGT declared a general strike in support of the striking SMATA workers. When the Concord and Materfer workers joined the strike in solidarity, the Concord workers undertaking their second factory occupation, the city seemed on the verge of a menacing working class insurrection. On June 4 the Cordoban police forcibly entered the Perdriel plant and arrested some 250 workers there, thereby prompting the autoworkers to abandon the other IKA-Renault plants. Torres was compelled to continue yet another strike campaign whose consequences he had not foreseen.[15]

For the rest of June the SMATA workers remained on strike and production in the IKA-Renault plants was suspended. Indeed production in the entire Cordoban automobile industry was seriously damaged, and provincial and national authorities put pressure on Torres to negotiate a settlement. As Córdoba lurched toward a state of anarchy, the real powers within the national government, General Alejandro Lanusse and the army, removed Onganía, who had been fatally weakened since the time of the Cordobazo and was definitively finished by the uprising's aftermath in Córdoba a year later. The immediate task of the new president, General Roberto Levingston, a relatively unknown military figure hastily flown to Buenos Aires from his position as military attaché in the Argentine embassy in Washington, was to achieve what had proved elusive to Onganía, namely the taming of Córdoba.

Torres was now eager to negotiate an end to a strike over which he had lost control and which rank-and-file militants, mostly from the left, were now sustaining. IKA-Renault accepted government mediation and demands for a grace period that allowed the workers to return to the plants while company and union officials negotiated a compromise.[16] Torres publicly remained belligerent but privately was mending his fences with the company. By early July most of the workers were back in the plants. The 1,500 or so firings that IKA-Renault had carried out during the strike, which had contributed to its bitter and prolonged nature, were negotiated to the mutual advantage of the *torristas* and IKA-Renault. Talks between Torres and company officials reduced the number of fired workers to some 600, a figure that included most of the left-wing activists in the Perdriel plant and elsewhere in the complex, thus eliminating a bumptious opposition and source of innumerable problems for the company and union alike. For the PCR and other left-wing parties, this was a serious blow, and it meant rebuilding their organizations on the shop floor. Despite its negative outcome, the strike was nevertheless fully within the calculations of the most active of the Marxist parties in Santa Isabel, the PCR, for it saw strikes as political weapons to be used to weaken the Torres union machinery and win over the workers to *clasista* positions, despite occasional setbacks such as this.[17]

Such party strategies were not present in the very different shop floor rebellion still germinating in the Fiat plants. In Ferreyra, as the SMATA strike was ending, the group of Concord workers who had emerged as the leaders of the movement to oust Lozano and establish effective union representation ran unopposed in the July 7 union elections. The generational rebellion that was so much a part of the *clasista* movements of the early 1970s was revealed unequivocally in the electoral results. The elected executive committee members and shop stewards were young men, mostly in their twenties and early thirties.[18] At thirty-seven, Masera, the SITRAC union's new secretary general, was known as *"el viejo."*

In the following months, these young workers rushed to change factory life and make the new SITRAC the instrument of a vigorous workplace democracy. Work problems were discussed openly in the departments and decisions were made through deliberation, sometimes in formal union meetings but more often in comradely consultations between the workers and shop stewards. Surly and formerly disrespectful foremen learned to treat the workers under their supervision gingerly, lest they risk a union response. Participation in union affairs, moribund just months before, slowly became more widespread. Open general assemblies held on the factory floor emerged as almost an institution of the new SITRAC. Organization of the open assemblies was greatly facilitated by SITRAC's character as a factory union, and such assemblies were held routinely to decide virtually all shop floor matters: problems with speedups, collective bargaining negotiations, even complaints over the poor quality of food being served in the factory cafeteria. The democratic spirit of the union was also encouraged by the fact that all the union leaders kept their jobs in the plant; there were no paid union positions, so SITRAC officials were therefore in constant contact with the rank and file. The tarnished reputation of union representation in the Fiat complex was quickly overcome. In a survey of the Concord forge for example, worker response showed that support for the new leadership was deep—nearly unanimous in the early months of the new SITRAC—although it was due mainly to the leaders' reputation as "honest comrades" and was not because of any revolutionary sympathies either on the part of the leadership or the rank and file.[19]

The new SITRAC won workers' loyalty because it proved to be a solicitous and effective advocate of their interests, despite the many obstacles against it. Specific problems in the Concord plant shaped the character of the union challenge there. Job stability was not a problem in these years for the Fiat workers, nor for that matter was it a problem generally for the Cordoban automotive proletariat, and labor problems revolved around the twin preoccupations of wages and working conditions. Had there existed highly unstable employment conditions with a floating mass of automobile workers moving in and out of the city's factories, the nature of the shop floor rebellion in Ferreyra might well have been quite different. Instead the workers' greatest frustrations grew from their daily relations with the company and from conditions in the plants. The situation was the same for the Materfer workers, who elected their new leadership the same month that the Concord workers did and whose union followed the lead of SITRAC on many issues. Wages were one area, however, in which the two unions' experiences were somewhat different.

Since the mid-1960s, the Concord workers had not had a collective bargaining agreement of their own and, instead, had been forced to accept Fiat's modified adoption of the UOM contracts. Fiat used the UOM agreements, which were generally less favorable than the SMATA agreements, despite the apparent inapplicability of job classifications in the metallurgical industry to automobile production. SITRAM, on the other hand, did have its own agreement, but its terms were even worse than those the Concord workers obtained under the bootlegged UOM contracts. The Materfer workers waited while the Concord workers made the first attempt to redress the situation. The SITRAC leadership formed a special committee of workers' representatives and union officials to draft an agreement of its own to present to the company, one that would meaningfully reform conditions in the Concord plant. Over the next year union members consulted previous SMATA agreements and laboriously assembled the contract it would propose to the company in January 1972.[20]

More than a conflict over wages, the union's insistence on drafting its own contract was a direct challenge to Fiat's absolute control over the factory and all questions related to production. The new SITRAC elicited company hostility for this very reason. Beyond the proposed collective bargaining negotiations, the union immediately began to preoccupy itself with long-standing shop floor grievances that had been ignored during the years of the UOM- and then company-controlled plant unions. One issue was the company forge, which was notorious for its hazardous working conditions but was where Fiat stonewalled any talk of improvement. In the early months of their administration of the union, the SITRAC leaders were in close contact with the Italian Fiat unions, and through them they learned that the technology used in the Ferreyra forge had been banned under Italian labor law for its deleterious effects on worker health; it had been found to cause everything from premature deafness to sexual disorders, resulting from the hammers' and hydraulic presses' incessant pounding.[21] The SITRAC leadership chose the forge problem as one of the principal issues on which to take a stand for effective union intervention on outstanding work-related grievances. Soon it was questioning the panoply of company production practices and wage policies.[22] Demands for overdue job reclassifications, respect for job categories, and a fixed salary independent of productivity struck at the heart of Fiat's control over the factory, and the lines were drawn for future confrontation between the union and the company.

As the union fashioned its challenge to Fiat around problems that all the workers shared, a more surprising development accompanied events in Ferreyra: the shop floor rebellion was evolving into a dissident political movement, *clasismo*. The term *clasismo* and the unions SITRAC and SITRAM have become all but synonymous in recent Argentine labor history. But in reality *clasismo* was not born in Ferreyra plants; as has been discussed, it had been present in left-wing party theorizing and, in embryonic form, on the shop floor in the IKA-Renault plants since the late 1960s. Indeed the term *clasista* had been a part of the Marxist lexicon since the 1920s, when the communists established the Comité Sindical de Unidad Clasista as a militant trade union alternative in the country's labor movement. The term had been resuscitated by the new left in the 1960s, and by 1970 it was being used by nearly all the Marxist parties and increasingly by certain sectors of the Peronist left. The fact that *clasismo* was already a part of working class discourse at the time helps explain how the rank-and-file rebellions of the early 1970s could identify themselves in such terms.

Nevertheless, *clasismo* was first expressed outside of the hermetic world of underground party debates and factory cells, and with national resonance in the labor movement, in the SITRAC-SITRAM union rebellion, and that curious development must be accounted for. The political education of Masera, Bizzi, and the other workers who had come to the forefront of the Fiat rebellion was a slow process that never was fully consummated. Some members of the executive committee and of the *cuerpo de delegados* embraced the *clasista* ideology intuitively, while others arrived at it through reading and political discussion. As the Fiat rebellion gained the attention of activists and intellectuals throughout the country, and especially in Córdoba itself, the left established contacts with many workers, particularly those exercising leadership positions. Party and student activists assumed a tutelary relationship with some of the workers, and the SITRAC-SITRAM union hall in the city center became a kind of political salon for the Cordoban left, a meeting place where they could analyze the daily reality workers were confronting in the plants and give it a political explanation and, eventually, an ideological expression.

The steps taken toward *clasismo* were halting. The union slogan adopted later that year, *¡Ni golpe, ni elección, revolución!,* was the creation of an anonymous intellectual or party activist and caught on in the Fiat unions' public discourse and its pamphlets at a time when genuine electoral possibilities appeared remote. The slogan expressed more disconnection with the general state of affairs in the country than it did widespread sympathy for revolution, or even socialism, among the Fiat workers. *Clasista* ideas were ancillary to the struggles being waged in the factories, and they only became dominant after late 1971, when SITRAC-SITRAM had been outlawed by the government. Then the former union leaders found themselves somewhat removed from the situation in the plants, and they were heavily dependent on the help of party activists to print their fliers, aid their imprisoned comrades, provide them with protection, and generally give the support necessary to sustain the now proscribed SITRAC-SITRAM. Rather than as a revolutionary workers' movement, the *clasismo* of these early months should be understood as a rank-and-file movement firmly rooted in the problems of work. It offered a dissident political message as a means to combat the enemies—both in and outside the plants—that some Fiat workers believed were attempting to frustrate the reforms they were advocating through their unions.

Though there was virtually no participation by diehard Peronist activists as leaders in the Fiat *clasista* unions, the new SITRAC and SITRAM did not emerge as explicitly anti-Peronist. Indeed, with a labor force that was nearly entirely Peronist and with a union leadership comprising many workers who had passed through Peronism, though few with an active militancy, a confrontation with the Peronist labor movement on ideological or political grounds was not initially contemplated. The bad blood between the Peronist labor movement and the Fiat *clasistas* resulted, rather, from the latter's active encouragement of other union recovery movements in the country, nearly all of which affected established Peronist leaderships. Changes in national labor politics were also behind the animosity between the *clasistas* and Peronist labor. The election of José Rucci of the UOM as secretary general of the CGT on July 2, 1970, presaged an attempt to reestablish the verticalist structure of the labor movement, which had not been restored since the time of the CGTA rebellion. The tense relations between SITRAC-SITRAM and the Cordoban Peronists resulted from the Fiat unions' support for dissident union slates in local unions and from the *clasistas'* resentment, in turn, of the local CGT's supposed kowtowing to Rucci and its unwillingness to support the Fiat workers in what they saw as the eminently working class, nonpartisan struggles taking place in the Fiat plants. The *clasistas'* opposition was not expressed in terms of *clasismo* versus *peronismo* but in terms of fighting for honest and democratic union leadership and the vindication of a leadership role for the working class in building socialism. The *clasista* message could draw on the Peronist working class's own traditions, including its anticapitalist currents, which had been submerged since the time of the Resistance and had reemerged after the Cordobazo. The object of *clasista* vituperation in the movement's public discourse was thus not the *peronista,* but the *traidor,* the *vendido,* the *burócrata.*

In the months following the July union elections, the Fiat unions gained confidence and eventually were able to offer assistance to other rank-and-file movements in Córdoba, particularly in the *ortodoxo* unions, who looked to their example in establishing legitimate and effective union representation. The example of SITRAC-SITRAM electrified the local labor movement in second half of 1970. For the first time in their history, the Ferreyra plants became the epicenter of Cordoban working class politics. The unions had successfully challenged Fiat on a number of issues and had adopted innovative militant tactics that were to become widespread in the Cordoban labor movement in the 1970s. Plant abandonments and factory occupations, the taking of company executives as hostages, hunger strikes, and street demonstrations were drastic tactics that had not been seen in the labor movement since the Peronist Resistance of the late 1950s. Other unions in the city followed the unions' example in their attempts to remove entrenched union leaderships. Workers and shop floor rebels in the Industrias Mecánicas del Estado plants (formerly IAME), and in the construction, dairy, and especially the shoe industries developed a close relationship with SITRAC-SITRAM, which provided them with access to union printing machinery, helped distribute union affiliation cards, and generally lent moral support.[23] These rank-and-file rebellions initially presented their movements as more "antibureaucratic" than *clasista*. Nevertheless as SITRAC-SITRAM emerged as the standard-bearer of both union democracy and *clasismo,* the two causes gradually became synonymous in the city, and the workers' movements increasingly adopted *clasista* identities.

The emergence of Cordoban *clasismo* took place just as changes in national labor politics were making causes such as union democracy particularly potent. Tosco's release from prison and his return to Córdoba in January 1970 had already put the national CGT leadership on guard. The government prohibited a January 31 national labor congress at which Tosco proposed to work out a "plan of national liberation." On February 4, the Luz y Fuerza headquarters was attacked with gunfire by the army and the union was again put under government control, forcing union leaders to hold the congress clandestinely.[24]

The Peronist labor bosses actually had their first real taste of the new antibureaucratic crusade in February 1970, when construction workers at the El Chocón power plant in Neuquén Province refused to accept their union central's expulsion of the union leaders who had attended Tosco's clandestine conference. The construction workers occupied the power plant for several days in protest, in what is now considered the first of the great antibureaucratic strikes of the decade. The Peronist labor movement found itself in a state of crisis. A fierce and often violent power struggle for control of the 220,000-member UOM that had started after Augusto Vandor's assassination was only resolved in early 1970, when Lorenzo Miguel, the treasurer of the UOM under Vandor, established his control of the union.[25] It was Miguel who later nominated Rucci, Vandor's former press secretary and a relatively unknown UOM leader from Santa Fe, for secretary general of the CGT at the July Congreso de la Unidad Augusto Timoteo Vandor. Rucci, who had been expected to serve as Miguel's puppet, soon emerged as a powerful figure in his own right and as Perón's foil for the independently minded *vandorista* tendencies always latent in the UOM.

Rucci, Miguel, and the UOM immediately set about reestablishing the rigid chain of command in the labor movement—considered imperative by both Perón and the more ambitious labor bosses, such as Miguel—to reestablish labor's influence at the national level. These new powers in the labor movement obviously looked disapprovingly at SITRAC-SITRAM and the Cordoban labor movement generally, while the left was making more frequent and wounding attacks against the "labor bureaucracy," with the UOM a particular target of its criticisms.

Clasismo was not then the only development in Córdoba seen as a threat by the Peronist labor bosses. The Cordoban Peronists, divided as always between *legalistas* and *ortodoxos,* continued to worry Buenos Aires. Miguel slowly pressured Alejo Simó and the Cordoban UOM, and thus the *ortodoxo* unions under their sway, into the verticalist fold. The lessons of the CGTA and the Cordobazo had not been lost on Simó, who would eventually become the faithful representative of *verticalismo* in the city and would align his union with the powers in the labor movement rather than the mavericks, who now appeared to him to be unpredictable and dangerous. Simó led the UOM in a few more gestures of insubordination, and he would continue to seek the independence from Buenos Aires that would guarantee his own influence within labor and thus within the Peronist movement. Nevertheless the new currents in Cordoban labor now seemed more dangerous to him than the aggrandizing tendencies of the *porteños.* The Cordoban UOM was gradually being won to the cause of *verticalismo* and was pulling away from the radicals in the local labor movement. Rather than the *ortodoxos,* the *legalistas* now loomed as the principal obstacle to verticalism among the Cordoban Peronist unions.

The explanation for this change lies in the Cordobazo and the events that followed it. The *legalistas'* participation in the uprising and in the labor resistance in the following months made their alignment with Miguel,

Rucci, and the CGT, who were urging dialogue and compromise with the government, virtually impossible. The *legalistas'* first public statements following Miguel's victory in the UOM revealed a mixture of defiance, germinating Peronist left positions, anticapitalism, uncompromising militancy, and the familiar opposition to *porteño* centralism; they supported, among other things, a national law to prevent the further establishment of industry in the federal capital and a complementary law of industrial promotion for the provinces.[26] Atilio López was gradually emerging as the principal spokesman for the *legalistas,* and his own union, the Unión Tranviarios Automotor, served as the meeting place for Peronist left intellectuals, political activists, and the city's Peronist unions, who were combining Peronist labor's historical demands for the return of Perón and the relegalization of the Peronist party with an ideology of national liberation and a socialist project for Argentina.[27] The power struggle between the two factions of Peronist labor for control of the CGT would actually not be decided until later the next year, but both *legalistas* and *ortodoxos* were acquiring a clearer political profile throughout 1970, and they embodied in their own ranks the gathering polarization of their movement between left and right.

The relationship between SITRAC-SITRAM and local unions such as López's *legalistas* and Tosco's Independents was initially cordial but never more than formally supportive. Though both López and Tosco were at first sympathetic to the Fiat union recovery movement and supportive of the antibureaucratic cause, which was also effectively a revindication of Cordoban autonomy against *porteño* centralism, neither was pleased with the *clasista* positions that SITRAC-SITRAM increasingly identified with. Tosco's suspicions stemmed more from his poor understanding of what was taking place in Ferreyra than from genuine political differences. From the time the government took control of Luz y Fuerza in early February until the restoration of its legal status in September 1971, Tosco and the union leadership were working in hiding. For the bulk of the Fiat *clasista* experience, therefore, Tosco received information only through intermediaries, whose biased accounts of the Fiat workers' rebellion jaundiced his subsequent interpretations of the movement. The suspicions of López and the *legalistas,* on the other hand, were largely political. They objected to the Fiat unions' apparent indifference to the legalization of the Peronist movement.

On November 11, 1970, the major political parties, including the Peronist party, released a public statement demanding immediate direct elections and an end to military rule, with the Peronist movement's full participation. This democratic front, dubbed the Hora del Pueblo, received the support of nearly all of the city's unions save the Fiat *clasistas*. SITRAC-SITRAM was skeptical of the military's willingness to relinquish control to civilian parties, but genuine ideological and political differences were also starting to emerge. The struggle born in the factories and the political tutelage some workers were now receiving from the left were bringing the Fiat workers closer to positions inimical to the Peronist electoral solutions supported by the *legalistas,* closer to positions that could fairly be described as revolutionary.

In the final months of 1970 the Fiat rebellion grew stronger, and the unions found the company hesitant and ineffective in its attempts to thwart their movement. Workers who had once been submissive and afraid were now defiant. Unions that had formerly been the instruments of the Fiat's personnel department were now questioning company policy at every turn. Strikes and slowdowns were not daily affairs, as the unions' detractors would have it, but they were frequent. A strike campaign waged by the unions in September brought Fiat to the negotiating table and won a begrudging concession from the company that union grievances on wages and work practices were to be included in future collective bargaining negotiations. On November 26, SITRAC-SITRAM began a *plan de lucha* demanding a series of immediate shop floor reforms—among them a reduction of the work day in the company forge and the elimination of productivity clauses—that had been adamantly rejected by the company in previous negotiations. Hunger strikes by the SITRAC executive committee and Curutchet to protest the firing of two union delegates turned into a local cause célèbre, with marches and demonstrations in the city center and support from various local church, student, and political organizations.[28]

Fiat was now a company under siege, and it was paying for the failure of its previous labor policies and past duplicities in dealings with its workers. In early 1971 the company decided to act, hoping to eliminate the union rebellion and return to the peaceful labor relations, coerced but effective, it had known just months before. On January 14, as an intimidation tactic, Fiat fired seven workers, among them SITRAC union executive committee members José Paéz, Domingo Bizzi, and Santos Torres, and a shop steward and member of SITRAC's recently formed committee to reevaluate Fiat's job classifications, Gregorio Flores.[29] SITRAC responded with a factory occupation that included the taking of company officials as hostages. Levingston ordered the workers to abandon the plant within three hours and threatened that if they did not, Córdoba would be declared an emergency zone, giving the president full powers to order military intervention in the province; the union ignored the order.[30]

The Fiat crisis spread citywide when all the city's mechanical workers called a solidarity strike for the following day. In addition to the Materfer workers the SMATA-affiliated IKA-Renault and Grandes Motores Diesel workers, and the neighboring Perkins workers (who, like the Fiat workers, were organized in a plant union) joined the protest. For Torres, this was a last, desperate bid both to head off the internal opposition building in his own union and to adopt the militant tactics that would allow him to assume control of the "hard-line" Peronists, possibly making Córdoba and the SMATA the seat of power for the 62 Organizaciones, which was badly divided nationally between those who supported dialogue with the government and those who opposed it. Torres's loss of prestige that especially followed the strikes of May to July 1970 had caused him to once again adopt a militant position. He went so far as to publicly exhort the local CGT to call a labor congress to work out a *plan de lucha* against Levingston, and he demanded that Rucci adopt militant tactics that would place the labor movement squarely in opposition to the military government; meanwhile he secretly schemed with Simó and *ortodoxo* leader Mauricio Labat of the taxi drivers' union to support the moderate position of the CGT central and seek dialogue with the government.[31] Torres's ulterior motives notwithstanding, his public support for the strike had the effect of escalating the crisis. The government immediately ordered Fiat to reinstate the fired workers pending government arbitration. The striking Fiat workers abandoned the Concord plant at midnight on the fifteenth.[32]

Rather than the end of a conflict, the January strike was the first in a series of events that would culminate in Córdoba's second major working class protest and popular uprising in less than two years. SITRAC-SITRAM and Fiat were now locked in an escalating confrontation; possibilities for compromise were remote and the points of conflict were magnified by the mutual suspicions and animosities of the past. After six months of union representation, issues such as the forge and job classifications had still not been addressed by the company. Instead of negotiating, Fiat had reacted by harassing shop stewards, attempting to restrict union activities in the plants, and finally firing the most belligerent of the new union leaders. On January 29, SITRAC and SITRAM responded to the Levingston government's lifting of the ban on collective bargaining negotiations by presenting the Labor Ministry with its collective bargaining proposal, a contract modeled on the established SMATA agreements and that included wage increases that would bring the Fiat workers up to the wage scales paid in other automotive firms.[33]

Throughout February SITRAC, SITRAM, and other local unions awaited the outcome of the first collective bargaining negotiations to be held in over three years. By March all the workers in Córdoba's mechanical industries and those in other unions, such as the public employees and university teachers, were engaged in strike actions as they confronted the hostility of employers faced once again with the unpleasant prospect of negotiating agreements with their workers. Fiat reacted to the SITRAC-SITRAM proposal by insisting that negotiations be held in Buenos Aires, an impossible requirement for workers who held the unrecompensed SITRAC-SITRAM union positions and whose sole source of income was the pay they received from their jobs in the Fiat plants. Perhaps as a reprimand for the Italian company's intransigence, the Labor Ministry's March 11 arbitration of the January dispute revoked the company's firings and rejected Fiat's claims that the union officials had abused union responsibilities and needlessly promoted conflict in the Ferreyra factories.[34]

SITRAC-SITRAM's ongoing conflict with the company over establishing effective union representation and collective bargaining in the Ferreyra complex coincided with a particularly sensitive political moment. On March 1 Levingston named José Camilo Uriburu, scion of a renowned aristocratic family, as the new governor of Córdoba. The choice of the intolerant and intemperate Uriburu for the governorship of a province such as Córdoba was a political blunder of almost willful stupidity. Uriburu's appointment came just as unions were mobilizing throughout the city and preparations for yet another labor protest were being made.

The first two weeks of March were filled with daily political tremors. On March 2 a general strike of the Cordoban CGT shut down the city. On March 5 Tosco proposed the creation of a strike committee, which would include the wayward Fiat unions, for the preparation of a March 12 citywide worker occupation of factories and workshops, to protest the diverse union grievances in the city, among them the suspended legal status of his own Luz y Fuerza, and to demand an end to the dictatorship. On March 6 Elpidio Torres, discredited since the 1970 strike and besieged by the opposition in the union he had once ruled absolutely, finally resigned the presidency of the SMATA, leaving the city's most important union in the hands of less able and skittish union lieutenants. The following day, March 7, Uriburu made his infamous public speech to the Cordoban oligarchy at the Leones Wheat Festival, in which he pledged "to cut off the head of the poisonous snake that nests" in Córdoba. The target of the threat was not lost on the city's unions, and the strike committee proposed a March 9 meeting to plan their response.

The relationship of SITRAC-SITRAM with the city's other unions and the Cordoban CGT at this point became crucial. The Fiat unions had refused earlier invitations to join the local CGT. They had always defended their position on the grounds that they were unwilling to subordinate the Fiat workers' struggle to the dictates of a labor organization in which the undemocratic and in many cases right-wing *ortodoxo* unions still held the majority. This distant relationship had become more strained, almost acrimonious, after the Cordoban CGT had failed to support the Fiat workers with strike action in the midst of the conflict over the January firings. Of all the city's principal labor leaders, only Tosco had made a public statement in support of SITRAC. The Fiat unions had responded by publicly chiding the Cordoban CGT, and thenceforth SITRAC-SITRAM routinely included the local CGT in their tirades against the *"burocracia sindical."*[35]

The presence of representatives from SITRAC-SITRAM at the March 9 meeting therefore caused unease in a number of unions and barely disguised displeasure in others. Bizzi and Masera criticized the committee's plans for workplace occupations as being ill conceived, since giving notice of such plans to public authorities undermined any possibilities for success. Plant occupations also assured an effective repression by the police, a repression that most likely would fall particularly hard on the Ferreyra complex, as it was now the recognized center of labor militancy in the city. Instead they proposed a march of separate worker columns and a public demonstration in the city center, in other words a return to the broad strategy that had led to the Cordobazo. When their motion was voted down, the Fiat representatives refused to commit their unions to the CGT plan, but they agreed to participate in the protest after a compromise was reached for two sequential actions: first they would carry out the CGT's plans for plant occupations and then there would be a general strike, with worker columns to march and meet in the Plaza Vélez Sarsfield to stage a public demonstration against the government and employers.[36]

On March 12, the day of the proposed *tomas,* the Fiat workers chose not to occupy the Fiat complex but instead to abandon the Concord and Materfer plants and hold a demonstration outside the Materfer factory

gates. From the Fiat complex, they marched into the nearby neighborhoods, where police units sent to suppress the demonstration were waiting. The police fired on the protesters, killing one worker and providing
the others, just as the police repression in the Cordobazo had, with the
martyr they needed to galvanize collective anger into a mass protest.
Police and workers in Ferreyra clashed repeatedly through the afternoon
and evening until the security forces were ordered to withdraw from the
zone.

This conflict, the Ferreyrazo, as the Fiat workers subsequently called
it, signaled the start of a citywide working class insurrection. At the
March 14 funeral for Alfredo Cepeda, the Fiat worker who had been killed
two days before, an estimated ten thousand Cordobans accompanied the
funeral cortege in a silent repudiation of the police repression. The local
CGT meanwhile extended its protest and publicly criticized Rucci and the
CGT central for its "passive complicity" and its refusal to declare a national general strike in support of Córdoba.[37]

Thousands of angry Fiat workers abandoned the plants on Monday
morning, March 15. The SITRAC-SITRAM columns marched as planned
from Ferreyra to the city center, expecting to meet thousands of fellow
workers there for the demonstration. En route, they received the first of
many surprises they would experience that day. Passing near the Villa
Revol power plant, the principal source of electric power in the city, the
SITRAC-SITRAM columns learned of the presence of Luz y Fuerza workers positioned in and around the plant, a sign that the light and power
workers' union had undertaken a plant occupation instead of proceeding
to the Plaza Vélez Sarsfield, an act that occasioned the jeers of the passing
Fiat workers who saw it as a betrayal of the May 9 compromise.[38] When
the Fiat columns arrived in the plaza, they also discovered that neither a
podium nor loudspeakers had been set up by the CGT as agreed.

In fact, the SITRAC-SITRAM leaders had been out of communication
with Tosco and other labor leaders for several days, and the CGT unions
had made some decisions for the proposed rally independently. A majority of the *ortodoxo* unions had refused to participate, and *legalista* and
Independent unions participated individually, making strategic decisions,
notably Tosco's decision to occupy Villa Revol, that were never communicated to the Fiat unions. The result was a disorganized protest that,
though massive, lacked even the minimal tactical and organizational preparations of the Cordobazo.

The rally proceeded nonetheless, and the Fiat and IME workers, historically isolated from the Córdoba workers' movement and largely ab-

sent in the protests of May 1969, made up two of the largest working class contingents in the city center. After speeches by Masera and Florencio Díaz, the secretary general of SITRAM, and as word spread of Tosco's occupation of Villa Revol, discussion and debate erupted over what steps to take next. Ignoring the Fiat unions exhortations to remain in the plaza, one contingent, led largely by the Luz y Fuerza and SMATA workers who were in attendance, marched off to Villa Revol to support Tosco. Soon other unions left the plaza to occupy nearby neighborhoods such as Barrio Alberdi and Barrio Clínicas, the centers of protest in the Cordobazo. There they were soon joined by students and common citizens, and by early afternoon the city was once again engulfed in a wave of destruction, greater in terms of damage to property if not loss of human life than even the Cordobazo had been. Attacks on businesses spread, and by midafternoon the Banco del Interior, Banco Galicia, the Jockey Club, and scores of supermarkets were all in flames, the first of some one hundred businesses that would be burned or sacked that day. Meanwhile some SITRAC-SITRAM workers had occupied nearby Barrio Güemes while others marched backed to Ferreyra, where barricades were constructed and entrance into the city from Highway 9 was cut off. Unlike in the 1969 uprising, the immediate downtown district was not occupied; the protesters chose instead a strategy of withdrawal and fortification in adjacent neighborhoods. Barricades were built by the Fiat workers in Güemes as well as other neighborhoods such as Colón and San Vicente, and by evening the western districts in the city had once again been abandoned by police and security forces and left to the control of protesters. In Barrio Clínicas alone, some 200 barricades had been built.[39]

The failure of the unions to coordinate their protest assured a swift repression. The next day, March 16, a specially trained antiguerrilla brigade arrived from Buenos Aires and met little of the stiff street resistance that army troops had encountered in the Cordobazo. Within several hours the city was occupied and the street barricades abandoned. That same day the Labor Ministry announced that a number of unions, among them SITRAC-SITRAM, had been placed under government supervision, and the army released orders to capture and detain Tosco, Masera, and the other principal labor leaders in the city, who were now planning resistance through the CGT. On March 17, the Levingston government requested Governor Uriburu's resignation, put the province under military rule, and hastily reestablished the death penalty in the Argentine penal code. After a general strike of the Cordoban CGT on March 18, Córdoba was declared an emergency zone; troops were deployed in nearly every neighborhood in the city as well as in the Fiat and IKA-Renault complexes. Nevertheless the resistance continued, and Fiat workers abandoned the Concord and Materfer factories on March 19 to protest the presence of the army troops in the complex. The following days brought incessant army night patrols through the Córdoba's streets, raids on all the major union halls, and hundreds of arrests of workers and labor activists. The pleas of the Cordoban delegation for support from Rucci and the national CGT were ignored at the national labor congress held in Rosario on March 19 and 20.[40]

The SITRAC-SITRAM leaders who were still at large promised to continue clandestine labor resistance. That promise and the sight of Córdoba's still unquieted, insurrectional temper convinced the army commander, General Lanusse, to remove Levingston and assume control of Argentina's government on March 23. For the second time in less than two years, events in Córdoba had been decisive in toppling the central government.[41]

Despite some apparent similarities, the series of mobilizations and protests that took place between March 12 and March 16, afterward dubbed the *viborazo* in an allusion to Uriburu's scurrilous remark, displayed a number of significant differences from the Cordobazo. One was the predominantly working class character of the *viborazo;* participation by the city's university students and the general population was a much less important factor, and strictly working class interests were more determinative than in the 1969 uprising. Another difference was the more visible presence of the Argentine left, which had been small and underground in 1969 but was growing and defiant in 1971. The presence of the billowing PRT banners with the marching SITRAC-SITRAM columns, as well as those of the PCR, the Montoneros, and others in the Plaza Vélez Sarsfield demonstration of March 15, indicated that a significant political shift had taken place since the Cordobazo. The revolutionary left's confidence and capabilities had increased markedly since the May 1969 uprising, and it was allying itself openly with the dissident workers' movement. Another related difference was the ubiquity in the local working class of what might be termed the *clasista* vernacular. The presence of class animosities, and even the sense of class war, were greater in the *viborazo*. The destruction of businesses was more widespread and wanton; looting was more pronounced. The speeches by Masera and other union leaders at the downtown demonstration were more anticapitalist in tone, more critical of the system than the regime. The target of the working class ire in 1971 was less Levingston, who had at least shown some signs of easing the more repressive aspects of the military government, or even the business owners and their refusal to satisfy what the unions considered the fair demands of the workers; the enemy was coming to be capitalism itself. If the Cordobazo had articulated the peculiarities of Cordoban society and a local political culture at a particular historical moment, the *viborazo* exposed the new ideological currents and political alliances appearing in Argentine national life, many of which had received their inspiration and impetus from the earlier protest.

In the aftermath of the *viborazo,* the owners struck back. Fiat, especially, sought to redress the balance of power in its plants. Despite the workers' March 19 walkout, the presence of army troops in the Ferreyra complex and in the factories themselves prevented much of the formerly spirited union activity on the shop floor. The company also began to pressure the government to adopt legal measures against the SITRAC and SITRAM unions, claiming a serious drop in production and loss of profits as a result of labor problems.[42] As another intimidation tactic, Fiat hired a public notary to document conditions in the plant, to use as evidence for the suit it was preparing to bring against the union leadership.[43]

In spite of the establishment of martial law, the banning of their unions, and the company's offensives, the Fiat workers continued their mobilizations and protests, and the militancy of the Cordoban labor movement generally remained unbroken. The Cordoban CGT held general strikes on April 2 and April 15 and planned a third for April 29 to protest the government's repressive measures. On April 13, after an acrimonious debate in which epithets were hurled between the *ortodoxo* and *legalista* unions, an alliance between the *legalistas* and the Independents elected López and Tosco president and vice president, respectively, of the local CGT, giving Córdoba the most pluralist and militant regional body in the entire labor movement and effectively neutralizing the more conservative, verticalist local representatives of the Peronist labor movement, the *ortodoxos.*[44]

To prevent the April 29 strike, and especially as a reaction against the conformation of the new CGT, on April 28 General Lanusse personally visited Córdoba. Orders for Tosco's arrest were immediately given, and the light and power workers' leader was captured and flown to the Villa Devoto federal penitentiary in Buenos Aires, where he would share a cell with Raimundo Ongaro for the next several months. But Lanusse's presence and Tosco's arrest only served to heighten tensions in the city. The

April 29 strike proceeded as planned; not even such conciliatory gestures as the Labor Ministry's lifting of the union bans managed to dissuade the Cordoban unions, whose mobilizations had become a problem of national importance.[45] The insurrectional state of Cordoban labor was very much in Lanusse's mind when he announced from the province on May 1 the military government's sponsorship of the Gran Acuerdo Nacional, a proposed transition to civilian rule but also a strategic withdrawal of the military from power, to combat the growing threat of labor violence and guerrilla insurgency in the country.[46]

The Gran Acuerdo had no immediate effect in Córdoba, where the *legalistas, clasistas,* and Independents defied the government further and organized a National Labor Congress of Combative Unions to be held on May 22 and May 23. Some 117 unions participated in the congress and, despite the discord between the Peronist and *clasista* unions in attendance, reached agreement on a program of opposition to the government. The congress's final resolution called for the nationalization of all major sectors of the economy, supported central planning and worker participation in management, and represented an unqualified rejection of the economic programs sponsored by the military since 1966.[47] Its real significance, however, was that it served notice to the government that Cordoban labor would continue its opposition and, more ominously, attempt to gather all the dissident, combative currents of Argentine labor under its wing.

SITRAC-SITRAM had submitted a program of its own for the congress's approval, but the Fiat *clasistas'* more radical program had been voted down in favor of the Peronist-sponsored one, which was less Marxist in language and included a peremptory demand for the relegalization of the Peronist movement. The SITRAC-SITRAM program nonetheless indicated just how far the union recovery movement had developed ideologically and politically. Though it contained utopian elements, among them the proposed formation of a "popular assembly" instead of the reestablishment of a discredited "bourgeois parliamentary system," it also spelled out its socialist positions more clearly, citing the Cordobazo (as would all the *clasista* movements of the early 1970s) as having opened a new chapter in the Argentine working class's final struggle for socialism and calling for the abolition of private property.[48]

Despite their participation in the congress, for the SITRAC-SITRAM unions it marked a turning point in their deteriorating relations with the Cordoban CGT. The Fiat unions criticized the very organization of the congress, because the CGT had extended invitations only to the established union leaderships and not to any of the opposition groups or dissident slates that were now to be found in many unions throughout the country. SITRAC-SITRAM criticized the final program for not presenting any clear *plan de lucha* and for not going beyond the La Falda and Huerta Grande programs sponsored by the combative Cordoban CGT at the height of the Peronist Resistance of the late 1950s and early 1960s.[49]

The *viborazo* had had the effect of further politicizing the Fiat factories, and *clasismo*'s ideological and political component became more intertwined with the shop floor struggles that had sustained the rank-and-file rebellion in Ferreyra. The *viborazo* had especially convinced groups on the left, outside the factory walls, of the importance of the Cordoban industrial proletariat in any future revolutionary project. Many Marxist parties competed for influence in the Fiat factories, but the most successful was the PRT. In late 1970, shortly after the party's fifth national congress, party leader Roberto Mario Santucho had moved to Córdoba to make Argentina's rebel city the headquarters of the PRT's national operations. There, particularly in the aftermath of the *viborazo,* Santucho and the PRT reevaluated their previous emphasis on military strategies, demonstrated most recently in the formation of the party's military wing, the Ejército Revolucionario del Pueblo (ERP), and began to give greater attention to the possibility of cultivating a revolutionary role for the industrial proletariat—that is, to the revolutionary left's interpretation of *clasismo*.[50]

Santucho took a personal interest in the PRT cell established in IKA-Renault, but the party seems to have had greater success in winning supporters in the Fiat complex, though more at the level of the youthful *cuerpo de delegados* than in the SITRAC-SITRAM union executive committees. Measuring precisely how many militants were won to the party, however, is impossible, and it is important to remember that the Fiat *clasista* unions' principal preoccupations and source of worker support and participation continued to be their honest and effective leadership on work-related issues. Fiat *clasismo*'s increasing identification with a distinctly anticapitalist political program undoubtedly is not simply attributable to the precocious development of the workers who emerged out of the 1970 shop floor rebellion. The political tutelage by the Marxist left was a factor, but the Fiat *clasista* movement remained predominantly a rank-and-file movement rooted in the factories.[51]

In the wake of the *viborazo* and Fiat's campaign to eliminate the unions, the struggle in the factories, not ideology or politics, unquestionably remained the decisive motivation for the workers. Fiat's union-busting campaign worked at multiple levels, and it elicited a resolute union action to prevent its success. As the company had done during a similar radicalization in its Italian plants in the late 1960s, Fiat combined intimidation with apparently conciliatory gestures. The intimidation was expressed most nakedly by the continued presence of army troops in the Fiat complex and by the hard line adopted on the shop floor by the foremen. Fiat balanced such displays of authority with a concession to allow a gradual resumption of union activity in the plants, but even this was part of a calculated strategy to undermine SITRAC-SITRAM. Seeing that the era of pliant company unions had ended, Fiat requested that the government revoke the unions' *personería gremial,* their legal status, in preparation for an affiliation with a more tractable, Peronist industrial union—with the UOM, Fiat hoped, but the company was now even willing to accept a SMATA affiliation. Fiat trusted that a Peronist union affiliation would eliminate the *clasista* problem and return the plants to a tranquil state.[52] Though the government refused the company's request, uncertain of reaction it would elicit at this still-sensitive political moment, it did agree to uphold the arrests of those Fiat *clasistas* who had been in prison since the March uprising. Thus, after the May congress, the SITRAC-SITRAM unions were faced with a company intent on reestablishing absolute authority over its labor force, and they had few trustworthy allies in the local labor movement to support their cause.

By June the Fiat union leaders who remained free prepared for what promised to be arduous negotiations with the company over their collective bargaining proposal. For SITRAC, Masera and Curutchet negotiated with the company; SITRAM was represented by its secretary general, Florencio Díaz. Among the demands the Fiat workers presented were a 60 percent wage increase to bring wages up to the scales paid by other automobile companies, a reduced work day in the company forge, and the elimination of all productivity clauses.[53] A terror campaign was waged against the Fiat workers during the weeks of negotiations, including a bombing attack against the home of Curutchet, and the company balked at every one of the union demands.[54] Fiat refused to compromise because it realized that the powers of the state would support the company rather than grant a victory to the unions, who now loomed as the regime's principal labor opposition and the most vociferous critics of Lanusse's Gran Acuerdo Nacional. In fact, the government's compulsory arbitration of the contract produced exactly the kind of agreement that Fiat hoped and the union feared it would. Minimal wage increases were awarded, and the unions' demands regarding the elimination of productivity clauses and improved working conditions were ignored. SITRAC and SITRAM reacted angrily to the arbitration, calling it a mere reproduction of the company's offer, and prepared a series of strikes in protest.[55]

Strikes, slowdowns, and other forms of union resistance produced few results in July and August. In addition to the unions' displeasure with the collective bargaining agreement, there remained the problems of the imprisoned union leadership, the harassment and firing of union activists, and the increasingly frequent terrorist attacks against them. The bombing of Curutchet's home was only the first of many such reprisals against the unions. Their tense relations with the local CGT meant there was little support from the combative local labor movement for the Fiat workers, and SITRAC and SITRAM were forced to look outside the city for allies.

On August 28 and 29 the Fiat unions held a Congreso de Sindicatos Combativos y Agrupaciones Clasistas in Córdoba, a national gathering of *clasista* unionists from throughout the country. Since the 1970 Fiat rebellion, and especially after the *viborazo,* other dissident union groups, particularly in the provinces, had adopted *clasista* positions in opposition to established union leaderships and in favor of socialist programs. In Tucumán, in Rosario, and especially in the Paraná industrial belt, which was the center of the country's steel industry and, like Córdoba, a region of recent industrial development, *clasista* unionists had emerged as influential minorities in many unions. Masera and Díaz called the congress in the name of SITRAC-SITRAM for two purposes: to provide a forum in which to debate and refine *clasismo*'s ideological and political positions, and to begin to establish a national alliance that would provide mutual support and protection that would somewhat compensate for the lack of support from the Peronist CGT.[56]

The gathering brought together not only trade unionists but also representatives from most of the country's Marxist parties, a fact that exposed it to Peronist criticisms of manipulation by the left. Indeed, the events of the congress gave some credence to such criticisms, as the workers in attendance found themselves subjected to endless debates on revolutionary praxis and socialist economics by the left-wing activists. To a great extent the parties, not the unions, dominated the proceedings. Nevertheless, the congress ended by approving the *clasista* program that had been presented but rejected at the Peronist-controlled labor congress of the previous May, which included a specific *plan de lucha* to be waged against the owners and the state.[57]

In light of the serious problems they were facing, the Fiat unions reacted to the passivity of the other Cordoban unions with particular bitterness. However, SITRAC and SITRAM did not have an altogether fair understanding of the realities of local labor politics, a fact that undoubtedly had much to do with the Fiat complex's many years of isolation from the Cordoban labor movement. Atilio López and the *legalistas'* position in the local CGT remained vulnerable, weakened by Tosco's imprisonment and unremitting pressures from the *ortodoxos* and Buenos Aires to break the alliance with the Independents and reform the CGT with strictly Peronist participation. The *ortodoxos'* withdrawal from the CGT precipitated intense pressures from José Rucci and the Peronist labor hierarchy to make López comply with the purge of the non-Peronist elements in Cordoban labor. López responded by resigning as the CGT's secretary general, a resignation that was later rejected by the unions in an open assembly, but the fact was that Peronists such as López who sought to make the CGT more representative, who allied with Tosco's Independents against the labor bosses and in opposition to the military government, were not in a position to ally themselves too closely with the more radical currents at work in Ferreyra.[58] But there was fault on both sides. López and other *legalistas,* and indeed Tosco himself, had never hidden their doubts about Fiat *clasismo* and had failed to respond constructively in those moments, such as in the planning of the March strikes, when SITRAC-SITRAM had sought to cooperate with the other unions in Córdoba. In public statements the SITRAC-SITRAM leaders had also lately taken greater pains to distinguish between the *legalistas* and Independents, acknowledged to be democratic unions with honest leaders, and the unions they regarded as corrupt preserves of the labor bureaucracy, locally the *ortodoxos* and nationally Rucci, the UOM, and the Peronist labor bosses who controlled the CGT and the 62 Organizaciones.[59]

The isolation of the Fiat unions proved disastrous when the state finally decided to eliminate the Cordoban *clasista* movement. The first victim was the Cordoban shoe workers' union, where *clasista* activists, with support from SITRAC-SITRAM, had led a rank-and-file rebellion that seemed poised to take power from the union's established Peronist leadership. The government banned the shoe workers' union on the eve of the August *clasista* congress and served notice that a reaction against Cordoban *clasismo* was imminent. In Ferreyra, a sense of expectancy hung over the Fiat plants through September and October. On October 26 the morning shift in the Concord and Materfer plants watched as army troops once again occupied their plants. In the Concord plant, shop stewards immediately stopped the production lines in their departments, and the workers abandoned their stations en masse to attend a general assembly in the factory, but the army troops swiftly dispersed them with tear gas and attack dogs.[60] By this time the Materfer workers had also stopped production. Shortly before ten o'clock that morning, the SITRAC-SITRAM leaders learned that the Ministry of Labor had cancelled their *personería gremial* the night before.[61]

The repression of the Fiat unions was swift and decisive. The government froze the SITRAC-SITRAM union funds, and army and police units occupied their downtown union headquarters. SITRAC's legal counsel, Curutchet, was arrested outside the door of the provincial court house just as he was about to enter and file suit against the company for the continued imprisonment of Fiat union leaders and the company's reputed intimidation campaign.[62] The company then finished what the state had begun. On October 30 it fired 259 workers, including nearly all the workers on the SITRAC-SITRAM executive committees and the shop floor stewards' commission. Fiat justified the firing of union representatives, illegal under Argentine labor law, with legal artifice: since SITRAC-SITRAM no longer had legal status, the fired workers were no longer union officials.[63]

When the fired workers later filed suit against the company, Fiat offered an indemnity in return for signed resignations. The offer signaled that the company feared that a favorable court decision, even under a military government, was by no means assured.[64] SITRAC and SITRAM sought to resist the government's and company's union-busting measures, but they were hampered by their isolation from the other Cordoban unions. Though the SMATA workers had called a strike and abandoned their plants on the morning of the army's occupation of the Ferreyra complex, the Fiat unions found little support in the local labor movement in the following weeks. López had agreed to include the SITRAC-SITRAM interventions on a list of grievances to accompany the local CGT's fourteen-hour general strike on October 29, but this was a feeble gesture of solidarity; the *legalista* leader, in particular, did little to support them at a critical moment. In an open assembly of the local CGT on November 3, the SITRAC-SITRAM motion for a general strike specifically in support of the Fiat unions was voted down, and the issue of SITRAC-SITRAM was left to be resolved by the hardly sympathetic CGT central.[65] After the Cordoban CGT released a document critical of the Fiat *clasista* movement, SITRAC drafted an open letter to the organization, which was ultimately never sent, accusing it of passiveness that bordered on complicity with the repression of the *clasista* movements at Fiat, in the Perkins factory, and in the shoe workers' union.[66] Privately the union leadership reacted bitterly to the "treachery" of the other Cordoban unions and to the decision of the *legalistas* and Independents alike to refer the Fiat union controversy to Buenos Aires, which they fairly interpreted as a virtual abandonment of SITRAC-SITRAM by the local unions.[67]

Isolated within the Cordoban labor movement, vilified by Rucci and the Peronist-controlled CGT central, with all of its leadership either in jail or fired, and with army troops and tanks occupying the Ferreyra factories, there remained few possibilities for union resistance. A November 3 strike called by the union leaders failed miserably. Despite their unbroken support for the union leadership, the workers in the plants were frightened, demoralized, and incapable of acting resolutely. The sight of thousands of applicants outside the factory gates after Fiat announced the opening of some 400 jobs to fill the positions left by the imprisoned or dismissed union activists discouraged them even further. Fiat also increased production rhythms in the plants and returned to its hated piece work system of remuneration as a way of reducing worker contact on the shop floor and undermining rank-and-file resistance.[68] Though the SITRAC and SITRAM executive committees held firm, even some of the union leaders lost heart in the face of such overwhelming opposition. Several accepted the company's indemnity offer, a fact that caused the greatest despair among the other union leaders.[69]

Yet it was only a small minority of the union leadership that succumbed to the temptation to abandon SITRAC-SITRAM. On December 30, SITRAC undersecretary Domingo Bizzi filed suit against the company for unlawful firing. The names of some twenty other fired SITRAC-SITRAM union activists were added to the suit, and over the next three months the fired Fiat workers opted for a legal strategy to reestablish their unions.[70] They took this action despite the precarious situation in which nearly all the fired workers now found themselves. Union blacklists, reputedly compiled by Fiat and distributed by the military and intelligence agencies, had made their way not only into the IKA-Renault and IME factories, but also into the hundreds of small metallurgical workshops in the city. Despite their long work histories and, in some cases, highly coveted skills, none of the fired workers were able to find work in either the mechanical complexes or the metallurgical workshops, nor would they ever work again in the local automobile industry.[71] Meanwhile Fiat's repression in the plants continued. The unions protested the piecemeal firings *(despidos hormigas)* of workers with suspected union sympathies and accused the company of devising a new strategy of hiring workers from Santiago del Estero, Jujuy, Formosa, and Corrientes in the hope of fashioning a submissive labor force out of the agricultural workers from the country's poorest and most backward provinces.[72]

The possibility of a successful resolution to their conflict with the company through the court system had always been remote, but even that small possibility completely disappeared with the ERP's kidnapping of Fiat's Italian president, Oberdán Sallustro, on March 10, 1972. Sallustro's kidnapping was an action taken independently by the guerrilla organization. Whatever silent sense of retribution some workers may have felt at a reprisal made in their behalf, the union leadership recognized that it did irreparable damage to their cause. Fiat immediately attempted to implicate SITRAC-SITRAM in the terrorist act and request that the unions and their imprisoned legal counsel intercede and negotiate the release of Sallustro directly with the ERP.[73] Any agreement by the fired union leaders would have compromised SITRAC-SITRAM, sullied its reputation, and given credence to the company's accusations of ties to the guerrilla left. The union leaders and Curutchet condemned and rejected the company's request and insisted it was an affair strictly between Fiat, the government, and the ERP. However, the public nature of the dispute, and then Sallustro's death in a Buenos Aires shootout between his ERP captors and the police, cast a shadow over the Fiat unions and effectively ended their chances of regaining their legal status.

Fiat's request had had a clear strategic and political intent in its then unresolved conflict with the fired union officials. But the attempt to use SITRAC and SITRAM as intermediaries may also have been based on the company's genuine but mistaken belief that there were organic links between the PRT-ERP and the Fiat unions. As has been discussed, since the emergence of the Fiat workers' rebellion in March 1970 it was undoubtedly true that militants from nearly all Argentina's left-wing parties had concentrated their efforts in Córdoba. Overnight the Fiat workers had become the hope of the Argentine left, and there had developed a kind of cult of the worker in the city that was centered on SITRAC-SITRAM.

Working class status immediately connoted a moral superiority and an innate revolutionary predisposition in the eyes of left-wing militants. Volunteers had appeared at the unions' hall, offering to type the SITRAC-SITRAM fliers and comuniqués, edit their newspapers, run errands, and perform any of the other miscellaneous tasks necessary to administer the industrial unions, whose memberships numbered in the thousands. More significantly, the slow and difficult process of politicizing the rank and file had been started, and significant gains had been made. Among the left-wing parties represented in the rank and file and the union leadership by early 1972 was the PRT.[74] Despite the widespread belief that the PRT had dominated the Fiat *clasista* movement, it is now clear that the party was only one of a number of Marxist parties, albeit the most important one, that competed for influence in Ferreyra, and that its greatest success in incorporating union activists as party militants occurred after the banning of SITRAC-SITRAM. The Fiat *clasista* movement, moreover, never advocated armed struggle as a strategy for building socialism, and its "revolutionary" message, never fully elaborated by the unions, was ultimately more of a call for a democratic, socialist workers' movement than for a forcible seizure of state power by the working class.[75]

The Fiat workers' rebellion has generally been interpreted by scholars and union and political activists alike as a laudable experiment in union democracy that ultimately failed because of SITRAC-SITRAM's political intransigence. Fiat *clasismo* was supposedly crippled by the unions' insistence on revolutionary postulates and their scorn for electoral solutions on the eve of the relegalization of the Peronist movement, as well as by their unwillingness to cooperate with the more combative sectors of Cordoban labor, Lopez's *legalistas* and Tosco's Independents.[76] The intelligence with which the Fiat unions challenged the relations of production in the plants was reputedly not matched by their political judgment, and their insistence on a revolutionary purism supposedly isolated them even within the very militant Cordoban labor movement. The inexperience of the *clasista* leaders undoubtedly caused them to commit many errors. Their criticisms of the *legalistas* and especially of Tosco and the Independents were sometimes needlessly provocative, despite the legitimate dissatisfaction the SITRAC-SITRAM leaders felt with their lack of support from the local labor movement. They also failed to appreciate the significance of Lanusse's Gran Acuerdo Nacional and the fact that the changing political circumstances that followed the *viborazo* called for different tactics and perhaps a different political program altogether.[77] Yet to have foreseen the political opening that resulted from Lanusse's blatant attempt to concede minimal political participation in the hope of defusing the type of mounting popular opposition that had been unleashed in the Cordobazo would have required a political prescience that few other groups or individuals then displayed.

Accusations that the labor union had become confused with the political party also need to be put in the context in which Fiat *clasismo* first emerged. After years of authoritarian rule, and indeed given the lack of a bona fide workers' party to represent strictly working class positions, not to mention socialist ones, some confusion of union and party roles was probably unavoidable. SITRAC and SITRAM were faced with the daunting task of addressing the long-standing work related problems in the Fiat plants and rebuilding a working class tradition that had virtually disappeared after the rise of Peronism—a tradition that the Fiat workers themselves only imperfectly understood, which undoubtedly led to many political, ideological, and tactical errors. Yet the mistakes were also a product of the reaction unleashed against the unions. With the powers of the state, the company, and the Peronist labor bureaucracy fully arrayed against them, a siege mentality set in that hardened their positions, undermined their willingness to compromise, and made their language more truculent. However, if the tactical and political decisions of Fiat *clasismo* are open to debate, the unions' insistence on an unavoidable involvement in politics cannot be. SITRAC and SITRAM trenchantly criticized detractors who pointed to their meddling in politics as the cause of their downfall. They noted that abstention from politics was not only an impossible position but also a dishonorable one to take in the face of a repressive regime carrying out a systematic assault on working class interests.[78]

The Fiat workers' rebellion failed not because of any rightful involvement in politics—nearly all the country's unions were involved in politics in some fashion—but because it seriously challenged one of the country's most powerful and influential foreign companies, and because the unions briefly emerged as the country's most serious working class threat to the state. That threat was made all the more real when the Fiat unions gained national prominence after the *viborazo.* SITRAC-SITRAM loomed as a disturbing precedent, and other *clasista* movements, inspired by the Fiat workers' example, had begun to appear throughout the country, particularly in the provinces.

Fiat *clasismo*'s most enduring legacy, however, and the source of continued support for SITRAC-SITRAM among the Fiat rank and file in the coming years, was not its political message but the sense of power the union rebellion had instilled in the Fiat workers. For the first time in its history, the company had been forced to accept legitimate union representation of its labor force. Throughout the months that SITRAC and SITRAM existed, the unions' publications were filled with such terms as *dignity, respect,* and *self-worth.* The example of honest union leadership and a functioning workplace democracy were important aspects of Fiat *clasismo,* but it was perhaps in the subtler changes—precisely, in their sense of dignity and the begrudging respect they commanded from a formerly intransigent company—that SITRAC and SITRAM achieved their most significant gains and provided the workers' movement, especially in Córdoba, with an example on which to build. In the aftermath of the banning of their unions, the workers who had defied Lozano, Cassanova, and the company in the 1970 shop floor rebellions and come to power in the first honest union elections ever held in the Ferreyra complex considered those very changes to be SITRAC-SITRAM's most enduring achievements: "What we most achieved is that nobody, as in the past, could level fines against us, fire us, or do anything else to us just as they pleased. During all this time, we stood up to whoever we had to, from the most important company executive to the lowliest foreman with a boss' pretensions."[79]

· III ·

The Peronist Restoration

Were the last battles of the Comintern fought in Córdoba?

Antonio Marimón, *El antiguo alimento de los héroes*

SEVEN

Tosco and Salamanca

From the Villa Devoto Prison in Buenos Aires, Agustín Tosco released a steady stream of letters and public statements through 1971 and early 1972. The most prominent figure in Córdoba's dissident labor movement relied on his lawyers and the many Argentines now moving routinely in and out of Argentine jails to smuggle out his forbidden political missives. Despite his loss of visiting privileges, his poor health, bouts of solitary confinement, and the threats of more severe punishment, Tosco continued to play a decisive role in leading the labor opposition to the government. His writings alternately offered exhortative, fulminating criticisms of José Rucci, the national Confederación General del Trabajo, and the labor leaders who sought dialogue with the dictatorship and prodigal encouragement for the labor resistance that had been building from the time of the Cordobazo. General Alejandro Lanusse's Gran Acuerdo Nacional was also now a target, and Tosco demanded a full restoration of democratic rights instead of the carefully conditioned transition to civilian rule that the military commander offered.[1]

Strategically, Tosco now put all his hopes in Córdoba's regional CGT as the bulwark of an alternative labor movement. The failure of the alternative Confederación General del Trabajo de los Argentinos had been instructive. The power of the Peronist labor bosses in the CGT national and in the union centrals was still too great to challenge in the ambitious terms of a parallel CGT. Supporting the pluralism of the labor movement nationally and the autonomy of the Cordoban unions appeared to be more realistic goals. Tosco's membership in the Movimiento de Unidad y Coordinación Sindical, the Communist-party–sponsored political trade union alliance that was a counterpart to the Peronists' 62 Organizaciones, was one attempt to encourage ideological and political diversity in the country's labor movement. That cause, Tosco believed, would actually best be furthered by protecting Córdoba, since it was there that the full panoply of the labor movement's ideological and political diversity was most evident.[2]

The keys to assuring Córdoba's autonomy, as had been apparent from the time of the Cordobazo, were Atilio López and the combative Peronists grouped in the *legalistas.* As Peronists, the Cordoban *legalistas* were the most effective opponents of Rucci and the trade union philosophy Tosco saw embodied in the national CGT. In their opposition to Rucci and *verticalismo,* López and the *legalistas* were favored by Perón's tactical stratagems of the early 1970s, which were intended to keep pressure on the military governments and to restore Peronism, and especially Perón himself, in the country's political life. The pressure came especially from the newest arrivals to the movement, the Peronist youth groups, particularly the Montoneros, but it also could come from the militant sectors of the labor movement. By mid-1970, Perón was once again encouraging Raimundo Ongaro to lead an active labor opposition to the government, and after Ongaro's release from Villa Devoto in early 1972, the print workers' leader attempted to resuscitate his combative, dissident CGT.[3] López himself began to be courted by Perón and the entourage surrounding the exiled leader in Madrid. By early 1972, the *legalistas* could rightly claim official approval from Perón's virtual court in exile for their opposition to Rucci.[4]

Despite Perón's apparent change of heart and his consistent, fulsome praise for diversity within the labor movement, the impending exit of the military from power and the possibility Peronists foresaw of a lifting of the proscription of their movement also encouraged a hardening of lines between Peronists and non-Peronists in the labor movement, in Córdoba as well as elsewhere. The tensions within certain unions and between unions, the perennial dialectic of Cordoban labor politics, were becoming stronger and were influencing the fate of a Córdoba-based dissident labor movement. This change, still nascent, was nonetheless perceptible even in Tosco's own union. The rebirth of the Peronist opposition in Luz y Fuerza was, however, fundamentally the result of the disarray caused first by the union's early 1970 proscription and then by Tosco's long imprisonment following the *viborazo.* Moreover there existed an ideological affinity between Tosco's positions and those of a large number of Luz y Fuerza Peronists, a number of whom were of the *ongarista* tendency, were stalwart running mates on the Tosco slates, and were longtime members of the union's central committee. These Luz y Fuerza Peronists collaborated closely with the Marxists in the union and supported the union's increasing role as one of the trade union movement's principal advocates of socialism.[5] Opposition to Tosco came not from this group but from a small clique of more traditional Peronists.

The conservative Peronists in the union had long had a tendency to downplay their traditional sympathies, regarding them as a liability in a union that had as its banner opposition to at least some aspects of Peronist trade unionism. From the time of the Cordobazo on, however, their discontent had been mounting. These Peronists, led by Sixto Ceballos, were uneasy with the union's increasingly prominent political role, with what they viewed as a needlessly belligerent attitude toward the Peronist labor hierarchy, especially in the Federación Argentina de Trabajadores de Luz y Fuerza, and with Tosco's galling indifference to the prospect of a re-legalization of the Peronist movement.[6] Hoping to capitalize on Tosco's absence, the conservative Peronists presented their first serious opposition slate in almost a decade. Tosco's slate won easily—1,100 votes to Ceballos's 653—but it was a sign that the polarization within the labor movement between Peronist and non-Peronist was appearing even in this redoubt of union democracy and political pluralism.[7]

The Peronist opposition to Tosco was nonetheless still a relatively minor affair, and the union's political development toward socialist positions was uninterrupted. Though he would not publicly proclaim his Marxism until 1973, Tosco left little doubt of his identification and the union's with a socialist project. When the union reoccupied its headquarters in late 1971, the interim secretary general, Ramón Contreras, proclaimed the union's rejection of bread-and-butter trade unionism (*"sindicalismo de reinvindicación"*) and declared Luz y Fuerza's adherence to a political role for the working class, a *"sindicalismo de liberación,"* that broadly shared the *clasista* positions on private property, the state, and the need to build a socialist movement in Argentina.[8]

The union's role as a leading working class opponent of the government and Tosco's growing notoriety as labor dissident finally precipitated Lanusse's long threatened reprisal, and on April 9 Tosco was transferred from Villa Devoto to Rawson Prison. Lanusse hoped the isolation of Argentine Patagonia would silence his hectoring and formidable adversary, but letters and communiqués, continued to arrive in Córdoba, though with less frequency, signed by the Luz y Fuerza leader. After the move to Rawson, Tosco continued to direct his efforts toward fashioning Córdoba into the bulwark of the labor opposition to the government and, ultimately, into an alternative to Rucci and the CGT. National politics and developments within the Peronist movement temporarily favored such plans. The unremitting pressures placed on the government from the Peronist left, and Perón's now frank support for the tactics of "revolutionary war" adopted by his youthful cadres, unleashed a national wave of popular effervescence that had Peronism at its center. The consequence for Córdoba was that the *ortodoxos*—who represented tendencies within Peronism that seemed to have been eclipsed in Perón's heart by the Peronist left—were paralyzed, and the *legalistas* were permitted to cooperate with the Independents and share power in the local CGT. Although even in Córdoba the militant Peronists were committed to remaining within the Peronist labor movement nationally and attempting to gain control of the 62 Organizaciones, their local working alliance was with Tosco.[9]

The great unresolved question in Córdoba remained *clasismo*. The demise of SITRAC-SITRAM did not bring an end to *clasismo* in Cordoban working class politics, nor did it hinder the development of a Marxist alternative in the Cordoban labor movement that was free from the nonsectarian preoccupations of Tosco and the Independents. The various parties of the Marxist left had elaborated a clear "provincial" strategy since the time of the Cordobazo, and the experience of SITRAC-SITRAM had only encouraged them further. The Marxist left regarded the Peronist identity of the new working class of the interior, especially in the modern industrial sectors, as the weak link in the Peronist labor movement. Thus Córdoba, as the industrial center of the interior and the site of its most modern industries, had a special strategic priority.[10] Differences existed among the Partido Comunista Revolucionario, Partido Revolucionario de los Trabajadores, Vanguardia Comunista, and other Marxist organizations on the most appropriate method of establishing a following among the industrial proletariat in the city, but there also existed a broad consensus on some issues. Generally there was agreement on the need to link workers' daily struggles with a socialist political program, to win the workers' trust through honest and effective union representation, to practice a genuine workplace democracy, and to begin political tutelage slowly and always to center it on concrete, workplace problems.

One issue *clasista* slates almost unanimously adopted, for example, was the reform of collective bargaining negotiations. Though the SMATA had more transparent collective bargaining procedures than many unions, with contracts subject to greater scrutiny by the workers and considerable consultation of workers through their shop stewards, most of the final negotiating process nonetheless remained in the hands of a small group of union officials. The left's *clasista* strategy saw the collective bargaining process as a potentially useful politicizing tool. Marxist parties proposed a thorough democratization of the collective bargaining process. Shop stewards were to encourage the free discussion of workers' demands and grievances in their departments; then open assemblies would be held to discuss the workers' positions and to elect the committees that would draft the union's proposal. A voice vote would then be held, again in open assembly, on the final contract that the union would present to management and also to elect the worker representatives who would negotiate directly with the company.[11]

Of all the Marxist organizations, the small Vanguardia Comunista was perhaps the most fecund source of theorizing on *clasista* tactics. It was the first to suggest the political utility of the collective bargaining process and to urge the left to adopt the cause of "union democracy" against entrenched labor leaders; it offered the best and most elaborated programs for the formation of the *clasista* cells, the *comisiones obreras* that would link the workers' shop floor struggles to a socialist project. The VC stressed the vulnerability of the Peronist leadership on such shop floor issues as production rhythms and job classifications in the modern industrial sectors. It argued for the need to maintain the clandestine nature of the *comisiones obreras* to avoid reprisals by management and the union bureaucracies, and to work discreetly until such time as party activists enjoyed sufficient rank-and-file support to run for election as shop stewards and eventually to form separate union slates to bid for control of the union executive committee.[12] In summary, the left would use the issues of union democracy and effective shop floor representation to win power in the unions and take the first step toward a political tutelage of the industrial proletariat.

If the Vanguardia Comunista was the most sophisticated theoretician of *clasismo,* its most effective practitioner in Córdoba was the PCR. The PCR had been established in 1968, when disaffected militants from the Partido Comunista abandoned the pro-Soviet, reformist PC and formed a pro-Chinese, revolutionary Marxist party.[13] The party apparatus in Córdoba included the ablest of the PCR activists, and the city's industrial proletariat was a special priority for the PCR.

The PCR's greatest efforts were undoubtedly directed toward the IKA-Renault complex. From the late 1960s, and particularly following the

Cordobazo, the PCR's Córdoba committee, under the leadership of César Gody Alvarez, began to accumulate detailed information on conditions in the plants, systematically and with great skill identifying those departments where the *torrista* union apparatus was "soft" and where party activists could enter and begin *clasista* work.[14] The PCR certainly had been the first to perceive the weakness of Torres in the Perdriel plant, where Renault had undertaken a wholesale technological restructuring of the factory and converted many of the formerly highly skilled tool and die makers there into mere assembly line workers, without the slightest opposition from the union. Party members led the 1970 Perdriel factory occupation that triggered the great 1970 strike, and it was largely due to the PCR's efforts that the left recovered from the strike's disastrous outcome and was able to rebuild the anti-*torrista* union recovery movement in the IKA-Renault plants.[15]

Thanks in great measure to the proselytizing activities of the apparently tireless polemicists on the left, *clasismo* was gradually becoming synonymous in Córdoba, and elsewhere in Argentina, with the antibureaucratic union democracy cause that Ongaro's 1968 union rebellion had first crystallized but that had since lost momentum within the ranks of Peronist labor. The Peronist left also made it a cause, but the left was predominantly a movement of middle-class university students that had only limited resonance in the labor movement, despite the hasty formation of the Juventud Trabajadora Peronista (JTP), designed to cultivate ties with the working class. The "counter-discourse" that historians of Argentine labor have come to speak of, the championing of militant tactics in a *línea dura* Peronist vernacular, was actually much more than that. It was an ideologically charged assault on the bastions of power in the labor movement that appeared, after the adoption of *clasista* programs by left-wing parties that also advocated armed struggle, to represent a subversive threat to some and a revolutionary possibility to others. In that historical moment, neither view was mistaken.

Clasista slates in unions throughout the Argentine interior were winning elections. In the northwest sugar provinces, for example, the VC was particularly active and largely responsible for the formation of Armando Jaime's *clasista* CGT in Salta.[16] In the Paraná industrial belt the PRT's efforts were producing promising results, and a number of *clasista* shop stewards had won election in the Villa Constitución, San Nicolás, and Zárate steel plants.[17] Even in such bastions of the Peronist labor boss as the Unión Obrera Metalúrgica, *clasista* activists were appearing in Santa Fe as well as in Córdoba and in other cities of the interior. To coordinate these diverse *clasista* movements the left in Córdoba established the Frente Unico Clasista, which was never effective, owing to the ideological and tactical positions that divided the Marxist organizations, but which was an important symbol of the vibrancy of *clasismo* in those years.

Córdoba remained the center of the *clasista* movements. Despite the grave setback *clasismo* suffered with the government's repression of SITRAC-SITRAM, the *clasista* activists in Santa Isabel recovered from the 1970 strike and prepared to challenge Torres's successors in the 1972 elections in IKA-Renault and the other SMATA-affiliated factories (Thompson Ramco, Ford-Transax, Grandes Motores Diesel, Ilasa). In late 1971 the left-wing challengers organized the Movimiento de Recuperación Sindical (MRS), a loose alliance of strange bedfellows that included activists from the PC, the PCR, the Trotskyist Palabra Obrera, El Obrero, Peronismo de Base, Vanguardia Comunista, and many independents—leftists not aligned with any specific Marxist party as well as nonleftists, including a number of former Peronist supporters of Torres who were sympathetic to a program of honest and effective union representation and unhappy with the sclerosis that now afflicted the *torrista* union machinery.[18] Although the MRS had received early support from SITRAC-SITRAM and had even published its first fliers in the Fiat workers' union hall, after the government's busting of the Ferreyra unions, the SMATA activists sought to distance themselves from their former allies and present a more moderate image, going so far as to expunge the word *clasismo* from their union program.[19]

The MRS framed its challenge to Torres's successor, Mario Bagué, and the *torrista* union apparatus not in political terms but strictly in terms of the work-related issues of effective and honest representation and union democracy. The tactics of the MRS were twofold. The movement activists conducted an unrelenting campaign of propaganda against Bagué and caustic criticism of the leadership where the *torrista* union machinery was most vulnerable: on shop floor issues. They also called numerous wildcat strikes in late 1971 and early 1972 to increase their visibility among the workers and to highlight the perfunctory representation that union shop stewards offered there, a tactic whose effectiveness was evidenced by the SMATA union leadership's increasingly shrill criticism of their actions.[20]

The SMATA Peronists, ironically, attempted to outflank the union dissidents' challenge by riding the wave of political radicalization that had taken hold of the city since the Cordobazo. Bagué and the *torrista* leaders strengthened their ties with the more combative sectors of Cordoban labor in the hopes that it would deflect some of the criticisms of the MRS. Although the MRS activists did not present their program in political terms, the SMATA leadership was aware that the temper of the local working class had changed enormously as a result of the 1969 and 1971 uprisings, the SITRAC-SITRAM experience, political changes at the national level, and the leftward shift that had taken place in Argentine society in general. The old *torrista* brand of militancy would no longer bestow legitimacy; traditional Peronist militancy—strikes and mobilizations against the company and the government for improved wages—was not sufficient, at least not in Córdoba. Unions were now almost obliged to take an anticapitalist stance to retain their prestige among the rank and file. As a result, the political language of Bagué and the *torristas* changed, literally within a span of months. The targets of the union's attacks were now the "procapitalist" regime, and the union went so far as to demand the future nationalization of IKA-Renault by the government.[21] The influence of *clasismo* was seen subtly but clearly as the SMATA union hierarchy sought to appropriate the *clasistas'* own political program and assume the role of the opposition.

Bagué also sought to align the SMATA with the *legalistas* and the Independents, to counter the disrepute into which *torrismo* had fallen since the time of the 1970 strike. The widespread belief that Torres had betrayed the workers in that strike had tainted the entire leadership. Bagué's decision to participate in the March 1971 mobilizations that culminated in the *viborazo* was intended to repair the damage that had been done to the leadership by the vacillations and eventual resignation of Torres in days preceding that uprising and indicated an early awareness of the leaders' vulnerability. The rise of the MRS only confirmed such beliefs. Thus the SMATA became a regular fixture at CGT assemblies and generally supported the *legalista*-Independent positions against those of the *ortodoxos*. Finally, in desperation, Bagué also abandoned the Córdoba SMATA's historic pretensions to independence and sought help from the SMATA central.

The powers in Buenos Aires, Dirk Kloosterman and José Rodríguez, the presidents, respectively, of the SMATA central and the Buenos Aires SMATA, recognized the potential threat of an MRS victory in Córdoba, not only to Bagué and the Cordoban Peronists but also to themselves. The generally tranquil labor-management relations that had characterized the first decade of the Buenos Aires–based firms ended in the early 1970s with a series of mobilizations, including a prolonged and bitter strike in the Citroën plants in 1971.[22] A victory of the MRS might encourage shop floor militants in the Buenos Aires plants to capitalize on worker discontent and mount union challenges of their own. To support Bagué, the SMATA national undertook a national publicity campaign in late 1971 to support Peronist leadership in the automobile workers' union. Under the motto ¡*Violencia no, justicia sí* the SMATA attacked *clasismo* and attempted to link the growing political violence in the country with a subversive left, a left that it intimated was working on many levels of Argentine society, including from within the ranks of labor. SITRAC-SITRAM were especially singled out for their supposed brinksmanship and irresponsibility, their having engaged in *"gimnasia subversiva,"* as the Peronist labor hierarchy thenceforth would deprecatingly refer to any sign of worker militancy independent of its control. The real targets of the campaign, however, were not the defunct Fiat *clasista* unions but the MRS and other shop floor movements that were threatening Peronist control of the autoworkers' union, as well as the traditional pretension of the Cordoban unions to leadership of the national labor movement.[23]

In fact the SMATA central had already, unwittingly, done much to make a union recovery movement possible in Córdoba. The ability of the *clasistas* to mount a serious challenge to Peronist control of the union was largely due to the 1968 SMATA reforms that, under pressure from Córdoba, had greatly decentralized the union's structure. Among those reforms were more circumscribed powers for the SMATA central in disciplining union branches, greater powers for the union locals to appeal any such disciplinary action, and, most important, broad financial decentralization that gave locals almost complete control of union funds.[24] Thus, despite the admonitions and veiled threats from the SMATA central to the shop floor dissidents, in Córdoba and elsewhere the members of the MRS understood the restrictions that Buenos Aires was now under. The *clasistas* knew that, should they come to power, the SMATA central would be hampered in its dealings with Córdoba and unable, at least legally, to impose its wishes. Union power offered real possibilities for autonomous administration of Cordoban SMATA affairs and the chance to implement a reform program that would strengthen rank-and-file support and make an important advance for *clasismo*. The success of the opposition campaign against Bagué and the sense that the MRS members had of widespread worker discontent with the leadership encouraged the SMATA dissidents in late January 1972 to form a union slate, the *lista marrón,* to run against the *torrista* slate, the *verde y celeste,* in the upcoming April union elections.[25] Shortly thereafter the *lista marrón* presented its electoral platform, a proposed series of union reforms with a deliberately apolitical tone, in which the word *clasista* did not appear.[26]

The city's combative unions received news of the rebirth of left-wing opposition in the local automobile industry with some suspicion. The discordant relations between them and the Fiat *clasistas* and the bilious criticisms local labor leaders had occasionally been subjected to from SITRAC-SITRAM had made them wary of what they perceived as the ideological purism and maximalist tactics inherent in *clasismo*. For the Fiat *clasista* activists, their union rebellion had meant a vigorous defense of the Fiat workers' interests and eventually a commitment to a specific political program; it had not been caprice or conceit. The *clasistas* considered themselves to be the genuine realists in Córdoba's labor movement, the only ones who realized that immediate work-related gains would be ephemeral and militancy so much wasted effort unless the working class had a socialist project as its final purpose. Nevertheless, given the unusual configuration of the local labor movement, there is no doubt that Fiat *clasismo* had damaged the cause of the local labor movement at particular conjunctures, and there was an understandable wariness toward the MRS and the *lista marrón*. The perception was widespread among the *legalistas* and Independents that the victory of the *lista marrón* in the SMATA might again disrupt positive developments that were taking place in the Cordoban labor movement.

Atilio López and the *legalistas'* suspicions of the SMATA Marxist opposition were certainly influenced by the changing political fortunes of the Peronist movement. Since announcing the proposed transition to civilian rule under the Gran Acuerdo Nacional, Lanusse had been besieged by a wave of guerrilla violence that prompted the military's hastened exit from power and favored a full restoration of democratic rights, including a lifting of the proscription of the Peronist movement. The source of this violence came partly from the Marxist left, from the Ejército Revolucionario del Pueblo and the Fuerzas Armadas de Liberación, but also now from the Peronist left, the *formaciones especiales* that were awarded an increasingly important position within the movement by Perón.

The changes within Peronism were not solely of Perón's choosing. The Peronist left erupted as a force in Argentine revolutionary politics in 1970, independent of the *caudillo,* with the Montoneros' kidnapping and execution of former military president General Pedro Aramburu. However, it had been germinating since the time of the Resistance and had never been completely subservient to the exiled leader. To maintain the discipline of his movement, and to further his own political ends, Perón chose not to repudiate their tactics but to pose as the guerrillas' champion. He increasingly employed the political vocabulary of the hoary revolutionary and implicitly accepted his youthful followers' attacks against José Rucci, Lorenzo Miguel, and the *"burocracia sindical."* Perón's words were exhilarating for the *legalistas,* who were interested in seeing the power of the labor bosses curbed and developing ideologically left-wing positions but were unwilling to break with their Peronist identity or affiliate with a left-wing Marxist party. In March 1972 they received more encouragement when Perón announced his movement's formation of an electoral front, the Frente Justicialista de Liberación (FREJULI), thereby frustrating Lanusse's hopes for a limited democratic restoration and for his own candidacy in the 1973 presidential elections.

The leftward shift of the Peronist movement profoundly affected the subsequent history of Cordoban labor. It committed the *legalistas* and their Independent allies to supporting—the *legalistas* enthusiastically and the Independents cautiously—a democratic restoration in which the Peronist movement would inevitably occupy a prominent position. It also made immediate cooperation with the SMATA Marxists unlikely. *Clasista* critiques of Peronist trade unionism lost their force with signs that Peronism was moving toward more left-wing positions, a political evolution that many on the left believed would make it more of a factor for revolutionary change than any of the small Marxist parties that promoted *clasismo.*

Once again Tosco held the key to which way labor would turn. Though under no illusions about Perón's real intentions and skeptical of the Peronist left's ability to transform the movement into a genuinely revolutionary party, Tosco assessed the immediate political circumstances in cold, unromantic terms. The future of an alternative labor movement and the democratization of the country's unions depended on the preservation of the *legalista*-Independent alliance. The strength of that alliance had been proved in the January 15 and 16, 1972, congress of the Agrupaciones Peronistas Combativas, a national gathering of dissident Peronist unions presided over by López and the Cordoban *legalistas* that had elected the non-Peronist Tosco as its honorary president, a decision lambasted by Rucci and the CGT as a betrayal of Peronist labor. Tosco knew that the well-being of this ecumenical spirit on the part of the combative Peronist unions depended on maintaining a certain distance from *clasismo*. As had been the case with the Fiat *clasistas,* Tosco preferred to trust his erstwhile *legalista* allies rather than the as yet little-known SMATA Marxists.

Tosco's imprisonment prevented him from seeing signs that were already nonetheless apparent that cooperation between the Peronist and non-Peronist sectors of Cordoban labor might not be as possible to maintain as he believed. The ongoing crisis in the local metalworking industry and the early 1972 bankruptcy of the Del Carlo factory, a manufacturer of seat frames for IKA-Renault and the Cordoban UOM's largest single source of union members, indicated that Simó would have to rely increasingly on Rucci, Miguel, and the CGT central to maintain the UOM's influence in the local labor movement and any future role for himself within the Peronist movement. The UOM needed to recover jurisdiction over the Fiat workers, or it would sink to the level of a middling union in the local labor movement.[27] In addition, despite the local CGT's drafting of a new *plan de lucha* and the general strikes it held on April 7 and April 28 to demand Tosco's release from prison, there were other reasons for concern. Perón was already meddling in Córdoba, attempting to restrain the alliance between the Peronist and non-Peronist unions in the city. His tolerance and even encouragement of the Peronist left did not mean he was prepared to accept a potential loss of control over the unions. Since Córdoba was the most visible and real threat to a verticalist, Peronist CGT, the city's maverick labor movement became an issue of concern. In late April Perón received a delegation of local *ortodoxo* unions who brought complaints of a Marxist infiltration of Cordoban labor and generally encouraged the unification of the Cordoban Peronists and the isolation of the *clasistas* and Tosco's unions.[28]

Perón's and the *ortodoxos'* fears had been heightened that same month by two events: the April 9 Cordoban CGT elections and the victory of the *lista marrón* in the April 26 through 28 SMATA elections. The CGT elections demonstrated once again the exceptional character of the local labor movement. The *legalistas* and Independents strengthened their alliance and elected López and Tosco the secretary general and adjunct secretary, respectively, giving the two combative sectors of Cordoban labor an unassailable position in the local CGT's executive committee.[29] The election of the SMATA Marxists several weeks later reaffirmed that the Cordoban labor movement was acquiring a configuration that served the purposes of neither Lanusse nor Perón. The Peronist-controlled SMATA central had done everything in its power to discredit the Marxist union slate, and Kloosterman especially had intensified the publicity campaign against the *clasista* militants, attacking everything from their youthful inexperience to their grandstanding *(tremendismo)* and the divisive threat they supposedly represented for the country's labor movement.[30] Despite such intimidations, the *lista marrón* upset the Peronist slate in an electoral victory of 3,089 votes to 2,804, a stunning turn-around for the left, which had maintained a presence in the SMATA factories through the long years of *torrismo* but had never before come close to regaining control of the union it had lost in the late 1950s.[31]

For the first several months of their leadership, the SMATA *clasistas* concentrated on problems in the plants and played a minimal role in local labor politics. Problems with production rhythms, working conditions, and layoffs in the plants occupied nearly all their attention. They gave some early signs of wishing for better relations with the *legalista* and Independent unions than the Fiat *clasistas* had experienced. The union's new secretary general, thirty-one-year-old Renée Salamanca, had publicly chided his own party, the PCR, for claiming credit for the *lista marrón* victory and expressed the SMATA leadership's intention to follow a nonsectarian policy in administering and to cooperate with all the "progressive" sectors of Cordoban labor.[32] Nevertheless the SMATA *clasistas* responded coolly to an invitation from the CGT several weeks later to participate in a fourteen-hour general strike to commemorate the Cordobazo, stating they were unwilling to engage in a strictly political strike, though they did respect the SMATA workers' vote to support the strike.[33]

Rather than involve the union excessively in Cordoban labor politics, the SMATA *clasistas* began a long campaign over the Argentine winter months to address the many workplace grievances that had been accumulating since Renault's takeover of IKA. As the Fiat *clasistas* had done, the SMATA leadership chose the hazardous working conditions in the company forge as an early issue on which to confront management's authority on the shop floor. In early August, the union brought in a team of medical experts to observe and document working conditions in the plants. On August 20, Salamanca held a press conference to present the medical team's findings of unsatisfactory working conditions in both the forge and the painting tunnels and to announce the union's intentions to undertake the laborious task of preparing detailed reports on working conditions in each of the SMATA-affiliated plants.[34]

What little time the new leadership could spare away from problems in the plants was not devoted to local CGT affairs but to the still unresolved question of the Fiat *clasista* movement and SITRAC-SITRAM. Fiat management continued its intimidation campaign in Ferreyra. The systematic firing of suspected union sympathizers, the shuffling of workers from department to department, increased production rhythms, and a return to tight factory discipline all indicated the Italian company was determined to reassert absolute control over the shop floor. The SITRAC-SITRAM *clasista* activists, many of whom were in hiding and others still in prison, resumed their propaganda work as unrest mounted in Ferreyra.[35]

Nevertheless even the most determined within their ranks recognized the hopelessness of resuscitating SITRAC-SITRAM. With the victory of the *lista marrón,* resistance and the future of *clasismo* seemed most promising through an affiliation with the SMATA. From Rawson Prison, former shop steward Gregorio Flores expressed the general belief of the imprisoned union leadership that the demise of the Fiat unions was a fait accompli and urged that a grassroots movement be organized to force the company to accept a SMATA affiliation.[36] Several days later, from his own jail cell in Rawson, Alfredo Curutchet expressed a similar opinion and stressed that affiliation with the SMATA was an absolute necessity, given the imminent collective bargaining negotiations. The lack of effective union representation in these talks, he suggested, would be disastrous for the Fiat workers and would leave the door open for a UOM affiliation.[37]

Simó and the UOM, in fact, had already begun their campaign to recover the workers they had only begrudgingly given up in the mid-1960s. Within weeks of the dissolution of SITRAC-SITRAM, UOM men were found distributing affiliation cards at the factory gates, a fact that drew bitter criticism from the SITRAC leadership.[38] With the Cordoban UOM hemorrhaging and his own political future at stake, Simó eagerly jumped at the prospect of adding several thousand new members in the city's second most important industrial complex to his union's thinning ranks. He could now count on the full support of Rucci and the Peronist labor hierarchy in his cause. With the election of the predominantly Marxist union slate in the SMATA, the prospect of the Cordoban automobile workers being united in a single union behind a *clasista* leadership was unacceptable to Peronist labor. Support from Fiat and Buenos Aires allowed Simó to move quickly, and by July a UOM committee *(comisión provisoria)* was already operating in the Materfer plant.[39] Simó's fitful alliance of convenience with the combative sectors of Cordoban labor was irrevocably ruptured with the Fiat affiliation controversy, and he returned to the fold of mainstream Peronist trade unionism. Thenceforth Simó and the Cordoban UOM would be the most faithful lieutenants of Rucci, Miguel, Perón, and *verticalismo* in the city.

Salamanca and the new SMATA executive committee agreed to resist the UOM's plans and to support the affiliation of the Fiat workers, despite the widespread misgivings from the SITRAC-SITRAM experience that existed in their ranks. Salamanca's own party, the PCR, was an especially outspoken critic of Fiat *clasismo*. The PCR had long depicted the Fiat workers' rebellion as a well-meaning and honest rank-and-file movement that had been marred by its political ingenuousness and "isolationism," specifically by its supposed refusal to cooperate with the progressive elements of Cordoban labor in the local CGT.[40]

In reality, the criticisms of the Fiat unions derived from two very different conceptions of *clasismo*. The PCR, the VC, and other parties that made up the SMATA leadership had bristled at accusations hurled at them by the Fiat unions that the formation of *comisiones obreras* and *agrupaciones sindicales* constituted examples of a neo-Bolshevik opportunism that threatened the workers with manipulation by the left-wing parties. The SMATA *clasistas* countered that the Fiat unions had a "Trotskyist" aversion to organization and political discipline that had cost them their opportunity to lead an alternative workers' movement.[41] The SMATA *clasistas* were certainly politically a much more disciplined group than the Fiat union leaders. The MRS was the product of individuals who had served long political apprenticeships in their respective parties. The SMATA *clasista* movement included many hardened party militants, the representatives of organizations that had been engaged in painstaking shop floor work over a period of several years. They were also in a much larger union, a union that had a long history of militancy and that enjoyed a great sense of legitimacy among the rank and file. The union machinery and established procedures therefore had to be respected to a considerable extent, and a certain professional union style had to be maintained, which caused a small group of Fiat *clasistas* to regard them rashly and mistakenly as just another group of union bureaucrats and to oppose affiliation.[42]

The principal difference between the Fiat and SMATA *clasistas* was rooted in their the conception of the limits and purposes of *clasismo*. The SMATA *clasistas* envisaged the dissident workers' movement as part of a broader scheme of political participation for the working class, but also to a certain extent as subordinate to the party apparatus. SMATA *clasismo*'s party orientation was no doubt influenced by the the PCR's roots in the Communist party. Both parties were highly centralized and hierarchical. Central committee directives were expected to be carried out uncritically, and not only by their paid party functionaries but also by their working class members. Salamanca's stormy relationship with his party, already apparent from the time of the 1972 election, was essentially due to his independence and the disregard he often showed for the PCR's apparatus and party procedures.

The differences between Fiat and SMATA *clasismo* were also the result of historical circumstance. SMATA *clasismo* emerged in a political context very different from the Fiat movement's. Union dissidents no longer faced a military dictatorship but an impending democratic restoration, which appeared to offer new opportunities for the country's left-wing parties. The PCR and other left-wing organizations represented in the SMATA were jockeying for political position, which caused them to temper their behavior in the union.

Despite their differences, the overwhelming majority of the Fiat *clasistas* put aside their differences and urged affiliation with the SMATA. For most of the SITRAC-SITRAM loyalists, with the possibility of recovering their unions gone, only affiliation in SMATA promised competent union representation and protection of the gains already made. The Fiat *clasistas* sought to extend an olive branch to the SMATA and dropped the controversial slogan, *"¡Ni golpe, ni elección, revolución!"* from their union communiqués and fliers because it was needlessly provocative and obviously inappropriate in the very different political circumstances of early 1972. Similarly, in their public statements they sought to emphasize that *clasismo* was a commitment to honest leadership, union democracy, and generally progressive politics rather than an immediate identification with any revolutionary socialist project.[43] The Fiat leaders characterized the new SMATA leadership as honest and democratic if not yet *clasista,* and held that affiliation would not only safeguard the interest of the Fiat workers but would also have a positive influence in the SMATA and help to define its own *clasista* identity. Nevertheless the discord between the two concepts of *clasismo* remained latent and lurked behind the affiliation campaign. In an August ceremony held in the SMATA's downtown headquarters to welcome the recently released SITRAC-SITRAM prisoners, Carlos Masera expressed the continued interest of the Fiat workers in a SMATA affiliation but also some dissatisfaction with the handling of the problem by the union leadership, failures he diplomatically attributed more to a lack of experience than bad faith. But the gathering generally marked a serious setback for the cause of a united Cordoban autoworkers' union. Criticisms from the Fiat ranks of the SMATA's membership in the local CGT were voiced, and Salamanca remained evasive on the Fiat affiliation issue while emphasizing the SMATA's commitment to cultivating amicable relations with the other, non-*clasista* unions in the Cordoban CGT.[44]

The Fiat workers nonetheless threw themselves into the affiliation campaign with abandon in these months. SMATA affiliation cards were distributed at the factory gates and through fellow workers in the Fiat plants. The SITRAC-SITRAM activists ably resisted a UOM affiliation that enjoyed the blessing of the company, and they warned of phony union communiqués that were really the work of the UOM or Fiat and were meant to sow confusion in their ranks.[45] Though considerable progress was made, there were also signs of exhaustion by late in the year.

The position of Salamanca and the SMATA executive committee remained clear: an overwhelming show of support in favor of affiliation was necessary to convince the Ministry of Labor of the justness of the SMATA's jurisdiction. At an October 1972 assembly to discuss the status of the affiliation drive, Salamanca warned that time was running out and more signatures were needed to overcome the opposition of Fiat and the government. The position of Masera and other Fiat *clasistas,* on the other hand, was that although more than 1,200 affiliation cards had been filled out, the obstacles to further canvassing work by the leadership were insurmountable, that progress depended on what the workers themselves were capable of in the plants.[46] The Fiat workers, in turn, found that a vigilant management obstructed their efforts; they appealed to the Cordoban CGT for help. Indeed there was little chance of overcoming the combined powers of the government, Fiat, and the UOM without support from the other Córdoba unions.[47]

Political antipathies lingered among the unions; and the CGT had remained silent on the Fiat issue. Future support became possible, however, after Salamanca moved the SMATA closer to an alignment with the other Córdoba unions, showing a political realism that had been sadly lacking in Fiat *clasismo.* In the August labor mobilizations called by the CGT to demand Tosco's release from prison, the SMATA had played a prominent role. On August 22 the SMATA leadership, accompanied by several perhaps contrite former SITRAC-SITRAM leaders, had made an unexpected appearance at a CGT emergency session and pledged support for any strike action intended to secure Tosco's freedom.[48] The general strikes of August 26 and September 7 had the backing of all the Independent unions and the majority of the *legalista* unions, but it was the participation of the SMATA that had turned the strikes into major labor protests. Any sign of labor unrest in Córdoba was now received nervously by the government, and it had responded by assuming control of the local CGT and issuing warrants of arrest for the principal organizers of the strikes, among them López and Salamanca.[49] But the government, unnerved by promises of further labor violence from the *legalista*-Independent unions and the SMATA, had quickly relented and on September 22 had announced its intention to release Tosco.

Tosco arrived to cheering throngs of workers and students at Córdoba's airport on September 26. Beyond the immediate drama of the event, it marked a turning point in the history of the dissident Cordoban labor movement. Tosco returned to Córdoba a revolutionary. As it was for many labor activists who passed through Argentine jails in these years, prison had been a deeply politicizing experience for him. In prison, Tosco's prestige as the dissident labor movement's most important national figure had drawn him into many political discussions with members of the guerrilla left in both Villa Devoto and Rawson. His opposition to armed struggle as a legitimate political option in Argentina did not prevent him from building strong friendships and gaining respect for what he saw as the mistaken but idealistic *guerrilleros,* with whom he shared certain common enemies. But it had been precisely to avoid any association between the dissident labor movement and the guerrilla left that Tosco had refused to accompany the ERP, Fuerzas Armadas Revolucionarios, and Montonero militants in their planned escape from Rawson Prison, which ended tragically with the capture and execution in nearby Trelew of sixteen of the escapees on August 22. The "Trelew massacre" was a national scandal and political controversy, and it was in fact one of the precipitants of the Córdoba CGT's August 26 general strike, but it was also a personal trauma for Tosco. After Trelew, the light and power union leader increasingly saw no middle ground and felt that Argentina was on the verge of a decisive confrontation between the left and the right. In his homecoming speech he made what amounted to a virtual declaration of war against Rucci and the labor bureaucracy and announced his pledge to promote and protect the alternative labor movement centered in Córdoba.[50]

Tosco had a new ally waiting for him in Córdoba. Political necessity and personal empathy would make Tosco and Salamanca close collaborators over the next several years as they sought to build a new political program for the workers' movement. For Tosco, as for most of the labor leaders in the city, Salamanca was an enigma, a man who had risen from obscurity to the leadership of the city's most important union virtually overnight.

Salamanca's dusky complexion and vaguely Indian features hinted at his origins as country boy turned proletarian and Marxist militant. His career as a labor activist had begun in the 1960s when he unsuccessfully ran for shop steward of his small metal workshop against the official Simó slate. Predictably, he lost the election and, sometime later, his job. His ties to the PCR were established in those same years, and shortly after the Cordobazo, he entered the highly skilled die shop of the IKA-Renault forge as a party activist. He was one of many PCR militants who sought to find employment in the more skilled SMATA-affiliated factories as part of the party's strategy of inserting itself into the local labor movement.

Though he quickly joined the anti-*torrista grupo 1º de mayo,* Salamanca did not assume an open involvement in union affairs until 1970, when he successfully defeated Torres's candidate for a shop steward position. The union refused to recognize his election on the grounds that he had not yet been a member for one year, which SMATA bylaws required for holders of union offices. In 1971 he ran again for the relatively minor office of *subdelegado,* and this time his election was recognized by the union. Salamanca was by now one of the leading figures of the MRS, and when MRS decided in early 1972 to challenge the *torrista* slate, he was a natural selection to head the politically pluralist *lista marrón.*[51]

The alliance between Tosco and Salamanca would become one of the cornerstones of the dissident Cordoban labor movement. The factor that complicated their efforts to build an alternative labor movement and that would continue to influence the dynamic of local labor politics was national politics. The prospects for the Córdoba unions depended largely on whether favorable political circumstances nationally would continue to protect them from Buenos Aires. In that regard the impending legalization and full participation of the Peronist movement in the March 1973 elections was a mixed blessing.

Within Peronism, the power struggle between the movement's left and right wings seemed to have been finally settled in favor of the former. Once elections were assured, the Peronist labor bosses staked their prestige on securing a majority of the candidates on the FREJULI ticket. The CGT and the 62 Organizaciones had spared no effort in criticizing the Peronist left, denigrating its members as the *"recién llegados,"* or upstarts, and the *"izquierda gorila y aristocrizante."* But for the moment, Perón's interests were best served by a continued courting of the Peronist left. The left-wing of the movement exerted the more effective pressure on the government for a full restoration of Peronism. Moreover, Perón's youthful cadres had political alternatives: potential allies in the form of the reinvigorated Marxist left, should the movement suddenly veer to the right.

The loyalty of Peronist labor was less problematic. The *vandorista* tendencies within labor remained strong, and many Peronist labor leaders, particularly in Buenos Aires, continued to seek dialogue with the conciliatory Lanusse and were reluctant to confront the government over political questions. Despite tough talk from labor leaders such as Miguel, Perón knew that those who were really willing to do battle in his behalf were in his youth wing. At the same time, no labor leader could appear to oppose Perón or a Peronist restoration and maintain his prestige among the Peronist rank and file.

Assured of labor's fealty and intent on maintaining the support of his left-wing, Perón formalized his favor in the FREJULI candidate selection. In consultation with Montonero and Juventud Peronista leaders, Perón chose candidates heavily weighted in favor of the movement's left. The selection of Hector Cámpora as the FREJULI presidential candidate was a major concession to the Peronist left and was followed by similar choices for other positions. A bitter struggle between the youth sector and the 62 Organizaciones over the governorship of Buenos Aires province, the former supporting Oscar Bidegain and the latter UOM leader Victorio Calabró, ended with Perón's selection of Bidegain. Left-wing candidates were subsequently favored over labor men among the movement's governorship candidates for all the major provinces. The reaction from labor was mixed. The more conservative *participacionista* unions, which for years had favored their relations with the state and captains of industry over Perón, refused to accept the ascendancy of the left. Union czars such as Roger Coria of the construction workers' union and the UOM's Manuel de Anchorena and Luis Guerrero resigned from the 62 Organizaciones, withdrew their support for the FREJULI. They were only the most outspoken of the labor leaders who called for a Peronist ticket purged of left-wing elements.[52]

Perón's immediate repudiation of such a ticket stripped it of any possibility of success and cautioned other labor leaders about undertaking similar actions. Rucci and Miguel, the UOM leaders who represented the sentiment of the majority of the Peronist labor bosses, counseled acceptance of Perón's orders and their "junior partner" status within the movement while they bided their time. Perón's return to caustic verbal attacks against the labor bureaucracy during the election campaign influenced this decision. So too did the appearance of *clasista* union challenges in a number of union strongholds, including Rucci's own UOM local representing the Sociedad Mixta Siderúrgica Argentina (SOMISA) steelworkers in San Nicolás, where a majority of the 6,700 workers had voted to withdraw from the UOM in repudiation of its conservative leadership.[53] The Paraná industrial belt, especially, was beginning to loom as a dangerous center of opposition to the established powers within the labor movement, second only to Córdoba. The efforts of Marxist and Peronist left activists had mobilized the workers in the metalworking factories there against their established union leaderships and threatened a virtual rebellion of the industrial unions of the interior against Buenos Aires. With such a lack of discipline within its own ranks, Peronist labor could not hope to confront the movement's left-wing for control and had no choice but to accept the battle as lost.

The immediate significance for Córdoba of the power struggle within Peronism was that it strengthened the position of that faction of Peronist labor most closely allied with *"la tendencia,"* or the Peronist left, the *legalistas,* and thus temporarily favored the dissident labor movement there. Córdoba was the only province where the youth sector had prevailed completely and denied the labor bureaucracy an electoral slot for the vice governorship. Rucci and Miguel had initially urged that Simó be placed on the FREJULI ticket as the candidate for vice governor, as UOM candidates had been placed in many provinces, along with the JP-Montonero gubernatorial candidate, Ricardo Obregón Cano. However, the deal that had been cut elsewhere in the country was unnegotiable in Córdoba. In no other province did the Peronist left have the solid base of support in the local labor movement that it had in Córdoba; Obregón Cano had an opportunity not available to the other left-wing Peronist candidates in the upcoming elections. In Córdoba, the Peronist left's candidate could retain the majority of labor's support, and especially that of its most powerful unions, without accepting a representative of Rucci or Miguel on the ticket. The imposition of UOM men could be avoided thanks largely to the unusual configuration of the Cordoban labor movement. Obregón Cano and his youth sector supporters refused to accept Simó as a running mate and insisted instead on López, head of the *legalistas,* to represent Peronism's labor wing on the ticket, a decision that Rucci, Miguel, and the UOM were reluctantly forced to accept.[54]

López's selection displeased the *ortodoxos* and also disconcerted the Independents and the SMATA *clasistas.* For the *ortodoxos,* the candidacy seemed to rule out any possibility that they would recover the local CGT soon. In the weeks leading up to the December 19 nomination of the

Obregón Cano–López ticket, rumors were rife of an imminent move against the Cordoban CGT by Rucci. Such a move at this point, would have been more than a purely internal labor affair: it would have had enormous political consequences for the power struggle taking place within Peronism, perhaps even jeopardizing the elections themselves. Disciplining the maverick Cordoban CGT was therefore a great risk. The strength of the *legalistas* and Independents had been proven repeatedly, and now that formidable union bloc had been joined by the *clasista* SMATA. Any meddling in local labor affairs would elicit a reaction from these unions, perhaps leading to another massive labor protest, for which Córdoba now had a national reputation. Rucci and his *ortodoxo* allies argued for disciplining the Cordoban unions anyway, and Perón himself continued to show an interest in keeping his left-wing and labor sectors separate, but the political circumstances of the moment and the need to retain the support of his left wing prevented further action. Despite his displeasure with Cordoban labor Perón had no choice but to accept the López candidacy, though he counted on the countervailing influences of Simó's *ortodoxos* to leave open the possibility of a future purge of the Cordoban labor left.[55]

The outcome that had favored the Peronist left and the *legalistas* did not necessarily enhance the prospects of a Cordoban-led dissident labor movement. Tosco would subsequently lament the damage done by these political developments.[56] The nascent labor alliance between the *legalistas,* the Independents, and the SMATA would operate under severe restraints if the *legalistas* participated in the government; the *clasistas* remained intransigent in that regard. To give the working class a revolutionary role, it was believed necessary to adopt a revolutionary program, something that was all but impossible given the contradictions of Peronism and the FREJULI alliance. Tosco nonetheless insisted on maintaining the *legalista*-Independent axis as the cornerstone of alternative labor movement and on supporting the FREJULI ticket in Córdoba, while allowing for a certain distance from its national slate.

It was this insistence that sparked criticisms of Tosco from *clasista* groups and the Marxist left generally. Tosco was seen to be holding back the cause of *clasismo* and adopting "reformist" positions in his determination to uphold the alliance with the *legalistas.*[57] Tosco refused to back many *clasista* proposals that the Marxist left promoted to cultivate a revolutionary consciousness in the Cordoban working class. For example, many *clasistas* urged that citywide collective bargaining negotiations be established via a special committee of the CGT with representatives from all the city's unions. Such a committee, the *clasistas* believed, would enable the labor movement to present a united working class front to the employers, to protect the rank-and-file interests of the weaker unions, and to create a spirit of solidarity among the workers that would be the first step toward the formation of a *clasista* Cordoban CGT. Tosco saw such a proposal as impractical and politically rash and refused to support the idea, a position that drew bitter criticism from at least some *clasistas*.[58]

Tosco was not the only labor leader to oppose such ideas. For Salamanca and the SMATA executive committee, in positions of authority and responsible for running the affairs of the city's largest industrial union, the luxury of revolutionary theorizing gave way to the practical considerations of administering the autoworkers' union. The SMATA leadership was engaged at the moment in contract talks for the Transax and Ilasa workers, and ceding authority to a virtual Cordoban soviet was out of the question; their established labor alliances held precedence. In the final months of 1972, the SMATA *clasistas* showed an effectiveness and pragmatism, as well as a conciliatory spirit, that did not always characterize other supporters of *clasismo* in the city. Rather than expending energy in enervating and needless quarrels with the other Cordoban unions or in woolly, utopian projects for workers' assemblies, Salamanca and the SMATA *clasistas* put their efforts into uniting the city's automobile workers.

A federal court decision and a review by the Labor Ministry granting the UOM jurisdiction over the Fiat workers did not dissuade the SMATA. The UOM jurisdiction was dismissed by the SMATA as a politically inspired maneuver by the military government, in alliance with the labor bureaucracy and Fiat, to prevent the consolidation of *clasista* representation for the Cordoban automotive proletariat. In response, in early November SMATA activists began a three-day plebiscite at the Concord factory gates that produced an important victory for *clasismo:* 1,339 of the Fiat Concord workers voted for a SMATA affiliation and only 164 voted for the UOM.[59] Though the UOM rejected the results on a number of technicalities and refused to allow a planned plebiscite of the Materfer factory, the vote was a moral victory for the SMATA and one more sign that the city's left-wing unions held the initiative, that the mainstream Peronist labor movement could resist its advance only in alliance with the powers of the state.

In the Córdoba plants, however, the SMATA Peronists began to resist the *clasista* leadership of their union almost immediately upon the April

1972 SMATA union election defeat. The displeasure of Kloosterman, Rodríguez, and the other *porteño* leaders with the *clasistas* was aggravated by the Cordoban unionists' policy of supporting other dissident groups, many of them *clasista,* in the automobile industry. For example, after a big Peugeot strike in 1972, fired *clasista* union activists had come to Córdoba, where they had been warmly received by the SMATA leadership and had been offered the union hall for a press conference in which the Peronist leadership's handling of the strike was highly criticized. When the SMATA central had protested his harboring of their opposition, Salamanca had curtly replied that the union's actions were perfectly appropriate and that Córdoba would continue to offer its facilities to all political groups in the automobile industry.[60] Within the plants, the *torristas* had regrouped and were on the offensive by the time of the Fiat plebiscite. The *clasista* leadership was subjected to a mounting barrage of criticism from the Peronist shop stewards, who were a weakened but still formidable presence in the SMATA factories, particularly in the IKA-Renault plants, and who could distribute almost daily tirades against the *clasistas* among the workers.[61]

Local labor alliances prevented the attacks against the SMATA *clasistas* from going beyond insults and recriminations for the time being. Salamanca had increased the SMATA's participation in the local CGT, and he eventually received the backing of both the *legalistas* and the Independents in the SMATA's dispute with the UOM over the Fiat affiliation. He could reasonably count on the support of both in the event of more menacing forms of intimidation, whether from *clasismo*'s opponents in the Córdoba plants or from the SMATA headquarters in Buenos Aires.

Nevertheless the first signs of fissures in the frail alliance between the combative sectors of Cordoban labor appeared at the end of 1972. Political and ideological discord intervened, as it had in the past, to polarize diverse currents of the maverick trade union movement into opposed camps. The SMATA publicly criticized López's decision to accept a position on the FREJULI ticket and questioned Tosco's attempt to walk an ideological tightrope at such a crucial political juncture, to sacrifice a revolutionary project, once again, in favor of an alliance with the *legalistas.*[62]

Political differences were highlighted by Perón's return to Argentina on November 17, more than eighteen years after the overthrow of his government. It was an emotional event of enormous importance for the Peronist working class, a fact that the *clasistas* did not understand or at least underestimated. With the great wave of Peronist sentiment sweeping the country, the *clasistas* might have adopted a more fruitful position similar to Tosco's and supported the palatable Cordoban FREJULI ticket while maintaining a critical distance from Cámpora and the national FREJULI ticket. Yet their unwillingness to do so was understandable. Their suspicions of Perón's motives and of the ability of left-wing Peronists such as López to remain free of the compromising entanglements of the Peronist movement once they were in power were not groundless.

López's fealty to the Peronist movement became more demanding after he entered the political arena. His hasty and unsuccessful attempt to organize a Peronist labor congress, the Plenario Nacional de Gremios Peronistas para el Regreso del General Perón, was regarded as an unnecessary and unseemly concession to Rucci, the Peronist labor bosses, and their local *ortodoxo* allies. Even more troublesome was López's decision not to attend the Tosco-chaired third national congress of the communist-sponsored trade union alliance Intersindical in the Salon Verdi, the historic Buenos Aires meeting hall of the country's anarchist, socialist, and communist unions.[63] His absence warned that perhaps López's and the *legalistas'* sympathies for a pluralistic, anti-*verticalista* Cordoban labor movement were succumbing to pressures from Perón or were simply wilting in the midst of the Peronist euphoria surrounding their movement's return to power.

Political developments within the Peronist movement had allowed the left-wing Cordoban labor movement to flower in 1972, and by early 1973 political developments were conspiring against it. López resisted pressures to reform the Cordoban CGT, to purge its leadership of non-Peronist unions, but a rightward shift within Peronism, especially with regard to its labor wing, was already apparent. In early February Rucci arrived from Madrid, where Perón had returned after his brief visit to Argentina, with a recorded message from the *caudillo* for his working class followers. The Cordoban labor movement, and specifically Tosco, *"el dirigente de la triste figura,"* as he was derisively referred to by Perón, were singled out for special criticism, and *verticalismo* was defended.[64] Perón's words were ominous. Córdoba would be one of the first targets should Peronism reestablish its conservative priorities, and the *legalistas* would be hamstrung in any future confrontation between their movement and the city's left-wing unions. The *ortodoxos* could count on Perón's blessing, perhaps his active encouragement, in any purge of the dissident factions in Cordoban labor.[65]

The prospects for dissident groups, however, did not yet appear so grim when the electoral campaign got under way in late 1972. The country's fickle political culture had momentarily shifted sharply to the left, and a

234 · The Peronist Restoration

reaction in the other direction would succeed only if the circumstances changed suddenly, before the Cordoban unions could consolidate their position and move outside the city to unite the growing but dispersed and disorganized working class militancy that was appearing throughout the country, particularly in the interior. The dissident Cordoban unions needed time, time that depended, to a great extent, on which way Perón would turn.

· EIGHT ·

Peronists and Revolutionaries

In the tumult of national and local politics surrounding the Peronist restoration, Renée Salamanca and the left-wing union leaders in the SMATA continued to advance the principles of *clasista* unionism. Unlike the old-guard leftist SMATA activists, who were mainly members of the Partido Comunista, the majority of the *clasista* executive committee members and shop stewards aspired to more than just winning union elections against their Peronist rivals. The conquest of the union was regarded as the first step toward the development of a socialist project for the working class. The SMATA *clasistas* saw their movement as a continuation and a refinement of the ideas first put into practice by the Fiat unions, and Salamanca himself implicitly recognized the lineage to Fiat *clasismo* when he defined himself as a "neo-*clasista*."[1]

The shadow of SITRAC-SITRAM hung heavily over the *clasista* SMATA. Its achievements were a source of inspiration and its failures a sobering reminder of the vulnerability of any union that tried to balance effective union representation with a radical political project. The early successes of SITRAC-SITRAM and the open encouragement of the Fiat *clasistas* had been the decisive factors in consolidating the SMATA dissidents into the union recovery movement, the Movimiento de Recuperación Sindical; during the months of Fiat *clasismo,* Ferreyra had been their most fecund source of ideas and tactical advice. But admiration had turned to disillusionment, and the Fiat experience served as the SMATA *clasistas'* touchstone as they attempted to work out what for them would be a more constructive version of *clasismo.* If any single issue preoccupied the SMATA *clasistas,* it was the determination not to repeat what they saw as the fatal mistakes of their predecessors in the Fiat unions.

235

Among those perceived mistakes was political myopia in the form of maximalist tactics that had isolated SITRAC-SITRAM from other sectors of the labor movement. Another was the SMATA *clasistas'* belief that SITRAC-SITRAM had rushed its political work in the plants before the unions' workplace gains had been consolidated. Though this was not an altogether fair assessment of the actions of the Fiat *clasistas,* the perception nonetheless exercised a powerful influence on the decisions of the SMATA leaders. Their caution was also the result of their conviction that it would take many years of tutelage to wean the workers away from Peronism and inculcate a *clasista* consciousness. "The idea," said SMATA undersecretary Roque Romero, "was not to make the revolution right away but to recover the union for the left and then see what happened."[2] The SMATA *clasistas* were resolved not to hasten the political work and especially to avoid a politicization of the union recovery movement. They chose to concentrate on shop floor and work-related issues with an almost professional scrupulousness. This policy was also the product of their realistic assessment of the overwhelmingly Peronist loyalties of the rank and file and the sensitive political conditions that existed after the *clasistas'* electoral victory, with Peronism poised for a triumphant return to power.

However, if the SMATA *clasistas* showed a greater moderation in their handling of union affairs, it was also due to the absence, until relatively late, of a systematic management campaign to bust the union, such as the one Fiat had stealthily implemented against SITRAC-SITRAM. Unlike the Italian company, Renault had long been accustomed to union representation in both its French and Cordoban plants that was more than merely formal, and the company first sought a course of compromise with the new union leadership. Though the points of friction between the company and the union were many, a decidedly less tense atmosphere existed in Santa Isabel than in Ferreyra, and the victory of the predominantly Marxist slate in the 1972 SMATA elections did not unduly rattle the French executives, who were accustomed to communist leadership among their workers in France. Management believed that IKA-Renault's most serious problems were not the *clasistas* but the worsening crisis in the country's automobile industry and, especially, nationalistic economic policies.

The June 1971 automotive legislation passed under the Lanusse government, for example, had limited foreign companies' access to local credit and established higher domestic content requirements for manufactured products—policies that threatened IKA-Renault's very solvency. The company's problems were so severe that management had even explored the possibility of turning over a majority of its stock to Argentine shareholders—of undertaking an "Argentinization" of the company to insulate it from the effects of further nationalist measures.[3] In addition the greater expenses it incurred as a result of its location in Córdoba, calculated as leading to 2.5 percent higher prices on average over those of its Buenos Aires–based competitors as a result of transport costs and higher provincial taxes, persuaded IKA-Renault that its market position was declining. In the light of such problems, IKA-Renault actually welcomed the possibility of a Peronist government, anticipating that, despite some nationalist legislation and much nationalist rhetoric, the Peronists would nevertheless allow the auto companies to raise prices in accordance with any wage increases it granted. IKA-Renault was especially hopeful that it would be in a privileged position to gain access to Perón and perhaps to receive favored treatment, given the fact it was the heir to the original Kaiser investment, the only auto manufacturer established under Perón's first presidency.[4] Thus, with all of these issues to consider, the *clasista* victory initially appeared to be a relatively minor affair.

The SMATA *clasistas* took advantage of the company's momentary goodwill and its preoccupation with other problems to carry out the reforms promised in their 1972 electoral platform. As mentioned in the preceding chapter, the *lista marrón* slate had run a campaign that stressed above all else the establishment of a genuine union democracy. When the MRS first announced its plans to challenge the *torrista* leadership, honesty, not *clasismo,* had been its banner.[5] Once in power, the *clasistas* set about dismantling the legacy of *torrismo.* As was the case in many Cordoban unions that came under radical leadership in these years, democratic reform was as much a question of style as it was structural change. In the case of the Cordoban SMATA, union leaders expressed democratization by abandoning *torrismo*'s bureaucratic aloofness; making the union hall more accessible to workers; holding frequent open assemblies on the shop floor itself, to assure maximum worker participation; and especially by employing a tactic that Torres himself had successfully used in the first years of his leadership: cultivating loyalties in the departments through closer daily contacts with the executive committee, which heard complaints, took suggestions, and kept the rank and file informed through almost daily union broadsides.[6]

Some important reforms in the union machinery and practices were made. A participatory union democracy was encouraged by making the resolutions of the shop stewards' committee binding for the executive committee and by requiring that Labor Ministry election overseers be empowered to monitor electoral procedures instead of merely standing as ceremonial "observers." Access to union office was opened up by amending SMATA bylaws that required a minimum length of union membership to hold a shop steward's position (a measure also obviously intended to facilitate the entry of *clasista* activists into the union apparatus).[7]

The most important structural changes involved the executive committee itself. To prevent the formation of a labor bureaucracy removed from the workers and to enhance union accountability, the *clasistas* not only reduced the number of paid union officials but also made union salaries equivalent only to what the SMATA leaders received in their respective jobs in the plants.[8] The most significant reform along these lines was certainly the establishment of a rotating system for union officials. All members of the executive committee were required to serve three-month stints in rotation, to minimize the prolonged absences from the shop floor that had become notorious under the *torristas*.[9] The new leadership's resolve to remain in close contact with the rank and file, a principle that was also consonant with its long-range political goals, was evidenced when Salamanca himself returned to his job in the forge in early 1973.[10]

The union reforms not only represented a challenge to the old-guard *torrista* leadership and enhanced the *clasistas'* possibility of consolidating rank-and-file support, they also ultimately represented important changes on the shop floor. The balance of power in the SMATA plants was shifting, putting the union on more equal terms with management and making a return to the deliberative union style of Elpidio Torres increasingly unlikely. The *clasistas* challenged the company on many fronts. Union collective bargaining negotiations and a series of strikes in late 1972, culminating in an unprecedented open assembly ratification of the final agreement, forced IKA-Renault to reestablish the *sábado inglés,* thereby providing the *clasistas* with an enormously valuable prestige-building victory. The *clasistas'* successful campaign to include the company's administrative employees under union jurisdiction also shifted the balance of power in the plants and made successful, prolonged strikes more feasible in the future. In the event of such a strike, the company would no longer be able to hold out for weeks, perhaps months, relying on existing stock to carry on with business as usual, as it had in the great 1970 strike, for example. With both administrative employees and assembly line workers on strike, production and distribution would simply be paralyzed.[11]

The SMATA leadership sought to establish a workplace democracy and strengthen the union as the first step in its *clasista* project. Partido Comunista Revolucionario, Vanguardia Comunista, and other *clasista* activists initially avoided abstract discussions of class struggle and revolutionary praxis and concentrated on issues immediately relevant and intelligible to the workers. Honest leadership was such an issue, and the *clasistas* harped incessantly on the reputed corruption of the deposed *torrista* leadership. The *clasistas* frequently complained about the union's 150 million peso deficit, the union staff of thirty administrative employees who were presumed *torrista* cronies, the union's fleet of cars, and the state of near inoperativeness of the shop stewards' grievance committee (Comisión Interna de Reclamos), which was presented as a policy deliberately designed to facilitate Torres's deal-cutting style.[12] This soft-pedaling of the political tutelage of the workers caused some dissent within the *clasista* ranks. Groups such as the Núcleo de Activistas Clasistas and the Vanguardia Obrera Mecánica criticized the timorousness of the leadership and its hesitancy in undertaking deeper political work in the plants. Nevertheless the strategy of the executive committee was accepted by all the principal left-wing parties represented in the SMATA executive committee, and it explains much of how they were able to build such deep rank-and-file support in so unpropitious a political moment.[13]

Though politicization of the rank and file was postponed, the union could not avoid an involvement in politics altogether, and it was ultimately drawn into the political whirlwind preceding the March 11, 1973, elections. The Marxist left regarded the return of a Peronist government with displeasure; it was an unwelcome event with a counterrevolutionary intent. Most of the left-wing parties represented in SMATA *clasismo* staked out positions critical of the elections that ultimately had repercussions in the union. Salamanca's name and those of other *clasista* members of the SMATA executive committee and shop stewards' commission, for example, figured prominently in a flier distributed in the plants urging the workers to cast blank votes in the upcoming elections, an unusually impolitic move that drew choleric attacks from the *torrista* activists in the plants, who correctly saw it as an issue to exploit.[14] Salamanca's actions also caused dissent within the *clasista* ranks, as members from both the Peronismo de Base and the PC supported the Frente Justicialista de Liberación slate. The SMATA workers themselves ignored Salamanca's exhortations.

After the workers voted in open assembly to reject the executive committee's suggestion and to support the FREJULI ticket, the *clasistas* avoided future forays into the electoral campaign that might offend the Peronist sensibilities of the rank and file. As the FREJULI's inevitable victory drew nearer, the SMATA *clasistas* chose the role of sober union negotiators rather than electoral spoilers and again concentrated on workplace issues, resigned to a Peronist victory. Nevertheless it would not be the last time that the *clasistas* allowed their anti-Peronist sentiments to adversely affect their political judgment under restored Peronist rule.

Salamanca's abstention call had been costly in other ways. For Dirk Kloosterman, José Rodríguez, and the SMATA union central it was a welcome provocation, a chance to intensify a defamatory campaign that would grow even more scurrilous in the coming sixteen months.[15] However, the SMATA central's inability to use these tactics indiscriminately against the Cordoban leadership was demonstrated when representatives of the SMATA hierarchy attempted to distribute fliers critical of the *clasistas'* handling of the election issue to workers arriving at the plants. The workers reacted angrily, a scuffle ensued, and gunshots were fired by the bodyguards who accompanied the SMATA representatives. After word spread of the incident, the IKA-Renault workers abandoned the plants en masse to stage a rally to protest interference by the *porteños* in local union affairs.[16] Buenos Aires responded by declaring an inquiry into Salamanca and the *clasista* leadership and refusing SMATA-Córdoba permission to participate in the autoworkers' annual national convention.[17] But in truth Kloosterman and Rodríguez were not yet interested in a frontal assault against their dissident union local. In their long-standing rivalry with the UOM for control of the Peronist labor movement, the SMATA central leaders to a certain extent needed the *clasistas.* On January 19, 1973, the SMATA central announced a *plan de lucha* to contest the Labor Ministry's awarding jurisdiction of the Fiat workers to the UOM. Despite the outcome of the late-1972 Ferreyra plebiscites, the government had followed its previous October 25, 1972, decision on the Fiat Materfer workers with a January 1, 1973, decision assigning the Fiat Concord workers to the UOM. Its displeasure with the Cordoban *clasistas* notwithstanding, the SMATA central publicly pledged its support for the Cordoban SMATA against what was considered an inexcusable intrusion of the rival UOM into the autoworkers' rightful preserve.[18]

The immediate reasons for Buenos Aires's forceful rebuke of Salamanca's abstention call were essentially political. Kloosterman, Rodríguez, and the powers in the national union looked more favorably on the FREJULI ticket than did most other Peronist unions, because they saw a victory as likely to lead to a diminution in the power of its arch rival, the UOM. Sensing the new winds blowing within Peronism after the Cordobazo, the SMATA had changed the name of the union magazine from the homely *El Mecánico,* to the revolutionary sounding *Avance,* adopted a fulminating anti-imperialist discourse, and showed a certain sympathy for the Peronist left that was utterly absent in the UOM.[19] Buenos Aires's support for Córdoba in the Fiat affiliation controversy actually masked a power struggle between the autoworkers' union and the UOM for control of the 62 Organizaciones and ultimately the CGT. But since Kloosterman's and Rodríguez's support was based on self-interest, their reliability was taken for granted by the *clasistas;* it made little difference to the Cordoban local that a SMATA jurisdiction would serve the political interests of the labor bosses in their union. The *clasistas* were under no illusions about their ability to contest the UOM for control of the Fiat workers without support from Buenos Aires. For that reason, the union central's churlish behavior alarmed SMATA *clasistas.* It served to put them on guard of the political considerations involved in administering the most important union in the Argentine interior.

Salamanca and members of the SMATA *clasista* leadership suffered other consequences of the abstention call in the following months. The autoworkers' relations with the left-wing sectors of the Peronist movement were strained, and Salamanca himself was roundly jeered by the Montonero columns at a public demonstration held in the city center to commemorate the fourth anniversary of the Cordobazo.[20] To the Peronist left, particularly in Córdoba, it appeared that the movement's revolutionary wing had established its dominance within Peronism and that criticisms from the Marxist left were simply the envious carping of the outsider. On this particular occasion, Salamanca shared the platform with Tosco, López, and an honorary guest, Cuban president Osvaldo Dorticos. The presence of Dorticos, who had been invited by Hector Cámpora to attend the May 23 presidential inauguration and celebrate the renewal of diplomatic relations between Cuba and Argentina, was perhaps the most graphic testimony of the revolutionary spirit, the "culture of resistance" as José Aricó would later describe it, that then dominated the city. In the minds of most who attended the demonstration, that spirit had a Peronist and not a Marxist face. In such dramatic circumstances, the SMATA *clasistas* did indeed seem guilty of the kind of fussiness that had often characterized the Marxist left, which had been marginalized in Argentine political life for the past thirty years.

Nor was the *clasistas'* position helped by Tosco's temporizing. Though he had for the first time publicly declared himself a Marxist in a nationally televised debate with Rucci in February, Tosco was also making statements clearly intended to appeal to the Peronist left, championing the anti-imperialist struggle and speaking more of the "popular sectors" and not exclusively of the working class in the struggle for Argentine socialism.[21]

Tosco's endorsement of the Cordoban FREJULI ticket, and his statements that seemed to evidence a certain sympathy for the Peronist left's nationalist perspective as opposed to a class perspective, were perfectly consistent with his past behavior. Since the failure of the CGTA and especially since his release from prison, Tosco's overriding concern had been to maintain the integrity of the Cordoban labor alliance. Though Tosco's light and power workers' union was clearly associated with the left, a rigid adherence to ideology had never characterized his actions; a sectarian stance might have offended Peronists within Luz y Fuerza and in other combative unions and had always been carefully avoided. Yet Tosco's realpolitik had damaged his relations with the Fiat *clasistas* and was doing the same with the SMATA.

Political discussions among the SMATA *clasistas* focused on this lack of ideological clarity, on the significance of the Peronist restoration and the positions of the PC and labor leaders such as Tosco, who urged greater pragmatism. For the PCR and other "new left" parties represented in the SMATA leadership, the FREJULI alliance was simply a last-ditch attempt by the country's propertied classes to restore order and defuse the prerevolutionary conditions that had developed in the country since the Cordobazo. The actions of the guerrilla organizations and especially the revolutionary currents germinating within the labor movement presented Argentina's capitalist order with the most serious threat in its history. Peronism had subordinated the revolutionary potential of the Argentine working class to an ersatz anti-imperialist program once before, and it now had willing collaborators within the supposedly progressive sectors of the labor movement.[22]

Tosco's support of the FREJULI alliance, though it was confined to the Cordoban ticket, caused the left again to question the current he represented in the labor movement. What Tosco justified as political pragmatism smacked of naïveté and even opportunism to many of the young SMATA *clasistas*. New doubts arose concerning the compatibility of *clasismo* with the nonsectarian brand of left-wing unionism advocated by Tosco and the Independents. Charges of Tosco's "Guevarist" approach to the labor movement rang in party discussions, and the working relationship with the Independents that the *clasistas* had encouraged since late 1972 was questioned. Also questioned was whether unions in the service sector and the small-scale, light industries that comprised the Independents were capable of a genuine understanding of the ability of the working class to effect revolutionary change. There was a widespread belief that these unions had not known that sense of power that the members of large industrial unions had acquired, and thus they had an unfortunate propensity to fall for the multiclass, *"movimientista"* temptations of the Peronists. In short, the Independents' perceived lack of a strictly proletarian and revolutionary point of view persuaded some of the *clasistas* that it would be difficult to collaborate closely with Tosco's group.[23]

The SMATA *clasistas* did not go their own way as their predecessors in Ferreyra had, partly due to the changes unleashed by Cámpora's electoral victory on March 11. Despite the ambiguous nature of the FREJULI alliance, the end of military rule and the return of Peronism to power unleashed a radical wave in the country that indicated the government would have a limited ability to control the popular mobilizations and radical currents at work in Argentine society. This popular frenzy spanned Argentina geographically and socially. In Buenos Aires, the militant youth sector of the Peronist movement had gained a sense of its power and was apparently in a position to play an influential and perhaps dominant role in the new government, having won several cabinet positions, eight congressional seats, and a dominant position in the administration of the universities.[24] In the backward northeastern provinces, the steamy land of *yerba mate* and cotton plantations, agricultural workers rose in a powerful movement for stable tenancies and land reform. Using as their inspiration the Brazilian peasant leagues of the early 1960s, Marxist and Peronist-left activists and especially radical parish priests mobilized the agricultural workers of the region and occupied large landholdings in Corrientes, Formosa, Misiones, and Chaco in the weeks following the FREJULI victory.[25]

The most significant mobilizations in this highly urbanized and industrial country, however, were those of the working class. The factory occupations that spread after Cámpora's May 23 inauguration gave a certain credence to the arguments of those, like Tosco, who were unenthusiastic at the prospect of Peronist rule but felt that it nevertheless offered certain possibilities; it was, at any rate, the freely chosen government of the democratic majority and therefore could not be dismissed offhandedly by the left. In Córdoba, Cámpora's victory encouraged many unions to attempt to settle old scores with their employers. Atilio López's own Union Tranviarios Automotor used the victory of the FREJULI ticket and the election of López as vice governor as a signal to undertake strike action that had been postponed during the long years of military rule. As would be the case with much of the labor protest during the stormy months of the Cámpora presidency, the UTA strikes were prompted by specific workplace grievances but were really motivated by deeper, long-term concerns over the workers' vulnerability in a capitalist enterprise and the desire to somewhat redress the balance of power in relations between management and labor that had been heavily weighted in favor of the former since the time of the Onganía dictatorship.[26]

The Cordoban bus drivers, for example, had never been reconciled to the collapse of their cooperatives and the full reestablishment of private ownership in the city's public transportation system at the end of the 1960s. Their grievances with the twelve private companies that controlled the bus system were many: failure to invest in equipment, inadequate service, poor maintenance of the buses, dangerous working conditions for the night shift, and unheeded calls to provide protection for drivers assigned the more dangerous routes. Particularly resented was the *socios mulas,* which a number of companies practiced, in which they pressured rookie drivers to accept a small share of company stock that, in return for a paltry dividend check and bogus partner status, allowed the company to withdraw costly social benefits that had been won in previous collective bargaining agreements.[27] The bus drivers' strikes and their demands for a return of public ownership of the urban transport system initiated a bitter feud between the UTA and the provincial government on one side and the bus owners on the other that would reach a tragic conclusion a year later in the events of the Navarrazo.

The UTA strikes of May and June 1973 galvanized the Cordoban CGT and renewed its fighting spirit, which had been dormant since the nomination of López and during the months of the electoral campaign. Roberto Tapia, López's principal union lieutenant and his successor, resumed the UTA's participation in the CGT and strengthened ties with the city's non-Peronist unions. By late June, the Cordoban CGT was once again resting on the familiar triumvirate that had emerged in late 1972 but had appeared doomed with the Peronist restoration: the UTA-led *legalistas,* Tosco's Independents, and the *clasista* SMATA were all again participating regularly in the CGT's general assemblies and committees and were determining its policies. Tosco attempted to allay the fears of the SMATA leaders about his reformist political sympathies, even employing the once anathema word *clasista,* in his public statements.[28] More important, he proved his determination to protect the pluralist Cordoban labor movement from interference from Buenos Aires.

In June the CGT central prepared to reassert its control over the labor movement, to strengthen its position in the the power struggle taking place within the Peronist movement. Rucci announced the revocation of the executive committees of all the CGT locals, effective July 1, with new elections to be held on an as yet unspecified date. The principal target of Rucci's action was obviously Córdoba, and Tosco's response was unequivocal. The Cordoban CGT rejected the interference of the *"burocracia porteña"* in its affairs and not only refused to comply with the decision but also said it would actively resist its implementation.[29]

Outside of Córdoba, political changes at the national level contributed to the spread of a working class militancy that permitted Córdoba to remain defiant. Workers and shop floor activists, their confidence and sense of power buoyed by Cámpora's victory, undertook some 176 factory occupations in the first twenty days of the new government, to oust entrenched union leaderships.[30] These "antibureaucratic struggles" were not a utopian attempt to establish worker control of industry. Rather, they were dispersed and spontaneous rank-and-file movements to transform the relationship between business and organized labor that had developed under the recent military governments and had manifested itself at the workplace level. The wage increases and, to a certain extent, labor stability that had been gained by the Peronist labor bureaucracy in the years following Perón's fall, as a tradeoff for management's absolute control over the workplace and all questions related production, had led to atrophied shop stewards' organizations and a gradual loss of genuine union protection in the workplace. Thus shop floor conditions and effective union representation, "union democracy" as the latter would be frequently called, served as the catalyst for rank-and-file discontent. Challenges to management's unfettered control of production rhythms, job classifications, working conditions, and other work-related issues allowed workers such as those at the General Motors plant to bypass their union representatives, force concessions from management (in GM's case, to dismantle rationalization schemes and reduce production rhythms), and disrupt the structures of power and authority in the labor movement and in the workplace.[31]

The SMATA *clasistas* remained skeptical of the Peronist restoration, but it appeared that they could not simply ignore the events surrounding it. The sight of the strongholds of Peronist labor bosses coming under attack from their own rank and file, with workers raising issues similar to those pioneered by the Cordoban *clasista* movements and actually succeeding in winning control of a number of unions, was a change too significant to dismiss, it called for a less critical attitude toward Tosco's strategy. However, their initial suspicions were borne out after this first wave of working class unrest.

The momentary ascendancy of the Peronist left, the factory occupations and rank-and-file mutinies, could not hide the fact that the FREJULI alliance had drawn much of its legitimacy if not outright support from sectors of Argentine society that expected a restored Peronist government to end social and political strife in the country, not to foment it. The conservative priorities of the Peronist restoration soon reappeared. In June Cámpora's government passed the Pacto Social in an attempt to reestablish the government's authority and carry out Perón's plan for economic stability. The Pacto Social froze prices for all goods and services and received in return from labor a pledge to suspend collective bargaining for two years. Cámpora immediately granted the workers an across-the-board wage increase of 200 pesos, but he also wrangled an agreement from labor that thenceforth annual wage increases would depend on increases in productivity and would be negotiated in a centralized collective bargaining process, the Gran Paritaria Nacional.[32] For the highly paid SMATA workers, the 200 peso wage increase was far less significant than it was for the poorly remunerated sectors of the working class, but it was generally bad pottage for most of the labor movement—a lopsided agreement that forfeited union autonomy and collective bargaining rights in return for very little.

Even more ominously, Perón was denouncing the anarchy in the country and insinuating that the left was responsible for much of it. A massacre that took place at the Ezeiza Airport on June 20, 1973, when dozens of Perón's followers awaiting the *caudillo*'s arrival were killed and hundreds wounded, was placed squarely on the shoulders of the left, despite considerable evidence that right-wing sectors of the Peronist movement were most likely responsible.[33] In mid-July, Perón withdrew his support from Cámpora and replaced him with provisional president Raúl Lastiri—a political cipher but the son-in-law of José López Rega, the former police officer and Rasputin-like adviser of Perón—giving a clear indication of a rightward shift in the Peronist government. Elections were scheduled for September, with Perón this time running as a candidate. The left's political alliances, despite the government shake-up, remained in a state of flux. Admonitions from Perón did not discourage the Peronist left, which doubted their authenticity and generally attributed them to López Rega. Nor did they affect the Marxist left, which was generally indifferent to Perón's political designs. In the labor movement, the struggle between the dissidents and the *verticalistas* was also far from decided.

Córdoba remained the crucible of the dissident trade union movement. The first showdown took place over the lingering Fiat affiliation issue. The Cordoban UOM had responded testily to the SMATA's continued claims to the Fiat workers and its recent occupations of the Concord and Materfer plants, calling it a conspiracy of *"gorilas y trotskistas"* and refusing to allow another plebiscite in Ferreyra.[34] In the months of Cámpora's and Lastiri's government, the Fiat affiliation controversy gained new significance for the warring factions within organized labor. For the SMATA *clasistas* and the left-wing labor movement in general in Córdoba, unification of the Cordoban automobile workers would ensure a powerful resistance against pressures from the *porteño* labor bureaucracy and would promote a pluralist and combative labor movement nationally. But it was equally important for Perón and Rucci to keep that from happening. Upholding the UOM's jurisdiction over Ferreyra—though it could not significantly affect the balance of power in the city, which was still weighted heavily in favor of the left—could at least keep it out of the hands of the *clasistas.* For that reason the Peronist governments of 1973, Cámpora's, Lastiri's, and finally Perón's, all refused to consider the Cordoban SMATA's appeals.

The situation was further complicated by the union central's actions. The rivalry between the SMATA and the UOM for control of the Peronist labor movement continued. It had reached a new level of rancor after the May 22 assassination of SMATA president Dirk Kloosterman, and some autoworkers suspected that the UOM was in some way involved.[35] Each union was now competing for Perón's blessing, a blessing that he would undoubtedly bestow on the strongest. The SMATA central's strained relations with its Cordoban local had kept it away from the Fiat affiliation drive, which resumed after Cámpora's election. Yet in the autoworkers' rivalry with the UOM, it remained in the SMATA's best interest to contest the metalworkers' jurisdiction over Ferreyra. Moreover, the national leadership could not withdraw its support for the Cordoban local without making an indecorous exit that would appear spiteful and leave it open to charges of the very autocratic abuses on which it currently based its challenge to the UOM. In resisting the UOM claim, it had stated on one occasion that "the SMATA is the only legitimate representative of the automobile workers in the country," and called several solidarity strikes in support of a SMATA affiliation for the Fiat workers.[36] Despite its displeasure with the *clasistas,* the local's decision to press the issue meant that the central would, at least for the moment, be forced to support Córdoba's claims.

Salamanca simply ignored the Ministry of Labor's awarding of the Fiat workers to the UOM and held a second referendum in late June. As they had in the previous election in November 1972, the Fiat workers showed an overwhelming preference for the SMATA: 1,502 for a SMATA affiliation and only 153 for the UOM in Concord; 652 and 44, respectively, in Materfer.[37] On July 11 Salamanca held a press conference and announced his union's intention to formally affiliate the Concord and Materfer Fiat plants and the small Perkins plant with the SMATA. The union's first goals, he stated, would be to improve working conditions in the Fiat forge and to extend the *sábado inglés* law and the SMATA job classifications and wage scales to them.[38] Two weeks later he announced that a shop stewards' commission in the plants would soon be formed.[39]

Resistance within the plants to Fiat's and the government's disregard for the referendum's outcome and to the continued UOM jurisdiction raged throughout August. On August 21 the Concord workers occupied the plant and demanded the SMATA affiliation. Workers in the Perkins plant and the other SMATA plants walked off the job in support.[40] The controversy now clearly pitted the Fiat workers, the Cordoban SMATA, and Tosco's Independents, the latter actively supporting the SMATA through solidarity strikes, against Rucci, the CGT central, the UOM, and the national government, with the Cordoban provincial government of Ricardo Obregón Cano and Atilio López in the middle. This battle, however, masked a deeper political struggle being conducted between the right and left nationally and especially in Córdoba. The Fiat Concord occupation ended three days later, after Obregón Cano and López interceded and won an agreement from Fiat to allow Salamanca to travel to Buenos Aires and discuss the union representation issue with labor minister Ricardo Otero.[41] Otero's promise to resolve the issue within ninety days was received with suspicion by the *clasista* leaders, who began preparations for additional strikes over the issue, which was far from resolved.

As the political atmosphere in the city rarefied, Kloosterman's successor, José Rodríguez, wrestled with a momentous decision. Support for Salamanca and the Cordoban local would strengthen his hand in future dealings with the UOM but would also make Córdoba a serious rival within the autoworkers' union and solidify a Marxist bloc in the heart of the Peronist labor movement. After Cámpora's sacking and the rightward shift of the government, such an outcome loomed as a liability to any future influence the SMATA might have in the government. For weeks Rodríguez stalled and hedged his bets, verbally supporting the local while, in effect, doing nothing to help it. But as the conservative nature of the Peronist government and its ostracism of the movement's left wing became more apparent, the central's language with regard to the Cordoban CGT grew frosty, then recriminatory. It cast doubts on the real intentions of the *clasistas* and withdrew its support for the Fiat affiliation, attacking the Cordoban leadership openly and accusing the local of passivity during the former military government's rule.[42]

The SMATA central's calumnies notwithstanding, no Argentine union had struggled against the military dictatorships more than the SMATA-Córdoba. Rodríguez's attacks revealed how the dynamic of labor politics in the city had changed with Cámpora's removal. Statements of support were belied by the SMATA central's immobility. The freedom that the Cordoban unions had enjoyed over recent months was ending. Pressures built on union centrals to get control of their rebellious locals all over the country, and Córdoba naturally received the greatest attention. In labor circles, the talk was increasingly of the perfidy of the *"bolches," "zurdos,"* and *"trotskos,"* and the begrudging tolerance of recent years turned into open hostility. While Juan José Taccone, Peronist president of the Buenos Aires branch of the light and power workers' union, berated Tosco and the Cordoban union for their independent ways, Rucci was moved to make wild accusations about fifth columns, alleging on one occasion that "the Cordoban workers' movement has been infected by elements that are in the service of the international Sinarchy whose true representative goes by the name of Agustín Tosco."[43] Perhaps most affected of all was López, caught between incompatible loyalties to the Peronist movement and to his local allies in the unions. From mid-July until his removal as vice governor in early 1973, López was under unremitting pressure to purge Cordoban labor of all its left-wing elements.[44]

Perón well knew that the success of the verticalist campaign depended on Córdoba. Reestablishing the CGT's central authority was necessary both to control the working class militancy spreading throughout the country and to ensure the success of the Pacto Social and the government's conservative economic program. Only Córdoba was capable of harnessing working class opposition to the program and fashioning it into a movement of national weight. The SMATA could be attacked through its union central, but that approach was less feasible in the case of the largely federal unions that made up the Independents. Tosco's light and power workers, at any rate, had been outcasts within the FATLYF for many years, and the union had much experience in working independently.

Tosco had abandoned any sort of working relationship with his central during the Onganía dictatorship. Since then, the FATLYF's decisions had carried little weight with the Cordoban local, unlike the situation in the SMATA local, which had remained very much a part of the national organization, despite the victory of the *clasista* slate in 1972. Mainstays in Tosco's left-wing labor alliance, such as Juan Malvár's print workers, also enjoyed virtual independence from Buenos Aires. Malvár was especially favored by the high degree of democratic decentralization in the print workers' union and the strong *ongarista* sentiment that lingered among the union leadership in Buenos Aires. It allowed him not only to adhere to the Independent alliance but also, later, to use the union hall as the clandestine meeting place for the dissident labor movement after the removal of the union leadership of Luz y Fuerza and the SMATA in 1974.[45] Such freedom characterized nearly all the Independent unions; they were organizations that had long been beyond the reach of *verticalismo*.

With Tosco's group immune to manipulations from meddlesome union centrals and the SMATA *clasistas* still strong enough to fend off Rodríguez's sorties, the *legalistas* were the weak link in the left-wing labor alliance that still dominated the Cordoban CGT. Thenceforth the policy of Perón and Labor Minister Otero was to exert greater pressure on Córdoba's combative Peronists to purge the Cordoban labor left. López himself, stiff-necked in his business suits and no match for the professional politicians in whose circles he now moved, had already succumbed to entreaties to cooperate with the *ortodoxo* unions in the 62 Organizaciones. During the Cámpora months he had been able to profess loyalty both to the Peronist movement and to his local labor allies. But in the vastly changed political climate that followed Cámpora's fall, that position was increasingly untenable. In early July López was still resisting *ortodoxo* demands that he withdraw the *legalistas* from the local CGT and form a parallel CGT comprised strictly of Peronist unions, while at the same time he was criticizing accusations of Cuban infiltration of the local labor movement and the red-baiting tactics that were intended to serve as a justification for a move against the Cordoban labor movement.[46] Still, in meetings with Perón and Rucci he had pledged to cooperate with the *ortodoxos* for Perón's candidacy in the September elections. The noose was tightening.

The turning point came at the national convention of the 62 Organizaciones, held in July at the UOM's vacation colony, Augusto Timoteo Vandor, in Villa Hermosa in the Cordoban mountains. Presided over by Lorenzo Miguel, president of the 62 Organizaciones, and Otero, it was largely an occasion to dress down López and the Cordoban delegation, to chide them for their past cooperation with the left-wing sectors of Cordoban labor, and to make veiled threats should the Cordoban Peronists fail to put their house in order. Otero lambasted Tosco, saying, "A union leader from this province has said Córdoba will be the capital of a socialist Argentina. We accept the challenge and say Córdoba will be the capital of a Peronist Argentina." López was forced to agree to a reunification of the warring camps in the Cordoban Peronist labor movement through a reunited 62 Organizaciones.[47] The *legalistas* were now in the position of sharing power with unions whose stated aim was the recovery of the Cordoban CGT for the Peronist labor movement and the purging of its refractory Independent and *clasista* members.

For the left-wing unions, López's decision was shattering. The Independents especially were incredulous at the vice governor's eleventh-hour capitulation, his readiness to bolt from the labor alliance, even if he had been under duress. Tosco responded to the news by warning, "Under no circumstances can this combative and revolutionary CGT ally with groups that just a short time ago were attacking their fellow workers," while Salamanca emphasized that the autoworkers' union would only cooperate in the CGT with those Peronist unions that supported ideological pluralism in Cordoban labor.[48]

For the *clasistas,* at least, the outcome of the Villa Hermosa convention was probably not unforeseen. With the SMATA acting as host, the PCR just days before had held in Córdoba its own national conference of *clasista* trade unionists and had openly defied Peronist labor by declaring one of the party's priorities to be the development of a *clasista* current within the UOM, urging an alliance with the sizable Peronismo de Base groups that already existed in at least the Cordoban metalworkers' union.[49] López's action was undoubtedly more traumatic for Tosco; his great hopes for an alternative labor movement based in Córdoba were suddenly dashed. When, days later, López sharply criticized his former comrades, saying that the unification of the 62 Organizaciones was a closed matter and that Tosco and Salamanca, at any rate, had no say in

Peronist affairs, it was clear that their close relationship was breaking down under the weight of the Peronist restoration. The countervailing pressures of commitment to the success of a Peronist government and loyalty to Perón had made the alliance impossible for López.

Tosco attempted to salvage the left-wing Cordoban labor movement by strengthening his ties with the *clasistas* and forming, along with Salamanca, the Movimiento Sindical Combativo (MSC).[50] The *clasista* leadership in the SMATA, and particularly Salamanca himself, would serve as Tosco's principal allies in the difficult coming months, and both sides preferred to ignore the ideological and political differences that had separated them in the past for the sake of resisting further advances of the Peronist right in Córdoba. In the full blush of the Peronist restoration, Tosco was thus once again emerging as the dominant figure in the country's dissident labor movement. He had badly underestimated the hold that Peronist loyalties exercised on his *legalista* allies and had himself more than once fallen victim to his own tactical and even ideological contradictions, as when he gave support to the ostensibly left-wing Peronist government in the province for the greater good, he had believed, of the Cordoban labor movement and ultimately of the Argentine left. But he had also been the first to perceive the vulnerability of the Cámpora government and the ascendancy of Peronism's right-wing sectors after the June massacre of the Montonero–Juventud Peronista columns at Ezeiza and with the promulgation of the Pacto Social, and now he had no hesitation in confronting Perón himself, if necessary, to protect Córdoba.

Within his own union, Tosco's initially conciliatory attitude toward the new Peronist government had caught the small coterie of opposition Peronists off guard and prevented them from capitalizing on the changed political circumstances. The May 1973 Luz y Fuerza elections were handily won by Tosco's slate, just as they had been, consistently, since 1958.[51] But the schism produced in the Cordoban labor movement after the Villa Hermosa conference, and Tosco's opposition to the Lastiri "caretaker" government in the weeks that followed—his repeated accusations that a *franquista* spirit animated the Peronist government and his increasingly harsh criticisms of the Pacto Social—bred unrest. A palpable unease within the union had been apparent since the Rucci debate and Tosco's public proclamation of his Marxist sympathies, which was considered by Sixto Ceballos and the more conservative Peronists in the union to have been an indiscreet admission that somehow placed all the Cordoban light and power workers in a non-Peronist posture. For the first time in the union's history, grumbling—of an albeit small but vocal minority—could be heard in the union hall. Ceballos' Peronists abandoned their critical support of Tosco's leadership and considered ways to challenge the *tosquistas'* seemingly unassailable position in Luz y Fuerza.[52] Perhaps not unexpectedly, the polarization of political life that was taking place throughout the country and especially in the Cordoban labor movement had finally appeared in Luz y Fuerza, and it was creating animosity where there had previously been friendly rivalry.[53]

Tosco and the union generally appeared unruffled by the small opposition group huddled around Ceballos as they moved toward an open confrontation with the government. The light and power workers' militancy, however, continued to be confined to the labor movement and was not directed politically toward the creation of a broad working class front independent of ties to any opposition party. In part this was due to Tosco's appreciation of the deep Peronist loyalties of the working class and its inability emotionally to oppose Perón's return to the presidency. It was also perhaps a final act of loyalty to the Partido Comunista. Tosco's fitful but close relationship with the PC had always had much to do with his desire to encourage political pluralism in Argentina and with the personal friendships he had developed over the years with some of the leading figures in the party. In the past he had often agreed with the PC's strategies and interpretations of Argentine politics. Though he never became a party member, and despite the fact that he had some important differences with the PC, its cautious policies often coincided with his own, notably its misgivings about *clasismo* and its opposition to armed struggle as a legitimate revolutionary strategy for the Argentine left.

In early August the principal new left party that supported a military strategy, the Partido Revolucionario de los Trabajadores, was the driving force behind the formation of the Frente Antiimperialista por el Socialismo. At an August 18 convention the Frente Antiimperialista nominated Tosco and the leader of Salta's *clasista* CGT, Armando Jaime, as an alternative, left-wing workers' ticket to run against Perón, in the hastily organized Partido Socialista de los Trabajadores (PST).[54] Tosco declined the nomination, certain of its imprudence and the baleful effects a political opposition to Perón would be likely to have on the dissident workers' movement. His analysis was also tempered by the unenthusiastic reception the idea received from the Alianza Popular Revolucionaria, a coalition of left-wing parties dominated by the PC that supported Perón's candidacy.[55] Tosco's path would later stray far from that of the PC, but he agreed with the party's pessimistic analysis of his candidacy and that of any political opposition to Perón. From the time of the September 23, 1973, election that restored Perón to the presidency until Perón's death less than a year later, Tosco would nevertheless be the principal working class foil to the conservative Peronist governments in power.

After his election Perón moved quickly against the insubordination in working class ranks as he sought, above all else, a unified labor movement that could neutralize the left and assure his government social peace. Perón used the recent coup in Chile as a reminder of the potentially disastrous consequences of unrestrained partisan politics and as a justification for the imposition of order. Shortly after his election, a spate of labor legislation was pushed through the congress with the intent of reestablishing an effective, centralized labor bureaucracy that would be able to punish transgressors and award the compliant with all the power the state could muster. The Ley de Seguridad banned factory occupations and virtually strikes while the Ley de Asociaciones Profesionales, extended the length of elected national union office from two to four years, thereby granting union centrals almost unlimited power to meddle in their locals as well as unilateral power to reverse decisions taken by independent factory committees and shop stewards' commissions.[56] Such measures were intended to restore the now rickety verticalist structure of the trade union movement to a position of strength. The legislation did strengthen the hand of the Peronist labor bureaucracy and made independent action, at least within the prescribed legal limits of the labor movement, exceedingly difficult. By fiat, Perón had reestablished a clear chain of command within organized labor and reduced shop floor activists and dissident union leaders to the status of virtual criminals.

The first targets of the government's campaign, predictably, were Tosco and the Cordoban light and power workers. The FATLYF's admonitions and votes of censure had been singularly ineffective in the past, but they were employed time and again in the final months of 1973 as the Cordoban union's criticisms of the government became more outspoken. At times the pressure coming from Buenos Aires was subtle. In early August for example, the FATLYF had sent a telegram to the local requesting that it nominate delegates to the local 62 Organizaciones to represent its Peronist members. This attempt to aggravate existing tensions and to hem in Luz y Fuerza by entangling it in local Peronist labor politics was not lost on Tosco, however, nor was it lost on the union, which voted against the request and sent back a caustic reply, an act which won it yet another vote of censure from the FATLYF.[57] Shortly thereafter the

FATLYF formally suspended the Cordoban local to emphasize its pariah status within the labor movement.

The salvos against Tosco and the Cordoban light and power workers were merely one component of Perón's campaign against the labor left. The attacks of the Peronist death squads and assassinations of labor militants did not attract widespread attention, but those of the Peronist labor bosses did. José Rucci's assassination on September 25, along with the murders of other Peronist labor bosses such as Augusto Vandor, José Alonso, Dirk Kloosterman, and Marcelino Mansilla, president of the Mar del Plata CGT, were used by the government to justify its heavy hand in dealing with the labor dissidents.

Though some of these assassinations were undoubtedly the result of power struggles within Peronist labor, most were perpetrated by leftist guerrilla organizations, often in unauthorized retribution for acts against the maverick Cordoban unions and the government's labor opposition. The guerrilla left took a characteristically condescending attitude toward the dissident labor movement, blithely assuming that political assassination would be approved by the workers and would help build support for a revolutionary movement within their ranks. In addition to conducting a terrorist campaign against the *"burocracia sindical,"* the guerrilla organizations somewhat cynically sought to exploit conditions in the workplace for political ends and to justify terrorist acts against company officials in the name of *clasismo.* The Fuerzas Armadas Peronistas' April 1973 kidnapping and execution of Fiat personnel director Francisco Klecker was presented to the Fiat workers as the revolutionaries' retribution for the increased production rhythms, piecework schemes, and generally harsh working conditions in the Ferreyra plants.[58] The ERP, one of the principal perpetrators of this kind of action, rarely failed to include some reference to problems in the plants in its frequent comuniqués to the workers in Santa Isabel.[59]

Just as the Fiat *clasistas* had repudiated the ERP's execution of Fiat president Oberdan Sallustro, so the Independents and SMATA *clasistas* strongly disapproved of such tactics and moved swiftly to disassociate themselves from the guerrillas' terrorist acts. The implication of a link between the dissident union movement—which was for the vast majority of the rank and file preeminently a struggle for effective union representation, union democracy, and workers' rights on the shop floor—and such political violence nevertheless could not be avoided, and it facilitated reprisals against the dissidents from the government and the trade union leadership.

Perón did not act right away. His labor wing was still too cautious, having been only recently restored to official favor, and the power of the Cordoban unions was still too formidable to risk an open confrontation. The nonproletarian left was an easier target, particularly its non-Peronist variants, and Rucci's assassination was followed by the proscription of the most important of the Marxist guerrilla organizations, the ERP, and attacks by Perón on "antinational" ideologies that recalled the days of the first presidency when the Justicialist doctrine was flaunted as a national, and hence superior, answer to Marxian socialism.[60] Nor was Peronism's own left wing exempt from attacks. Perón, sallow, doddering, and often in great pain from a number of maladies, still had the strength to preside over the first stages of the dismantling of that current within Peronism he had done so much to create. Throughout October Perón held several well-publicized meetings with labor leaders to discuss tactics for purging the movement's "antinational, capitalist and Marxist influences," a classic example of Peronist verbal legerdemain since, in addition to his daily tirades against the left, his close contacts with the Confederación General Económica and his government's conservative economic program showed that Perón considered the left the only real enemy that remained.[61] In November he oversaw a reorganization of his movement that virtually excluded the youth sector by appointing a provisional executive committee comprising only representatives from the labor and political wings of Peronism. Perón had taken the first steps toward eliminating what had become a serious liability in his movement, now that political power had been recovered.

A thornier problem was working class mobilization, which continued unabated. The workers could not legally mobilize on the wage issue, and indeed they had relatively few pressures to do so, since the price freeze held for several months and inflation was kept to tolerable levels until the end of the year. Rather, for the remainder of the year discontent continued to be expressed over union democracy and workers' control issues. Specifically, opposition to the entrenched union leaderships centered on the near absence of union protection on the shop floor, the factory committees' state of virtual inoperativeness, and the indifference of the shop stewards to problems involving increased production rhythms, plant rationalizations, hazardous working conditions, and job classifications.[62] To the government, this working class unrest was ominous and potentially destablizing because Córdoba loomed as a pole of working class militancy, the seat of an alternative labor movement with the potential to fashion the dispersed and inarticulate mobilizations into a united opposition. Nor were such fears unfounded.

Particularly in the Cordoban mechanical industries, *clasismo* was making serious advances throughout 1973. In the Perkins plant, the British engine manufacturing company in Ferreyra, the *clasista* slate's victory in the SMATA had sparked a movement to incorporate the plant union into the Cordoban autoworkers' union. The *clasista* activists in the plant partly justified membership by pointing to the greater possibility it offered for resolving long-standing problems with working conditions and job classifications.[63] But the Perkins affiliation drive was also linked to the growing strength of Cordoban *clasismo* as a political movement. By 1973 the Cordoban labor movement's "counterdiscourse," antibureaucratic, anticapitalist, and to a great extent anti-*porteño,* was thus appearing even in formerly tranquil preserves such as the Perkins plant. The *clasista* SITRAP adopted an ideological posture and political language that could reasonably have been interpreted by the traditional sectors of Peronist labor as provocative, replete as it was with scathing attacks against the *"burócratas y traidores"* both in the local *ortodoxo* ranks and at the level of the national leadership.[64]

Clasismo spread throughout the city in 1973, encouraged by a political climate, especially locally, that favored radical ideologies, and by the efforts of able militants who had been working in the plants for years and who now saw an opportunity to realize what once must have seemed to be the unobtainable reveries of the revolutionary. The *clasista* SMATA, for example, consolidated its position in the factories outside the Santa Isabel complex. The shop stewards' commission elected in the Ilasa plant in June 1973 had clear *clasista* leanings, and *clasista* activists within the local rubber workers' union were also petitioning for membership in the SMATA.[65] Even more worrisome to the government was the fact that many *ortodoxo* Peronist unions were under internal assault by rank-and-file movements with leftist leaderships. In the construction workers' union, long a local redoubt of job brokering, corruption, and union thuggery, a forceful grassroots movement attempted to throw out an entrenched union leadership regarded as the puppet of local construction firms.[66] In the state workers' union, the Asociación de Trabajadores del Estado, which was one of the largest unions in the city and a traditional Peronist stronghold, the threatened victory of a *clasista* slate in the upcoming union elections, albeit one comprising primarily members of the

Peronist left Juventud Trabajadora Peronista, was more ominous and disconcerting for the Peronists. In the ATE-affiliated plants of the Industrias Mecánicas del Estado, *clasista* militants of the VC, PCR, and JTP had been working stealthily since the Cordobazo. As early as 1972, the Vanguardia Comunista could fairly claim success with its *clasista* proselytization in the IME factories, where members of the collective bargaining committee were virtually ignoring the authority of the ATE secretary general, Héctor Castro.[67] By the time of Perón's election, militants from the Peronismo de Base, whose positions were now virtually indistinguishable from those of the Marxist *clasistas,* were also active in the military factories. In fact they were the principal promoters of the *clasista* union slate that challenged the *ortodoxo* Castro in what the Peronismo de Base, particularly, was soon denouncing as the rigged union elections of the Peronist right.[68]

The most serious working class opposition to the government elicited the most drastic response. Shortly after his election, Perón appointed UOM lawyer Luis Longhi as the regional delegate for Córdoba in the revamped CGT executive council, thereby providing a powerful ally for the chief exponent of *verticalismo* in the city, Simó's UOM. And while the attacks on Tosco and Luz y Fuerza from the FATLYF continued, the government undertook a campaign to eliminate the Cordoban labor opposition, occasionally resorting to individual acts of intimidation. An October 4 attack on the CGT headquarters, which left several wounded and prompted an October 9 general strike supported by all the Córdoba unions save the *ortodoxos,* was the most dramatic example of the government's violent approach.[69] But more characteristic of this stage in the government's labor policies was not its use of terrorist tactics but its resorting to institutional means. To control the growing threat of the *clasista* movement in the IME factories, for example, the government used a hastily passed redundancy law for government employees, the Ley de Prescindibilidad, to fire some 250 workers in the IME complex, including nearly the entire militant shop stewards' commission, though the response of the city's left-wing unions swiftly forced the government to rescind the firings.[70]

A settling of scores from the Fiat affiliation controversy was also part of the government's campaign to tame Córdoba. Since the Concord and Materfer plebiscites, former SITRAC-SITRAM *clasista* activists had made frequent visits to the SMATA and local CGT headquarters to plead for an open challenge to the UOM's spurious claim to the Fiat workers. *Clasista* activists drawn from all the city's unions in the Frente Unico Clasista made the Fiat workers' affiliation's with the SMATA one of its principal objectives. Salamanca's ardor had cooled, however, as pressures from Perón had definitively eliminated any possibility of support from Rodríguez and the SMATA central on the issue.[71] In the rarefied political climate of late 1973, the SMATA *clasista* leadership undoubtedly believed that pressing the issue constituted an unnecessary provocation to Perón and the Peronist labor movement, who were looking for any pretext to eliminate the Cordoban union. Masera, the former SITRAC president, was personally informed by Salamanca that the Fiat affiliation remained a long-term goal but that political circumstances made impossible any immediate action on the issue.[72] The Fiat affiliation controversy died a quiet death soon thereafter, and the UOM reestablished unfettered control of the Fiat workers.

The government's intimidation campaign was soon extended to those groups that could reasonably be expected to support the Cordoban unions against the government. Córdoba was the scene in the following months of a furious power struggle within Peronism, between its left and right wings. The Montoneros and the Fuerzas Armadas Revolucionarias united to defend themselves against an impending reaction, an alliance that was perhaps more significant in Córdoba than anywhere else in the country, since the balance of power between the two, generally heavily weighted in favor of the Montoneros, was somewhat more even there. This alliance provided the principal sustenance for the left-of-center provincial government as it was besieged by the Peronist right and Perón's now hostile national government. On October 22 the central committee of the Justicialist party and the 62 Organizaciones publicly condemned Governor Obregón Cano for supposedly permitting Córdoba to be used as a base of antigovernment agitation and for participating, himself, in Montonero rallies where Perón was openly criticized.[73]

The right-wing sectors of Peronism regarded both Obregón Cano and López as relics from the Cámpora months; they were painful reminders of the brief ascendancy of the Peronist left within the movement and thus obstacles to be removed. Among Simó and other *ortodoxo* leaders, there was little sentiment for a genuine reconciliation with the *legalistas*. Despite his contrite behavior, López was a suspect figure in the eyes of most of them. Perón had personally berated the vice governor at the October 2 congress of the Peronist provincial governments, and the specter of direct action against López's union was raised when the Labor Ministry began to assume control of various provincial branches of the UTA where the Peronist left, specifically the JTP, was well established.[74]

The linchpin in any strategy to break Cordoban labor was the *clasista* SMATA. Tosco remained the single commanding figure in the left-wing labor movement, and the Independents were a source of preoccupation for the government, but the existence of a left-wing leadership in the region's major industrial union was more troublesome. The Cordoban automobile workers' union loomed as a potentially more dangerous adversary, and it was also an annoying symbol, the only branch of any major industrial union not in Peronist hands. Besides the support it could lend Tosco, the Cordoban SMATA could directly jeopardize the government's economic program through prolonged work stoppage. The government was also sensitive to the threat the SMATA represented to the interests of a powerful foreign multinational corporation. On several occasions IKA-Renault had communicated its displeasure with the union to the government. It cited as a consequence of its grave labor problems the loss in production of some 6,000 cars between October 1972 and July 1973. In that period, the company claimed to have had only 215 work days compared with 232 for the Buenos Aires companies, a fact that was making its ability to compete in the tight automotive market even more difficult and threatening IKA-Renault's very survival.[75]

Aware of their vulnerability and the hostility that the government, Rodríguez, and the company had for them, the SMATA *clasistas* drew closer to Tosco and the MSC. Tosco's own political development facilitated this. After the break with López, the Luz y Fuerza leader inched toward an alliance with the Marxist left. Tosco led the Cordoban delegation, which included representatives from the SMATA, to the November 24 and 25, 1973, congress, Frente Antiimperialista por el Socialismo, held in the Chaco. The congress brought together all the country's *clasista* and revolutionary unions, and under Tosco's guidance, the Cordobans presented an anticapitalist, revolutionary program, which the attending members actually voted down for being too radical.[76]

The *clasistas* accepted Tosco's aid but were aware that their real strength had always resided in their reputation among the rank-and-file SMATA workers as vigilant custodians of worker interests on the shop floor. It was in the Cordoban car plants that the *clasistas* naturally sought to resist any campaign against them, and in this they were aided by the company itself. With the weight of the Pacto Social behind it, Renault began to whittle away at its labor costs, allowing working conditions to slip and increasing production rhythms, hopeful that the SMATA central would prevent the Cordoban union from undertaking strike action that would discredit the government and undermine its economic program. This proved to be a serious miscalculation on the company's part.

Throughout November and December, *clasista* shop stewards and the union's executive committee denounced the deterioration of working conditions and especially the changes in line speeds and job assignments that were occurring with greater frequency in numerous departments. The death of a worker on November 8 due to dehydration and exhaustion (the sultry Cordoban summer took its toll in the poorly ventilated Santa Isabel plants) prompted a strike the following day. A month later Salamanca held a press conference to denounce the company's recent policies and present an extensive report on the deteriorating state of working conditions in the plants since the onset of the Peronist restoration. The union attributed increased numbers of daily faintings, heat stroke, dehydration, and dizziness to Renault's new boldness with its labor force and the silent complicity of the government and the SMATA central.[77] Wildcat strikes, slowdowns, and soldiering in the plants, not provocative and proscribed general strikes, were more often the *clasistas'* response to the company's policies, but to Renault the effects were much the same: decreased labor productivity and declining profits for a company heavily in debt to both suppliers and the home office and on the edge of financial ruin.

Because of such actions, Rodríguez and the SMATA central were under almost daily pressures from Perón and the rest of the labor movement to get control of Córdoba. In response, the union central had refused to support the November 9 strike and had stepped up the SMATA's press campaign against Córdoba, including accusations of a mishandling of union funds for medical and social welfare programs.[78] More significantly, Rodríguez for the first time publicly accused the Cordoban leadership of subversive activities. In the past, displeasure with the Cordoban local had always been expressed somewhat circumspectly. Even at the nadir in relations between Córdoba and Buenos Aires, in the days following the SMATA central's withdrawal from the Fiat affiliation campaign, Rodríguez had avoided public criticisms that might discredit the autoworkers' union generally. But the *clasistas* obstreperous repudiation of the Pacto Social and their apparent disregard for the fate of the Peronist government were now looked on as an intolerable state of affairs and as acts of outright insubordination that drew the Cordoban autoworkers' union further away from the Peronist labor movement and too close to Tosco and the left.

Rodríguez's displeasure was compounded by the *clasistas'* unrelenting

criticism of the "labor bureaucracy" and the SMATA leader's own handling of the 1973 General Motors strike, notably for the fact that only
minimal gains had been won by the GM workers in one of the longest
and bitterest strikes in the history of the Argentine automobile industry.
In a public statement released to all the SMATA locals in December,
Rodríguez accused Córdoba of "attempting to discredit the executive
committee, which is Peronist, in order that comrade Salamanca, who is
anti-Peronist, can engage in revolutionary stratagems alongside the group
of malcontents who are encouraging him" and attempted to portray
clasismo as a personal attack against Perón. He tried to appeal to the
Argentine working class's nationalist sensibilities by saying, "We have
some political differences with comrade Renée Salamanca. We're for the
revolution of General Juan Perón while he is for the counterrevolution
that serves the interests of imperialism and dependency."[79]

Salamanca and the *clasista* union activists responded to these and other
philippics by stepping up political work in the plants. Winning out over
the objections of the communist members and some Peronist members
of the executive committee, the *clasistas* now openly encouraged political
discussions on the shop floor, undoubtedly convinced that the rightward
drift of the Peronist government was inexorable and that socialism now
had to be advanced directly, that somehow the workers had to be convinced to reject Peronism if they hoped to obtain socialism. Despite the
protests of the communists and the Peronists, meetings in the departments and especially the factories' open assemblies increasingly became
forums for political discussion, even indoctrination. *Clasista* shop stewards and activists, and the voluminous party literature that entered the
SMATA factories virtually every day, were less circumspect in their criticisms of Peronism. But with excitement still running high among the
workers in the weeks following Perón's election, conditions were hardly
propitious for such a campaign. The union rank and file remained staunch
supporters of the *clasistas'* daily handling of union affairs and would
oppose any attempt by the *porteños* in the SMATA central to interfere in
the local, but they were resolutely unwilling to break with Perón.

Rather than inculcating a *clasista* perspective and strengthening the
union's position, the political work only served to exacerbate tensions
within the *clasista* ranks and to provide ammunition for the Peronist
opposition. Former *torristas* organized the Frente Justicialista Sindical de
Afiliados de SMATA and began preparations, with *ortodoxo* support, to
challenge the leadership in the upcoming May 1974 union elections. It
also emboldened the Peronist right and the paramilitary organizations

that were beginning to act in the city. An abortive December 11 attempt on Salamanca's life and the murder of IKA-Renault worker and PCR activist Arnaldo Rojas that same month initiated a terror campaign that would claim dozens of victims in Córdoba in the next months.

Only a unified Cordoban CGT would be capable of resisting the combined power of the government, the labor bosses, and the death squads, but the Cordoban labor movement was now hopelessly divided between Peronist and non-Peronist camps. López and the *legalistas* still clung to a comforting loyalty to Perón, though the UTA leader had occasional moments of doubt. Following the attempted assassination of Salamanca, he agreed to support a December 14 general strike to protest the terror campaign being waged against the left. For the first time in many months, López and the *legalista* unions marched alongside the Independents and the SMATA *clasistas*. It was a public repudiation of the *ortodoxo* unions, which were believed in most political and labor circles to be behind the attacks.[80]

The vice governor's presence in the protest represented a sentimental, almost nostalgic gesture more than a change of political loyalties. Even López realized there was no longer any middle ground. The triumph of the Peronist right meant Córdoba was soon to feel the full weight of a hostile state. The radical trade union movement was still a formidable adversary and retained the potential to execute major working class mobilizations like those that had paralyzed the city in 1969 and 1971. But the unions now had to contend with the divisions from within and without that had accompanied Perón's presidency. Opposed to Perón's conservative program and hounded by the government and, in the case of the autoworkers, by their union central, the Independents and the SMATA chose the path of open confrontation. López chose simply to obey the government, unwilling to follow any course that implied opposition to Perón and a possible, perhaps irrevocable, break with the Peronist movement.

For Perón, the dream of reviving the alliances of the 1940s and 1950s haunted the remaining eight months of his life. The return to Peronism's authentic roots was complicated by the continued existence of a powerful and bumptious left-wing, one that swaggered with youthful confidence and annoyingly refused to break camp simply on Perón's word. Even more prickly were the divisions appearing within the labor movement, in which Córdoba played a central role, as the diverse currents of the country's recent history came to a climax in the working class.

The Peronist restoration's relations with the unions were complex and worked on multiple levels. Working class opposition to a simple return to the status quo, even under Peronist rule, was expressed in many ways, from rank-and-file challenges to entrenched leaders in individual factories, to challenges encompassing entire industries, to local CGT rebellions. Of the CGT rebellions, Córdoba's was by far the most significant, but the great majority of the working class mutinies that were to plague the governments of Perón and his widow, Isabel, would be taking place in provinces other than Córdoba. In many ways, the Argentine working class was catching up to ideas and experiences that already had a long history in the city. Córdoba remained the center of the dissident workers' movement, but it would no longer be its sole protagonist.

Nationwide, working class agitation was stoked by the heady political climate but also by the effects of the Pacto Social. By the early months of 1974, the failings of the government's economic program were already apparent, and the union hierarchies' inability to control the dissident unions and rank-and-file mobilizations was increasingly manifest. The wage freezes of the Pacto Social were now as prominent in working class grievances as the complaints of undemocratic union structures and the abuse of authority by entrenched leaderships that had dominated factory occupations during the Cámpora months. The June 1973 agreement between the CGT and the CGE had traded a price freeze from business in return for a pledge from labor not to push for wage increases. But the working class mobilizations of the Cámpora period had wrung a number of costly concessions from management on working conditions and had generally shaken the business sector's confidence in the agreement. Moreover, in accepting the Pacto Social, business had not shackled itself to any commitment to maintain or increase investment. This led first to a sharp decline in production and then to a flourishing black market. From this point an increase in prices was just a step away, as business would be able to justify violating the agreement on price ceilings by citing the losses incurred due to the rising costs of imports, the concessions awarded to workers in the Cámpora months, and a healthy demand as proven by the vibrancy of the black market.[81]

Inflation put greater pressures on the labor leadership, and activists now had another issue on which to base their antibureaucratic campaign. In the first two months of 1974, a series of strikes and rank-and-file mobilizations pushed a reluctant CGT into a more spirited defense of working class interests. Led by Miguel and the UOM, the Peronist union leadership pressed Perón for a wage increase. The hike was granted, and

along with it an agreement to let industry increase prices at rates set by
the government. But the increases were lower than those demanded by
the CGE and led to a virtual withdrawal from the Pacto Social by business,
a rash of price increases, and an inflationary spiral that would gather
steam throughout the remainder of the year.[82] Predictably, the workers
responded. Between March and June, the monthly national average number of strikes was the highest it would be in the entire three years of
Peronist government, and unlike the strikes of 1973, they had wage
demands as their principal cause.[83] Working class militants challenged
the union leadership in this second great wave of strikes, threatening not
only the labor bosses' control over organized labor but also their recently
won position within the Peronist movement and the government. Although the strikes were not, strictly speaking, political, and indeed the
organizers were usually Peronists themselves, they soon took on political
significance because they echoed the very criticisms being made by the
left-wing unions against the government and the CGT labor hierarchy.

From Córdoba came the call in early 1974 for an active opposition to
the government's economic program. The maverick shop stewards and
activists who mobilized the workers in the strikes of these months looked
to Córdoba, not the national CGT, for inspiration. More than any other
sector of organized labor in the country, the Cordoban labor movement
remained the bulwark of labor opposition, willing and able to fend off
attacks from Buenos Aires. If increased pressures from Perón and the
labor hierarchy had made it impossible to maintain the old alliance with
López, Tosco hoped at least some of the *legalistas* would prefer to side
with the MSC rather than with the *ortodoxos*. In this belief he was encouraged by the conspiracies of the Peronist right against the provincial
government.

The *ortodoxo* unions, in particular, were widely known to be negotiating
with the government for a move against the Cordoban CGT, even demanding the ousting of the provincial government, and they had already
assumed control of the local 62 Organizaciones.[84] With such a threat in
the air, a curious spectacle emerged of leftist union leaders protecting a
Peronist provincial government from a Peronist national government,
even threatening general strikes should the Obregón Cano–López government be removed. Nearly all the city's left-wing parties and student
organizations adopted this position. Its disillusionment with López notwithstanding, the Cordoban left, particularly the proletarian left, saw the
maintenance of the government as essential to its own interests. Tosco
interpreted the fortunes of the provincial government in broader terms:

any attack against the Obregón Cano–López government would have as its primary objective the breakup of the combative Cordoban labor movement.

López's hedging and his capitulation to the Peronist right in 1973 had paralyzed the *legalistas* to the point that they were incapable of mustering enough support to save their own government. After his belated and reluctant participation in the December general strike, López had moved the *legalistas* further away from their former allies and finally signed the unification agreement with the *ortodoxos* in January that formalized the breach between the *legalistas* and the left. Dissent within the *legalista* camp, particularly from López's own UTA, where the new secretary general, Roberto Tapia, continued to oppose an alliance with the *ortodoxos,* kept the accord from being implemented in practice. But the agreement's very existence obstructed the dialogue and coordinated action necessary for the *legalistas* to resist the advances of the Peronist right.[85]

Shortly after the agreement was signed, the *ortodoxos* demanded that López dissolve the CGT and call new elections that would proscribe the left and return the local to the ranks of Peronism. López held back from such a drastic step, however, perhaps partly out of loyalty to his former comrades but no doubt mainly due to his realization that they were capable of shutting down the city at will. In the final weeks of January 1974, as the left-wing Peronist governor of Buenos Aires province, Oscar Bidegain, was being sacked, the eight Peronist left congressmen were being pressured to resign, and rumors were rife of an imminent move against Córdoba, López retreated into a kind of morbid silence. He was incapable of taking the kind of action that could save his provincial government, out of loyalty to a movement that was giving every sign of repudiating his brand of Peronism.

In February the situation in Córdoba deteriorated further and finally collapsed. The *ortodoxos,* still a minority current within Cordoban labor, began to conspire with other disgruntled local opponents of the government, to plot its forcible removal. On February 9, the local 62 Organizaciones released a public statement entitled, "An Agreement between the Peronist Labor Leaders," which ignored certain *legalista* objections and called for a CGT executive committee comprising only Peronists and a pledge of respect for the principal of *verticalismo* and the decisions made by both the national leadership of the CGT and the 62 Organizaciones.[86] The *legalista* unions, including the UTA, did not publicly endorse the document, but they did not repudiate it either, or immediately criticize the *ortodoxos'* announcement of a "normalizing congress" to be held that month to carry out the proposed restructuring of the local CGT. However, the combination of the *ortodoxos'* conspiracies against the government and their galling assumption of authority in the Peronist labor movement led to grumbling within the *legalista* ranks—especially within the UTA, where the JTP and the Peronist left remained strong—and to complaints that López had grown unduly obliging in his efforts to appease Perón. Tapia and the UTA led a silent *legalista* exodus out of the 62 Organizaciones shortly after the *ortodoxo* announcement, and in a matter of weeks the *legalistas,* Independents, and SMATA *clasistas* were offering a united labor resistance to Buenos Aires's interference in the provincial government.

The reconciliation of the unions in the dissident labor movement, however, came too late to forestall the demise of the Cordoban Peronist government. The local opposition to the Obregón Cano–López government was at least as menacing as the hostility of the *ortodoxos* and Perón. In fact, the overthrow of the Cordoban Peronist government at the end of February had diverse roots in local political wars not directly attributable to Buenos Aires. For example, the bus owners' federation, Federación Empresaria del Transporte Automotor de Pasajeros (FETAP), had had an ongoing and acrimonious feud with López over the vice governor's plan to expropriate the private bus companies and reassert public ownership of the city's urban transport system. López's plan was not only a response to the wishes of his own union, but it also expressed widespread public dissatisfaction over the years of slipshod service that had been provided by the local transport monopolies. In the months leading up to the Cordoban government's overthrow, the FETAP had allowed service to deteriorate even further, contributing to the already palpable state of unrest in the city.[87] The local police department, where a series of corruption scandals threatened a thorough shake-up of the constabulary, was similarly aligned against the government.

It was Obregón Cano's rumored intention to remove the principal figure in the corruption scandals, the chief of police, Lieutenant Colonel Domingo Navarro, triggered the series of events that would lead to his government's downfall. Navarro, a shadowy figure with close ties to both the more extreme sectors of the Peronist right and the local underworld, unexpectedly arrested Obregón Cano and López on the eve of the *ortodoxos'* rump CGT congress, and the police occupied the city, forcing Tosco, Tapia, and others into hiding and taking over the CGT headquarters. A week later the governor and vice governor resigned at Perón's insistence, while the MSC released a communiqué inciting popular resistance to Navarro's suspension of constitutional government.[88]

Perón had not organized the "Navarrazo," as the virtual coup d'etat in miniature was later derisively called, but it did fit neatly into his government's purposes. Navarro's and the *ortodoxos'* claims of a near state of insurrection in the city, replete with false accusations about the distribution of arms to workers and students by the government's left-wing sympathizers, as well as the less fanciful warnings of a power vacuum created by the imprisonment of the governor and vice governor, were the perfect pretext for decreeing government intervention in the province on March 12. The Navarrazo marked a turning point for the Perón government. Thenceforth it would be openly at war with the left, particularly with the still formidable left-wing sectors within Peronism.

The Cordoban unions responded by publicly implicating Perón in the fall of the provincial government and stepping up their resistance to the gathering rightist reaction, which promised to fall particularly hard on Córdoba. Tosco elaborated a plan to call a national labor congress, to coordinate working class resistance to the Pacto Social and the government's labor policies, and also to combat locally the central government's actions in the province and the *ortodoxos'* control of the Cordoban CGT. Meanwhile the *ortodoxos* feuded over the spoils of the provincial government, and Perón assumed the customary role of disinterested arbiter and urged the *legalistas* to return to the Peronist fold.[89]

Coincidentally, the events in Córdoba occurred just as a major crisis was erupting in the bastion of *verticalismo* and Peronist trade union orthodoxy, the UOM. In Villa Constitución, a grimy young steel town on the banks of the Paraná River, some 6,000 steelworkers at the Acindar, Marathom, and Metcon plants (Metcon was a Ford parts factory) undertook yet another of the factory occupations that had become commonplace since the restoration of the Peronist government. At the root of the occupations was a catastrophic 1970 strike that the companies and government had defeated and that had led to a virtual ban on union activities in the plants. The UOM had continued to collect its handsome union dues after the strike and had retained formal jurisdiction over the workers, but union activity had virtually ceased until shop floor activists, among them a large number of *clasistas,* had organized union elections in January 1974. The first round of elections had resulted in the overwhelming victory of the self-styled "antibureaucratic" slate, which had ran on a platform of honest and democratic union representation and the immediate suspension of further voting by the UOM central. On March 8, led by shop floor activist Alberto Piccinini, workers in the Acindar plant occupied their plant en masse. Their occupation was soon followed by similar actions in the Marathom and Metcon factories. Within days, unions throughout the entire Paraná industrial belt had called sympathy strikes, and the small businesses that depended on the steelworkers as customers declared a lockout in support of the occupations.[90]

As news traveled to Córdoba of the steelworkers' strikes, the momentary gloom following the Navarrazo was replaced by renewed hope. The *clasistas* were particularly encouraged. The *clasista* position had always been that the future of the revolutionary trade union movement depended on its ability to win a following in the country's large industrial unions. Their skepticism of the Independents had been due, at least in part, to the Independents' scant resonance among those unions with real strategic weight in the country's labor movement, Tosco's light and power workers being a notable exception. The insubordination of an important UOM local was heartening, and the Villa Constitución rebellion was a boon to the Cordoban dissident labor movement in general. It not only deflected the attention of Buenos Aires away from Córdoba, it also gave the city's left-wing unions a common point of reference in their opposition to the government. If resistance to the government was difficult for the moment in Córdoba, it might be encouraged elsewhere in the country.

Tosco, especially, saw the advantages in such a strategy. Throughout the nine days of the factory occupations, which culminated in the government's capitulation to all the workers' demands, the combative Cordoban unions transformed Villa Constitución into a local cause célèbre. Tosco made almost nightly appearances at union halls and student rallies to speak on the strike. On April 20, Tosco, Salamanca, and the Salta *clasista* leader, Jaime, paid a dramatic visit to Villa Constitución, where they had been invited by the steelworkers to attend a Plenario Antiburocrático, along with representatives of the JTP, Peronismo de Base, and other *clasista* unionists.[91] Once again Tosco suggested the possibility of building an alternative trade union movement that would include those sectors of the Peronist working class, such as the local steelworkers, that were at odds with the sectarianism and abuses of authority of the Peronist labor bosses.[92] By late April the events in Villa Constitución had so galvanized the Cordoban labor movement that some forty unions were adhering to the MSC, and the *ortodoxos* were once again on the defensive.[93]

Despite the respite offered by the events in Villa Constitución, the purge of the left-wing unions that had begun with the Navarrazo had been only stalled, not stopped. Yet in Córdoba the months that followed Villa

Constitución seemed full of promise, and the final outcome apparently still hung in the balance. Tosco and Tapia had actually returned from hiding to rejoin their unions in the days before the steelworkers' rebellion and had jointly announced a program demanding worker representation on the boards of all provincial banks, industries, hospitals, and public utilities; reforms in public housing and education; the creation of a thorough health and welfare system; and a popular resistance to Navarro's putsch.[94] The *legalistas* reasserted their independence from the *ortodoxos* and distanced themselves from the Peronist government's turn to the right by maintaining the integrity of their "62 Organizaciones Legalistas." Villa Constitución reaffirmed Tosco's belief in the depth of working class disaffection with the government and the labor bureaucracy. At the same time, it did not dissuade him from following a strategy that emphasized Córdoba's central role in building a socialist movement within the working class, or from maintaining his alliances with those sectors of the Peronist labor movement whose indispensability he, more than any other left-wing labor leader, had always recognized.[95]

Córdoba, however, presented greater divisions than perhaps even Tosco appreciated. In the SMATA, the *torristas* had regrouped and organized their slate, the *lista gris,* to challenge the *clasistas lista marrón* in the upcoming May union elections. The *clasista* leadership, in turn, had split into two separate camps: the new left parties (the PCR, PRT, VC, JTP, and part of the Peronismo de Base) with the surprise addition of the small, Trotskyist Palabra Obrera, had broken with the more conservative members of the original *lista marrón* coalition (the PC, the Radicals, and another Peronismo de Base faction).[96]

The PC was, in fact, the principal instigator of the left-wing split. The communists prided themselves on their reputed pragmatism and political realism, regarded in new left circles as crass opportunism. The communists had been disenchanted with the *lista marrón* since Salamanca's 1973 electoral abstention call, they also disliked the local's increasingly discordant relations with the Peronist government. Although the PC objected to such sectarianism, however, its break with the new left was due more to its displeasure with its "junior partner" status in the *clasista* alliance and to having been eclipsed by the upstart PCR than to questions of principal or political differences. The communists were also offended by the PCR's outspoken anti-Soviet stance, which they not unreasonably took as an indirect criticism of the strongly pro-Soviet Argentine communists. Within the *lista marrón,* ideological and political differences had also started to appear that hindered the leadership's ability to effectively administer the SMATA. Objections to the PRT's military strategy as a complement to *clasismo* and its attempts to cultivate the "worker-soldier" in the plants, for example, had already created discord and grave tensions among the union leadership.[97]

The government and the Peronist labor leadership placed great hopes in these divisions within the *clasista* ranks, and in an effective campaign by the *torristas* that would return the autoworkers to the Peronist ranks. Rodríguez and the autoworkers' central in Buenos Aires were almost desperately anxious that Salamanca's slate be defeated. Indeed, the SMATA *clasistas* loomed as an ever-increasing threat to the union central. In February the Cordoban workers had voted to extend the period of union office from two to four years so if the *clasista* slate won reelection, they would be in power for the length of the Peronist government and beyond. Even more ominously, the *clasistas* were now openly encouraging an opposition slate to contest Rodríguez in the upcoming elections for the SMATA national executive committee.[98] Though they were hardly yet in a position to challenge the Peronists at the national level, a sizable electoral victory in Córdoba and alliances with autoworker dissidents in Buenos Aires could make them serious rivals at a later date.

Supported by Rodríguez but also mindful of keeping the *porteño* SMATA bureaucracy at arm's length, the Peronists in Córdoba's SMATA waged a bitter electoral campaign from March through early May, portraying the *clasistas* as quixotic and divisive leaders who had needlessly antagonized the government and made possible the advances of the right-wing sectors of Peronism. But these were inappropriate times for such arguments, and as events in the Navarrazo had shown, the government itself had been a willing collaborator in the rightist reaction. Charges of political sectarianism, moreover, had lost their force with the rank and file, who had seen the real gains made under the *clasista* stewardship of the union. The *clasistas* had acted on every one of the planks in the 1972 *lista marrón* platform. In addition to improvements in working conditions and production rhythms, which were continuously under assault by the company but protected by vigilant shop stewards and an effective use of strike actions, the *clasistas* had also won job classifications for some 2,500 workers, forced the company to restore the *sábado inglés*, extended benefits and wage scales to Renault dependencies such as the Ilasa and Thompson Ramco factories, brought the administrative employees into the union, expanded union social services, and taken important steps toward establishing a genuine, participatory union democracy in the Cordoban local.[99]

In the face of meager prospects for the SMATA Peronists, Rodríguez and the SMATA central plotted to ensure their electoral victory. Despite the *clasista*-sponsored opposition slate, Rodríguez knew that his union machinery was sufficiently strong and that the Cordoban *clasistas* were too weak to upset the Peronist slate in the elections for the national executive council. He therefore scheduled the national elections to coincide with those of the Cordoban local, obviously hoping in that way to sweep in an anti-*clasista* slate in Córdoba along with the assured victory of the Peronist candidates at the national level.[100] The SMATA central and the government harassed the local in myriad ways in the weeks leading up to the election, accusing it of electoral procedure irregularities (never specified), sending out union ballots that excluded the names of many *clasista* shop stewards who were up for election, and arresting Salamanca for a minor traffic violation on May 6.[101] Only the Peronist slate's criticism that the union central's heavy-handed behavior was increasing anti-*porteño* sentiment in the union and actually aiding the opposition seemed to warn that Rodríguez's meddling tactics might backfire.

In reality, with or without Rodríguez there were ample reasons for optimism among the *clasistas*. The *torrista* challengers had failed utterly to win over the majority of the Peronist rank and file. Worker resentment of the *torrista* union practices lingered, and the *clasistas'* solid list of achievements was a source of great prestige for Salamanca's group among the SMATA workers. The *torrista* slate, moreover, was known to be favored by the *ortodoxos* and other right-wing sectors of the Peronist movement and was thus associated in the minds of many workers with the recent events in the Navarrazo. Even though the *lista gris* had the advantage of Peronist credentials at a particularly propitious political moment, with Perón in power and heightened expectations among the working class that his government would resolve the country's critical problems, an association with Perón proved insufficient for victory, and the election results confirmed the workers' overwhelming support for the *clasistas*. Salamanca's slate won 4,027 of the votes and the Peronists 2,770 (the PC polled a paltry 793).[102] Renault noted that the decisive *clasista* victory was due especially to the great gains made in the other SMATA-affiliated factories, such as Ford-Transax, Thompson Ramco, and Grandes Motores Diesel.[103]

Amid the euphoria of their spectacular victory there were also reasons for concern, had Salamanca's group chosen to look for them. The size of the *clasista* victory stunned Rodríguez and the SMATA central authorities, and they apparently abandoned all hope of removing the Cordoban leadership by electoral means. The central's defamation campaign intensified, and whether out of spite or to rethink his previous strategy, Rodríguez stalled for weeks on the investiture of the reelected *clasistas,* as a delegation from the central was required by union statute to oversee the swearing-in ceremony.[104] The *clasistas* regarded such behavior as a blatant provocation, but they limited their response to letters of protest and refrained from more drastic action, which they felt could trigger reprisals from Buenos Aires.[105] But they did not always display such prudence. Their overwhelming victory had created a sense of overconfidence and led many to believe that their power in both the union and the labor movement was greater than it really was. The *clasistas'* standing among the rank and file was due to their honesty and effectiveness as union leaders. The workers could be counted on to support them in any confrontation with the *porteño* SMATA bureaucracy, but that support was conditional on their judicious exercise of union authority. The ideological diversity and competing interpretations of national politics that existed both within the *clasista* ranks and between the union leaders and the vast majority of the rank and file, long a latent source of weakness, would now become a fatal contradiction.

· N I N E ·

Patria Metalúrgica, Patria Socialista

Much of Argentine labor history in the final two years of the Peronist government can be best explained through the Unión Obrera Metalúrgica's ongoing attempts to buttress the labor movement's position in the Peronist coalition, to assure the metalworkers' union's own ascendancy within organized labor, and to eliminate or at least control the opposition and dissident currents within the labor movement. The predominance that the UOM had come to enjoy in the twenty years since Perón's fall, during its checkered, often contradictory history of militancy, hard-nosed negotiating, aggrandizement, and opposition to power sharing, reached its culmination in this period. Political analysts and opponents of the regime alike now began to speak of the *"patria metalúrgica,"* a virtual corporatist pact between the business groups that controlled the Confederación General Económica, dominated by the industrialists in the metal trades who were the principal architects and beneficiaries of the government's economic program, and the metalworkers' union, the recognized power within the Confederación General del Trabajo that was expected to control the other unions and maintain social peace in return for a greater voice in government decisions.[1]

The term *patria metalúrgica,* stripped of its conspiratorial connotations, revealed a great deal about the character and alliances within the Peronist government. Since their near demise under Onganía's government, the industrialists who comprised the CGE, the "national bourgeoisie" so often extolled by Peronists, had climbed back to a position of considerable influence and power by the early 1970s. The CGE grouped all the country's medium and small industrialists, but it had become particularly influenced by the domestic auto parts manufacturers. The president of

274

the CGE in 1971 and now the minister of economy, José Ber Gelbard, was the former president of the country's only national tire company, and the CGE's subsequent president, Julio Broner, was the owner of a major auto parts empire. Carlos Coquegniot, the president of the Asociación de Industrias Metalúrgicas de Córdoba and the Federación de Industrias Metalúrgicas del Interior, would be named president of the Confederación Industrial Argentina (CINA), after the government's 1974 merger of the CGE and the Unión Industrial Argentina (UIA).[2]

These industrialists, who made products strictly for the domestic market, had long relied on the state to ensure their well-being. To halt the growing bill for imported parts and components, the Illia government had passed separate automotive decrees in 1964 and 1965 establishing stricter domestic content requirements for Argentine automotive manufacturers. A domestic parts sector grew rapidly in those two years, though the great majority were relatively small operations that did not sell directly to the automobile manufacturers but to the replacement market.[3] Under Onganía, an increasing number of these auto parts firms had been bought up by foreign capital and been concentrated in large, technologically sophisticated operations. By 1974, fewer than 8 percent of the auto parts firms were producing more than half the country's parts, essentially serving the automotive manufacturers directly.[4] Nevertheless, through lobbying and state intervention, the domestic manufacturers had recovered somewhat from the shakedown caused by the Onganía government's economic legislation. These manufacturers in the CGE had been the principal promoters of Lanusse's 1971 automotive law 19135. They were determined to push nationalist legislation in the automotive sector even further under Peronist rule and to serve as the spokesmen, generally, for the economic groups that could hope to benefit from nationalist economic programs under Perón.

The source of the UOM's influence in the government was its perceived ability to reestablish the verticalist structure of Argentine trade unionism as it had been perfected by Augusto Vandor. The UOM's power continued to rest on its status as the country's largest industrial union, its financial resources, the support it enjoyed from much of the UOM rank and file, and especially on the political influence it wielded in the Peronist coalition. The union had gone from being just one of half a dozen influential members in the labor movement during the 1946 to 1955 Peronist governments to being the final arbiter in all labor affairs. Its network of health clinics and vacation colonies and its handsome collective bargaining agreements gave it status within the labor movement, and despite the

276 · The Peronist Restoration

often nefarious workings of its labor bosses, it had a legitimacy among much of the rank and file that only the SMATA and Luz y Fuerza could match. And now it was once again a full partner in the political wing of the Peronist movement, occupying political office and wielding political influence to an extent unknown to the country's other unions. The naming of UOM leader Ricardo Otero as labor minister was only the most exalted symbol of the influence it had regained with Perón's return to power, and examples abounded of the UOM's power once Perón had definitively broken with his movement's left wing.

The UOM was thus the only union in a position to restore hierarchy and discipline to the labor movement. As the dropping of the Fiat affiliation campaign had shown, resistance to the UOM's hegemony from rivals such as the SMATA had become sporadic and was at least temporarily subordinated to the possibility of sharing the spoils in labor's restored position in a Peronist government. The policies that characterized the UOM, moreover, were also those of the union hierarchies in the SMATA and Luz y Fuerza; indeed, the term *patria metalúrgica* covered a set of values that were shared by the leadership in all the country's most powerful unions, not just the metalworkers' union. Opposition such as the SMATA's to the UOM had been due to venal power struggles and not ideological disputes or fundamental differences about the way unions and the labor movement should be run.

The UOM had also enjoyed the benefit of being, until Villa Constitución, somewhat less affected by the dissident rank-and-file movements and radical winds blowing from Córdoba. As the menace of Córdoba loomed larger, not only for *verticalismo* but also for the very success of Perón's government, it naturally fell to the UOM's Cordoban local to assume a leading role in the campaign against the city's maverick unions. Alejo Simó and the UOM local's past policy of verbally adhering to the verticalist line but avoiding a too-aggressive policy toward the city's non-*ortodoxo* unions was now untenable and was abandoned. Perón named Simó to serve as the government's plenipotentiary to head the provincial department of labor, thus giving the UOM leader enormous power to reshape the balance of power in the city's labor movement. Alfredo Martini, who was elected president of the local after Simó's appointment, was subjected to pressures and threats of a cutoff of union funds unless he adopted a harder line toward the left-wing unions, and he therefore obediently cooperated in isolating the city's non-Peronist unions from the rest of the Cordoban labor movement.[5]

Compliance with Buenos Aires's mandates was all the more necessary given the crisis in the local metallurgical industry and the Cordoban UOM's greatly weakened position. Since the late 1960s the demise of the city's parts industry had been a subject of constant comment and lamentation in the local press, and in the official statements of the metallurgical industrialists' association (Cámara de Industrias Metalúrgica) and the Cordoban UOM. During the Onganía government, the owners had pressed the government for legislation that would allow them to continue to prosper in the shadow of the automotive boom. They had unsuccessfully attempted, for example, to obtain legislation to prevent decentralization programs such as Fiat's that would transfer production facilities to other regions of the country and result in a loss of markets for the local industry.[6]

Moreover, the Cordoban industry seemed to have recovered little from the nationalist legislation of the early 1970s and to have suffered more than the industry as a whole, given its lesser reliance on the replacement parts market and its character as a direct supplier for the local automotive complexes. Industrial census figures taken at decade intervals do not reveal the full magnitude of the crisis, since the 1964 census occurred before the enormous growth in the local industry, largely due to the Illia legislation, that took place between 1964 and 1966. At worst, the census reveals lackluster growth for the ten years from 1964 to 1974, compared with the previous decade (Table 9.1). Nevertheless, the closings of the city's larger metallurgical establishments, such as the Del Carlo factory in 1972, and the enormous instability in the thousands of small workshops where bankruptcies were frequent, labor turnover was endemic, and working conditions already poor, testified to an industry in decline. Though in late 1973 IKA-Renault was still buying 33 percent of its basic metallurgical components from some 250 local suppliers, this was a drastic drop from the early Kaiser years, when the Santa Isabel complex, despite vertical integration, had a near complete dependence on such suppliers for certain of its simpler parts and components.[7] The crisis was

Table 9.1 Cordoban metallurgical industry

Year	Number of firms	Number of workers
1954	452	1,115
1964	1,555	7,953
1974	2,043	8,945

Source: Industrial census, 1954, 1964, and 1974, Ministerio de Hacienda, Economía y Previsión Social, Provincia de Córdoba.

so severe that the local CGT made numerous direct appeals to the local population to support a government response.[8]

As the crisis in the Cordoban metallurgical industry worsened, the UOM's influence in the local labor movement diminished and the need for the union's labor leaders to court official favor increased. The past policy of tepid support for *verticalismo* and effective independence, often pursued in alliance with those very unions most opposed to the centralist policies of the *porteño* labor bureaucracy, had been abandoned long before the Peronist restoration. But now the UOM was prepared to buttress its authority even at the expense of an open confrontation with other local unions, first in its campaign to regain jurisdiction over the Fiat workers and then by scrupulously following directives from Buenos Aires and heading the Peronist government's attempt to reestablish a thoroughly Peronist, subordinate CGT local. Simó would preside over a purge of Cordoban labor during the next eighteen months by supporting union busting, making favorable decisions for unions with compliant Peronist leaderships in industrial disputes, and generally bestowing a legal, union mantle on the government's often heavy-handed reprisals against the wayward Cordoban unions.

While the *patria metalúrgica* struggled to maintain its ascendancy within Perón's government, the forces working to fulfill the dream of a *patria socialista* remained a formidable adversary. The Peronist left and especially the Marxist left had been critical of the government since the establishment of the Pacto Social.[9] Once the verticalist program became clear, and particularly with the government's rightward shift after the Navarrazo, those criticisms intensified, and many groups on the fractured Argentine left called on the revolutionary Peronists to break with the government and cast their lot in a common revolutionary front.[10]

On May 1, 1974, Perón made his historic break with the Peronist left when he publicly rebuked and dismissed the jeering Montonero columns during the May Day rally held in the Plaza de Mayo.[11] The significance of the event was not in Perón's repudiation of his movement's left wing, as the true colors of the Peronist restoration had long been apparent. Rather, it was in how the act was perceived by the Peronist right, including sectors within the labor movement. The right saw it as a signal to intensify its attacks against the left. The murder of three activists from the Partido Socialista de los Trabajadores and a spate of attacks against the Juventud Peronista headquarters were part of the repressive wave that followed. Working class organizations were also targets. The raid on the Peronismo de Base headquarters and the arrest of one hundred of its members there initiated a four-month campaign to weed out the left from the unions in greater Buenos Aires. The Labor Ministry's subsequent revoking of the *personería gremial* of the Buenos Aires journalists' union and Ongaro's print workers was also a part of the purge.

To a certain extent the labor bosses were simply taking advantage of the opportunity to nip in the bud the grassroots movements and growing opposition to the Pacto Social that were mushrooming in greater Buenos Aires. The purge of the left served to eliminate union rivals and protect the bosses' positions within the unions that were under assault by rank-and-file movements. But the purge also reflected a genuine ideological and political struggle taking place within Peronism. It undoubtedly relied on at least the silent complicity of many workers—workers who had been reared on a steady diet of Peronist litanies and who were concerned for the future of Perón's government, which was under siege, they were told, by leftist infiltrators in their own ranks.

Córdoba awaited a similar purge as the Argentine winter commenced. The city's labor movement remained the greatest obstacle to the verticalist strategy, and thus the government's most formidable adversary. All attempts to neutralize the city's left-wing unions by Ricardo Otero and the Labor Ministry, by the CGT and the union centrals, and even by Perón himself had failed. Their only real accomplishment had been the creation of a loose alliance of the Peronist unions in the Cordoban 62 Organizaciones, a reunification that had remained little more than an administrative fiction after Roberto Tapia and the UTA had led an exodus of the *legalista* unions out of the organization following the Navarrazo. Similarly, the decisive victory of the *clasistas* in the recent SMATA union elections had been a major blow to the verticalist campaign in Córdoba. The struggle within the labor movement drew an unwelcome response from both the right and left in the city, and political assassination became commonplace. Company executives and *ortodoxo* union leaders received their share of the attacks, but most were directed against the antiverticalist unions. Assassination attempts against Tosco and Salamanca had been bungled, but bomb attacks against the Luz y Fuerza and UTA union halls in June caused considerable damage and managed to sow a climate of fear in the city that only contributed to the growing animus between the unions. The labor bosses in Buenos Aires and their lieutenants in Córdoba meanwhile had to stick by Perón's unpopular Pacto Social, which only made them more vulnerable to the labor dissidents' criticisms.[12]

In the power struggle going on in the local labor movement during this period of violence, the city's dissident unions gave every indication of strengthening their hand. López himself had somewhat reconciled with his former allies, and he formed the 62 Organizaciones Legalistas Leales a Perón in May as a way of maintaining a formal association with the Peronist government while in reality taking tentative steps toward reentering the labor alliance he had abandoned earlier under pressures from Buenos Aires.[13] Similarly, the *clasistas* and Tosco's Independents reached the high point of their cooperative relationship in the weeks following the May SMATA elections. The Cordoban dissident unions' disagreement with the Peronist government and their opposition to the government's closely linked economic and labor policies lost its former ambiguity. In public statements, Tosco emphasized the lineage between the government's programs and the *"participacionismo"* of Vandorism and the craven, obsequious behavior of the trade union hierarchy under Onganía. The Movimiento Sindical Combativo was now openly speaking of a "betrayal" of working class interests by the Peronist government in power. As had often been the case since 1969, the Cordobazo was used as the touchstone for the working class's historical role: not subordination to a neocorporatist regime but active participation in behalf of a socialist transformation of Argentine society. The MSC used the fifth anniversary of the Cordobazo, for example, to draw the distinction for the first time between the real interests of the working class and those of the Peronist movement.[14]

The MSC now dominated Cordoban labor, and the many components of the local working class opposition to the Pacto Social and the verticalist campaign seemed to be coalescing once again into a serious adversary for the labor bureaucracy. But Perón died suddenly in July, and that event put greater powers into the hands of the most hard-line sectors of the government, thereby making the Cordoban unions more vulnerable. Among other measures, the government passed the Ley de Seguridad, which gave the Labor Ministry almost unfettered powers to intervene in strikes.[15] Authority in labor affairs was essentially handed over to Otero and his allies in the labor movement, as Perón's successor, his wife Isabel, virtually relinquished decision-making power in such matters.

Perón's death and the subsequent changes within the government were particularly ominous for the Cordoban SMATA. The *clasistas* had unilaterally defied the government when the union had voted on June 5 to reduce production in the Cordoban plants through a soldiering strike *(trabajo a convenio)* in demand of a 60 percent wage hike and the resolution of some outstanding workplace grievances. Renault had responded by suspending some 2,000 workers, and Otero had labeled the strike as "political" and threatened to take away the local's legal status.[16]

The strike revealed the political vulnerability of the *clasista* leadership. The anti-Peronist sentiment of much of the SMATA leadership had always been a fundamental contradiction and a potential source of weakness in their relationship with the overwhelmingly Peronist rank and file. After the 1973 abstention call, *clasista* positions had been presented more circumspectly but still insistently. *Clasista* shop stewards encouraged political discussion, and voluminous political literature circulated on the factory floor. The factory bathrooms served as virtual Marxist bookstores where the competing parties of the left peddled their parties' missives.[17] After the Navarrazo and the government's shift to the right, the criticisms of Peronism and even Perón himself became more caustic, and at least some of the *clasistas* set about to destroy the myth of Perón. The very decision to call the June 5 strike had responded to Partido Comunista Revolucionario stratagems for that purpose. At a union meeting held in Villa Allende shortly after the *lista marrón*'s electoral victory, *clasista* leaders from other parties had listened incredulously as Salamanca urged a frontal assault against the Pacto Social, to break free of the "tightening noose" *("romper el cerco")* against the dissident labor movement and rally working class opposition to the government's economic program. Most incredibly, Salamanca voiced the PCR's well-known, and in other left-wing organizations notorious, position on the putative Soviet connection of the Peronist government—that there was a supposed conspiracy to destroy the anti-Soviet, revolutionary parties of the Argentine left—as further justification for an open challenge to the government.[18]

Both the government and the company perceived that there were unquestionably political motivations lurking behind the strike and that therefore any strike call was ultimately vulnerable among the SMATA rank and file.[19] The union's demand for a wage increase and for company attention to hazardous working conditions in certain departments had widespread rank-and-file support, and the strike had been voted on in open assembly and received the endorsement of both the opposition *torristas* and the communists.[20] Nevertheless, the company's position might reasonably have appeared legitimate to some of the workers, namely that it was bound by law not to grant the wage increase under the provisions of the Pacto Social and that company officials could only give in on the issue if the government changed its economic program.[21]

Though the union's action was technically within the limits of the Pacto Social, since it was not an outright strike but a slowdown, its deleterious effects on an already troubled company were much the same. Unlike most industries, automobile manufacturers could not resort to hoarding and a black market to compensate for a price freeze while other costs, particularly electric power and the never thoroughly controlled small parts industry, were rising despite the government's Pacto Social. Sales, on the other hand, had fallen off precipitously after a brief consumer boom in 1973. The company was also faced with a critical financial situation. It was heavily in debt to both the home office and local suppliers; new loans were not forthcoming from either local or foreign banks; management was jittery over declining sales and the potential repercussions of its labor problems; and the burden of the old loans had become more onerous with the onset of hyperinflation.[22]

The actions of the Cordoban union had implications beyond the local economy; they hurt the entire Argentine automobile industry. The crucial role that the Cordoban plants played especially as suppliers of parts to other automobile firms meant that its effects spread well beyond Córdoba. The IKA-Renault forge, for example, was the most important in the country and did the casting work for many automobile firms while, the Ford-Transax plant supplied axles for most of the companies. Renault noted that the strike was especially hurting the Peugeot, Ford, Mercedes-Benz, General Motors, and Chrysler plants.[23] Any prolonged crisis in the automobile industry, moreover, would adversely affect other dependent industrial sectors, particularly the steel and rubber industries.

The gravity of strike, which was threatening the government's very economic program, was heightened when Renault suspended more than 1,000 workers on July 19, followed by an additional 2,800 a week later.[24] Now Rodríguez and the SMATA central had the provocation and the opportunity they had been waiting for: the coveted slip by the *clasistas* that would enable them to deal a mortal blow to the Córdoba union. Rodríguez had intimated from the very first days of the strike that a suspension of the local from the autoworkers' union was possible. After the July layoffs, the SMATA central rebuffed all of the *clasistas* overtures to declare an emergency SMATA meeting, insisting that the Cordoban leaders travel to Buenos Aires instead, and stressing the risk of reprisals that Córdoba was exposing the entire union to. It was becoming increasingly apparent that the central would accept nothing less than the full capitulation of the local and the resignation of the *clasista* leadership.[25]

On August 3 Renault announced that it was declaring a lockout, indefinitely shutting down the Santa Isabel complex. The following day the government sent national guard troops to occupy the plants in a repeat of the measures applied to the Fiat plants during the final days of the *clasista* movement in Ferreyra. Yet unlike SITRAC and SITRAM, the SMATA was not isolated in the local labor movement and could count on the support of a majority of the Cordoban unions in their conflict with the company and the SMATA central. With Tosco and Tapia's collaboration, the *clasistas* could mount a formidable working class opposition. Tosco himself saw the SMATA conflict as an opportunity to rally local working class support against the Pacto Social and to integrate the remaining prodigal *legalista* unions into a rejuvenated, combative, and antiverticalist Cordoban CGT. On August 6 Tosco spoke at an open assembly of some 6,000 SMATA workers and pledged the MSC's support for the auto-workers' strike.[26] The possibility of a conflict with the government and SMATA central increased when Salamanca, at the same assembly, re-jected the government's decreed obligatory arbitration and made menac-ing sounds about the *clasistas'* resolve to resist pressures from Buenos Aires; the workers voted overwhelmingly to continue the strike.[27]

Renault, the government, and the SMATA central were equally re-solved to break the strike and remove the troublesome *clasista* leader-ship. For the government, this was no ordinary industrial dispute. Capit-ulation by the company to the *clasistas'* wage demands would put in jeopardy the government's anti-inflation program and increase the *clasistas'* standing within the labor movement at the expense of the Per-onist labor leadership. As a result, throughout the conflict IKA-Renault director general Jacques Leroy, and Labor Minister Otero were in almost daily contact. The lockout at the Cordoban plants had been closely coor-dinated between the company and the government.[28] Rodríguez was also drawn into the conspiratorial circle. As a result of the broader implications for the government of the Cordoban local's actions, the SMATA central took the Labor Ministry's threats of a loss of legal status for the auto-workers' union with the utmost seriousness, compounding the deep an-tipathy it already felt for the Cordoban *clasistas* and making a response from the central obligation; it was only a matter of time.[29] On August 6 company officials, Otero, and a SMATA delegation headed by Rodríguez met to discuss the Cordoban situation. On August 8, the day a strike was called by the Cordoban SMATA and the MSC to protest the plant clo-sures, the SMATA central expelled Salamanca and the remaining twenty-two members of the Cordoban executive committee from the union and decreed the local union suspended, naming a caretaker committee from Buenos Aires to assume control. On government orders, the Central Bank froze the local's union funds in accounts throughout the country, while

Simó and the Cordoban Labor Ministry ignored entreaties to contest the SMATA central's actions.[30]

Rodríguez moved quickly to carry out the intervention against the SMATA-Córdoba. The same day, the SMATA central took out full-page ads in newspapers in Córdoba and Buenos Aires to denounce the *clasistas* and revive rumors of what seemed shopworn but were still apparently useful accusations of Córdoba's supposed sinister connections with foreign interests. The strike was characterized as "a defense of foreign ideologies," and Rodríguez implicated the entire Cordoban labor movement when he alleged it had poisoned the SMATA local and was involved in "a conspiracy of the traitorous left" *("la izquierda cipaya")* in the service of big business. Promising to "finish off" Córdoba, the SMATA president sought to justify the intervention not on the basis of the local leaders' demands, which he knew were supported by the rank and file, but through an appeal to the members' Peronist loyalties.[31] Complicating his position, however, were rumors of growing worker discontent in several of the Buenos Aires–based auto companies, including his own Ford plant, and sentiment was running high for the Cordoban strike among the country's autoworkers. Certainly working class disillusionment with the Pacto Social was widespread, and wildcat strikes were proliferating, especially in the automobile industry.[32]

Decisive action by the Cordoban labor movement might have frustrated Rodríguez's actions, but such decisiveness was not forthcoming for a variety of reasons. The August 8 strike by the Cordoban CGT had been only a modest success, since Atilio López and the UTA were embroiled in their own internal power struggle and the *legalistas'* participation had therefore been greatly weakened. López was attempting to win reelection in the bus workers' union and regain control of the militant, antiverticalist Peronist unions in the city, a fact that won him the enmity of the Peronist right. With the backing of the *ortodoxos,* López's union rivals formed an opposition slate to oppose him in August 17 union elections. The MSC's allies within the UTA had thus been preoccupied with internal union affairs at a crucial juncture and had not committed themselves to a strike that would have exposed them to even further charges of disloyalty to the Peronist government by the opposition slate. The absence of the *legalistas* at the public demonstration in the Plaza Vélez Sarsfield August 8 weakened the effectiveness of the strike, a fact noted with some bitterness in the speech delivered there by Salamanca.[33]

The MSC strike failed for other reasons, as well. As Tosco was to note later, a general mobilization of the working class proved impossible because the SMATA leadership, in an effort to remain within the legal limits of the Pacto Social, had decreed a production slowdown instead of an outright strike. There were considerable technical difficulties in many of the smaller SMATA-affiliated factories with conducting a slowdown as opposed to an outright suspension of production, and workers in the Ford-Transax, Grandes Motores Diesel, and Ilasa plants were forced to remain on the job.[34] Yet the lackluster results of the strike were not simply attributable to such fortuitous factors; they also had a political explanation. The unrelenting propaganda campaign by both the government and the Peronist labor bureaucracy was clearly having some effect on the overwhelmingly Peronist Cordoban working class. In every union where there existed a Peronist opposition, relations between it and the left-wing leadership had deteriorated sharply in the past year of Peronist rule. Even in the pluralist Luz y Fuerza, Ceballos's Peronists had virtually broken off dialogue with Tosco and entered into negotiations with the CGT leadership in Buenos Aires (this would culminate, ignominiously, in their cooperation with the government's takeover of the union in October). As was the case in many unions, the Luz y Fuerza Peronists opposed a solidarity strike with the SMATA *clasistas* because they regarded it as an essentially political strike directed against the Peronist government.[35] The result was a disappointing strike at a time when a convincing show of force was necessary to restrain both the government and the union centrals from interfering in Cordoban labor affairs. From this point on, the MSC effectively ceased to exist, and the militant Cordoban unions were fragmented into their traditional *legalista,* Independent, and *clasista* trinity.

Rodríguez confined his purge of Córdoba to the SMATA executive committee, preferring to ignore for the moment the thornier problem of the many *clasista* shop floor delegates. The Cordoban SMATA was thus spared the massive expulsion of union activists that had followed the collapse of the Fiat *clasista* movement. In Ferreyra, Fiat had used the opportunity both to deal a mortal blow to unionism in the complex and to effect a major restructuring of its labor force. Rodríguez and the SMATA central were aware of the risks of such a drastic response. Though the central wished to see all traces of *clasismo* expunged from Santa Isabel, it would hardly be served by dismantling the entire union apparatus in its most important local in the interior, much less by overseeing a massive company firing that would be certain to galvanize rank-and-file support for the ousted *clasista* leader. The central's policy over the following weeks was to continue its political campaign against the *clasistas,* denouncing their antinational designs and their sabotaging of the government's economic program, while attempting to forestall a company reaction, trying to keep Renault at bay until the union could bring to bear all the pressures of the Peronist government and wring concessions from the company that might raise its prestige among the workers. Rumors were already rife in the plants that the removal of their union leadership was really a ploy to reduce labor costs though firings and abrogate the gains that had been won by the *clasista* leadership over the past two years. The workers' suspicions were given graphic credence on August 14, when Renault announced plans to lay off some 2,800 workers in response to the production slowdowns and shop floor resistance that the union stewards continued to coordinate.[36]

In reality, gaining control of the SMATA in Córdoba was far more complicated than Rodríguez could have imagined. Beyond the continued strength of the *clasista* shop stewards and the company's precipitous behavior with the layoffs, the intervention was jeopardized by the union's very deep regional identity and members' suspicions of *porteño* interference in the Cordoban SMATA's affairs, which had always characterized the union, *clasistas, torristas,* and communists alike. Numerous incidents in the early months of the SMATA central's administration of the local indicated that the feelings of the *torristas* and communists were running far stronger against the *porteños'* intervention than for any shared need for retribution against Salamanca and the deposed *clasista* executive committee. In the Ford-Transax factory, where workers had assumed control of the plant to protest the SMATA central's removal of the union leadership, the Ford workers decried the company's policy of giving preference to its own Buenos Aires plants in the greatly reduced production of axles that had accompanied the strike. The workers controlling the plant, in an exercise of the *autogestión* so often championed in *clasista* discourse, announced that preference in the supply of axles would henceforth be given to Cordoban companies, specifically IME and IKA-Renault.[37] An abortive occupation of the union hall by the SMATA central representatives on August 23 and a subsequent police raid against the autoworkers' headquarters triggered a citywide strike of the Cordoban SMATA and violent confrontations with the police.[38] Widespread rank-and-file participation in the soup kitchens *(ollas populares)* organized by the *clasistas* for the laid-off workers created a community of solidarity around the conflict that strengthened rank-and-file resolve to resist the company, the government, and the SMATA central.[39]

Despite these encouraging signs, however, there was also cause for concern on the part of the *clasistas*. The Fuerzas Armadas Peronistas' assassination of IKA-Renault personnel director Ricardo Goya on August 27 had precisely the same negative effect on the *clasistas'* position as the Ejército Revolucionario del Pueblo's kidnapping and murder of Oberdán Sallustro had had in the final days of SITRAC-SITRAM. Unable to control the actions of the guerrilla left and opposed to its violent tactics, the local union leadership was nonetheless implicated in the press and by government and company spokesmen, an association that undoubtedly raised the suspicion in the minds of at least some workers that the accusations bruited about by Rodríguez against the *clasistas* were true. More seriously, despite nearly three months of conflict, Salamanca and the ousted executive committee seemed to have little appreciation for the weariness that had set in among the workers. In part, this was due to the reduced contact they had with the plants. The police occupation of the union hall had not only been a serious psychological blow but more importantly, it also attenuated the ties between the leadership and the workers. Tosco allowed the SMATA leadership to use the light and power workers' union hall, where they continued to coordinate resistance through the shop stewards' committee. But their prolonged absence from the plants and the loss of union facilities, union funds, and authority hampered their efforts and slowly undermined their position.

Throughout September, the deposed *clasistas* struggled to confront both the company and the union central but met with increasing difficulty. A closely coordinated strategy between Renault, Otero, and Rodríguez produced an agreement in which the company promised to rescind most of the recent firings, grant the workers a 28 percent wage hike, and meet virtually all the other union demands from the recent strike.[40] This conciliatory behavior stood in sharp contrast to the frightening reprisals for continued opposition. In September and October, José López Rega and his recently organized Alianza Anticomunista Argentina (AAA) unleashed a wave of terror and repression against the Cordoban workers' movement on a scale never before imagined. One of its first victims was Alfredo Curutchet, the *compañero abogado* of SITRAC who had continued to do legal work for dissident Cordoban unions, including the *clasista* SMATA. He was murdered on September 11 in one of the very first acts of the AAA.[41] Following the viewing of Curutchet's body in the Luz y Fuerza union hall, Tosco marched in the long funeral procession to the San Jeronimo Cemetery, his hand resting on the casket and his gaze grim and fixed ahead, perhaps with some premonition of the deaths that would follow.

Any presentiment he and other Cordoban workers may have had at that moment of an ominous future was heightened less than a week later by another murder. Since his defeat in the recent union elections, Atilio López had returned to work as an ordinary bus driver. Though out of power in the UTA, where he had been narrowly defeated by a well-financed, government-backed *ortodoxo* slate, López remained a symbol, somewhat sullied from his days as vice governor but still powerful, of the Córdoba's combative Peronist working class tradition. He was one who had been closely linked from the time of the Cordobazo to the city's left-wing unions. On September 16 the AAA kidnapped him and left his bullet-riddled body in an empty lot on the outskirts of Buenos Aires.[42]

Tosco's funeral orations at the grave of Curutchet and then of López were major public events, popular outpourings of grief in which the political differences of the past between the *legalistas,* Independents, and *clasistas* were forgotten. His eulogies were more than gestures of respect for two fallen comrades. They were warnings to all the city's dissident unions that these deaths were the start of a systematic campaign of extermination. The murders of Curutchet and López were the inauguration of what Tosco would subsequently describe as the "fascist reaction" by the right-wing sectors of Peronism, the start of a nationwide terror campaign that had its epicenter in Córdoba.[43]

Indeed, few doubts remained that Córdoba had been targeted for a bloody political purge. The counterrevolutionaries were proving to be more effective than the revolutionary left, proletarian or guerrilla. Party and labor activists were murdered by the dozens, and a sense of fear and desperation took hold of even the most seasoned and experienced veterans of what had long been a tempestuous political environment. Córdoba had experienced repression in the past, but this new situation was hardly comparable to anything seen before. Systematic political assassination had rarely been resorted to, even after the uprisings of 1969 and 1971. Yet since August, and with a furious intensity thereafter, violence became a common method of confronting political opposition, and it was especially directed from the right against the left.

It was in such a climate that the *clasistas* attempted to resist the SMATA central's actions and salvage their union mandate. The results were predictable. On September 23, workers in the Ford-Transax, Ilasa, Thompson Ramco, and Grandes Motores Diesel factories voted to approve Salamanca's proposal to continue the soldiering strikes in the plants but, more significantly, the IKA-Renault workers narrowly voted to return to work for a period of ten days, to give the company the opportunity to make good on its promised wage increase.[44] On October 4 the remaining SMATA workers joined them. Sensing a momentary weakness in the *clasista* ranks, army units raided the Luz y Fuerza union hall shortly thereafter and arrested SMATA undersecretary general Roque Romero and several other members of the former Cordoban SMATA executive committee who were working out of the union's makeshift headquarters there. Salamanca, who had just recently returned to his job in the forge, and the remaining SMATA *clasistas* immediately went into hiding.[45]

The SMATA strike had been a catastrophic tactical blunder by the *clasistas,* Salamanca in particular. They had nearly squandered the deep reservoir of goodwill and rank-and-file support earned through tough negotiating and honest leadership since their election in early 1972. The strike had provided their enemies in the company, the government, and the SMATA central with a perfect pretext to plot and carry out their demise. Badly underestimating the workers' susceptibility to accusations that their leaders were sabotaging the Peronist government, they had rashly embroiled the union in a prolonged, enervating dispute that it had been doomed from the start.

Yet the two years of *clasista* leadership had left a legacy that the SMATA workers would not easily forget. The *clasistas'* vigilance in protecting the workers on the shop floor, their successful efforts in reestablishing the *sábado inglés,* and their genuine workplace democracy were sources of untarnished prestige. Moreover, the workers' resentment of Rodríguez and the *porteño* delegation sent to run the union grew as news of the arrests spread. The strong regional identity that had been an important element in Cordoban working class history in the CGTA mobilizations, in the Cordobazo, and in the history of *clasismo* itself had resurfaced. Indeed, by the early 1970s the terms *porteño, traidor,* and *burócrata* had become virtually synonymous in local working class argot and expressed attitudes of mistrust and disdain that were widely shared by Cordoban workers but that were especially strong among the city's autoworkers.

Respect for the achievements of the *clasistas,* combined with the SMATA central's callous disregard for regional sensibilities, quickly rallied the Cordoban SMATA workers in support of their beleaguered former leaders. On October 10 the recently appointed military governor of Córdoba, General Raúl Oscar Lacabanne, visited the SMATA central's headquarters where he basked in Rodríguez's encomiums for having "finished with the image of a Marxist Córdoba which is really Peronist from head to toe," in response to which the general gratefully acknowledged that "without the support of the 62 Organizaciones and the CGT local nothing could have been done" and pledged that they "were cleaning up the city of the little that remains."[46] On November 6, however, the Cordoban SMATA workers gave the *clasista* leadership a badly needed vote of confidence when they abandoned their jobs in most of the SMATA-affiliated plants to demand the withdrawal of Rodríguez's union emissaries and the return of the local's elected leaders.[47] The workers' September decision to return to the plants had been a reprimand but not a repudiation of the executive committee. The shop stewards' movement remained strong on the factory floor, and though Rodríguez could occupy the local's union hall and impound its assets, he could not control the IKA-Renault workers' hearts and minds or break the resolve of activists in the SMATA plants to resist where it would be most effective: at the point of production.

Tosco, meanwhile, was attempting to rebuild yet another dissident labor alliance. In September he had hosted a national labor congress in Tucumán, the Plenario Nacional de Gremios en Conflicto, and had invited such mainstays of combative trade unionism as Ongaro's print workers and the Tucumán sugar workers, as well as those unions, such as the Rosario state workers and the Buenos Aires journalists' union, in which the Peronist left, either the Juventud Trabajadora Peronista or the Peronismo de Base, had a strong presence. Once again Tosco was assuming the realistic political position. Sensing that *clasismo*'s political fortunes had waned considerably with the return of a Peronist government to power, he sought to encourage the antiverticalist currents then at work within Peronist labor to compensate for the combative trade union movement's relative political weakness.

The government's last-minute proscription of the sugar workers' union, which was involved in yet another of a long series of strikes with the owners of the *ingenios,* and the arrest of the principal FOTIA leaders there, forced the congress to be held clandestinly. The congress produced a national resistance committee, the Coordinadora de Lucha Sindical, to coordinate opposition to the government's economic program and the CGT's verticalist measures.[48] Though this committee would be unable to coordinate labor opposition effectively at the national level, it would spawn the numerous resistance committees known as the *coordinadoras,* which would work effectively at the local and, in the case of Córdoba, at the provincial level in 1975.

With its status intact as the leading labor opponent to the government and the labor bureaucracy, the Cordoban light and power workers naturally became a principal target for the terrorist attacks of the AAA and the Peronist right. An outright prohibition of the union by the government, however, was problematic. In addition to the fact that Luz y Fuerza was protected by its membership in a federal union, a move against it was a great risk because of Tosco's national reputation and the union's prestige among the Cordoban working class, including much of the Peronist rank and file. The legitimacy of his leadership, his stature as a union leader of reputed incorruptibility and proven skill, had been demonstrated in his slate's decisive electoral victories ever since the late 1950s. Any intervention by the government would thus be repudiated in many political and union circles. By the same token, the government could not tolerate Tosco indefinitely. More than any other figure, he had sustained the labor opposition and had contributed to the resiliency of the city's dissident union tradition. So long as the Cordoban light and power workers' local continued to function with relative freedom, there would be a sizable, perhaps preponderant radical wing in Cordoban labor. After weeks of indecision, the government took action against the union on the grounds of its alleged involvement in "subversive activities" and sent army troops to occupy the union hall on October 10, the day following the SMATA union arrests.[49]

Direct intervention by the Peronist government rather than by a mediating union central, as in the case of the SMATA, assured more severe repression. Tosco and the executive committee narrowly escaped arrest and went into hiding, and the government's actions were thus directed against the union itself rather than just the leadership. Córdoba's governor, General Lacabanne, banned all union assemblies, permitted the sacking of the union archive and library, and oversaw the virtual suspension of all union activities, including its social welfare activities.[50]

The government's reprisals against light and power workers meant the dissident Cordoban labor movement had lost its spiritual mainstay. By year's end, the once formidable militant trade union alliance apparently lay in a shambles. Lacabanne used the absence of Tosco and the momentary weakness of the left-wing unions to annul the legal status of the Independents, and Simó and the UOM presided over the restructuring of the theretofore pluralistic Cordoban labor movement, purging the local CGT of its non-Peronist elements and fully integrating it into the national CGT's verticalist structure.

The purge of the labor movement was facilitated by the furious political violence in the city, which gave credence to the government's insistence that Córdoba was in a near insurrectionary state and seemed to justify drastic remedies. The assassination of leftist labor leaders continued, but the left now responded to the AAA and the government's terror campaign with one of its own. Most of the violence was between the Peronist right and the leftist guerrilla organizations. In the first two months of 1975, more than a dozen assassinations of police officials, military officers, and political figures were carried out, culminating with the February 26 kidnapping and subsequent murder of the American consul in Córdoba, John Patrick Egan. The resiliency of the guerrilla left in the city proved greater than that of the dissident labor movement, and the government seemed powerless to stop it.[51]

The union purge campaign, in contrast, seemed to be an unqualified success by early 1975. Labor dissidents all over the country had been eliminated, removed, or intimidated into silence. The cynosure of the labor opposition, Córdoba, had been at least temporarily neutralized. The strict verticalist structure of the Peronist labor movement seemed invulnerable, and even the most sanguine of the militant labor leaders had given up all hope of forming an alternative labor confederation. Between November 1974 and March 1975, labor strikes fell to their lowest levels in the three years of Peronist government, and the Labor Ministry was able to use the Ley de Seguridad to prevent further factory occupations of the sort that had proliferated in the first six months of Peronist rule.[52]

In 1975 the radical trade union movement was once again partially resuscitated by conflicts taking place within the metalworkers' union, specifically the unruly Villa Constitución local's ongoing feud with the UOM central. In March, the steel towns along the Paraná River exploded for the second time in less than a year. The steelworkers had demanded wage increases and union control of production rhythms; they also rose in protest against Lorenzo Miguel, the UOM central, and the government's efforts to withhold power from Alberto Piccinini's opposition slate, which had been elected in late 1974. The government responded immediately. To justify the elimination of a disturbing opposition in the heart of its most important labor ally, the UOM, the Peronist government claimed to have discovered a conspiratorial plot to destabilize the country, involving Villa Constitución and the Cordoban unionists who were at large. In March, it arrested more than forty union activists, including Piccinini and the union local's elected executive committee.

The arrests sparked a week-long popular protest in Villa Constitución on the scale of the great Cordoban urban rebellions of 1969 and 1971.

Afterward, strike committees organized in preparation for a prolonged confrontation with the Peronist government. From his hiding place in a monastery in the Cordoban *sierra,* Tosco sent a letter expressing his solidarity with the striking workers and stated his belief that the fate of the alternative trade union movement would be decided in Villa Constitución.[53] The strike ended on May 19, when the government released some of the imprisoned union activists and Piccinini opted for a tactical retreat and urged the workers to return to the plants. But two months of defiance had been a major achievement and had helped to check the verticalist campaign, as Tosco had foreseen. The strike and the support it had garnered from the left as well as from the Peronist working class, including several other UOM locals, cautioned a more vigilant policy from Miguel.[54]

More than by Villa Constitución strike, however, the belligerent labor opposition was saved by a ground swell of rank-and-file frustration with the Peronist restoration itself. Working class discontent had reached a critical state by mid-1975. The cost of living rose 21 percent in June and 35 percent in July, and a series of wildcat strikes, generally in defiance of union leaders, swept the country. The government's attempt to intervene in the collective bargaining negotiations of key unions created generally unfavorable union agreements and sparked widespread protests and union recovery movements among the workers. The automobile industry was the most affected by these rank-and-file movements, and its wage increases, which were far below what the UOM had acquired, prompted work stoppages, hostage taking, and demands that union leaders resign at Ford, GM, and other Buenos Aires plants.

In early July, the floodgates of discontent were opened by the CGT itself when, in an attempt to reestablish control of the unions, it called a forty-eight-hour general strike for July 7 and 8. Subsequently called the Rodrigazo in reference to the austerity program of new minister of economy, Celestino Rodrigo, that triggered it, the strike paralyzed the country.[55] The Rodrigazo revealed that it would be increasingly difficult for the government or the labor bureaucracy to uphold labor discipline on strictly political grounds, that loyalty to a Peronist government had glaring limitations under an economic program that adversely affected working class interests and that shop floor activists from both the Peronist and Marxist left were prepared to exploit. The CGT itself had made the resignation of José López Rega, President Isabel Perón's hated adviser and the presumed architect of the new plan, one of its principal demands in the general strike, and thus showed that the trade union hierarchy, besieged by rank-and-file movements, had begun to oppose the government out of the need for self-preservation.

In Córdoba, still the undisputed center of working class radicalism and opposition to *verticalismo,* the dissident labor movement had recovered from the setbacks of late 1974 and was again active in mobilizing the workers. Though the warrant for Tosco's arrest remained in effect, on August 13, 1975, a federal judge lifted all charges against Luz y Fuerza's executive committee, and the traditional *tosquista* union slate prepared to run for reelection in the September union elections. In ill health and on the run, Tosco himself had formed the Movimiento de Acción Sindical (MAS) to coordinate labor opposition among the more recalcitrant anti-verticalists. However, Tosco also abandoned his long-standing insistence on the necessity of maintaining the independence of the labor opposition from military strategies and moved closer to the guerrilla left.

The close friendships that Tosco had developed with members of the ERP during his long months of imprisonment in the Rawson penitentiary had never before led to more than a discreet sympathy with and a respectful if slightly chary attitude toward the *vía armada.* Unquestionably, the light and power workers' leader's priority had always been to build an alternative labor alliance free from ties to non–working class organizations. But cut off from close contact with both his own union and the Cordoban labor movement and with the bitter results of Peronist restoration still fresh in his mind—the abandonment by López in 1973 and then the government's repressive measures in 1974—Tosco cast his lot with those groups making the most serious bid to capture state power. Though he had repeatedly expressed misgivings about armed struggle in the past, Tosco now sought the unity of the left and the participation of the radical unions in a revolutionary struggle.

The Cordoban labor resistance, however, developed largely independently of Tosco's reformulated strategic designs. Resistance committees, or *coordinadoras,* had emerged in opposition to Miguel, Rodríguez, and the CGT hierarchy generally, in Córdoba and throughout the country, but were not associated with the guerrilla left. In early June, activists in the Fiat and SMATA-affiliated plants had formed the most important of these resistance committees, the Mesa Provisoria de los Gremios en Lucha, and the long-desired unity of the Cordoban autoworkers was at last somewhat achieved, though in a clandestine, subterranean fashion.[56] Most important, this autoworker-led *coordinadora* served as a kind of parallel CGT to draw together dissident local unions. In Córdoba, the rank and file did not actively participate in the *coordinadora,* and membership was largely confined to the *clasista* shop stewards and union activists. But the workers did rally independently behind numerous *coordinadora*-led strikes in the latter half of 1975, in behalf of higher wages and, in the case of the SMATA workers, to demand the release of the imprisoned executive committee and the lifting of the warrant for Salamanca's arrest.[57] In the SMATA plants, the continuing power of the *clasista* shop stewards was evidenced by the central steering committee, the Comisión Normalizadora's frequent references to them and its criticism of their role in encouraging shop floor agitation and organizing the wildcat strikes in the plants.[58] Indeed, 1975 witnessed the greatest number of work stoppages seen in the IKA-Renault plant complex during the tumultuous period between 1966 and 1976 (Table 9.2).

Rodríguez's stewardship of the SMATA local had proved to be a failure. The union emissaries sent from Buenos Aires had used a panoply of methods to root out the *clasista* presence in the plants, including an intensive indoctrination campaign and a suggestive attempt to claim Peronist responsibility for the Cordobazo, aware of what a powerful symbol it had become for the *clasistas* and for the SMATA workers generally.[59] But the central's efforts to reassert control of the union had been impeded by the Peronist labor hierarchy's defense of the government's conservative economic program and also by Renault's unwillingness to negotiate further concessions to the interventors beyond the September 1974 wage hike. Shortly after the removal of the *clasistas,* Renault had bristled at the SMATA's demand that all automobile manufacturers make a contribution of 1 percent their annual profits to the autoworkers' social welfare pro-

Table 9.2 Work stoppages, IKA-Renault complex, Santa Isabel, 1967–1976

Year	Work stoppages	Hours lost
1967	27	451,498
1968	—	—
1969	54 (Jan.–Oct.)	882,585
1970	132	1,353,924
1971	46	613,344
1972	49	583,061
1973	61	670,447
1974	120	947,289
1975	219	1,755,596
1976	61	414,249

Source: Industrial Relations Department, Company Records on Work Stoppages, Renault S.A. Santa Isabel, Argentina.

grams and that they accept a union delegate's participation in future meetings with the government.[60] Indeed, from the point of view of the French multinational, the struggles between the Peronists and the *clasistas* receded to an issue of secondary importance as the company wrestled with the government's erratic economic policies, runaway inflation, and disastrous market conditions. Renault also perceived the imposed union leadership's lack of legitimacy among the workers and therefore its inability to serve as an ineffective shop floor disciplinarian. By mid-1975, the company was virtually ignoring the union interventors and dealing directly with unofficial plant committees comprising both *clasistas* and *torristas* that were for all practical purposes now representing the IKA-Renault labor force.

Company officials realized the Peronist union leaders, under siege from the rank and file, would attempt to make the companies pay in their effort to shore up their eroded authority among the workers. IKA-Renault, at least, was in no position to make such concessions. In late 1975, company officials noted that no gains in productivity had been made in the past five years. Working conditions had seriously deteriorated in the plants over the past year; at the same time the erratic supply of parts and components, and thus the daily adjustments made in the production process that caused the repeated moving of workers in and out of job classifications, had occasioned absentee rates of alarming proportions, between 15 and 20 percent.[61] IKA-Renault teetered on the edge of bankruptcy, because to all these problems was added the more than $64 million in outstanding loans it owed to the home office. The widening exchange rates resulting from galloping inflation made repayment at a time of slumping sales virtually impossible.[62]

With the shop floor threat posed by the *clasistas* seeming to be less serious than the lack of an effective union interlocutor, Renault proved to be an unwilling partner in the SMATA central's attempt to reestablish its authority in the Cordoban plants. The SMATA's urgent need to establish control of the Cordoban local was heightened by the imminent threat that the autoworkers' union would lose its power and influence within the Peronist labor movement. Since the automobile industry remained a hotbed of militancy and therefore a liability for its economic program, the government gave signs in early 1975 of its intention to assign jurisdiction of the country's some 120,000 automobile workers to its principal labor ally and a potentially more effective working class disciplinarian, the UOM.[63]

In response to both Renault and the government, the SMATA central changed tactics after the upheavals of the Rodrigazo. It began to criticize the government's economic plan, and it embraced a militant campaign for wage increases for the SMATA workers, which were won in November of that year.[64] The *clasistas'* influence in the SMATA plants began to decline sharply in these same months. In part this resulted from the central's changed tactics, but mainly it represented the exhaustion of the charged political environment in the local that had begun with the CGTA rebellion and intensified in the aftermath of the Cordobazo. A certain fatigue had set in among the Cordoban autoworkers, and as rumors began to circulate of an impending military coup and the fall of a bitterly disappointing Peronist government, they grew reconciled to the idea that the central afforded them some measure of protection that the *clasistas,* out of power and now clearly with little chance of recovering it, could not give them.

Salamanca's personal history was the most eloquent testimony of *clasismo's* demise. His ties to the workers grew weaker in 1975 while those to the PCR party apparatus in Córdoba tightened and became more restrictive. Without the union, Salamanca could find an outlet for his opinions but not his ambitions, much less his revolutionary dreams. His outspokenness and renegade personality did not sit well with the PCR hierarchy in Buenos Aires, which had barely tolerated his ways when he had been secretary general of the most important industrial union in the Argentine interior and the party member with the greatest political profile in the country. Soon there were rumors circulating that he had Soviet connections, an accusation more damning than any other in the conspiratorial world of the PCR. By late 1975, Salamanca had become a prisoner of his own party's contradictions. Though he was not one of the architects of the party's astonishing volte-face to support Isabel Perón's government, he was not a critic of it. In his last letter to the SMATA workers, he parroted the conspiratorial obsessions of his party, being either oblivious to reality or following party directives to ignore what were the real concerns of the SMATA workers. But his words were by that point largely hollow politically, no more than the feeble death rattle of Cordoban *clasismo.*[65]

The other commanding figure of the Cordoban working class, Agustín Tosco, died before he would have to witness the collapse of the dissident labor movement he had done so much to create. The long years of imprisonment and his final months on the run had sapped Tosco's once robust figure and reduced him to frailty. Suffering from a number of illnesses, his last torment was a neck boil that, left unattended, had abscessed and poisoned his blood system. As his condition steadily worsened in October, plans to smuggle him out of the country to Mexico were changed; Tosco insisted that he remain in the country. Accepting an offer from the ERP to transport him to Buenos Aires, he moved to the capital city. There he received a massive dose of antibiotics that proved too much for his weakened system and caused a fatal heart attack on November 5.[66] The public viewing of Tosco's body and the funeral cortege, a march of tens of thousands through the Cordoban streets, was one of the greatest outpourings of public grief in Córdoba's history, comparable to Perón's, which had taken place less than a year before. At the grave site in the San Jerónimo Cemetery, near the neighborhoods where just six years before he had stood at the barricades during the Cordobazo, workers, students, and common citizens listened to the funeral eulogies and watched as police and army troops filed into the cemetery grounds. The events in the cemetery themselves became a kind of metaphor for the death of the Cordoban labor left. The jeers of the crowd directed against the security forces were answered with gunfire that scattered the mourners, and Tosco's casket was left to await a solitary burial in the Luz y Fuerza mausoleum later that day.[67]

The significance of Tosco's death was naturally most immediately felt in his own union. There, many of the workers who had endured the persecution of their union while Tosco was alive were reluctant to transfer their allegiance to his successors. The despondency was great, although a certain relief that the union's prominent political involvement had come to an end may also have been felt by many workers, as one scholar has suggested.[68] The dejection and confusion of Tosco's collaborators, the loss of their leader and moral conscience, and the renewal of the terror campaign against them, now ominously directed by the military rather than the AAA and the Peronist right, forced a number of Luz y Fuerza activists into hiding and intimidated the majority of the workers into silence. The light and power workers had repudiated the government's intervention of their union just shortly before, in the victory of Tosco's slate in the September 11 union elections, demonstrating that support for the union's general policies remained as strong as ever. But the will to resist was gone, and many prepared for the worst as the ineffectiveness of Isabel Perón's government almost willfully seemed to invite yet another military coup.

The Cordoban automobile workers were also affected by the gloom surrounding the government's final days in power. The crisis that had erupted in the labor movement, the mutinies in Villa Constitución and other union locals, the rank-and-file mobilizations and repudiation of *verticalismo,* the *patria metalúrgica* and the fight against government's economic program—all of which had gone on throughout the nearly three years of Peronist rule—certainly could not be sustained by the Fiat or SMATA *clasistas.* By early 1976 the *coordinadoras* had disintegrated, and the *clasistas* who were still active on the shop floor were increasingly isolated. The working class mobilizations that took place in the city's automotive plants thereafter were not in opposition to *verticalismo,* and much less did they aspire to the overthrow of Argentine capitalism. Now they would be strictly defensive, in direct response to runaway inflation and inadequate wages; they would be led by the UOM and SMATA centrals themselves, as they tried to strengthen their position among the rank and file and force a change in direction on the part of the government, which was increasingly indifferent to the pleas of its labor allies.

The Cordoban strikes had lost their former power. By early 1976 Renault was far more concerned with its efforts to either "Argentinize" its operations and convince the government to become its partner through a merger of the IME and IKA-Renault operations or disengage itself altogether from Argentina than it was concerned with labor problems.[69] Indeed, it was now almost grateful for strikes, which helped the company reduce costs at a time of slumping sales and meager profits.[70]

Nationally, the Peronist labor movement's internal power struggles and increasing estrangement from the government undermined any hope that the labor bosses had of reestablishing the kind of influence and power they had wielded in the days of Vandor. The third great figure of the dissident trade union movement, Raimundo Ongaro, abandoned the country to live in exile in Peru when he was released from prison in August. The threat to the labor bosses, however, no longer came from the likes of Ongaro but from their struggles against each other.

After it had become apparent that the UOM would monopolize union power and influence as the Peronist government's principal labor interlocutor, the SMATA had renewed its long-standing feud with the metalworkers' union. Rodríguez had made considerable progress in centralizing the autoworkers' union apparatus, thereby enabling the SMATA to make a respectable challenge to the metalworkers. In addition to removing dissident currents from within, particularly by getting control of the troublesome Cordoban local, he had further centralized the collective bargaining process in the agreement the autoworkers had signed in the days following the Rodrigazo that established an industrywide wage scale for all job classifications. The traditional source of power for autoworkers' union locals such as the Cordoban SMATA, direct negotiations with the company and independence from Buenos Aires, had thus been eliminated.[71] Nevertheless, the fierce rivalry between the UOM and the SMATA for control of the labor movement obstructed efforts by both unions to reassert control over their rank and file via centralized collective bargaining negotiations. Each had tried to outdo the other in the 1975 contract talks, thereby stalling final agreements and creating conditions that had allowed shop floor activists to exploit the uncertainty and agitation in the workplace, notably in Córdoba but also in other plants such as the Ford complex, a traditional stronghold of antibureaucratic sentiment and rank-and-file militancy among the Buenos Aires factories.[72] By the end of the year, though the shop floor dissidents were fewer in Córdoba they remained active in the Buenos Aires plants; the SMATA central's control had only formally been buttressed.

The final reckoning came on November 14, 1975, when the SMATA's deepest fears were at last realized and the government awarded jurisdiction over the autoworkers to the UOM. The Labor Ministry's decision (*laudo* 29/75) had been hovering over the autoworkers since early that year. On November 26 an estimated 40,000 SMATA workers met in Luna Park and marched to the Congress to protest the encroachments of the UOM on their union and the government and Lorenzo Miguel's attempts to annex the autoworkers' union.

That annexation was consummated just as the Peronist government entered the last days of a tumultuous and crisis-ridden three years in power.[73] The principal of *verticalismo* had been taken to its ultimate end; union power had been centralized. But it was not enough to prevent a moribund and discredited government from falling on March 24, 1976. The verticalist, Peronist labor movement was not able, in fact, to offer the feeblest resistance against a military coup that would establish a savagely repressive regime—a regime that would take the lives of thousands of workers and persecute and harass the labor movement into a position of marginality in the country's political life for years to come.

In Córdoba a series of events, some premeditated and some fortuitous, had conspired to defeat the city's dissident unions and undermine its militant working class tradition. The Cordoban labor movement was incorporated into that of the nation, and the possibilities it once offered to the working class and the left vanished. By the time of the coup, few remained free and alive who still seriously envisioned an alternative to Peronist trade unionism based on the Cordoban unions. When the most important of the still-active *clasista* leaders, Salamanca, fell into government hands the very day of the coup, it was more significant for its metaphorical poignancy than its political relevance. By the time of Salamanca's disappearance and subsequent murder in the La Perla death camp several weeks later, not only *clasismo* but also the Cordoban unions had ceased to represent any threat to the Peronist labor bosses or Argentina's battered but hardly expiring capitalist order. The combined powers of the state, their working class brethren in the Peronist labor movement, and the dissident Cordoban labor movement's own contradictions and fatal weaknesses had been enough to ensure that if the revolution came to Argentina, it would be without the Cordoban unions.

· IV ·

The Politics of Work

The factory occupations had less to do with the workers'
grievances than the need to be in control for once.

Simone Weil, *Expérience de la vie d'usine*

· T E N ·

Work and Politics in Córdoba

An upsurge in militancy and the political radicalization of at least some sectors of the local labor movement characterized Cordoban working class history after 1966, particularly following the Cordobazo. The local working class was broadly affected by this process, but its greatest impact was felt in the two automotive complexes. Ferreyra and Santa Isabel were the sites of another expression of Cordoban labor politics, not the power politics of the trade union movement, but a politicization that was rooted in the workplace and alternately complemented and clashed with the power rivalries, tactical jockeying for bargaining muscle, ideological disputes, and broader political designs that explained much of the labor militancy in the city. In the Fiat and IKA-Renault plants, labor and capital confronted each other in a struggle for control of the workplace that was occasioned by the particular production context found in Cordoban automotive manufacturing. There, the connection between work and the emergence of a radical union leadership was more direct than anywhere else in the local trade union movement. The shop floor politics in the Fiat and IKA-Renault plants not only deepened the militancy of the Cordoban working class, but also contributed to the articulation of an ideological alternative to Peronist trade unionism, *clasismo*.[1]

The origins of the Cordoban autoworkers' militancy and the *clasista* movement are therefore not only found in union and revolutionary politics, Córdoba's distinct political culture, and the Cordobazo but also in the market conditions, production processes, and management practices of the Cordoban automobile industry. The most salient characteristic of the automobile industry everywhere is its hypersensitivity to changes in the business cycle. Auto sales are always extremely volatile, subject to sud-

305

den jumps and slumps in demand and affected by both seasonal and cyclical fluctuations.[2] This natural fragility becomes chronic instability when to this characteristic there are added the periodic crises that plague a weak capitalist economy such as Argentina's. Because automotive production was almost totally dependent on domestic demand, it is not surprising that the fortunes of the Cordoban automobile industry closely mirrored the general health of the country's economy and that sales, particularly after 1965, were notoriously erratic while the decade-long automotive boom began to lose steam.[3] Though the annual volume of automobile production and sales increased in Argentina and in Córdoba between 1960 and 1976, profit figures for the industry were unstable, and good years alternated with catastrophic ones (Table 10.1).

In addition to market volatility and industrial doldrums, Fiat and IKA-Renault were faced with the slow but stubborn deterioration of the Cordoban automobile industry with regard to their Buenos Aires competitors. In the late 1950s, with demand still far exceeding supply, the Frondizi government's courting of foreign automotive investment had completely restructured the industry. Among the new investors, Ford, General Motors, Chrysler, Mercedes-Benz, Citroën, and, slightly later, Peugeot, established manufacturing operations in and around Buenos Aires in the early 1960s, thereby ending the dominance of the market by the Cordoban-based companies, Fiat and especially IKA, that had characterized the first years of the industry. This rush of investment soon overwhelmed demand, and of the twenty-one companies producing motor vehicles at the start of the decade only eleven remained in 1967.

The new market conditions changed the very nature of the industry. In a reduced and now highly competitive market, manufacturers adopted a policy of model diversification and frequent, stylistic changes—producing more and flashier models though not necessarily improving the cars' technology—to serve the conspicuous consumption habits and fickleness of the privileged pool of car buyers. The automobile industry now found its customers among the country's upper income groups, and the workers who built the cars could rarely afford to buy them in the firsthand market. The industry's exceptionally high price inelasticity, the inability to prime demand through price manipulations, was just one proof that the industry was thenceforth serving a small pool of relatively affluent customers.[4]

As one scholar of the industry notes, these changes led to scale inefficiencies and raised the costs of production, leading to a "high-cost, high-price, low-volume" industry.[5] Nevertheless demand remained unstable, highly erratic in fact, and vulnerable to the vagaries of government policy and the volatile Argentine economy. Even those who were relatively

Table 10.1 Annual profits, automobile industry, 1960–1976 (in millions of pesos; includes trucks and jeeps)

	1960	1961	1962	1963	1964	1965	1966	1967	1968	1969
IKA-Renault	504	746	703	131	615	1,791	1,591	483	-2,182	242
Fiat	143	323	108	660	998	1,208	3,319	2,061	2,043	5,325
Ford	901	761	38	-699	1,031	2,104	3,319	1,233	5,016	4,331
General Motors	712	889	-99	-724	589	1,407	1,752	1,644	3,991	4,771
Chrysler	45	131	221	199	47	24	397	526	493	2,356
IAFA-SAFRAR	—	283	527	-132	—	114	109	295	465	795
Citroën	—	9	18	-27	-54	-110	-163	44	152	366
Mercedes-Benz	101	104	-31	-97	73	-95	65	-51	153	397
IASF	3	75	4	-75	-69	34	-67	-323	—	—
Di Tella Automotores	244	456	198	112	256	-1,971	-1,197	—	—	—

	1970	1971	1972	1973	1974	1975	1976
IKA-Renault	-729	84	153	-2,870	-11,428	-210,020	-517,980
Fiat	6,048	1,870	1,160	-666	-7,162	2,090	83,250
Ford	720	4,146	3,070	4,603	-23,153	-121,670	469,400
General Motors	1,009	496	-12,396	-15,300	-27,000	-194,690	-508,300
Chrysler	172	-526	2,412	-4,082	-11,008	-11,010	87,200
IAFA-SAFRAR	324	65	-2,424	-5,849	-3,260	2,680	-43,100
Citroën	-300	-1,942	293	-8,440	-7,963	6,700	-212,230
Mercedes-Benz	45	244	260	-2,697	-5,000	4,280	132,890

Source: Juan V. Sourrouille, *El complejo automotor en Argentina* (Mexico City: Editorial Nueva Imagen, 1980), pp. 60–61.

affluent, particularly buyers in the middle class, could be scared away from the considerable investment that an automotive purchase represented in Argentina by government economic policies that raised interest rates or by social and political turmoil and economic uncertainty. An industry subject to such cyclical volatility also required flexibility with regard to its labor costs. Argentine automobile manufacturers would have preferred to adjust production and labor costs according to sales, by laying off workers in times of slumps and hiring them back when demand recovered, much as automobile companies all over the world have historically done. The North American automobile industry managed to do this through a system of recall rights based on plant-level seniority agreements, which were complemented by the generous supplementary unemployment benefits won by the United Auto Workers union in the early postwar years.[6] In Mexico and especially Brazil, hire and fire practices were an accepted part of the industry's labor policy and were made possible by the relative weakness of the labor movements and the strength of the state in those countries.[7]

Hire and fire practices did not characterize the Argentine automobile industry, and Córdoba's in particular, for various reasons. The price-inelastic market for automobiles meant that the companies, within certain limits, had more leeway to pass on greater costs through price increases without affecting demand. After 1966, moreover, the state generally refrained from interfering in the industry's price policies. A 1971 IKA-Renault company report, for example, recorded with considerable calm a recent wage increase for its labor force, noting that the government could be counted on to agree to price increases to compensate for the higher wages, a situation that would only be reversed in 1973 with the price freezes under the Pacto Social.[8] The hefty indemnities for fired workers that Argentine law required cautioned other strategies as well. In 1974, in the midst of the most serious crisis in its history, IKA-Renault allotted money only for indemnities due to death on the job and none for firings, an obligatory indemnity for thousands of laid-off workers that the company regarded as too costly an option in any attempt to reduce its labor bill.[9] Finally, the latent power of the labor movement in Argentina and especially in Córdoba in these years, made untenable hire and fire policies such as those routinely practiced by automobile companies operating in Brazil and Mexico. After an attempt at following such policies in 1968 sparked bitter labor protests and severe social disturbances in Córdoba, IKA-Renault decided that the reduction of its labor costs would be very difficult and thenceforth possible only in piecemeal fashion, through a slow reduction of its labor force and gradual industrial reconversion, not through periodic mass layoffs adjusted to changes in the business cycle.[10] Several years later, when the position of the company was seriously eroded, the tense political and social conditions in Córdoba again forced IKA-Renault officials to dismiss the possibility of sizable reductions of its labor force to alleviate its grave business problems.[11]

The situation in Argentina, particularly in Córdoba, was thus quite different from the automobile industry in other parts of Latin America. In the 1960s periodic attempts were made to resort to what might be termed the Brazilian model. But the 1962 IKA layoffs, those of Fiat in 1965, and the several attempts undertaken by IKA-Renault between 1966 and 1968 to sizably reduce its labor force in times of reduced profits were frustrated by a combination of union vigilance, company temerity, and the quick recovery of auto sales. Mass firings before 1976 were rare and tended to follow major confrontations between the unions and the companies, such as those following the great 1970 IKA-Renault strike or the final banning of SITRAC-SITRAM in late 1971. Layoffs were thus episodic rather than routine. One result was that the Cordoban automobile industry was characterized by a high degree of labor stability. In IKA-Renault plants, union demands in the 1960s were concerned predominantly with wage issues, not job stability.[12] IKA-Renault's company records, moreover, show a remarkably stable labor force between 1966 and 1976 (Table 10.2), and among the long list of worker grievances championed by the *clasista* Fiat and IKA-Renault unions, job security did not figure prominently.

Although Cordoban automobile workers were thus subject to fewer

Table 10.2 Employment figures and union affiliation, IKA-Renault

Year	No. of workers	Union members	Percent with union affiliation
1966	7,222	6,373	88
1967	6,591	5,949	90
1969	5,976	5,305	89
1970	5,266	5,068	96
1973	6,034	5,315	88
1974	7,350	5,839	79
1975	8,510	6,147	72
1976	7,656	5,845	76

Source: Industrial Relations Department, Employment Records, Renault Argentina S.A., Santa Isabel, Argentina.

layoffs than those in Brazil or Mexico, when they were laid off the workers tended to leave the industry permanently, finding employment in the nondynamic sectors of Cordoban industry (flour mills, textile plants, and the like), in the service sector, or, as one scholar has posited for the Buenos Aires–based companies, as independent mechanics with their own workshop, or *taller*.[13] Unlike his Brazilian counterpart, the Cordoban automobile worker did not bounce in and out of work or drift from company to company in accordance with an unstable business cycle and fickle company hiring policies but generally kept his job with either Fiat or IKA-Renault and stayed with the company for the length of his work life in the local automobile industry. The minority of workers who did lose their jobs often were paying the price for union activism and suffering management's reprisals in the form of outright firings, company black-lists, and banishment from the local automobile industry altogether.

If labor market strategies were not an option for IKA-Renault or Fiat, they nevertheless could not hope to compete with the Buenos Aires firms simply by maintaining the status quo. By the time of the 1966 Onganía coup, it was clear that Córdoba's preeminence in the country's automobile industry was being seriously threatened by the newly arrived firms in Buenos Aires. Particularly in the case of IKA, the competition from the major American manufacturers that had prompted the company's earlier move from the United States seemed to have reappeared in Argentina in even more threatening forms. IKA's total sales in 1965 were still the highest in the industry, but its market share had been declining since the arrival of the other firms at the start of the decade. In 1964, for the first time, IKA was not the industry leader in annual profits, surrendering that position to Ford. In 1966 it trailed behind both Ford and General Motors, as well as Fiat, and the company actually registered its first losses in 1968. Fiat fared somewhat better, but its rates of growth, until 1969, were well behind those of Ford and only slightly better than those of General Motors, a situation that greatly disappointed the Italian company, since it had only made the decision to reconvert its Concord tractor factory to automotive production when it had appeared that IKA and Fiat would be able to divide up the Argentine market between them.[14]

To meet mounting competition, IKA and Fiat undertook a series of financial and administrative reforms, but they depended most heavily on increasing labor productivity and lowering labor costs to survive in what had become a cutthroat market. In the Fiat plants, this entailed not so much plant rationalizations as it did deepening already established man-agement practices and labor processes that sought to maximize worker productivity. In the Kaiser plants, in turn, structural reforms that included changes in technology and the organization of production were adopted.

The sale of IKA to Renault in 1967 was the first step in a broad process of plant rationalizations and productivity reforms in the Santa Isabel terminals. As a small and essentially Argentine company, IKA lacked the financial resources and even the technological capacity to modernize its plants and overcome the advantages in access to capital and proximity to market that were enjoyed by the Buenos Aires–based companies. Reports from Renault technical teams that visited the Kaiser factories during the months of negotiations to buy the IKA complex included a mixture of praise for certain plants, notably the forge, and general disappointment with the lack of transfer equipment, absence of shop floor discipline, and primitive nature of the production and assembly line work in most of the plants.[15] Painfully aware of their own inability to undertake the reforms necessary to reestablish the company's leadership, Kaiser officials nonetheless convinced Renault of the French multinational's chances to rescue the beleaguered company through a broad modernization program.

To analyze and assess the significance of the companies' productivity schemes and their effects on the labor force, it is necessary to bear in mind the nature of auto manufacturing and auto work in general, as well as the specific shop floor conditions that existed in the IKA-Renault and Fiat complexes. Automobile manufacturing has represented industrial production on its largest and most integrated scale. Automobile plants rarely have labor forces of less than 2,500, thus making them larger than textile, chemical, shipbuilding, and nearly all other major industrial concerns. In Argentina, only the major steel complexes had labor forces comparable in size. In addition, the car plants were unique, as they are everywhere, in the diversity of functions workers performed, spanning a range of operations that included the forging of metals to sophisticated machine tool production to the simpler final assembly work (Figure 2). Automotive manufacturing is also unique for its organizational complexity and integrated nature. Henry Ford once remarked that his factories were a river nourished by streams. The forges, the smelting and stamping departments, were the river's sources, the production lines the streams, and final assembly the river. The metaphor accurately depicts the interdependent nature of automotive production. The automotive plants' web of parts- and materials-producing departments, each engaged in its own production processes, created a clockwork-like operation whose enormous manufacturing capacities were ironically offset by their vulnerabil-

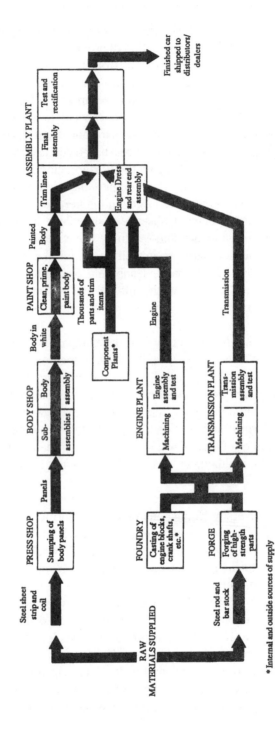

Figure 2 The manufacturing process in the automobile industry. *Source:* Central Policy Review Staff (1975), "The Future of the British Car Industry," London: HMSO.

ity, work stoppages in any one department being capable of paralyzing the entire line of production.

Autoworkers have shown an unusual propensity to undertake such actions, as work stoppages, a fact that can be attributed to the specific pressures that result from the relationship between production, costs, and profitability in this industrial sector. Lowering labor costs in the automobile industry has rarely been attempted simply by lowering wages. The higher skill levels required for relatively small but crucial parts of the production process (tool and die making, machinery repair, electrical work) and especially the rigorous working conditions autoworkers are subject to, make it a high-wage industry. Since the establishment of Ford's "five dollar day," managers have found higher than average wages necessary to attract workers to the monotony and general dreariness of work in a car plant and to avoid high levels of labor turnover.[16]

Instead of through wage cuts, automobile manufacturers have sought labor flexibility, the ability to respond quickly to the vagaries of the car market, through two methods: layoffs and what can generically be called the speedup. Production is adjusted according to profits through the use of one or both of these methods and not, for example, through overtime. Indeed, overtime is handed out stingily in an automobile plant. The overtime differential frequently nullifies production gains and has historically been used only when greater output is needed in one department to balance it with that in other plant departments.[17]

In the course of the 1960s, inefficiency and inflated labor costs, real or imagined, became the source of company grumbling at both IKA-Renault and Fiat. Getting control of their labor bills was unquestionably a more decisive variable for them than it was for the European or American automobile industries, which enjoyed access to vast consumer and capital markets, were constantly undertaking technological innovations, and were able to prime demand through price reductions, advertisement, and creative installment plans. Since hire and fire policies were precluded, the Cordoban companies had only one realistic alternative: the speedup. Labor costs historically have been attacked in the automobile industry, in Argentina and elsewhere, by constant efforts to reduce the labor time spent on a unit, to maximize labor's cost efficiency. The less time spent on one unit the greater the profit margin, as surplus value will have been enhanced by maximizing production.[18] The time study therefore has been one of the hallmarks of management practice in the industry. "Fordism," the application of strictly timed work to the mechanical rhythms of the line, was the method whereby the diversity and scale of automobile production were reconciled. Fordism took the Taylorist principle of the subdivision into minute and repetitive tasks and adapted it to the moving line. Such a system allowed Ford and his successors to create the acme of twentieth-century industrial capitalism, the car plant. It also permitted a unique system of labor control, which management sought to put to use in the inexorable drive for profits.

Time studies have not always met with the opposition of automobile workers or their unions, since occasionally they have been used to increase production without placing an added burden on the workers. But for the most part the time study has been perceived by automobile workers—correctly perceived—to be the handmaiden of the speedup. It is because of the power that time and motion engineers wield over the workers in automobile plants that a near universal demand of autoworkers' unions has been to have a say in determining production rates. The unions have sought to standardize these rates to avoid abuses in the speedup and have therefore presented their grievances in terms of demands for the abolition of piece rates (a precipitating factor in the Fiat *clasista* movement, for example), the use of fixed wage rates, and the establishment of a standard procedure for relief work, to be determined by the workers themselves.[19]

The speedup can, of course, simply mean increased production rhythms, that is, reallocating the tasks on the line into smaller units and then raising the speed of the line. More specifically it has meant one of two things: increasing the speed of the line without altering the operations or the number of workers on the line, thereby making the workers work faster, or removing workers from the line and giving the remaining workers more tasks to perform, thus again making them work faster to fulfill their line responsibilities. The latter type has been particularly common in the industry and has been called the "stretch-out" in the U.S. automobile factories. Both practices were widespread in the Fiat and IKA-Renault plants by the late 1960s.[20]

The United Auto Workers secretary general Walter Reuther's famous description of automobile plants as "chrome-plated sweat shops" pithily captured the rigorous conditions inherent in automotive production. Yet a simple correlation between difficult working conditions and labor militancy has glaring limitations as an analytical tool and does little to explain the reasons for the militancy of autoworkers generally and those of the Cordoban unions in particular. The arduous working conditions in the industry are only relevant when put into their specific social and shop floor context. Nevertheless, it is possible to sketch broadly the relations between labor and capital from the workers' point of view before discussing the specific cases of the Cordoban companies.

The integrated nature of automotive manufacturing, the complex weave of production, subassembly, and final assembly subject autoworkers not necessarily to greater pressures than workers in other industries, but to different ones. At the mercy of the time study and erratic market demand, instability of one form or another characterizes auto work; it can mean either the ever-present threat of a layoff or uncertainty on the job itself. Frequent model changes, for example, have unsettled workers and created tensions on the shop floor. The restructuring of production methods that this requires, with machine tools having to be rebuilt and rearranged to produce new parts, presses fitted with new dies, work rhythms and sequences modified, can disrupt established work practices and foment conflict in the workplace.[21] Autoworkers thus have had to contend to a far greater extent than most industrial workers with the impersonal demands of time and machine. As one scholar has noted, the only freedom the autoworker can expect comes through a concerted effort to get ahead of the work flow; but that creates a "burnout" situation, which may afford the worker some ephemeral sense of retribution but can only be sustained in short bursts.[22]

Disputes exist about the role played by foremen in the shop floor politics surrounding production. In some cases a company's centralized control over work speeds and job assignments has relegated the foreman to a secondary role as a troubleshooter; others have stressed the foreman's continued importance as the "pusher," a labor disciplinarian who is responsible for getting the work out on time and up to standards and who is also management's most vital link to the rank and file and its most important source of information on shiftless, insolent, or rebellious workers.[23] In Córdoba, with its lower incidence of machine-paced production and, in the case of Fiat, its piecework production practices, foremen played a crucial role, and the surly, authoritarian, often incompetent foreman became a recurring theme in the *clasista* discourse.

Historically, autoworkers have suffered instability or foremen's abuse only so long before they have expected their union representatives to intercede on their behalf. Shop stewards in autoworkers' unions are in an unusually sensitive position in this respect, compared with most industries. They have to intermediate on behalf of the workers in their departments, but they are also reluctant to let discipline break down and disrupt production, because of the serious implications such actions have for the dependent departments and the entire production process. The union steward is under the countervailing pressures to adopt militant tactics and also to moderate behavior that might be considered reckless or irresponsible by management. Ultimately, however, the shop steward owes his allegiance to the workers he represents, and he either stands up for them or loses their support.[24]

The struggle for job control was at the heart of the Córdoba autoworker factory rebellions in the 1970s. Why the workers' militancy should have assumed a certain political expression, *clasismo,* is an altogether separate question and has been discussed in the preceding chapters. But both the Fiat and IKA-Renault *clasistas* had certain work-related grievances to address that were rooted in the nature of automotive manufacturing, particularly in the common problems faced by the Cordoban industry after 1965. In addition each company had distinct managerial and production practices, greatly influenced by experiences with their labor forces in Europe, that were determinative in the history.

To appreciate the significance of work and the labor process in Córdoba's labor history, one must also understand the idiosyncratic nature of automotive production in Argentina, specifically in the IKA-Renault and Fiat plants.[25] In the 1960s and 1970s in Argentina, and in Latin America generally, automobile manufacturers were producing complete units for local markets and were not yet serving as international sources of component parts for their parent companies.[26] Standardization and international integration would not come to the Argentine industry until the end of the 1970s. Though Renault's long-range industrial strategy was to convert the IKA-Renault complex into the productive hub for its component plants in Chile, Colombia, and other Latin American countries, and thereby to gain access to the great commercial markets it mistakenly believed were taking shape in the continent through the 1969 Latin American Free Trade Association and the Pacto Andino, its plants in Córdoba continued to supply an essentially Argentine market.[27] Production practices and therefore shop floor relations in IKA-Renault and throughout the auto industry in Argentina differed significantly from company to company.

From the start, the Kaiser plants had had certain characteristics that set them apart from other automobile manufacturers. For instance they had a low incidence of classical Fordist production practices and a more informal style of work. The production volume in the IKA plants was well below what would have been found in similar plants in the United States and Europe. In addition, modifying Kaiser models and tinkering with those being built under license were permanent activities, undertaken to adapt the cars to the specific needs of the Argentine market. The resulting changes were generally cosmetic, but sometimes they were necessary adaptations to the exigencies of the local market. For example, given the poor quality of Argentine roads, the suspensions and metal tolerances had to be strengthened in the Renault Dauphine model built by IKA under license. Nevertheless, tinkering of this sort was often a source of friction between IKA and its licensors, the latter being convinced that such modifications were often gratuitous, due to IKA's "amateurishness" and the poor quality control in the plants. For example, IKA's changes in Renault's engine design, and thus all the components that made up the engine, greatly concerned the French company. This was yet another factor that convinced Renault that if its cars were going to be built in Córdoba, standardization and rationalization along stricter Fordist lines was necessary. Renault did recognize, however, that such tinkering by IKA management was partly due to the poor quality of the components from local suppliers, a weakness that it believed could only be overcome by deepening Kaiser's policy of vertical integration.[28]

Under IKA management, the production processes required an adaptability that implied a lower incidence of Fordism, of subdivided, integrated, strictly timed work. Instead, a considerable amount of work was "labor paced" and was frequently performed in batches rather on continuous-flow principles. For the labor force, especially for production as opposed to final assembly workers, this meant the operators had to be more flexible and slightly more skilled than in most automobile plants. IKA's use of three separate production lines allowed for greater flexibility; the lines moved more slowly than in most car plants, and workers had a greater number of more varied tasks to perform.[29] For example, on a typical processed machine line workers would use mills, drills, broaches, hones, pressure text fixtures, and inspection gauging stations, all tied together in one continuous line. In North American and European plants, such work would have been broken down into several different production classifications and numerous subclassifications, each worker performing a minute task, with a specialized machine tool, in the production flow.

In the Kaiser plants and those of Fiat as well, workers performed multiple tasks in separate work stations and then manually transferred the material to the next station in small trucks, automated machinery being almost completely absent in the complexes. The general-purpose machine tool, which required more highly skilled machinists and had been phased out in the more industrialized countries in favor of special-purpose, semispecial-purpose, and, finally, automated machinery, was still in wide use in the Cordoban plants. A number of IKA and Fiat workers had mechanical drawing and mathematical skills, could operate a wide variety of machine tools, and could perform assembly operations at the bench. This was particularly the case with the first wave of workers who were hired in IKA and Fiat and drawn mainly from the Industrias Aeronáuticas y Mecánicas del Estado plants. Even those who specialized in using a lathe or machine tool had some familiarity with other machine production operations. Indeed, automatic lathes with single speeds and single feeds were used less in these factories than in most automobile plants of the period, and worker discretion was of considerably greater importance. For IKA especially, maintaining flexibility of job classifications, in a labor process that was somewhat closer to the earlier stages of automotive production than to strict Fordism, thus became the guiding principle in all the company's contract negotiations with the union.[30]

By the late 1960s, IKA's production practices were considered an anachronism by Renault, the licensing company whose models in 1966 comprised more than half of IKA's sales.[31] After Renault's takeover of IKA in 1967, the French company insisted on the need to bring the organization, technology, and labor processes of the IKA-Renault factories closer to the standards of those in the industry internationally. Renault company reports between 1967 and 1973 would repeatedly stress the belief that profitability in a tight domestic market depended on industrial reconversion and lowering the costs of production.[32] Similarly, the decision to abandon IKA's single-model policy and begin producing a series of vehicles for a more competitive car market called for a different production process. In 1967, IKA-Renault produced twenty-three different models, a changeover that required stricter factory discipline and rationalization. As a result, in 1968 Renault began an ambitious modernization program that would last almost five years and cost the company in excess of $100 million—a considerable figure, taking into account the fact that IKA's original capital investment had been only $10 million.

Renault's reforms were not restricted to production and included finance and marketing. The company established some installment buying and financing plans, and it upgraded its dealerships as well. It also streamlined its operations and sold off the Transax axle plant to Ford. More significantly, it sought to resolve IKA's serious financial problems by making overdue royalty payments and buying out the licensing agreements of IKA's other licensors (American Motors and Kaiser itself), and integrating the company into the multinational's financial network of French and foreign creditors instead of relying on the unpredictable and often usurious capital sources in Argentina.[33] Renault's financial reforms were nonetheless contradictory, as it sold IKA the technology for reconversion, held the company strictly accountable for up-to-date payments, and generally maintained a policy of offering technical but not financial support for its Cordoban operations. This policy put IKA under extreme pressure and explains in great measure why the company teetered on the brink of bankruptcy between 1967 and 1976 and never managed to break free of local financing.[34]

The alacrity with which the production reforms were undertaken responded basically to IKA-Renault's need to quickly win the confidence of financial backers for the modernization program. The problem was not only to show robust sales but also to give an impression of direction and long-range planning. The scale of the modernization program was thus unusual in the Argentine automobile industry, as the local subsidiaries of the automotive multinationals were not generally considered profitable enough by their home offices to warrant costly overhauls. The Argentine branches of Ford, GM, Chrysler, Citroën, and other companies generally had to make do with the equipment and layout they were first established with, and there was minimal intentional technological transfer or investment in the industry after the mid-1960s.[35] Renault's investment, nevertheless, was in the public company's tradition of increasing its competitiveness by improving production and reducing labor costs rather than devising creative marketing strategies or investing heavily in advertising, a tradition reinforced by the peculiarities of the Argentine market.[36] For IKA-Renault, there was the added incentive of countering an increasingly belligerent labor force with reforms that would ultimately reduce the number of workers needed in the plants and impose tighter factory discipline. Such thinking was in keeping with the history of the industry in other parts of the world and with the tendency of management to undertake sweeping changes in technology and organization especially when labor presented problems and workers resisted increases in productivity through the mere intensification of work.[37]

The shop floor reforms of Renault were extensive and affected nearly every department in every plant in the Santa Isabel complex. One goal was simply to rationalize production along Fordist lines, to reduce the amount of "down time" in the production process and convert more tasks to discretely timed, machine-paced operations. Product reforms were also essential if the company were ever to break into the export market, as

Renault officials believed it eventually could, and such features as safety and exhaust requirements in the cars built in Córdoba were brought up to international standards.[38] Renault did not wish to completely change the productive process in the Kaiser plants. Some labor flexibility was essential in an industry that exported little and was servicing a predominantly local market, that depended significantly on local suppliers of parts and components, and in which frequent adjustments had to be made in product design and thus the labor process. Renault had been attracted to the IKA buyout partly because of its appreciation for the adaptability of the Kaiser labor force.[39] Moreover, in a low-volume, highly protected industry, competitive economies of scale were not as important as keeping labor costs as low as possible. Thus, though the company began replacing all-purpose machine tools with specialized machine tools in 1968, it continued to purchase some of the all-purpose tools that IKA workers had been using since the 1950s.[40]

Nevertheless, between 1968 and 1973 Renault converted the Kaiser plants to a Fordist production system to a significant degree, introducing transfer machinery in the die-casting plants, installing new and rationalized production and final assembly lines, completely transforming the paint department and quality control sections, adding a variety of stamping machines in the production lines, and introducing automatic equipment and new labor processes in the forge.[41] The modernization program, which lasted roughly until 1973, saw fundamental changes not only in organization and technology but also in the nature of work and specifically in increased work rhythms. At the start of the modernization program, Renault proposed a production goal of twenty cars per hour, fully aware that such a figure meant a highly subdivided process that would be a break with the Kaiser past.[42]

As shop floor conditions grew more regimented and severe, issues of working conditions became more important for the IKA-Renault workers, and they brought new pressures to bear on their union representatives. The company itself saw a relationship between rationalization and labor militancy in its Argentine plants in these years. For example, in an extensive report on the reconversion of its Perdriel plant, which once had produced high-precision machine tools and was reconverted to assembly line production *(unité de production de pièces en série),* Renault directly attributed worker discontent and the growth of support for the *clasista* leadership in the plant to new low-skill work and plant rationalization.[43] Similarly, Renault believed that changes in the labor processes and job reclassifications in numerous other plants and departments—

fabricaciones varias (assembly), *carrocerías en blanco* (chassis paint department), *mecanizado* (production), *inspección y producción* (quality control), *suministros* (parts)—triggered worker resistance and work stoppages throughout the early 1970s.[44]

Fiat also implemented modernization and rationalization programs in these years. In 1970, workers in Concord's Planta A saw their general-purpose machinery removed and automatic machinery requiring minimal skills introduced. Like Renault, the Italian company completely overhauled its painting department and converted from a labor intensive process in which workers hand-painted the chassis with spray guns to an automated process in which workers merely monitored machinery. Fiat also introduced automatic and high-precision tools for its machining operations, brought in transfer machinery to move engine blocks from station to station and perform machining operations on them, and generally specialized production, moving final car assembly in 1965 to a new plant in El Palomar (in the province of Buenos Aires) and truck and tractor assembly in 1973 to another in Sauce Viejo (Santa Fe province). This left the Fiat Concord factory strictly devoted to engine and component production for automobiles.[45]

However, in the case of Fiat, of greater significance than plant rationalizations, which were by no means as extensive as in the IKA-Renault plants, was the deepening of established company policies that sought to maximize worker productivity and reduce labor costs. The company's establishment of plant unions and its effort to isolate the workers from the dangerous influences of Argentine industrial unions, notably to obstruct their membership in the SMATA, were part of Fiat's intent to ensure only perfunctory union representation in its plants and to maintain absolute control over the shop floor. Nominal union representation allowed Fiat to implement and sustain a series of work and wage practices that would have been unthinkable in any other automobile company in the country. One such practice was a system of remuneration, the *premio de la producción* (productivity prize), that pegged wages to worker productivity, an anomaly in an industry in which hourly or monthly wages, depending on the job classification, were the standard form of payment.

The *premio de la producción* established production goals, revised on a monthly and sometimes a weekly basis, that the company calculated as a "130 percent production rate." The Fiat workers' final takehome pay depended on their success in meeting these productivity targets. Minimum wages were paid for meeting the "100 percent" rhythms, and a bonus was granted for any work performed within the additional 30 percent limit. The base-rate wages were far inferior to what other workers in the automobile industry received. Moreover when the bonus was paid, the company awarded it to the workers in the specific production lines in a lump sum, to be divided equally among them in a process the workers regarded as inscrutable and that was indeed never explained in the Fiat collective bargaining agreements. With good reason, the *premio de la producción* appeared arbitrary to the Concord workers; success or failure in exceeding the 100 percent rhythms seemed subject to the whims of foremen and management. Workers' frustrations with their unpredictable pay were exacerbated by the fact that they suffered from any decline in production, including those due to the breakdown of machinery or a shortage of components from suppliers. The benefits for the company, on the other hand, were obvious. The *premio* system allowed Fiat to adjust production and labor costs in accordance with market conditions and thereby to avoid the rigid wage scales that increased the labor costs for other automobile companies operating in Argentina.[46]

Fiat's production practices were also exceptional. One such practice, known in the Concord plant as the *acople de máquina* (machine yoke), was intended to assure maximum worker productivity regardless of the physical and mental stress it placed on the labor force. This particular practice applied to the workers operating production machines and consisted essentially of doubling a single worker's responsibility for tending machines. One machine, such as a press for cutting screws, might be the worker's primary responsibility. Time and motion studies, however, would often calculate down time for such workers, gaps in the labor process that industrial engineers deemed sufficient for tending to additional responsibilities. Thus the worker monitoring the screw-cutting press could be assigned an additional machine, perhaps a grinder, and sometimes a third, a honing machine, for example, with yet another unrelated function. Each machine required its own tending, and the strain placed on the worker was enormous. After ousting the too-compliant Fiat union representatives, the *clasista* SITRAC leadership, with strong backing from the rank and file, demanded that Fiat *"descoplar"* the machinery as complaints of physical and mental exhaustion became widespread in the plant.[47]

As in the case of IKA-Renault, Fiat's labor policies were greatly influenced by company traditions and established practices in its European plants. Fiat had a long history of hostility to unionism and even the slightest interference in its absolute control over questions of production. Of all the European automobile manufacturers, it was the company that most consistently preached and practiced a policy of paternalism as a method of achieving labor-management harmony. Fiat provided worker incentives for compliance through practices such as its no-strike bonus clause *(il premio antisciopero)* while doggedly resisting union encroachments on management prerogatives on the shop floor.[48]

Similarly, Fiat had a long tradition of squeezing its labor costs in times of flagging sales and downturns in the business cycle rather than investing directly in production to improve competitiveness. After the First World War Fiat had not adopted the strategy adopted by many European automobile firms to meet American competition, that of radically restructuring production through technological and organizational reforms. Instead, in 1929 it had introduced what American labor historian David Montgomery has described as the "Taylorism of the Great Depression," the Bedaux system.[49] The Bedaux system replaced time studies with more rigorous and precise motion studies; it stressed intensifying work loads, reducing the size of the labor force, and generally lowering labor costs to remain competitive, and it was in widespread use in the Fiat plants in Italy in the 1930s.[50] Certain hallmarks of Fiat's labor policies, remuneration based on worker output *(il cottimo)*, for example, reappeared in one form or another in its Cordoban plants. Following the great strikes of the *biennio rosso* (1919–20), Fiat had agreed to phase out the old, individually calculated piecework rates. But with defeat of their unions and the rise of fascism in the 1920s, the Fiat workers had been forced to return to the piecework system, which was thenceforth under constant revision by management and which brought a precipitous drop in wages in the 1920s.[51] The managerial philosophy underlying piecework, if not the precise mechanism for its calculation, reappeared in the Fiat Concord plant.

The most important of Fiat's labor policies for the Cordoban workers was undoubtedly its hostility to unionism. Fiat had used Italy's abolishing of the shop floor workers' councils *(commissioni interne)* under the 1927 Carta del Lavoro to implement its paternalist, antiunion company philosophy in its factories there. As it would in Ferreyra, Fiat had jealously guarded its control over production rhythms and job assignments, routinely fired shop floor activists, and never attempted to ameliorate shop floor tensions by giving workers even a symbolic say in productivity questions.[52]

The Italian postwar industrial revolution owed much to the weakness of the labor movement on the shop floor. This had been particularly important in the automobile industry, the linchpin of Italian postwar economic development, where piecework and bonus systems were the rule and where labor did not mount a serious resistance to management until the late 1960s.[53] After the defeat of the Confederazione Generale Italiana del Lavoro (CGIL), the communist and socialist labor confederation, in the 1955 union elections, the company had launched a counterattack against the union and minimized union activity in its plants. In Italy, Fiat complemented its intransigence on the shop floor with the highest wages in any sector of the Italian working class and with an ostentatious paternalism.

The calm period in labor-management relations ended in Turin in the late 1960s. By that point, worker disenchantment with the "privileges" of belonging to the "famiglia Fiat" and discontent with shop floor conditions and the company's labor policies could no longer be held in check by the combination of weak union representation and company vigilance. The Fiat workers in Turin exploded in 1969, just as the Fiat workers in Córdoba did a year later. The company confronted the two challenges in different ways: with automation and shop floor reforms in the Italian plants, and with a frontal attack enlisting the powers of the state to destroy the *clasista* movement in Argentina.[54]

The significance for Córdoba of Fiat's management practices in its Turin plants is obvious. The Italians had a wealth of experience and a guiding managerial philosophy that they brought with them to Argentina. The company also had a panoply of specific production practices that it simply transferred to its Cordoban operations in Ferreyra. One of these was the use of incentive wages as the basis of its remunerative system. The practice whereby entire departments, much less individual workers, received payment on the basis of output, though once widespread in the industry, was by the 1960s extremely rare. In the North American automobile industry, for example, the UAW had won its elimination and replacement with straight-time wages in all the major automobile companies by 1950. Renault in France had also begun converting to straight-time wages in the 1950s; piecework was eventually completely abolished in its plants.[55] Nevertheless Fiat adopted the system for its Cordoban plants. Similarly, with its establishment of the Cordoban plant unions in the early 1960s, Fiat continued its unyielding opposition to independent union activity, which had been an unstated but understood company policy in its Turin plants between 1955 and 1969. And it also followed its own example by decentralizing production in Argentina, moving assembly operations to El Palomar and Sauce Viejo just as it had dispersed production in Italy and moved some plants to southern Italy to get them away from the corrupting influences of Turin.[56] Most important, it took advantage of a state hostile to the labor movement to tighten factory discipline and implement practices such as the *acople de máquina,* speedups of various sorts, and a reliance on labor costs as the manipulable variable in its profitability.

In contrast to the hard line Fiat adopted with its labor force in Ferreyra, Renault adopted a more cautious approach with its workers in Santa Isabel. This was partly due to the disparity in union power between the two complexes. The SMATA had taken advantage of Kaiser's inexperience in handling a labor force independently and had early on consolidated a position that was simply unknown to the Fiat workers in Ferreyra. The significance for Renault of its belated assumption of control of the Santa Isabel complex was that the parameters of labor-management relations had already been established, and the French company was not in as strong a position as Fiat was to assert absolute control over the shop floor. Kaiser was a second-rank American company accustomed to dealing with its work force through a union intermediary, and it had had few pretensions about forming plant or company unions. By the time of the Renault buyout, the SMATA had established its role as an interlocutor with management and had become a reasonably effective guardian of the workers' interests. Renault thus was more cautious in its dealings with its labor force, and even in its attempt to rationalize production and tighten up shop floor discipline it was unwilling to adopt the blatant union-busting tactics that Fiat employed.

But as was the case with Fiat, Renault's labor policies were also the result of the French company's experience in dealing with its labor force in Europe. Like Fiat founder Giovanni Agnelli, Louis Renault had made his pilgrimage to Detroit to study Fordist production methods but had been forced, largely because of the small size of the French domestic market, to adopt a modified version of Fordism. From the start, European companies such as Fiat and Renault stressed greater flexibility with their labor forces than was common in the North American industry. Unable to adopt high wages and Ford's five-dollar-day scheme, they showed a preference for piece rates and a greater proclivity for using speedups to play with labor costs and adjust to fluctuations in demand.[57]

Nevertheless there were important differences of degree in this general tendency. Renault had shown a greater willingness to innovate technologically and had been less inclined to rely strictly on its labor costs to meet competition. It had not adopted the Bedaux system, for example, as Fiat had. Moreover at Renault, unlike Fiat, the 1930s had been a decade of growing union power, with the French communists taking the lead in organizing the car workers and the Renault workers playing a prominent role in negotiating the agreements won during the Popular Front government that recognized worker factory councils, thereby establishing a formidable shop floor presence and winning workers a hand in establishing productivity rates.[58] Though there had been a company reaction and a union purge after the great November 1938 general strike, Renault was never able to assert the kind of tightfisted control over its labor force that was practiced by Fiat. Indeed, in the postwar period French autoworkers in general and the Renault workers in particular had managed to develop into a powerful force within the French trade union movement and to resist the more notorious kinds of shop floor manipulation that was common fare in Turin.[59]

The general tenor of management-labor relations in Santa Isabel partly reflected the stalemate between capital and labor that existed in the home plants in France, a situation that was more palatable to Renault than it would have been to Fiat, given the French company's long history of dealing with a formidable union adversary. Nonetheless, at Renault and Fiat alike economic reality defined the limits of compromise. Management in the two Cordoban companies was under similar market pressures and was forced to bring production costs in line with sales and profit figures. IKA-Renault and Fiat, each in its own way, relied heavily on reducing its labor bills to survive the shakedown in the Argentine automobile industry of the mid-1960s and to remain competitive with the Buenos Aires–based companies. Between 1966 and 1973, years of declining sales and then lackluster growth, company profits depended heavily on plant rationalizations, increased productivity, and lower labor costs.[60]

The IKA-Renault labor force that experienced the first effects of the French company's rationalization program in 1968 had been formed by years of struggle, militancy, and close identification with the autoworkers' union. As in most car plants, the workers in the Santa Isabel complex were stratified along the following lines: unskilled workers engaged in assembly operations; semiskilled workers involved in semi-automatic machine operations; skilled workers who built, repaired, and maintained machinery. In 1969 the IKA-Renault labor force roughly broke down as follows: 48 percent in the unskilled positions, 35 percent in the semiskilled ones, and 16 percent in the skilled jobs.[61] The labor force continued to be a young one of only recent proletarian origins: in 1969 the average age of the low-skilled workers was 27; of the semi-skilled, 29; and of the skilled, 32. Whereas a majority of the skilled workers (52 percent) were second-generation workers, only 37 percent of the low-skilled and 42 percent of the semiskilled were. In addition, 87 percent of the workers had grand-fathers with agricultural backgrounds, and only a low percentage of each group (27 percent of low-skilled, 18 percent of semiskilled, and 23 percent of skilled workers) had fathers who were urban-born. In addition to giving a clearer picture of the character of the labor force in the Renault plants, these figures also shed light on the predominantly rural origins of the postwar internal migrations to Córdoba.[62]

In 1969, shortly before the Cordobazo, a prominent American sociolo-gist conducting a survey of autoworkers found that the IKA-Renault workers' predominant concerns lay with the social mobility issues of wages and job advancement. Political questions, such as the relegalization of the Peronist movement or the ending of nondemocratic rule, and even concerns with monotonous work or hazardous working conditions were of notably less importance; in this the workers' attitudes were similar to those that had been reported by another American sociologist several years before, prior to the establishment of the Onganía dictatorship.[63] Furthermore, though a high percentage of workers lived within the city limits (80 percent of the low-skilled workers, 79 percent of the semi-skilled, and 91 percent of the skilled), they had a very low rate of involve-ment in community organizations, a testimony to the weakness of the working class neighborhoods in Córdoba and yet another refutation for those who would look outside the workplace for the source of the mili-tancy of the Cordoban car workers in the late 1960s and in the 1970s.[64]

The American sociologists were undoubtedly correct in perceiving that politics, narrowly defined, was the preoccupation largely of the labor leadership. Nevertheless political and wage issues became inextricably bound after 1966, and the mobilizations of the IKA-Renault workers be-tween 1966 and 1969 that culminated in the Cordobazo defy definitions of the labor force as an economistic labor aristocracy or even an upwardly mobile, privileged sector of workers that lacked a collective identity. The greater concern for wages as opposed to working conditions was natural in the context of the company's abrogation of collective bargaining nego-tiations and its direct assault on workers' income through reduced work days and production suspensions. But with the onset of the Renault rationalization program and in the midst of increasing inflation and de-clining wages, the marked militancy of the IKA-Renault workers in the 1970s, modernization theories notwithstanding, fed on the workers' very real concerns with conditions in the plants as well as on political influences.

This tendency for issues of work and politics to blur became even more pronounced following the Cordobazo. Rank-and-file animus toward the company had been growing since the time of the 1966 coup. The suspension of collective bargaining rights under Onganía, the massive though largely unsuccessful layoffs undertaken by the company between 1966 and 1968, the abolition of the *sábado inglés,* and management's general attempt to ignore the union as an interlocutor had raised workplace grievances to the level of politics. Elpidio Torres and the Peronist *torrista* leadership of the SMATA had ridden this wave to the events of May 1969. The combined effects of the Cordobazo and the Renault rationalization program were to take the politicization of work a step further. By coincidence, the political changes that occurred nationally and locally following the Cordobazo took place just as factory discipline was tightening, production rhythms were increasing, and the IKA-Renault complex was going through a deep restructuring. *Clasismo* and rank-and-file opposition to company policies dovetailed and produced the factory rebellions of the early 1970s.

The rank-and-file rebellion against rationalization actually preceded the Cordobazo and had circumvented Torres and the *torrista* leadership. Throughout the 1960s the leftist labor opposition to Torres had based its criticisms precisely on those issues where the Peronists were most vulnerable: job control and shop floor protection.[65] Between 1966 and 1969, Torres and the SMATA Peronists were spirited and able protectors of rank-and-file interests, so long as the problems they confronted remained within traditional limits. But once the problems in the workplace went beyond issues of wages and job stability and raised issues at the heart of the relationship between labor and capital in the automobile industry, the limits of their ideology and of Peronism, not defined as a working class culture or political movement but as a trade union style and a practical system of running union affairs, became apparent. In the face of the Renault rationalization programs and the intensification of work, the union proved timorous and ineffective. For example, in March 1969 the workers, encouraged by leftist activists, protested rationalization in various departments, especially in the stamping section *(chapa),* that would eliminate the number of line workers and increase production rhythms.[66] The union meanwhile muted its criticisms and failed to respond with a work stoppage. Torres and the SMATA leadership in fact only belatedly recognized the problems resulting from Renault's rationalization program, in part because they were preoccupied with other issues in those months but also because they were unprepared to deal with such problems and to confront the company on terrain they had long since abandoned.[67]

The Peronist leadership of the SMATA had never challenged more than verbally management's right to absolute control over the workplace or on questions related to production. Indeed, though the shop stewards' movement during the Peronist governments of the 1940s and 1950s had gained considerable strength and achieved some influence in determining production rhythms and job assignments, by the early 1960s Peronist trade unionism had abandoned all pretensions to shop floor authority.[68] In the Cordoban SMATA there was a long-standing demand during the Torres years for "comanagement" *(cogestión)*, in which the union and the company would share, among other things, responsibility on the shop floor. But the calls for comanagement were strictly rhetorical and were never seriously presented to IKA officials as a union demand in collective bargaining negotiations. Nor, more important, did the issue concern the union leadership in the day-to-day workings of union affairs, as the low incidence of strikes over shop floor issues before 1970 attests.

In the agreements reached with IKA, in fact, the union had effectively abandoned all rightful claims to a comanagement role. Torres's consistent refusal to work in behalf of a union affiliation for the IKA-Renault administrative employees was part and parcel of this trade union style. Torres's position was an astute one, since those same employees handled figures on production, sales, work rhythms, job assignments, and the like, which if obtained by the rank and file would have jeopardized his *caudillo* union style. When the administrative employees were finally affiliated with the union during the period of Salamanca's leadership, that wealth of information was made available to the *clasistas*, and it was undoubtedly a factor in the shop floor struggles that were waged in the 1970s. The employees in the Contaduría General alone, the "brain center" of the IKA-Renault complex, were able to provide invaluable information to the *clasistas*.

The *clasista* activists took advantage of the old guard Peronist leadership's silence and built their union opposition on issues directly related to the problems that the workers were facing in the IKA-Renault factories.[69] The greatly expanded number and role of the shop stewards that accompanied their rise facilitated a more confrontational union style in the workplace, and the *clasistas* challenged the company on many fronts. Renault's attempt in the early 1970s to hire temporary workers with three-month contracts, the first tentative step toward creating a non-unionized labor force that might eventually have permitted a reproduction of Mexico's rotating employment system in the local automobile industry, was successfully resisted by the *clasistas*.[70] The hazardous working conditions that existed in many departments were also subject to greater union vigilance. In late 1973 the *clasistas* formed the Comisión de Insalubridad to investigate problems with working conditions and to coordinate a united shop steward front on such issues to the company.[71]

The most important *clasista* challenges, and those most doggedly resisted by the company, were not on these issues, however, but involved two issues stemming from Renault's rationalization program: job classifications and production rhythms. During the Kaiser years, the production process had combined maximum labor flexibility with loosely defined job classifications.[72] The role of the shop steward had atrophied under such conditions, since classification crossings had been left vague in collective bargaining agreements and were therefore not subject to union grievance procedures. Indeed the shop stewards commission during the Kaiser years had served essentially as Torres' parliament rather than as a zealous protector of workers' interests on the factory floor, and the *caudillo*'s link to the rank and file had a vocal but only token minority opposition among the left-wing Trotskyist and Partido Comunista activists. Renault's rationalization process in this sense was a double-edged sword. To break the labor force's common identity, born of a compressed wage structure, Torres's union-building strategies, and the SMATA workers' history of militancy and struggle, Renault bureaucratized the wage structure and introduced precisely defined gradations in job classifications. This it hoped would fragment the labor force and direct their efforts into ascending the job ladder rather than taking collective action.[73]

Renault's need to maintain a considerable degree of labor flexibility, however, meant that the job classifications *(categorías)* could not in practice be respected. In 1969 a study of conditions in the IKA-Renault plants showed an extraordinarily high incidence of job transfers, with 40 percent of the assembly line workers, 30 percent of machine operators, 39 percent of test inspection–repair workers, and 45 percent of craftsmen subject to monthly job changes.[74] These numbers are not particularly significant for the skilled workers, for whom a certain variety of work is not only expected but often desired. But for the line worker who had a well-defined sense of the hierarchy of unpleasant jobs and a corresponding expectation of appropriate payment, such changes could be bitterly resented, and even the skilled workers could resent the occasional moves from their departments out to the machines on the production lines that the company practiced.

Renault's job transfer policies opened the door for shop stewards to initiate grievance procedures and strengthened their position on the shop floor. During the two years of *clasista* control of the SMATA (1972 to 1974), shop stewards repeatedly filed grievances over job crossings. The company's refusal to respect classifications, in fact, became the most common cause of shop stewards' grievances, and in one month alone, July 1973, shop stewards filed more than one hundred grievances on that issue (Table 10.3). This contrasted with the virtual absence of such grievances during the period from 1956 to 1969. Ultimately the *clasistas* began to take the problem a step further, to question the classifications for entire departments, not just individual workers, a policy that drew the harshest criticisms from the IKA-Renault personnel department.[75]

The *clasistas'* efforts to control production rhythms was an even more direct assault on management's shop floor authority. The long-standing demand of the left-wing activists in the IKA-Renault plants for union control over the pace of work became a source of numerous work stoppages after the Cordobazo. The *clasistas'* defiance on the production rhythms issue was expressed in multiple ways. Generally it was purely reactive, as with a protest led by shop stewards in specific departments simply to reduce the speed of the line considered by the workers to be too fast.[76] It could also be expressed as a broader union demand for a role in determining the rhythms, such as it pushed for in the painting department after the company repeatedly refused to entertain formal union complaints of excessive rhythms or to respond to wildcat strikes there.[77] Whatever its precise expression, the *clasistas* used the production rhythms issue more than any other to strengthen rank-and-file support. *Clasista* references to problems with the pace of work were constant in union publications, and indeed the problem seemed literally tailor-made to raise class consciousness on the shop floor.[78] The production rhythms issue became so explosive, and the *torristas* vulnerability on the issue so manifest, that the Peronists themselves were forced to adopt a more

Table 10.3 Union grievances, Comisión Interna de Reclamos, SMATA-Córdoba, 1972–1974

Year	Job classifications	All other issues
1972–73	187	146
1973–74	216	84

Source: SMATA archive, SMATA-Córdoba, volumes "Reclamos de Comisión Interna," 1972–73 and 1973–74.

aggressive stance and eventually to take a card from the *clasistas* and accuse the union leadership of lax vigilance on the issue.[79]

The problems of work were the issues on which the *clasistas* based their attempt to garner rank-and-file loyalties and reestablish the position of the Marxist left in the workers' movement that it had lost with the rise of Perón. Under the *clasistas* the union adopted an openly tutelary role and, often employing hortatory language, attempted to link the problems of work with a critique of capitalism and the cultivation of a revolutionary role for the working class.[80] Most significantly, the strike record of the IKA-Renault complex between 1967 and 1976 reveals a change, albeit a rough one, in union behavior under the *clasistas*. Differences appear in the frequency and nature of strikes between 1969, the last year of absolute Peronist control over the union machinery, and the *clasista* period, which includes both the actual years of *clasista* administration of the union (1972 to 1974) and the years that immediately preceded and followed, when *clasista* activists were the principal promoters of strikes and work stoppages in the IKA-Renault plants. Under the *clasistas* there was an increased tendency to strike, especially when one considers that 1969, the year of the Cordobazo, was an unusually active one for the Peronist leadership, and to strike over questions of production and issues of job control (production rhythms, hazardous working conditions, and job classifications), not just wage demands. There was a particularly pronounced tendency under the *clasistas* to protest speedups. Such changes in the line often precipitated partial work stoppages in specific departments. Occasionally work stoppages would emerge in one department and spread to others where similar problems existed, unleashing plant-wide protests.[81] Mostly, however, the work stoppages of the *clasista* period were what were known in the American automobile industry as "quickies," production shutdowns or slowdowns confined to specific departments and lasting only a few hours. The compartmentalization of factory life in automobile plants, where the lines of communication between the various departments were often poor, historically has encouraged this kind of work stoppage in automobile industries where the shop stewards have a powerful and vigilant presence.[82]

IKA-Renault company papers do not always specify the precise causes of these work stoppages, often attributing them to the generic speed up *(ritmos de producción)*. But the specific practices that triggered worker protest are not the crucial variable. As has been discussed, *speedup* is a term that applies more to an end than a means. The management employed a gamut of practices to enhance worker productivity and satisfy company needs. A detailed tracing of the precise speed up measures it adopted in each case would not only be impossible, it would also be pointless. Rather, what is clear from company records, diverse union sources, and worker testimony, as well as what is historically significant, is a general pattern of behavior. Specifically, between 1969 and 1975 work-related issues were the predominant causes of work stoppages; such stoppages tended to be brief and confined to specific departments, not unionwide strikes; and the number of strikes greatly increased in the 1970s, at the height of both Renault's rationalization program and *clasista* power in the IKA-Renault plants. Similarly, lower strike figures and a lesser propensity to strike over job-control issues between 1967 and 1969 and in 1976, by which point the remaining *clasistas* had largely been purged from the Santa Isabel factories and a Peronist leadership was securely back in power (although under a harsh and intimidating military government), reflect the *torrista* style of running union affairs.

A dramatic increase in the number of quickie strikes naturally suggests serious shop floor problems, but it also often means a breakdown in union discipline, with shop stewards ignoring time-consuming strike procedures and circumventing the established union machinery.[83] In the United States, where in the 1930s union activists rode the wave of rank-and-file discontent with retimed jobs and arbitrary changes in job assignments, the use of departmental strikes to shore up one union faction's position or discredit another was a notoriously prominent feature of the UAW's early history.[84] In Córdoba the rivalries and bad blood existing between the Partido Comunista Revolucionario, Partido Comunista, Partido Revolucionario de los Trabajadores, Peronists and other political-ideological tendencies among the shop stewards made such motivations very common in the strike record in the IKA-Renault plants as well. Company complaints of anarchy in the plants therefore were not totally unfounded, as union rivals often seemed to be engaged in political brinksmanship, attempting to outdo one another in their displays of militancy.

The danger this situation represented to the company was also not mere hyperbole. In late 1972 IKA-Renault was already complaining that *"actitudes de incumplimientos, paros parciales, y trabajo a desgano"* ("insubordination, departmental strikes, and slowdowns") were responsible for a monthly drop of production of 500 cars and were undermining the company's modernization program, and indeed between 1973 and 1974 production dropped from 40,760 complete units to 35,952.[85] In France, company officials noted that the *clasistas'* vigilance over production rhythms had lowered output to what it considered an unacceptable rate of 200 to 240 cars manufactured a day.[86] As a result of union opposition, Renault decided that production could only be increased by hiring temporary labor or through overtime work, that increased production rhythms were sure to elicit an unwanted shop steward reaction.[87] But the union's opposition to the hiring of temporary workers and the severe financial burdens that overtime imposed on the company meant that IKA-Renault continued to employ speedups.

Causes for strikes were never lacking in these years, and the workers demonstrated broad support for the *clasistas'* handling of shop floor problems, a fact that must qualify partisan politics as an explanation for the stormy labor-management relations of these years. The *clasistas'* decisive 1974 electoral victory and the workers' continued support for the *clasista* shop floor stewards after the local's *clasista* leadership was removed showed the depth of rank-and-file identification with the *clasistas'* more confrontational union style in the workplace. Blatantly partisan strikes, moreover, could never have been sustained over a period of years unless there had also existed a ground swell of discontent among the workers over problems directly related to production. More than political rancor or revolutionary designs, the explosion in worker militancy also may have had much to do with the *clasistas'* increasing of the number of shop stewards after the 1972 union elections, which coincided with the changed working conditions stemming from Renault's rationalization program.

In the daily skirmishing over the control of production, shop stewards were naturally more sensitive to shop floor problems and were more likely to call wildcat strikes than the union's executive committee. They also had a greater ability and more authority to do so. The policy of the *clasista* SMATA executive committee was to cede the initiative on work-related problems to the shop stewards instead of requiring that they work through the cumbersome union machinery or grievance procedures, as they had during the *torrista* years. The power of the shop stewards reached the point where there were built-in pressures—increased numbers of shop stewards and changes in the nature of work—that encouraged work stoppages that were beyond the control of the executive committee. The rising incidence of work stoppages between the 1974 removal of the *clasista* union executive committee and late 1975, for example, reflected a situation in which shop stewards continued to respond to rank-and-file pressures and formulate effective responses to work-related problems, despite the union interventors' considerable efforts to centralize the decision-making process and to calm the waters in the union.

The history of the work stoppages in the IKA-Renault complex between 1967 and 1976 demonstrates the important influence of work in the rise of *clasismo* and in the shop floor rebellions of the automobile workers in the early 1970s. Political mythology has represented the Cordoban car workers as a political vanguard, an advanced sector of the working class that developed a radical political program that served as the basis of its union demands and the inspiration for its militancy. Certainly "politics" as a precipitating factor in some of the work stoppages cannot be dismissed offhandedly. Many strikes, particularly those involving the entire union as opposed to partial work stoppages in isolated departments, were undertaken for broadly political reasons: in opposition to Confederación General del Trabajo policies, to protest a political assassination, in support of the Cordoban labor movement's independence from Buenos Aires, and so on. Nor can the politics of work be separated entirely from the revolutionary politics of the Marxist and Peronist left. It was undoubtedly a *clasista* tactic to keep the plants in a high state of agitation, to attempt to raise worker consciousness by confronting management at every available opportunity. Company accusations of *paros guerrilleros,* gratuitous strike actions with purely subversive designs, were overstated, but Renault's belief that the *clasistas'* shop floor politics was closely linked to their revolutionary program was correct.

Nevertheless, the strike record indicates that partisan and revolutionary politics were secondary to the politics of work in the IKA-Renault plants, that political issues influenced union behavior and exacerbated tensions on the shop floor but were subordinate to the problems related to production that the workers experienced in the plants. Those problems, in turn, were filtered through a more general sense of workers' rights that drew on the legacies of Peronism, as it contributed to the Argentine working class's conception of its lawful birthright, and also on the SMATA workers' own history of struggle. Both legacies were heightened in the city's charged political atmosphere following the Cordobazo and during the Peronist restoration.

The company interpreted the labor agitation as a purely politically inspired, subversive movement manipulated by the revolutionary left and intended to sow discord in the workplace—in effect, as a kind of industrial terrorism. Management doggedly resisted union attempts to increase its power on the shop floor and generally dismissed union complaints on production rhythms and working conditions, using diverse strategies to suppress unwelcome union encroachments on its authority in the plants.[88] Renault singled out the skilled workers as the core of labor opposition (and in fact skilled workers have historically played a leading role in labor organizing activities and as foils to management in the automobile industry, as the history of the UAW particularly demonstrates).[89] In Córdoba, the Perdriel tool and tie makers did provide a large contingent of the left-wing opposition to Torres during the 1960s and immediately following the Cordobazo, but they were the principal victims of Torres and the company's negotiated settlement following the great 1970 SMATA strike. Thereafter, though the Perdriel workers mounted a stiff resistance to the rationalization of their plant, they cannot be said to have in any way dominated the *clasista* movement. The *clasista* union slate, the *lista marrón,* drew workers from diverse job categories, skilled and unskilled, and its work stoppages affected all departments in all the plants, including the less skilled production and assembly line departments. Thus company arguments that the skilled workers served as political agitators provide a convenient scapegoat but clarify little about the reasons for the deep rank-and-file support of the *clasistas.*[90] Support for the *clasistas* had more to do with Renault's rationalization program and the perception of deteriorating conditions on the shop floor—heightened, undoubtedly, by the *clasistas'* didactic union discourse—than purely revolutionary politics.

The Fiat *clasista* movement, similarly, was firmly rooted in workplace problems. The workers who led the 1970 shop floor rebellion that ousted the company henchmen running the SITRAC and SITRAM plant unions had no immediate political program. As previous chapters have made clear, *clasista* positions were adopted only later and as a result of the workers' own search for a political education and an ideology to explain the struggles they were experiencing with the company.[91] In Ferreyra, the workers' rebellion grew out of rank-and-file discontent with Fiat's unique management practices. The Fiat workers' isolation from the labor movement in Córdoba had allowed the Italian company to establish a highly idiosyncratic factory regime characterized by management's absolute control over production and a nominally paternalistic but in actual practice highly authoritarian style. The existence of the piecework system of payment or production practices such as the *acople de máquina,* introduced elements in labor-management relations that were absent at IKA-Renault and in automobile firms in general in Argentina.

The role of the foreman in Fiat plants was especially different from that found in other automobile companies. Responsible for determining if workers had met the production rates necessary to receive the *premio* and for assigning extra tasks, the foreman was in the delicate position of balancing the company's needs with the workers' expectations. Not surprisingly, foremen generally were more concerned with the former than the latter, and the relationship between foremen and workers was unusually acrimonious in the Concord plant. The strikes that periodically erupted in the plant during the *clasista* period in objection to a manager's disrespectful tone or apparently capricious behavior on the lines were attempts to establish the shop floor rights that a lack of effective union representation had denied the workers. Throughout the fifteen months of the *clasista* SITRAC, more than *clasismo* or *revolution,* the words most often found in union publications and in *clasista* discourse were *respect, dignity,* and *fairness,* often expressed in relation to the treatment received from company foremen.

The slogan of SITRAC-SITRAM, *¡Ni golpe, ni elección, revolución!* has bequeathed Fiat *clasismo* an ultraleftist, slightly utopian, almost chiliastic image as a movement at odds with the general tenor of Argentine working class history after 1945. This image has encouraged some to see in it not the product of the workers' movement at all, but of leftist ideologues and even of infiltrators from one of the myriad revolutionary organizations of the early 1970s. Even sympathetic critics have lamented its reputed ideological and political intransigence.[92] In reality, for the great majority of the workers the Fiat *clasista* movement, like its counterpart in the SMATA, was a struggle more for workplace rights and union protection than it was for socialism. The factory rebellions grew out of the concrete experiences of common workers, and the new union leadership received its support from the rank and file because it addressed problems confronted by the workers in the factory that the previous union leadership had been unwilling or unable to address. In addition to its general commitment to more democratic union structures, it pledged to resolve specific, deeply resented management practices. The union campaign against the *premio de la producción* and its efforts to convert to a straight hourly wage was certainly a greater source of prestige than *clasismo*'s political program.[93]

The poor working conditions that existed in certain departments—in the forge, for example—also became an issue that galvanized the workers behind the *clasista* SITRAC. Though it was a small plant containing only slightly more than one hundred highly paid workers, the forge had been notorious in the Fiat complex as the "graveyard department," where the excessive heat and the incessant pounding of the thirty-ton hydraulic presses caused dehydration and nervous disorders. In the early 1960s Fiat had repeatedly dismissed worker complaints about the hazardous working conditions there, claiming that they were unavoidable occupational

338 · The Politics of Work

risks and ones, moreover, that the workers were compensated for in the form of higher wages. Thereafter, Jorge Lozano and the company-union SITRAC leadership had brandished those arguments to discourage the periodic demands of the forge workers for improved conditions. The *clasista* SITRAC converted the forge question into a unionwide issue and won a major prestige-building victory when the company agreed to reduce the work day there, reversing its long-standing refusal to even negotiate on the matter.[94]

The *clasistas'* further successes in winning the abolition of the *acople de máquina* practice and, after a hard-fought battle, a promise from Fiat to begin the gradual phasing out of the *premio* system were other major achievements for the new union. The *clasista* SITRAC expanded the parameters of workers' authority on the shop floor in myriad ways. For example, the union fought for, and won, a role in overseeing the quality control section. This particular department had been a source of great friction between the labor force and the company during both the UOM and Lozano years, since parts had often been rejected as unacceptable with no apparent criteria, in the process hurting the workers' chances of meeting the quotas necessary to gain the *premio*.[95]

The *clasista* movement in the Fiat Concord plant was not characterized by the highly fractious situation that accompanied the rise of the militant shop stewards' movement at IKA-Renault. The circumstances surrounding the emergence of the *clasista* movement in Ferreyra, which was the only belated introduction of political organizations there, partly explain this. The nature, scale, and organization of production in the Concord plant were also factors. With production confined to machining operations, there was less variety in the grievances to be dealt with. Thus, there was less "grievance brokerage," fewer departmental shop stewards competing to get their problems resolved first and putting corresponding pressure on the union executive committee to choose which issues to champion. The union had tighter control over the shop floor, and there was a lesser tendency for independent departments to call strikes or for shop stewards to take matters into their own hands because of their impatience with working through established union procedures.

The lighter weight of partisan politics in the Concord plant, combined with the plant's specific workplace context, lay behind the differences in the two *clasista* movements. Though the Concord plant was an exceptionally politicized factory between 1970 and 1971 and there were numerous "political" strikes by the *clasista* SITRAC, they were generally strikes called by the union, not independently by the shop stewards. Departmental strikes did occur, but their motivations appear to have been generally freer of the political rivalries that were so common in IKA-Renault.[96] The smaller size of the Fiat plant also permitted more direct and fluid contact between the union leadership and the rank and file. Despite the efforts of the SMATA *clasistas* to prevent it, the greater scale and complexity of the IKA-Renault operations had made a continuation of some of the bureaucratic distancing of the *torrista* period unavoidable. One result had been the breakdown of shop floor authority, which appears in the IKA-Renault strike record for these years.

Despite these differences, however, the automobile companies' need to reduce labor costs and the policies they adopted to remain competitive in the peculiar Argentine automotive market subjected the Cordoban car workers to different pressures than their counterparts in Buenos Aires. The struggle for job control, which developed out of an aggravated conflict between labor and capital in the workplace, lay behind the *clasista* movements in Ferreyra and Santa Isabel. Resistance to factory life could be and was expressed individually, through quitting or loafing on the job for example, rather than in a collective, much less class-conscious, act. If collective challenges to the "managerial functions" were more characteristic than individual resistance in Cordoban car plants in the 1970s, it was partly due to the workers' previous history of struggle and to the particular conditions existing in Argentina and especially in Córdoba that had created a sense of community among the local autoworkers. But there were also elements specific to automobile manufacturing—the integrated nature of production and the ubiquity of timed, repetitive work—that encouraged labor militancy on job control issues such as the hours and conditions of work, job assignments, and production rhythms. This is demonstrated by similarities in the postwar history of autoworkers in countries with very different political cultures from Argentina's, such as Great Britain and the United States.[97] The Cordoban autoworkers had an usually pronounced history of militancy for all the reasons discussed in this book, but autoworkers the world over have been characterized by their confrontations with management on these issues, and the history of the IKA-Renault and Fiat workers must be put squarely within that tradition in industrial capitalism in the twentieth century.

The workplace struggles of the Cordoban autoworkers certainly should dispel any notion that they were a labor aristocracy. Despite their relatively high wages and the considerable job stability they enjoyed, the Cordoban car workers all confronted problems involving management's absolute control over the labor force, whether in the form of speedups, increased work loads, or productivity schemes. The application of a theory of labor aristocracy seems of limited use when analyzing the history of autoworkers in Latin America. Indeed the general concept appears to be the result of some glib assumptions based on isolated historical precedent: specifically, the postwar history of the United Auto Workers and UAW president Walter Reuther's success in capitalizing on the prosperity of the American auto industry to win high wages, five-year contracts, cost of living adjustments, and lavish pension programs, which has influenced many interpretations of autoworkers' unions since. Undoubtedly, the UAW was transformed into a privileged union and the American autoworkers, arguably, into a kind of labor aristocracy. Collective bargaining was centralized and reduced to wage issues, while the union abandoned any pretensions to authority on the shop floor, though job control issues continued to fuel many work stoppages called by shop stewards, as opposed to by the national union.[98]

But the history of the UAW is hardly representative of autoworkers' unions generally and was made possible only by the exceptionally prosperous state of the American automobile industry in the postwar period, as well as by the influence of the Cold War on the labor movement's relationship with the state. The tactical options that were therefore available to the UAW leadership helped to transform the union in what one historian has called, "a combination political machine and welfare bureaucracy which 'serviced' the membership and 'policed' the national contract."[99]

Rather than accommodation, the history of automobile workers in other parts of the world, and indeed of the UAW before the 1950s, was one of continuous conflict. One reason for the militancy was the industry's compressed wage structure. Though automobile companies introduced bureaucratized wage structures as a means of labor control, they could not prevent the inexorable move toward more compressed wages, and wages in the industry leveled off steadily as the work became less skilled. Thus, though greatly divided spatially and to a certain extent by skill in the workplace, autoworkers tended to see improvements in their incomes in collective terms.[100] In Córdoba, this was the real community that bound the autoworkers together, one forged not in the neighborhoods but in the factories where they spent most of their waking hours and the better part of their lives.

Other factors peculiar to the industry reinforced the Cordoban autoworkers' militancy. The strategic importance of automobile manufacturing was one. As it was a chief sector in industrial production, with other industries such as steel and rubber greatly dependent on its well-being, automobile workers had a considerable amount of power. Because the automobile industry was highly interdependent in Argentina, work stoppages such as the 1974 SMATA strike had a chain effect on the economy, and the autoworkers could make their presence felt with an authority that most other sectors of the industrial working class simply lacked. In a country like Argentina, which had not experienced diversified industrial development and had made the automotive complexes the nexus of their postwar industrial programs, strikes were capable of precipitating national economic and even political crises, as the history of the Cordoban autoworkers between 1969 and 1976 repeatedly shows. In the hierarchy of powerful unions, the autoworkers thus ranked high, a fact that encouraged their leadership and the rank and file to undertake strike action when other unions might have hesitated.

It is clear that the *clasista* movements in the IKA-Renault and Fiat Concord plants emerged partly in response to shop floor grievances unresolved by previous union representation. Where the Peronist SMATA and the Fiat company union officials had been deferential and hesitant to question the companies' control over the production process, the *clasistas* practiced confrontation and intransigence in the plants. The class struggle was taken to the factory floor and expressed in terms that the workers not only understood but supported. At Fiat, formerly surly foremen learned to treat workers with greater respect, or they risked the reaction of the newly vigilant and captious union. At IKA-Renault, management practices were challenged at every turn, and the clear demarcation of the workplace as the exclusive zone of management authority, a line that had existed during the *torrista* years, was ignored by the *clasistas.*

Certain characteristics unique to Córdoba perhaps led the workers to a deeper questioning of the relations of production than automobile workers elsewhere. One such characteristic was the high stability of employment in the Cordoban automobile industry. Another could have been the absence of ethnic or racial cleavages among the local automotive proletariat. The fact that there was a homogeneous labor force in Córdoba may also have made management-labor conflict more direct and kept it from moving onto the other tracks that complicated and confused such conflicts in other automobile industries.[101]

The problems of work, however, did not perforce occasion either worker resistance or *clasismo.* Rather, it was those problems as they were perceived subjectively by the workers, through an emotional lens made of the manifold influences in Argentina and Córdoba that were their common intellectual property and that focused on a redefined worldview, an ideology that contained certain elements that could be shared by both the *clasista* leadership and the Peronist rank and file. Society and the factory interacted in a dynamic process to give meaning and direction to *clasismo*. The legacy of the Peronist Resistance, the struggles of the 1960s, the Cordobazo all infused the local working class with a heightened sense of rights and power that underlay the factory rebellions of the 1970s. Influences of ideology and politics weighed heavily in this history, thereby creating the romanticized image of the Cordoban car worker and the Cordoban labor movement in general.

The potential for militancy most likely never would have been realized, however, had not certain workplace influences intervened to catalyze it among the rank and file. The Cordobazo was undoubtedly the starting point for the politicization of the young workers who led the union recovery movements, but those union recovery movements were sustained by workplace issues, and without an understanding the dynamic interplay between the market, production processes, and management practices, their true significance will be missed. The struggle over job control, a naked if complex conflict between labor and capital in the automobile plants—not the exogenous influences of student-workers, the alienating effects of sudden industrialization, or the frustrated mobility aspirations of a supposed labor aristocracy—was at the heart of the factory rebellions in Santa Isabel and Ferreyra during the 1970s. Politics and work were inextricably bound for the Cordoban autoworkers, and it was in the history of working class politics on the shop floor and its interaction with Argentine and Cordoban society that the historian can find the best explanation for the unique role played by Córdoba's unions in recent Argentine labor history.

· E L E V E N ·

Conclusion: The Sources of Working Class Politics in Córdoba

Nearly since the genesis of the industrial world, intellectuals studying the development of the state and social classes have been concerned with the role of the working class in politics and the labor movement's relationship to civil society. Assertions by nineteenth-century intellectuals of the working class's growing political power became a reality in the twentieth. Though the working class's role in the great social revolutions of the twentieth century has often been ambiguous, or even of little consequence, its importance in the political life of societies as different as those in Germany, the United States, and Argentina has never been in doubt. Studies of the working class in politics have been elaborated in a rich philosophical and historical literature, which has elevated but hardly resolved a debate that was never strictly scholarly and has often been closely linked to political disputes in the authors' own societies. On a purely theoretical level, the primacy given to economic factors and the social relations of production as described in early Marxist thought were refined by later Marxist intellectuals such as Gramsci, who also acknowledged the importance of national political traditions and general cultural factors in working class politics. In recent years, academic scholars have contributed to the debate by demonstrating the influences of the labor market, management philosophies, and work in this history.[1]

Among scholars, it is the historians who have fleshed out the theories of the working class and applied them to the real-life experience of workers in specific cultural and temporal settings. The research and writings of E. P. Thompson, Eric Hobsbawm, William Sewell, Herbert Gutman, David Montgomery, and others have not only established labor history in Europe and North America as a respectable field for scholarly study,

343

they have also illuminated the complexity of the working class's relationship to civil society under capitalism.[2] In Latin America, the study of the working class lagged behind that in Europe and North America, partly due to a dearth of archival sources on labor topics and partly due to the prejudices of scholars who stressed the region's predominantly agrarian character and discounted the working class and the labor movement's importance in modern Latin American history.[3] In recent years, historians have overcome such glib and groundless assumptions and presented broad interpretive studies, heavily influenced by dependency and world system theories, that have stressed Latin America's particular place in the world economy as an explanation for the history of the Latin American working classes and their labor movements.[4]

While I do not deny that the particular character of Latin American capitalist development and the structure of its export economies are factors of supreme importance in the region's history, the pressures and constraints imposed on the Cordoban unions by the postwar international economy are also important themes in this volume. However, domestic influences are the most determinative variables in Latin America's working class history, particularly after the era of export capitalism and in the years of industrial expansion that followed 1929. In that respect a detailed study of Córdoba's labor movement has utility not only for understanding the history of Argentina in the 1960s and 1970s, but also for a better understanding of the relationship between organized labor and politics in modern Latin American history and for tracing the sources of working class politics in general. At first glance the Cordoban unions' prolonged history of militancy and even political radicalism might seem to suggest that their experience was exceptional. As essentially products of the state and with the logic of the industrial relations system behind them, the other modern Latin American labor movements have certainly been more reformist than revolutionary or even combative, more inclined toward integration than resistance, to use the paradigm of one historian of Latin American labor.[5]

In Argentina, Brazil, and Mexico, the Latin American countries with the largest and most important labor movements, the trade unions abandoned the insurrectional policies that anarchists and anarcho-syndicalists had followed in the late nineteenth and early twentieth centuries for a more pragmatic approach. This more conservative tendency was most pronounced in Brazil and Mexico where, during the governments of Getúlio Vargas and Lázaro Cárdenas, the states redoubled their efforts to integrate the once fractious trade unions. Labor affairs increasingly became the preserve of the *pelegos* and the *charros*, the perennial union officials and professional trade union bureaucrats who moved with ease in the labor ministries, alternately negotiating small favors for the unions and cajoling the government into action when concessions no longer appeased their unions and rank-and-file discontent threatened to spill over into working class protest. It is not surprising that in these countries the tightly controlled labor movements for many years represented no threat to the established order. They were, in fact, one of the principal props for that order.

In Argentina, the government's co-optation of the labor movement was more problematic and never fully realized. The unique configuration of the country's class structure, the proportionally greater weight of the working class and its significantly higher levels of unionization, made the working class a more formidable adversary than in either Brazil or Mexico. To this was added the more visible hostility of the state in Argentina after 1955 to working class interests. The visceral anti-Peronism of the upper classes and large sectors of the middle class, and especially the animus of the military toward Perón and Peronism, naturally obstructed the integration of the Peronist labor movement into the state. The working class, in turn, had a symbol in an exiled Perón, who served to galvanize working class opposition to the successively hostile governments.

Though under Augusto Vandor's tutelage the labor movement inched toward a slow reconciliation with the state, even in this period Argentina's differences are apparent, as *vandorismo* ultimately aspired to create a worker's party that was independent of Perón and that had a close relationship with but not necessarily organic links to the state. Also, as a working trade union system, *vandorismo* displayed greater working class autonomy than was thinkable in either Brazil or Mexico. The Peronist labor bosses were to some degree accountable to the rank and file—a rank and file, moreover, which by the early 1960s had formed a consensus for a certain amount of dialogue and cooperation with the state and employers that was fully in keeping with the ideological underpinnings of the Peronist movement.[6] By the same token, the latent tendency for militancy and resistance in the Argentine working class always remained present, and any union leaders who refused to recognize that fact courted opposition, as the history of the labor movement after 1966 would make vividly clear.

Despite the state control in the Latin American labor movements, there were other grassroots movements contemporary with the Cordoban unions that developed in opposition to entrenched labor bureaucracies and government policies favoring the dominant classes' interests over those of the workers. In Mexico, dissident movements among the railroad, light and power, and autoworkers unions challenged the legitimacy of the Mexican labor confederation, the Confederación Trabajadores de México, and the Mexican state's labor policies in the early 1970s.[7] In Brazil, there was an even more significant union rebellion. In 1978, that country's metalworkers' union, a union dominated by the Brazilian autoworkers, unleashed the first serious labor protests in a decade against the military government and began a process that would see all currents of dissent rally around the workers' protests. As in Córdoba, the Brazilian autoworkers were compelled by a series of workplace demands to break with the military governments' labor policies, a break that perforce entailed political opposition, since opposition to any facet of the military's authoritarian program questioned the legitimacy of the regime itself. This working class disaffection ultimately moved beyond strictly sectarian interests and embraced causes such as free elections, agrarian reform, and amnesty for the regime's political prisoners, a fact which explains the appeal it elicited from sectors of Brazilian society outside the working class.[8]

The importance of these two cases of labor militancy notwithstanding, neither seems to have represented either as great a threat to the state or as complete a disruption of the established ways of conducting union affairs as did the dissident labor movement in Córdoba. A major difference, and one generally ignored by those who have studied working class militancy in the city, was its heterogeneous character. Labor militancy was not confined to the "modern sectors," the autoworkers' unions that postdated the populist labor structures. Also, the role of Peronism was crucial in its formation.

Labor militancy in Córdoba was not confined to the autoworkers, and, indeed, the unions with the longest history of militancy were ones that had existed prior to Córdoba's industrial boom. Unions such as Luz y Fuerza and the bus drivers' union had been the leaders of working class militancy years before the *clasista* trade unionism of the early 1970s emerged in the Fiat and IKA-Renault complexes. Nor had their militancy been inconsequential, despite being confined to relatively small unions. Agustín Tosco's light and power workers were capable of effecting city-wide blackouts and had a strategic weight unknown to most of the city's other unions, as the Cordobazo had frighteningly shown. Similarly, the Union Tranviarios Automotor was strategically positioned: since Córdoba had no alternative means of urban transportation, a bus strike invariably precipitated a major urban crisis. In general, there existed a solid block of trade unions in the city drawn from the mainstream working class movement in Argentina, Peronism, which after 1966 opposed both the military governments and the *porteño* labor leadership and played a leading role in the attempts to establish militant, alternative working class alliances nationally, as with the Confederación General del Trabajo de los Argentinos, and in the city itself.

In this light, the entire question of Peronism and its role in the dissident Cordoban labor movement must be reassessed. The few existing studies of Cordoban unionism have given short shrift to the importance of a combative Peronism in the history. Some have even suggested that the "new" working class that emerged after 1955 had only attenuated ties to Peronism, which permitted it to stay free from Peronist tutelage and develop an alternative working class ideology.[9] In addition to displaying a poor understanding of the importance of the Peronist period in Cordoban labor history, when key unions such as Luz y Fuerza and the UTA were either established or greatly expanded, this view confuses the sympathies of a minority of left-wing militants with those of the majority of workers in the local automobile industry. As this volume should have made clear, the Cordoban working class, including the young automotive proletariat, had an overwhelmingly Peronist identity. One *clasista,* Carlos Masera, the secretary general of SITRAC, estimated that at the height of the *clasista* movement in Fiat, more than 90 percent of the workers in the Concord factory still considered themselves *peronistas.* Roque Romero, the undersecretary general of the *clasista* SMATA, estimated a similar figure for his union. The Cordoban autoworkers seem to have had no trouble reconciling their deep Peronist loyalties with support for a *clasista* and, in the main, Marxist union leadership. The key to understanding Cordoban labor militancy is therefore to be found not in a fruitless search for an ideological conversion of the local working class to *clasismo,* but rather in analyzing those conditions in Córdoba that allowed the reconciliation of a Peronist identity with a non-Peronist union leadership and led workers to support more militant tactics than those advocated by Vandor and his heirs nationally.

The influence of independence in the Cordoban labor movement, the Cordoban workers' strong regional identity and opposition to *porteño* interference in local labor affairs, is one such condition. The Cordoban working class thought of itself as *cordobés* as much as *peronista.* The local Peronist leaders, in turn, considered themselves to be worthy rivals of the *porteño* labor bosses, and both union leadership and the rank and file deeply resented centralist policies that ignored local interests and expected blind obedience to the directives coming from Buenos Aires. *Ortodoxos* and *legalistas* alike frequently ignored the orders of their union centrals and allied with supposed political adversaries in the local labor movement as tactical considerations warranted it, to remain free of Buenos Aires. The Cordobazo was the most dramatic example of this pluralism and the potential for nonpartisan cooperation. The alliance of the *legalistas* with left-wing, non-Peronist unions throughout the early 1970s was another. The militant tendencies that were always latent within Peronist trade unionism, with its roots in the struggles of the Resistance, which had been particularly strong in Córdoba, facilitated this cooperation. So did the changes Peronism itself was experiencing in these years, specifically the strong revolutionary, anticapitalist currents within it. As a result, the return of Perón became the only issue of real dispute between the *legalistas* and the left-wing unions, and they worked together for a period of time in a kind of revolutionary syndicalist alliance. With the restoration of Peronist government and the reestablishment of *verticalismo,* however, these independent gestures became more difficult, and ultimately impossible. But for much of the history of the maverick Cordoban labor movement, a combative Peronism was an important factor.

Just as Peronism's resonance within the Argentine working class was the product of deep and complex historical influences, so too were the militancy and political radicalism of the Cordoban labor movement. Though the issue of honest and effective leadership undoubtedly weighed heavily in the election and support for non-Peronist union slates, it would be an oversimplification to reduce Cordoban labor history in these years to such instrumentalist factors alone. In Luz y Fuerza, for example, Tosco undoubtedly enjoyed the advantages bestowed by recognition of his adamantine integrity and reputation as an effective negotiator with Empresa Pública de.Energía Córdoba. But Tosco's leadership clearly represented something more than honest union leadership and good collective bargaining agreements. From the time of the Onganía coup, Tosco's slates presented themselves in what were essentially political terms. Though he scrupulously avoided attacking Perón by name, Tosco's tirades against the "labor bureaucracy" and against attempts by the Peronist trade union movement to subordinate organized labor to its own political stratagems were as much a part of his union platforms, and as great a source of prestige among the rank and file, as was his ability to protect the workers' interests and win better collective bargaining agreements.

Union independence, an independence that led to Luz y Fuerza's suspension from the Federación Argentina de Trabajadores Luz y Fuerza in 1968 and its virtual outcast status within the national labor movement thereafter, was a unifying issue that lost the support of only a small number of light and power workers with the onset of the Peronist restoration in 1973. Political unionism in Luz y Fuerza did not mean a complete acceptance of Tosco's socialist convictions, much less a rejection outright of Peronism. Rather, it meant support for the union's participation in specific political acts such as the CGTA campaign; solidarity for imprisoned political activists; participation in major working class mobilizations, such as the Cordobazo and *viborazo;* and generally a tradition of union democracy that often implied criticism of and even open breaks with some of the tenets and many of the practices of Peronist trade unionism. Moreover, though there was no rank-and-file unity behind Tosco's socialist project, neither was there political apathy. The workers did not simply surrender the union apparatus to Tosco and his lieutenants in return for effective representation. Many light and power workers, Peronists and non-Peronists alike, identified with the ideological assumptions underlying Tosco's *sindicalismo de liberación.*

The case of the automobile workers is more complex. In both the Fiat and IKA-Renault complexes, the *clasista* leaders initially launched their union challenges strictly over work-related issues. The SITRAC-SITRAM rebels who eventually came to power in Ferreyra and slowly adopted *clasista* positions, as well as the more partisan *clasista* SMATA slate that won the 1972 union elections, spoke of such problems as corruption, union democracy, excessive production rhythms, and hazardous working conditions, but not socialism. Indeed such notions as anti-imperialism, national liberation, *cogestión,* and even socialism itself, albeit defined by the Peronists as "national socialism" to distinguish it from its Marxist variants, were the common intellectual property of many factions within the workers' movement by the time of the *clasista* movements, among them the Peronist, and would not have served as the basis for any effective union challenge.

But as in the case of Luz y Fuerza, there is considerable evidence that the workers who supported the *clasista* unions were aware that they were repudiating a trade union style and not just backing a resolution of specific shop floor problems. From the time of the Cordobazo there existed in Córdoba in general, and in the automotive complexes especially, a considerable degree of sympathy for shop floor renegades, those militants who were arguing for a fundamental change in the way the country's trade unions were run. Though they made little headway in winning over the majority of the workers from Peronism to *clasismo,* the *clasistas* had considerable success in gaining the tacit approval of the workers for their political leadership. Such support seems attributable to more than mere gratitude for the workplace problems effectively resolved and might well have had much to do with a rough understanding of the *clasistas'* position on political trade unionism, or at the very least a respect for it. The grassroots resistance to the suppression of SITRAC, SITRAM, and the *clasista* SMATA, the massive Fiat mobilizations in the series of strikes that culminated in the *viborazo,* and the support of the SMATA workers for the alliance with Tosco suggest a nascent if unarticulated political sympathy. Of course it was very much influenced by the particular circumstances existing in Córdoba at that historical moment, but it was more than mere gratitude for services rendered on the shop floor.

Nevertheless the importance of the relationship between labor militancy and shop floor problems in the local automobile industry should not be underestimated. Had there not been problems with hazardous working conditions, work-incentive rules, assembly line speedups, and other grievances, it is doubtful that the union rebellions of the early 1970s would ever have taken place. *Clasismo* itself might never have emerged. In Ferreyra, the birthplace of the Cordoban *clasista* movement, the nature of the workplace problems and the effects of specific Fiat management practices encouraged a socialist perspective among a small number of workers. In Santa Isabel, tightening factory conditions and ineffective union protection at the shop floor level underlay the union recovery movement in the IKA-Renault plants and allowed the left to achieve a relationship with the local working class that had previously eluded it.

Clasismo in its most fundamental sense represented the workers' attempt to break with the trade union style that had emerged under *vandorismo* and to assert some degree of control in the factory. Daniel James notes that the contradiction between the real-life experience of the working class after the Resistance, particularly in the workplace, and Peronism's loudly proclaimed commitment to social justice was not so great in these years that the workers felt compelled to reject it. There were other things that contributed to their continued identification with Peronism, among them the movement's proscribed status and the unremitting hostility of certain sectors of Argentine society to it.[10] But in Córdoba the contradiction was acutely felt, and *clasismo* was both an ideological and practical response to the failings of Peronist trade unionism. If the *clasistas* underestimated the depth of the Peronist loyalty among the rank and file, the Peronist labor bosses likewise underestimated the degree of workers' discontent with a trade union style that stressed protection for the workers only in collective bargaining negotiations (and there with increasing ineffectiveness after 1966) and not on the shop floor.

Other factors often singled out as explanations for Córdoba's militant trade union movement seem decidedly less convincing. Arguments of creeping immiserization or of heightened working class tensions due to the combined effects of rapid industrialization and sudden industrial decline are highly questionable.[11] Though some services in Córdoba compared unfavorably with those in Buenos Aires, particularly those in urban transport, others, such as housing, were far better. Nor was unemployment a major problem in the city during the period in question. As the Cordoban automotive boom lost strength, new workers were absorbed by the city's more traditional industries, and they also found employment in government and services. Broad sociological explanations for Córdoba's labor militancy, in short, seem facile and misleading. Similarly, those who posit that the greater working class militancy among Argentine autoworkers was due to the short-term boom and slump cycle, as opposed to a sustained depression in its automobile industry, which presumably preserved a core of labor activists who were able to move in and out of the car plants, have incorrectly applied the experience of the Brazilian industry, and perhaps of the Buenos Aires factories, to the industry as a whole.[12]

The hire and fire practices that may have existed in Buenos Aires were almost unknown in Córdoba, where in actual fact it was slow deterioration, not wild swings in the business cycle, that characterized the local automobile industry, and where the power of the local labor movement cautioned management against such policies. Furthermore, something approaching dual labor markets appears to have existed. Workers only rarely moved between the Fiat and IKA-Renault plants—those who did were principally skilled workers—and the existence of company blacklists prevented the movement of activists between Ferreyra and Santa Isabel.

Finally, those who have looked for the source of the local working class's militancy in the city's character as a university town, and in the reputed existence of part-time student workers who encouraged student radicalism in the automobile plants, have little to support their claim.[13] The first empirical study of the social origins of the SMATA workers in the 1950s and 1960s does not show any significant presence of university students in the plants.[14] Indeed, given the labor surplus that existed in the city after 1965, as well as a predominantly middle-class student body and a local student culture that, in fact, displayed a certain distaste for manual labor, such arguments appear to provide a convenient scapegoat for Cordoban working class militancy rather than a satisfying explanation. Though the city's university students were important political allies in the workers' movement throughout these years, the radicalizing influence of student-workers among the Cordoban autoworkers seems a greatly exaggerated if not altogether mistaken claim.

The history of the dissident Cordoban labor movement suffers in general from much confusion on the crucial distinction between labor militancy and political radicalism. Certainly one of the arguments of this book has been that there is no simple correlation between the two, that although militancy informed and nurtured a heightened politicization of the local working class, it would be an error to ascribe a *clasista* ideology to the local working class as a whole, to assume that the Cordoban labor movement's notable combativeness responded to a radical ideology fully elaborated and commonly shared. In this respect, the myth of the Cordobazo is revealing.

The widespread assumption that the uprising was led by revolutionary Marxist leaders in the autoworkers' unions completely distorts the true nature of the event. What best explains the Cordobazo's causes within the working class (though not its ultimate consequences, which were indeed potentially revolutionary) is a series of more mundane crises that occurred in a number of local industries, combined with the power rivalries between the Cordoban Peronists and their union centrals in Buenos Aires, and especially the local political and cultural influences that the workers were subject to. In addition, there were the more explicitly political motives of Tosco and the various student and left-wing political organizations that participated, the latter belatedly, in the uprising. What the Cordobazo most definitely was not is what it is often assumed to have been: a sort of revolutionary strike led by *clasista* autoworkers' unions. The SMATA was firmly in Peronist hands at that point, and Fiat's company-controlled plant unions, SITRAC and SITRAM, did not take part to any significant degree in the uprising.

The Cordobazo reflected the multiple and variegated influences that were responsible for Cordoban labor militancy. In this respect, political rivalries and the power politics of the labor movement seem to be the one great factor most often overlooked in the history. From the late 1950s on,

Cordoban union leaders had been formulating their tactics with political considerations in mind. In part they were jockeying for power within the Peronist labor movement itself, as Peronist union leaders such as Elpidio Torres and Alejo Simó attempted to retain their independence and resist the verticalist pressures coming from Buenos Aires. Both Torres and Simó were at various moments rumored to be possible candidates for leadership positions in the national Confederación General del Trabajo and the 62 Organizaciones, and neither was willing to sacrifice his own ambitions for the sake of the unity of Peronist labor, until they were given no choice by Perón. Internal union politics was also a factor of supreme importance in the leadership's calculations for outflanking any internal opposition, leftist or Peronist, that could undermine its authority and threaten its control of the unions. The history of a union such as the Cordoban Union Obrera Metalúrgica, for example, which oscillated between outright insubordination and an almost slavish obedience to Buenos Aires, illustrates the dynamic at work in Cordoban labor politics. The ups and downs of the local metalworking industry and the need to adjust strategy in accordance with self-interest best explain the Cordoban UOM's checkered history. Similar considerations explain the behavior of the SMATA and a number of other Cordoban Peronist unions, particularly before the 1973 Peronist restoration.

The image of Córdoba as a hotbed of political and specifically Marxist trade unionism is therefore only half true, and Peronist union politics must also be included as a factor in Cordoban labor militancy. Peronist union politics was part of an ongoing process, as the behavior of individual unions was subject to myriad influences—rivalries within the union, its relationship with its union central and the Peronist labor bosses in Buenos Aires, pressures from Perón, the balance of power in the labor movement locally and nationally, and, of course, national politics. There was always considerable room for the fortuitous and the unexpected in this process, and nothing in Córdoba's recent history, neither its sudden and fragile industrial development nor the rapid transformation of its class structure, led ineluctably, as some of the scholars who have studied Córdoba seem to suggest, to the intense and prolonged militancy of Cordoban labor.

If some broad sociological explanations are of little utility in explaining Córdoba, however, other sociological variables are more relevant. One was simply the small size of the city and the centrality of the factory in Cordoban life. The concentration of the Cordoban automobile workers in two great industrial complexes made worker mobilizations easier to organize and generally more effective than in Buenos Aires, where industry was physically dispersed and sectorially diverse and the working class lacked a common identity. When the Fiat unions abandoned their plants to protest poor working conditions in the forge, the IKA-Renault workers had a point of reference that made such action immediately intelligible. Similarly, problems with production speeds in the Ford-Transax factory struck a responsive chord among the Fiat Concord workers. The many solidarity strikes called by the two automobile complexes for each other during the early 1970s were made possible by the empathy workers felt for others engaged in a similar industry, confronting similar problems, and sharing a common workplace idiom.[15]

The relatively small size of the city and the geographic concentration of the headquarters of all the leading Cordoban unions (see Figure 1 in Chapter 1) also made the coordination of strike actions and labor mobilizations easier to effect. The union leaders saw one another frequently, and personal friendships developed even among those who differed politically. With the principal union headquarters situated within five minutes' walking distance of one another and with nearly all the other unions concentrated within a six-block radius in the city, daily contact between union officials was routine and last-minute union deliberations and decisions were more common than in Buenos Aires. Cordoban trade unionism was characterized by improvisation and its tendency to dispense with formal, drawn-out procedures for approving strikes and demonstrations, and this was partly the result of the ease with which union officials could move from one union hall to the next, present their point of view, and coordinate action in a personal way. The last-minute preparations that went into the Cordobazo and the alacrity with which decisions were reached the night before the uprising were illustrative of a more informal union style that allowed for a quicker resolution of problems and a greater propensity to act and to adopt militant tactics. Finally, the greater independence from meddling union centrals enjoyed by leading unions such as the SMATA, Luz y Fuerza, and the *clasista* SITRAC-SITRAM reinforced the local character of Cordoban trade union politics.

Other factors often singled out as contributing to Cordoban labor militancy are more difficult to gauge and seem to have been less decisive. The development of new working class neighborhoods such as Ferreyra and Santa Isabel does not appear to have had the profound influence on class consciousness that is generally attributed to it.[16] Working class neighborhood organizations were few, and Córdoba, unlike Buenos Aires, did not produce anything resembling an authentic proletarian culture that was separate from the workplace and the union. The new working class neighborhoods may have given the unions some logistical advantage in terms of mobilizing the workers for strikes or demonstrations, but the loci of power and class identity for the new Cordoban working class were the union and factory, not the neighborhood. The suddenness of its industrial development and the quick formation of its industrial working class worked against the flourishing of a working class culture of the *barrio* and the informal ties of class found in other Latin American cities. The simple facts that the new neighborhoods, despite their rapid growth in the late 1950s and early 1960s, held relatively small populations and that the working class shared its neighborhoods with students and middle-class residents all over the city undermined class solidarity at that level.

The absence of a countervailing and powerful local bourgeoisie, on the other hand, does seem to have been significant, but this is another case in which the precise effects are difficult to measure. The local business associations, the Bolsa de Comercio, Cámara de Industrias Metalúrgicas, and Centro Comercial e Industrial de Córdoba, did not represent the employers of note in the city, that is, the two automobile multinationals and the provincial and federal governments. Instead they included the owners of the small industrial establishments, the small parts factories, and especially the city's retail stores, and thus they were not serious interlocutors with the labor movement. The kind of ongoing, familiar contacts that the *porteño* labor bosses had with the Confederación General Económica or the Unión Industrial Argentina were unknown in Córdoba. The automobile workers dealt with their employers directly, and the public-sector unions with agencies of the federal, provincial, or municipal government. The lack of a powerful and reasonably united local bourgeoisie may have encouraged a certain recklessness among some Cordoban unions. As Juan Malvár, secretary general of the Cordoban print workers and one of the leading Independent activists remarked, "There was big money involved in Buenos Aires, the stakes were much higher there than in Córdoba. The *porteño* labor leaders were dealing with interests that represented lots of money, which naturally made them more cautious. To a certain extent, we in Córdoba didn't feel we had anything to lose."[17] Though such feelings could not be said to represent Cordoban labor as a whole, and indeed the car workers were very conscious of dealing with powerful economic interests, they did represent the situation of at least a sizable proportion of the local unions.

Cordoban labor militancy can thus be traced to several headwaters.

One was certainly the dynamic relationship between the factory and Cordoban society and the character of the local trade union movement. The Cordoban working class was exceptionally militant because of unresolved workplace problems, particularly in the crucial automobile industry, that could be more immediately confronted there than elsewhere thanks to the greater independence of the local unions and the heterogeneity of the local labor movement. The existence of plant unions, federal unions, and even unions such as the SMATA, formally part of a centralized structure but effectively independent of Buenos Aires, encouraged a combative union style. There were also intangible sources, such as the spatial characteristics of the city and the absence of a powerful local industrial bourgeoisie, that could have contributed to its maverick character. But another question remains: Why, in the case of some unions, was militancy complemented by a radical, often revolutionary political program?

It was the coincidence of militancy and politics that made the city so explosive and gave the Cordoban unions a power unmatched in the country, allowing them not only to challenge the labor movement hierarchy and practices of Peronist trade unionism but also to forge an alternative trade union movement that briefly threatened the Argentine state itself. In the case of the automobile workers' unions, the strategies used by the revolutionary left to win a following in the industrial proletariat were important factors. Also influential, however, were elements that have been suggested by two students of the Argentine labor movement, in a theory that is broadly applicable to the new industrial working class in Latin America in general but is of considerable utility for explaining the particularities of recent Cordoban labor history. Juan Carlos Torre and Elizabeth Jelin have criticized the "reductionism" of scholars—their preoccupation with the workplace at the expense of the reigning sociopolitical culture as a factor of considerable weight in working class politics.[18]

Cordoban labor history of the 1960s and 1970s does indeed need to be put in its cultural, intellectual, and political context. A confluence of factors, not the least of which was the growing radicalization of Argentine political and intellectual life in the 1960s and early 1970s, influenced labor politics in the city. Such factors were aided by Córdoba's unique cultural context: its tradition as Argentina's rebel city and its character as a university town, a place where politics and political discussion formed a vital part of civic culture. The impact of ideology on union politics is difficult to weigh precisely, but its significance does appear to have been greater in Córdoba than in other parts of the country.

Córdoba's reputation as Argentina's radical city was well deserved. Various political currents—the Third World priests' movement, student radicalism, a revitalized Cordoban left, and a solid core of Marxist and Peronist left labor activists—all came together to produce a climate conducive to the radicalization of at least part of the working class. The bitter disputes between Peronist left, Maoist, and pro-Soviet communist parties that found expression in the Cordoban trade union movement attest to the importance of ideology in the city. Political debates that had not survived the 1940s in most Latin American labor movements were still alive and well in Córdoba in the 1970s, and when Antonio Marimón asked whether in Córdoba the last battles of Comintern had been fought, it was not an idle question. Such ideological squabbles gave local labor politics a slightly musty air in some respects, but they were also testimony to the vitality of the local labor movement and Córdoba's political culture. More significant than the divisions and bickering within the left was the fact that Córdoba showed that there was nothing immutable about mainstream Peronism's hold on the working class, that there still existed room for dissent and debate both within Peronism and outside of it.

One of the chief proponents of a critical assessment of mainstream Peronism's relationship with working class, and an actor too often ignored in the history, was the Cordoban left. The Cordoban left built on its ideological differences with the putative heirs of Juan Perón to forge an effective challenge to the trade union practices of the Peronist labor bosses that were by then widespread in the Argentine labor movement. It managed to do this by succeeding precisely where Peronism had always bested it before, by marrying effective union representation with the workers' emotional needs, by speaking to them in an idiom that more faithfully responded to the moment in which the Cordoban working class was living. Leftist denunciations of the betrayals of "bureaucrats" resonated with the workers because they were verified by their own experience. Declining wages, an absence of union protection in the workplace, the loss of a sense of self-worth and even a sense of historic mission, which the Peronism of the 1940s and 1950s and the Resistance had instilled in them, were all issues appropriated by the left. The leftist upstarts, moreover, whether by instinct or design, were able to frame their challenge in an appeal to regional sensibilities. *Clasismo* itself became a kind of Cordoban working class identity, and the Cordoban working class was presented in leftist discourse as embodying the virtues of purity, integrity, and solidarity, in contrast to the corrupt and venal values of working class politics in the federal capital, especially as personified by the labor bosses.

In this light, the dissident Cordoban labor movement failed not simply because it clashed with the Peronist sensibilities of the working class. Peronism was a very malleable concept in those years, and there was much in the *clasista* message that was fully acceptable even to the most stalwart Peronist worker. Rather, *clasismo* failed for very specific reasons. The failure was largely political, owing to the inability or unwillingness of the Marxist left to resolve its chronic factionalism and effectively ally with the dissident currents in the Peronist working class nationally. But the failure was not wholly of the left's own making, as the absence of a bona fide workers' party hindered its efforts from the start. In that sense the restoration of Peronism to political power was fatal, because it undermined the very real possibility that the dissident Cordoban labor movement had had of uniting a sizable portion of the Argentine working class behind a socialist program, whether such a program declared itself *peronista* or *clasista*.

Instead the Cordoban unions were forced to perform a function for which they were ill-suited and which they were ultimately unable to carry off. In the absence of a workers' party of national stature, the Cordoban unions had to assume the formidable task of combining political work with effective union representation. The presumed political errors of the *clasistas* become more understandable when the obstacles to reforming the labor movement while simultaneously rebuilding an alternative workers' political movement, first under military rule and then under a Peronist government, are taken into account. Particularly after 1973, politically the dissident Cordoban unions could only react to events, watch from the sidelines, and attempt to consolidate their trade union alliance before the contradictions of the Peronist government eroded its own popular support and invited yet another military coup. When they did attempt to precipitate the course of events, such as with the 1974 SMATA strike, they invariably failed.

The inability of the Cordoban unions to fulfill their goals and the scarce resonance that *clasismo* has in the Argentine labor movement today have led to a widespread interpretation of the militant trade union movement as having been an aberration, as an interesting but exceptional chapter in recent Argentine working class history. The uniqueness of much of Córdoba's recent labor history is undeniable, and the distinct character of the city's trade union politics is obvious. But the importance of the Cordoban unions and, I would argue, their relevance today, as Argentina attempts to build a stable participatory democracy, overshadow Córdoba's eccentricities.

The lasting significance of the Cordoban unions lies, above all, in their scrupulous practice of a rigorous union democracy and in their frank recognition of the continued existence of social classes in capitalist society, and ultimately of the conflicting class interests that tend to characterize an underdeveloped country like their own. Finally, the unions have contemporary relevance because they were determined to build a party that would represent faithfully, free from manipulation by the state and charismatic populists, that class to which they belonged. If their revolutionary élan and their blind faith in the ability of socialism to resolve the inequities of capitalism seem a bit ingenuous and stale today (a product, it should be remembered, of the historical moment in which they emerged), their democratic spirit and faithful advocacy of workers' rights do not. The Cordoban unions made the concept of ideological and political pluralism within the Argentine labor movement respectable once again. Union democracy was interpreted as unobtainable without a workplace democracy, and *verticalismo,* unquestioning fealty to the Peronist trade union hierarchy, was no longer sacred. All these ideas are worthy contributions to the future of any organized workers' movement in Argentina.

Whatever their legacy to the labor movement and Argentine political life, the importance of the Cordoban unions in the country's history between 1966 and 1976 hardly seems questionable. Virtually every dissident movement and shop floor rebel after 1966 looked to Córdoba for some kind of inspiration, if not outright support. The power of the Cordoban unions became so great and their opposition to both military government and unrepresentative union leaders so outspoken and effective that even working class mavericks in Buenos Aires looked to their example and depended on their encouragement. Their influence among labor dissidents in the Argentine interior was preponderant. The Cordoban unions were the source of moral and practical sustenance for nearly all the great union democracy movements of the period, from Raimundo Ongaro's CGTA in 1968 to the great 1975 Villa Constitución strike, profoundly affecting the power struggles within the labor movement and thus national politics. They were also a power in their own right. The two greatest working class protests in contemporary Argentine history, the 1969 Cordobazo and the 1971 *viborazo,* occurred in Córdoba and precipitated the fall of two military governments, paving the way for the restoration of civilian government in 1973.

The power of the Cordoban unions, their ability to shut down Argentina's second-largest industrial city virtually at will after 1969 and the potential that their protests always had of developing into full-fledged national crises, made them an even more formidable opposition to the governments in power than the myriad guerrilla organizations operating in those years. The association made by the Peronist government, the Peronist labor hierarchy, and the military between the guerrilla organizations and the Cordoban unions and *clasista* movements greatly hurt the dissident trade unions' cause. The relationship of the Cordoban unions with groups such as the Fuerzas Armadas Peronistas, Ejército Revolucionario del Pueblo, and Montoneros was always distant and critical, though there is no question that a minority of *clasista* activists were drawn toward armed struggle as the repression of their unions grew more severe. But the guerrilla left's own incorporation of the dissident trade union movement into its revolutionary praxis ultimately did great damage to the workers' cause. As their self-appointed protectors and avengers, the guerrillas may have elicited some sympathy among the workers. Abusive foremen and intransigent company officials paid the price for their actions, often with their very lives, thanks to the guerrilla left's patronage of the unions, and the workers may have felt a silent sense of retribution at the punishment meted out. But mostly the Cordoban union leaders were displeased and frightened by the guerrillas' actions, and they realized that too close an association between what were in reality two separate movements would have high political costs. Indeed, by the end of the Peronist government they found themselves isolated as popular concern with the guerrillas and the political violence mounted and many associated the "subversives" excoriated in military pronouncements with the union dissidents.

The military had held back for many years from suppressing the Cordoban unions, aware of the risks of any attempted purge of Cordoban labor. One of the factors that persuaded the military to relinquish its state control to a civilian government was the explosive situation in Córdoba and specifically, one may presume, the militant workers' movement there.[19] The Peronist governments of 1973 to 1976 did what no military government could have achieved without paying a high political price.

Perón, Ricardo Otero, and Lorenzo Miguel justified the destruction of the Cordoban labor movement as being in the interests of preserving working class unity and protecting a democratically elected government, adorning their claims with the nationalist and populist fustian of the past. In their dealings with the working class during Perón's "second coming," repressive tactics that had only occasionally been resorted to in the Peronist governments of the 1940s and 1950s became commonplace. Redbaiting and the suppression of democratically elected unions, the harassment and murder of independently minded labor leaders, including a number, such as Atilio López, drawn from their own Peronist ranks, unmasked a regime intent on subordinating the country's unions to its own need to ensure labor stability as part of its conservative economic program. Only the Peronists could have followed such policies and still hoped to remain in power.

The baleful effects of Peronism on working class politics came home to roost in the early 1970s and brought an end to the Cordoban union rebellion that had begun shortly after the Onganía coup and gathered force after the Cordobazo. The Cordoban unions had been pushed into an adversarial relationship with the state and the labor bureaucracy by multiple factors. The problems of the local economy that resulted from its undiversified industrial development were certainly involved. The automobile workers, largely unskilled and therefore unable to protect their interests without a united union front, were also forced into political opposition by state policies that were unremittingly hostile to working class interests after 1966. Other sectors of the local working class felt the effects of the governments' policies as well, but they lacked the size and power of the automotive proletariat. Of all the city's unions, only the light and power workers held as strategic a position in the local economy, and the leadership role both assumed was largely in response to their importance in Córdoba's particular economic and social setting.

The social underpinnings of Cordoban working class politics are evident and do indeed need to be examined, because they formed the bedrock without which the Cordoban labor movement would not have developed as it did.[20] But the Cordoban unions also had a history, and in the details of that history, in the ebb and flow of events, lies much of the explanation and all of the drama of their struggle against Onganía, the labor bosses, and ultimately Perón himself. By analyzing that struggle historically, the question of their reputed failure also becomes more relative. The inability of the Cordoban unions to achieve their goals does not invalidate the historical circumstances that produced their movement any more than it diminishes their achievements or justifies their errors. In their own day, no one doubted their importance or dismissed their struggle as inconsequential and the outcome as preordained. And certainly this historian, whose sympathy for their movement is by now obvious, does not want to defend their mistakes. But the supposed failure of the Cordoban unions is understood fully only when looked at historically. The historical circumstances that at first made possible their movement later turned against them. Yet the final outcome, like the history of the Cordoban labor movement itself, was the result of many factors, including their own mistakes and some bad luck. It was certainly nothing predetermined by the Argentine working class's Peronist identity.

The success of any political movement, moreover, lies as much in the opportunities exploited as in the chances missed. Apparent victories are often illusory and defeats only temporary setbacks. Though the future of the Argentine labor movement might well vindicate the Cordoban unions, from the historian's point of view and even, I would argue, from their own, the point is incidental. The political history of the Latin American working class is certainly more than merely episodic, and that of the Cordoban unions is more than simply an interesting episode. The process by which a slightly stodgy university town was transformed into the country's second industrial city, a young working class was formed in the space of a few years, and a powerful and democratic labor movement was forged almost overnight is part of that history. So too were Atilio López's personal conflict between loyalty to his movement and to his conscience, the *clasistas'* impassioned political discussions, the Cordoban autoworkers' daily work lives in the plants, and Agustín Tosco's lifelong, exemplary struggle to build a democratic trade union movement. Together they make the Cordoban unions a point of reference in the history of modern Latin American labor movements rather than an interesting oddity. Certainly few of the workers who participated in the events of those years consider the outcome to have dishonored the struggle itself.

The post-1976 military governments' loudly proclaimed neoliberal economic policies were particularly consequential for the Argentine automobile industry and for Córdoba. In an effort to dispense with the "irrationalities" of the country's economic structure, to dismantle protectionism and the legacies of a statist economy, as well as to eliminate what had become a particularly troublesome sector of the industrial working class, the military repealed industrial legislation that dated from the Frondizi years and opened up the country to automobile imports. By the early 1980s, Chrysler, General Motors, Citroën, and Peugeot had all abandoned their plants in Argentina. In 1982 Fiat, which by then had already shifted the bulk of its Latin American manufacturing establishments to Brazil, sold all but 15 percent of its stock in the Ferreyra complex to Argentine investors. The automobile companies that remained in the country deepened the rationalization programs they had begun before the coup and sought to convert their Argentine plants into suppliers for their global operations. In Córdoba 6,876 jobs disappeared in the Santa Isabel and Ferreyra complexes between 1976 and 1981. An additional 1,670 jobs were lost in July 1980, when the government closed down the IME factories, the progenitors of Córdoba's automobile industry.[21]

The military's repression of the labor movement was part and parcel of its deindustrialization program. The post-1976 juntas abolished the right to strike, outlawed the CGT and the 62 Organizaciones, busted dozens of unions, among them the UOM, Luz y Fuerza, and SMATA centrals, and abducted and murdered thousands of labor leaders, activists, and simple working men and women. The military's economic program and labor policies succeeded in doing what the Peronists, the automobile companies, and the previous military governments had been unable to do—namely, to tame Córdoba.

Source Materials

Company Archives

Archives des Usines Renault, Boulogne-Billancourt, France:
  Direction des Affaires Internationales (D.A.I.) 0200
  Direction du Budget et des Affaires Financières (D.A.I.) 0212, 0295
  Direction des Services Financiers (D.F.) 0764
  Direction Générale (D.G.) 0272
  Direction Juridique (D.J.) 0263, 0734
  Direction des Usines à l'Etranger (D.U.E.) 0070, 0295, 1290, 9030

Archivio Storico, Fiat S.p.A., Turin, Italy:
  Argentina-Progetto-Viaggi-1947–1958 Fondo "ex CM13"-III/9/C
  Servizio Collegamento Società Estere Fondo CG89-IV/8/E
  Direzione Partecipazioni Estere Fondo CG86-XI/1/6
  Coordinamento Affari Internazionali, Fiat Concord Fondo CG-87-XIV/1/F
  Pianificazione e Controllo Fondo CG89-XVIII/9/C

Company Papers

Empresa Pública de Energía de Córdoba (EPEC), *Informe Estadístico, 1966–1976*
Industrial Relations Department, Renault Argentina, S.A., Santa Isabel, selected
  papers related to labor force, 1966 to 1976
Memoria y Balance, Fiat Concord, 1956 to 1975
Memoria y Balance, Grandes Motores Diesel, 1956 to 1964
Memoria y Balance, Industrias Kaiser Argentina, 1956 to 1965
Memoria y Balance, Industrias Mecánicas del Estado, 1968 to 1976

Union Archives

Archivo del Sindicato de Trabajadores Concord (SITRAC), Buenos Aires (files):
  A. Documentos de SITRAC
  B. Elecciones Internas

C. Discusiones paritarias y convenio de 1971
D. Congreso Nacional de Sindicatos Combativos, Agrupaciones Clasistas y Obreros Revolucionarios
E. Documentos administrativos y contables
F. Despidos de dirigentes y activistas de 1971
G. Documentos relacionados con los presos
H. Listas de expedientes tramitados en la delegación del Ministerio de Trabajo
I. Juicio por reincorporación
J. Relaciones de los despidos de Fiat con SMATA y UOM
K. Intentos de reorganización del SITRAC
L. Materiales para reconstruir la historia
M. Recortes de Prensa
N. Cronología diaria (1970–71)
O. Publicaciones

SMATA Archive, Sindicato de Mecánicos y Afines del Transporte Automotor, Seccional Córdoba (volumes):
Confederación General del Trabajo. Notas enviadas y recibidas, 1970–71
Diarios del Sindicato del SMATA, 1971–72
Diarios del Sindicato del SMATA, 1972–73
Diarios del Sindicato del SMATA, 1973–74
Diarios, Revistas y Publicaciones Diversas, 1971–72
Notas sobre Escalas Salariales, 1970 to 1972
Notas de Comisión Interna de Reclamos y Respuesta de IKA-Renault, 1972–73
Notas de Comisión Interna de Reclamos y Respuesta de IKA-Renault, 1973–74
Notas y Comunicados Enviadas del SMATA, 1971–72
Volantes Varios, 1972
Volantes Varios, 1975
Volantes y Comunicados, 1969
Volantes y Comunicados, 1970
Volantes de Agrupaciones Varias, 1973–74
Volantes, Diarios y Revistas, 1973

Union Publications

Avance. Monthly union magazine of the Sindicato de Mecánicos y Afines del Transporte Automotor, 1969 to 1976.
CGT. Weekly newspaper of the Confederación General del Trabajo de los Argentinos, 1968–69.
Electrum. Weekly publication of the Sindicato de Luz y Fuerza de Córdoba, 1966 to 1974.
Memoria y Balance. 1964 to 1974. Sindicato de Luz y Fuerza de Córdoba.
Informe. Servicio de Documentación e Información Laboral, 1968 to 1976.
Memoria y Balance. Sindicato de Mecánicos y Afines del Transporte Automotor, 1966 to 1976.
SITRAC: Boletín de los Trabajadores Concord, 1971.
SITRAC-SITRAM: Boletín de los Trabajadores Concord y Materfer, 1971–72.

SITRAP: Boletín Informativo del Sindicato de Trabajadores de Perkins, 1973.
SMATA, SMATA-Córdoba. Weekly union newspaper, 1969 to 1976.
UTA. Monthly union magazine of the Unión Tranviarios Automotor, Seccional Córdoba, 1969 to 1976 (collection incomplete).
La Voz del SMATA, SMATA-Córdoba. Weekly union newspaper, 1960 to 1969.

Government Documents

Anuario Estadístico de la Ciudad de Córdoba. Dirección de Estadística y Control. Municipalidad de Córdoba, 1955 to 1976.
Archives du Ministère du l'Industrie, Paris. Report "Le conflit I.K.A.-Renault à Cordoba, 13–08–1974."
Cámara de Diputados. Provincia de Córdoba. Diario de Sesiones, 1973–75.
Censo Industrial, 1954, 1964, 1974. Ministerio de Hacienda, Economía, y Previsión Social. Provincia de Córdoba.
Dirección General de Estadística, Censos e Investigaciones. Reports:
"Población, 1869–1960." Córdoba, 1961.
"Estadísticas Demográficas y Vitales: Población, 1901–1970." Córdoba, 1970.
"Encuesta sobre empleo y desempleo en la ciudad de Córdoba." Córdoba, 1973.
"Incremento Edilicio." Secretaría de Estado de Planeamiento, Córdoba, 1975.
"Indice de precios a nivel del consumidor. Costo de vida en la ciudad de Córdoba." Subsecretaría de Planeamiento, Córdoba, 1975.
Dirección General de Rentas. Ministerio de Hacienda, Economía y Previsión Social. "Boletín," 1955 to 1976.
Ministerio de Desarrollo. Area Planeamiento. "Informe ecónomico de la provincia de Córdoba, 1971."
U.S. Department of State. Papers Relating to the Internal Affairs of Argentina, 1955 to 1976.
U.S. Military Intelligence Reports. Argentina, 1918–1941.

Oral Sources

In the course of almost a decade of research on Córdoba, I had many interviews with workers in the city, particularly with autoworkers from the Fiat and IKA-Renault plants, light and power workers employed by EPEC, and metalworkers from the city's numerous parts factories and workshops. Those interviews nearly always yielded interesting and sometimes useful information on the unions and on working conditions in the local industrial establishments. Nevertheless, since this book is not an analysis of the local working class's "popular memory" but a study of labor politics in the city, it was my opinion that most of the workers' recollections were often too sketchy or incomplete to use as historical evidence. Though these interviews undoubtedly have influenced my interpretation of the history, I chose not to rely on "rank-and-file testimonies" for this study except in my reconstruction of the Cordobazo, about which workers' personal memories, sharpened by the dramatic events of the uprising, seemed of some evidential worth. Instead,

I decided to concentrate my efforts on the key figures in the Cordoban labor movement, the dominant individuals for whom union affairs and labor politics were ongoing, almost daily concerns. Similarly, my attempt to analyze political consciousness through oral testimony is based on interviews with such individuals. These oral sources thus might appear to recapture the experience only of a labor elite. But in a labor movement such as Córdoba's, where the unions' bureaucratic apparatuses were weak and where ordinary workers commonly achieved positions of union leadership, the distinction between leaders and rank and file is less important than is the case in other trade union movements. Though oral testimonies are always problematic and vulnerable to both a shaded rendering and a biased interpretation, the relationship of trust and confidence that I believe I was able to establish with nearly all of these individuals has persuaded me that such oral sources can be cited as evidence. Multiple interviews were conducted with each of the following individuals, over a period of several years. I was able to evaluate their testimony critically, to challenge them on points that were unconvincing or inconsistent, and to reach conclusions I believe are historically sound.

The majority of the oral testimonies of the Cordobazo were recorded by Mónica Gordillo, with some follow-up interviews by myself, when she worked as my research assistant during 1989–90. The questions posed to the participants loosely followed a questionnaire I had prepared, but essentially we decided to let the individuals just tell their story. I have only begun to explore the meaning of the Cordobazo in this volume, and future historians can consult these rich testimonies in the offices of the Fundación Pedro Milesi in Córdoba, where the tapes have been stored for their safekeeping.

UNION OFFICIALS

Felipe Alberti, Secretary of Culture and Social Welfare, Luz y Fuerza de Córdoba, 1966 to 1976

Oscar Alvarez, Secretary of Technical Affairs, Luz y Fuerza de Córdoba, 1968 to 1976

Domingo Bizzi, Undersecretary General, SITRAC, 1970 to 1971

Juan Canelles, communist construction workers' union leader, 1958 to 1976

Sixto Ceballos, leader of Peronist opposition, Luz y Fuerza de Córdoba, 1960 to 1976

Ramón Contreras, Secretary General of Luz y Fuerza de Córdoba, 1966 to 1968

Miguel Angel Correa, Secretary General of CGT de los Argentinos, Córdoba branch, 1968 to 1969

Gregorio Flores, *clasista* SITRAC shop steward, 1970 to 1971

Pedro Gómez, Secretary General of Cordoban textile workers' union

Juan Malvár, Secretary General of Cordoban print workers' union, 1958 to 1976

Antonio Marimón, Press Secretary of SMATA-Córdoba, 1972 to 1974

Alfredo Martini, Secretary General of Cordoban UOM, 1973 to 1976

Carlos Masera, Secretary General of SITRAC, 1970 to 1971

Robert Nágera, *clasista* SMATA shop steward, Ford-Transax factory, 1972 to 1974

José Páez, *clasista* shop steward and member of executive committee, SITRAC, 1970 to 1971
Roque Romero, Undersecretary General of SMATA-Córdoba, 1972 to 1974
Alejo Simó, President of Cordoban UOM, 1962 to 1974
Elpidio Torres, President of SMATA-Córdoba, 1958 to 1971

PARTICIPANTS IN THE CORDOBAZO

The following individuals were all interviewed between 1989 and 1991. They are listed in the chronological order in which they were interviewed. Many of those interviewed request anonymity, and therefore only their first names are recorded. All of these interviews can be consulted at the Fundación Pedro Milesi in Córdoba.

Nora, university student; Carlos Bustos, EPEC employee; Adolfo Mena, textile worker, Dante Antonelli, EPEC employee; Pablo, IKA-Renault worker; Carlos Palumbo, IKA-Renault worker; Manuel J. Cabrera, IME worker; José M. Descalzo, EPEC employee; Graciela García, EPEC employee; Humberto Brondo, IKA-Renault worker; Pedro Diserio, IKA-Renault worker; Eduardo, student; Arturo Weiss, IKA-Renault worker; Héctor Olmedo, EPEC employee; Fernando Solís, IKA-Renault employee; Juan Baca, IKA-Renault worker; Raúl Pepi, ILASA worker; Marita Mata, journalist; Aldo J. Serafino, Fiat employee; Juan A. Peleteiro, IKA-Renault employee; Jorge Sanabria, university student; Roque Ionadi, businessman; Mizael Bizzotto, IKA-Renault worker; Francisco Cuevas, IKA-Renault foreman; Carlos Ríos, university student; Nino Chávez, IKA-Renault worker; Humberto R. Blasco, IME worker; Alberto Nicoli, IKA-Renault worker; Armando Franceschini, businessman; Fernando, university student; Isabel Rins, university student; Horacio Blanco, university student; Victor, bank employee; Norma, university student; Gustavo Orgaz, university student; Rodolfo, priest; Osvaldo, student and IKA-Renault worker; Delinda Olmos de Di Toffino, EPEC employee; José Nezara, IKA-Renault foreman; I. Massuets, IKA-Renault foreman; José Quinteros, IME worker; Juan, factory owner; María García, homemaker; Luis, university student; Aristides Albano, Fiat worker; Erio Vaudagna, priest; Alberto, EPEC employee; Gonzalo Fernández, lawyer; Matilde, university student; Bernardino Taranto, architect; Omar Córdoba, university student; Carlos Masera, Fiat worker; Juan, metallurgical worker; Raúl Argüello, Fiat worker; José Lipari, IKA-Renault worker; Luis Rubio, university student; Carlos Merelli, IKA-Renault worker; Alfredo Ceballos, state worker; Julio Lescano, IKA-Renault worker; Manuel Horacio Pelliza, UTA worker; Lidia Alfonsina *("la tucumana")*, owner of student boarding house; José Campellone, IKA-Renault worker; Eduardo Flores, construction worker; Juan Carlos Toledo, journalist; Oscar Alvarez, EPEC employee; Horacio Obregón Cano, student; Héctor Maisuls, university student; Dante Véliz, Fiat worker; Enrique Fernández, university student; Ramón Romero, Fiat worker; Raúl Belistelle, Fiat worker; Erminio, IKA-Renault worker; Eduardo Bischoff, journalist; Guillermo, university student; José Ponce, Fiat worker; Miguel Contreras, metallurgical worker.

Memoirs, Documentary Collections, Miscellaneous Sources

Archive Fermín Chávez, Buenos Aires. Private collection of Peronist materials, 1968 to 1976.

Gregorio Flores. Unpublished, untitled history of SITRAC.

James McCloud, President of Industrias Kasier Argentina, 1956 to 1967. Our personal correspondence, 1989 to 1991.

Agustín Tosco. Recorded oral testimony of Cordobazo, circa 1972. Luz y Fuerza headquarters, Córdoba.

Los programas obreros, "La Falda," "Huerta Grande," "1º de Mayo." CGTA publication, May 1971.

Pasado y Presente. Oral history project of 1965 Fiat workers' strike.

Tippetts-Abbett-McCarthy-Stratton, Engineers and Architects, Kennedy and Donkin Consulting Engineers. "Study of Argentine Power Problems," 2 vols, Buenos Aires, 1960 (Baker Library, Harvard University).

Notes

Introduction

1. Norbert MacDonald, "Henry J. Kaiser and the Establishment of an Automobile Industry in Argentina," *Business History,* vol. 30, no. 3 (July 1988), pp. 329–345; Stephen Meyer, "The Persistence of Fordism: Workers and Technology in the American Automobile Industry, 1900–1960," in Nelson Lichtenstein and Stephen Meyer, eds., *On the Line: Essays in the History of Auto Work* (Urbana and Chicago: University of Illinois Press, 1989), p. 91.

2. Anthony Rhodes, *Louis Renault: A Biography* (New York: Harcourt Brace, 1969), pp. 174–202.

3. Palmiro Togliatti, *Lectures on Fascism* (New York: International Publishers, 1976), pp. 59–86; Luisa Passerini, *Fascism and Popular Memory: The Cultural Experience of the Turin Working Class* (Cambridge: Cambridge University Press, 1988), pp. 129–149.

4. Emilio Pugno and Sergio Garavini, *Gli anni duri alla Fiat: La resistenza sindicale e la ripresa* (Turin: Guilio Einaudi editore, 1974), pp. 5–14; Giovanni Contini, "The Rise and Fall of Shop Floor Bargaining at Fiat, 1945–80," in Stephen Tolliday and Jonathan Zeitlin, eds., *The Automobile Industry and Its Workers* (Cambridge: Polity Press, 1986), pp. 144–146.

5. For example, the military-administered airplane factory in Córdoba entered into many licensing agreements to build German-model planes, and German industrial consultants were apparently not uncommon in the Cordoban armaments factories in the 1930s. U.S. Military Intelligence Reports from Argentina, 1918–41, Lamont Library, Harvard University: Report No. 5812, "Current Events, May," May 31, 1938; No. 5867, "Military Aviation-General: German Company Offers to Operate Córdoba Army Factory," August 29, 1938, from Lester Baker, Military Attaché, U.S. Embassy, Buenos Aires; No. 2048–195, "Comments on Current Events," from M. A. Devine, Jr., Military Attaché, U.S. Embassy, Buenos Aires, October 16, 1939.

6. Carlos F. Díaz Alejandro, *Essays on the Economic History of the Argentine Republic* (New Haven, Conn.: Yale University Press, 1970), pp. 166, 256–262;

371

Peter Waldmann, *El peronismo, 1943–1955* (Buenos Aires: Editorial Sudamericana, 1981), pp. 193–200.

7. U.S. Dept. of State, Correspondence Related to the Internal Affairs of Argentina, U.S. Embassy in Buenos Aires, "With Reference to the Plans of the Argentine Government for Industrial Projects and for Increased Industrialization of the Country," letter from Ambassador George S. Messersmith to William L. Clayton, Undersecretary of State for Economic Affairs, 835.60/8–2146, August 21, 1946.

8. William C. Smith, *Authoritarianism and the Crisis of the Argentine Political Economy* (Stanford, Calif.: Stanford University Press, 1989), pp. 26–30; Paul H. Lewis, *The Crisis of Argentine Capitalism* (Chapel Hill: the University of North Carolina Press, 1990), pp. 184–188.

9. Alain Rouquié, *Poder militar y sociedad política en la Argentina, 1943–1973,* vol. 2 (Buenos Aires: Emecé Editores, 1978), p. 81.

10. Díaz Alejandro, *Essays on the Economic History of the Argentine Republic,* pp. 166, 256–262.

11. Eduardo F. Jorge, *Industria y concentración económica* (Buenos Aires: Siglo XXI, 1970); Jorge Niosi, *Los empresarios y el estado Argentino (1955–1969)* (Buenos Aires: Siglo XXI, 1974); Jorge Schvarzer, *Empresarios del pasado: La Unión Industrial Argentina* (Buenos Aires: CISEA/Imago Mundi, 1991).

12. María Beatriz Nofal, *Absentee Entrepeneurship and the Dynamics of the Motor Vehicle Industry in Argentina* (New York: Praeger Publishers, 1989), pp. 14–16.

13. David Rock, "The Survival and Restoration of Peronism," in David Rock, ed., *Argentina in the Twentieth Century* (Pittsburgh: University of Pittsburgh Press, 1975), p. 187.

14. Rock, "The Survival and Restoration of Peronism," p. 191.

15. Daniel James, *Resistance and Integration: Peronism and the Argentine Working Class, 1946–1973* (Cambridge: Cambridge University Press, 1989). James's introductory chapter, and particularly his discussion of Peronism's broadening of the concept of citizenship, is the most perceptive account of the cultural underpinnings of this complex movement.

16. Alberto Ciria, *Política y cultura popular: la Argentina peronista, 1946–55* (Buenos Aires: Ediciones de la Flor, 1983), pp. 273–318.

17. Hiroshi Matushita, *El movimiento obrero argentino, 1930–1945: Sus proyecciones en los orígenes del peronismo* (Buenos Aires: Siglo XXI, 1983). This is only one of a number of studies that posit the now widely accepted argument of the existence of certain affinities between Perón's labor policies and those of the government's of the 1930s and early 1940s. Nevertheless, the co-optive strategy of the earlier governments, the willingness to negotiate and compromise with labor, especially with key, strategic unions, lacked the depth of Perón's reforms, which undoubtedly had the effect of strengthening the institutions of the labor movement and establishing organic links between the state and the unions. Collectively, Perón's policies clearly represent a significant change in the history of organized labor in Argentina.

18. Walter Little, "La organización obrera y el estado peronista," *Desarrollo Económico,* vol. 19, no. 75 (October–December 1979), pp. 338–339.

19. Louise Doyon, "La organización del movimiento sindical peronista,"

Desarrollo Económico, vol. 24, no. 94 (July–September 1984), pp. 210–212. By the same token, it was the degradation of the Peronist shop stewards' organization in the 1960s that fomented the *clasista* movements and the shop floor rebellions of the 1970s.

20. Waldmann, *El peronismo, 1943–1955,* pp. 149–178.
21. Little, "La organización obrera y el estado peronista," p. 370.
22. Clarence Zuvekas, "Argentine Economic Policy, 1958–62: The Frondizi Government's Development Plan," *Inter-American Economic Affairs,* vol. 22, no. 1 (1968), pp. 45–75.
23. Gary Wynia, *Argentina in the Postwar Era* (Albuquerque: University of New Mexico Press, 1978), pp. 209–210.
24. Nofal, *Absentee Entrepeneurship and the Dynamics of the Motor Vehicle Industry in Argentina,* pp. 16–30.
25. Zuvekas, "Argentine Economic Policy," 1958–62, pp. 45–75; Nofal, *Absentee Entrepreneurship and the Dynamics of the Motor Vehicle Industry in Argentina,* pp. 18–34.
26. Rhys Owen Jenkins, *Dependent Industrialization in Latin America: The Automobile Industry in Argentina, Chile and Mexico* (New York: Praeger Publishers, 1977), p. 10.
27. One distinguished American labor historian, David Brody, has noted that unions and unionism have comprised only a relatively small part of the experience of the American working class; that influences of ethnicity, gender, religion, the family, and the community, among others, have been at least as important to workers as their unions. While this can probably be said about the history of any working class, it was perhaps less true of the Argentine working class in those years. Peronism created a working class culture that broke down whatever ethnic and religious differences—never as strong in Argentina as in many countries—had formerly divided Argentine workers. Similarly, women never represented as great a percentage of the working class in Argentina as in the United States, and this was especially true in the post-1955 heavy industrial era. The working class community, particularly in the new industrial cities of the interior, was also weaker. I contend that if unions and the workplace were not the universe of the Argentine and specifically Cordoban working class experience, they were nonetheless the most important influences.

1. Industry, Society, and Class

1. Adolfo Dorfman, *Historia de la industria argentina* (Buenos Aires: Solar/ Hachette, 1971), pp. 278–279.
2. Juan Carlos Agulla, *Eclipse de una aristocracia: Una investigación sobre las élites de la ciudad de Córdoba* (Buenos Aires: Ediciones Libera, 1968), pp. 30–31, 37–38, 72–73.
3. U.S. Military Intelligence Reports for Argentina, 1918–1941. Edmond C. Fleming, Military Attaché, U.S. Embassy, Report no. 4029, "Current Events for the Month of August," August 31, 1929, p. 4.
4. U.S. Military Intelligence Reports for Argentina, 1918–1941. Military Attaché, Argentina, Report no. 4489, "Military Supply: Government Production of Mili-

tary Supplies," January 16, 1932. This intelligence report provides an extensive description of the Cordoban plants.

5. U.S. Military Intelligence Reports from Argentina, 1918–1941. Lester Baker, Military Attaché, Buenos Aires, Report no. 5663, "Current Events, Argentina," October 30, 1937, p. 2.
6. Roberto A. Ferrero, *Sabattini y la decadencia del yrigoyenismo,* 2 vols. (Buenos Aires: Centro Editor de América Latina, 1984). For an important new study of *sabattinismo,* see César Tcach, *Sabattinismo y peronismo. Partidos políticos en Córdoba, 1943–1955* (Buenos Aires: Editorial Sudamericana, 1991).
7. Ferrero, *Sabattini y la decadencia del yrigoyenismo,* vol. 2, p. 134.
8. Efraín Bischoff, *Historia de Córdoba* (Buenos Aires: Editorial Plus Ultra, 1979), pp. 556–558.
9. María del Carmen Angueira and Alicia del Carmen Tonini, *Capitalismo de Estado (1927–1956)* (Buenos Aires: Centro Editor de América Latina, 1986), pp. 72–73.
10. Mónica B. Gordillo, "Características de los sindicatos líderes de Córdoba en los '60: El ámbito del trabajo y la dimensión cultural," Consejo de Investigaciones Científicas y Tecnológicas de la Provincia de Córdoba, *Annual Report,* 1991, p. 48; Rinaldo Antonio Colomé and Horacio Palmieri, "La industria manufacturera en la ciudad de Córdoba," Instituto de Economía y Finanzas, Facultad de Ciencias Económicas, Universidad Nacional de Córdoba, pp. 4–13.
11. Fernando Ferrero, "Localización industrial en la Provincia de Córdoba," *Revista de economía y estadística,* Universidad Nacional de Córdoba, no. 2 (1964), pp. 7–42.
12. "La industria en la Provincia de Córdoba." *Córdoba,* May 1974, pp. 4–13.
13. Colomé and Palmieri, "La industria manufacturera en la ciudad de Córdoba," pp. 8–10.
14. María Beatriz Nofal, Absentee *Entrepeneurship and the Dynamics of the Motor Vehicle Industry in Argentina* (New York: Praeger Publishers, 1989), p. 15.
15. María del Carmen Angueira and Alicia del Carmen Tonini, *Capitalismo de Estado (1927–1956),* p. 77; U.S. Dept. of State, Papers Related to the Internal Affairs of Argentina, U.S. Embassy in Buenos Aires, "Installation of Fiat Plant for Motor Car Production," 835.3331/11–658, November 6, 1958.
16. U.S. Dept. of State, Papers Related to the Internal Affairs of Argentina, U.S. Embassy in Buenos Aires, "Conversation with Edgar Kaiser, February 21, 1955," 811.05135/2–2155, February 21, 1955.
17. U.S. Dept. of State, Papers Related to the Internal Affairs of Argentina, U.S. Embassy in Buenos Aires, "Letter from Henry J. Kaiser Companies to U.S. Dept. of State," 811.05135/1–2055, January 20, 1955
18. Letter from James McCloud, president of Industrias Kaiser Argentina 1956–1967, July 24, 1989. McCloud contends that Kaiser's establishment in Córdoba was solely the result of pressures coming from San Martín and the Argentine military. McCloud's claims have been confirmed in a recent study of the Kaiser negotiations: Norbert MacDonald, "Henry J. Kaiser and the Establishment of an Automobile Industry in Argentina," *Business History,* vol. 30, no. 3 (July 1988), p. 336. Neither Fiat nor Kaiser was interested in the early

1950s in establishing plants in Buenos Aires, viewed as the stronghold of the Peronist working class, because of the labor problems they foresaw there. Both companies wished to establish plants in the interior, but Córdoba was the second choice for each.

19. U.S. Dept. of State, Papers Related to the Internal Affairs of Argentina, U.S. Embassy in Buenos Aires, "Market Report on Electric Motors-Argentina," 835.333/11–2858, November 28, 1958.

20. U.S. Dept. of State, Papers Related to the Internal Affairs of Argentina, U.S. Embassy in Buenos Aires, "Investigation of Industrias Kaiser Argentina, S.A. by the Provincial Government," 835.3331/12–1955, December 19, 1955.

21. U.S. Dept. of State, Papers Related to the Internal Affairs of Argentina, U.S. Embassy in Buenos Aires, "Kaiser to Manufacture Alfa Romeo Automobiles," 835.3331/12–2358, December 23, 1958.

22. Joseph Geschelin, "Argentina's Automotive Industries, Part III: The Kaiser Empire," *Automotive Industries,* vol. 132, April 1, 1965, p. 50.

23. Letter from McCloud; U.S. Dept. of State, Papers Related to the Internal Affairs of Argentina, U.S. Embassy in Buenos Aires, "Industrias Kaiser Argentina," 335.3331/10–1955, October 19, 1955.

24. Joseph Geschelin, "Argentina's Automotive Industries, Part I," *Automotive Industries,* vol. 132, February 15, 1965, p. 58.

25. Industrias Kaiser Argentina S.A., *Memoria y Balance General,* 1961.

26. Gilles Gleyze, "La Régie Nationale des Usines Renault et l'Amerique Latine depuis 1945. Brésil, Argentine, Colombie" (M.A. thesis, Université de Paris X—Nanterre, 1988), pp. 48–49; Michel Freyssenet, "Les processus d'Internationalisation de la production de Renault: 1898–1979," *Cahiers de l'institut de recherche èconomique et de planification du développement,* no. 6, 1984, pp. 15–49.

27. The growth of the Cordoban metallurgical industry was nonetheless extraordinarily rapid. In 1954, many other industries in the city had larger labor forces: the railroad workshops (3,373), food processing industries (21,952), and even the leather industry (1,189) were all larger. Ten years later, only the automobile companies would have larger labor forces. Industrial census (1954, 1964, 1974), Ministerio de Hacienda, Economía, y Previsión Social, province of Córdoba.

28. Industrias Kaiser Argentina S.A., *Memoria y Balance General,* 1961; Delbert Miller, "Community Power Perspectives and Role Definitions of North American Executives in an Argentine Community," *Administrative Science Quarterly* (December 1965), pp. 364–380.

29. Geschelin, "Argentina's Automotive Industries, Part III," p. 47; "Instituto IKA: En abril inicia las clases," *Gacetika,* no. 45 (October 1961), p. 1.

30. Industrias Kaiser Argentina S.A., *Memoria y Balance General,* 1962. The company report lists 6,300 workers directly engaged in production, 2,390 employees at the Santa Isabel complex, and another 590 in the central office in Buenos Aires. The executive staff consisted of 313 people, many of them Americans (50 of the 62 "technical advisers" on the staff were Americans), though IKA had by then incorporated a sizable number of Argentines for upper-level positions.

31. Juan V. Sourrouillee, *El complejo automotor en Argentina* (Mexico City: Editorial Nueva Imagen, 1980), pp. 60–61; Nofal, *Absentee Entrepreneurship and the Dynamics of the Motor Vehicle Industry in Argentina,* pp. 32–34.

32. *La Voz del Interior,* September 28, 1963, p. 13.

33. U.S. Dept. of State, Papers Related to the Internal Affairs of Argentina, U.S. Embassy in Buenos Aires, "Fiat Proposes to Manufacture Automobiles in Argentina," 835.3331/11–2458, November 24, 1958; Grandes Motores Diesel, *Memoria y Balance General,* 1958.

34. Grandes Motores Diesel, *Memoria y Balance General,* 1958.

35. Grandes Motores Diesel, *Memoria y Balance General,* 1959.

36. Sourrouille, *El complejo automotor en Argentina,* pp. 60–61. Fiat was also favored by its initial decision to specialize in one sector of the automotive market, the manufacturing of small, economical cars, and to forgo the production of trucks and luxury cars; U.S. Dept. of State, Papers Related to the Internal Affairs of Argentina, U.S. Embassy in Buenos Aires, "Fiat Car and Truck Manufacturing Investment Approved," 838.3331/9–2959, September 29, 1959.

37. Even after the buyout, Renault was hindered by the licensing agreements and found itself in a prolonged and costly lawsuit to revoke the IKA agreements with American Motors. Archives des Usines Renault, Boulogne-Billancourt, Direction Juridique, file 3400 "Argentine," dossier "Rachat actions AMC/KJC," and 4436, "IKA Status Contrats Renault. KJC/AMC/WILLIS."

38. U.S. Dept. of State, Papers related to Argentina, U.S. Embassy in Buenos Aires, "Investment Projects in Argentina," 811.05135/2–259, February 2, 1959.

39. Colomé and Palmieri, "La industria manufacturera en la ciudad de Córdoba," pp. 25–38; Aldo A. Arnaudo, "El crecimiento de la ciudad de Córdoba en el último cuarto de siglo," *Economía de Córdoba,* vol. 8, no. 2 (December 1970), pp. 7–11.

40. Colomé and Palmieri, "La industria manufacturera en la ciudad de Córdoba," p. 35.

41. Nofal, *Absentee Entrepreneurship and the Dynamics of the Motor Vehicle Industry in Argentina,* p. 32.

42. Arnaudo, "El crecimiento de la ciudad de Córdoba en el último cuarto de siglo," pp. 18–19.

43. Nofal, *Absentee Entrepreneurship and the Dynamics of the Motor Vehicle Industry in Argentina,* p. 44.

44. Gleyze, "La Régie Nationale des Usines Renault et l'Amerique Latine depuis 1945," pp. 58–60.

45. Carlos E. Sánchez, "El desempleo juvenil en la ciudad de Córdoba," *Economía de Córdoba,* Universidad Nacional de Córdoba, Facultad de Ciencias Económicas. Instituto de Economía y Finanzas (December 1971), p. 13.

46. Sánchez, "El desempleo juvenil en la ciudad de Córdoba," pp. 3–20. José Nun's survey findings on unemployment in the industry in the two cases studied in Buenos Aires in 1967—specifically the tendency he discovered for laid-off automobile workers to find work in services, in industry, and as independent mechanics but not in the car plants where they had previously worked or even in the automobile industry generally—were true for Córdoba as well. See José Nun, "Despidos en la industria automotriz argentina: Estudio de un

caso de superpoblación flotante," *Revista mexicana de sociología,* vol. 40, no. 1 (1978), pp. 55–106.

47. Anna Segre, "La localizzazione dell'industria automobolistica in America Latina: I casi di Belo Horizonte (Brasile) e Cordoba (Argentina)," *Rivista Geografica Italiana,* vol. 80, no. 2, (June 1983), pp. 262–264.

48. Municipalidad de Córdoba, Dirección de Estadísticas, "Censo Nacional de Población: Familias y Viviendas," Departamento Capital, 1970, vol. 1. Mónica Gordillo's study of the Cordoban Sindicato de Mécanicos y Afines del Transporte Automotor (SMATA) has shown that a large percentage of the workers who settled in the new industrial neighborhoods adjacent to the automotive complexes were migrants to the city. Though these were the fastest growing districts in the city, it should be emphasized that only a minority of the SMATA workers lived in the new neighborhoods (38.1 percent for the period 1956–1960, with similar percentages for the 1960s), the majority residing in the traditional downtown neighborhoods in the city and a sizable number in small towns outside the city limits; Gordillo, "Características de los sindicatos líderes de Córdoba en los '60," pp. 10–12.

49. Rinaldo A. Colomé, "Construcción y vivienda en la ciudad de Córdoba, 1947–1965," *Revista de Economía y Estadística,* vol. 11, nos. 3 and 4 (1967), pp. 68–69.

50. Carlos E. Sánchez, "La situación de la vivienda en la ciudad de Córdoba," *Economía de Córdoba,* vol. 8, no. 2 (1970), pp. 2–11.

51. Arnaudo, "El crecimiento de la ciudad de Córdoba en el último cuarto de siglo," p. 15; Juan Carlos Agulla, "Aspectos sociales del proceso de industrialización en una comunidad urbana," *Revista mexicana de sociología,* vol. 15 (May 1963), pp. 762–763.

52. Charles Bergquist, *Labor in Latin America* (Stanford, Calif.: Stanford University Press, 1986), p. 188.

53. *La Voz del Interior,* November 20, 1960, p. 11.

54. Carlos E. Sánchez and Walter E. Schulthess, *Población e immigración en la ciudad de Córdoba, 1947–1966,* Facultad de Ciencias Económicas, Universidad Nacional de Córdoba, 1967, p. 3.

55. Joseph Geschelin, "Argentina's Automotive Industries. Part VI," *Automotive Industries,* vol. 132 (February–June 1965), p. 53.

56. Sánchez, "El desempleo juvenil en la ciudad de Córdoba," pp. 3–20.

57. Edith Aostri, "El mercado de trabajo en la ciudad de Córdoba," *Comercio y Justicia,* no. 87 (May 28, 1971), pp. 11–12.

58. Francisco J. Delich, *Crisis y protesta social: Córdoba, mayo de 1969* (Buenos Aires: Ediciones Signos, 1970), pp. 24–25.

59. Gleyze, "La Régie Nationale des Usines Renault et l'Amerique Latine depuis 1945," pp. 160–163.

2. Union Politics

1. The tutelage of the dissident Cordoban union leaders by an older generation of union activists is a little known but interesting part of the history of the Cordoban labor movement in these years. One such later mentor, the legendary anarcho-syndicalist union leader Pedro Milesi, would have a great per-

sonal influence not only on Tosco and others in the light and power workers' union, but also on the Fiat *clasistas* of the early 1970s.

2. Iris Marta Roldán, *Sindicatos y protesta social en la Argentina: Un estudio de caso de Luz y Fuerza de Córdoba, (1969–1974)* (Amsterdam: Center for Latin American Research and Documentation, 1978), pp. 118–119.

3. Jorge O. Lannot, Adriana Amantea, and Eduardo Sguiglia, *Agustín Tosco, conducta de un dirigente obrero* (Buenos Aires: Centro Editor de América Latina, 1984), p. 12.

4. Los programas obreros, "La Falda" "Huerta Grande" "1º de mayo de 1968," CGTA publication, May 1971.

5. *La Voz del Interior,* January 16, 1957, p. 5.

6. Interview with Elpidio Torres, secretary general of SMATA-Córdoba, 1958–1971, Córdoba, July 25, 1985.

7. The IKA workers hired between 1956 and 1960 were predominantly young men (67.3 percent were between 21 and 25 years of age) for whom employment in the Kaiser automobile plants was their first experience with factory life. One study contends that the delay in union affiliation (only 34.8 percent joined the union on entering the factory) indicates a certain indifference in the early years toward the union on the part of this young labor force, an argument that is supported in Elpidio Torres's testimony. Mónica B. Gordillo, "Características de los sindicatos líderes de Córdoba en los '60: El ámbito del trabajo y la dimensión cultural," Consejo de Investigaciones Científicas y Tecnológicas de la Provincia de Córdoba, Annual Report, April 1991, pp. 6–9.

8. Industrias Kaiser Argentina, *Memoria y Balance General,* 1959.

9. Interview with Elpidio Torres.

10. Ibid.

11. Ibid.

12. *La Voz del Interior,* December 16, 1958, p. 9.

13. Industrias Kaiser Argentina, *Memoria y Balance General,* 1959; U.S. Dept. of State, Papers Related to the Internal Affairs of Argentina, U.S. Embassy in Buenos Aires, "Visit to Córdoba," 835.3331/4–1858, April 18, 1958.

14. *La Voz del Interior,* June 13, 1958, p. 9.

15. Ibid., August 18, 1958, p. 9.

16. Interview with Elpidio Torres.

17. Ibid.; Mónica B. Gordillo, "Los prolegómenos del Cordobazo: Los sindicatos líderes de Córdoba dentro de la estructura de poder sindical," *Desarrollo Económico,* vol. 31, no. 122 (July–September 1991), p. 171.

18. *La Voz del Interior,* March 12, 1960, p. 9; Gordillo, "Características de los sindicatos líderes de Córdoba en los '60," p. 29. As a result of this wage adjustment clause, IKA later claimed that the workers received across-the-board wage increases eight times between 1960 and 1964. Industrias Kaiser Argentina, *Memoria y Balance,* 1964.

19. Daniel James, *Resistance and Integration: Peronism and the Argentine Working Class, 1946–1973* (Cambridge: Cambridge University Press, 1988), pp. 161–166.

20. Emilio Pugno and Sergio Garavini, *Gli anni duri alla Fiat: La resistenza*

sindicale e la ripresa (Turin: Guilio Einaudi editore, 1974), p. 14; Giovani Contini, "The Rise and Fall of Shop Floor Bargaining at Fiat, 1945–80," in Steven Tolliday and Jonathan Zeitlin, eds., *The Automobile Industry and Its Workers* (Cambridge: Polity Press, 1986), pp. 144–146.

21. Grandes Motores Diesel, *Memoria y Balance General,* 1959.

22. Mónica B. Gordillo, "Los prolegómenos del Cordobazo," p. 169; "Algunas consideraciones preliminares sobre el conflicto de Fiat," *Pasado y Presente,* vol. 3, no. 9 (April–September 1965), p. 64; Judith Evans, Paul Hoeffel, and Daniel James, "Reflections on Argentine Auto Workers and Their Unions," in R. Kronish and K. Mericle, eds., *The Political Economy of the Latin American Motor Vehicle Industry* (Cambridge, Mass.: MIT Press, 1984), p. 149.

23. Within a decade, the Cordoban UOM was one of the arbiters of the local labor movement and the city's second largest union, after the SMATA, with more than 6,000 members—although they were dispersed in some 600 workshops and small factories. "El sindicalismo cordobés en la escalada," *Aquí y ahora,* vol. 3, no. 26 (May 1971), pp. 11–14.

24. Cordoban Peronism had a decidedly conservative cast to it. In a still overwhelmingly agrarian province with only a small working class (70 percent of the population was rural in Córdoba in 1947 compared with 32 percent rural in Buenos Aires province), Peronism in Córdoba had drawn the bulk of its strength from three groups: local political *caudillos* formerly in the service of the oligarchical Partido Demócrata; the nationalist, antiliberal *sabbitinista* faction of the Cordoban Radical party; and especially the Catholic church, an institution at least as powerful in Cordoban society in the years of Perón's first government as the labor movement and one that mobilized a sizable number of the Cordoban citizenry through the Acción Católica. See César Tcach, *Sabbitinismo y peronismo* (Buenos Aires: Editorial Sudamericana, 1991), p. 82.

25. *La Voz del Interior,* July 15, 1957, p. 9.

26. Francisco Delich, *Crisis y protesta social: Córdoba, mayo de 1969* (Buenos Aires: Ediciones Signos, 1970), p. 35.

27. Carlos E. Sánchez, "Estrategias y objetivos de los sindicatos argentinos," Universidad Nacional de Córdoba, Instituto de Economía y Finanzas, Working Paper no. 18, 1973, p. 19.

28. Gordillo, "Los prolegómenos del Cordobazo," pp. 172–173; Sánchez, "Estrategias y objetivos de los sindicatos argentinos," pp. 30–37.

29. Gordillo, "Características de los sindicatos líderes de Córdoba en los '60," pp. 31, 84–94.

30. In his study of Renault, Gleyze notes that the French company was well aware of this arrangement and sought to put a stop to it with the 1967 buyout, regarding it as one of the factors most responsible for IKA's inability to keep its labor costs in line with its profits. Gilles Gleyze, "La Régie Nationale des Usines Renault et l'Amerique Latine depuis 1945. Brésil, Argentine, Colombie" (M.A. thesis, Université de Paris X—Nanterre, 1988), p. 182.

31. Gordillo, "Características de los sindicatos líderes de Córdoba en los '60," pp. 41–42.

32. Industrias Kaiser Argentina, *Memoria y Balance,* 1962.

33. *La Voz del Interior,* December 2, 1962, p. 11; December 16, 1962, p. 19.
34. *Informe,* Servicio de Documentación e Información Laboral, no. 35 (January 1963), p. 11; no. 36 (February 1963), p. 8.
35. *La Voz del Interior,* May 2, 1964, p. 9.
36. Ibid., July 5, 1964, p. 9; September 21, 1964, p. 11.
37. Ibid., May 28, 1964, p. 13.
38. Roldán, *Sindicatos y protesta social en la Argentina,* pp. 133–134.
39. Sindicato de Luz y Fuerza de Córdoba, *Memoria y Balance,* 1964–65, pp. 34–37.
40. Ibid.
41. Fifty percent of incoming workers were now joining the union at the time they were hired, and an additional 27 percent did so within the first year of employment; rank-and-file identification with the union was also deepening. Gordillo, "Características de los sindicatos líderes de Córdoba de los '60," p. 7.
42. *Informe,* Servicio de Documentación e Información Laboral, no. 51 (May 1964), pp. 51–52.
43. "Informe preliminar sobre el conflicto Fiat," *Pasado y Presente,* vol. 1, no. 4 (1964), pp. 64–65.
44. The GMD workers would not actually join the SMATA until September 15, 1966, when the government finally recognized the SMATA's jurisdiction over that Fiat plant. *La Voz del SMATA,* Córdoba, vol. 3, no. 20 (November 1966), pp. 2–7.
45. Interviews with Fiat workers Carlos Masera, Córdoba, July 18, 1990; Doming Bizzi, Córdoba, July 22, 1987; José Paez, Buenos Aires, July 11, 1989; Gregorio Flores, Buenos Aires, November 12, 1985. See also *La Voz del Interior,* May 9, 1965, p. 21; May 18, 1965, p. 9.
46. The attempt to "make over" the mass production worker—to acculturate him and instill in him a close personal identification with the company that would increase productivity, undermine worker solidarity, and reduce the likelihood of industrial conflict—was a hallmark of Fiat's labor policies, but it cannot simply be attributed to some Latin form of culturally embedded paternalism. The pioneer of such policies was Henry Ford himself, specifically in the paternalist intent of his famous "five dollar day" and in the activities of Ford's sociological department in the first years of the American automobile industry. See Stephen Meyer III, *The Five Dollar Day: Labor Management and Social Control in the Ford Motor Company, 1908–1921* (Albany: State University of New York Press, 1981), pp. 95–168.
47. Interview with Elpidio Torres.
48. *Informe,* Servicio de Documentación e Información Laboral, no. 75 (May 1966), p. 35.

3. The Factory, the Union, and the New Industrial Worker

1. E. P. Thompson, *The Making of the English Working Class* (London: Vintage Books, 1963); Herbert G. Gutman, "Protestantism and the American Labor Movement," in Gutman, *Work, Culture and Society in Industrializing America* (New York: Vintage Books, 1977), pp. 79–117; David Montgomery, *The Fall of*

the House of Labor (Cambridge: Cambridge University Press, 1989); Michelle Perrot, "On the Formation of the French Working Class," in Ira Katznelson and Aristide R. Zolberg, eds., *Working Class Formation: Nineteenth Century Patterns in Western Europe and the United States* (Princeton, N.J.: Princeton University Press, 1986), pp. 71–110.

2. A representative statement of this pre-Cordobazo consensus is Henry A. Landsberger, "The Labor Elite: Is It Revolutionary?," in Seymour Martin Lipset and Aldo Salari, eds., *Elites in Latin America* (Oxford: Oxford University Press, 1967), pp. 256–300.

3. For a summary of the labor aristocracy versus vanguard arguments, see Elizabeth Jelin and Juan Carlos Torre, "Los nuevos trabajadores en América Latina: Una reflexión sobre la tesis de la aristocracia obrera," *Desarrollo Económico,* vol. 22, no. 85 (April–June, 1982): 4–23.

4. Silvia Sigal, *Attitudes ouvrières en Argentina: Rapport d'enquête* (Paris: Centre d'Etudes des Mouvements Sociaux, 1974).

5. John Humphrey, *Capitalist Control and Workers' Struggle in the Brazilian Auto Industry* (Princeton, N.J.: Princeton University Press, 1983); Ian Roxborough, *Unions and Politics in Mexico: The Case of the Automobile Industry* (Cambridge: Cambridge University Press, 1984); Kevin Middlebrook, "The Political Economy of Mexican Organized Labor, 1940–1978" (Ph.D. diss., Harvard University, 1988).

6. Daniel Labbe, "Travail formel et travail réel: Renault-Billancourt, 1945–1980" (M.A. thesis, Ecole des Hautes Etudes en Sciences Sociales, 1990), pp. 44–58.

7. The best general study of the labor process in this stage of automotive manufacturing remains Alain Touraine, *L'évolution du travail ouvrier aux usines Renault* (Paris: Centre de Recherche Scientifique, 1955). My analysis of the specific production processes and shop floor relations found in the IKA-Renault and Fiat plants is drawn primarily from the company archives of Renault and Fiat and is given a fuller treatment in Chapter 10.

8. James J. Fink, "Mass Production," in George S. May, ed., *Encyclopedia of American Business History and Biography: The Automobile Industry, 1920–1980* (New York and Oxford: Bruccoli, Clark, Layman, 1989), pp. 323–325.

9. "Fiat Someca Concord" and "Industrias Kaiser Argentina," Archivo Storico di Fiat, "Viaggio nella Repubblica Argentina, June 11–14, 1958," pp. 4–7. By contrast, in Fiat's Turin plants, production machining was already being performed by automated machinery such as that found in the leading American manufacturers at the time, "Italian Production: A Survey of the Fiat Factory Layout, Methods and Equipment," *Automobile Engineer,* vol. 40, no. 531–532 (September–October, 1950), pp. 335–341.

10. "Italian Production: A Survey of the Fiat Factory Layout, Methods and Equipment," p. 337.

11. "Fiat Someca Concord," Archivio Storico di Fiat, "Viaggio nella Repubblica Argentina, June 11–14, 1958," p. 4.

12. "Visita alla fabbrica Industrias Kaiser Argentina," Archivio Storico di Fiat, "Viaggio nella Repubblica Argentina, June 11–14, 1958," p. 5.

13. William H. Form, *Blue-Collar Stratification: Auto Workers in Four Countries* (Princeton, N.J.: Princeton University Press, 1976), pp. 42–43.

14. The importance of the autonomy of the Cordoban autoworkers' unions and of the more democratic internal union practices that resulted from greater independence was first suggested by Juan Carlos Torre in *Los sindicatos en el gobierno, 1973–76* (Buenos Aires: Centro Editor de América Latina, 1983), pp. 58–60, and has been explored more deeply by Judith Evans, Paul Hoeffer, and Daniel James "Reflections on Argentine Auto Workers and Their Unions," in R. Kronish and K. Mericle, eds., *The Political Economy of the Latin American Motor Vehicle Industry* (Cambridge, Mass.: MIT Press, 1984), pp. 138–146, and especially by Mónica B. Gordillo, "Los prolegómenos del Cordobazo: Los sindicatos líderes de Córdoba dentro de la estructura de poder sindical," *Desarrollo Económico,* vol. 31, no. 122 (July–September 1991), pp. 168–172.

15. Certainly the existence of either plant or company unions does not perforce define any kind of working class politics. In the Japanese automobile industry, for example, the company unions in firms such as Nissan and Toyota were the very instruments by which class tensions were ameliorated in the industry. The Japanese company unions worked not on the basis of a shop steward system, but rather as a management council system, in which both the union and management participated more or less as equal partners. These company unions were also stepping-stones to managerial positions for the workers who held union office, something that facilitated the philosophy of cooperation and class harmony after the decline of industrial unionism in the Japanese automobile industry in the early 1950s. See, Michael A. Cusumano, *The Japanese Automobile Industry: Technology and Management at Nissan and Toyota* (Cambridge, Mass.: Harvard University Press, 1985), pp. 165–171. In Córdoba, the factory regime found in the company-controlled Fiat plant unions was very different. The extreme, exclusionist philosophy of management with regard to labor at first bred worker apathy toward union affairs and later led to a furious reaction and perhaps an equally intransigent posture on the part of the SITRAC-SITRAM *clasista* unions in those plants in the early 1970s.

16. The differences between the Cordoban local and the Buenos Aires locals were significant in this respect. Though the SMATA, like the UOM, had a centralist union structure, SMATA bylaws that required locals within a 60-kilometer radius of the federal capital to send their union dues directly to the SMATA central, and that similarly required all strike and slowdown measures to be decreed by the national executive, did not apply to Córdoba. The Cordoban local therefore occupied a uniquely independent position within the autoworkers' union structure. See Evans, Hoeffel, and James, "Reflections on Argentine Auto Workers and Their Unions," pp. 145–146.

17. Ibid., p. 139; Gordillo, "Los prolegómenos del Cordobazo," p. 175.

18. Gordillo, "Los prolegómenos del Cordobazo," pp. 176–180.

19. Gordillo has documented a number of interesting incidents that took place in these years and that highlight the very different character of the Fiat plant unions compared with the SMATA. One such incident was the 1967 visit of Onganía to Córdoba, a visit that caused strong protests by the city's other unions and violent demonstrations especially by the SMATA, yet was warmly received by the SITRAC-SITRAM leadership. Onganía paid a personal visit to

the Materfer plants, where SITRAM secretary general Hugo Cassanova made a florid speech praising the government's economic program. Mónica B. Gordillo, "Características de los sindicatos líderes de Córdoba en los '60: El ámbito del trabajo y la dimensión cultural," Annual Report, Consejo de Investigaciones Científicas y Tecnológicas de la Provincia de Córdoba, April 1991, pp. 44–45.

4. Córdoba and the "Argentine Revolution"

1. Oscar Anzorena, *Tiempo de violencia y de utopía (1966–1976)* (Buenos Aires: Editorial Contrapunto, 1988); Guillermo O'Donnell, *Modernization and Bureaucratic Authoritarianism* (Berkeley and Los Angeles: University of California Press, 1979); Gregorio Selser, *El onganiato,* 2 vols. (Buenos Aires: Hyspamérica Ediciones Argentinas, 1986).
2. William C. Smith, *Authoritarianism and the Crisis of the Argentine Political Economy* (Stanford, Calif.: Stanford University Press, 1989), pp. 74–100; Paul H. Lewis, *The Crisis of Argentine Capitalism* (Chapel Hill: University of North Carolina Press, 1990), pp. 281–286.
3. John Humphrey, "Auto Workers and the Working Class in Brazil," *Latin American Perspectives,* vol. 6, no. 4 (Fall 1979), p. 71.
4. Daniel James, *Resistance and Integration: Peronism and the Argentine Working Class,* 1946–1973 (Cambridge: Cambridge University Press, 1988), pp. 174–175.
5. *Informe,* Servicio de Documentación e Información Laboral, no. 77, (July 1966), pp. 6, 7.
6. Interview with Felipe Alberti, former union affairs secretary, Luz y Fuerza de Córdoba, July 22, 1985.
7. Guy Bourde, "L'Etat-patron et les luttes des cheminots en Argentine (1947–1967)," *Le Mouvement Social,* no. 12 (October–December 1982), pp. 7–43; Silvia Sigal, "Crise économique et action ouvrière: Les travailleurs du sucre de Tucuman (1966–1968)," *Le Mouvement Social,* no. 12 (October–December 1982), pp. 45–69.
8. Anzorena, *Tiempo de violencia y de utopía (1966–1976),* p. 36.
9. *Informe,* Servicio de Documentación e Información Laboral, no. 80 (October 1966), pp. 21–30.
10. Ibid., no. 84 (February 1967), pp. 17–19.
11. Ibid., no. 85 (March 1967), pp. 12–23.
12. U.S. Dept. of State, Papers Related to the Internal Affairs of Argentina, U.S. Embassy in Buenos Aires, "Biographic Report: Raimundo José Ongaro," A-908, June 19, 1968. Also present at the meeting was Rodolfo Walsh, soon to be Ongaro's principal intellectual collaborator in the Confederación General del Trabajo de los Argentinos movement. Perón did not make public his support for Ongaro until several months later.
13. *Informe,* Servicio de Documentación e Información Laboral, no. 98 (April 1968), pp. 20–35.
14. Raimundo Ongaro, *Solo el pueblo salvará al pueblo* (Buenos Aires: Editorial de Las Bases, 1970), p. 15.

15. *Informe,* Servicio de Documentación e Información Laboral, no. 97 (March 1968), pp. 23–24.

16. Ibid., no. 102 (August 1968), pp. 6–7.

17. Archives des Usines Renault, Boulogne-Billancourt, Direction Juridique 0734, 3400 "Argentine," file "Situation IKA," memorandum from J. M. Palacios to M. Maison, January 16, 1967.

18. Ibid., memorandum from A. Compain Mefray to M. Maison, February 3, 1967.

19. Gilles Gleyze, "La Régie Nationale des Usines Renault et L'Amerique Latin depuis 1945: Brésil, Argentine, Colombie" (M.A. thesis, Université de Paris X—Nanterre, 1988), pp. 181–182.

20. Archives des Usines Renault, Boulogne-Billancourt, Direction des Affaires Internationales 0200, 1071 file "Personnel IKA," document "Réduction des effectifs et salaires d'IKA-Renault," April 22, 1968. Renault eliminated, for example, 262 jobs in its tool and die plant in these months.

21. Ibid., Direction des Services Financiers 0764, 113 file "IKA-Renault S.A.," letter from M. Lavaud, President IKA-Renault, to M. Maison, June 24, 1968.

22. *Informe,* Servicio de Documentación e Información Laboral, no. 89 (July 1967) p. 6.

23. *La Voz del Interior,* September 20, 1967, p. 19.

24. Ibid., April 27, 1967, p. 13.

25. Agustín Tosco, "El congreso votó no, la Historia votó sí," in A. Lannot, ed., *Agustín Tosco: Presente en las luchas de la clase obrera* (Buenos Aires: Jorge Lannot y Adriana Amantea, 1984), p. 86.

26. Iris Marta Roldán's study of the Cordoban Luz y Fuerza, *Sindicatos y protesta social: Un estudio de caso del sindicato de Luz y Fuerza de Córdoba, 1969–1974* (Amsterdam: Center for Latin American Research and Documentation, 1978), is an insightful analysis of the union and offers an especially interesting glimpse of internal union politics at a crucially important political moment. The weakness of the book is its general ahistoricity, Roldán's conclusions being largely based on her personal, albeit often very cogent, observations. Roldán's fieldwork was conducted between September 1973 and October 1974, which was a period of transition for the union as a result of the restoration of Peronist rule and a certain exhaustion that existed after almost seven years of uninterrupted struggle. Some of her conlusions, as a result, seem excessively lapidary and subjective.

27. Empresa Provincial de Energía de Córdoba (EPEC), *Informe Estadístico, 1966–1976.*

28. Carlos E. Sánchez, "Estrategias y objetivos de los sindicatos argentinos," Universidad Nacional de Córdoba, Instituto de Economía y Finanzas, Working Paper no. 18, 1973, p. 31.

29. Roldán, *Sindicatos y protesta social,* pp. 110–111.

30. Interview with Felipe Alberti.

31. These characteristics were not unique to Córdoba and are representative of the light and power industry in general. International Labor Office, *Conditions of Work and Employment in Water, Gas and Electricity Supply Services* (Geneva: ILO Offices, 1982).

32. Sindicato de Luz y Fuerza de Córdoba, *Memoria y Balance,* 1964–65, pp. 67–70; *Memoria y Balance,* 1966–67, pp. 69–71.
33. Sánchez, "Estrategias y objetivos de los sindicatos argentinos," p. 73.
34. Ibid., p. 67.
35. Roldán, *Sindicatos y protesta social,* pp. 110–111.
36. Sánchez, "Estrategias y objetivos de los sindicatos argentinos," pp. 33–37.
37. Sindicato de Luz y Fuerza de Córdoba, *Memoria y Balance, 1966–67,* pp. 73–75.
38. Tippets, Abbett, McCarthy, Stratton, Engineers and Architects; Kennedy and Donkin, Consulting Engineers, "Study of Argentine Power Problems," company report, 2 vols., Buenos Aires, 1960 (Baker Library, Harvard Business School), vol. I, p. 44.
39. "La situación económica-financiera de la Empresa Provincial de Energía de Córdoba: Una contribución sindical a su solución," *Eléctrum,* vol. 16, no. 65 (August 1972), pp. 6–11.
40. *Electrum,* vol. 4, no. 109 (March 17, 1967), pp. 1–4.
41. Sindicato de Luz y Fuerza de Córdoba, *Memoria y Balance,* 1966–67, pp. 69–71.
42. *CGT,* vol. 1, no. 1 (May 1, 1968), p. 1.
43. Ibid., no. 2 (May 3, 1968), p. 1.
44. Los programas obreros, "La Falda," "Huerta Grande," "1º de Mayo," CGTA publication, May 1971, pp. 6–12.
45. *Informe,* Servicio de Documentación e Información Laboral, no. 99 (May 1968), p. 44.
46. Carlos Ceballos, *Los estudiantes universitarios y la política (1955–1970)* (Buenos Aires: Centro Editor de América Latina, 1985), pp. 19–20; Ramón Cuevas and Osvaldo Reicz, "El movimiento estudiantil: De la Reforma al Cordobazo," *Los libros,* vol. 2, no. 1 (August 1971), pp. 16–19.
47. Mónica B. Gordillo, "Características y proyección nacional de los sindicatos líderes de Córdoba (1966–1969)," Annual Report, Consejo de Investigaciones Científicas y Tecnológicas de la Provincia de Córdoba, April 1990, p. 22.
48. Anzorena, *Tiempo de violencia y de utopía (1966–1976),* pp. 83–84.
49. Gordillo, "Características y proyección nacional de los sindicatos líderes de Córdoba (1966–1969)," p. 65.
50. *La Voz del Interior,* May 3, 1968, p. 13.
51. Ibid., May 5, 1968, p. 25.
52. Ibid., May 11, 1968, p. 16.
53. Interview with Miguel Angel Correa, Secretary General of the CGTA de Córdoba, 1968–69, Córdoba, July 3, 1985.
54. Interview with Elpidio Torres, secretary general of the SMATA de Córdoba, 1958 to 1971, Córdoba, July 12, 1987; Judith Evans, Paul Hoeffel, and Daniel James, "Reflections on Argentine Auto Workers and Their Unions," in R. Kronish and K. Mericle, eds., *The Political Economy of the Latin American Motor Vehicle Industry* (Cambridge, Mass.: MIT Press, 1984), p. 144; Mónica B. Gordillo, "Características de los sindicatos líderes de Córdoba en los '60: El ámbito del trabajo y la dimensión cultural," Annual Report, Consejo de In-

vestigaciones Científicas y Tecnológicas de la Provincia de Córdoba, April 1991, p. 79.

55. One crucial public gesture of support was the widely publicized letter from Perón to Ongaro (June 27, 1968), first published in *Cristianismo y Revolución,* declaring Ongaro to be the sole legitimate leader of the workers' movement. Roberto Baschetti, *Documentos de la Resistencia Peronista (1955–1970)* (Buenos Aires: Puntosur Editores, 1988), pp. 285–286.

56. *La Voz del Interior,* July 2, 1968, p. 11.

57. *Review of the River Plate,* vol. 143, no. 3678, (June 22, 1968), p. 11.

58. *Informe,* Servicio de Documentación e Información Laboral, no. 101 (July 1968), p. 34.

59. *CGT,* vol. 1, no. 10 (July 4, 1968), p. 2.

60. Ongaro declared open war against Vandor: "We workers must now throw ourselves into the reconquest of the industrial belt of Buenos Aires, where some powerful unions, once combative, continue to be manipulated by a half-dozen traitorous leaders. For that there is only one road open to us. A general mobilization in each of the groups that oppose the *'camarilla,'* a battle in each internal commission, an assembly in every factory." *CGT,* vol. 1, no. 12 (July 18, 1968), p. 1.

61. *La Voz del Interior,* September 11, 1968, p. 18.

62. *Informe,* Servicio de Documentación e Información Laboral, no. 105 (November 1968), p. 42.

63. *CGT,* vol. 1, no. 26 (October 24, 1968), p. 2.

64. U.S. Dept. of State, Papers Related to the Internal Affairs of Argentina, U.S. Embassy in Buenos Aires, "Recent Activities of Trade Unionist Raimundo Ongaro," A-37, February 3, 1969.

65. Mónica B. Gordillo, "Los prolegómenos del Cordobazo: Los sindicatos líderes de Córdoba dentro de la estructura de poder sindical," *Desarrollo Económico,* vol. 31, no. 122 (July–September 1991), p. 185.

5. The Cordobazo

1. Ernesto Laclau, "Argentina: Imperialist Strategy and the May Crisis," *New Left Review,* no. 62 (July–August 1970), pp. 3–21; Paul H. Lewis, *The Crisis of Argentine Capitalism* (Chapel Hill: University of North Carolina Press, 1990), pp. 371–380; Robert Massari, "Le cordobazo," *Sociologie du Travail,* no. 4 (1975), pp. 403–418; and James Petras, "Córdoba y la revolución socialista en la Argentina," *Los libros,* vol. 3, no. 21 (August 1971), pp. 28–31, are representative of these overly schematic interpretations of the Cordobazo. Argentine sociologists have stayed closer to the historical record, but are also guilty of too closely associating the character of the city's industrial development with the uprising. See Francisco Delich, *Crisis y protesta social: Mayo de 1969* (Buenos Aires: Ediciones Signos, 1970); Francisco Delich, "Córdoba: la movilización permanente," *Los libros,* no. 21 (August 1971), pp. 4–8; and Juan Carlos Agulla, "Significado de Córdoba," *Aportes,* no. 15 (January 1970), pp. 48–61.

2. *Clarín,* May 12, 1969, p. 24.

3. *Jerónimo,* vol. 10, no. 10, (May 20, 1969), p. 1; SMATA archive, "Volantes, Comunicados y Diarios del SMATA, 1969," union flier, "La lucha por nuestros derechos debe proseguir," May 19, 1969. It is clear from union publications and communiqués in the weeks leading up to the Cordobazo that the *sábado inglés* problem was a galvanizing issue for the SMATA workers. Nevertheless it was the culmination of some three years of general anti–working class measures on the part of the government, and implicit in the autoworkers protest was certainly a political repudiation of the regime. See James P. Brennan and Mónica B. Gordillo, "Working Class Protest, Popular Revolt, and Urban Insurrection in Argentina: the 1969 *Cordobazo,*" *Journal of Social History,* vol. 27, no. 3 (Spring 1994), pp. 477–498.

4. Ramón Cuevas and Osvaldo Reicz, "El movimiento estudiantil: De la Reforma al Cordobazo," *Los libros,* no. 21 (August 1971), pp. 17–18.

5. Cuevas and Reicz, "El movimiento estudiantil," pp. 17–18; A. Pérez Lindo, *Universidad, política y sociedad* (Buenos Aires: Editorial Universitaria de Buenos Aires, 1985).

6. *La Voz del Interior,* April 27, 1964, p. 9.

7. From 1966 onward, the Cordoban light and power workers' weekly publication, *Electrum,* was replete with references to the students' use of union facilities.

8. *La Voz del Interior,* March 23, 1969, p. 34; Agustín Tosco, "Testimonio del cordobazo," *Presente en las luchas de la clase obrera: Selección de trabajos* (Buenos Aires: Jorge Lannot y Adriana Amantea, 1984), pp. 37–55.

9. *La Voz del Interior,* May 7, 1969, p. 21.

10. *Electrum* 213, March 28, 1969, p. 1.

11. Tosco, "Testimonio del Cordobazo," pp. 37–55; Agustín Tosco, tape-recorded testimony of the Cordobazo, Luz y Fuerza headquarters, Córdoba.

12. Interviews with Elpidio Torres, Córdoba, July 25, 1985; Miguel Correa, Córdoba, July 3, 1985; Alfredo Martini, Córdoba, July 20, 1987. Narrative histories of varying accuracy that purport to recount the events of the Cordobazo can be found in Roque Alarcón, *Cordobazo* (Buenos Aires: Editorial Enmarque, 1989); Jorge Bergstein, *El cordobazo* (Buenos Aires: Editorial Catargo, 1987); Beba C. Balvé and Beatriz S. Balvé, *Lucha de calles, lucha de clases (Córdoba 1971–1969)* (Buenos Aires: Editora La Rosa Blindada, 1973); M. Bravo Tedin and G. Sarria, *El cordobazo: Un grito de la libertad* (La Rioja: Editora del Nordeste, 1989); and Daniel Villar, *El cordobazo* (Buenos Aires: Centro Editor de América Latina, 1971).

13. See, for example, Agustín Tosco, "El Cordobazo: Rebelión obrera y popular," reprinted in *Democracia sindical* (June, 1984), p. 6. The degree to which workers were aware of the strategy devised for the protest undoubtedly differed greatly from union to union. In the small and highly democratic light and power union, it appears that nearly all the workers had been apprised of the plans. In the SMATA, on the other hand, the union directive that was passed out to the three shifts on May 28 gave only general instructions. The workers on the morning shift were told to wait for the word from their shop stewards and to abandon the plants around eleven, assembling at the factory gates for the march downtown shortly thereafter. Afternoon and night shift workers

were instructed to meet at the union's downtown headquarters at ten and make their way to Vélez Sarsfield directly from there. At no point were the SMATA workers informed of plans to occupy the city, and every indication was given that the plan was for a peaceful demonstration and then dispersal at the CGT headquarters; SMATA archive, SMATA-Córdoba, volume "Volantes, Comunicados y Diarios del SMATA, 1969," union directive "Paro Nacional," May 28, 1969.

14. U.S. Department of State, Papers Related to the Internal Affairs of Argentina, U.S. Embassy in Buenos Aires, "Córdoba, Ex-Governor's Views on May Uprising," A-464, September 15, 1969.

15. *La Voz del Interior,* May 31, 1969, p. 13; June 1, 1969, p. 16; June 4, 1969, p. 21.

16. SMATA archive, SMATA-Córdoba, "Volantes, Comunicados y Diarios del SMATA, 1969," union directive "A los compañeros del gremio," June 4, 1969.

17. U.S. Dept. of State, "Vandor's Assassination and Funeral," A-366, July 21, 1969. Theories of Vandor's murder include everything from assassination by rivals within the UOM to the first elimination of a "traitorous" labor leader carried out by the Peronist left's youth wing, a practice that would indeed become common in the following decade.

18. Oscar Anzorena, *Tiempo de violencia y de utopía* (Buenos Aires: Editorial Contrapunto, 1988), p. 89.

19. "Desde el encierro envía un mensaje al gremio el compañero Elpidio Torres," *La Voz del SMATA,* SMATA-Córdoba, vol. 6, no. 35 (June 30, 1969), p. 3.

20. *La Voz del Interior,* October 1, 1969, p. 10.

21. In 1966 Fiat, for the first time, had overtaken IKA-Renault in sales figures. In 1969 it was the leading profit maker in the industry. Juan V. Sourrouille, *Transnacionales en América Latina: El complejo automotor en Argentina* (Mexico City: Editorial Nueva Imagen, 1980), pp. 60–61.

22. "Conflicto GMD: El triunfo de la solidaridad y la lucha," *La Voz del SMATA,* SMATA-Córdoba, vol. 6, no. 36 (October 14, 1969), p. 7.

23. The importance of the May uprising for the Cordoban *clasistas* was quite simple: it was regarded almost unanimously as nothing less than the first act of the socialist revolution in Argentina. This interpretation can be found in any of the *clasista* publications of the 1970s. See, for example, "La caída de la 'Revolución Argentina: La ensenañza del Cordobazo," *SMATA,* SMATA-Córdoba, no. 103, (May 29, 1973), p. 3. The Maoist group Vanguardia Comunista stated in its annual party report in 1971 that the Cordobazo had demonstrated the "inexhaustible revolutionary spirit of our people with the industrial proletariat in the lead," Vanguardia Comunista, Political Report, 1971, SITRAC archive, file "Vanguardia Comunista."

6. *The* Clasistas

1. In addition to Oscar Anzorena, *Tiempo de violencia y de utopía* (Buenos Aires: Editorial Contrapunto, 1988), other valuable sources for the history of the Marxist and Peronist left, respectively, in these years are Luis Mattini, *Hombres y mujeres del PRT-ERP* (Buenos Aires: Editorial Contrapunto, 1990), and

Richard Gillespie, *Soldiers of Perón: Argentina's Montoneros* (Oxford: Oxford University Press, 1984).

2. SITRAC archive, Buenos Aires, file "PCR," documents "Programa del primer congreso del Partido Comunista Revolucionario." The word *clasista* appears in party publications for the first time in late 1968, in "Los comunistas revolucionarios ante la actual situación política nacional e internacional," report of the national committee, November 1968, pp. 19–20. Gordillo has found the term used by PRT activists in the SMATA as early as 1967; Mónica B. Gordillo, "Características de los sindicatos líderes de Córdoba en los '60: El ámbito del trabajo y la dimensión cultural," Annual Report, Consejo de Investigaciones Científicas y Tecnológicas de la Provincia de Córdoba, April 1991, pp. 87–88.

3. SITRAC archive, file "Desgrabaciones: Rafael Clavero/Santos Torres," transcribed series of interviews with two former Fiat workers, Córdoba, July 15, 1984.

4. Ibid.

5. Ibid.; *La Voz del Interior,* April 5, 1970, p. 32; April 30, 1970, p. 18.

6. SMATA archive, SMATA-Córdoba, volume "Confederación General del Trabajo: Notas enviadas y recibidas, 1970–71," letter from Jorge Emilio Lozano, secretary general of SITRAC to Elpidio Torres, secretary general of the CGT Córdoba, May 5, 1970.

7. Ibid., letter from Jorge Emilio Lozano, secretary general of SITRAC, to the executive committee, CGT Córdoba, May 8, 1970.

8. SITRAC archive file AI "Volantes, Impresos o Mimeos," fliers "A los compañeros de Fiat Concord" and "Expulsemos a Lozano: Ni un paso atrás."

9. *Informe,* Servicio de Documentación e Información Laboral, no. 123 (May 1970), pp. 40–41; *La Voz del Interior,* May 15, 1970, p. 19; May 17, 1970, p. 14.

10. Interviews with Carlos Masera, secretary general of SITRAC, 1970–71, Córdoba, July 18, 1990; Domingo Bizzi, undersecretary general of SITRAC, 1970–71, Córdoba, July 22, 1987; José Páez, member of SITRAC executive committee, 1970–71, Buenos Aires, July 11, 1989; Gregorio Flores, union shop steward, SITRAC, Buenos Aires, November 12, 1985.

11. Interview with José Páez.

12. SMATA archive, "Confederación General del Trabajo," SITRAM communiqué, May 26, 1970; *La Voz del Interior,* May 28, 1970, p. 20.

13. Interview with Antonio Marimón, former press secretary for the *clasista* SMATA (1972–1974), Buenos Aires, June 30, 1990. The "new left" parties had increased their efforts to gain influence in the SMATA and had been placing activists in IKA-Renault plants since the late 1960s, a policy that became a priority only after the events of May 1969. The PCR, for example, only fully worked out its strategy of insertion into the local working class in the months following the Cordobazo. Militants would be placed in the various IKA-Renault plants, where they would establish *"comisiones de lucha,"* cells of shop floor militants who would politicize the workers by linking political discussions to daily work problems. The goal was generally to establish a few delegates in strategic factories and then to link *clasismo* with union democracy

movements. This strategy was first presented in the PCR's 1969 party manual (Chapter 8, "Desarrollar una poderosa corriente sindical clasista") and then was refined by two party theoreticians, Jorge Zapata and Alberto Troncoso, shortly before the Perdriel *toma;* "El partido y la lucha sindical," *Teoría y política* 4 (March–April 1970), pp. 1–8.

14. *Informe,* Servicio de Documentación e Información Laboral, no. 123 (May 1970), pp. 39–40; *La Voz del Interior,* May 13, 1970, p. 20; May 14, 1970, p. 20; IKA-Renault company memorandum, "Resumen de los hechos que culminaron con las tomas de planta," June 6, 1971, Renault Industrial Relations Dept., Santa Isabel. The *clasistas* gave their account of the events in Perdriel in "Cómo fue y que enseña la lucha de Perdriel-IKA," report of the Agrupaciones 1º de mayo, June 1, 1970, SMATA archive, SMATA-Córdoba, volume "Volantes y Comunicados 1970."

15. *Informe,* Servicio de Documentación e Información Laboral, no. 124 (June 1970), pp. 53–59.

16. Ibid., no. 125 (July 1970), pp. 61–71.

17. "IKA-Perdriel: Un camino y un método," *Nueva hora,* no. 46 (June 1970), p. 4.

18. SITRAC archive, file "Elecciones: Comisión directiva y delegados," photocopy of union slate "azul y blanco," Ministerio de Trabajo y Seguridad Social.

19. SITRAC archive, Francisco Delich, "Condición obrera y sindicato clasista," paper presented to the Seminar on Labor Movements in Latin America, San José, Costa Rica, November 12–18, 1972, p. 5.

20. SITRAC archive, file AI "Volantes, Impresos o Mimeos," document "Situación de las paritarias—plan de lucha," May 18, 1971.

21. SITRAC archive, "Esto pasa en Forja," *Boletín del Sindicato de Trabajadores Concord,* no. 1 (January 13, 1971), p. 2. Union contacts with the Turin Fiat unions remained strong for the length of the SITRAC-SITRAM *clasista* experience; interview with José Páez.

22. SITRAC archive, file "Juicios de Reincorporación," document "Bizzi, Domingo Valentín, y sus acumulados c/Fiat Concord," letter from Arturo Curutchet, SITRAC legal counsel and Domingo Valentín Bizzi, undersecretary of SITRAC to the Secretaría de Trabajo, November 24, 1970.

23. SITRAC-SITRAM supported these unions with strikes on several occasions. SITRAC archive, file AII-37 "Comunicado de prensa de SITRAC: Abandono de planta y manifestación en las calles de San Vincente," August 13, 1971.

24. Anzorena, *Tiempo de violencia y de utopía,* p. 101; U.S. Dept. of State, Papers Related to the Internal Affairs of Argentina, U.S. Embassy in Buenos Aires, "Government Cancels Cordoba Opposition Meeting Sponsored by Some Labor Elements," Telegram 376.41356Z, February 4, 1970.

25. U.S. Dept. of State, Papers Related to the Internal Affairs of Argentina, U.S. Embassy in Buenos Aires, "Labor Developments in January," A-57, February 15, 1970. A "Chicago-style shooting," as the U.S. embassy reported it, left two dead and nineteen arrested in the UOM power struggle and finally established Miguel's control of the union.

26. SMATA archive, "Confederación General del Trabajo," document "Declaración y resolución del plenario de gremios confederados de Córdoba, normalizador de la CGT Regional," Córdoba, March 3, 1970.

27. The UTA's union magazine, *UTA,* was the most important union publication in the city between 1970 and 1974 and was where the positions of the Peronist left were distilled. Its political language, support for *"liberación nacional"* and *"la lucha anti-imperialista,"* may not have been so different from that of the *ortodoxos,* but its political alliances and the degree to which discourse reflected actual union behavior certainly were. In any given issue of the magazine during these years, there can be found articles on Tosco and the Independents, the Cuban Revolution, interviews with liberation theologians, and fulminating criticisms of Miguel, Rucci, and the *porteño* labor leadership, all expressing ideas that were by then anathema to the *ortodoxos.* See, for example, the May 1971 issue, *UTA: Revista Mensual de la Unión Tranviarios Automotor,* and also the union's political program published in *La Voz del Interior,* September 13, 1970, p. 25.

28. Natalia Duval, *Los sindicatos clasistas: SITRAC (1970–71)* (Buenos Aires: Centro Editor de América Latina, 1988), pp. 32–38. The late-December hunger strike also brought the first public support for the Fiat *clasistas* from guerrilla organizations such as the Ejército Revolucionario del Pueblo (ERP) and the FAL; "Una Navidad combatiente," *Cristianismo y revolución* 4, no. 27 (January–February 1971), p. 14.

29. SITRAC archive, file AI "Volantes, Impresos o Mimeos," document "A la clase obrera y al pueblo de Córdoba," Córdoba, January 14, 1971.

30. *Informe,* Servicio de Documentación e Información Laboral, no. 131 (January 1971), p. 9.

31. SMATA archive, volume "Confederación General del Trabajo," letter from Elpidio Torres, secretary general of SMATA-Córdoba, to Delegación Regional Córdoba de la Confederación General del Trabajo, January 8, 1971; letter from Elpidio Torres to José Rucci, secretary general, Confederación General del Trabajo, December 14, 1970; U.S. State Dept. Papers Related to the Internal Affairs of Argentina, U.S. Embassy in Argentina, "Labor Developments in Rosario and Córdoba," A-561, December 3, 1970; "The Argentine Labor Movement-1970," A-111, March 23, 1970.

32. *Informe,* Servicio de Documentación e Información Laboral, no. 131 (January 1971), pp. 9–11.

33. One source of considerable worker animosity toward the company was the knowledge that Fiat paid the lowest wages in the industry. In the union's second bulletin, SITRAC compared the Fiat wage scales with those paid by Ford, which were correctly shown to be significantly higher for every job category. SITRAC, "Paritarias: No nos van a doblegar," *Boletín del Sindicato de trabajadores Concord,* no. 2 (June 1971), p. 8.

34. SITRAC archive, file 2 "Pruebas," Ministerio de Economía y Trabajo, arbitration award, Secretaría de Estado de Trabajo, Delegación Regional Córdoba, March 11, 1971.

35. SITRAC archive, file AI "Volantes, Impresos o Mimeos," flyer "Llaman a luchar contra la dictadura entreguista, la patronal explotadora, la burocracia sindical cómplice," Córdoba, January 27, 1971. SITRAC-SITRAM here accused the Cordoban CGT of being, "completely under the thumb of José Rucci and his gang."

36. *La Voz del Interior,* March 14, 1971, p. 26; *Panorama* 8, no. 206 (April 6–12, 1971), p. 13.

37. Duval, *Los sindicatos clasistas,* p. 47.

38. B. Balvé and B. Balvé, *Lucha de calles, lucha de clases: Elementos para su análisis (Córdoba, 1969–1971)* (Buenos Aires: Ediciones La Rosa Blindada, 1973), p. 62. Luz y Fuerza's later account of the uprising interpreted it as a largely spontaneous response on the part of the city's unions to its occupation of the Villa Revol power plan. No mention is made of the alternative SITRAC-SITRAM plan; Sindicato de Luz y Fuerza de Córdoba, *Memoria y balance,* 1971, p. 93

39. *Clarín,* March 13, 1971, p. 21; *La Voz del Interior,* March 17, 1971, pp. 20–22.

40. *La Voz del Interior,* March 20, 1971, p. 15. The Cordoban representatives to the congress, Ramón Contreras of Luz y Fuerza and Manuel Cabrera of the UTA, had been shouted down during the proceedings with cries of *"¡Ni Yanquis, Ni Marxistas, Peronistas!"* and had in turn lambasted the UOM's "armed thugs" *("matones a sueldo").* The relationship between Rucci and Córdoba was thenceforth one of mutual contempt and open hostility; the bitter feud would end only with Rucci's death in 1973.

41. Alejandro Lanusse, *Mi testimonio* (Buenos Aires: Lassere Editores, 1977), pp. 199–208.

42. SITRAC archive, file "Expedientes: Ministerio de Trabajo: Despidos, Paritarias, Denuncias Fiat de baja producción," telegram, Fiat Concord to Secretary of Labor San Sebastián, April 13, 1971. In a letter sent to the Cordoban Ministry of Labor a few weeks earlier, the company figures that were included showed that production in all the departments except the forge had actually increased between July 1970 and March 1971. Production had only begun to decline as of January 1971, the month that Fiat fired the union leadership; ibid., letter from Fiat Concord to the regional delegate of the Ministry of Labor, Dr. Hector Mende, March 31, 1971.

43. This stratagem actually backfired, as the SITRAC union leadership would later use the notary's reports as evidence for their own suit for damages that they brought against Fiat for unlawful firings after the union was banned in late 1971. The suit was brought under the post-1976 military government, and the court predictably did not award the union leaders damages. It did, however, cite the notarized accounts as proof that Fiat's claims that the union leaders had acted as provocateurs in its plants were unfounded, and accepted the union leaders' position that the labor upheavals of the *clasista* period were the result of general conditions in the plants. SITRAC archive, file "Juicios de Reincorporación, III, IV," Superior Court, Secretaría Laboral, Provincia de Córdoba, sentence no. 69, November 29, 1976.

44. *Informe,* Servicio de Documentación e Información Laboral, no. 134 (April 1971), pp. 25–26; U.S. Dept. of State, Papers Related to the Internal Affairs of Argentina, U.S. Embassy in Buenos Aires, "Cordoba CGT Reorganized," A-165, April 18, 1971.

45. "El sindicalismo cordobés en la escalada," *Aquí y ahora* 3, no. 26 (May 1971), pp. 6–15.

46. Anzorena, *Tiempo de violencia y de utopía,* pp. 177–180.

47. *La Voz del Interior,* May 27, 1971, p. 17; U.S. Dept. of State, Papers Related to Internal Affairs of Argentina, U.S. Embassy in Buenos Aires, "Cordoba CGT Calls National Meeting," 2375 241154Z, May 21, 1971.
48. "Ponencia de SITRAC-SITRAM," *CGT: Regional Córdoba* (May 1971), p. 6.
49. "Nosotros y la CGT cordobesa," *Boletín SITRAC,* no. 2 (June 1971), p. 3.
50. Luis Mattini, *Hombres y mujeres del PRT-ERP* (Buenos Aires: Editorial Contrapunto, 1990), pp. 105–123.
51. Though other parties gained some influence in the Fiat plants, notably the Maoist Vanguardia Comunista and the Trotskyist Palabra Obrera, the PRT's visible presence in the *viborazo* and in all subsequent Fiat public demonstrations, as well as its subsequent outspoken vindication of the SITRAC-SITRAM *clasista* experience—and concomitantly the virulent criticisms of the PC and the PCR by SITRAC-SITRAM—indicate that it was the PRT that had the greatest influence among the Fiat workers. See the PRT party publication, "Sindicalismo clasista: Sus perspectivas, sus desviaciones," 1972, SMATA archive, volume "Volantes, Diarios, Revistas, 1973."
52. *Panorama,* vol. 8, no. 206 (April 6–12, 1971), p. 10.
53. "Paritarias: No nos van a doblegar," *Boletín SITRAC,* no. 2 (June 1971), p. 8.
54. *La Voz del Interior,* July 5, 1971, p. 11.
55. *Informe,* Servicio de Documentación e Información Laboral, no. 137 (July 1971), pp. 77–79.
56. "SITRAM y SITRAC a los trabajadores y al pueblo argentino," *Boletín SITRAC,* special edition, August 1, 1971, pp. 2–3.
57. *La Voz del Interior,* August 31, 1971, p. 11. SITRAC secretary general Carlos Masera has related the widespread dissatisfaction with the August 1971 congress that existed among the Fiat *clasistas.* The congress convinced them of the necessity of distinguishing in the future between the role of a workers' party and those functions that should be the rightful and sole preoccupation of a union. Interview with Carlos Masera, Córdoba, July 22, 1987.
58. Iris Marta Roldán, *Sindicatos y protesta social en La Argentina: Un estudio de caso: El Sindicato de Luz y Fuerza de Córdoba, 1969–1974* (Amsterdam: Center for Latin American Research and Documentation, 1978), pp. 192–193.
59. SITRAC archive, file AII "Comunicados y conferencias de prensa; proyectos de solicitudes," document 32 "Respuesta de los sindicatos al cuestionario de la revista *Panorama,*" August 3, 1971.
60. *Los Principios,* October 27, 1971, pp. 10–11.
61. The government justified its measure by alleging that "both unions have repeatedly called wildcat strikes and failed to follow the procedural norms established by the law . . . a situation that is manifested in the holding of open assemblies in the workplace, plant abandonments, and a refusal to cooperate with the company, all of which has led to a notable drop in production," and also citing strikes undertaken for "political reasons"; SITRAC archive, file "Juicios de Reincorporación," document "SITRAC/Amparo," Labor Ministry, Buenos Aires, Federal Court No. 2, October 25, 1971.
62. SITRAC archive, file "Documentos Relacionados con los Presos," letter from Alfredo Curutchet to SITRAC, Villa Devoto Prison, Buenos Aires, October 30, 1971.

63. SITRAC archive, file "Juicios de Reincorporación," document "SITRAC/ Amparo," Federal Court No. 2, letter from Dr. Haroldo H. A. Ferrero, Dirección de Personal, Fiat Concord, to Federal Court No. 2., Córdoba, May 31, 1972.

64. SITRAC archive, file AIII, "Comunicado, Comisiones Directivas de SITRAC-SITRAM," document "Las Comisiones Directivas y la Gran Mayoría de los Delegados Queremos la Reincorporación," Córdoba, November 18, 1971.

65. *La Voz del Interior,* November 4, 1971, p. 12.

66. SITRAC archive, file AII "Comunicados y Conferencias de Prensa; proyectos de solicitadas," document "Carta abierta de SITRAC a la CGT cordobesa," December 1971.

67. SITRAC archive, file "Documentos Relacionados con los Presos," letter from Carlos Masera to Gregorio Flores, Rawson Prison, Córdoba, December 22, 1972.

68. "Sí: Fracasaron los paros en Fiat," *Boletín SITRAC-SITRAM,* no. 1 (November 8, 1971), p. 1. After the proscription, the Fiat unions began publishing their formerly separate union newspapers together.

69. SITRAC archive, file "Documentos Relacionados con los Presos," letter from Gregorio Flores to SITRAC, Rawson Prison, December 12, 1971. Flores, a shop floor steward in prison since the time of the *viborazo,* wrote, "Unfortunately, the betrayals of those who accepted the union indemnifications, thus recognizing that the company fired them for 'just cause,' have not in any way helped to continue the struggle; indeed, they have greatly hurt our chances by having made the workers skeptical of all the leadership because we told them right from the start, we did not assume the responsibility of union leadership just to cut ourselves the best deal . . . it's useless to talk tough and assume a combative posture if we later practice just the opposite."

70. SITRAC archive, file "Volantes, Impresos o Mimeos," union flyer "En el mes del viborazo: SITRAC en pie," Córdoba, March 15, 1971.

71. SITRAC archive, file "Historia," unpublished letter from Carlos Masera and Domingo Bizzi to the newspaper *La Opinión,* Córdoba, January 14, 1972.

72. SITRAC archive, file "Volantes, Impresos o Mimeos," SITRAC-SITRAM communication "¡Basta de Despidos en Fiat!" Córdoba, February 2, 1972.

73. SITRAC archive, file "Comunicados y Conferencias de Prensa; proyecto de solicitadas," press releases "SITRAC denuncia maniobra concertada Fiat-Fuerzas de Seguridad," Córdoba, March 30, 1971; "Denuncia campaña difamatoria contra asesor legal, Dr. Alfredo Curutchet," Córdoba, April 2, 1971.

74. The most important left-wing influences were those "new left" parties that had emerged in the 1960s—the PRT, the PCR, and the Vanguardia Comunista. Because of the Communist party's cautious policies and hopes of building bridges to the Peronist movement, the country's principal Marxist party had little involvement in the Fiat *clasista* movement, a fact that explains its many calumnies against SITRAC-SITRAM and its repeated accusations of *"infantilismo de izquierda"* at work in Ferreyra. See the PC publication, "¿Clasismo o aventurismo? SITRAC-SITRAM, experiencias y enseñanzas," Buenos Aires, 1972.

75. I was among those who exaggerated the influence of the PRT-ERP on the

SITRAC-SITRAM leadership. In my doctoral dissertation, "Peronismo, Clasismo, and Labor Politics in Córdoba, 1955–76" (Harvard University, 1988), I restated the Fiat *clasista*–PRT link. The subsequent discovery of the SITRAC union archive, hidden and stored by the union's former secretary throughout the difficult years that followed the government's outlawing of SITRAC-SITRAM, forms the basis for the revised interpretation of Fiat *clasismo* found in this chapter. The SITRAC archive has been microfilmed, and a copy is now housed in Harvard University's Lamont Library.

76. Ronald Munck, Ricardo Falcón, and Bernardo Galitelli, *Argentina, from Anarchism to Peronism: Workers, Unions, and Politics, 1855–1985* (London: Zed Books Ltd., 1987), p. 178; Roberto Reyna, "La izquierda cordobesa," *Crísis*, no. 64 (1988), pp. 44–45. See the response to Reyna's article by former SITRAC secretary general Carlos Masera, "SITRAC y SITRAM: la autonomía obrera," *Crísis*, no. 67 (1989) pp. 78–79.

77. Shortly after the *viborazo*, Tosco personally approached the SITRAC-SITRAM union leadership and asked them to "put the brakes on" the Fiat *clasista* movement, as he feared they would destroy the goodwill of the Peronist rank and file and the more combative Peronist Cordoban unions for the broad workers' front he was trying to build. Though to a great extent the Fiat unions were responding to events over which they did not have absolute control, especially in their conflict with the company, many union officials were later to regret that they had failed heed Tosco's advice to temper the unions' public political and ideological positions; interview with José Páez.

78. SITRAC archive file "Volantes, Impresos o Mimeos," union flier "Sí, Todos hacemos política: La empresa, el gobierno, los dirigentes vendidos y SITRAC, todos tenemos una política," Córdoba, December 1, 1971.

79. SITRAC archive file "Juicios de Reincorporación," union comuniqué "SITRAC-SITRAM en la Resistencia," Córdoba, October 28, 1971.

7. Tosco and Salamanca

1. Letter from Tosco to Julio Guillán, Mesa de Gremios Peronistas Combativos, February 12, 1972, Villa Devoto Prison, in Agustín Tosco, *Presente en las luchas de la clase obrera: Selección de trabajos* (Buenos Aires: Jorge Lannot y Adriana Amantea, 1984), pp. 213–216.

2. Tosco's support for the MUCS actually may have hurt his efforts to further both pluralism in the labor movement and the unity of Cordoban labor, since the presence of the Communist party, considered conservative and reformist, and of the Radicals, regarded as representative of bourgeois interests, made it anathema to the *clasistas*. Tosco himself seemed to have realized this, and he devoted most of his efforts after 1971 to developing Córdoba as the cornerstone of the alternative labor movement rather than to the MUCS.

3. Archive Fermín Chávez, Buenos Aires, letters from Perón to Ongaro, Madrid, June 25, 1970, and November 26, 1970; U.S. Dept. of State, Papers Related to the Internal Affairs of Argentina, U.S. Embassy in Buenos Aires, "Ongaro Returns," A-026, January 19, 1972.

4. After a late-1971 visit to Madrid at Perón's invitation, López wrote: "I've spo-

ken recently to Perón and he congratulated me that the Cordoban CGT is comprised of Peronist and non-Peronist workers, both of whom are working for the liberation of the country from imperialism. Those who assert that the CGT ought to be made up only of Peronist workers . . . are the ones who have bought into Peronism as a business and do not accept it as a revolutionary movement," "Córdoba: La CGT convoca para la lucha," *Intersindical,* vol. 1, no. 1 (December 1971), pp. 4–5.

5. The prominent role played by the Cordoban light and power workers in the Congreso Nacional en Defensa de las Empresas Estatales held in Buenos Aires May 18 to 20, 1971, made clear its importance as a leading union advocate for socialist positions. Luz y Fuerza now unequivocally supported public ownership of energy, transport, communications, and banking, as well as basic industries. Sindicato de Luz y Fuerza de Córdoba, *Memoria y Balance,* 1971, p. 112.

6. Interview with Sixto Ceballos, leader of Peronist opposition in Luz y Fuerza, Córdoba, July 10, 1985.

7. Sindicato de Luz y Fuerza de Córdoba, *Memoria y Balance,* 1971, pp. 120–121; Iris Marta Roldán, *Sindicatos y protesta social en la Argentina, un estudio de caso: El Sindicato de Luz y Fuerza de Córdoba, 1969–1974* (Amsterdam: Center for Latin American Research and Documentation, 1978), pp. 193–194.

8. Sindicato de Luz y Fuerza de Córdoba, *Memoria y Balance,* 1971, p. 125.

9. U.S. Dept. of State, Papers Related to the Internal Affairs of Argentina, U.S. Embassy in Buenos Aires, "Combative Peronist Union Plenary," A-029, January 24, 1972, and "Peronist Control of Labor Waning," A-306, June 26, 1972.

10. "Córdoba: El corazón rojo de la patria," *No transar,* no. 90 (June 22, 1971), pp. 10–11.

11. "12% de aumento: Otro Gran Atraco Nacional," *No transar,* no. 114 (September 28, 1972), pp. 5–7.

12. "Construir comisiones obreras," *No transar,* no. 70 (September 1, 1968), pp. 1–4; SITRAC archive, Buenos Aires, file "Vanguardia Comunista," party document "Sobre la construcción de las comisiones obreras," March 22, 1970. The VC was also among the first to propose democratization of the collective bargaining process *(paritarias)* to win worker allegiance. Party reports on the situations in the Perkins, Ford-Transax, and IKA-Renault factories suggested that the *clasistas* should exploit widespread discontent with the lack of rank-and-file participation in the process by championing the election of union representatives *(paritarios)* and voting on union proposals *(anteproyectos)* in open assemblies on the shop floor. "Democracia sindical en las paritarias de Córdoba," *Desacuerdo,* no. 13 (November 1972), p. 8.

13. Both the PCR and the VC defined themselves as Maoist parties, though the PCR identified itself as pro-Chinese and the Vanguardia Comunista as pro-Albanian. The Maoism of the PCR reflected only its position on the Sino-Soviet rift and did not imply an adherence to Maoist postulates in actual practice. Though it rhetorically supported Maoist concepts of insurrection and popular revolutionary warfare, in its actions it was closer to a strictly Marxist-Leninist party than a Maoist one. Other left-wing parties that supported the *"vía armada"* came to regard it as a reformist party not very different from the PC

itself. The PCR, in fact, feuded with the Vanguardia Comunista precisely on the issue of revolutionary praxis, and it belittled the VC's support of the *"del camino del campo a la ciudad"* as inappropriate for Argentina. Indeed the VC's party programs were a strange mixture of sober pragmatism, as in its directives on the formation of the *comisiones obreras,* and a bizarre parroting of Maoist litanies. The PCR's support for the creation of a revolutionary workers' party, in turn, won it accusations of being putschist by the VC. See "Polémica con Vanguardia Comunista," *Nueva hora,* no. 59 (January 1971), p. 7.

14. The PCR's secretary general, Otto Vargas, discusses the party's strategy for moving into the Cordoban SMATA during the period in Jorge Brega, *¿Ha muerto el comunismo? El maoismo en la Argentina: Conversaciones con Otto Vargas* (Buenos Aires: Editorial Agora, 1990), pp. 213–232.

15. Virtually every Marxist party of any standing in Córdoba had some presence in the IKA-Renault plants by the early 1970s. In addition to the PCR, the other left-wing parties—the PC, VC, the Trotskyist Palabra Obrera, El Obrero (a small, local Marxist-Leninist party), the PRT, and the *ongarista* Peronismo de Base—all had activists on the shop floor. Nevertheless the leadership role of the PCR was clear from the time of the Perdriel *toma,* and PCR members dominated the executive committee and controlled the majority of the *clasista* shop floor stewards in the SMATA.

16. Given the VC's Maoist orientation, the agricultural workers of Tucumán, Salta, and Jujuy received special attention from the party. As early as 1969, VC activists were working to establish a foothold in the sugar workers' union. In party publications, the VC compared the importance of the sugar industry in that region to the automobile industry in Córdoba. As it did in Córdoba, the VC sought to build up support for *clasista* positions on the basis of effective union representation on rank-and-file grievances. First, as a politicization tool, it supported the participation of the workers in the collective bargaining process. In addition party militants championed specific reforms—resistance to the rationalizations and mill closings and demands for industry guarantees of a minimum 120-day work year—that it knew would draw broad rank-and-file support. SITRAC archive, Buenos Aires, file "Vanguardia Comunista," document "Para la próxima zafra"; *Norte obrera: Regional noroeste de la tendencia 29 de mayo* (a regional VC party publication), no. 10 (June 1971), pp. 1–2.

17. Luis Mattini, *Hombres y mujeres del PRT-ERP* (Buenos Aires: Editorial Contrapunto, 1990), pp. 277–283.

18. Interviews with Roque Romero, undersecretary general of the *clasista* SMATA Córdoba, 1972 to 1974, Córdoba, August 13, 1985, and Roberto Nágera, *clasista* SMATA shop steward, Ford-Transax factory, July 18, 1991, Córdoba.

19. SMATA archive, SMATA-Córdoba, "Volantes Varios, 1972," MRS–Lista Marrón flier "Próximas elecciones generales," March 15, 1972.

20. "Canalizar las decisiones por las vías orgánicas," *SMATA,* SMATA-Córdoba, no. 79 (January 27, 1972), p. 1.

21. "¡Nacionalización!" *SMATA,* SMATA-Córdoba, no. 77, (January 13, 1972), p. 1. Torres had also made periodic calls for the nationalization of IKA-Renault, but the new frequency of the union's demand and the incendiary language it used were something truly novel.

22. "1970: Acción y lucha," *Avance* 2, no. 5 (January 1971), pp. 4–5; "Masiva adhesión por el conflicto en Citroën," *Avance* 2, no. 6 (February 1971), pp. 1–4.

23. *Memoria y Balance,* Sindicato de Mecánicos y Afines del Transporte Automotor, Buenos Aires, 1971, pp. 88–89. After the obstreperous behavior of Cordoban *clasista* militants at a SMATA congress, the nettled Peronist leadership of the SMATA central wrote in *Avance,* the autoworkers' union monthly magazine, "In the Central Committee we listened respectfully to the inflammatory and overwrought [*"exaltado"*] words of a Cordoban comrade, demanding for the long-suffering working people of that province special praise for their heroism in the political and union struggle. Shortly before, the Cordoban CGT had declared a strike to protest, among other things, the 'sellout leadership of the national CGT' . . . which only serves to create divisions under the pretext that workers' interests are better defended in the interior of the country than in the federal capital," *Avance,* vol. 3, no. 9 (February 1972), pp. 4–5.

24. *La Voz del SMATA,* SMATA-Córdoba, no. 32 (November 1968), p. 6.

25. *La Voz del Interior,* January 26, 1972, p. 9.

26. The electoral platform proposed by the *lista marrón* in all the SMATA-affiliated plants comprised the following planks: 1) reduce the number of paid union officials from thirteen to four, with the requirement that all union officials work in the plants on a rotation basis; 2) allow for the removal of any shop steward from his union position if so voted in open assembly; 3) require all union resolutions be voted on in open assembly; 4) full union support for the restitution of the *sábado inglés;* 5) union affiliation for administrative employees in all the SMATA plants; 6) a single collective bargaining agreement for all Cordoban SMATA workers, with mandatory four-month wage adjustments; 7) a demand that the company recognize "hazardous" working conditions in the forge, as well as in the painting, electroplating *(galvanoplastía),* thermal treatment, and casting departments; 8) reduction of production rhythms, and union participation in the future in determining the appropriate pace of work. SMATA archive, SMATA-Córdoba, volume "Volantes Varios, 1972," flier "A los compañeros de Transax," February 1972, Lista Marrón GTT (Grupo Trabajadores de Transax).

27. *Primera Plana* 10, no. 471 (February 8, 1972), pp. 14–15. The actions of Peronist labor bosses such as Simó must always be understood in this light. Control of powerful unions was a source of wealth and power in their relationship with employers, but it also assured them political influence within the Peronist movement; with the prospect of a Peronist victory in elections in 1973, it might even, in Simó's case, make possible the recovery of a political career abruptly suspended with the 1966 coup.

28. U.S. Dept. of State, Papers Related to the Internal Affairs of Argentina, U.S. Embassy in Buenos Aires, "Peronist Control of Córdoba Labor Waning," A-306, June 26, 1972.

29. *Clarín,* April 15, 1972, p. 18.

30. *Avance,* vol. 3, no. 9 (February 1972), p. 4.

31. *Memoria y Balance,* Sindicato de Mecánicos y Afines del Transporte Automotor, Buenos Aires, 1972, p. 80. The victorious *lista marrón* included members of the PCR, PC, VC, and Peronismo de Base, and independent leftists as well

as anti-*torrista* Peronists. Out of respect for Tosco's strategy of cultivating support from the combative sectors of Peronist trade unionism rather than backing a separate, *clasista* workers' movement, the PC did not publicly express its support for the *lista marrón*. Nevertheless, members of the *clasista* executive committee such as Hugo Rivera (Secretario Gremial) and Miguel Leiva (Secretario Administrativo) were either PC members or closely associated with the communists.

32. *La Voz del Interior,* May 6, 1972, p. 15.

33. Ibid., May 28, 1972, p. 14.

34. Ibid., August 21, 1972, p. 11.

35. SITRAC archive, Buenos Aires, file A II "Comunicados y conferencias de prensa," communique "¡Basta de Despidos en Fiat!," Córdoba, February 2, 1972.

36. Ibid., file "Documentos relacionados con los presos," letter from Gregorio Flores to fired Concord union leaders, Rawson Prison, May 27, 1972.

37. Ibid., letter from Alfredo Curutchet to Domingo Bizzi, Rawson Prison, June 1, 1972.

38. Ibid., file "Volantes, Impresos o Mimeos," union flier "Por un Nuevo 23 de Marzo. ¡Fuera Alejo Simó de la Planta!," Córdoba, March 23, 1972. The SITRAC leaders astutely perceived not only that was this an attempt to reestablish the Fiat-UOM connection, but also that there was a deliberately political objective for the Peronist movement behind it, since if Peronism could not show that it controlled the working class, its utility to the Argentine bourgeoisie would be nil and the possibility of the FREJULI participating in the elections promised by the Gran Acuerdo Nacional would be undermined. A very different observer, the U.S. embassy in Buenos Aires, reached the same conclusion; U.S. Dept. of State, Papers Related to the Internal Affairs of Argentina, U.S. Embassy in Buenos Aires, "Current Labor Assessment," 5726–141647Z, September 14, 1972.

39. SITRAC archive, Buenos Aires, file "Volantes, Impresos o Mimeos," flier "A los compañeros de Fiat Concord," Córdoba, July 21, 1972.

40. "Fuerzas clasistas y sindicatos," *Nueva hora,* no. 61 (February 1971), p. 3.

41. Salamanca's criticisms of the Fiat unions echoed those of the SMATA leadership genrally, save the neo-Trotskyist Palabra Obrera, which looked favorably on SITRAC-SITRAM: "I think they [SITRAC-SITRAM] confused the union with the political party. There was a fundamental reason for that: the influence of nonproletarian elements with petit bourgeois approaches. That influence led to the isolation of SITRAC-SITRAM in the workers' movement. When the moment came to make important decisions, they were alone. And that happened despite the fact that they were the ones who really developed a step further the struggle against the dictatorship and the labor bureaucracy," *Panorama,* vol. 10 (December 14–20, 1972), p. 20.

42. "The new bureaucrats in the SMATA are not *clasistas.* They're opportunists and traitors to the revolutionary proletariat. In order to win the elections, they claimed to represent a continuation and even an advance over our experience, but once in power they demonstrate behavior which increasingly reveals them to be no more than the true bourgeois agents of the workers' movement," SMATA archive, SMATA-Córdoba, volume "Volantes Varios, 1972,"

Grupo Obrero Clasistas flier "Rescatar SITRAC-SITRAM," Córdoba, October 25, 1972.

43. "A union is *clasista* as a result of practicing a genuine union democracy and undertaking a political struggle against the Right and reformism, and when in actual practice and through concrete measures it shows itself to be guided by a *clasista* philosophy," SITRAC archive, Buenos Aires, file "Comunicados y Conferencias de Prensa," SITRAC-SITRAM union communiqué, Córdoba, August 30, 1972.

44. Ibid., file "Actas y Reuniones y Asambleas," document "Notas del acta en la sede del SMATA," Córdoba, August 14, 1972. It was also at this gathering that the first calls in support of armed struggle were heard from the Fiat ranks. Indeed imprisonment had been a radicalizing experience for a number of Fiat workers, many of whom had been in close, daily contact with members of the PRT-ERP, the Montoneros, and other left-wing militants in Rawson Prison. However, this represented a distinctly minority position among the Fiat *clasistas*.

45. Ibid., file "Volantes, Impresos o Mimeos," SITRAC-SITRAM flier "A los compañeros de Concord y Materfer," Córdoba, September 20, 1972.

46. Ibid., file "Actas de Reuniones y Asambleas," transcript of open assembly held in SMATA headquarters, Córdoba, October 21, 1972.

47. SMATA archive, SMATA-Córdoba, volume "Confederación General del Trabajo: Notas enviadas y recibidas, 1971–72," letter from Grupo de Obreros de Fiat por la Afiliación al SMATA to the Secretariat, CGT Córdoba, December 17, 1972. The Fiat workers reported overwhelming support in the plants for SMATA affiliation as opposed to UOM affiliation but described an intimidation campaign by the company that included firings of known union sympathizers and increased production rhythms of "almost 100 percent," which were making canvassing and the affiliation drive all but impossible.

48. *La Voz del Interior,* August 24, 1972, p. 11.

49. Ibid., August 27, 1972, p. 23; September 9, 1972, p. 11. By this time labor mobilizations confronted greater obstacles to developing into citywide insurrections on the scale of the Cordobazo and the *viborazo*. The police and the Third Army Corps, after the March 1971 rebellion, had coordinated their riot control tactics and drawn up contingency plans that were effectively applied in all subsequent general strikes. The city was now systematically partitioned off by police before any strike began. Some one hundred city blocks of the downtown area would be sealed off; people could leave the area but no one would be permitted to enter. The army in the meantime would proceed to Santa Isabel and Ferreyra, where Highways 9 and 36 would be cut off, thus denying the autoworkers entrance to the city. U.S. Dept. of State, Papers Related to the Internal Affairs of Argentina, U.S. Embassy in Buenos Aires, "Peronist Control of Córdoba Labor Waning," A-306, June 26, 1972.

50. *La Voz del Interior,* October 4, 1972, p. 9.

51. Enrique Arrosagaray, "Renée Salamanca, Secretario General de los Mecánicos Cordobeses, 1972–74," *Hechos y protagonistas de las luchas obreras argentinas,* no. 1 (Buenos Aires: Editorial Experiencia, 1984); Brega, *¿Ha muerto el comunismo?* pp. 213–238. Vargas, the longtime president of the

PCR, gives the most complete biography of Salamanca and details of the PCR's activities in Córdoba. Specific details of Salamanca's career have also been provided by Antonio Marimón and Roque Romero. The majority of the *clasista* leaders, especially at the shop steward level, however, were not seasoned party activists, and they adopted *clasista* positions in the plants before joining left-wing parties; many in fact never joined a party at all. A more typical *clasista* militant than Salamanca would be Roberto Nágera, a young worker in the Ford-Transax factory who began there in 1970, was swept up in the social and political ferment following the Cordobazo, won election as a *clasista* shop steward at the tender age of twenty-three in 1972, and subsequently joined a Marxist party, in his case the Vanguardia Comunista. Interview with Roberto Nágera, *clasista* shop steward, Ford-Transax factory, 1972 to 1975, Córdoba, July 25, 1991.

52. *Análisis-Confirmado,* vol. 12, no. 617 (January 9–15, 1973), p. 16; Jorge Luis Bernetti, *El peronismo de la victoria* (Buenos Aires: Editorial Legasa, 1983), pp. 62–68; Juan Carlos Torre, *Los sindicatos en el gobierno,* 1973–76 (Buenos Aires: Centro Editor de América Latina, 1983), p. 47.

53. *Análisis-Confirmado,* vol. 12, no. 619 (January 23–29, 1973), p. 8.

54. *Análisis-Confirmado,* vol. 12, no. 616 (January 2–8, 1973), p. 14; Richard Gillespie, *Soldiers of Perón: Argentina's Montoneros* (New York: Oxford University Press, 1984), pp. 132–133.

55. U.S. Dept. of State, Papers Related to the Internal Affairs of Argentina, U.S. Embassy in Buenos Aires: "Córdoba CGT Reopened," A-490, September 20, 1972.

56. Christopher Knowles, "Revolutionary Trade Unionism: An Interview with Agustín Tosco," *Radical America,* vol. 9 (May–June 1975), pp. 17–37.

57. "Tosco: ¿A qué jugamos?" *El clasista,* boletín no. 1 (December 18, 1972), pp. 7–8.

58. "Las paritarias, la CGT y el movimiento obrero," *El obrero,* vol. 1, no. 1 (December 22, 1972), pp. 2–5.

59. *La Voz del Interior,* November 29, 1972, p. 13; U.S. Dept. of State, Papers Related to the Internal Affairs of Argentina, U.S. Embassy in Buenos Aires, "Córdoba—The Achilles Heel of Peronist Labor," A-661, December 18, 1972

60. SMATA archive, SMATA-Córdoba, volume "Notas y comunicados enviados del SMATA Secc. al SMATA-central, 1971–72," letter from Renée Salamanca to Justo Maradonna, Secretario del Interior del SMATA central, Córdoba, October 30, 1972.

61. An example of the tone of the Peronist broadsides can be found in a November flier distributed by the *torristas* at the time of Perón's return from exile: "We want to point out and denounce the petty and sectarian mentality of those who, despite calling themselves *clasistas,* do not hesitate to demonstrate now—as they had before in 1945 and 1955—their alliance with the reactionaries and the oligarchy through a defamatory campaign against Perón and the members of our Movement . . . it's hypocritical then [*clasistas'* criticism of Perón's return], this small-minded attempt to pass judgment on Perón and assert that there are 'two kinds of Peronists,' as did the union newspaper of November 16, 1972, published by the current SMATA leadership, a collection

of Bolsheviks, Trotskyists, and others of similar tendencies, áll of whom respond to to the same Communist ideology," SMATA archive, SMATA-Córdoba, volume "Volantes Varios, 1972," flier "Perón en la patria: Día de júbilo
nacional," Agrupación Unidad Mecánicos 9 de Setiembre, Córdoba, November 20, 1972.

62. "Una entrevista con Renée Salamanca," *Panorama,* vol. 10 (December 1972),
p. 20. The *clasistas* objected specifically to Tosco's public support for the
Obregón Cano–López ticket and suggested that the appropriate response
should have been an alliance with the local Peronist unions and abstention
from the 1973 elections.

63. *Panorama,* vol. 10, no. 288 (November 2–8, 1972), p. 15, and no. 290 (November 16–22, 1972), p. 18; U.S. Dept. of State, Papers Related to the Internal Affairs of Argentina, U.S. Embassy in Buenos Aires, "Formation of Opposition
Labor Movement Hits Peronist Roadblock," A-589, November 15, 1972.

64. *La Opinión,* February 11, 1973, pp. 8–9.

65. In early December, at Rucci's urging, Perón refused to receive Atilio López in
Buenos Aires shortly after meeting with Simó's delegation of *ortodoxo* leaders,
thereby giving a symbolic nod to the latter in the internal power struggle
among the Cordoban Peronists. *La Voz del Interior,* December 2, 1972, p. 18;
U.S. Dept. of State, Papers Related to the Internal Affairs of Argentina, U.S.
Embassy in Buenos Aires, Subject: "Córdoba—The Achilles Heel of Peronist
Labor," Airgram A-661, December 18, 1972.

8. *Peronists and Revolutionaries*

1. *La Opinión,* April 11, 1973, p. 10.

2. Interview with Roque Romero, Undersecretary of SMATA 1972 to 1974, August 13, 1985, Córdoba.

3. Archives des Usines Renault, Boulogne-Billancourt, Direction des Affaires
Internationales 0200, 1070 "A. Lucas, Argentine 1973," file "Argentinisation
d'IKA," document "Memorandum sur l'Argentinisation de IKA-Renault,"
March 22, 1971.

4. Ibid., 1067 "A. Lucas, Argentine 1973," company report "Situation Politique
et Perspectives Economiques de l'Argentine," May 23, 1973. Though Fiat
had also begun manufacturing during Perón's presidency, its Ferreyra plants
did not begin to produce cars until 1960.

5. SMATA archive, SMATA-Córdoba, volume "Volantes Varios, 1972," flier
"Próximas Elecciones Generales," MRS-Lista Marrón, March 15, 1972.

6. Interview with Roque Romero; Carlos E. Sánchez, "Estrategias y objetivos de
los sindicatos argentinos," Universidad Nacional de Córdoba, Instituto
Economía y Finanzas, Working Paper no. 18, 1973, p. 115.

7. SMATA archive, SMATA-Córdoba, volume "Volantes Varios, 1972," flier
"¿Por qué queremos modificar los Estatutos?" Movimiento de Recuperación
Sindical, March, 1972.

8. Ibid., flier "A los compañeros del gremio," Movimiento de Recuperación
Sindical, July 7, 1972.

9. Sánchez, "Estrategias y objetivos de los sindicatos argentinos," p. 115.

10. "Rotación de Directivos: El compañero Salamanca se incorporó a la planta," *SMATA,* SMATA-Córdoba, no. 101 (May 9, 1973), p. 3.

11. SMATA archive, SMATA-Córdoba, volume "Volantes Varios, 1972," flier "¿Por qué queremos a los Empleados en el Sindicato?" Lista Marrón, March 1972; "A un año del triunfo de la lista marrón," *SMATA,* SMATA-Córdoba, no. 100 (April 30, 1973), p. 1.

12. "La herencia de Torres y Bagué," *Consejo obrero: Periódico de los obreros mecánicos comunistas revolucionarios,* vol. 1, no. 1 (June 15, 1972), pp. 4–5.

13. The precise extent to which worker identification with the *clasista* leadership increased as a result of the *lista marrón*'s strategy cannot be determined simply on the basis of the written historical record. The resistance offered by the workers at the time of the union leadership's removal from office by the SMATA central in 1974 and my many discussions with IKA-Renault workers of the period indicate that their identification ran deep. Moreover, the Cordoban press recorded enough instances of workers' appreciation of the reforms to allow one to posit that the reforms had their intended effect.

14. SMATA archive, SMATA-Córdoba, volume "Volantes, Diarios y Revistas, 1973," fliers "Repudie la Trampe, Vote en Blanco," Córdoba, March 1973; "Imperdonable Indiferencia por el Futuro Nacional," Agrupación, September 9, 1973. The *clasistas'* abstention call was not presented as a rejection of the FREJULI ticket per se but rather as a protest against the military government's attempt to defuse growing working class militancy through elections. The abstention call nonetheless clearly revealed an anti-Peronist bias and was a serious tactical blunder.

15. SITRAC archive, file "SMATA," flier "SMATA por la liberación nacional," Consejo Directivo Nacional del SMATA, April 1973. The union lambasted "an evil called 'revolutionary trade unionism' that, hiding behind the hollow sloganry of leftist eggheads, has chosen Dependency and the status quo by advising the workers to cast blank votes."

16. *La Opinión,* April 11, 1973, p. 10.

17. "Atropello de la Central: El SMATA Córdoba fue expulsado de un plenario," *SMATA,* SMATA-Córdoba, no. 99 (April 23, 1973), p. 1.

18. *La Voz del Interior,* January 20, 1973, p. 13; SMATA archive, SMATA-Córdoba, volume "Volantes, Diarios y Revistas, 1973," flier "1945–24 de febrero 1973," SMATA Consejo Directivo Nacional, Buenos Aires, February 1973.

19. Unlike the case of many Peronist unions, notably the UOM, the SMATA's references to Hector Cámpora in the weeks preceding and following the 1973 elections were glowingly favorable, and he appeared several times on the magazine's cover. See, for example, *Avance* 2, no. 17 (May 1973).

20. *Clarín,* May 30, 1973, p. 22.

21. "Entrevista con Agustín Tosco: La socialización progresiva," *Análisis-Confirmado* 12, no. 621 (February 6–12, 1973), pp. 16–18. Tosco offered his interpretation of that struggle in terms that would have been acceptable to any member of the Peronist left: "I'm for the anti-imperialist struggle as a step toward socialism. Socialism in Argentina is still a little far away, but the liberating, antimonopolist, anti-imperialist struggle is closer. In that struggle

are found all the popular sectors, and among them, of course, are bourgeois sectors, owners of small and medium-size businesses, but without either the big bourgeoisie or the oligarchy, who are tied to the imperialist order. . . . Also small- and medium-size landowners, all these have a role to play. . . . We believe that the goal is a nationalist, anti-imperialist, anti-oligarchic road."

22. Interview with Roque Romero. The *clasistas* had learned their lesson with the abstention controversy, however, and their public statements during the rest of the campaign (unlike their private discussions) were far more circumspect.

23. Ibid.

24. Richard Gillespie, *Soldiers of Perón: Argentina's Montoneros* (New York: Oxford University Press, 1984), p. 130–135.

25. Francisco Ferrara, *¿Qué son las ligas agrarias?* (Buenos Aires: Siglo XXI Editores, 1973).

26. The character of these rank-and-file movements in the country generally are discussed in Juan Carlos Torre, "The Meaning of Current Workers' Struggles," *Latin American Perspectives,* vol. 1, no. 3 (1974), pp. 73–81.

27. *La Voz del Interior,* May 29, 1973, p. 6.

28. After Cámpora's election, and influenced no doubt by the upsurge in popular fervor, Tosco increasingly employed the language of the revolutionary. In preparation for the fourth national congress of the Intersindical, he stated that its purpose was to work out a revolutionary program and baptized the congress in honor of the Cordobazo: "As a reaffirmation of its *clasista* and revolutionary character, as an homage to all the comrades who have fallen in the sacred struggle for national liberation and the building of the Socialist Fatherland, the plenary will be called 'the Heroic 29th of May' in honor of that great popular and working class event: the Cordobazo." SMATA archive, SMATA-Córdoba, volume "Volantes de Agrupaciones Varias, 1973–74," Agustín Tosco, "Comunicado de Prensa," Córdoba, May 15, 1973.

29. SMATA archive, SMATA-Córdoba, volume "Volantes, Diarios y Revistas, 1973," press release, Sindicato de Luz y Fuerza de Córdoba, June 27, 1973.

30. Ronaldo Munck, *Argentina: From Anarchism to Peronism: Workers, Unions and Politics, 1855–1985* (London: Zed Books, Ltd., 1987), p. 189.

31. Torre, "The Meaning of Current Workers' Struggles," p. 76–77; "Conflicto General Motors," *Avance* 4, no. 22 (October 1973), p. 18.

32. Pedro Aguirre, "La reforma de la Ley de Asociaciones Profesionales," *Pasado y Presente,* vol. 4, nos. 2–3 (1973), pp. 283–301.

33. Gillespie, *Soldiers of Peron,* p. 152; Jorge Luis Bernetti, *El peronismo de la victoria* (Buenos Aires: Editorial Legasa, 1983), pp. 154–162; Horacio Verbitsky, *Ezeiza* (Buenos Aires: Editorial Contrapunto, 1987).

34. SMATA archive, SMATA-Córdoba, volume, "Volantes, Diarios y Revistas, 1973," union flier "El Caso Fiat y la Verdad Peronista," Unión Obrera Metalúrgica, Seccional Córdoba, June 3, 1973. In a separate UOM comuniqué to the Fiat Concord workers, the UOM announced that it considered its jurisdiction "irrevocable" and warned of *clasista* activists in the plants, "traitors in the service of the red master" *("apátridas al servicio del amo rojo"),* who it also claimed were in the service of the company, the very company that had presided over the demise of the *clasista* unions and

hounded *clasista* activists on the shop floor for the past two years. Communiqué, Comisión Gremial Provisoria, Fiat Concord UOM, Córdoba, June 22, 1973.

35. "SMATA al pueblo argentino" and "Asesinos a sueldo de la antipatria," *Avance,* vol. 2, no. 17 (May 1973), supplement. The SMATA's references to the perpetrators were, at first, suggestively vague. Neither its own public statements nor those of the CGT, which the autoworkers' union naturally had an important hand in drafting, attempted to attribute it directly to the left; they implicated both the "ultra left and right" in the assassination. After Perón's break with Cámpora and the Peronist left and the Peronist government's rightward shift, sole responsibility was explicitly placed on the shoulders of the left. However, with the recrudescence of its rivalry with the UOM in 1975, the SMATA would again speak of the "evil forces" responsible for the assassination and cast doubts on its authorship. See "Kloosterman," *Avance,* vol. 4, no. 33 (May–June 1975), p. 3.

36. *Memoria y Balance,* Sindicato de Mecánicos y Afines del Transporte Automotor, Buenos Aires, 1973, p. 39.

37. U.S. Dept. of State, Papers Related to the Internal Affairs of Argentina, U.S. Embassy in Buenos Aires, "SMATA Sweeps Fiat Union Elections in Córdoba," A-314, July 5, 1973; *La Voz del Interior,* June 30, 1973, p. 6.

38. *La Voz del Interior,* July 12, 1973, p. 16.

39. *La Voz del Interior,* July 26, 1973, p. 11. The Fiat affiliation drive is discussed at length in the union's weekly newspaper. Especially useful is the August 27, 1973, article, "El estallido de Fiat Concord," *SMATA,* SMATA-Córdoba, no. 110, p. 1–5.

40. *La Prensa,* August 22, 1973, p. 7, U.S. Dept. of State, Papers Related to the Internal Affairs of Argentina, U.S. Embassy in Buenos Aires, "Inter-Union Rivalry Threatens Uneasy Cordoba Labor Truce," D730032–1086, August, 1973.

41. *Clarín,* August 25, 1973, p. 8. SMATA *clasista* activists were highly critical of López after he had refused to receive their delegation in the midst of the Fiat occupation, the first of many confrontations the former UTA leader and now vice governor would have with the Marxists in the local autoworkers' union. See SMATA archive, SMATA-Córdoba, volume "Volantes, Diarios y Revistas, 1973," "¡Viva la ocupación de Fiat Concord!" Frente Unico Clasista, Córdoba, August 22, 1973.

42. "It frankly appears suspicious that the Cordoban leadership, the self-proclaimed *clasista,* combative, and revolutionary communist leadership, should mobilize just now and create problems for a popularly elected government when it refused to struggle against the military dictatorship with the very union [the SMATA national] that by decision of the executive committee and a national congress of all the union locals had resolved to mobilize in favor of the Fiat comrades to demand their legitimate union affiliation," *Avance,* no. 21 (September 1973), p. 16.

43. *La Voz del Interior,* July 1, 1973, p. 17.

44. U.S. Dept. of State, Papers Related to the Internal Affairs of Argentina, U.S. Embassy in Buenos Aires, "Peronist-Marxist Showdown Developing in Córdoba," July 1973, D730048–0288. Some of the best analyses of labor politics

in Córdoba for this period are the U.S. embassy dispatches such as this one, presumably based on the reports of the American consul in the city, John Patrick Egan, a perceptive observer of events in the city. He would later be kidnapped and executed by the ERP in 1975.

45. Interview with Juan Malvár, secretary general of Cordoban print workers' union 1958 to 1976, Córdoba, June 10, 1987.
46. *Informe,* Servicio de Documentación e Información Laboral, no. 162 (August 1973), pp. 26–28.
47. *La Voz del Interior,* July 28, 1973, p. 11; *La Opinión,* July 29, 1973, p. 11; U.S. Dept. of State, Papers Related to the Internal Affairs of Argentina, U.S. Embassy in Buenos Aires, "Peronists Agree to Truce in Córdoba," D730052–0196, July 1973.
48. *Clarín,* July 28, 1973, p. 10.
49. "Plenario de las 1º de Mayo," *Nueva hora* 6, no. 121 (July 1973), pp. 4–5. *Clasista* activists in Córdoba had actually already been at work in that stronghold of Peronist labor for several years. In 1970, activists from the Vanguardia Comunista formed the clandestine Grupo Organizador de Comisiones Obreras Metalúrgicas (GOCOM) and established cells in various metalworking shops and factories in the city. The alliance with the Peronismo de Base groups was more feasible after Cámpora's fall, at which point the Peronismo de Base took a sharply critical attitude toward the rightward shift within Peronism and adopted positions identical (save one, the idea of a "captive" Perón in the clutches of a reactionary circle) to those of the Marxist *clasistas.* SMATA archive, SMATA-Córdoba, volume "Volantes, Diarios, Revistas, 1973," flier "Combatir los enemigos de adentro," Peronismo de Base, Regional Córdoba, July 25, 1973.
50. *Electrum,* no. 412, (August 3, 1973), p. 8.
51. Ibid., no. 402, (May 24, 1973), p. 1.
52. *La Voz del Interior,* May 11, 1973, p. 17; interview with Sixto Ceballos, leader of Peronist opposition in Luz y Fuerza, Córdoba, July 20, 1985.
53. It was in these months that Iris Marta Roldán was conducting the fieldwork that would lead to her important study of Luz y Fuerza, *Sindicatos y protesta social.* Roldán's conclusions, as previously noted, must be put in the broader context of the union's history. What she records of the criticisms of Tosco's leadership and the internal opposition is best understood as a reflection of union affairs at a particularly sensitive political moment and not necessarily a faithful portrayal of the tenor of union affairs throughout the long years of Tosco's leadership.
54. Luis Mattini, *Hombres y mujeres del PRT-ERP* (Buenos Aires: Editorial Contrapunto, 1990), pp. 273–274.
55. *La Voz del Interior,* August 15, 1973, p. 7.
56. Elizabeth Jelin, "Conflictos laborales en la Argentina, 1973–76," *Revista mexicana de sociología,* no. 2 (April–June 1978), p. 425; Aguirre, "La reforma de la Ley de Asociaciones Profesionales," pp. 283–301.
57. *Informe,* Servicio de Documentación e Información Laboral, no. 164 (October 1973), p. 241.
58. SMATA archive, SMATA-Córdoba, volume "Volantes de Agrupaciones

Varias, 1973–74," flier "A los trabajadores de Fiat," Fuerzas Armadas Peronistas, April 4, 1973, Córdoba.

59. For an example of this, see a 1973 ERP flier that criticized unhealthy working conditions in the forge, painting tunnels, and other departments, as well as increased production rhythms in the Ilasa plant. SMATA archive, SMATA-Córdoba, volume "Volantes, Diarios y Revistas, 1973," flier "Ninguna tregua a las empresas explotadoras," Ejército Revolucionario Popular, 1973.

60. Gillespie, *Soldiers of Perón,* pp. 144–153; U.S. Dept. of State, Papers Related to Internal Affairs of Argentina, U.S. Embassy in Buenos Aires, "Labor Policy Towards Incoming Peronist Government," A-400, October 4, 1973.

61. Gillespie, *Soldiers of Perón,* 144–153.

62. Torre, "The Meaning of Current Workers' Struggles," pp. 74–75.

63. "Nuestra incorporación al SMATA," *SITRAP: Boletín Informativo del Sindicato de Trabajadores del Perkins,* no. 4 (August 1973), p. 2; "Comienza la lucha por las categorías," *SITRAP: Boletín Informativo del Sindicato de Trabajadores del Perkins,* no. 5 (October 1973), p. 1.

64. "SMATA: Extraordinaria manifestación de repudio de las bases de ese gremio al ataque del burócrata Kloosterman," *SITRAP: Boletín Informativo del Sindicato de Trabajadores del Perkins,* no. 1 (April 1973), p. 3.

65. SMATA archive, SMATA-Córdoba, volume "Volantes Varios, 1972," flier "Movimiento de Recuperación Sindical: A los compañeros del gremio," Córdoba, 1972.

66. SMATA archive, SMATA-Córdoba, volume "Volantes de Agrupaciones Varias, 1973–74," flier "Fraude, con Provocaciones y Balas," Comisión Provisoria del Gremio de la Construcción–Córdoba, Córdoba, October 1973.

67. "Industrias Mecánicas del Estado: La 'perra' Castro perderá su sillón," *Desacuerdo,* no. 16 (December 20, 1972), p. 2. As were most of the local left-wing parties and organizations, by late 1973 the VC was voicing mordant criticisms of Perón and lambasting the rightward veering of his government. At the same time, the VC attempting to appeal to the Peronist rank and file, to convince the them that the real struggle in Argentina was no longer between Peronists and anti-Peronists but between the genuine advocates of workers' interests and the counterrevolutionaries, among whom was Perón himself. SMATA archive, SMATA-Córdoba, volume "Volantes de Agrupaciones Varias, 1973–74," flier "Ante Otro Aniversario del 17 de Octubre," Vanguardia Comunista, Córdoba, October 16, 1973.

68. "¿Qué pasó con las elecciones de ATE?" *Evita: Organo del Peronismo de Base–Regional Córdoba,* no. 14 (September 1973), p. 5. The Peronismo de Base's opposition to the Pacto Social, its support for incorporation of the Fiat workers into the SMATA, its socialist program, and its attacks against the labor bureaucracy put it squarely in the camp of the *clasista* opponents of the rightward shift in the Peronist government.

69. *La Voz del Interior,* October 9, 1973, p. 11.

70. Jelin, "Conflictos laborales en la Argentina, 1973–76," p. 437; U.S. Dept. of State, Papers Related to the Internal Affairs of Argentina, U.S. Embassy in Buenos Aires, "Fired Workers Reinstated in Córdoba," D730143–0057, December 1973.

71. "SMATA Consejo: Directivo Nacional a los Mecánicos Argentinos," *Avance,* no. 21 (September 1973), p. 16. Though the SMATA central was still demanding SMATA jurisdiction over the Concord workers as late as August, it also criticized Salamanca's plebiscite and the *clasista* leadership's supposed use of the affiliation issue to discredit the government. This would be the central's last mention of the Fiat controversy. Shortly thereafter it initiated disciplinary action against the Cordoban local for the March electoral abstention call and its refusal to support Perón's candidacy in the September elections, and the central began its campaign to unseat the *clasistas.* See "Sanción Córdoba: Congreso Mar del Plata," *Avance,* no. 22 (October 1973), p. 27.

72. Interview with Carlos Masera, secretary general of SITRAC 1970 to 1971, Córdoba, July 22, 1987.

73. *La Voz del Interior,* October 26, 1973, p. 9.

74. *Informe,* Servicio de Documentación e Información Laboral, no. 164 (October 1973), p. 263–264.

75. Archives des Usines Renault, Boulogne-Billancourt, Direction des Affaires Internationales 0200, "A. Lucas, Argentine, Finance et Stratégie," file "Politique," letter from Ingeniero Eduardo M. Huergo, President of IKA-Renault, to Dr. Gabriel Martínez, Subsecretary of Foreign Trade, November 7, 1973.

76. "FAS: Balance del V Congreso," *El obrero,* no. 6 (December 14, 1973), pp. 3–5.

77. *La Voz del Interior,* December 8, 1973, p. 11.

78. *Informe,* Servicio de Documentación e Información Laboral, no. 165 (November 1973), pp. 320–321; U.S. Dept. of State, Papers Related to the Internal Affairs of Argentina, U.S. Embassy in Buenos Aires, "Officialist Labor Moves Against Cordoba Trotskyite Unions," D730109–0908, November 1973.

79. *Memoria y Balance,* Sindicato de Motores y Afines del Transporte Automotor, Buenos Aires, 1974, p. 26.

80. U.S. Dept. of State, Papers Related to the Internal Affairs of Argentina, U.S. Embassy in Buenos Aires, "Attempt to Assassinate Labor Leader, Renée Salamanca, Fails," D730137–0208, December 19, 1973; *La Voz del Interior,* December 15, 1973, p. 14.

81. Juan Carlos Torre, "Sindicatos y trabajadores en la Argentina, 1955–76," in *Primera Historia Integral,* vol. 58 (Buenos Aires: Centro Editor de América Latina, 1980), pp. 160–161; Guido Di Tella, *Perón-Perón, 1973–76* (Buenos Aires: Editorial Sudamericana, 1980), pp. 196–204.

82. Di Tella, *Perón-Perón, 1973–76,* pp. 198–199.

83. Torre, "Sindicatos y trabajadores en la Argentina, 1955–76," pp. 162; Jelin, "Conflictos laborales en la Argentina, 1973–76," pp. 433–440.

84. *La Voz del Interior,* January 6, 1974, p. 17; January 10, 1974, p. 11; U.S. Dept. of State, Papers Related to Internal Affairs of Argentina, U.S. Embassy in Buenos Aires, "Orthodox Sector Seizes Control of Cordoba 62 Organizaciones," D730148–0273, December 1973.

85. *La Voz del Interior,* January 20, 1974, p. 13; U.S. Dept. of State, Papers Related to the Internal Affairs of Argentina, U.S. Embassy in Argentina, "Normalization of Cordoba CGT Postponed," D740004–0317, January 1974.

86. *La Voz del Interior,* February 10, 1974, p. 23.
87. U.S. Dept. of State, Papers Related to the Internal Affairs of Argentina, U.S. Embassy in Buenos Aires, "Bus Drivers' Strike in Córdoba has National Repercussions," D730157–0360, January 1974; "National Government and Labor Leadership Counter-Attack in Aftermath of Córdoba Bus Drivers' Strike," D730160–0981, January 1974. The SMATA *clasistas* likened the behavior of the FETAP to the destabilizing efforts of the Chilean truck owners' association during a particularly sensitive moment in Allende's Unidad Popular government; see "Transporte urbano: La negra historia de un caos," *SMATA,* SMATA-Córdoba (April 1, 1974), pp. 4–5.
88. Iris Marta Roldán, *Sindicatos y protesta social en la Argentina, un estudio de caso: El Sindicato de Luz y Fuerza de Córdoba, 1969–1974* (Amsterdam: Center for Latin American Research and Documentation, 1978), pp. 372–373.
89. U.S. Dept. of State, Papers Related to the Internal Affairs of Argentina, U.S. Embassy in Buenos Aires, "Perón on Córdoba Labor Situation," D740078–0603, April 1974.
90. SMATA archive, SMATA-Córdoba, volume "Volantes de Agrupaciones Varias, 1973–74," flier "Informe del Comité de Lucha de Villa Constitución," Villa Constitución, March 1974; Jelin, "Conflictos laborales en la Argentina, 1973–76," p. 437.
91. SMATA archive, SMATA-Córdoba, volume "Volantes de Agrupaciones Varias, 1973–74," flier "A toda la clase obrera," Comisiones Internas de Acindar, Marathom y Metcon, Villa Constitución, April 1974.
92. *Electrum,* no. 448 (April 26, 1974), pp. 4–5.
93. *La Voz del Interior,* April 26, 1974, p. 17.
94. Ibid., March 4, 1974, p. 4; March 6, 1974, p. 9.
95. *Electrum,* June 7, 1974, p. 4.
96. *La Voz del Interior,* March 8, 1974, p. 12.
97. SMATA archive, SMATA-Córdoba, volume "Volantes, Diarios y Revistas, 1973," see PRT party manual "Sindicalismo clasista: Sus perspectivas, sus desviaciones," Partido Revolucionario de los Trabajadores, Córdoba, 1972.
98. "Elecciones generales," *SMATA,* SMATA-Córdoba (April 1, 1974), p. 1. The union announced that "meetings are being held with other progressive, antibureaucratic forces for purposes of forming an opposition slate that will be able to confront the national bureaucracy that Rodríguez heads. In this undertaking, it is of vital importance to reach an agreement with revolutionary Peronism, especially the JTP, given its standing in Buenos Aires province. All our efforts are devoted to the formation of this antibureaucratic front, the only possible way to recover the union from a small clique and put it at the service of the workers."
99. Sánchez, "Estrategias y objetivos de los sindicatos argentinos," p. 115.
100. "Convocatoria a Elecciones," *Avance,* no. 25 (February 1974), p. 39; "Triunfo masivo de la lista verde que propició el 'Movimiento de Unidad Automotriz,'" *Avance,* no. 27 (May 1974), pp. 4–11.
101. *La Voz del Interior,* May 6, 1974, p. 9; U.S. Dept. of State, Papers Related to the Internal Affairs of Argentina, U.S. Embassy in Buenos Aires, "Automobile Workers in Union Elections," D740111–0775, May 1974.

102. *La Voz del Interior,* May 12, 1974, p. 27.
103. Archives des Usines Renault, Boulogne-Billancourt, Direction des Affaires Internationales 0200, 1067 "A. Lucas, Argentine, 1973," file "Comité Argentine," document "Réunion du Comité Général no. 4, May 13, 1974."
104. U.S. Dept. of State, Papers Related to the Internal Affairs of Argentina, U.S. Embassy in Buenos Aires, "Labor Unrest," D740134–0049, May 1974.
105. Interview with Roque Romero.

9. Patria Metalúrgica, Patria Socialista

1. Oscar Anzorena, *Tiempo de violencia y de utopia* (Buenos Aires: Editorial Contrapunto, 1988), p. 291; Ronaldo Munck, *Argentina: From Anarchism to Peronismo: Workers, Unions, Politics, 1855–1985* (London: Zed Books Ltd., 1987), p. 196.
2. María Beatriz Nofal, *Absentee Entrepreneurship and the Dynamics of the Motor Vehicle Industry in Argentina* (New York: Praeger Publishers, 1989), pp. 53–54.
3. Ibid., pp. 37–38.
4. Ibid., p. 47.
5. Interview with Alfredo Martini, secretary general of Cordoban UOM 1974 to 1976, Córdoba, July 27, 1987; *Informe,* Servicio de Documentación e Información Laboral, no. 181 (May 1975), p. 21.
6. Nofal, *Absentee Entrepreneurship,* p. 125.
7. Archives des Usines Renault, Boulogne-Billancourt, Direction des Affaires Internationales 0200, "A. Lucas, Argentine, finances et stratégie," file "Politique," letter from Ing. Eduardo M. Huergo, President of IKA-Renault, to Dr. Gabriel Martínez, Subsecretario de Comercio Exterior, November 7, 1973.
8. SMATA archive, SMATA-Córdoba, volume "Confederación General del Trabajo, 1970–71," CGT open letter "Al pueblo de Córdoba," April 21, 1970. The CGT described the state of the crisis: "We demand immediate and decisive action on the part of the government to combat the catastrophe through which the metallurgical industry is passing . . . workshops closed or working at minimum capacity, layoffs and firings of workers, violation of labor legislation, all testify with eloquence to a stubborn decline." On the crisis in the Corodoban industry and its effects on the UOM, see "El sindicalismo cordobés en la escalada," *Aquí y ahora* 3, no. 26 (May 1971), pp. 11–14.
9. SMATA archive, SMATA-Córdoba, volume "Volantes de Agrupaciones Varias, 1973–74," flier "¿Qué es el Pacto Social y hasta dónde llega su contenido?," Peronismo de Base, Regional Córdoba, January 13, 1974, is an example of the increasingly bitter criticisms of the Peronist government coming from the most important Peronist member in the SMATA *clasista* alliance.
10. "Al peronismo revolucionario," *El obrero,* no. 8 (March 28, 1974), p. 12, is representative of the appeals made to the Peronist left from Marxist organizations during these months.
11. The Peronismo de Base movement, whose slogan at this point was, *Desde las bases peronistas hacia la patria socialista,* did not attend the May Day rally as a protest against the anticipated presence of recognized representatives of the

Peronist right (José López Rega, Raúl Lastiri, and others) alongside Perón. Nevertheless, it still held back from openly criticizing Perón himself; *La Voz del Interior,* May 7, 1974, p. 14.

12. U.S. Dept. of State, Papers Related to the Internal Affairs of Argentina, U.S. Embassy in Buenos Aires, "CGT Congress," D740125–0646, May, 1974; "Perón-CGT Meeting," D740158–0718, June, 1974.

13. *La Voz del Interior,* May 25, 1974, p. 14.

14. "El Movimiento Sindical Combativo frente al quinto aniversario del Cordobazo," *Electrum* 453 (May 31, 1974), p. 6.

15. Juan Carlos Torre, *Los sindicatos en el gobierno, 1973–76* (Buenos Aires: Centro Editor de América Latina, 1983), pp. 118–119.

16. *Informe,* Servicio de Documentación e Información Laboral, no. 173 (July 1974), p. 287.

17. Interview with Roberto Nágera, *clasista* shop steward, Ford-Transax plant 1972 to 1974, Córdoba, July 25, 1991. I was given access to the Renault Industrial Relations Department's collection of political literature from these years. The sheer volume of the material, which was never collected systematically by company officials and which undoubtedly represents only a fraction of what actually appeared in the plants, clearly reflects a situation in which the political debates and the polarization of Argentine political life that were taking place generally in the country were also appearing on the shop floor.

18. Interview with Roberto Nágera; Jorge Brega, *¿Ha muerto el comunismo? El maoismo en la Argentina: Conversaciones con Otto Vargas* (Buenos Aires: Editorial Agora, 1990), pp. 183–208.

19. Archives du Ministère du l'Industrie, Paris, report of French Embassy, Buenos Aires, to Jean Sauvegnargues, Minister of Foreign Affairs, "Le conflit IKA-Renault à Córdoba," August 13, 1974. The French embassy noted that additional union demands, such as the release of all political prisoners, were clearly beyond the company's powers and that the strike was basically intended to discredit the Pacto Social, the Peronist union leadership that supported it, and ultimately the Peronist government, something it astutely perceived was a potentially fatal source of conflict for the Peronist IKA-Renault workers.

20. *Informe,* Servicio de Documentación e Información Laboral, no. 174 (August 1974), p. 326.

21. Renault made its position clear in an open letter to the workers: "A todo el personal," Industrial Relations Department, Renault Argentina, Santa Isabel, July 10, 1974.

22. Archives des Usines Renault, Boulogne-Billancourt, Direction des Services Financiers, file "Financement International, 1974," internal company document "Le Problème Syndical et ses Répercussions Bancaires," August 23, 1974.

23. Ibid., Direction des Affaires Internationales, "A. Lucas, Argentine," file "Comité Argentine," document "Réunion du Comité Général Nº 8," August 23, 1974. The U.S. embassy also expressed concern for the damage the strike was causing to the American auto companies, since Ford, General Motors, and Chrysler all depended on the IKA-Renault forge for their own assembly facto-

ries; U.S. Dept. of State, Papers Related to the Internal Affairs of Argentina, U.S. Embassy in Argentina, "Economic Implications of Conflict in IKA-Renault," D740215–0924, August 1974.

24. *La Voz del Interior,* July 19, 1974, p. 9; July 23, 1974, p. 13.

25. Ibid., July 30, 1974, p. 9; August 4, 1974, p. 25.

26. *Informe,* Servicio de Documentación e Información Laboral, no. 174 (August 1974), p. 328; U.S. Dept. of State, Papers Related to the Internal Affairs of Argentina, U.S. Embassy in Buenos Aires, "Labor Implications of Closure of IKA-Renault Automobile Plant," D740214–0421, August 1974.

27. U.S. Dept. of State, Papers Related to the Internal Affairs of Argentina, U.S. Embassy in Buenos Aires, "Cordoba Union Defies Ministry of Labor Ultimatum," D740216–0286, August 1974. Salamanca stated, "There may be an intervention of the union, but we are going to mobilize the workers and Rodríguez is not going to be allowed in, and that leaves him two options, with the workers or against them . . . the status of the labor ministry is that of the company and any decision in favor of arbitration is unilateral because we were never consulted. We totally reject any verticalist attempts within the labor movement," *Córdoba,* August 6, 1974, p. 2.

28. Gilles Gleyze, "La Régie Nationale des Usines Renault et L'Amerique Latine depuis 1945: Brésil, Argentine, Colombie," M.A. thesis, Université de Paris X—Nanterre, 1988, p. 175.

29. *Memoria y Balance,* Sindicato de Mecánicos y Afines del Transporte Automotor, Buenos Aires, 1974–75, pp. 50–52. In one of many telegrams it sent to the Cordoban local in these weeks, the central warned, "It is necessary to emphasize how your attitude hurts the interests of the workers, the risk that the Cordoban local has put the entire union in as we are faced with the threat of a loss of our *personería gremial* which will leave thousands of auto workers all over the country without union representation."

30. *Informe,* Servicio de Documentación e Información Laboral, no. 174 (August 1974), pp. 330–331; U.S. Dept. of State, Papers Related to the Internal Affairs of Argentina, U.S. Embassy in Buenos Aires, "National Automobile Workers Union Intervenes Cordoba Local," D740221–1148, August 1974.

31. "Una seccional, Córdoba: Plenarios, asambleas, congresos, resoluciones," *Avance,* no. 29 (September 1974), pp. 4–9; *La Voz del Interior,* August 8, 1974, p. 9.

32. Elizabeth Jelin, "Conflictos laborales en la Argentina, 1973–76," *Revista mexicana de Sociología,* no. 2 (April–June 1978), pp. 442–443; Judith Evans, Paul Hoeffel, and Daniel James, "Reflections on Argentine Autoworkers and Their Unions," in R. Kronish and K. Mericle, eds., *The Political Economy of the Latin American Motor Vehicle Industry* (Cambridge, Mass.: MIT Press, 1984), p. 153.

33. *Clarín,* August 9, 1974, p. 16.

34. Christopher Knowles, "Revolutionary Trade Unionism in Argentina: Interview with Agustín Tosco," *Radical America* 9 (May–June 1975), p. 29.

35. Iris Marta Roldán, *Sindicatos y protesta social en la Argentina, un estudio de caso: El Sindicato de Luz y Fuerza de Córdoba, 1969–1974* (Ambserdam: Center for Latin American Research and Documentation, 1978), pp. 440–441.

36. *Informe,* Servicio de Documentación e Información Laboral, no. 174 (August 1974), pp. 331–332.
37. *La Voz del Interior,* September 24, 1974, p. 11.
38. *Informe,* Servicio de Documentación e Información Laboral, no. 174 (August 1974), p. 333.
39. *Córdoba,* August 24, 1974, p. 3.
40. Jelin, "Conflictos laborales en la Argentina, 1973–76," pp. 442–443; *La Voz del Interior,* September 21, 1974, p. 13; U.S. Dept. of State, Papers Related to the Internal Affairs of Argentina, U.S. Embassy in Buenos Aires, "Cordoba Automobile Workers Strike," D740267–0940, September 1974.
41. Ignacio González Janzen, *La Triple-A* (Buenos Aires: Editorial Contrapunto, 1986), pp. 128–129; *La Voz del Interior,* September 12, 1974, p. 9.
42. *La Voz del Interior,* September 17, 1974, p. 16; U.S. Dept. of State, Papers Related to the Internal Affairs of Argentina, U.S. Embassy in Buenos Aires, "Legalist Peronist Labor Leader Assassinated," D740378–0478, September 1974.
43. Knowles, "Revolutionary Trade Unionism in Córdoba: Interview with Agustín Tosco," p. 34.
44. *La Voz del Interior,* September 24, 1974, p. 11.
45. U.S. Dept. of State, Papers Related to the Internal Affairs of Argentina, U.S. Embassy in Buenos Aires, "Arrest Order for Tosco and Salamanca," D740289–0078, October 1974.
46. "SMATA recibió la visita del Gobernador Interventor de Córdoba, Compañero Brigadier Mayor Raúl Oscar Lacabanne," *Avance,* no. 30 (October 1974), pp. 40–41.
47. *Clarín,* November 8, 1974, p. 15.
48. *Electrum,* no. 469 (September 20, 1974), p. 2; *La Voz del Interior,* September 16, 1974, p. 6.
49. Roldán, *Sindicatos y protesta social,* p. 402. The government arrested Ongaro and took control of the Buenos Aires print workers' union on the same day.
50. Ibid., pp. 403–404.
51. U.S. Department of State, Papers Related to the Internal Affairs of Argentina, U.S. Embassy in Buenos Aires, "Terrorism in Córdoba," D750244–0699, July 1975.
52. Jelin, "Conflictos laborales en la Argentina, 1973–76," pp. 441–442; Torre, *Los sindicatos en el gobierno, 1973–76,* pp. 118–119.
53. Agustín Tosco, "Carta a los compañeros de Villa Constitución," in Alberto J. Pla, ed., *Historia de América, Proclamas y Documentos,* vol. 3, no. 46 (Buenos Aires: Centro Editor de América Latina, 1985), pp. 164–168.
54. U.S. Dept. of State, Papers Related to the Internal Affairs of Argentina, U.S. Embassy in Buenos Aires, "Villa Constitución Strike," D750159–0118, May 1975; "La lucha por la democracia sindical en la UOM de Villa Constitución," *Hechos y protagonistas de las luchas obreras argentinas,* no. 7 (Buenos Aires: Editorial Experiencia, 1984–85), pp. 50–75.
55. *Informe,* Servicio de Documentación e Información Laboral, no. 185 (July 1975), pp. 52–69; U.S. Dept. of State, Papers Related to the Internal Affairs of Argentina, U.S. Embassy in Buenos Aires, "Labor's Confrontation with Gov-

ernment," D750228–0931, July 1975; "Renewed Strike Activity Declared Subversive," D750244–0529, July 1975.

56. *La Voz del Interior,* June 13, 1975, p. 13. The *"coordinadoras"* have been extensively studied by André Thompson in "Labour Struggles and Political Conflict, Argentina: The General Strike of 1975 and the Crisis of Peronism through an Historical Perspective," M.A. thesis, Institute of Social Studies, The Hague, 1982.

57. *La Voz del Interior,* June 26, 1975, p. 9; October 14, 1975, p. 15.

58. SMATA archive, SMATA-Córdoba, volume "Volantes Varios 1975," union communiqué "A todos los compañeros de planta," Comisión Normalizadora, SMATA-Córdoba, May 8, 1975. Like the government, the SMATA central also saw the *clasistas'* hand in the labor unrest in Villa Constitución: "What is happening is that the people in Córdoba want to exploit the situation existing in Villa Constitución. But the SMATA is not going to allow that. We'll never allow that. What's more, Salamanca and his people, never again in Córdoba. That's all over"; "La verdad sobre lo que ocurre en Córdoba," *Avance,* no. 33 (May–June 1975), p. 29.

59. SMATA archive, SMATA-Córdoba, volume "Volantes Varios 1975," union communiqué "A los compañeros en el aniversario del Cordobazo," Comisión Normalizadora, SMATA-Córdoba, May 29, 1975. The union missive stated, "The historical fact is that in the Cordobazo, the People were the true protagonist, a people who were, are, and always will be Peronist. For that reason we can claim that the Cordobazo was Peronist."

60. Archives des Usines Renault, Boulogne-Billancourt, Direction des Affaires Internationales 0200, 1069 "A. Lucas, Argentine," file "Rapports Missions Argentine," letter from IKA-Renault to Alfred Lucas, head of Latin American Division, Renault, October 4, 1974, Córdoba.

61. Ibid., 1066 "A. Lucas, Argentine, finances et stratégie," file "Stratégie," document "Confidential Report of M. Carlier for A. Lucas," April 15, 1975. The report states, "Output will correct itself the day the cars start to come off the line complete. At any rate, it is useless at the present moment to take a hard line with the personnel since the conditions that they have to operate under are such that they have every reason not to work."

62. Ibid., Direction des Services Financiers 0764, 108 "IKA 1975," letter from Jacques Graviere, Treasurer, IKA-Renault to Banco Central, Buenos Aires, October 16, 1975.

63. The first rumblings with regard to the jurisdiction issue appear in early 1975; they recur with growing intensity thereafter "Encuadramiento Sindical," *Avance,* no. 31 (January 1975), p. 30.

64. SMATA archive, SMATA-Córdoba, volume "Volantes Varios, 1975," union communiqué "A todos los compañeros," Comisión Normalizadora, SMATA-Córdoba, November 19, 1975.

65. Renée Salamanca, "A los compañeros mecánicos," in *Hechos y protagonistas de las luchas obreras argentinas,* no. 1 (Buenos Aires: Editorial Experiencia, 1984), p. 24.

66. The details of Tosco's final days are based on the testimony of Luz y Fuerza activists and also that of Juan Canelles, who had been a communist union ac-

tivist in the Cordoban construction workers' union at the time of the Cordobazo and was Tosco's close personal friend and the go-between in arranging
the ERP's transport of Tosco to Buenos Aires.

67. *La Voz del Interior,* November 8, 1975, pp. 15 and 17; U.S. Dept. of State, Papers Related to the Internal Affairs of Argentina, U.S. Embassy in Argentina,
"Leftist Labor Leader Tosco Dead," D750388–0490, November 1975; Tosco's
obituary is given in Christopher Knowles, "On the Death of Agustín Tosco,"
Radical America, vol. 10 (March–April 1976), pp. 71–74.

68. Roldán, *Sindicatos y protesta social,* p. 413.

69. Archives des Usines Renault, Boulogne-Billancourt, Direction Juridique 0734,
3686 file "Argentine: Etudes sur IKA-Renault," letter from Marcel Calier to M.
Lucas, April 30, 1976. Renault abandoned the idea of the IME-IKA merger
when it became apparent that the air force was unwilling to abandon its traditional bailiwick and the Peronist government was not prepared to make the
investment in the IME works necessary to convert it to the manufacture of
motors for the Renault plants as the French envisioned it. The decision to
abandon Argentina was forestalled as the company placed its hope in the willingness of the new military government to reverse the deleterious Peronist
legislation with regard to the automobile industry and stabilize the economy.

70. Ibid., Direction des Services Financiers 0764, 276 Finance Internationale, "Argentine, 1976," letter from Renault Argentina, S.A., to A. Lucas, Buenos Aires,
January 22, 1976. "We've been helped by a series of strikes that have had the
effect of practically adjusting our production levels to our sales and of therefore avoiding significant expenditures by the company."

71. "Un objetivo logrado," *Avance,* Extra (July 1975), p. 9.

72. Archives des Usines Renault, Boulogne-Billancourt, Direction des Affaires Internationales 0200, 1069 "A. Lucas, Argentine," file "Rapports Missions Argentine," internal IKA-Renault company document "Renovación Convenios Col-
ectivos de Trabajo," June 27, 1975. Just a week before the Rodrigazo, the
company noted this contradiction: "With regard to the labor situation, there
exists a strong rivalry between the UOM and the SMATA to obtain better
agreements, a fact which causes delay and difficulty in negotiations." The
SMATA central berated the shop floor activists for exploiting this contradiction and undermining its efforts to strengthen its hand in its struggle with the
UOM. See "A los trabajadores mecánicos y a la opinión pública del país," *Avance,* Extra (July 1975), p. 9.

73. U.S. Dept. of State, Papers Related to the Internal Affairs of Argentina, U.S.
Embassy in Buenos Aires, "Representation Issue Threatens UOM-SMATA
Conflict," D750407–0598, November 1975; "SMATA-UOM Conflict Worsens,"
D750419–0231, November 1975; "Conflicto de encuadramiento sindical," *Avance,* no. 36 (February 1976), pp. 48–73. The new military government, to prevent the consolidation of union power and as part of a program to weaken the
labor movement generally, eventually overturned the Labor Ministry's award
and restored the autoworkers' representation to the SMATA. The automobile
companies had opposed the UOM jurisdiction, since Miguel's union, having
taken full advantage of its close relationship with the government, had better
contracts and higher wages than the SMATA workers. Moreover, with collec-

tive bargaining agreements now centralized, the threat of rank-and-file movements such as those that had taken place in Córdoba appeared more remote.

10. Work and Politics in Córdoba

1. A detailed analysis of the IKA-Renault and Fiat plants has utility beyond explaining the dynamic of Cordoban working class politics. By 1975, Fiat was Argentina's second largest company in terms of annual sales, while IKA-Renault was seventh. Among the top seven, the remaining five companies were all state-owned enterprises (Yacimientos Petrolíferos Fiscales; Empresa Nacional de Telecomunicaciones; Servicios Eléctricos del Gran Buenos Aires; SOMISA, the public steel company; and Gas del Estado). Fiat and IKA-Renault's status as Argentina's leading private companies thus made them important barometers of what was occurring throughout the country in terms of national economic policy, labor relations, and industrial politics, although there were also conditions unique to Córdoba that made their histories exceptional.
2. Marjorie T. Stanley, "The Interrelationships of Economic Forces and Labor Relations in the Automobile Industry," Ph.D. diss., Indiana University, 1953; John Humphrey, "Labour Use and Labour Control in the Brazilian Automobile Industry," *Capital and Class,* no. 12 (Winter 1980), pp. 48–49.
3. Rhys Owen Jenkins, *Dependent Industrialization in Latin America: The Automotive Industry in Argentina, Chile, and Mexico* (New York: Praeger Publishers, 1977), p. 133. Jenkins notes the slowdown in Argentine automotive production after the mid-1960s. While production grew at an annual average of 27.2 percent between 1960 and 1965, it fell to 6.4 percent between 1965 and 1973.
4. Jenkins, *Dependent Industrialization in Latin America,* p. 63. To serve this new market, both IKA-Renault and Fiat increased significantly the number of models they produced. IKA-Renault gradually expanded from a six-model line in 1959 to twenty-three-model line in 1967, and Fiat went from a three-model line in 1960 to a sixteen-model line in 1972; María Beatriz Nofal, *Absentee Entrepreneurship and the Dynamics of the Motorvehicle Industry in Argentina* (New York: Praeger Publishers, 1989), p. 40. The companies sometimes adopted this model-diversification policy with great reluctance and as a strictly defensive measure. In a 1968 Fiat company report, for example, the Italian multinational stated that "the expansion of the model line is not only necessary to diversify our production but perhaps chiefly and peremptorily so as not to lose out to our competitors (avoiding having others beat us in the launching of new models) and therefore to dissuade them from moving into models with characteristics similar to what we already manufacture." Archivio Storico di Fiat, Turin, file "Planificazione e Controllo," Fondo CG89-XVIII/9/C, document, "Previsioni Economico-Finanziarie delle Aziende Fiat in Argentina per il Triennio 1969–1971," July 11, 1968, p. 13.
5. Nofal, *Absentee Entrepreneurship,* p. 42.
6. Harry C. Katz, *Shifting Gears: Changing Labor Relations in the U.S. Automobile Industry* (Cambridge: MIT Press, 1985), pp. 22–23.

7. Ian Roxborough, *Union Politics in Mexico: The Case of the Automobile Industry* (Cambridge: Cambridge University Press, 1984); John Humphrey, *Capitalist Control and Workers' Struggle in the Brazilian Automobile Industry* (Princeton, N.J.: Princeton University Press, 1983). Automobile plants cannot simply reduce production if they are to remain profitable. The need to run machinery at full capacity is the result of the high level of capitalization in an automotive plant. Defraying production costs entails getting the most out of the machinery, and the workers, in periods of peak demand. Companies prefer to run machines at full capacity, build up stock to certain levels, and then reduce their labor costs, through layoffs if possible, and if not, through reducing work days, through the generic speedup, and through generally fiddling with their labor bill.

8. Archives des Usines Renault, Boulogne-Billancourt, Direction des Affaires Internationales, 0200, 1067 "A. Lucas, Argentine 1973," company report, "Situation de IKA-Renault au 1er Janvier 1971."

9. Ibid., Direction Juridique 0263, 4396 "Argentina-IKA Renault," file "IKA, 1974."

10. Ibid., Direction des Services Financiers 0764, 113 file "Finance International," document "Grèves de IKA-Renault à Córdoba," August 28, 1968. A recent study of Renault's history in Latin America contends that the company's policy of employment stability and its rejection of hire and fire practices were considered necessary by Renault to simultaneously attack its labor costs and generally weaken the power of the SMATA in the Santa Isabel plants. See Gilles Gleyze, "La Régie Nationale des Usines et l'Amerique Latine depuis 1945: Brésil, Argentine, Colombie," M.A. thesis, Université de Paris X—Nanterre, 1988, p. 181.

11. Archives des Usines Renault, Boulogne-Billancourt, Direction des Affaires Internationales 0200, 1069 "A. Lucas, Argentine," file "Rapports Missions Argentine," company report "Argentine—Activités Industrielles," January 1973, p. 2.

12. Mónica B. Gordillo, "Características de los sindicatos líderes de Córdoba en los 60: El ámbito del trabajo y la dimensión cultural," Annual Report, Consejo de Investigaciones Científicas y Tecnológicas de la Provincia de Córdoba, 1991, p. 49.

13. José Nun, "Despidos en la industria automotriz argentina: Estudio de un caso de superpoblación flotante," *Revista mexicana de sociología* 40, no. 1 (1978), pp. 81–90.

14. Archivio Storico, Fiat S.p.A., Turin, file "Argentine-Progetto-Viaggi-1947–1958," Fondo "ex CM13"-III/9/C, documents "Viaggio nella Repubblica Argentina—Visita alla Fabbrica Fiat 'Grandes Motores Diesel' e alla Fabbrica 'Someca Concord'" and "Visita alla Fabrica 'Industrias Kaiser Argentina,' 1958"; U.S. Dept. of State, Papers Related to the Internal Affairs of Argentina, U.S. Embassy in Buenos Aires, "Fiat Proposes to Manufacture Automobiles in Argentina," 835.3331/11–2458, November 24, 1958; "Fiat Car and Truck Manufacturing Investment Approved," 835.3331/9–2959, September 29, 1959. Fiat began automotive production in 1960 on the basis of the promising market conditions it perceived in the late 1950s.

15. Archives des Usines Renault, Boulogne-Billancourt, Direction Juridique 0734, 3400 file "Situation IKA," document "Visite à IKA, à Buenos Aires et à Córdoba les 5, 6, 7, 8, 9 Décembre 1966."

16. Stephen Meyer, *The Five Dollar Day: Labor Management and Social Control in the Ford Motor Company, 1908–1921* (Albany: State University of New York Press, 1981), pp. 80–85, 108–121; David Gartman, *Auto Slavery: The Labor Process in the American Automobile Industry, 1897–1950* (New Brunswick, N.J.: Rutgers University Press, 1986), pp. 203–208; John Humphrey, "Labor in the Brazilian Motor Vehicle Industry," *The Political Economy of the Latin American Motor Vehicle Industry* (Cambridge, Mass.: MIT Press, 1984), pp. 109–113. The fact that the automobile industry's control over labor was exercised through a high-wage strategy meant that there was little incentive to hire women as a cheaper labor force for the unskilled tasks required in the production process and explains the historically low numbers of women autoworkers. See Ruth Milkman, "Rosie the Riveter Revisited: Management's Postwar Purge of Women Automobile Workers," in Nelson Lichtenstein and Stephen Meyer, eds., *On the Line: Essays in the History of Auto Work* (Urbana and Chicago: University of Illinois Press, 1989), p. 132.

17. William Heston McPherson, *Labor Relations in the Automobile Industry* (Washington D.C.: Brookings Institution, 1940), pp. 71–72.

18. Gartman, *Auto Slavery,* p. 55.

19. McPherson, *Labor Relations in the Automobile Industry,* p. 146.

20. These broad categories do not give a full understanding of the myriad practices that are included in management's use of the speedup. As one scholar of labor relations in the automobile industry has noted, "The question of the speed-up is not merely a matter of the speed of the assembly line. It is affected also by the number of employees working on the line and the number of relief men available to give the men an occasional respite from their task. Many other possible practices are classed by union officials as types of the speed-up. Among these are: failure to leave an occasional blank space on the assembly line to give the faster workers a brief pause and the slower ones an opportunity to catch up; failure in timing a job to make sufficient allowance for the handling of materials and other actions that enter in when the task is performed continuously over a long period of time; refusal to inform the worker of the results of the time study in the hope that the standard can be set higher on the basis of the performance; providing materials that are harder to work on than those used in the timing of the job; and replacement of a broken gear with one of a different ratio." McPherson, *Labor Relations in the Automobile Industry,* p. 143. Another scholar has gone so far as to state that the generic speedup could also be considered, under certain circumstances, to encompass grievances about pay: "Workers judged the adequacy of their wages in relation to the work demanded of them, thus calculating a common-sense rate of exploitation. And most workers judged their pay to be inadequate for the intensity of work they were forced to perform." Gartman, *Auto Slavery,* p. 260.

21. Gartman, *Auto Slavery,* p. 177.

22. Ely Chinoy, "Manning the Machines: The Assembly Line Worker," in Peter

Berger, ed., *The Human Shape of Work: Studies in the Sociology of Occupations* (New York: Macmillan, 1958).

23. Gartman, *Auto Slavery,* pp. 196–200; Al Nash, "Job Stratification: A Critique," in B. J. Widick, ed., *Auto Work and Its Discontents* (Baltimore: Johns Hopkins University Press, 1976), pp. 76–77; Nelson Lichtenstein, "The Man in the Middle: A Social History of Automobile Foremen," in Nelson Lichtenstein and Stephen Meyer, eds., *On the Line: Essays in the History of Auto Work* (Urbana and Chicago: University of Illinois Press, 1989), pp. 155–158.

24. H. Benyon, "Controlling the Line," in Tom Clarke and Laurie Clements, eds., *Trade Unions under Capitalism* (Atlantic Highlands, N.J.: Humanities Press, 1978), p. 253. "The position of the steward in the car plant is rooted in this clash . . . the day to day life was virtually one endless battle over control. The establishment of a steward in a particular section was clearly related to the attempt by the workers to establish job control in that section. If the steward wasn't up to the job he was replaced, or he stood down leaving the section without a steward for awhile."

25. The following discussion of shop floor politics in the *clasista* movements addresses only conditions in the IKA-Renault plants and the Fiat Concord factory. The other SMATA-affiliated plants (Ford-Transax, Thompson Ramco, the two Ilasa factories, and Fiat Grandes Motores Diesel) and the Fiat Materfer factory are not included in the analysis. The availability of source material for IKA-Renault and Fiat Concord, as well their importance both as the automobile plants that contained the largest concentrations of the local automotive proletariat, and as the epicenters of the *clasista* movements would seem to justify this focus.

26. Jenkins, *Dependent Industrialization in Latin America,* p. 27.

27. Gleyze, "La Régie Nationale des Usines et l'Amerique Latin depuis 1945," p. 65, pp. 135–136.

28. Archives des Usines Renault, Boulogne-Billancourt, Direction des Usines à l'Etranger 1290, 458 file "IKA," report of Pierre Souleil to Renault, November 29, 1960; Direction Juridique 0734, 3400 file "Argentine," letter from M. Maison to IKA president James McCloud, December 16, 1965; Direction des Usines à l'Etranger 0295, 458 file "IKA," report of Lucien Combes to Renault, June 12, 1961, pp. 3–4.

29. Ibid., Direction des Usines à l'Etranger 0295, 458 file "IKA," report of Pierre Souleil to Renault, June 22, 1961; William H. Form, *Blue-Collar Stratification: Autoworkers in Four Countries* (Princeton, N.J.: Princeton University Press, 1976), pp. 42–43; Nofal, *Absentee Entrepreneurship,* pp. 90–94.

30. Letter from James McCloud, former president of Industrias Kaiser Argentina, September 4, 1989. All the IKA collective bargaining agreements between 1956 and 1967 support McCloud's claim that the company held firm on the issue of labor flexibility and that the Peronist leadership of the SMATA traded off job classifications for good wages, employment benefits, and job stability. The relative weakness of the shop stewards in the Santa Isabel plants during the IKA years, compared with the power they would wield after Renault acquired control of the company in 1967, had much to do with the lack of strict job classifications. After 1969, and especially during the

years of the *clasista* leadership of the union, shop stewards had an important new role on the shop floor in monitoring company compliance with job classifications, and, as will be discussed, they repeatedly filed grievances on classification violations in a production process that was now basically Fordist. The great increase in the number of job subclassifications can be found in any of the IKA-Renault agreements from the early 1970s. See, for example, SITRAC archive, file B-2 "Paritarias y Convenios, 1971," document BX-3 "IKA-Renault/SMATA: Convenio Colectivo de Trabajo, 1971–72," pp. 23–69.

31. Gleyze, "La Régie Nationale des Usines et l'Amerique Latine depuis 1945," p. 94. In 1961, the Renault cars represented 35.9 percent of IKA's sales. By 1964 the figure had risen to 41.7 percent and by 1966 to 54.2 percent. As more of its cars were being built in Córdoba, Renault's involvement in company affairs increased, and little by little it asserted control over management until it finally purchased the company outright in October 1967.

32. Archives des Usines Renault, Boulogne-Billancourt, Direction des Usines à l'Etranger 0070, 216 file "Argentine: 1970 à 1975," document "Rapport de gestion, 1971–72, IKA-Renault."

33. Ibid., Direction des Services Financiers 0764, 113 file Finance International "Memorandum: Augmentation du capital d'IKA," document "Note complémentaire au résumé du rapport de mission de M. M. Pierre du Sert et Borghetti," September 11, 1968. The company reported that three-fourths of IKA's borrowing was being done outside the Argentine banking system, in the black market. These *"societés financières"* were reputedly imposing burdensome terms, but apparently better ones than could be obtained from Argentine banks.

34. Gleyze, "La Régie Nationale des Usines et l'Amerique Latine depuis 1945," p. 61.

35. Nofal, *Absentee Entrepreneurship,* pp. 95–96.

36. Patrick Fridenson, *Histoire des usines Renault: Naissance de la grande entreprise* (Paris: Le Seuil, 1972), pp. 167–175.

37. Gartman, *Auto Slavery,* 102–127; Stephen Meyer, "The Persistence of Fordism: Workers and Technology in the American Automobile Industry, 1900–1960," in Nelson Lichtenstein and Stephen Meyer, eds., *On the Line: Essays in the History of Auto Work* (Urbana and Chicago: University of Illinois Press, 1989), pp. 84–88. Meyer notes that in the American automobile industry, the machine tool innovations before 1929 were motivated by management's concern to get control of an increasingly belligerent labor force and were followed by a period of technological dormancy in the depression of the early 1930s, when workers offered little shop floor resistance to management. Similarly, the development of automated machinery after 1945 was a response to the established power of the UAW and the rebirth of worker opposition and industrial unionism; it was an effort by management to regain absolute control over production.

38. Archives des Usines Renault, Boulogne-Billancourt, Direction des Services Financiers 0764, 113 file "Finance Internationale," document "Argentine: Engineering et Assistance Technique," 1974.

39. Gleyze, "La Régie Nationale des Usines et l'Amerique Latine depuis 1945," pp. 77–78.
40. Archives des Usines Renault, Boulogne-Billancourt, Direction des Services Financiers 0764, 113, file "Finance International," document "Investissements Programme 118: Commandes des Machines," May 15, 1968. In the first order that the company made to replace old machinery in the Kaiser plants, it requested twenty-five specialized machine tools but nineteen additional all-purpose tools.
41. Ibid., Direction des Affaires Internationales 0295, 717, file "Argentine," document "Argentine: Vente de biens d'équipement et d'engineering à IKA-Renault," January 6, 1969; Direction Juridique 0263, 4444 file "IKA," document "Augmentation du capital d'IKA-Renault," November 6, 1970; Direction des Usines à l'Etranger, 0070, 216, file "Argentine: 1970 à 1975," document "Compte Rendu d'Activité 1968–1969: IKA-Renault."
42. Ibid., Direction des Affaires Internationales 0295, 715 file "Constructions-Installations-Equipements-Lay Out et Capacité de Production, 1963–1970," document "Etude IKA-Argentine," February 22, 1968.
43. Ibid., Direction des Affaires Internationales 0200, 1070 "A. Lucas, Argentine, 1973," file "Perdriel S.A.," document "Perdriel S.A. Situation au 1er Mars 1973."
44. IKA-Renault, *Informe Mensual,* July 1973, pp. 29–30. Renault reported that work stoppages led to decreases in production of the following percentages in these departments: 25 percent in assembly, 25 percent in chassis paint departments, and between 20 percent and 60 percent in production, depending on the component produced.
45. Nofal, *Absentee Entrepreneurship,* pp. 98–99, 125–126. Only the opposition of the provincial government and the local parts manufacturers kept Fiat from moving its Grandes Motores Diesel plant, the SMATA-affiliated manufacturer of diesel engines, to Santa Fe as well; *La Voz del Interior,* July 18, 1974, p. 15.
46. The *premio de la producción* also served to deflect workers' hostility away from the company and toward fellow workers. Under this system, one line frequently would be at odds with another for its failure to keep the pace necessary to win the bonus, and even within lines animosities developed between the faster workers who were able to maintain the production rhythms and the slower workers who lagged behind. Elimination of the *premio* system was one of the principal demands presented in the *clasista*'s collective bargaining proposal, never accepted by the company, that sought to bring Fiat closer to the standards and practices of the other automobile firms. SITRAC archive, "Convenio colectivo de trabajo para el personal de la empresa Fiat Concord S.A.I.C.," Córdoba, May 1972.
47. *SITRAC: Boletín del Sindicato Trabajadores Concord,* vol. 1, no. 1, (January 13, 1971), p. 2, discusses the problems with the *premio de la producción,* the *acople de máquina,* and working conditions generally in the Concord plant. The *acople de máquina* was one of many company practices that the *clasistas* learned through Italian trade unionists had been abolished in Fiat's Italian plants. Unlike the *premio de la producción,* which Fiat agreed in principle to

phase out of the plant but never did, the *clasistas* managed to have the *acople de máquina* practice abolished. However, following the October 1971 suppression of SITRAC-SITRAM, and as part of the reaction against the workers, Fiat began to double up the machinery responsibilities again.

48. Gianfranco Guidi, Alberto Bronzino, and Luigi Germanetto, *Fiat: Struttura aziendale e organizzazione dell sfruttamento* (Milan: Gabriel Mazzotta editore, 1974), pp. 165–166; Giuseppe Bonazzi, *In una fabbrica di motori: Organizzazione del lavoro, potere padronale e lotte operaie* (Milan: Giangiacomo Feltrinelli editore, 1975).

49. David Montgomery, *The Fall of the House of Labor: The Workplace, the State, and American Labor Activism, 1865–1925* (Cambridge: Cambridge University Press, 1987), p. 440.

50. Duccio Bigazzi, "Management and Labor in Italy, 1906–1945," in Steven Tolliday and Jonathan Zeitlin, eds., *The Automobile Industry and Its Workers* (Cambridge: Polity Press, 1986), p. 86. As in the British automobile industry, the Fiat workers initially supported piece rates as a means of broadening the union's shop floor authority but opposed them once management had established unilateral authority in establishing those rates.

51. Bigazzi, "Management and Labor in Italy, 1906–1945," p. 87.

52. Guidi, Bronzino, and Germanetto, *Fiat*, pp. 165–166; Giovanni Contini, "The Rise and Fall of Shop Floor Bargaining at Fiat, 1945–1980," in Steven Tolliday and Jonathan Zeitlin, eds., *The Automobile Industry and Its Workers* (Cambridge: Polity Press, 1986), pp. 144–146.

53. Giovanni Contini, "Politics, Law and Shop Floor Bargaining in Postwar Italy," in Steven Tolliday and Jonathan Zeitlin, eds., *Shop Floor Bargaining and the State* (Cambridge: Cambridge University Press, 1985), p. 210.

54. Guidi, Bronzino, and Germanetto, *Fiat*, pp. 92–98; Vincente Comito, *La Fiat: Tra crisi e ristrutturazione* (Rome: Editori Riuniti, 1982), p. 237–242.

55. Gartman, *Auto Slavery*, p. 281; Patrick Fridenson, "Automobile Workers in France and Their Work, 1914–1983," in S. L. Kaplan and C. J. Koepp, eds., *Work in France* (Ithaca, N.Y.: Cornell University Press, 1986), p. 540.

56. Comito, *La Fiat*, pp. 237–242.

57. Steven Tolliday and Jonathan Zeitlin, "Between Fordism and Flexibility," in Tolliday and Zeitlin, eds., *The Automobile Industry and Its Workers* (Cambridge: Polity Press, 1986), p. 4.

58. Sylvie Van de Casteele-Schweitzer, "Management and Labor in France, 1914–1939," in Steven Tolliday and Jonathan Zeitlin, eds., *The Automobile Industry and Its Workers* (Cambridge: Polity Press, 1986), pp. 72–73; J. P. Depretto and Sylvie Van de Casteele-Schweitzer, *Le Communisme à l'usine: Vie ouvrière et le mouvement ouvrier chez Renault, 1920–1939* (Paris: Roubaix, 1984).

59. Fridenson, "Automobile Workers in France and Their Work," pp. 534–536.

60. Nofal sees this as a tendency applicable to the entire industry (Nofal, *Absentee Entrepreneurship,* pp. 51–52) but it seems to have been more pronounced among the Cordoban companies. None of the Buenos Aires–based firms undertook a rationalization program as deep as Renault did in its newly acquired Kaiser plants. Nor were any companies as harsh in their dealings with

their labor force as Fiat was, in part because their workers' membership in the powerful SMATA prevented it. Strikes in 1973 in the Ford, GM, Chrysler, Peugeot, and Mercedes-Benz plants over work-related issues—speedups, company disregard for production classifications, and hazardous working conditions—offer proof enough that if these companies had fewer problems with their labor force between 1966 and 1972 than did IKA-Renault and Fiat, it was due to the advantages they enjoyed in the Argentine market rather than to any fundamental differences in their management philosophy or to the relations between capital and labor in those companies. Nevertheless, even during the great wave of strikes in the Buenos Aires–based firms from 1973 to 1976, wages, not working conditions, were the principal cause of work stoppages.

61. William H. Form, "Technology and Social Behavior of Workers in Four Countries: A Socio-technical Perspective," *American Sociological Review,* vol. 37, (December 1972), pp. 727–728.

62. William H. Form, "The Internal Stratification of the Working Class: System Involvement of Auto Workers in Four Countries," *American Sociological Review* 38 (December 1973), pp. 700–702; Form, *Blue-Collar Stratification,* pp. 78–80.

63. Form, *Blue-Collar Stratificiation,* pp. 160–163. In 1969 American sociologist William H. Form conducted a series of extensive surveys in automobile plants in diverse countries, one of which was the IKA-Renault complex in Córdoba. The data from Form's surveys appeared in a number of publications in the 1970s and comprise a rich corpus of material on the origins, stratification, and attitudes of the various labor forces. Coincidentally another American sociologist, Richard P. Gale, had conducted surveys of his own in the IKA-Renault plants in early 1966. His findings were published in "Industrial Development and the Blue-Collar Worker in Argentina," *International Journal of Comparative Sociology,* vol. 10, no. 1–2 (March–June 1969), and provide a useful complement to Form's data (see pp. 138–150).

64. Form, "The Internal Stratification of the Working Class," pp. 700–705; Form, *Blue-Collar Stratification,* p. 195. Form characterizes the IKA's workers' involvement in community organizations as "fairly high," a statement in fact belied by his own figures. His survey showed that only 36 percent of the respondents belonged to a community organization and a mere 15 percent were active participants in the same. The latter was the lowest such figure for all the companies he surveyed, and contrasts with the markedly higher rates of union affiliation and involvement in union affairs for the IKA-Renault workers in those years (reflected in indexes such as the 85 percent average participation in union elections, among others).

65. Gordillo, "Características de los sindicatos líderes de Córdoba en los 60," pp. 31–32, 84–90.

66. SMATA archive, SMATA-Córdoba, volume "Volantes, Comunicados y Diarios del SMATA, 1969," flier "Departamento 105: Incentivación a costa de la explotación obrera, no!" March 22, 1969.

67. "Problemas en Chapa," *SMATA,* SMATA-Córdoba, vol. 6, no. 39 (December 15, 1969), p. 15.

68. Daniel James, *Resistance and Integration: Peronism and the Argentine Working Class, 1946–1973* (Cambridge: Cambridge University Press, 1988), pp. 135–143.

69. The argument that the absence of shop floor protection and the importance of work partly explain the rise of *clasismo* seems even more applicable to the Fiat Concord workers. In the Concord plant, where the workers were nominally represented by a plant union before 1970 and were isolated from the protection that membership in a powerful industrial union might afford them, the possibility that the workers would challenge management on questions of production was even more remote. The struggle for job control and shop floor protection has apparently also been central to the emergence of *clasista* movements in other Latin American labor unions in this period. For the case of Peru, see Carmen Rosa Balbi, *Identidad clasista en el sindicalismo: Su impacto en las fábricas* (Lima: Centro de Estudios y Promoción del Desarrollo, 1989).

70. This system, which Renault was enjoying the benefits of in its Mexican plants, institutionalized labor instability in the industry by providing only a small percentage of workers, mostly skilled workers, with permanent employment while the great majority of replaceable production and assembly line workers were given temporary status as *eventuales,* short-term employees subject to dismissal at the company's discretion. See Ian Roxborough, *Union Politics in Mexico: The Case of the Automobile Industry* (Cambridge: Cambridge University Press, 1984), pp. 61–62.

71. "Insalubridad: En defensa de nuestra salud y nuestra vida," *SMATA,* SMATA-Córdoba, no. 117 (December 21, 1973), p. 1; *La Voz del Interior,* December 8, 1973, p. 11. As an example of their efforts on the working conditions issue, the *clasistas* undertook a major campaign to have the work day in the forge reduced to six hours. The heat and noise levels in that department had been declared hazardous by the provincial department of labor, and the work day had been reduced to six hours between 1965 and 1969. In the aftermath of the great 1970 strike, however Renault had reestablished the eight-hour day there, and the *torrista* leadership had been unable or unwilling to confront the company on the issue.

72. There existed ten job classifications (from highly skilled tool and die makers to low-skill sweepers and materials handlers) under both Kaiser and Renault management. The differences were not in the broad job classifications but in the way the classifications were defined (loosely under Kaiser, tightly under Renault) and in the numerous subclassifications. See the 1971–72 IKA-Renault collective bargaining agreement and SMATA archive, SMATA-Córdoba, volume "Notas sobre Escalas Salariales, 1971–72," document "Nueva Escala de Salarios Vigente desde el 1º de abril de 1971 en la Planta IKA-Renault."

73. Renault was merely conforming to management practices that were by this time in widespread use in the automobile industry, in Latin America and elsewhere. As Gartman notes, "Although the new technology rendered auto production jobs more and more alike technically, capitalists undertook to arrange these basically similar jobs into a fragmented hierarchy of occupa-

tional categories, each with a different rule-defined wage rate. By thus widening and bureaucratizing wage differentials, they hoped to undermine the basis of common worker action. Combined with a system of production, such a job structure could be doubly divisive, for not only would workers have their common interests hidden by largely artificial wage differentials, but their efforts to obtain higher wages and greater control could also be channeled away from collective struggle toward individual efforts to gain personal advantages through promotion," Gartman, *Auto Slavery,* pp. 233–234.

74. William H. Form, "Auto Workers and Their Machines: A Study of Work, Factory, and Job Stratification in Four Countries," *Social Forces,* vol. 52, no. 1 (September 1973), p. 12.

75. SMATA archive, SMATA-Córdoba, volume "Notas da Comisión Interna de Reclamos y Respuestas de IKA-Renault, 1972–73," letter from Dept. of Labor Relations to the grievance committee, Comisión Interna de Reclamos (CIR), second shift, July 5, 1973. Renault had a long history of ignoring job classifications, a practice that underlay the tense shop floor conditions and many work stoppages in the company's French plants in the 1970s. See Daniel Labbe, "Travail formel et travail réel: Renault-Billancourt, 1945–1980," M.A. thesis, Ecole des Hautes Etudes en Sciences Sociales, 1990, pp. 97–124.

76. SMATA archive, SMATA-Córdoba, volume "Notas de Comisión Interna de Reclamos y Respuestas de IKA-Renault, 1972–73," minutes of CIR meeting with Industrial Relations Dept., November 10, 1972. The union archive's collection of shop stewards' grievances is not the most fecund source for the speedup issue. Generally speedups, unlike problems with job classifications, are resolved on the factory floor in the moment they arise or are not resolved at all. Speedups only make it to the formal grievance procedures if they become a chronic problem. The strike record therefore is the most reliable source on union behavior on the question of production rhythms.

77. SMATA archive, SMATA-Córdoba, volume "Notas de la Comisión Interna de Reclamos y Respuestas de IKA-Renault, 1972–73," letter from CIR to Labor Relations Dept., October 31, 1972. In this particular case, worker complaints of excessive line speeds in the painting department had been ongoing; the shop stewards claimed that the company had stealthily raised production from 185 chassis per day to 240. Revealingly, it was not the shop stewards who were taking up the issue with the company but Renée Salamanca and Roque Romero themselves. The union demanded that "the verbal and psychological intimidation be ended, that the company eliminate control by the stopwatch and that the production rhythms be adjusted to the realistic capabilities of the workers."

78. SMATA archive, SMATA-Córdoba, volume "Volantes Varios, 1972," union flier "Por un SMATA clasista," Nucleo de Activistas Clasistas, October 30, 1972. In one of many *clasista* statements on the relationship between the company's need to maximize worker productivity and *clasismo*'s ability to win worker sympathy, this *clasista* opposition group to the *lista marrón* could fairly say that the worsening problems with production rhythms were "propitious" for the *clasistas* and would ultimately serve to strengthen their standing among the workers.

79. "Justificada protesta," *SMATA*, SMATA-Córdoba, no. 53 (July 22, 1971), p. 4. Torres's heirs had sensed the workers' susceptibility to *clasista* accusations of minimal union protection on the shop floor and reluctantly sponsored some work stoppages in various departments to deflect some of the criticisms. But it was the *clasistas*, not the Peronists, who were most inclined to stop production to protest work rhythms between 1970 and 1975.

80. "Como se gasta la gente," *SMATA*, SMATA-Córdoba, no. 117 (December 21, 1973), p. 4. This article, dealing with the problems of hazardous working conditions and production rhythms, is just one of numerous examples of *clasista* attempts to link work problems and political proselytism. After the union recovery movement had succeeded and the left had established a closer relationship with the SITRAC-SITRAM leadership, a similar attempt was made in the Fiat factories. See "Cómo funciona la máquina de enfermar" and "El obrero se usa y se tira," *SITRAC: Boletín del Sindicato de Trabajadores Concord*, vol. 1, no. 2 (June 1971), p. 2.

81. One example of a partial work stoppage that spread to other departments is a March 1974 strike that erupted in the upholstery department to protest company disregard for job classifications and then spread throughout the entire Santa Isabel complex. See "Planta IKA-Renault: Arbitraria actitud patronal en Tapicería," *SMATA*, SMATA-Córdoba, special supplement (March 25, 1974), p. 4.

82. Garfield Clack, *Industrial Relations in a British Car Factory* (Cambridge: Cambridge University Press, 1967), p. 19. As Clack notes, autoworkers historically have not produced vocational communities that are as tightly knit and distinct as those of miners, dockworkers, and many other sectors of the industrial working class. Autoworkers in one department are isolated from those in another and often know very little about what is happening even in nearby departments. Workers on the assembly and production lines, where the work is timed and the noise level high, have especially little opportunity for communication with other departments. The skilled workers, on the other hand, have the greatest opportunity to move around, both within their own department and in the plant generally. Form found the skilled workers to be the most actively involved in union affairs in Córdoba, and there is some evidence that the skilled workers served as the principal instigators of work stoppages in the plants. The unity of all the IKA-Renault workers, however exceptional, was nevertheless a reality, and a community emerged despite the obstacles automotive production presented. Form, *Blue-Colloar Stratification*, p. 173.

83. McPherson, *Labor Relations in the Automobile Industry*, pp. 61–66. The Peronists based their most cogent criticisms of the *clasistas'* more combative shop floor tactics precisely on this issue of partisanship and the breakdown of union discipline. See SMATA archive, SMATA-Córdoba, volume, "Volantes Varios, 1972," Flier "A los compañeros de IKA-Renault," Agrupación 24 de Febrero, October 23, 1972.

84. Nelson Lichtenstein, "Auto Worker Militancy and the Structure of Factory Life, 1937–1955," *The Journal of American History*, vol. 67, no. 2 (September 1980), p. 346.

85. SMATA archive, SMATA-Córdoba, volume "Notas da Comisión Interna de Reclamos y Respuestas de IKA-Renault, 1972–73," letter from José Castro, Director of Personnel and Social Relations, to IKA-Renault workers, December 6, 1972; *Review of the River Plate,* vol. 157, no. 3914 (January 10, 1974), p. 39.

86. Archives des Usines Renault, Boulogne-Billancourt, Direction des Affaires Internationales 0200, 1071 file "Rapports de Mission de M. Peyre," document "Voyage du 30/9 au 14/10/74."

87. Ibid., 1067 file "A. Lucas, Argentine, 1973," document "Reunions reparties sur les 2, 3, et 5 juillet, 1973."

88. A favorite company tactic was to suspend grievance hearings in response to shop steward belligerence on the factory floor: "Persistent strike measures in the plants, consisting of soldiering in departments such as the press shop, electroplating, and final assembly, undertaken in violation of established agreements and practices, hereby cause us to communicate to you that such a situation prevents us from being able to hold today's grievance hearings." SMATA archive, SMATA-Córdoba, volume "Notas de la Comisión Interna de Reclamos y Respuestas de IKA-Renault, 1972–73," letter from R. Goya, Labor Relations Dept., to CIR, December 29, 1972.

89. Thomas Klug, "Employers' Strategies in the Detroit Labor Market, 1900–1929," in Nelson Lichtenstein and Stephen Meyer, eds., *On the Line: Essays in the History of Auto Work,* (Urbana and Chicago: University of Illinois Press, 1989), pp. 63–66.

90. In response to an extensive questionnaire I prepared and submitted to the Industrial Relations Department of Renault in Santa Isabel, the company expressed the belief that the intense strike activity of the early 1970s had been due to the work of political agitators among the more skilled workers. For example, with regard to the question of whether certain departments presented more problems and were more inclined than others to adopt strike measures and eschew negotiation, the company replied, "Yes, the most strike-prone were the specialized departments that contained personnel with a higher educational level who undoubtedly, through a camouflaged indoctrination process, orchestrated a politicization of the plants." Though it is difficult say so with absolute certainty, oral testimony indicates that there was indeed a tendency for the more skilled workers to take the initiative in work stoppages, but they did not act exclusively and their motivations were far more complex than simply the "indoctrination" of the rank and file.

91. SITRAC archive, file AI "Volantes, Impresos o Mimeos," fliers "A los compañeros de Fiat Concord," "Expulsaremos a Lozano: Ni un paso atrás." The word *clasista* does not appear in the publications of the grassroots movement that overthrew the entrenched union leadership in the March to May 1970 factory rebellions; it would only be adopted at a later date.

92. Roberto Reyna, "La izquierda cordobesa," *Crísis,* no. 64 (1988), pp. 44–45. See the response of SITRAC's president, Carlos Masera, "SITRAC y SITRAM: La autonomía obrera," *Crísis,* no. 67 (1989), pp. 78–79.

93. There were a few workers who were initially opposed to SITRAC's pledge to work to abolish the *premio,* concerned that their earnings were going to decline sharply. Nonetheless the workers who were elected to leadership in

1970 came with a clear mandate from the rank and file to force the company to abandon the *premio* system and convert to an hourly rate comparable to that paid by other automobile companies operating in Argentina; interview with Carlos Masera, secretary general of SITRAC 1970–71, Córdoba, July 9, 1990.

94. Francisco Delich, "Condición obrera y sindicato clasista," paper presented at the Seminar on Labor Movements in Latin America, San José, Costa Rica, 1972, pp. 3–5.

95. Interviews with Gregorio Flores, SITRAC shop steward 1970–71, Buenos Aires, November 12, 1985, and Domingo Bizzi, member of SITRAC executive committee 1970–71, Córdoba, July 22, 1987.

96. A typical departmental strike was the one affecting a number of production lines on August 19, 1971, to protest company foot-dragging on the pledge to phase out the *premio de la producción*. SITRAC archive, file "Juicios de Reincorporación: Actas Nacionales, April 1970 to December 1971, Part II, Deposition 3300134." Among the handful of sources, beyond personal testimony, available to document conditions in the Concord plant during the *clasista* period, some of the most valuable are the reports of the public notary Ricardo Orortegui. Orortegui was hired by the company to document conditions in the plant, probably in preparation for a future lawsuit against the union. What emerged from the reports, no doubt unintentionally, was a picture of a vigorous but not excessively provocative or irresponsible union that enjoyed broad support from the workers. Ironically, the fired *clasista* union leaders would use these reports in the suit they would later bring against Fiat for unlawful firings.

97. Steven Tolliday, "Government, Employers, and Shop Floor Organization in the British Motor Industry," in Steven Tolliday and Jonathan Zeitlin, eds., *Shop Floor Bargaining and the State* (Cambridge: Cambridge University Press, 1985), pp. 131–132; Nelson Lichtenstein, "Reutherism on the Shop Floor: Union Strategy and Shop Floor Conflict in the USA, 1946–70," in Steven Tolliday and Jonathan Zeitlin, eds., *The Automobile Industry and Its Workers* (Cambridge: Cambridge University Press, 1986), p. 132.

98. Lichtenstein, "Reutherism on the Shop Floor," pp. 126–132.

99. Ibid., p. 126.

100. As one scholar of the industry has put it, "The objective leveling off of wage differentials, which indexed homogenization of working conditions, skill, status, and control, gave rise to a tendency to subjectively define themselves as a community with shared interests," Gartman, *Auto Slavery*, p. 175.

101. The problems of race and ethnicity have been notorious in the automobile industry. In France (native French workers versus North Africans and especially Algerians), Italy (northern versus southern Italians), and the U.S. (whites versus blacks), the existence of heterogeneous labor forces has often diverted attention away from work problems toward racial animosities and ethnic rivalries. For the U.S. industry, see Elliot Rudwick and August Meier, *Black Detroit and the Rise of the UAW* (New York: Oxford University Press, 1979) and James Geschwender, *Class, Race and Worker Insurgency: The League of Revolutionary Black Workers* (Cambridge: Cambridge University Press, 1977).

11. Conclusion: The Sources of Working Class Politics in Córdoba

1. Among the more recent noteworthy contributions to the debate are Michael Burawoy, *The Politics of Production: Factory Regimes under Capitalism and Socialism* (New York: Verso, 1987); Duncan Gallie, *Social Inequality and Class Relations in France and Britain* (Cambridge: Cambridge University Press, 1983); and Gary Marks, *Unions in Politics* (Princeton, N.J.: Princeton University Press, 1988).

2. E. P. Thompson, *The Making of the English Working Class* Eric Hobsbawm, *Labouring Men* (New York: Basic Books, 1965); William Sewell, *Work and Revolution in France: The Language of Labour from the Old Regime to 1848* (Cambridge: Cambridge University Press, 1980); Herbert G. Gutman, *Work, Culture and Society in Industrializing America* (New York: Vintage, 1977); David Montgomery, *The Fall of the House of Labor: The Workplace, the State, and American Labor Activism, 1865–1925* (Cambridge: Cambridge University Press, 1984).

3. Judith Evans, "Results and Prospects: Some Observations on Latin American Labor Studies," *International Labor and Working Class History,* vol. 16 (Fall 1979), pp. 29–39, provides an overview of Latin American labor history that still remains the best critical assessment of the first wave of scholarship in the field. For review essays on the historiography of the 1980s, see George Reid Andrews, "Latin American Workers," *Journal of Social History,* vol. 21 (Winter 1987), pp. 311–326; and Emilia Viotti da Costa, "Experience versus Structures: New Tendencies in the History of Labor and the Working Class in Latin America—What Do We Gain? What Do We Lose?" *International Labor and Working Class History,* vol. 36 (Fall 1989), pp. 3–24.

4. Hobart Spalding, *Organized Labor in Latin America: Historical Case Studies of Urban Workers in Dependent Socities* (New York: Harper and Row, 1977); Charles Bergquist, *Labor in Latin America: Comparative Essays on Chile, Argentina, Venezuela and Colombia* (Stanford, Calif.: Stanford University Press, 1986).

5. Daniel James, *Resistance and Integration: Peronism and the Argentine Working Class, 1946–1976* (Cambridge: Cambridge University Press, 1988).

6. Ibid., pp. 258–259.

7. Ian Roxborough, *Unions and Politics in Mexico: The Case of the Automobile Industry* (Cambridge: Cambridge University Press, 1984); Silvia Gómez Tagle, *Insurgencia y democracia en los sindicatos electricistas* (Mexico City: El Colegio de México, 1980).

8. John Humphrey, *Capitalist Control and Workers' Struggle in the Brazilian Auto Industry* (Princeton, N.J.: Princeton University Press, 1983); Isabel Ribeiro de Olivera, *Trabalho e Política: As origenes do Partido dos Trabalhadores* (Petrópolis, Brazil: Editorial Vozes, 1988).

9. James Petras, "Córdoba y la revolución socialista en la Argentina," *Los libros* 3, no. 21 (1971), p. 30.

10. James, *Resistance and Integration,* pp. 262–263.

11. Bergquist, *Labor in Latin America,* p. 188.

12. Judith Evans, Paul Heath Hoeffel, and Daniel James, "Reflections on Argen-

tine Auto Workers and Their Unions," in R. Kronish and K. Mericle, eds., *The Political Economy of the Latin American Motor Vehicle Industry* (Cambridge, Mass.: MIT Press, 1984), p. 141–145. The authors assert this was the case in the Buenos Aires industry and seem to imply that the problems with employment instability and plant rotation were characteristic of Córdoba as well. My own research on the Buenos Aires–based firms leads me to believe that they have exaggerated the extent of the hire and fire policies there. For Córdoba, such practices clearly did not exist.

13. Bergquist, *Labor in Latin America,* p. 188; David Rock, *Argentina, 1516–1982: From Spanish Colonization to the Falklands War* (Berkeley and Los Angeles: University of California Press, 1985), p. 350.

14. Mónica B. Gordillo, "Características de los sindicatos líderes de Córdoba en los 60: El ámbito del trabajo y la dimensión cultural," Annual Report, Consejo de Investigaciones Científicas y Tecnológicas de la Provincia de Córdoba, April 1991, pp. 4–21.

15. The union archives of SITRAC and the Cordoban SMATA have extensive materials dealing with each other's workplace and union situations. The SMATA-affiliated Fiat plant, Grandes Motores Diesel, seems to have served as a kind of link between the Ferreyra and Santa Isabel complexes, allowing labor leaders and workers alike to keep closely abreast of the struggles in each other's plants.

16. Evans, Hoeffel, and James, "Reflections on Argentine Auto Workers and Their Unions," p. 145.

17. Interview with Juan Malvár, secretary general of the Cordoban print workers' union 1958 to 1979, Córdoba, June 10, 1987.

18. Juan Carlos Torre and Elizabeth Jelin, "Los nuevos trabajadores en América Latina: Una reflexión sobre la tesis de la aristocracia obrera," *Desarrollo Económico,* vol. 22, no. 85 (April–June 1982), pp. 3–23.

19. The architect of the Gran Acuerdo Nacional and the most powerful military figure in Argentina between 1966 and 1973, General Alejandro Lanusse, hints at this in his memoir, *Mi testimonio* (Buenos Aires: Lasserre Editores, 1977), pp. 263–264.

20. Labor sociology offers a number of interesting possibilities for explaining working class politics in Córdoba. For example, the relations of production in the Cordoban automobile industry would appear to closely resemble sociologist Michael Burawoy's description of "market despotism," the factory regime, according to his typology, most likely to foment worker militancy. The four conditions for what Burawoy calls "the despotic regime of factory politics" were all met in Córdoba: competition among firms (the Argentine automobile industry was highly competitive after the early 1960s); absolute subordination of workers to capital through the separation of conception from execution (the largely unskilled automotive proletariat exerted little job discretion); complete dependence on the employer, on the sale of labor power for a wage, with no alternative form of subsistence (the Cordoban factories were not industrial islands in a peasant economy, and a return to the village or farm was not an option for most workers, who by the late 1960s were thor-

oughly urbanized); the state does not regulate either the relations among capitalists or the process of production (the automobile multinationals had great autonomy). See Burawoy, *The Politics of Production,* pp. 89–90.

21. María Beatriz Nofal, *Absentee Entrepreneurship and the Dynamics of the Motor Vehicle Industry in Argentina* (New York: Praeger Publishers, 1989), p. 129.

Index

Agriculture, 4, 6, 7, 16, 23, 25, 47, 243. *See also* Exports: agricultural
Alberti, Felipe, 79, 157
Alianza Anticomunista Argentina (AAA), 287, 288, 291, 292, 298
Alonso, José, 66, 69, 74, 83, 105, 106, 129, 255
Anarchism, 10–11, 24, 55, 113, 233
Anticlericalism, 131, 146, 147
Aramburu, General Pedro, 56, 64, 218
Argentina, 1, 85; and Cuba, 241; fascism in, 3–4; history of, 23, 344; industrial development in, 341; political culture of, 162; surveys of worker attitudes in, 87
Asociación de Trabajadores del Estado (ATE), 152, 165, 257, 258
Automobile industry, 54, 113, 139, 282, 293; and business cycle, 305–306, 308–310, 351; competition in, 306, 310, 326, 339; foreign investment in, 15–16, 19, 30, 32, 33–42, 50–52, 56; labor costs of, 141–142, 308, 313; labor flexibility in, 313, 320, 330; labor force of, 46, 86, 311, 341; labor militancy in, 88–89, 171–172, 296, 305, 350, 356; management control in, 339–340; market conditions of, 306, 308; modernization in, 318–319; and nationalist policies, 236–237; in 1940s, 1–3; in 1980s, 362–363; North American, 308, 324, 325; and Perón, 6, 30, 56; power of, 341; and repeal of *sábado inglés* law, 142–143; role of foremen in, 315, 336–337, 341; time study in, 313–314, 315; and unions, 65, 84, 95; wages in, 71, 140, 175, 180, 189, 197, 198, 293, 309, 313, 322, 327, 339, 340; working conditions in, 114, 314, 350. *See also* Córdoba, city of; Cordobazo; Strikes; Unions: automobile workers'; *individual companies*

Banco Industrial, 30, 31
Bedaux system, 323, 325
Bidegain, Oscar, 228, 266

Bizzi, Domingo, 175, 182, 187, 190, 201
Brazil, 87, 103, 104–105, 308, 309, 310, 344, 345, 346, 351, 362
Buenos Aires, 24, 25, 34, 47, 93, 228; antagonism of provinces toward, 23, 125, 162, 167, 185, 186, 229, 240, 244, 245, 247, 267, 286, 347, 348; banks in, 51; effects of industrialization in, 50; employment opportunities in, 49; migration to, 1, 44, 45; population of, 44, 45, 49; slums of, 132; and trade unions, 55, 56, 57, 59, 60, 61, 63, 64, 67, 68, 73, 74, 77, 78, 79, 80, 81, 83, 95–96, 98, 105, 106, 108, 109, 113, 117, 118, 130, 133, 185, 216, 217, 351, 355; working class in, 43, 50, 354
burocracia porteña, 80, 245
burocracia sindical, 108, 190, 219, 255, 262

Caballero, Carlos, 147, 161, 164
Cámara de Industrias Metalúrgicas, 34, 50, 277, 355
Cámpora, Hector, 228, 233, 241, 243–244, 245, 246, 247, 249, 250, 252, 259, 264
Capitalism, 301, 332, 359; hostility toward, 96, 169, 186, 193–194, 216, 242; industrial, 50, 85, 103, 339; multinational, 15–16
Carrasco, Jerónimo, 74, 77–78
Cassanova, Hugo, 176, 177, 205
Catholic Church, 12, 13, 14, 17, 18, 24, 67; liberation theologians of, 145–147; and student movement, 145, 164. *See also* Priests, radical
Ceballos, Sixto, 72, 73, 211, 252, 253, 285
CGT de los Argentinos (CGTA), 109, 112, 122–123, 130, 174, 185, 242, 349; and Cordobazo, 142, 143, 144, 146, 157, 160, 164, 166, 167; rebellion of, 123–126, 127, 128, 129, 132, 133, 134, 135, 141, 183, 297, 359; and students, 131, 148
Chrysler, 2, 34, 38, 110, 282, 319, 362
Citroën, 38, 91, 110, 153, 217, 306, 319, 362

clasismo (revolutionary trade unionism), 18, 52–53, 165, 170–205, 212, 268–269, 324; in automotive industry, 224, 316, 331, 336, 346, 350; and control of production rhythms, 331; demise of, 297–301; development of, 181–182, 350; electoral victory of, 272–273, 279, 334; and Independents, 269, 280; and opposition to company policies, 328–342 *passim;* origins of, 305; political discussions of, 362; and SMATA, 217, 222, 223, 224, 230, 231, 235, 237, 285–286, 287, 289, 297, 331; split in, 270–271; spread of, 214–215, 216, 257–263; strategies of, 213, 214, 290, 329; vs. *peronismo,* 52, 53, 139, 168, 183, 219, 220–221, 228–229, 239, 251, 252, 296, 342, 350; and working class, 357–358

cogestión (comanagement), 97, 116, 329, 349

Collective bargaining, 73, 74, 81, 82, 98, 110, 113, 142, 181, 198, 222, 238, 244, 275, 322, 348; in autoworkers' unions, 87, 95; centralization of, 299, 300, 340; committees *(comisiones paritarias)* for, 62, 75, 95, 106, 230–231, 258; and communism, 57, 59; and EPEC, 116–117; government intervention in, 293; and Gran Paritaria Nacional, 246; lifting of ban on, 188–189; and Perón, 11, 55; reforms in, 212–213; suspension of, 41, 51, 88, 106, 107, 111, 121, 246, 327, 328; and wage adjustment clause *(cláusula gatillo)*, 95; and working conditions, 115, 173, 180, 187, 197. *See also* Wages; *individual unions*

Communism, 55, 63, 70; and *clasistas,* 262; French, 236, 325–326; and PCR, 270; and Torres, 58–60, 61; and unions, 10, 57, 64, 72, 182, 233, 286, 357. *See also* Marxism

Communist party, 15, 75, 123, 127, 146, 209, 223

Companies, multinational, 39–40, 51, 81, 88, 140, 176, 177, 260, 296, 319, 355

Concord factory (Fiat), 36, 65; automation at, 91, 92, 310, 321; company policies at, 321–322, 323, 338; elections at, 248, 258; occupation of, 247, 248; and Peronism, 347; rebellion at, 173–175, 176, 177, 178, 179, 181, 188, 193, 199, 337, 354; role of foreman in, 336–337; and UOM, 74, 81, 82, 180, 231, 240. *See also* SITRAC-SITRAM

Confederación General del Trabajo (CGT), 10, 53, 72, 87, 98, 110, 113, 183, 184, 185, 210, 212, 220; agreement with CGE, 264–265; attack on headquarters, 258; and *clasistas,* 214, 231, 241, 250, 251, 258, 279, 290; congresses of, 119, 124, 128, 267; Cordoban, 69, 80, 83, 283, 291; and Cordobazo, 148, 149, 150, 151, 152, 154, 157, 158, 160, 166, 167, 186, 353; Declaración de Córdoba of, 134; and elections, 220; executive council of, 258; and Fiat company unions, 174, 176–177, 188, 190, 191, 198, 199, 201, 223; and government, 274, 278, 285, 363; and Onganía, 105, 112, 123; and Perón,

11, 108; and Peronism, 12, 107, 209, 219, 227, 229, 230, 233, 245, 249, 266, 267, 268, 294, 347; and SITRAC-SITRAM, 195–196, 198; and SMATA, 178, 216, 224–225, 232; and strikes, 189, 193, 194, 200, 221, 226, 244, 248, 284, 293, 335; and change led by working class, 131, 141, 264. *See also* CGT de los Argentinos

Confederación General Económica (CGE), 5, 256, 264, 265, 274–275, 355

Confederazione Generale Italiana de Lavoro (CGIL), 63, 324

Congreso Amado Olmos (March 1968), 107–108, 111, 112, 123, 130

Contreras, Ramón, 79, 105, 211

Cooke, John William, 124–125

coordinadoras, 290, 294–295, 299

Córdoba, city of, 1, 3, 18, 19, 23–24; Barrio Alberdi in, 42, 140, 153, 155, 156, 192; Barrio Clínicas in, 42, 140, 144, 148, 150, 153, 155, 156, 157, 158, 192; as center of *clasista* movement, 215, 247, 354–356; as center of dissident labor movement, 188, 210, 265, 276, 353–354; character of, 354, 356–357; class structure in, 42, 49, 50–52; defeat of dissident labor movement in, 300–301; as government adversary, 279, 363; housing in, 43, 44; importance of labor movement in, 110, 342, 359, 361–362; increase in population of, 42, 44–45, 49; industrial growth in, 38–39, 44, 50; industrial politics in, 33, 34, 39, 137; industrial workers in, 85–86, 140; and the left, 357; local culture in, 33, 356; Los Plátanos in, 146; municipal services in, 44; neighborhoods in, 42–44, 140, 151, 153, 156, 157, 158, 192, 327, 354–355; politics as way of life in, 162; radicalism of, 127–128, 131, 212, 352–354, 356–357; rivalry with Buenos Aires, 128; terror campaign in, 288, 291–292, 298; university students of, 126. *See also* Working class: in Córdoba

Córdoba Province, 1, 23, 24, 25, 47, 137, 229; as center of labor movement, 128, 129, 130–131; and electric power, 120; hydroelectric projects in, 25, 26; public works projects in, 25, 26; road-building in, 25

Córdoba Sport Club, 62, 75, 124, 143

Cordobazo, 136–169; anniversaries of, 176, 221, 241, 280; effect on Argentine left, 138–139, 163, 168, 170, 171; effect on working class, 138–139, 164, 169, 175, 280, 289, 328, 342, 352, 361; end of, 158–159; and labor unions, 139, 159, 168, 185–186, 190, 305, 331, 332, 346, 348, 349, 354; myths of, 159–160, 163, 164, 168, 352; political effect of, 138, 168–169, 170, 194, 212, 240, 242, 258, 288, 295, 297, 335, 336, 359–360; from protest to rebellion, 152–159; working class participation in, 159–160, 195, 327, 352

Coria, Roger, 134, 228

Coronel Moldes (Córdoba), 1, 44

Correa, Miguel, 128–129, 149, 154, 157
Coups, military, 103, 104, 105, 300
Cuban Revolution, 127, 168
Curutchet, Alfredo, 174, 175, 187, 197, 198, 200, 202, 222, 287; murder of, 287

Dean Funes (power plant), 29, 42
Del Carlo factory, 220, 277
Democracy, 138, 359; and unions, 72, 73, 95, 96, 98, 118, 131, 172, 179–180, 184, 203, 205, 209, 211, 212–213, 214, 219, 224, 237, 238, 245, 255, 256, 271, 289, 349, 359
Díaz, Florencio, 192, 197, 198
Dirección General de Fabricaciones Militares, 3, 5
Di Toffino, Tomás, 79, 157

Economic Commission on Latin America (ECLA), 14, 15
Economic development, 4, 15, 28, 38–39, 49–50, 84, 120, 121, 139
Ejército Revolucionario del Pueblo (ERP), 196, 202, 218, 226, 255, 256, 287, 294, 298, 360
Elections: national, 16, 186, 219, 246, 251, 262, 272; union, 70, 75, 78, 95, 105, 119, 172–179 *passim*, 183, 205, 218, 230, 235, 248, 257, 268, 284, 294, 324. *See also individual unions*
Electric power, 26, 29, 32, 49, 72, 148, 282
Electrum (newspaper), 118, 120, 168. *See also* Luz y Fuerza
Elite, 4, 8, 15, 23, 24, 50
Empresa Pública de Energía de Córdoba (EPEC), 26, 29, 70, 71, 114–117, 121, 148, 149, 150, 152, 159, 348
Exports, 4, 5, 6, 23; agricultural, 4, 7, 14, 16, 26
Ezeiza Airport, massacre at, 246, 252

Fábrica de Motores y Automotores, 26, 29
Factories, 1, 27, 45; airplane, 24; ammunition, 25; armaments, 3, 5, 6, 24–25, 30, 40; consolidation of, 26, 39, 40; ILASA, 33; modern, 85; production processes in, 90–94; takeovers of, 174–175, 177–178, 184, 190, 243, 245, 246, 264, 268–269, 292; tractor, 27, 30–31, 36
Federación Argentina de Trabajadores de Luz y Fuerza (FATLYF), 72, 105, 106, 113, 117, 119, 133, 211, 250, 254–255, 258, 349; Comisión Paritaria Nacional of, 121. *See also* Luz y Fuerza
Ferreyra, 27–28, 64, 74, 81, 93, 150, 172, 181; army occupation of, 200, 201; *clasista* movement in, 182, 203, 236, 243, 338, 339, 349, 350; and Fiat company, 30, 36–37, 42, 51, 63, 82, 97, 169, 247, 285; labor force at, 351, 354, 363; management practices at, 324; politicization at, 184, 305; workers' rebellion at, 174, 177, 179, 180, 186, 196, 336, 342; working conditions at, 255. *See also* SITRAC-SITRAM union rebellion

Fiat company, 2–3, 6, 49, 51, 52, 59, 121, 193; affiliation controversy in, 80–83, 224–225, 232, 241, 247–248, 249, 258, 259, 261, 276; Centro Cultural at, 97; *clasistas* at, 196, 217, 218, 220, 221, 222, 223, 224, 225, 235, 236, 240, 242, 255, 259, 283, 285, 299, 316, 336, 337, 338, 341, 346, 347, 349, 350; competitors of, 306, 310; and Cordobazo, 160, 169; and decentralization, 277, 324; factories of, 19, 30, 31, 33, 36, 42, 150; labor policies of, 40, 41, 63–64, 65, 66, 71, 97, 142, 173–175, 187, 197–198, 200, 204, 221–222, 236, 255, 309, 310, 313, 314, 322–324, 326, 350; paternalism at, 63, 82, 97, 175; plant unions of, 69, 74, 81, 82–83, 95, 124, 129, 160, 169, 172–175, 176, 181, 184, 190, 201, 352; politics in, 305, 339; production practices at, 34, 315, 316, 317, 318, 322, 324, 336; production process in, 89–91, 92, 93; reforms at, 310–311, 321; resistance committees at, 294; sale of Ferreyra complex, 362; union recovery movement in, 172–177, 183, 186, 187, 188, 189, 195, 199, 203, 204–205, 217, 235, 278, 342; and *viborazo*, 194; working conditions at, 337
Flores, Gregorio, 175, 187, 222
Ford, Henry, 311, 314
Ford company, 2, 6, 30, 33, 38, 92, 110, 282, 284, 293, 300, 306, 310, 319
Fordism, 313–314, 316, 317, 318, 319, 320, 325
Ford-Transax plant, 33, 34, 272, 282, 285, 286, 288, 318, 354
Frente Antiimperialista por el Socialismo, 253, 260
Frente Estudiantil Nacional, 144
Frente Justicialista de Liberación (FREJULI), 219, 227, 228, 229, 230, 232, 233, 239–240, 241, 243, 246
Frente Unico Clasista, 215, 258–259
Frondizi, Arturo, 15, 16, 30, 37, 38, 39, 58, 59, 64, 68, 306, 362
Fuerzas Armadas de Liberación (FAL), 163, 170, 218, 360
Fuerzas Armadas Peronistas (FAP), 127, 171, 255, 287
Fuerzas Armadas Revolucionarias (FAR), 127, 226, 259

Gelbard, José Ber, 275
General Motors, 2, 30, 38, 245, 262, 282, 293, 306, 310, 319, 362
Gerardo Seel factory, 111–112
Government: military, 362, 360; and trade unions, 88, 98, 105, 107, 108, 109, 281–283, 294; and working class, 112
Gramsci, Antonio, 86, 128, 343
Gran Acuerdo Nacional, 195, 197, 203, 209, 218
Grandes Motores Diesel (GMD; Fiat), 36, 37, 65, 81, 82, 151, 169, 188, 272, 285, 288
grupo 1° de mayo, 177, 227

Guerrilla organizations, 127, 144, 195, 202, 218, 219, 226, 242, 360; leftist, 170–171, 255, 256, 287, 292
Guevarists, 127, 163, 170, 242
Guillán, Julio, 109, 123–124

Hostage taking, 174, 177, 178, 184, 187, 293
Hydroelectric power, 25, 26, 29, 120

IKA-Renault: calls for nationalization of, 216; and *clasismo*, 52, 182, 196, 213–214, 215, 232, 236, 238, 240, 260, 287, 290, 295–296, 316, 335, 338, 341, 346, 349; competitors of, 306; and Cordobazo, 151, 156, 158, 160, 161, 165; and IME, 299; job classifications *(categorías)* in, 330–331; labor force of, 41, 89, 138, 148, 173, 227, 263, 326, 351, 354; labor policies at, 142, 178, 179, 282, 283, 288–289, 308–309, 310, 311, 314, 319, 326, 329; labor protests at, 110, 128, 188, 193, 309; and left wing, 112, 172, 178, 201; markets of, 316–317; modernization at, 318–319, 321, 333; and parts industry, 121, 220, 277, 282, 286; Perdriel factory of, 143; politics at, 305, 327; problems of, 236–237; production practices at, 89, 316, 317, 318; production process in, 89–91, 93, 320; reforms at, 310, 311, 318–320, 328; strikes at, 110, 137, 149, 150, 332, 333, 339; union recovery movement at, 214, 342, 350; working conditions at, 111, 136, 296, 320, 335; work stoppages at, 295, 332–333, 334–335. *See also* Renault Company
Ilasa factories, 33, 271, 285, 288
Illia, Arturo, 17, 65, 79, 103, 104, 105, 146, 275, 277
Imports, 4, 6, 16
Independents, 69, 74, 128, 218, 229, 242–243, 244, 250; and Buenos Aires, 267, 355; and *clasistas*, 221, 269, 280, 288; and government, 260, 291; and guerrillas, 255; and *legalistas*, 194, 195, 199, 201, 203, 216, 219, 220, 226, 230, 232, 251, 263, 288; and Peronism, 70–72, 134, 219, 250; *plan de movilización* of, 112; and strikes, 225, 248. *See also* Tosco, Agustín
Industrialists, 6, 7, 12, 15, 50–51, 52, 274–275. *See also* Confederación General Económica
Industrialization, 14, 25, 29, 30, 50, 85, 94, 98, 120, 342, 351; automotive, 90, 139; politics of, 28, 43, 104
Industrias Aeronáuticas y Mecánicas del Estado (IAME), 5, 27, 29, 40, 49, 76, 89, 92, 138, 318; and Cordobazo, 150, 160; and IKA, 31, 32, 33, 36, 58, 136; products of, 28, 39. *See also* Industrias Mecánicas del Estado
Industrias Kaiser Argentina (IKA), 31, 32–36, 37, 39, 51, 64, 65, 75, 76, 111; community service programs of, 35, 97; 1960 agreement with union, 62–63; productivity campaign at, 76–77; vertical integration of, 33–34; workers at, 56,

57, 58, 59, 60–61, 62, 71, 92, 94, 95, 96–97, 111, 126, 136, 175. *See also* IKA-Renault
Industrias Mecánicas del Estado (IME), 26, 184, 191–192, 201, 258, 286, 299, 363
Industry: aeronautical, 30, 136; armaments, 3, 25; brewery, 23, 29, 41; cement, 25, 29; chemical, 5, 71; construction, 10, 11, 49, 184; consumer goods, 5; diary, 184; electric power, 26, 119–121; food-processing, 39, 42, 66; heavy, 4; heavy metals, 5; light, 4, 5, 15, 25, 29, 30, 42, 65, 242; mechanical, 29, 30, 32–35, 39, 40, 41, 44, 49, 50, 51, 53, 56, 65, 138, 257; medium-size, 5; metallurgical, 33–34, 41–42, 52, 71, 78, 111–112, 114, 130, 141, 181, 201, 220, 274, 277–278, 353; parts, 16, 33, 142, 151, 274, 275, 277, 282; petroleum, 16, 133; rubber, 282; service, 65; steel, 5, 16, 34, 198, 214, 229, 268, 282; textile, 25, 29, 39, 41, 42, 47, 52, 56, 66
Inflation, 104, 264, 296, 299, 327
Investment: American, 15; British, 15; foreign, 6, 15, 16, 29, 31, 50; public, 14
Italy, 1, 30, 37, 92, 197, 324

Jaime, Armando, 214, 253, 269
justicialista doctrine, 9, 10, 26, 30, 256, 259
Juventud Trabajadora Peronista (JTP), 214, 228, 258, 259, 267, 269, 278, 290

Kaiser, Henry J., 1, 31, 38, 91, 92, 277, 330
Kaiser-Frazier Automobile Company, 19, 31
Kloosterman, Dirk, 216, 220–221, 232, 240, 241, 247, 248; assassination of, 255

Labor movement, 15, 64, 94–95, 98, 105, 109, 265, 294; in Brazil, 104–105; chain of command in, 185; national, 53, 110; and national liberation, 80; Peronist, 10–13, 19, 94, 113, 161, 167, 171, 183, 184–185, 186–187, 188, 194, 195, 197, 199, 203, 210, 211, 212, 215, 216, 217, 220, 222, 229, 231, 233, 235–273, 299, 300, 301, 348, 353; politics of, 17, 18, 53, 54–55, 68, 69, 78, 80–83, 98, 103–104, 106, 128, 143, 263, 344–345, 352, 358; and revolution, 168; study of Cordoban, 55, 344; transformation of, 128–129. *See also* Córdoba, city of; Strikes; Unions
Lacabanne, General Raúl Oscar, 289–290, 291
La Fraternidad (railway workers' union), 12, 109
Lanusse, General Alejandro, 178, 193, 194, 195, 197, 203, 209, 211, 218, 219, 220, 228, 236, 275
Lastiri, Raúl, 246, 247, 252
legalistas, 279, 348; and CGT, 199, 244, 250–251; and Independents, 70, 79, 194, 195, 199, 201, 203, 212, 216, 219, 220, 226, 230, 263; and *ortodoxos*, 194, 259, 265, 270; and Peronism, 185, 186, 187, 210, 229, 230, 233, 252, 284, 348; rebirth of, 165, 186, 195, 200, 201, 203; and SMATA, 78, 83, 152, 216, 218, 221, 232; and strikes, 191, 225

Legislation: industrial, 33, 37–38, 39, 40, 236, 275, 277, 362; labor, 12, 61, 64, 65, 104–105, 110, 181, 200, 254, 258, 280
Levingston, General Roberto, 178, 187, 188, 189, 192, 193, 194
Ley de Seguridad, 254, 280, 292
López, Atilio, 78, 362; and CGT, 194, 199, 200, 220, 230, 233, 244, 250–251; and *legalistas,* 186, 199, 203, 210, 218, 219, 229, 232; murder of, 288, 361; and Peronism, 241, 249, 250–252, 259, 263, 266, 267, 280; and strikes, 149, 200, 226, 248; and Tosco, 260, 265–266, 294; and UTA, 67, 68, 70, 148, 165, 243, 284. *See also legalistas*
Lozano, Jorge, 173, 174, 175, 176, 179, 205, 338
Luján Hornos factory, 111–112
Luz y Fuerza, 73, 78–80, 106, 114–116, 117, 191, 276; attacks on, 279, 291, 298; and Cordobazo, 149, 152, 153, 156, 157, 164, 165, 167, 186; elections of, 252, 298; and FATLYF, 250, 349; headquarters of, 119, 149, 184, 289; independence of, 354; and Independents, 69, 70, 71, 131; Mutual Unión Eléctrica of, 116, 117; and Peronists, 210–211, 242, 254, 285, 291, 294, 347, 348, 349; publication of, 118, 120; shop stewards in, 118–119; suspension of, 255, 363; and working class militancy, 148, 346. *See also* Federación Argentina de Trabajadores de Luz y Fuerza; Tosco, Agustín

Malvár, Juan, 70, 78, 79, 250, 355
Maoism, 163, 170, 357
Martini, Alfredo, 149, 276
Marxism, 8, 127, 128, 139, 146, 163, 170, 177, 179; and *clasistas,* 182, 195, 196, 198, 203, 215, 230, 258; and Cordobazo, 161, 168, 352, 353; and Peronism, 211, 212, 218, 219, 228, 229, 241, 246–247, 248–249, 256, 278, 281, 289, 332, 347, 349, 358; and politics of work, 335, 343, 357; and return of Perón, 239; and students, 137, 144; and union leaders, 71, 96, 123, 147, 176, 227; and unions, 72, 213, 220, 222, 236
Masera, Carlos, 173, 174, 175–176, 193, 224, 225, 259, 347; and SITRAC, 160, 179, 182, 190, 192, 197, 198
Materfer factory (Fiat), 36, 65, 82, 222, 231, 240; elections at, 248, 258; occupation of, 199, 247; rebellion at, 176, 177, 178, 180, 181, 188, 190–191, 193, 200
McCloud, James, 31, 75, 111
Mercedes-Benz, 38, 282, 306
Mesa Provisoria de los Gremios en Lucha, 294
Mexico, 87, 308, 310, 329, 344, 345, 346
Migrants, 1, 23, 44–47, 49, 58
Miguel, Lorenzo, 251, 292, 293, 294, 300, 360; and Perón, 219, 228, 264; and UOM, 185, 186, 220, 222, 229
Military, 17–18, 28, 43, 186, 187, 188, 249; and

Cordobazo, 153–154, 155–157, 158, 159; and factories, 25, 28, 200; and fascism, 3; hatred of, 137; and Peronism, 4, 5, 12, 13, 14, 26, 345; repression of labor movement, 193, 289, 291, 363; terror campaign by, 298
Modernization, 15, 18, 104, 318, 319. *See also* Industrialization
Montoneros, 164, 193, 210, 218, 226, 228, 241, 259, 278, 360
Montoneros-Juventud Peronista (JP) axis, 171, 228, 229, 252
Movimiento de Recuperación Sindical (MRS), 215, 216, 217, 218, 223, 227, 237
Movimiento de Unidad y Coordinación Sindical (MUCS), 171, 177, 209
Movimiento Sindical Combativo (MSC), 252, 260, 265, 268, 269, 280, 283, 284, 285

Nationalism, 3, 6, 13, 17, 25, 31, 37, 40, 67, 94, 130, 237
Nationalization, 4, 6, 68, 195, 216; of public utilities, 4, 26, 120; of railroads, 4
Navarrazo, 244, 268, 269, 270, 271, 272, 278, 279, 281
Navarro, Lieutenant Colonel Domingo, 267, 268, 270

Obregón Cano, Ricardo, 229, 230, 248, 259, 265, 266, 267
Olmos, Amado, 107, 108
Onganía, General Juan Carlos, 105, 107, 108, 112, 134, 250, 280, 327; and Cordobazo, 138, 158, 159, 160, 162, 164, 166, 167, 169, 178, 179; economic policies of, 109, 113, 141; and industrialists, 110, 244, 274, 275; 1967 visit to Córdoba, 112; opposition to, 88, 125, 128, 129, 138, 144, 145, 148, 160, 168, 170, 177, 361; Plan Nacional of, 132; seizure of power, 18, 103, 104; student protests against, 126, 127, 147; suspension of collective bargaining, 106, 107, 111, 121; and universities, 137–138, 155; and UOM, 277
Onganía coup, 79, 103, 104, 105, 111, 130, 137, 142, 310, 328, 348, 361
Ongaro, Raimundo, 122–123, 126, 131–132, 194, 279, 290; and CGTA, 107, 109, 112, 128, 129, 130, 133, 134, 135; and Cordobazo, 149, 166; May Day speech of, 124–125, 127, 128; and Perón, 108, 210; release from prison, 299; union rebellion (1968) of, 214, 359
ortodoxos, 216, 250, 266–268, 272, 279, 284, 288, 348; and CGT, 188, 229; and Fiat, 184, 190, 191; and Independents, 79, 199; and *legalistas,* 194, 259, 265, 270; and Peronism, 67, 68, 185, 212, 220, 233, 257, 284; and strikes, 191, 258, 263, 269; and UOM, 69, 74, 83, 130, 276
Otero, Ricardo, 248, 250, 251, 276, 279, 280, 281, 283, 287, 360

Pacto Social, 246, 249, 252, 260, 264, 282, 284, 285; opposition to, 261, 265, 268, 278, 279, 280, 281, 283

Palabra Obrera, 127, 215, 270

Paraná industrial belt, 198, 214, 229, 269, 292

participacionistas, 83, 106, 134, 167, 228

Partido Comunista (PC), 170, 171, 213, 215, 235, 239, 242, 253, 270, 272, 330, 333

Partido Comunista Revolucionario (PCR), 127, 212, 213, 221, 223, 224, 227, 242, 281, 333; *clasistas* in, 214, 215, 238–239, 258, 263, 297; and Cordobazo, 163, 171; and demonstrations, 193; national conference of, 251; and Onganía, 170; and PC, 270; and strikes, 177, 179

Partido Revolucionario de los Trabajadores (PRT), 127, 163, 164, 170, 171, 193, 196, 202, 203, 212, 253, 271, 333

Partido Socialista de los Trabajadores (PST), 253, 278

Perdriel plant, 34, 177–179, 214, 320, 336

Perkins factory, 36, 49, 188, 201, 248, 257

Perón, Eva, 9–10, 124

Perón, Isabel, 264, 280, 293, 297, 298

Perón, Juan, 3–5, 18, 168; and automobile industry, 30, 55, 58, 60; death of, 254, 280, 298; economic programs of, 14, 264, 265, 275; and electric power companies, 26, 120; exile of, 73; and Henry Kaiser, 31, 38; industrial programs of, 26, 32, 38; and labor leaders, 67, 108, 185, 267, 353; and the left, 218–219, 220, 222, 227–228, 230, 247, 255, 256, 259, 262, 278, 279, 332, 357; and military, 345; as minister of labor, 3, 10–11, 12; myth of, 281; and Onganía, 105; and Ongaro, 129; overthrow of, 17, 19, 28, 56, 97, 103, 113, 126, 146, 245, 274; and Peronism, 256, 268, 353; portraits of, 9; return of, 56, 66, 171, 186, 232–234, 235, 237, 246, 250–251, 253–254, 258, 276, 290, 348, 361; social welfare programs of, 9; and students, 126; and trade unions, 66, 67, 69, 108, 125, 126, 132, 210, 212, 220, 222, 249, 250, 252, 254, 256, 261, 263, 360, 361; and Vandor, 108, 134, 141; and working class, 6–7, 8–11, 13, 14, 19, 272, 345

Peronism, 4, 103; and capitalism, 15, 96, 169; and the Church, 18; conservative priorities of, 13, 130, 256, 263; and the left, 182, 218–221, 227, 229, 230, 236, 252, 259, 263, 265, 266, 267, 268, 278, 290, 335, 348, 357, 1144; and Perón, 256, 268; political culture of, 9; power struggle within, 259, 279–280, 299, 352; restoration of, 210, 235, 236, 239–240, 242, 243, 244, 245, 246, 252, 261, 264, 268, 278, 293, 294, 327, 335, 349, 353; right-wing, 252, 258, 259, 262–263, 265, 266, 267, 268, 270, 271, 272, 278, 284, 288, 291, 292, 298; role in dissident labor movement, 347–349; structure of, 13; and students, 126, 144; and trade unions, 52,

53, 55, 56, 57, 58–60, 61, 62, 63, 64, 65–66, 67, 68–69, 70, 71, 72–75, 76, 78, 80, 81, 83, 94, 95, 96, 97, 105, 109, 110, 116, 119, 123, 125, 129, 135, 136, 139, 141, 146, 148, 161, 163, 183, 186, 227, 328, 347, 348, 349, 350, 356; and working class, 7, 8, 10, 14, 15, 17, 52, 126, 144, 204, 234, 346, 350, 357, 358, 361, 362

Peronismo de Base, 215, 239, 251, 258, 269, 279, 290

Peronist Resistance, 56, 57, 73, 96, 183, 184, 196, 218, 342, 348, 350, 357; and Peronist unions, 65, 67, 125, 170; waning of, 61, 64, 104

Peugeot, 39–40, 110, 232, 282, 306, 362

Piccinini, Alberto, 269, 292, 293

Police, 151, 152, 153, 156, 158, 159, 164, 178, 191, 267, 287

Political parties, 8, 17, 104, 146, 186, 270

Politics, 4; intra-union, 72; labor, 53, 54–55, 56–63, 73–79, 87, 88, 94, 98–99, 114, 121–122, 149, 169, 305, 327, 352, 356; language of, 8–9; national, 227, 233–234, 353; parliamentary, 103; participation in, in Argentina, 162; party, 254; revolutionary, 18; and social mobility, 86; and work, 305–342. *See also* Working class: and politics

Priests, radical, 129, 132, 158, 161. *See also* Third World priests' movement

Privatization, 68, 121, 148

Production: automotive, 316–317; damage from strikes, 178; decline in, 264; mass, 24, 33, 36, 85, 86, 89–94, 95, 311, 313–315, 320; transport, 15; weapons, 3

Production rhythms, 89, 136, 213, 221, 245, 271, 315, 330, 349; increase of, 61, 110, 201, 222, 255, 256, 260, 314, 320, 328; union control of, 292, 323, 329, 331, 333–334, 335

Productivity, 15, 77, 104, 311–328

quitas zonales system, 111, 160

Radical Party, 8, 17, 24, 25, 65, 70, 81, 105, 120, 144

Rationalization, 112, 148, 245; of factories, 51, 256, 319, 320–321, 326, 336, 363; and labor militancy, 320–321, 328, 333, 334; under Onganía, 106, 110, 121; of Renault Company, 111, 327, 328, 330

Rega, José López, 287, 293

Renault, Louis, 2, 325

Renault Company, 19, 51, 214, 271, 272, 318; buyout of IKA, 35, 37, 40, 311, 318–319, 320, 325; and IKA, 32, 34, 40, 221, 317; labor policies of, 236, 260–261, 280–281, 324, 325–326, 327, 328, 333; and rationalization, 111, 327, 328, 330. *See also* IKA-Renault

Reuther, Walter, 314, 340

Revolución Libertadora, 126

Rodrigazo, 293, 297, 299

Rodríguez, José, 248–249, 262, 271; and *clasistas*, 232, 241, 250, 260, 272, 273; opposition to, 294; and SMATA, 216, 240, 259, 260, 261, 282, 283, 284, 285, 287, 289, 290, 295, 299

Romero, Roque, 236, 289, 347

Rosario, 31, 49, 55, 124, 125, 130, 141, 148, 166, 193, 198, 290

Rucci, José, 185, 201, 210, 220, 222, 228, 229, 233, 247; assassination of, 255, 256; and CGT, 183, 186, 188, 191, 193, 199, 230, 245, 248, 250; and Tosco, 209, 212, 219, 226, 241, 249, 252

sábado inglés law, 57, 142–143, 160, 238, 248, 271, 289, 328

Sabattini, Amadeo, 25, 26, 28, 120

Sacerdotes del Tercer Mundo. *See* Third World priests' movement

Salamanca, Renée, 225, 227, 238, 259, 261, 329; attempt to assassinate, 263, 279; murder of, 301; and PCR, 221, 223, 224, 227, 297; and Peronism, 262, 270, 271, 272, 281, 283, 284, 286, 287, 288, 289, 295; and SMATA, 232, 235, 239, 240, 241, 248; and Tosco, 226, 231, 251, 252, 269

Sallustro, Oberdán, 202, 255, 287

San Martín, Brigadier General Ignacio, 26, 29, 32

San Sebastián, Rubén, 108, 134

Santa Isabel, 59, 60, 64, 65, 93, 165, 177, 261, 342; and IKA, 35, 57, 77, 110, 111, 282, 311, 350; Kaiser plants at, 31, 32, 33, 34, 136, 277; labor force at, 149, 151, 351, 363; left-wing activists at, 168, 172, 179, 215, 236, 255, 257, 285, 339; and Renault, 319, 325, 326; as working class neighborhood, 354–355

Shop stewards *(cuerpo de delegados)*, 62, 118–119, 176, 182, 196, 213, 214, 227, 232, 239, 257, 258, 272; in autoworkers' unions, 315–316, 330–331, 333, 334, 338, 340

Simó, Alejo, 79, 130, 185, 188, 227, 229, 230, 259, 276; and Cordobazo, 142, 143, 149, 157, 160, 163, 353; and Ongaro, 133; and Peronism, 278, 284; and UOM, 74, 77, 78, 83, 108, 111, 124, 128, 149, 151, 220, 222, 258, 291; and Vandor, 81, 112, 129, 132, 141

Sindicato de Trabajadores de Concord (SITRAC), 65, 81, 175; leaders of, 176, 179, 180, 187, 193, 200, 259, 287, 322, 347; and local unions, 169, 186, 189, 190, 191, 198, 200–201; and strikes, 82, 160, 337, 338, 352; suppression of, 194, 350

Sindicato de Trabajadores de Materfer (SITRAM), 65, 82, 169, 172, 176–177, 181, 194, 350, 352

Sindicatos de Mecánicos y Afines del Transporte Automotor (SMATA), 59, 74, 87, 95–96, 217, 296

Sindicatos de Mecánicos y Afines del Transporte Automotor (SMATA; Córdoba), 57–67 *passim*, 72, 76, 77, 78, 80, 81, 82, 128, 141–142, 276,

280–299 *passim*, 300, 329, 334, 349, 350, 352, 353; and *clasismo*, 216–299 *passim*, 331, 337, 339; and collective bargaining, 212–213; and Cordobazo, 142, 143, 149, 150, 151, 152, 153, 154, 157, 160, 161, 164, 165, 167, 169; and elections, 80, 83, 220–221, 232, 236, 239, 243, 248, 271, 272, 279, 280, 349; and Fiat company, 64, 81, 82, 83, 97, 180, 197, 223, 225, 247–248, 259, 321; and government, 249, 260, 280; independence from union central, 354, 356; leaders of, 75, 76, 77, 80, 108, 112, 124, 128, 129, 216; Marxism in, 218, 219, 220, 222, 227; Peronists in, 57, 58, 59, 60, 65, 72, 74, 75, 78, 94, 95, 96, 328, 329; reforms in, 217–218, 237–239; and strikes, 61–63, 110–111, 179, 188, 189, 192, 200, 226, 280–285, 336, 341, 358; tactics of, 297, 325. *See also* Torres, Elpidio Angel: and SMATA

SITRAC-SITRAM union rebellion, 182–205, 216, 217, 225, 236, 354; and *clasismo*, 215, 218, 221, 223, 235, 258, 337, 349; demise of, 212, 222, 224, 287, 309

62 Organizaciones, 57, 209–210, 228, 254, 259, 279, 290; control of, 59, 98, 199, 212, 241; and Cordobazo, 353; national convention at Villa Hermosa, 251, 252; and *ortodoxo* unions, 199, 250, 265, 266, 267, 270; outlawing of, 363; and Perón, 125, 227; split of, 129, 188. *See also* Peronism: and trade unions

Socialism, 8, 15, 24, 55, 63, 127, 163, 233; and *clasistas*, 182, 195, 198, 203, 224, 262, 349, 358; and Cordoban unions, 121, 131, 164, 168, 211, 359; national, 349; and Peronism, 70, 262, 349; and students, 137, 144, 146; and working class, 183, 218, 270. *See also* Marxism

Sociedad Mixta Siderúrgica Argentina (SOMISA), 5, 34, 229

Strikes, 12, 41, 61–63, 64, 137, 214, 217, 232, 238, 243–244, 264, 292, 350; active *(paro activo)*, 61, 62, 149, 156; of Communists, 59; general, 79, 107, 108, 112, 113, 122, 130, 149, 157, 159, 163, 176, 189–190, 191, 194, 200, 220, 221, 225, 258, 261, 263, 265, 266, 292–293, 326; General Motors (1973), 262; hunger, 184, 187; and issues of job control, 332, 333, 339, 342; of metal workers, 111–112; 1970 SMATA, 336; of oil workers, 133; political, 122, 179, 281, 335, 338, 341; prohibition of, 110; quickie, 332, 333; at SMATA-Córdoba, 280–284, 289; soldiering *(trabajo a convenio)*, 280–281, 288; solidarity, 127, 147–158, 167, 178, 188, 248, 269, 354; of steelworkers, 268–269, 292; student, 148; Sunday or stay-at-home *(paro matero* or *paro dominguero)*, 62, 149; violence in, 153; wildcat, 215, 261, 284, 293, 295, 331, 334. *See also* Cordobazo; Villa Constitución strike; SITRAC-SITRAM union rebellion; *individual companies; individual unions*

Students, university, 51, 126–127, 129, 131, 132, 134, 135, 137, 193; and Cordobazo, 140, 143–145, 155, 163–164; left-wing culture of, 144; organizations of, 144; radical influence of, 351–352, 357. *See also* Worker-student alliance

Taccone, Juan José, 106, 118, 121, 134, 249
Tapia, Roberto, 244, 266, 267, 270, 279, 283
Technology, 4, 16, 26, 32, 34, 37, 38
Third World priests' movement, 127, 131, 138, 145, 148, 158, 357
Thompson Ramco factory, 33, 271, 272, 288
Torres, Elpidio Angel, 57–63, 76, 78, 79, 80–81, 82, 175; and CGTA, 128, 129; and Cordobazo, 143, 149, 150, 151, 153, 155, 157, 159, 160, 163, 164, 165, 167, 353; leadership style of, 96; and Ongaro, 128; opposition to, 177, 227, 237, 238, 239, 336; and Perdriel plant, 177, 178, 179, 214; and Peronism, 80, 161; and shop stewards' commission, 330; and SMATA, 65, 74, 75, 77, 83, 94, 108, 110–111, 112, 124, 129, 177, 178, 188, 189, 215, 328, 329; and Vandor, 128
Tosco, Agustín, 1, 3, 6, 18–19, 26, 44, 47, 52, 143, 362; attempt to assassinate, 279; and Catholic Church, 146, 147; and CGT, 79, 109, 110, 119, 192, 194, 231, 245, 246, 283; and CGTA, 128, 134; and Cordobazo, 149, 152, 153, 154, 155, 157, 158, 159, 163, 164, 167, 168, 172, 352; and Curutchet, 287, 288; death of, 297–298; imprisonment of, 199, 209, 210, 211, 220, 294; and Independents, 69, 70–73, 74, 78, 80, 82, 83, 112, 124, 130–131, 148, 161, 165, 167, 168, 169, 171, 186, 194, 199, 203, 212, 242–243, 244, 248, 260, 280; and López, 260, 265–266, 288, 294; and Luz y Fuerza, 108, 113, 116, 118, 129, 131, 174, 189, 249, 250, 253, 254, 255, 258, 269, 285, 291, 298, 346, 348; and Marxism, 252, 253, 260; and Navarrazo, 268; and Onganía, 105–106, 121, 123; and Ongaro, 123, 132–133; and PC, 253; and Peronism, 55, 210, 211–212, 219–220, 230, 232, 233, 241–242, 243, 249, 250, 251, 252, 254, 261, 267, 348, 349; release from prison, 184, 220, 225, 226, 242; and SITRAC-SITRAM, 190, 191, 192; and SMATA, 287, 350; and union alliances, 290; and Villa Constitución strikes, 269, 270, 293. *See also* Luz y Fuerza
Trotskyists, 75, 127, 129, 163, 170, 215, 223, 270, 330
Tucumán, 125, 141, 148, 198, 290; sugar workers *(ingenios)* of, 106, 109, 133, 290
Turin (Italy), 2, 3, 37, 51, 63, 64, 92, 324, 326. *See also* Fiat company

Unión Ferroviaria, 107, 109
Unión Industrial Argentina (UIA), 5, 143, 275, 355
Union leaders, 12, 55, 62, 70, 74–75, 77–78, 80,

121, 123, 345; *clasistas* as, 273; coordination of, 354; in Cordobazo, 154–155, 157–158, 161, 162–163, 353; and guerrillas, 360; harassment of, 192–193, 361; imprisonment of, 200; Peronist, 66–67, 76, 79, 107, 185, 256. *See also individual leaders*
Unión Obrera Metalúrgica (UOM), 34, 66, 111, 112, 117, 124, 128, 148, 228, 229, 251, 258; and CGT, 130, 183, 291; and *clasismo*, 214, 222, 223, 240, 241, 268, 269; Cordoban, 277, 278, 353; and Cordobazo, 149, 151, 160, 166; and Fiat company, 59, 64, 74, 77–78, 83, 173, 180–181, 197, 220, 225, 231, 232, 247, 248, 259, 338; and government, 275, 296, 299, 363; loss of legal status of, 107, 108; and Perón, 67, 264–265; power struggle in, 185, 186, 199, 292, 293; *quitas zonales* controversy, 142; and SMATA, 56–57, 80, 81, 300; and Vandor, 68, 69, 82, 108, 126, 129, 132, 275
Unions, 10–11, 15, 18, 37, 52; automobile workers', 52, 53, 54, 56, 64, 74, 81, 84, 87, 88, 94, 95, 98, 129, 160, 165, 217, 222, 224, 231, 240, 247, 251, 261, 283, 349, 356, 361; in Buenos Aires, 130; carpenters', 129; and *comisiones obreras,* 213, 223; Communist, 3, 10, 11; construction workers', 10, 11, 108, 128, 134, 184, 228, 257; cooperation between, 149; dock workers', 106; federal, 69, 72; "generation of 1953" in, 55; and government, 88, 98, 105, 107, 109; hierarchy of, 113; industrial, 95; journalists', 279, 290; left-wing activists in, 55–60, 61, 63, 74, 75, 118, 124, 129, 136, 144, 168, 198, 202, 260, 262; legal status *(personería gremial)* of, 11, 81, 107, 197, 200, 279; light and power workers', 55, 56, 65, 69, 70, 71, 72, 79, 105, 106, 112–113, 114–118, 119–120, 122, 131, 133, 134, 146, 147, 150, 152, 157, 158, 164, 191, 194, 242, 249, 252, 253, 254, 269, 291, 294, 346, 349; local autonomy of, 98; and mass firing, 41; meatpacking, 10, 11; membership of, 13; merchant marine, 109; metalworkers', 13, 59, 64, 66, 67, 78, 82, 111, 151, 247, 251, 274–276, 292; municipal workers', 108; national industrial, 10; and negotiation, 66, 67; new left, 270; petroleum workers', 108, 133; plant *(sindicatos de planta),* 64–65, 74, 81, 82–83, 95, 97; political pluralism in, 72, 73, 79, 98, 131, 211; postal and telegraph workers', 69; print workers', 55, 56, 69, 70, 107, 133, 210, 250, 279, 290, 355; railroad workers', 12, 55, 56, 106, 109, 150; rubber workers', 257; sanitation workers', 69, 70; shipyard workers', 109; shoe workers', 10, 166, 184, 199, 201; and shop stewards' movement *(comisiones internas),* 12, 95, 248, 290, 323, 329; socialist, 3, 11, 12; state workers', 13, 66, 109, 165, 166, 257, 290; sugar workers', 106, 109, 133, 290; syndicalist, 11; taxi drivers', 188; telephone

Unions *(continued)*
  workers', 109, 123–124, 166; textile, 10, 13, 66; tradition of, 84, 99; transport workers', 66, 67, 68, 244, 267, 284, 346; and violence, 11, 18, 78, 140, 162. *See also clasismo;* Peronism: and trade unions; *individual unions*
Unión Tranviarios Automotor (UTA), 108, 243–244, 259, 288, 346, 347; and Cordobazo, 148, 149, 165; and *legalistas,* 67, 68, 70, 152, 186, 263, 266–267, 279
United Auto Workers (UAW), 314, 324, 333, 336, 340
United States, 32, 38, 86, 90, 310, 313, 333, 339, 340
Universities, 23, 24, 27, 104
University reform movement, 24, 126, 145
Urbanization, 5, 42, 43–44, 46
Uriburu, José Camilo, 189, 190, 192, 193

Vandor, Augusto, 63, 77, 79, 105, 106, 107, 109, 112, 122, 128, 251, 347; assassination of, 166, 167, 185, 255; and CGT, 123, 149; and CGTA, 130, 132, 133, 141; opposition to, 125–126, 128, 129, 130; and Perón, 108, 134, 141, 345; and Peronist unions, 67, 68, 69, 73, 110, 165, 166, 299; and SMATA, 74, 78, 80, 81, 83, 135, 165; and UOM, 66, 78, 82, 142, 275
vandorismo, 63, 65, 66, 68, 69, 129, 130, 131, 132, 157, 165, 167, 185, 228, 280, 345, 350
Vanguardia Comunista (VC), 127, 163, 170, 171, 212, 213, 214, 215, 223, 239, 258
Vasena, Alberto Krieger, 104, 143
verticalismo, 130, 185, 250, 266, 292, 300, 359; campaign for, 73, 80, 82, 83, 105, 222, 249, 279, 280, 293; opposition to, 71, 78, 79, 124, 210, 220, 233, 247, 290, 294, 299, 353; reestablishment of, 69, 131, 134, 254, 348; and UOM, 258, 268, 275, 276, 278
viborazo, 69, 193–194, 196, 198, 203, 204, 210, 216, 349, 350, 359
Villa Constitución strike, 268–270, 276, 292, 293, 299, 359

Wages, 16, 97, 115, 181, 187, 246; in Córdoba, 44, 71, 88, 114, 136; declining, 8, 357; freezing of, 106, 264; increase in, 7–8, 9, 62–63, 75, 76,
86, 87, 104, 111, 173, 245, 246; and productivity prize *(premio de la producción),* 321–322, 337, 338; strikes for, 216, 265, 281, 287, 295, 297, 299. *See also* Automobile industry: wages in
Walsh, Rodolfo, 124, 125–126
Women: in automobile industry, 46, 93; as migrants, 45
Workers: agricultural, 202, 243; lay-offs of, 76–77, 110, 111, 112, 117, 130, 142, 169, 221, 281, 282, 286, 308, 309–310, 313, 315, 328; maintenance, 89; male vs. female, 45–47, 50; new industrial, 85–86; and piece rates, 314, 315, 323, 325, 336; *porteño,* 109, 132, 142, 153; semiskilled, 89, 114, 326–327; skilled, 32, 35, 49, 89, 90, 92, 114, 121, 136, 176, 214, 313, 318, 326–327, 330, 335–336, 351; speedup of, 313, 314, 325, 332–333, 334, 350; unskilled *(peones),* 86, 89, 114, 176, 326–327, 361; white-collar, 49, 51; and workplace relationships, 54. *See also* Unions
Worker-student alliance, 131, 135, 138, 146, 147–148, 151, 152, 153, 154, 158, 342, 351
Working class, 8–9, 18, 28, 88; and capitalism, 344; and *clasismo,* 352, 357–358; in Córdoba, 24, 33, 42–44, 49, 50, 51, 53, 56, 71, 72, 99, 113, 119, 134, 135, 139, 141, 202, 264, 285, 291, 305, 342, 354–356; and Cordobazo, 138–157, 159; formation of, 85; growth of industrial, 25, 50, 85–86; history of, 343–344, 345, 356, 359, 361–362; and left, 126, 127, 164, 171, 193, 202–203, 216, 217, 223, 224, 270, 350; mobilization of, 256–257, 263–264, 284–285, 294, 299, 349, 353–354; and Peronism, 5, 6–7, 10, 13, 14, 17, 212, 232, 243, 253, 280, 288, 335, 347; and politics, 50, 53, 54, 104, 109, 135, 234, 343–363; radicalization of, 357; and revolutionary change, 243; slang *(lunfardo)* of, 8; and student movement, 126, 131, 135, 138; and *viborazo,* 193
Working conditions, 88, 94, 97, 136, 180, 221, 245, 257, 264; hazardous, 114–115, 181, 255, 256, 281, 327, 330, 337–338, 349, 354; improvements in, 198, 248, 271; in metallurgical industry, 277. *See also* Collective bargaining: and working conditions; *individual companies*